CW00726594

Companies and other Business Structures

IN SOUTH AFRICA

COMMERCIAL LAW

THIRD EDITION

Companies and other Business Structures

IN SOUTH AFRICA

COMMERCIAL LAW

DENNIS DAVIS (Editor)
WALTER GEACH (Managing Editor)
TSHEPO MONGALO ı DAVID BUTLER
ANNELI LOUBSER ı LINDI COETZEE
DAVID BURDETTE

OXFORD
UNIVERSITY PRESS

SOUTHERN AFRICA

OXFORD
UNIVERSITY PRESS
SOUTHERN AFRICA

Oxford University Press Southern Africa (Pty) Ltd

Vasco Boulevard, Goodwood, Cape Town, Republic of South Africa
P O Box 12119, N1 City, 7463, Cape Town, Republic of South Africa

Oxford University Press Southern Africa (Pty) Ltd is a subsidiary of
Oxford University Press, Great Clarendon Street, Oxford OX2 6DP.

The Press, a department of the University of Oxford, furthers the University's objective of
excellence in research, scholarship, and education by publishing worldwide in

Oxford New York

Auckland Cape Town Dar es Salaam Hong Kong Karachi
Kuala Lumpur Madrid Melbourne Mexico City Nairobi
New Delhi Shanghai Taipei Toronto

With offices in

Argentina Austria Brazil Chile Czech Republic France Greece
Guatemala Hungary Italy Japan Poland Portugal Singapore South Korea
Switzerland Turkey Ukraine Vietnam

Oxford is a registered trade mark of Oxford University Press
in the UK and in certain other countries

Published in South Africa
by Oxford University Press Southern Africa (Pty) Ltd, Cape Town

Companies and Other Business Structures in South Africa
Third Edition

ISBN 978 019 905260 8

© Oxford University Press Southern Africa (Pty) Ltd 2013

The moral rights of the author have been asserted
Database right Oxford University Press Southern Africa (Pty) Ltd (maker)

First published 2008
Second edition 2011
Third edition 2013

Publisher: Penny Lane
Project manager: Marguerite Lithgow
Editor: Helena Janisch
Proofreader: Annette de Villiers
Indexer: Clifford Perusset
Cover designer: Judith Cross and Cathy Watts

Set in Utopia Std Regular 9.5 pt on 12 pt by Barbara Hirsch
Printed and bound by ABC Press, Cape Town
120424

Acknowledgements
The authors and publisher gratefully acknowledge permission to reproduce copyright material
in this book. Every effort has been made to trace copyright holders, but if any copyright
infringements have been made, the publisher would be grateful for information that would
enable any omissions or errors to be corrected in subsequent impressions.

To Michael Blackman
No one could wish for a better
teacher of company law

Dennis Davis

To my friends and colleagues in the Department of Accounting at the
University of the Western Cape who are dedicated to the upliftment of others
through providing quality tertiary education

Walter Geach

Contents in brief

Contents

Preface

The introduction of comprehensive new legislation to govern companies in South Africa constitutes the single most important legislative innovation in the area of commercial law since the advent of democracy in 1994. It is trite to argue that the new Companies Act will materially affect economic intercourse in South Africa. In essence, the core of our company law has remained broadly the same since 1926. All amendments that followed the 1926 Companies Act, including the 1973 Act, were no more than alterations and modifications to a structure that had lasted for more than three-quarters of a century.

The Companies Act 71 of 2008, as amended, introduced significant changes to that structure. It incorporates developments that have worked with considerable success in other jurisdictions, including the United States of America, Australia, New Zealand and the United Kingdom. It introduces into South African law a number of new concepts that will demand innovative legal thinking and will prompt significant development to this area of law.

Expressed differently, the 2008 Act challenges practitioners, who are now required to adapt to legislation that is different from that which has governed their professional lives to date. It also provides challenges to academic lawyers as they educate a new generation of company lawyers.

This third edition is a comprehensive attempt to come to terms with the challenges posed by the 2008 Act and the published regulations as well as by other new legislation such as the Financial Markets Act, 2012. It seeks to analyse, interpret and explain the new body of company law and related legislation and to comment on their application. The interpretation and analysis are based on existing precedent where applicable, and on comparative law where required. The work also guides the reader through the intricacies of the 2008 Act, the regulations and related legislation by means of practical examples that elucidate the content of the key concepts contained in the legislation. Each chapter also has useful summaries that highlight the critical points made in each chapter. Thus, this book is designed to assist the reader to discover a new and essentially revised field of law. Accordingly, it aims to contribute significantly to the education of existing practitioners as well as to a new generation of legal and accounting professionals, which will ensure that the practice of company law remains congruent with the objectives of this legislation. The book also deals with business structures other than companies, and highlights the most recent position regarding close corporations, business trusts and partnerships and the extent, if any, to which the 2008 Companies Act affects them.

Dennis Davis
Walter Geach

Foreword

The Companies Act, 2008 introduces far-reaching changes to company law in South Africa, both of a substantive and a procedural nature.

Perhaps the most fundamental aspect of the new legislation is its flexibility in recognition of the fact that a single Companies Act will regulate all companies, from the biggest to the smallest. New concepts have been established, and existing legislation and common law have been refined to take cognisance of developments in company law worldwide, as well as economic factors and issues that have been problematic in practice or have formed the basis of important litigation.

The legislation replaces all existing statutes governing company law. This legislation, together with the applicable common law, now constitutes South Africa's company law system. It will thus be readily appreciated that the significance and practical impact of most of these changes require a knowledge of the existing Companies Act and common-law principles. It is this factor that is the real strength of *Companies and other Business Structures in South Africa*. Each of the chapters deals separately with the most important concepts and issues of company law. Where any topic under discussion has been the subject of litigation, the leading reported cases are referred to, and the fundamental principles that were the basis of the judgments are outlined. The provisions in the 2008 Act are described, accompanied by an analysis of how these provisions change previous legislation and, where relevant, the applicable common-law principles.

The book does not profess to be a major treatise analysing in detail case law or philosophies or theories of company law. What it seeks to achieve, it does very well – it provides a practical analysis of the nature and impact of the changes to South African company law arising from the 2008 Act. This it does comprehensively and in an easily readable manner using simple language and well-structured material. The manner in which the text highlights the practical application of the law by means of the Practical Issue boxes is particularly useful. Sometimes these consist of extracts from, or descriptions of, important cases; at other times they contain a useful summary of the relevant principles described in the text.

The book will be a useful reference for anyone concerned with South African company law and a useful guide to the practical impact of the new laws – not only students, but also practitioners, primarily in the legal and accounting fields.

Michael M Katz
Chairman: Edward Nathan Sonnenbergs Inc.

The one fascinating thing about the advent of our constitutional democracy is the space it has created for fresh conversation on issues of society, law and economic justice. Much of the conversation appears to be animated by the ideal of creating a better society. It is our abiding challenge to convert this ideal into reality.

It is fair to say that much of the present-day flourish and innovation in the area of the law, society and justice is compelled by our collective choices to re-enact the way we transact our lives. These shared choices are mirrored in our supreme law – the Constitution. Seen against this wide backdrop, it is somewhat inescapable that the way we transact business, and the norms and vessels through which we do business would themselves become the object of critical scrutiny and renovation. Put simply, the re-writing of the Companies Act is somewhat inescapable. It is compelled by our very deep sense of historic change even in an area as sometimes sheltered and austere as company law.

Well into the adolescence of our democratic dispensation, the question arises as to which core values and objectives inform company law. Because company law always invokes issues of social and economic policy and equity, it is inevitable that corporate law reform in present-day South Africa would be informed by debate on what are appropriate objectives of company law. In our case, it does seem that organised business, organised labour and government at national level have generated considerable consensus on the objectives of the Companies Act, 2008.

Unlike in past Companies Acts, one of the objectives of the Companies Act, 2008 is to ensure the broader constitutional and economic well-being of South Africa and its citizens. This is a noticeable departure from the notion that corporate entities exist only to advance the peculiar and narrow interests of their shareholders or beneficial owners.

Other objectives of the Companies Act, 2008 include the promotion of compliance with the Bill of Rights in the Constitution in the application of company law, as well as the development of the South African economy by measures such as promoting entrepreneurship and enterprise development. The 2008 Act sees innovation and investment in South African markets as a valuable objective. The concept of a company and the creation and use of companies are seen as methods of enhancing the economic welfare of South Africa and its citizens in the global economy.

The Act places a high premium on the aggregation of capital for productive purposes and for investments. Another noble objective is to bring into being a company law that is flexible enough in terms of the design and the organisation of companies to satisfy the obvious need for appropriate diversity of corporate entities.

It appears that the 2008 Act facilitates corporate efficiency by migrating from a capital maintenance regime to one that relies on solvency and liquidity as critical criteria. The efficiency requirement covers several aspects of the existing companies legislation, such as board structure, directors' responsibilities, the position of minority shareholders (particularly in inefficient companies), the reformation of mergers and takeover regimes, and the regime necessary to ensure an effective rescue system for failing companies.

Additional targets of the Companies Act, 2008 appear to be an enhancement of corporate governance, high levels of transparency and an insistence on minimum accounting standards for annual reports. In this way, the new law appears to be bent on advancing shareholder activism to enhance the protection of minorities and to increase standards of corporate governance. Another important consideration appears to be finding harmony between our company law requirements and the best practice observed by other jurisdictions internationally.

Companies and other Business Structures in South Africa represents a remarkable aid in understanding the Companies Act, 2008 through the tinted lenses of its manifest and tacit purposes. This book reflects the rational internal cohesion of the Companies Act, 2008 and is written in accessible language that allows novices and seasoned practitioners alike to come to terms with the new legislation. In a very helpful manner, the text examines the new provisions against the backdrop of case law developed over the last hundred and fifty years. This legal precedent is contrasted with the new legislative provisions in a way that enriches the reader's understanding of the changes envisaged in the Companies Act, 2008. The book properly recognises the underlying and continuing role of the common law that complements company law and must, in itself, be consistent with the dictates of our Constitution.

I have no doubt that this book constitutes a valuable addition to the body of company-law writing, particularly because of the care taken by the authors to ensure that the Companies Act, 2008 is seen within the prism of the new legal, economic and social context of South Africa as a constitutional democracy, an open economy, and as a people who are striving for genuine social equity.

Dikgang Moseneke
Deputy Chief Justice of South Africa
Constitutional Court of South Africa

List of authors

Judge Dennis Davis

Judge Davis is the Judge President of the Competition Appeal Court and a Judge of the High Court of South Africa (CPD). He is an Honorary Professor at the University of Cape Town, where he teaches tax, constitutional and competition law. Judge Davis assisted in drafting the Companies Act, 2008.

Professor Walter Geach

CA (SA) BA, LLB (University of Cape Town), MCOM FCIS.

Professor Geach is an admitted Advocate of the High Court of South Africa and a Chartered Accountant. He is a Professor in the Department of Accounting at the University of the Western Cape, and a Fellow of the University of KwaZulu-Natal. He is a non-executive director of Grindrod Ltd and Grindrod Bank, a non-executive director of CareCross Health (Pty) Ltd, an advisor to the accounting and legal professions, and the author of several distinguished legal and financial planning books.

Professor Tshepo Mongalo

BProc (*summa cum laude*), LLB (University of KwaZulu-Natal); LLM (University of Cambridge); Cert. in Legal Writing (Cape Town); Cert. in Law, Social Thought & Global Governance (Brown); Cert. in Global Law, Economic Policy & Social Justice (Harvard); PhD Candidate (Cape Town).

Professor Mongalo is an Associate Professor of Commercial Law at the University of Witwatersrand, Johannesburg, and the Deputy Chairperson of the Specialist Committee on Company Law in South Africa. As Project Manager for Company Law Reform at the Department of Trade and Industry, South Africa (2003–2008), he was instrumental in the development of the Companies Act, 2008. He is a Fellow of the Cambridge Commonwealth Society, and a member of an HSRC Think Tank in recognition of his outstanding scholarship in matters relating to the governance of cities.

Professor Anneli Loubser

BA, LLB (University of Pretoria); LLM in Corporate Law (University of South Africa); LLD (University of South Africa).

Professor Loubser is an Attorney, Notary Public and Conveyancer of the High Court of South Africa. She is a Professor in corporate law in the Department of Mercantile Law at the University of South Africa, and a member of the Litigation Committee of the Financial Services Board of South Africa. She is the contributing author of several books, including *Mars: The Law of Insolvency in South Africa* (ninth edition), and journal articles.

Ms Lindi Coetzee

BIuris, LLB (University of Port Elizabeth), LLM (University of South Africa).

Ms Coetzee is a Senior Lecturer in company law at the Nelson Mandela Metropolitan University, and an Advocate of the High Court of South Africa. She is the National Director of Street Law (South Africa), and a contributing author to several books and journal articles.

Professor David Butler

BCom, LLB, LLD (University of Stellenbosch).

Professor Butler is Emeritus Professor of Mercantile Law at the University of Stellenbosch, and an Attorney of the High Court of South Africa. He has taught company law to accountancy students at the University of Stellenbosch for more than thirty years. His particular research interests are company law, share blocks and arbitration.

Professor David Burdette

BIuris, LLB (University of South Africa); LLD (University of Pretoria).

Professor Burdette is a Professor of Law at Nottingham Law School, Nottingham Trent University (United Kingdom), and an Extraordinary Professor at the Faculty of Law, University of Pretoria. He is a co-author of the leading insolvency law publication by PM Meskin, *Insolvency Law and its Operation in Winding Up*, a contributor to *Henochsberg on the Companies Act 71 of 2008*, and the author of numerous journal articles and specialised reports. He is also a Senior Consultant for the World Bank and Director of the Centre for Business and Insolvency Law at Nottingham Law School.

Specialist contributors

The publisher and authors would like to express their sincere appreciation for the valuable contributions made to this book by the following persons:

Ms Siobhan Cleary, Director: Strategy and Public Policy, Johannesburg Stock Exchange: for the contribution of her expertise in relation to the Johannesburg Stock Exchange (chapter 19: Financial Markets).

Mr Etienne Swanepoel, Partner, Webber Wentzel: for his contributions relating to the Financial Markets Act (chapter 11: Insider Trading, and chapter 19: Financial Markets).

Professor RC Williams, Faculty of Law, University of KwaZulu-Natal: for his authorship of the glossary which is contained in this book.

Dr Maleka Femida Cassim, Attorney and Notary Public of the High Court of South Africa, Senior Lecturer at the University of Pretoria, and **Ms Rehana Cassim**, Attorney and Notary Public of the High Court of South Africa: for their preparation of the original content in the PowerPoint slides that form part of the ancillary materials.

Mr Craig Renaud, Faculty of Law, Rhodes University: for updating the original Power-Point slide ancillary materials, and for expanding the original question bank with updated and new problem question material.

About the book

Companies and other Business Structures in South Africa is a pedagogically rich learning resource. This book is designed to form a strong foundation of understanding, to develop the skills to engage independently and judiciously with legal and commercial principles, and to create skilled and proficient professionals.

Brief description of the features:

Key terms and concepts: The most important terms and concepts, which are essential to understanding the subject matter, are identified in each chapter and appear in bold. This feature assists students to comprehend the material clearly and effectively.

Practical issue: This feature demonstrates the relevance and practical application of the law. It provides context, insights and interest, building a better understanding of the dynamics of the legal system and its operation and impact in the business environment. This feature enlivens the subject matter, stimulates discussion, and develops the ability to engage meaningfully with relevant issues.

Contextual issue: This feature considers the development, underlying policy and ramifications of the law, its logic and consistency with other principles, possible alternatives, and other key issues. It instils a broader and deeper understanding of the subject matter and supports independent thinking.

Case study: This feature profiles extracts from key court judgments, which are relevant to the legal principles under discussion. Case studies demonstrate the practical relevance, meaning and application of the law in the business environment, and show how principles have been developed and applied in the courts. This feature enhances understanding of the legal principles, and supports the development of applied legal thinking.

Critical issue: This feature highlights specific criticisms, areas of controversy and differing perspectives in relation to the law just described. It may identify reform options and possible alternatives. It also supports the ability to think critically and flexibly. It assists students to understand legal issues from various perspectives, develops skills in formulating legal argument, and points to possibilities for the development of the law.

Diagrams: These provide visual overviews of some concepts in the book. This feature reinforces understanding, helps to clarify key concepts, and illustrates the interrelationship between distinct legal concepts.

Tables: These are used to distinguish content, and to assist with information management and conceptualisation.

Glossary: This contains explanations for the words and phrases that constitute the jargon, or terms of art, that are particular to the area of study covered in the book. Latin phrases and many others are explained and contextualised.

The extract from Carl Stein (page 31). SOURCE: Quote from Carl Stein with Geoff Everingham *The New Companies Act Unlocked* Cape Town: Siber Ink 2011 at 407, reprinted with the permission of Siber Ink.

Figure 3.1: Structure of the Grindrod group (page 63). SOURCE: Diagram originally from the website *http://www.grindrod.co.za/ Uploads/wheel_March_2010aW%20(2).jpg* and used with the permission of the Grindrod group.

Table 6.2: The difference between directors and managers (pages 113-14). SOURCE: Table based on the online factsheet: Institute of Directors 'The Key Differences Between Directors and Managers', with appropriate revisions to reflect the differences between company law in the UK and in South Africa, reproduced with the permission of the IoD *http://www.iod.com*.

The extract from Carl Stein (page 124). SOURCE: Quote from Carl Stein with Geoff Everingham *The New Companies Act Unlocked* Cape Town: Siber Ink 2011 at 245, reprinted with the permission of Siber Ink.

The extract from Carl Stein (page 127). SOURCE: Quote from Carl Stein with Geoff Everingham *The New Companies Act Unlocked* Cape Town: Siber Ink 2011 at 407, reprinted with the permission of Siber Ink.

The PRACTICAL ISSUE extract: Example of corporate governance statement (page 172). SOURCE: Extract from the Grindrod website *http://grindrod.investoreports.com/grindrod_iar_2012/sustainability/corporate-governance/, used with the permission of the Grindrod group.*

The PRACTICAL ISSUE extract: Strate and dematerialisation (pages 180-1). SOURCE: Extract from the website *www.strate.co.za/ aboutstrate/overview/dematerialisation.aspx,* reproduced with the permission of Strate Ltd.

The extract from Davids, Norwitz and Yuill (page 206). SOURCE: Quotes from E Davids, T Norwitz and D Yuill 'A microscopic analysis of the new merger and amalgamation provision in the Companies Act 71 of 2008' in T Mongalo (ed.) *Modern Company Law for a Competitive South African Economy* Cape Town: Juta & Co. Ltd. (2010) 337 at 343, reprinted by permission of the publisher.

The extract from Boardman (page 208). SOURCE: Quote from N Boardman 'A critical analysis of the new South African takeover laws as proposed under the Companies Act 71 of 2008' in T Mongalo (ed.) *Modern Company Law for a Competitive South African Economy* Cape Town: Juta & Co. Ltd. (2010) 306 at 314, reprinted by permission of the publisher.

The extracts from Davids, Norwitz and Yuill (pages 210-11). SOURCE: Quotes from E Davids, T Norwitz and D Yuill 'A microscopic analysis of the new merger and amalgamation provision in the Companies Act 71 of 2008' in T Mongalo (ed.) *Modern Company Law for a Competitive South African Economy* Cape Town: Juta & Co. Ltd. (2010) 337 at 344 and 345, reprinted by permission of the publisher.

The extract from Boardman (page 219, footnote 74). SOURCE: Quote from N Boardman 'A critical analysis of the new South African takeover laws as proposed under the Companies Act 71 of 2008' in T Mongalo (ed.) *Modern Company Law for a Competitive South African Economy* Cape Town: Juta & Co. Ltd. (2010) at 319, reprinted by permission of the publisher.

The PRACTICAL ISSUE extract: The market for corporate control (page 220). SOURCE: Quote from Rob Rose 'Liberty bonuses queried' *Sunday Times (Business Times)* report of 16 May 2010, p.4, reprinted with the permission of the publisher.

The PRACTICAL ISSUE extract: A cautionary announcement (page 226). SOURCE: Cautionary announcement from *http://www.fin24.com/Companies/Nedbank-issues-further-cautionary-20100930* on Sep 30 2010 15:52, but appeared originally on the I-Net Bridge website © I-Net Bridge (Pty) Ltd, reprinted with the permission of I-Net Bridge (Pty) Ltd.

The extract from Odendaal and De Jager's article (page 273). SOURCE: Quotation from EM Odendaal and H De Jager 'Regulation of the auditing profession in South Africa' (2008) 8 *The Southern African Journal of Accountability and Auditing Research (SAJAAR)* 1 © Southern African Institute of Government Auditors (SAIGA), used with the permission of SAIGA.

The PRACTICAL ISSUE extract: The IRBA (page 284). SOURCE: Extract from the IRBA website *www.irba.co.za*, reprinted with the permission of the IRBA.

The CASE STUDY: Universal partnership (page 369). SOURCE: Extract from HR Hahlo *The South African Law of Husband and Wife* 5 ed, Cape Town: Juta, 1985, reprinted with the permission of the publisher.

Chapter 1

Introduction: the Companies Act 71 of 2008

1.1   The Companies Act, 2008: a new approach

South Africa, as a unified country, has had a total of three Companies Acts. The first Companies Act was passed in 1926, the next in 1973 and the current Act, the **Companies Act 71 of 2008**, was introduced with effect from 1 May 2011.[1] It would, however, be wrong to think that there were no changes to the **1973 Act** before 2009. Virtually every year after 1973, amendments were made to the Companies Act, some of these changes being more significant than others. These amendments by and large ensured that South African company law remained in tune with changing business trends and developments. For example, the Companies Amendment Act 37 of 1999[2] allowed a company to acquire its own shares from existing shareholders in certain circumstances, thereby modifying the previous strict capital maintenance rule. Another example of amendments introduced to ensure that the Companies Act kept abreast of new developments is the Companies Amendment Act 70 of 1984. This Act inserted sections into the 1973 Act,[3] allowing a close corporation to convert into a company in certain circumstances.

Why then was it necessary to draft a new Act – the Companies Act, 2008?

CRITICAL VIEWPOINT	**Why change?**
	It could be argued that a new Companies Act was unnecessary because the 1973 Act, through amendments, kept pace with changing needs and circumstances. Many statutes are much older than the 1973 Companies Act, and yet they have not been replaced in their entirety. The Income Tax Act 58 of 1962 is an example.
	However, one must not lose sight of the significant political changes in South Africa since 1973, and that South Africa now has the benefit of a new Constitution. It is perhaps only right that all Acts in South Africa should be subject to a complete overhaul, keeping in mind the spirit, principles and the purpose of the Constitution.
	Furthermore, there have been global changes in how businesses function and operate. It is appropriate that the corporate environment in South Africa should keep pace with international developments and trends to ensure that new business initiatives and company expansions can take place in South Africa.
	Another reason for the creation of a new Act is that in recent years there has been a growing recognition of the need for higher standards of corporate governance and ethics to apply and for greater responsibility to be taken by an entity towards the society in which it operates – for the benefit not only of investors, but of all stakeholders.[4] The 1973 Act, even in its amended form, did little to recognise the interests of a broader stakeholder community. The 2008 Act gives significant rights to a variety of stakeholders, including employees, trade unions and minority shareholders.

---

1   The effective date for the Act was 1 May 2011, to allow the Department of Trade and Industry additional time to publish the Amendment Bill and Regulations for comment, as well as allowing business some time to prepare for the implementation of the Act.

2   By amending s 85 of the Companies Act, 1973.

3   Sections 29A to 29D.

4   The concept of corporate governance was first introduced into South Africa in 1994 with the publication of the King Report on Corporate Governance. This has been followed by a second and then a third King Report on Corporate Governance for South Africa. These reports produced a Code of Corporate Practices and Conduct, the latest Code being King 3.

> Furthermore, the rise in international trade and foreign investment in South Africa since 1994 has also emphasised the need to modernise company law, and to take cognisance of international laws and practices, as well as to make specific provision for foreign companies to operate in South Africa.

South Africa is not unique in its initiative to produce a new Companies Act. In 2006, the United Kingdom (UK) introduced a new Companies Act following a review of company law commissioned by the UK Department of Trade and Industry in March 1998. The mandate to those who conceptualised the UK Act was similar to that of the South African initiative – that is, to develop a simple, modern, efficient and cost-effective framework for carrying out business activity in the twenty-first century.

Significantly, given that South African company jurisprudence has been so heavily influenced by earlier UK legislation, the UK company law review found that many of the existing features of UK company law were outdated. They represented arrangements put in place in the middle of the nineteenth century and had not kept up with changes in business practice. In addition, the law review emphasised the demands flowing from globalisation of the UK economy and the need for UK company law to accord with the growing global framework for corporate regulation.

An examination of the recent changes to Australian and New Zealand company law also supports the argument that an Act, the core of which is almost a hundred years old, is no longer suitable for an economy that must meet the challenges of global competition.

There has also been recent recognition from the courts that there is a need for the adoption of a new approach in the interpretation and application of company law in South Africa. As an example of this, the court in *Nedbank Ltd v Bestvest 153 (Pty) Ltd*[5] stated that a fresh approach must be adopted when assessing the affairs of 'Corporate South Africa'.

> **The Legislature has pertinently charged the Courts with the duty to interpret the Act in such a way that, firstly, the founding values of the Constitution are respected and advanced, and, secondly so that the spirit and purpose of the Act are given effect to. Fundamental to the Act is the promotion and stimulation of the country's economy through, inter alia, the use of the company as a vehicle to achieve economic and social well-being. This must be done efficiently and in accordance with acceptable levels of corporate stewardship, all the while, balancing the rights and obligations of shareholders and directors in the company, its employees and any outside parties with which a company ordinarily interacts in the course of its business …. Our company law has for many decades closely tracked the English system and has often taken its lead from the relevant English Companies Acts and the judicial pronouncements thereon. The Act now encourages our Courts to look further afield and to have regard, in appropriate circumstances, to other corporate law jurisdictions, be they American, European, Asian or African, in interpreting the Act.[6]**

---

5   2012 (5) SA 497 (WCC).
6   At paras. [20] and [26].

Section 7 of the Companies Act, 2008 sets out the purpose of the Act.[7] This purpose expresses a clear desire to encourage business activity and entrepreneurship by providing a flexible regulatory environment that eases the regulatory burdens on those who wish to take advantage of incorporation. At the same time, it recognises a need for sufficient regulation to make a company and its office bearers accountable to relevant stakeholders. In other words, there is an emphasis on stimulating growth, business activity and entrepreneurship, while achieving a balance between no regulation and over-regulation. These issues received little or no attention under the Companies Act, 1973.

In terms of the 2008 Act, there is also clearly a desire to make the formation of a company a right of all persons – not a privilege – and to do away with unnecessary hurdles that impede growth and entrepreneurship. The 1973 Act did little to simplify the formation and administration of the different types of company.

The 2008 Act also clearly desires a new procedure to ensure, as far as possible, the rescue of failing companies. The judicial management provisions of the 1973 Act were widely regarded as outdated and ineffective. These have now been replaced with business rescue provisions. The principles of liquidity and solvency are also entrenched in the 2008 Act, which largely removes the capital maintenance concept on which the 1973 Act was originally based.

A whole rethink on company law has accordingly taken place in South Africa. Rather than simply amend and build on the old, it was thought that a totally new approach was necessary. The rewriting of a Companies Act in its entirety has also facilitated input and comment from business and society at large,[8] and allowed free expression of new ideas and concepts, as well as a critical evaluation of existing provisions.

CASE STUDY	Courts adapting to the new approach of the 2008 Act

In *Welman v Marcelle Props 193 CC*,[9] the issue for determination was whether the development and implementation of business rescue proceedings would maximise the likelihood of a close corporation's continued existence on a solvent basis, thereby resulting in a better return for creditors or members than would be the case in liquidation proceedings. The court held that to:

> move away from the mind-set of the earlier regime of preferring liquidation to judicial management, and to promote compliance with the Bill of Rights as provided for in the Constitution, and to achieve the purposes of the Act as encapsulated in section 7 of the Act, it is necessary to determine the case made out by the applicant in this application ... [O]ne of the purposes of the Act as encapsulated in section 7, is to provide for the efficient rescue and recovery of the financially distressed (companies) and close corporations in a manner that balances the rights and interests of all the relevant stakeholders and to provide a practicable and effective environment for the efficient regulation of (companies) and close corporations.

Accordingly, the court held that courts faced with rescue applications must bear in mind that there are other stakeholders whose interests must be taken into account and respected. The court stated that, if it granted the application for business rescue

---

7 For a discussion of s 7, see para. 1.4.1 below.
8 See para. 1.3.2 below for a discussion of the National Economic Development and Labour Council (NEDLAC) and its input.
9 2012 JDR 0408 (GSJ); [2012] ZAGPJHC 32.

proceedings in this case, it 'would be to subvert the purposes of the Act and disregard the interest of other stakeholders'.

This is certainly a new approach and illustrates the changes brought about by the new Companies Act in South Africa.

1.2   The Close Corporations Act, 1984

In contrast to relatively minor changes brought about by the Companies Act, 1973, there was an innovative and important legislative development in 1984: the enactment of the Close Corporations Act 69 of 1984. This legislation was introduced alongside the Companies Act, 1973, and created a new form of business enterprise, being the close corporation. The Close Corporations Act was specifically designed to facilitate the incorporation of smaller business entities. The key principle underlying the Act was the incorporation of a simple and inexpensive entity. The **close corporation** was restricted to a membership of 10 natural persons. Corporate membership was excluded to prevent large companies from using the close corporation as a subsidiary vehicle. However, there was no restriction on the size of business being conducted or on turnover of the close corporation, and similarly no restriction on the number of employees or on the nature of business activities. The Close Corporations Act tried to simplify conducting business through an incorporated entity and to do away with complicated legal concepts that applied to companies – such as the *ultra vires* doctrine and the capital maintenance concept.

In terms of the Companies Act, 2008, close corporations that were in existence on the date that the 2008 Act became effective (1 May 2011) are allowed to continue to exist indefinitely, and there is no phasing out of the concept of the close corporation. However, no new close corporations may be formed after the effective date. The Close Corporations Act will continue to apply to close corporations, and certain provisions of the Companies Act, 2008 are also specifically made applicable to close corporations, such as the business rescue provisions.

CASE STUDY	**The Close Corporations Act**
	An example of the simplicity aimed at by the Close Corporations Act is found in the reported case of *J & K Timbers (Pty) Ltd v G L & S Furniture Enterprises CC t/a Tegs Timbers*.[10] In that case, the court made it clear that the intention of the legislature in enacting s 54 of the Close Corporations Act was that every member of a close corporation, merely as a member, should be an agent of the corporation for all purposes. In other words, any member (even a member who had the smallest or a minority interest in the close corporation) can act on behalf of a close corporation and can enter into a binding contract on behalf of that close corporation without the consent of other members. Therefore, third parties who deal with a member of a close corporation will know that any contract entered into between them and the member who is acting on behalf of a close corporation cannot be set aside by other members on the grounds that the contracting member had no authority to bind the corporation.

---

10   2005 (3) SA 223 (N).

1.3   Background to the 2008 Act

A number of different processes, forums, discussions and concerned interested parties played important roles in the lead-up to the drafting of the 2008 Act. These include a government policy paper published in 2004, formal agreements reached in the National Economic Development and Labour Council and pressure from the trade union movement to expand the rights in company law of a broad range of stakeholders.

1.3.1   The Department of Trade and Industry's policy paper of 2004: Guidelines for Corporate Law Reform

In 2004, the Department of Trade and Industry (dti) published a policy paper entitled *South African Company Law for the 21st Century: Guidelines for Corporate Law Reform*.[11] The paper promised significant development and reform of company law, while facilitating a predictable and consistent regulatory environment. The policy paper proposed that company legislation should promote both the competitiveness and development of the South African economy by encouraging entrepreneurship and enterprise development. Borrowing from the spirit of the close corporation, the paper promised a law in which the procedures for forming companies should be simplified and the costs associated with these formalities reduced significantly.

The policy document also committed the proposed new legislation to the promotion of innovation and investment in South African markets and companies by providing for flexibility in the design and organisation of companies and for a more predictable and effective regulatory environment. It argued that the law must promote efficiency of companies and their management, transparency and high standards of corporate governance.

While the policy document was concerned to reform corporate law, it gave the assurance that it would not want unreasonably to jettison the comprehensive body of company law that had been built up over a century. In other words, the common-law principles of company law that had been built up over many years would continue to apply, to the extent that they did not contradict specific provisions of the Companies Act, 2008. However, the latter did abolish certain parts of the common law, such as the common-law derivative action. Section 165 of the 2008 Act now provides for a statutory derivative action. The 2008 Act does not purport to codify company law in its entirety. The dti emphasised that the primary objective of the review was to ensure new legislation that would be appropriate to the legal, economic and social context of South Africa as a constitutional democracy and an open economy. The reform process then moved from the policy document to negotiations between government, business and labour at the National Economic Development and Labour Council (NEDLAC).

1.3.2   The National Economic Development and Labour Council (NEDLAC)

NEDLAC is the National Economic Development and Labour Council. It was set up to provide a forum for organised business and organised labour to meet with government at a national level to reach consensus on issues of social and economic policy. Manifestly, company law falls within this scope.

Five key objectives for corporate law reform in South Africa were agreed at NEDLAC, as illustrated in Table 1.1.

---

11   Published in *Government Gazette* 26493, General Notice 1183 dated 23 June 2004.

Table 1.1 *Corporate law reform objectives agreed at NEDLAC*

Objectives[12]	Explanation
1. *Simplification*: simplification of the procedures for forming companies and a reduction in the costs of company formation and maintenance	1. The law should provide for a company structure reflecting the characteristics of a close corporation as one of the available options. 2. The law should establish a simple and easily maintained regime for non-profit companies. 3. Cooperatives and partnerships should not be addressed in the reformed company law.
2. *Flexibility*: providing for flexibility in the design and organisation of companies	1. Company law should provide for 'an appropriate diversity of corporate structures'. 2. The distinction between listed and unlisted companies should be retained.
3. *Corporate efficiency*: promoting the efficiency of companies and their management	1. Company law should shift from a capital maintenance regime based on par value to one based on solvency and liquidity. 2. There should be clarification of board structures and director responsibilities, duties and liabilities. 3. There should be a remedy to avoid locking minority shareholders into inefficient companies. 4. The mergers-and-takeovers regime should be reformed so that the law facilitates the creation of business combinations. 5. The judicial management system for dealing with failing companies should be replaced by a more effective business rescue system.
4. *Transparency*: encouraging transparency and high standards of corporate governance	1. Company law should ensure the proper recognition of director accountability, and appropriate participation of other stakeholders. 2. Public announcements, information and prospectuses should be subject to similar standards for truth and accuracy. 3. The law should protect shareholder rights, advance shareholder activism, and provide enhanced protection for minority shareholders. 4. Minimum accounting standards should be required for annual reports.
5. *Predictable regulations*: company law should be compatible and harmonious with best-practice jurisdictions internationally	1. Company law sanctions should be decriminalised where possible. 2. Company law should remove or reduce opportunities for regulatory arbitrage. 3. Company law should be enforced through appropriate bodies and mechanisms, either existing or newly introduced. 4. Company law should strike a careful balance between adequate disclosure (in the interest of transparency) and over-regulation.

CRITICAL VIEWPOINT

Corporate efficiency: capital maintenance versus solvency and liquidity

Under the corporate efficiency objective, it is stated that company law should shift from the rigid framework of the capital maintenance regime to one based on solvency and liquidity. The **capital maintenance** law was established over a hundred years ago. The idea behind this rule is that creditors can look to a company's share capital funds for

---

12   Objectives as explained by the dti on 10 May 2007 to Parliament's Portfolio Committee on Trade and Industry. See *www.pmg.org.za/report/20070620-corporate-law-reform-briefing-department-trade-and-industry.*

payment and that creditors will be prejudiced if a company pays out some of its funds by returning share capital to its members. Share capital is seen on this basis as a permanent fund intended for payment of creditors and thus cannot be reduced nor returned to shareholders, except where legislation or common law permits. The point was well set out in the judgment in *Cohen NO v Segal*:[13]

> Whatever has been paid by a member cannot be returned to him and no part of the corpus of the company can be returned to a member so as to take away from the fund to which the creditors have a right to look as that out of which they are to be paid. The capital may be spent or lost in carrying on the business of the company, but cannot be reduced except in the manner and with the safeguards provided by the statute.

The capital maintenance rule prohibited the following:
1. A company could not buy back its own shares from existing shareholders.
2. A company could not declare dividends out of capital.
3. A company could not provide financial assistance for purchase of its own shares.

The Companies Act, 2008 has embraced the principles of **solvency and liquidity**, thus abandoning the strict capital maintenance rule, and, as will appear from ss 44 to 48 of the Act, it is against the policy of the Act that any portion of the capital should be returned to the shareholders without the statutory conditions of solvency and liquidity being met.

1.3.3   Corporate law reform and the stakeholder question

In any corporate law reform programme, one of the key questions to be asked is: for whose benefit does a company exist? There are three approaches to this question:

1. The **traditional shareholder-oriented model (or 'classic' model)** was prevalent in the United Kingdom and thus also in the 1973 Act in South Africa. In this model, only the interests of shareholders are considered as the focus of corporate activity. Other stakeholders, including employees, are thus excluded.
2. The **enlightened shareholder value approach** indicates that directors should have regard, where appropriate, for the need to ensure productive relationships with a range of interested parties – often termed 'stakeholders' – and have regard to the longer term, but with shareholders' interests retaining primacy. In other words, directors can take into account the interests of other stakeholders, such as the interests and rights of employees, but only if it ultimately promotes the success of the company for the benefit of the shareholders.
3. The **pluralist approach** asserts that cooperative and productive relationships will only be optimised where directors are permitted (or required by law) to balance shareholders' interests with those of others committed to the company. The adoption of a pluralist theory therefore invariably necessitates a dramatic change to the legal concept of 'interests of the company' from being identified solely with shareholders to the inclusion of other stakeholders, including employees, customers, creditors, and the community in which the enterprise is located. The pluralist approach therefore takes into account

---

13   1970 (3) SA 702 (W).

the interests of all stakeholders, and a company has to balance the interests of all stakeholders, and to prefer the interests of one stakeholder above those of another only where it is in the best interests of the general body of stakeholders to do so.[14]

The South African policy document went through a process of analysis. The authors of the policy document were under some pressure, particularly from the trade union movement, to adopt a pluralist model, thereby increasing the scope of key stakeholders in whose direct interests a company operates.

CONTEXTUAL	COSATU's input
ISSUE	On Monday, 18 October 2004, the Congress of South African Trade Unions (COSATU) made representations on the Corporate Law Reform Guidelines as contained in the policy document, and presented them to the Corporate Law Reform Task team at NEDLAC.
	COSATU stated that labour has a very specific interest in ensuring good corporate governance, since pension funds are major shareholders of listed companies in South Africa. COSATU stated in its representations that there is a 'need for stronger shareholder activism and tighter control of the board of directors' powers and functions'. It also made the point that 'given the huge inequalities and the exclusive nature of growth in South Africa, we should ascertain the role of other stakeholders, such as communities, labour, consumers and the public at large'.

Ultimately, the policy document preferred the enlightened shareholder value approach as a guide to directors when they consider how to act in the best interests of the company. The enlightened shareholder value approach suggests that the term 'company' (particularly when used in the phrase 'acting in the interests of the company') is to be associated primarily with the shareholders, with the possibility of others being included if their interests promote the interests of shareholders.

The adoption in the Companies Act, 2008 of the enlightened shareholder value approach ensures that directors are obliged to promote the success of the company in the collective best interests of shareholders. This would include, as the circumstances require, the company's need to foster relationships with its employees, customers and suppliers. Significantly, the UK went further, in that its policy document recommended the inclusion of stakeholders in the proposed enlightened shareholder value codification of directors' duties, as well as additional information requirements for companies in respect of stakeholders. On this basis, directors must take account of the long- as well as the short-term consequences of their actions, which may include the need to take account of employee relationships, the local community and the physical environment, in deciding how the interests of the shareholders are most effectively advanced.

Significantly, the South African counterpart has stopped short of extending directors' duties in that direction, although there are significant parts of the new Act that have taken express account of the possible need for protection of larger groups of stakeholders, other than shareholders.[15]

---

14 See C Stein *The New Companies Act Unlocked* (2011), chapter 30 and refer also to p.8.
15 See para. 1.7 below.

| **PRACTICAL** | **Stakeholders and the enlightened shareholder value approach** |
| **ISSUE** | Section 20(4) of the 2008 Act is an example of the adoption of the enlightened shareholder value approach. It provides that shareholders, directors, prescribed officers or a trade union representing employees may take proceedings to restrain a company from doing anything inconsistent with the Act. It is clear that a trade union representing employees now has rights in terms of the Act, and can play an important part in the governance of companies. |

1.3.4   The enlightened shareholder approach in the 2008 Act

The 2008 Act gives statutory effect to the enlightened shareholder approach and grants stakeholders significant rights that were not enjoyed under the 1973 Act. In particular, it gives many remedies and rights to employees (and to trade unions representing employees) and to minority shareholders.[16] For example, in the case of employees, special rights and preferences are granted in the event of business rescue.[17] Employees' representatives (that is, trade unions) may also apply for an order declaring a director delinquent or under probation.[18] Such employee representatives may also apply to court to restrain a company from doing anything inconsistent with the Act.[19] And employees may lodge complaints with the Commission or Takeover Regulation Panel.[20] There are a host of other sections granting rights and remedies to employees and trade unions.[21] Rights afforded to minority shareholders are provided for in a number of sections such as the granting of relief from oppressive or prejudicial conduct,[22] the new derivative action,[23] and the dissenting shareholders' appraisal rights.[24]

As far as directors are concerned, many provisions of the 2008 Act also ensure that 'it is not business as usual' for directors. There is a fundamental shift towards holding directors statutorily responsible and accountable. Apart from the fact that the common law duties (the fiduciary duty and the duty of care, diligence and skill)[25] are now specifically provided for in the Act, there are many provisions that ensure compliance with the provisions of the Act by making directors personally liable for losses, damages and costs of the company under a variety of circumstances.[26] More worrying for directors and others involved in company matters is the catch-all provision of s 218(2), a section that appears reasonable but which could have significant consequences leading to the lifting of the corporate veil and the personal liability of directors and others. Section 218(2) reads as follows: 'Any person who contravenes any provision of this Act is liable to any other person for any loss or damage suffered by that person as a result of that contravention.'

Section 218(2) could have severe financial repercussions for directors because it is wide enough to include a monetary claim by anyone against a director personally if that director

---

16 See C Stein *The New Companies Act Unlocked* (2011), chapter 30 and see also pp. 386–7.
17 See ss 131 and 136 for examples. (Business rescue is discussed in chapter 12 of this book.)
18 See s 162 (discussed in para. 14.2.1 below).
19 See s 20(4) (see practical issue in para. 1.3.3 above).
20 See s 168(1) (and para. 14.5.1.3 below).
21 Curiously, the Act is not consistent: trade unions are sometimes given rights that employees do not have, such as the right to apply for the delinquency or probation of a director.
22 See s 163(1) (and para. 14.3.1 below).
23 See s 165 (discussed in chapter 14 of this book and para. 14.2.2 in particular).
24 See s 164(2) (and para. 14.3.2 below).
25 See s 76 (and para. 6.7 below).
26 See s 77 (and para. 6.3.4.1 below).

contravened any provision of the Act and thereby caused that person to suffer monetary loss.[27] It should also be noted that s 218(2) will not only apply to directors but to 'any person' who fails to comply with the provisions of the Act.

1.4   Purpose and interpretation of the 2008 Act

The purposes of the 2008 Act are set out in s 7 and are the framework to be used for the interpretation of the Act as a whole. The manner in which the Act is to be interpreted is governed by s 5.

1.4.1   The purposes of the 2008 Act (s 7)

Section 7 sets out an impressive list of legislative purposes. The section reads as follows:

> The purposes of this Act are to–
> (*a*)   promote compliance with the Bill of Rights as provided for in the Constitution, in the application of company law;
> (*b*)   promote the development of the South African economy by–
>   (i)   encouraging entrepreneurship and enterprise efficiency;
>   (ii)   creating flexibility and simplicity in the formation and maintenance of companies; and
>   (iii)   encouraging transparency and high standards of corporate governance as appropriate, given the significant role of enterprises within the social and economic life of the nation;
> (*c*)   promote innovation and investment in South African markets;
> (*d*)   re-affirm the concept of the company as a means of achieving economic and social benefits;
> (*e*)   continue to provide for the creation and use of companies, in a manner that enhances the economic welfare of South Africa as a partner within the global economy;
> (*f*)   promote the development of companies within all sectors of the economy, and encourage active participation in economic organisation, management and productivity;
> (*g*)   create optimum conditions for aggregation of capital for productive purposes, and for the investment of that capital in enterprises and the spreading of economic risk;
> (*h*)   provide for the formation, operation and accountability of non-profit companies in a manner designed to promote, support and enhance the capacity of such companies to perform their functions;
> (*i*)   balance the rights and obligations of shareholders and directors within companies;
> (*j*)   encourage the efficient and responsible management of companies;
> (*k*)   provide for the efficient rescue and recovery of financially distressed companies in a manner that balances the rights and interests of all relevant stakeholders; and
> (*l*)   provide a predictable and effective environment for the efficient regulation of companies.

---

27   See C Stein *The New Companies Act Unlocked* (2011) at 407.

The purposes of the Companies Act, 2008 can be summarised as aiming to:
- promote development;
- encourage entrepreneurship;
- encourage enterprise efficiency;
- create flexibility and simplicity;
- encourage transparency;
- encourage high standards of corporate governance;
- promote innovation;
- promote investment;
- achieve economic and social benefits;
- enhance economic welfare;
- encourage productivity;
- balance the rights and obligations of shareholders and directors;
- encourage efficient and responsible management;
- provide for the efficient rescue and recovery of companies; and
- balance the rights and interests of all relevant stakeholders in rescues.

It is clear that the drafters of the Companies Act, 2008 followed the dti policy document and the NEDLAC agreement. The core of s 7 captures the balance that the new Act seeks to achieve – that is, between, on the one hand, creating a flexible regulatory environment that eases the burdens on entrepreneurs and others who wish to take advantage of incorporation (thereby encouraging business activity), and on the other hand, regulation that holds the corporation and its office bearers accountable to the interest bearers they are directed to serve.

1.4.2   Interpretation of the 2008 Act (s 5 read with s 7)

Section 5 contains a general interpretation clause. Of particular importance is the injunction that the Act must be interpreted and applied in a manner that gives effect to the purposes of the Act (as set out in s 7). In short, courts must interpret the language of the statute to promote the purpose of the legislation. Section 6 reinforces this objective. The key section is s 6(1), which provides as follows:

> **A court, on application by the Commission or Panel, may declare any agreement, transaction, arrangement, resolution or provision of a company's Memorandum of Incorporation or rules–**
>
> *(a)* **to be primarily or substantially intended to defeat or reduce the effect of a prohibition or requirement established by or in terms of an unalterable provision of this Act; and**
>
> *(b)* **void to the extent that it defeats or reduces the effect of a prohibition or requirement established by or in terms of an unalterable provision of this Act.**

Lawyers are often clever in the way they draft agreements. They may establish corporate structures to avoid legal prohibitions and then claim that the legal forms of the agreements and structures comply with the legal form required by the 2008 Act even if, read together, the agreements or structures achieve in substance an opposite result. In terms of the 2008 Act, a court is thus empowered to examine the substance of an arrangement. In its form, an arrangement may well not breach a legislative prohibition but when its substance is examined, it may become clear that the arrangement has been set up to circumvent a legislative prohibition.

CASE STUDY

Interpreting 'registered office' under the 2008 Act

In *Sibakhulu Construction (Pty) Ltd v Wedgewood Village Golf and Country Estate (Pty) Ltd*,[28] the court emphasised that questions of interpretation of the 2008 Act must be undertaken with the provisions of ss 5 and 7 in mind. The court in this case had to determine what was meant by 'registered office' (as used in s 23 of the 2008 Act) because a company resides at its 'registered office', and where a company resides will determine which division of the high court has jurisdiction in respect of a legal matter involving that company.

Section 23(3) of the 2008 Act provides that every company must maintain at least one office in South Africa and it must register the address of its office with the Commission. The court acknowledged that, in practice, a company's registered office under the 1973 Act was often an address chosen for convenience rather than an office of the company itself in the ordinary sense; frequently, the registered office of a company was, for example, that of the company's auditors.

The court held that in determining the effect of s 23 on the question of a court's jurisdiction it had to take into account the provisions of s 7*(k)* and *(l)*, which provide as follows:

> The purposes of this Act are to ... *(k)* provide for the efficient rescue and recovery of financially distressed companies, in a manner that balances the rights and interests of all relevant stakeholders; and *(l)* provide a predictable and effective environment for the efficient regulation of companies.

The court held that:

> it would give effect to the purposes set out in s 7*(k)* and *(l)* to interpret s 23 of the Act to the effect that a company can reside only at the place of its registered office (which must also be the place of its only or principal office). The result would be that in respect of every company there would be only a single court in South Africa with jurisdiction in respect of winding-up and business rescue matters ....

The court therefore found that a company can only reside in one place and a:

> material distinction between a 'registered office' under the 2008 Act and its predecessors ... is that under the current Act the registered office must be the company's only office, alternatively, if it has more than one office, its 'principal office'.

The court therefore concluded that whilst the 1973 Act expressly acknowledged the possibility of a distinction between a company's registered office and its 'main place of business', the 2008 Act requires the registered office and the principal place of business for jurisdictional purposes to be at one and the same address.

---

28 2013 (1) SA 191 (WCC).

1.5   Flexibility and the importance of a company's Memorandum of Incorporation

The founding document of a company in terms of the Companies Act, 2008 is the company's **Memorandum of Incorporation (MOI)**. It replaces both the Memorandum and the Articles of Association that were required for the formation of a company in terms of the 1973 Act.

An important feature of the 2008 Act is its emphasis on flexibility. It is a company's MOI that provides much of this flexibility. Note that a single Companies Act applies to all companies – whether they be private, public, listed, unlisted or other companies. What makes companies different from each other? It is the contents of a company's MOI that:

- distinguish one company from another;
- determine whether it is a public, private or other type of company;
- determine the rights of shareholders and the duties of directors; and
- determine what body has power in a company in respect of any transaction – whether the board is all-powerful, or whether the approval of shareholders or other stakeholders must first be obtained before certain transactions can take place.

The contents of a company's MOI is accordingly critical in determining the nature of the company, and the rights and duties of stakeholders. Those wishing to make use of the company form are given great flexibility when it comes to the contents and provisions of a company's MOI.

1.6   Structure of the 2008 Act

The Companies Act, 2008 has nine chapters and five schedules, and is structured as follows:

Table 1.2 Structure of the Companies Act, 2008

Chapter number	Content
1	Interpretation, purpose and application
2	Formation, administration and dissolution of companies
3	Enhanced accountability and transparency
4	Public offerings of company securities
5	Fundamental transactions, takeovers and offers
6	Business rescue and compromise with creditors
7	Remedies and enforcement
8	Regulatory agencies and administration of Act
9	Offences, miscellaneous matters and general provisions

The five schedules are as follows:

Schedule number	Content
1	Provisions concerning non-profit companies
2	Conversion of close corporations to companies
3	Amendment of laws
4	Legislation to be enforced by commission
5	Transitional arrangements

Relevant provisions of the Act are discussed in more depth elsewhere in this book. However, a brief overview of the contents of the Act is useful in the introductory stages of this subject.

1.6.1   Chapter 1: Interpretation, purpose and application (ss 1 to 10)

Section 1 is very important, since it defines key words used in the Act. Whenever a word is used in the body of the Act, it should be established whether that word has been defined in s 1. For example, when determining what is meant by an 'ordinary' or 'special' resolution of shareholders,[29] the definitions in s 1 become most important. Sections 2 to 4 similarly define certain important expressions used in the Act: s 2 ('related and inter-related persons', and 'control'), s 3 ('subsidiary relationships') and s 4 ('solvency and liquidity test').

Section 5 contains a general interpretation clause. Of particular importance is the injunction that the Act must be interpreted and applied in a manner that gives effect to the purposes of the Act (as set out in s 7).[30] In short, courts must interpret the language of the statute to promote the purpose of the legislation. Section 6 reinforces this objective. The key provision is s 6(1), which states:

> A court, on application ... may declare any agreement, transaction, arrangement, resolution or provision of a company's Memorandum of Incorporation or rules–
>
> (*a*)   to be primarily or substantially intended to defeat or reduce the effect of a prohibition or requirement established by or in terms of an unalterable provision of this Act; and
>
> (*b*)   void to the extent that it defeats or reduces the effect of a prohibition or requirement established by or in terms of an unalterable provision of this Act.

Lawyers often attempt to avoid legal prohibitions in the way they draft agreements and establish corporate structures. They then claim that the legal form of the agreements and structures complies with the legal form required by the 2008 Act – even if, when read together, the agreements or structures achieve, in substance, an opposite result. In terms of the 2008 Act, a court is empowered to examine the substance of an arrangement. In its form, it may not breach a legislative prohibition, but upon examination, it may become clear that the arrangement has been set up to circumvent a legislative prohibition. The court is then entitled to declare the arrangement void.

---

29   See chapter 5 of this book for a discussion of these concepts.
30   See para. 1.4.1 above.

1.6.2   Chapter 2: Formation, administration and dissolution of companies (ss 11 to 83)

Chapter 2 of the Act is a comprehensive and important chapter providing for a number of matters, including the following:
- the incorporation of a company (ss 11 to 21);
- the prohibition of reckless, grossly negligent or fraudulent trading (s22);
- the lifting of the corporate veil (s 20);
- financial statement requirements and record-keeping (ss 24 to 31);
- the capitalisation of profit companies, shares and securities (ss 35 to 56);
- the governance of companies, such as the holding of shareholders' meetings and the duties and liabilities of directors (ss 57 to 78); and
- the winding-up and deregistration of companies (ss 79 to 83).

1.6.3   Chapter 3: Enhanced accountability and transparency requirements (ss 84 to 94)

Public companies and state-owned companies are required to:
- appoint a company secretary;
- appoint an auditor; and
- have an audit committee.

Chapter 3 of the Act deals with these enhanced requirements.

1.6.4   Chapter 4: Public offerings of company securities (ss 95 to 111)

Chapter 4 of the Act deals with offers of shares to the public, and deals with matters such as the contents and form of a prospectus (ss 100 to 106) and the allotment of shares (ss 107 to 111).

1.6.5   Chapter 5: Fundamental transactions, takeovers and offers (ss 112 to 127)

Chapter 5 of the Act deals with so-called fundamental transactions, including the disposal of all or a great part of the assets of a company (s 112) and amalgamations, mergers and takeovers.

1.6.6   Chapter 6: Business rescue and compromise with creditors (ss 128 to 155)

One of the features introduced by the 2008 Act is the concept of **business rescue**. Chapter 6 of the Act has detailed provisions aimed at rescuing those companies that, although financially distressed, are possibly capable of being rescued in accordance with a business plan developed by a business rescue practitioner. The Chapter determines how an application to initiate business rescue must be made and highlights the rights of so-called 'affected persons'.

The business rescue provisions are a further example of the enlightened shareholder value approach of the 2008 Act since it is not only directors and shareholders who can initiate business rescue proceedings but also creditors, employees or trade unions representing employees. The purpose of business rescue proceedings is to put in place a process that could avoid the liquidation of a financially troubled company, thereby avoiding the consequences of a liquidation, such as unemployment and retrenchments.

1.6.7   Chapter 7: Remedies and enforcement (ss 156 to 184)

An important feature of the 2008 Companies Act is that disputes and the enforcement of rights do not have to take place in a high court. The Act contains provisions allowing for **alternative dispute resolution (ADR)**. In addition to providing for ADR (ss 166 to 167), Chapter 7 of the Act gives powers for the conduct of investigations and inspections (ss 176 to 179), and the establishment of a Companies Tribunal (ss 180 to 184). The Act to a large extent also decriminalises company law by providing for the issue of compliance notices by the Commission (s 171) as well as for other mechanisms that allow stakeholders to enforce their rights, such as a new derivative action (s 165), and relief from oppressive conduct (s 164).

1.6.8   Chapter 8: Regulatory agencies and administration of the Act (ss 185 to 212)

The 2008 Act provides for four institutions as follows:
1. The **Companies and Intellectual Property Commission** (ss 185 to 192): the main purpose of the Commission is to register companies and intellectual property rights, and to keep details of registered companies. Its function is also to ensure that companies and directors comply with the provisions of the Companies Act.
2. The **Companies Tribunal** (ss 193 to 195): the Tribunal is established inter alia to adjudicate on disputes that may arise between the Commission and companies, and it is also part of the alternative dispute resolution mechanism introduced by the 2008 Act.
3. The **Takeover Regulation Panel** (ss 196 to 202): the Panel oversees so-called affected transactions[31] and ensures that transactions are carried out in accordance with prescribed rules and procedures.
4. The **Financial Reporting Standards Council** (ss 203 to 204): the Council recommends appropriate reporting standards for different types of company.[32]

1.6.9   Chapter 9: Offences and general matters (ss 213 to 225)

Chapter 9 deals with a number of issues such as offences (for example, false statements or reckless trading), penalties, the power to make regulations, and transitional arrangements.

1.7   Key concepts and features of the 2008 Act

Some of the more fundamental issues arising from the provisions of the Companies Act, 2008 are listed below.
- The 2008 Act recognises the right of any person to form a company.
- There are minimal requirements for the act of incorporation.
- The sole document that governs the affairs of a company is the Memorandum of Incorporation (MOI). As highlighted in paragraph 1.5 above, a company's MOI is a flexible document and determines the nature of a company and the rights, powers and duties of stakeholders.
- The MOI must meet certain core requirements. These core requirements are provisions of the Companies Act that apply to all companies and cannot be changed in a company's MOI – they are known as the unalterable provisions of the Act. Thus, for example, all

---

31   Affected transactions are discussed in chapter 10 of this book.
32   See chapter 7 of this book for a discussion of differential reporting and annual financial statements.

companies must prepare annual financial statements. Beyond a minimum compulsory threshold, all issues and matters affecting a company and its stakeholders are default positions that can be altered to meet the needs and interests of stakeholders. These are known as the alterable provisions of the Act. For example, there is great flexibility when it comes to allocating rights to shares, and an MOI can vary the rights of shareholders in such matters as the right to receive dividends and to vote. However, every provision in the MOI must be consistent with the 2008 Act, unless the Act expressly allows a deviation. In other words, a company cannot contract out of the Act.

- In keeping with the principle of flexibility and simplicity, the Act has tried to provide as easy a regulatory system as possible for all companies. However, greater burdens of regulation fall upon state-owned companies, public companies, and certain private companies that have some public impact, (based on turnover, the size of their workforce and nature and extent of their activities). In other words, companies whose activities have a wider social and economic impact on the public are subject to greater regulation than companies whose activities do not have such impact. In practice, this means, for example, that not all companies will require an audit, and some companies will require neither an audit nor an independent review of their financial statements.[33] The Act also embraces the concept of differential reporting in that certain companies that have an impact on society at large (such as public companies) are required to prepare financial statements in accordance with International Financial Reporting Standards (IFRS), whereas other companies (such as owner-managed private companies) have far less stringent reporting requirements.

- The Act focuses not on the capital maintenance concept but on the principles of solvency and liquidity. Thus, for example, before a company can declare a dividend, or buy back its shares, the directors must apply the solvency and liquidity test. They must be satisfied that after the transaction has taken place, a company's assets will exceed its liabilities, and that the company will be able to pay its debts in the normal course of business for the next 12 months. The Act specifies what is meant by solvency and liquidity.

- The 2008 Act adopts the enlightened shareholder value approach. It tries to provide maximum protection of shareholders together with an increased emphasis on minority shareholder protection and the rights of other stakeholders, such as employees and their representatives. The Act extends the possibility of legal protection to other stakeholders even in circumstances where their interests may be subordinate to those of the shareholders. Thus, the Act provides for extended standing. This means that the right to approach a court (or any of the regulatory bodies established under the Act) for relief is not restricted to shareholders. Other interested parties may approach the court for relief in circumstances where their legally recognised interest or the interest of their members has been affected by the decision of the company.

- The Act introduces business rescue provisions that are aimed at rescuing financially distressed companies, rather than merely liquidating such ailing companies. Another example of the enlightened shareholder value approach is found in these provisions. The 2008 Act provides an opportunity for employees or their trade unions to make a business rescue initiative in circumstances where their proposal might be the only viable option available to rescue the company. In this way, the Act yet again extends its concerns beyond the traditional scope of shareholders.

---

33   See para. 13.2 below for a fuller discussion.

- Read as a whole, the 2008 Act promotes the objective that there should not be an over-regulation of company business. The Act grants directors the legal authority to run companies as they deem fit, provided that they act within the legislative framework. In other words, the Act tries to ensure that it is the board of directors, duly appointed, who run the business rather than regulators and judges, who are never best placed to balance the interests of shareholders, the firm and the larger society within the context of running a business.
- The regulatory provisions include a **partial codification** of the duties of directors. This draws on existing jurisprudence (from the common law) to set out the nature of the fiduciary duty of directors, as well as the duty to exercise reasonable care. The principle of accountability of directors is extended by means of a provision that empowers a court to declare a director who fails to perform in terms of the law to be delinquent, or to be placed on probation, where the actions do not justify an immediate declaration of delinquency.
- The sanctions imposed under the 2008 Act are **decriminalised** wherever possible. This means, for example, that the Act seeks to ensure compliance with its provisions, not by sending delinquent directors to jail, but by providing that they will be personally liable for losses incurred by the company in certain circumstances. While certain forms of conduct continue to carry a criminal sanction – such as falsification of records, publication of untrue or misleading statements and refusal to respond to a summons – the Act has largely moved from criminal to administrative remedies. An example of the use of administrative remedies to secure compliance with the Act is found in the provisions dealing with complaints that may be brought by any person whose rights under the Act or the MOI may have been infringed. The complaint may be lodged with the relevant regulator – that is, with the Companies and Intellectual Property Commission or the Takeover Regulation Panel. Following an investigation into a complaint, the Commission or Panel may:
  - end the matter;
  - urge the parties to attempt voluntary alternative resolution of their dispute;
  - advise the complainant of any right they may have to seek a remedy in court;
  - commence proceedings in a court on behalf of a complainant, if the complainant so requests;
  - refer the matter to another regulator, if there is a possibility that the matter falls within their jurisdiction; or
  - issue a compliance notice, but only in respect of a matter for which the complainant does not otherwise have a remedy in a court.
- The Act prohibits reckless, grossly negligent and fraudulent trading.
- The Act provides that if there has been an unconscionable abuse of the juristic personality of the company as a separate entity, there can be a 'lifting of the corporate veil' and those responsible for this abuse cannot be protected by the company form and can be held responsible and liable for their actions.
- All companies formed in terms of the earlier company law legislation are deemed to have been formed in terms of the Companies Act, 2008. In other words, the 1973 Act largely becomes irrelevant and a company's Memorandum and Articles of Association are deemed to be that company's MOI as envisaged by the 2008 Act. However, the provisions of the 1973 Act will continue to apply to the liquidation of insolvent companies until a new uniform insolvency law is introduced in South Africa.

1.8   Types of company

The 2008 Act recognises a range of companies. A primary distinction is drawn between a profit company and a non-profit company. There are four distinct types of for-profit company:

1. a public company;
2. a state-owned company;
3. a personal liability company; and
4. a private company.

The different types of company are discussed in detail in chapter 2 of this book.

1.9   The Companies Act, 2008 and the common law

Although it is often believed that South African company law is to be found exclusively in legislation, the Companies Act, 2008 does not comprise the entire body of South African company law. The legislation should be seen as the superstructure built on the foundation of the common law. However, the Companies Act, 2008 is not a codification of company law. Not all rules and principles of company law are sourced in legislation. The common law still applies and assists in the interpretation of the Act. Where the Act is silent, the common law will apply.

CASE STUDY	The common law on requiring security for costs lives on under the 2008 Act
	There is no equivalent in the 2008 Act of s 13 of the 1973 Act. Section 13 provided that:

where a company is plaintiff or applicant in any legal proceedings, the Court may at any stage, if it appears by credible testimony that there is reason to believe that the company or, if it is being wound up, the liquidator thereof, will be unable to pay the costs of the defendant or respondent if successful in his defence, require sufficient security to be given for those costs and may stay all proceedings till the security is given.

The court, in *Ngwenda Gold (Pty) Ltd v Precious Prospect Trading 80 (Pty) Ltd*,[34] made it very clear that there has been a policy shift with regard to an application for security. The court held that it would be inappropriate to assume that the absence of a provision similar to s 13 was as a result of an oversight on the part of the legislature, and, in fact by not having a section similar to s 13 in the 2008 Act, the legislature intended that there should be a new approach regarding the issue:

(t)he fact that the new Companies Act was promulgated after the inception of the Constitution of the Republic of South Africa, 1996, suggests that the legislature, in not retaining an equivalent provision to the previous section 13, was mindful of the provisions of section 34 of the Constitution of the Republic of South Africa, 1996, in terms whereof access to the courts is enshrined.[35]

---

34   2012 JDR 0397 (GSJ); [2011] ZAGPJHC 217.
35   At para. [12].

In this case, the respondents had sought an order directing the applicants to provide security for costs. The court held that, in the absence of a provision similar to s 13, an applicant in an application for security for costs must found its entitlement to security for costs on the principles of the common law.

In looking at the common law, the court stated that two conflicting considerations of public policy arise in instances where security for costs is sought from a plaintiff or an applicant.

On the one hand, it was recognised in the case law that the object of s 13 of the previous Companies Act was to protect the public against the cost of litigation by bankrupt companies. On the other hand, the court stated that it has often also been recognised that s 13 of the 1973 Act may have the undesirable consequence that an impecunious or insolvent company is precluded from recovering a valid claim. The court concluded that the:

> absence of an equivalent to section 13 suggests that the legislature placed greater emphasis on the entitlement of even impecunious or insolvent corporate entities to recover what is due to them in the courts without the obstacle of having to provide security in advance for the costs of the litigation. (See e.g. *Crest Enterprises (Pty) Ltd v Barnett and Schlosberg NNO* 1986 (4) SA 19 (C) at 20B-D, where the court stated that 'no hurdle should be permitted to stand in the way of any person's access to a court in seeking relief at its hands ...'.) A valid consideration in support of the approach of the legislature as reflected in the new Companies Act would be the fact that litigation can seldomly, if at all, be instituted and proceeded with on a risk-free basis. At the very least, those funding the litigation on behalf of the insolvent or impecunious corporate entity would normally be exposed to the deterrent that the funding provided would be irrecoverable in the event of unsuccessful litigation.[36]

South African common law consists of all law that is not found in legislation. It comprises a combination of rules drawn primarily from Roman-Dutch law and, to a lesser extent, from English law. In the case of company law, English law has been particularly influential. The English law rules have, over time, been analysed and adapted by the courts to meet the needs of South Africa. Hence, in the vast majority of cases, the common law is to be found in the decisions of the courts (which then act as precedents) built over more than a century. When courts need to adapt the common law to meet fresh situations caused by social or economic contexts, they may examine Roman-Dutch or English texts in an effort to preserve the spirit of the common law.

In the area of company law, the Companies Act, 2008 is extremely detailed, and thus much of the regulation of companies takes place at present through the Act.

---

36   At para. [14].

CONTEXTUAL **ISSUE**	**The application of common law** The Companies Act, 2008 sets out broad principles relating to the fiduciary duties and the duty of care and skill owed by directors of companies. Although the Act imposes a fiduciary duty and a duty of care and skill on a director, the content of those duties cannot be understood or interpreted without knowledge of the common-law principles pertaining to the range and scope of a director's duties. Therefore, in interpreting provisions such as s 76(3) of the Act ('standards of directors' conduct'), a court will have recourse to the principles of common law in order to give content to these statutory provisions.

For this reason, when the Act is studied, the underlying common law must be understood as being part of the law. Many of the concepts set out in the statute are in fact merely statements of the common-law position.

For example, in *MMA Architects v Luyanda Mpahlwa*,[37] the court referred to the case of *Phillips v Fieldstone Africa (Pty) Ltd*,[38] which summarised the position in South African law on fiduciary obligations inter alia as follows:

> [W]here one man stands to another in a position of confidence involving a duty to protect the interests of that other, he is not allowed to make a secret profit at the other's expense or place himself in a position where his interests conflict with his duty.
>
> The principle underlies an extensive field of legal relationship. A guardian to his ward, a solicitor to his client an agent to his principal afford examples of persons occupying such a position .... It prevents an agent from properly entering into any transaction which would cause his interests and his duty to clash. If employed to buy, he cannot sell his own property; if employed to sell, he cannot buy his own property; nor can he make any profit from his agency save the agreed remuneration; all such profit belongs not to him, but to his principal. There is only one way by which such transactions can be validated, and that is by the free consent of the principal following upon a full disclosure by the agent ....[39]

THIS CHAPTER IN ESSENCE

1. A new Companies Act, the **Companies Act 71 of 2008**, has been introduced in South Africa with effect from 1 May 2011. The 2008 Act replaces the **Companies Act 61 of 1973**, except for those provisions of the 1973 Act specific to the liquidation of insolvent companies, which will continue to apply.
2. The 2008 Act aims to encourage business activity by providing a flexible regulatory environment, while ensuring sufficient regulation to make a company and its office bearers accountable to relevant stakeholders.
3. The 2008 Act introduces **business rescue** provisions in place of judicial management. The principles of **solvency and liquidity** are also entrenched as the key test for various transactions, in place of the capital maintenance concept.

---

37   [2011] ZAWCHC 259.
38   2004 (3) SA 465 (SCA).
39   At para. [13] of *MMA Architects.*

4. The Close Corporations Act 69 of 1984 was designed to facilitate the incorporation of smaller business entities with a membership of up to 10 natural persons. In terms of the Companies Act, 2008, existing **close corporations** will be allowed to continue indefinitely. However, no new close corporations may be formed after 1 May 2011.

5. The drafting of the 2008 Act was preceded by a number of processes, forums, discussions and input from concerned interested parties. These include a government policy paper published in 2004, formal agreements reached in the National Economic Development and Labour Council (NEDLAC) and pressure from the trade union movement to expand the rights in company law of a broad range of stakeholders.

6. Five key objectives for corporate law reform in South Africa were agreed at NEDLAC – namely, simplification, flexibility, corporate efficiency, transparency and predictability.

7. After some debate, the 2008 Act adopted an **enlightened shareholder value approach**, which ensures that directors are obliged to promote the success of the company in the collective best interests of shareholders, but with due regard for the need to foster positive relationships with employees, customers and suppliers. Stakeholders are now given extensive statutory rights in terms of the 2008 Act.

8. An important feature of the 2008 Act is its emphasis on **flexibility** and this is reflected in allowing a company to regulate itself through its **Memorandum of Incorporation (MOI)**, the contents of which can be varied to a significant degree from company to company.

9. The regulatory provisions of the 2008 Act include **a partial codification** of the duties of directors.

10. The sanctions imposed under the 2008 Act are **decriminalised** wherever possible.

11. The 2008 Act prohibits reckless trading and also prohibits a company from trading in a grossly negligent or fraudulent manner.

Chapter 2

Legal personality, types of company and company formation

2.1   Why incorporate a business?

A person does not have to form a company in order to trade or to open a business. In some cases, it makes good business sense for a person to trade in his or her own name. However, naïve or misinformed entrepreneurs may believe that the use of a close corporation or a company is mandatory if a person wishes to embark on a business venture. This is not true.

There are a number of matters that require careful consideration prior to deciding which business entity will be the most appropriate for a particular business. These include the number of persons who will be involved in the business, the extent of their involvement, the capital required to commence business, the sources of that capital, the requirements of customers and clients, and the strategic objectives of those involved. A number of choices are available when choosing a trading or business form. Any of the following can be used: company; close corporation; business trust; partnership; or any combination. An example of a combination choice is a company that carries on business using assets in its trading activities that are not owned by the company itself but are held in a trust that leases the assets to the company. The shareholders of the company could be the same people who are the beneficiaries of the trust. This book deals with all of these business structures: companies (part one), close corporations (part two), partnerships (part three) and business trusts (part four).

Tax issues must also be taken into account when considering the most appropriate business entity, because the South African tax system is not entity-neutral. For example, the effective tax rates of individuals are different from the rates that apply to a company or close corporation.[1] Moreover, although the Companies Act, 2008 recognises different types of

---

1   For example, in computing the tax liability of an individual, a sliding scale of tax applies which, together with the tax rebates (which are available only to natural persons), results in certain tax thresholds for individuals. This means that an individual who is below the age of 65 years can have a taxable income of R63 556 (based on 2013 rates) per year and pay no tax (that is his or her tax threshold), while a person who is 65 to 74 years old has a tax threshold of R99 056 (and a person of 75 years or older R110 889) per year. However, the tax threshold of a company (other than a small business corporation) is R1,00.

company[2] and allows great flexibility in company structure as expressed in a company's Memorandum of Incorporation (MOI),[3] the Income Tax Act[4] also recognises a variety of different companies for tax purposes, and grants favourable tax treatment to some (such as small business corporations and micro businesses) and penalises others (such as employment and personal service companies and trusts).

PRACTICAL ISSUE	**Tax considerations**
	The normal tax rates for various types of company, as recognised by the Income Tax Act, are as follows:
	• for non-mining companies, 28% of taxable income;
	• for personal service providers, 33% of taxable income;
	• for qualifying small business corporations, tax rates are on a sliding scale from 0% to 28% of taxable income; and
	• micro businesses can pay tax based on taxable turnover, not on taxable income.

2.2   Legal personality

A company is a legal person. Unlike a partnership, a company is not simply an association of persons; it is itself a separate legal person.

In terms of s 14(4), a registration certificate is conclusive evidence that the requirements for incorporation have been complied with and that a company is incorporated in terms of the 2008 Act as from the date, and time if any, stated in the certificate.[5]

A **legal person** is regarded as an entity that can acquire rights and duties separate from its members. In *Airport Cold Storage (Pty) Ltd v Ebrahim*,[6] the court confirmed that one of the most fundamental consequences of incorporation is that a company is a juristic entity separate from its shareholders. Accordingly, the assets of a company are the exclusive property of the company itself and not of its shareholders. Thus, although a company has no physical existence, it can acquire ownership in assets and is liable to pay its own liabilities. In *Dadoo Ltd v Krugersdorp Municipal Council*,[7] the court found that the property vests in the company and cannot be regarded as vesting in any or all of the shareholders of the company. In *Salomon v A Salomon & Co Ltd*,[8] the court found that once a company is legally incorporated, it must be treated like any other independent person with its rights and liabilities appropriated to it; the motives of the promoters of a company during the formation of the company are irrelevant when discussing the rights and liabilities of such a company.

Although incorporation and limited liability are different concepts,[9] generally speaking, incorporation also entails **limited liability** of shareholders, with the result that shareholders are generally not liable for the debts of the company. However, certain companies can have

---

2 See para. 2.6 below.
3 See para. 2.10.2 below.
4 58 of 1962.
5 See also para. 2.10.14 below.
6 2008 (2) SA 303 (C).
7 1920 AD 530 at 550–1.
8 [1897] AC 22 (HL).
9 John J Farrar & Brenda M Hannigan *Farrar's Company Law* (1998) 4 ed 79; JT Pretorius et al *Hahlo's Company Law through the Cases* (1999) 6 ed 13.

legal personality, but unlimited liability.[10] For example, if a personal liability company were registered in terms of the Companies Act, 2008,[11] the MOI of such a company would state that the directors are jointly and severally liable with the company for contractual debts and liabilities incurred during their period of office.[12] Such a company has legal personality despite the fact that the directors can be held personally liable for payment of the company's debts. Professional persons, such as attorneys, often incorporate their practice in this manner.[13]

Section 19(1) of the Act reinforces the common-law position as outlined, in that it provides: 'From the date and time that the incorporation of a company is registered, ... the company – *(a)* is a juristic person ...'.

This statutory provision brings the law into line with accepted judicial pronouncements, particularly that of Innes CJ in *Dadoo v Krugersdorp Municipal Council*:[14]

> A registered company is a legal persona distinct from the members who compose it ... Nor is the position affected by the circumstance that a controlling interest in the concern may be held by a single member. This conception of the existence of the company as a separate entity distinct from its founders is no merely artificial technical thing. It is a matter of substance; property vested in the company is not, and cannot be, regarded as vested in all or any of its members.

Section 19(1) contains two concepts that need to be examined. The Act distinguishes between **incorporation**, which is effected by the actions of the incorporators as provided for in s 13(1) of the Act, and **registration**, which is effected by the Companies and Intellectual Property Commission (the Commission) as soon as practicable after the act of incorporation has been perfected by the incorporator, who files a notice of incorporation (the Notice).[15]

Given this distinction between incorporation and registration, there may be a gap in time during which the company will notionally exist but not enjoy legal personality. In practice, this will generally be a brief period – that is, between the completion of the act of incorporation by the filing of the Notice and the issue of the certificate, which the Commission is required to do as soon as practicable after accepting the Notice. Questions of liability may well arise during this period if a person purports to conduct business in the name of the company. Significantly, the 2008 Act has not included a provision similar to s 172 of the 1973 Act, which made it an offence for a company with share capital to commence business or exercise any power of borrowing until it was issued with the certificate by the Registrar.

2.3   Lifting the corporate veil: common law and statute

Although incorporation can provide for the limitation of liability of those persons behind the company, this principle may not be abused. The courts have made it clear that the law looks at the substance of things, rather than at mere legal form. Courts will not allow a legal entity to be used 'to justify wrong, protect fraud or defend crime'.[16]

In *Cape Pacific Ltd v Lubner Controlling Investments (Pty) Ltd*,[17] it was said that if a company has been legitimately established and is legitimately operated, but is misused in

---

10   Pretorius supra at 13.
11   A personal liability company is discussed in para. 2.6.3 below.
12   Sections 1 and 8(2)*(c)* of the Companies Act, 2008.
13   See para. 2.6.3 below.
14   Supra at 550–1.
15   Section 14(1)*(b)*(iii).
16   See *Cape Pacific Ltd v Lubner Controlling Investments (Pty) Ltd* 1995 (4) SA 790 (A).
17   Supra.

a particular instance 'to perpetrate a fraud, or for a dishonest or improper purpose, there is no reason in principle or logic why its separate personality cannot be disregarded in relation to the transaction in question'.

In *Airport Cold Storage (Pty) Ltd v Ebrahim*,[18] the court held that the directors and members of a company ordinarily enjoy extensive protection against personal liability. However, 'such protection is not absolute, as the court has the power – in certain exceptional circumstances – to "pierce" or "lift" or "pull aside" "the corporate veil" and to hold the directors and others personally liable for the debts of the company'.

The Companies Act has basically adopted the common-law position (as described above) relating to the **lifting of the corporate veil**. Section 20(9) of the Act provides that if, on application by an interested person or in any proceedings in which a company is involved, a court finds that the incorporation of the company, any use of the company, or any act by or on behalf of the company, constitutes an 'unconscionable abuse of the juristic personality of the company as a separate entity', the court may do the following:

    (*a*)   declare that the company is to be deemed not to be a juristic person in respect of any right, obligation or liability of the company or of a shareholder of the company or, in the case of a non-profit company, a member of the company, or of another person specified in the declaration; and

    (*b*)   make any further order the court considers appropriate to give effect to such declaration described in (*a*) above.

The 2008 Act has been largely decriminalised, in that non-compliance with the provisions of the Act is not a criminal offence (as was often the case in terms of the 1973 Act). However, an offending person can be held personally liable in a variety of circumstances for losses caused by his or her wrongdoing. This is also a form of 'lifting the corporate veil'. Thus, for example, a director (including an alternate director, prescribed officer, or member of a committee) can be held liable for any loss, damages or costs sustained by the company as a direct or indirect consequence of the director having acted in a manner (as set out in s 77) in contravention of the provisions of the Act.

Moreover, s 218(2) provides that 'any person' who contravenes any provision of the Act is liable to any other person for any loss or damage suffered by that person as a result of that contravention. In Stein's view:

> Section 218 (2) could have severe financial repercussions for directors, because it is wide enough to include a monetary claim by anyone against a director personally if that director contravened any provision of the Act and thereby caused that person to suffer monetary loss.[19]

It should also be noted that s 218(2) will not only apply to directors but to 'any person' who fails to comply with the provisions of the Act. Thus, for example, s 22 prohibits 'reckless trading'[20] and a person who causes a company to act in a manner prohibited in that section could face personal liability in terms of s 218(2).

---

18 Supra.

19 See Carl Stein with Geoff Everingham *The New Companies Act Unlocked* Cape Town: Siber Ink (2011) at 407.

20 Section 22 provides that a company must not carry on its business recklessly, with gross negligence, with intent to defraud any person or for any fraudulent purpose. Obviously a company, being an artificial person, cannot act in this way: it is the people behind the company who can therefore fall foul of this section.

Lifting the corporate veil in terms of the common law

In *Airport Cold Storage (Pty) Ltd v Ebrahim*,[21] a creditor of a close corporation had sold and delivered imported meat products and frozen vegetables to the corporation on account. The close corporation was some time later put into provisional liquidation at a time when it owed the creditor R278 377.

On the liquidation of the corporation, the creditor proved a claim against it for the amount outstanding, but it received no dividend in the liquidation because the corporation had no assets. The creditor (the plaintiff) then sought to hold the member and his father (who assisted in running the business, even though he was not a member) personally liable for the debt.

The court held that it does not have a general discretion simply to disregard the existence of a separate corporate identity whenever it considers it just or convenient to do so, and acknowledged that the circumstances in which a court will disregard the distinction between a corporate entity and those who control it are 'far from settled'. The starting point is that veil-piercing will be employed only where special circumstances exist indicating that a company or close corporation is a mere façade concealing the true facts. The court held that fraud will be such a special circumstance, but the existence of fraud is not essential. In certain circumstances, the corporate veil will also be pierced where the controlling shareholders do not treat the company as a separate entity, but instead treat it as their alter ego or 'instrumentality to promote their private, extra-corporate interests'.

The court concluded that the defendants operated the business of the corporation as if it were their own, and without due regard for, or compliance with, the statutory and bookkeeping requirements associated with the conduct of the corporation's business. The court held that when it suited them, the defendants chose to ignore the separate juristic identity of the corporation. 'In these circumstances, the defendants cannot now choose to take refuge behind the corporate veil' of the corporation in order to evade liability for its debts.

The defendants were therefore held to be jointly and severally liable to the plaintiff for the amounts owed to the plaintiffs at the time of liquidation.

In another case involving the lifting of the corporate veil, *Die Dros (Pty) Ltd v Telefon Beverages CC*,[22] the court held that where fraud, dishonesty or other improper conduct is present, the need to preserve the separate corporate personality of a company has to be balanced against policy considerations favouring the piercing of the corporate veil. The court held that separate personality may be disregarded, for example, when a natural person, who is subject to a restraint of trade, uses a close corporation or company as a front to engage in the activity that is prohibited by an agreement in restraint of trade.

This is precisely what happened in *Le'Bergo Fashions CC v Lee*,[23] where Mrs Lee had personally signed a restraint of trade contract, and had then proceeded to trade through a company of which she was the sole shareholder and director. The court held that she had signed the restraint personally and the company was not a party to that contract. The court held that notwithstanding the fact that the company had not been

---

21　Supra.
22　2003 (4) SA 207 (C).
23　1998 (2) SA 608 (C).

party to the restraint, its competition with the plaintiff in this case amounted to intentionally assisting Mrs Lee to breach her agreement, and such assistance was regarded in law as wrongful, and could thus be interdicted.

2.4   Branches and divisions of a company

The **branches** or divisions of a company are part of the company itself and a division or branch does not have its own separate legal existence. In *ABSA Bank Ltd v Blignaut and Four Similar Cases*,[24] the court acknowledged that a company can decide for practical reasons to have separate operating divisions, but that this separation of divisions does not in law result in different businesses that exist separately from its other divisions. Although a business arm of ABSA may have been called United Bank and it conducted business under the name of United Bank, that division had not been registered as a separate entity in terms of the 1973 Act. Accordingly, although the impression might have been created for an outsider that he or she was working with two different businesses, in fact and in law there was only one entity, namely ABSA Bank Ltd.[25]

2.5   Key features of a company's juristic personality

The fact that a company is a separate legal person, separate and distinct from its shareholders, has a number of practical implications including the following:

- Incorporation entails limited liability of shareholders, with the result that shareholders in the capacity of shareholders are not liable for the debts of the company.
- The assets of a company are the exclusive property of that company; the assets of a company do not belong to its shareholders.[26]
- Where a wrong is alleged to have been committed against a company, it is the company that must seek redress and not the shareholders of the company.[27]

CASE STUDY	**Limitation of powers of shareholders**
	In *Letseng Diamonds Ltd v JCI Ltd; Trinity Asset Management (Pty) Ltd v Investec Bank Ltd*,[28] the critical issue was whether two shareholders had the right to have certain agreements, to which neither of them was a party, declared invalid, one-and-a-half years after their implementation.
	The court made it clear that strangers cannot interfere in contracts, and in this case this principle meant that as a general rule 'a shareholder is a stranger to the company

---

24   1996 (4) SA 100 (O).

25   At 101.

26   See chapter 4 of this book, where it is pointed out that while s 1 of the Act defines 'share' as one of the units into which the proprietary interest in a profit company is divided, this does not mean that a share entitles the holder thereof to the assets of the company. The company itself, being a separate legal entity, owns its assets. The number of shares held by a shareholder is therefore simply an indicator of the extent to which a holder has an interest in the company itself.

27   This is why s 165 – discussed in chapter 14 of this book – provides for a so-called 'derivative action' in terms of which certain persons may serve a demand upon a company to commence or continue legal proceedings, or take related steps, to protect the legal interests of the company. This action will be particularly relevant in cases where a company that has been wronged has not taken any action because the wrongdoers control the company.

28   2007 (5) SA 564 (W).

in its dealings with third parties'. The consequence of the rule is that an individual shareholder cannot bring an action to complain of an irregularity (as distinct from an illegality) in the conduct of a company's internal affairs, provided that the irregularity is one that can be cured by a vote of the company in general meeting.

If the general body of shareholders has no confidence in the board of directors, it is open to it to elect a new board, which can then act as it chooses, but shareholders, as shareholders, have no rights in this regard. The court stated that if each shareholder had the right to take it upon him- or herself to act in a way that he or she thought was in the best interests of the company, there would be chaos.

2.6   Types of company

The 2008 Act provides for two types of company – namely profit companies, and non-profit companies. A company is a **profit company** if it is incorporated for the purpose of financial gain for its shareholders.[29] A profit company may be incorporated by one or more persons. The Act does not restrict the maximum number of shareholders in a profit company, not even in the case of a private company. Historically, in terms of the 1973 Act, a private company could not have more than 50 shareholders. There are four types of for-profit company:

1. a public company;
2. a state-owned enterprise;
3. a personal liability company; and
4. a private company.

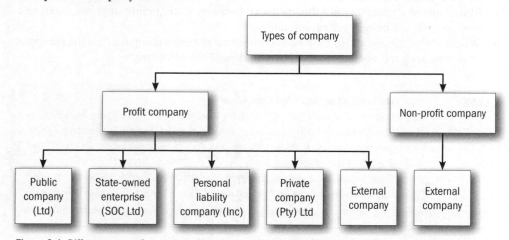

Figure 2.1 *Different types of company allowed in terms of the Companies Act, 2008*

29 This is the definition of a 'profit company' in s 1, which appears at first to contradict the principles of the 'enlightened shareholder' approach – see para. 1.3.3 above – because it focuses on the interests of shareholders as opposed to embracing the interests of other stakeholders. But see the discussion in para. 1.3.3 above as to how the enlightened shareholder approach has been firmly entrenched in the Act. See also C Stein *The New Companies Act Unlocked*, chapter 2.

2.6.1   The public company

A **public company**[30] is any profit company that is not a state-owned enterprise, a private company or a personal liability company. In a public company, shares may be offered to the public and are freely transferable. A public company could be listed (on a stock exchange) or unlisted. The recognition of public company status is essentially sourced in the MOI of a company, which is the sole governing document of a company. Its provisions will determine whether a company enjoys public company status.

2.6.2   The state-owned company

A **state-owned company** (SOC)[31] is a profit company that is either listed as a public entity in Schedule 2 or 3 of the Public Finance Management Act,[32] or is owned by a municipality. A SOC is therefore a national government business enterprise. It is a juristic person under the ownership and control of the national executive that has been assigned financial and operational authority to carry on a business activity. The principal business of a government business enterprise or SOC is that it provides goods or services in accordance with ordinary business principles and is fully or substantially financed from sources other than the National Revenue Fund or by way of tax, levy or any other statutory money.

PRACTICAL ISSUE	**State-owned companies**
	Examples of SOCs are the following: Albany Coast Water Board, Amatola Water Board, Aventura, Bloem Water, Botshelo Water, Bushbuckridge Water Board, Council for Mineral Technology (Mintek), Council for Scientific and Industrial Research (CSIR), Export Credit Insurance Corporation of South Africa Limited, Ikangala Water, Inala Farms (Pty) Ltd, Khula Enterprises, Lepelle Northern Water, Magalies Water, Mhlathuze Water, Namakwa Water, Ncera Farms (Pty) Ltd, Onderstepoort Biological Products, Overberg Water, Pelladrift Water Board, Public Investment Corporation Limited, Rand Water, SA Bureau of Standards (SABS), Sasria, Sedibeng Water, Sentech, State Diamond Trader, Umgeni Water and the Umsobomvu Youth Fund.
	It may be of interest to note that the Public Investment Corporation Ltd (PIC), an SOC, is the largest single investor in shares on the Johannesburg Stock Exchange and invests funds on behalf of public sector entities, including the Government Employees Pension Fund (GEPF).

2.6.3   The personal liability company

A **personal liability company**[33] is a private (profit) company used mainly by professional associations such as attorneys, entrepreneurs and stockbrokers who wish to exploit some of the advantages of corporate personality such as perpetual succession. A personal liability company's MOI will state that it is a personal liability company, which usually means that the directors are jointly and severally liable together with the company for all contractual debts and liabilities incurred during their terms of office.

---

30   Section 1 defines 'public company'.
31   Section 1 defines 'state-owned company'.
32   1 of 1999.
33   Section 1 defines 'personal liability company'.

CASE	**Personal liability companies**
STUDY	In *Sonnenberg McLoughlin Inc v Spiro*,[34] a personal liability company (this company was incorporated under the 1973 Act as a s 53 company, which is essentially a personal liability company) wanted to hold a previous director personally liable for his share for company liabilities contracted during his period of office. The company had paid debts due to its creditors. These debts had been incurred during the respondent's term of office as director. The company contended that, having discharged those debts, it had a claim against the previous director in his capacity as co-debtor for his proportionate share. In terms of the company's memorandum, 'all past and present directors of the company shall be liable jointly and severally with the company for the debts and liabilities of the company contracted during their period of office'.
	The court held that the purpose of a 'personal liability company' was to allow a private company to include in its memorandum a provision that the directors and past directors would be jointly and severally liable, together with the company, for debts and liabilities of the company that were contracted during their periods of office. The court, however, held that the section did not provide a company with a right of recourse against its directors where the company had already paid its debts.

The Companies Act, 2008 provides that if an amendment to the MOI of a personal liability company has the effect of transforming that company into any other category of company, the company must give at least 10 business days' advance notice of the filing of the notice of amendment to the following:
- any professional or industry regulatory authority that has jurisdiction over the business activities carried on by the company; and
- any persons who, in their dealings with the company, may reasonably be considered to have acted in reliance upon the joint and several liability of any of the directors for the debts and liabilities of the company, or who may be adversely affected if the joint and several liability of any of the directors for the debts and liabilities of the company is terminated as a consequence of the amendment to the MOI.

2.6.4   The private company

A **private company** is a profit company[35] whose MOI prohibits the offering of its shares to the public and restricts the transferability of its shares. There is no restriction on the number of shareholders of a private company in terms of the 2008 Act. Under the 1973 Act, shareholders of a private company were restricted to a maximum of 50.

In *Smuts v Booyens; Markplaas (Edms) Bpk v Booyens*,[36] the court stressed that the restricted transferability of a company's shares is an essential attribute of a private company, and a shareholder's right to transfer shares at all must be restricted by the company's articles.

---

34   2004 (1) SA 90 (C).
35   Section 1 of the Companies Act, 2008 defines 'private company'.
36   2001 (4) SA 15 (SCA).

CASE **STUDY**	**Pre-emptive right** In *Sindler NO v Gees and Six Other Cases*,[37] one of the two equal shareholders in a private company entered into an agreement with a third party for the sale of its 50 per cent shareholding to the third party. As was required by the company's articles of association, the sale was subject to the suspensive condition that the remaining 50 per cent shareholder must have failed to exercise its pre-emptive rights over the shares that were the subject of the sale agreement. Upon being offered the shares, the second shareholder indicated that it would not purchase all the shares that had been offered to it, but only three of the shares offered for sale, and tendered payment for the three shares based on the price at which the 50 per cent shareholding had been offered. The offeror adopted the attitude that it was not open to the second shareholder to purchase only three of the shares offered, and that it was therefore entitled to sell the shares to the would-be buyer. The court held that the notice addressed to the other shareholder indicated clearly that the offer was for the offeror's entire interest in the company, consisting of its shares and loan account – not just for three shares. The court therefore held that where a member offered to sell some or all of his or her shares in the company to an existing member or members of the company, the proposed selling price was the price for the total number of shares offered and could not be converted into a price for each share offered. The court held that provisions in the articles limiting the right of transfer must be restrictively interpreted, which means that a court will only prevent a shareholder from freely selling shares held in a company where it is quite clear that such a sale would be in contravention of a clause in the company's MOI. A common method of giving effect to the restriction on transferability is a clause in a company's MOI that gives the directors of the company a discretionary right to refuse to recognise a transfer of shares.

2.6.5   The non-profit company

A **non-profit company** is a company that was previously recognised in terms of s 21 of the Companies Act, 1973. The 2008 Act provides for the regulation of non-profit companies in Schedule 2. Briefly stated, such companies must have as at least one of their objectives a public benefit object or an object relating to one or more cultural or social activities or communal or group interests.[38] All assets and income of a non-profit company must be used to further the company's stated objective.

A non-profit company may acquire and hold securities issued by a profit company, or directly or indirectly, alone or with any other person, carry on any business, trade or undertaking consistent with or ancillary to its stated objects. An incorporator, member or director, or person appointing a director, of a non-profit company may not directly or indirectly receive any financial benefit or gain from the company, other than reasonable remuneration for work done, or compensation for expenses incurred, to advance the stated objects of the company. When a non-profit company is being wound up or dissolved, no member or director of that company is entitled to any part of the net value of the company after its

---

37   2006 (5) SA 501 (C).
38   See item 1 of Schedule 1 of the 2008 Act.

obligations and liabilities have been paid. The entire net value of the company must be distributed to one or more non-profit companies, external non-profit companies carrying on activities within the Republic, voluntary associations, or non-profit trusts having objects similar to the company's main object.

A non-profit company is not required to have members, but the provisions of its MOI may provide for the company to have members. Two categories of member are provided for – namely, voting and non-voting members. Voting members of a non-profit company will each have at least one vote. The word 'members' is used for non-profit companies, whereas the word 'shareholders' is used for profit companies.

The incorporators of a non-profit company are its first directors and its first members – if its MOI provides for it to have members.

2.7   Transitional provisions and close corporations

Schedule 5 to the Act contains **transitional provisions** designed to make the transition between the Companies Act, 1973 and the Companies Act, 2008 as seamless as possible.

The 2008 Act ensures that the incorporation of a company is made accessible and easy. It has also been designed to facilitate the formation and maintenance of small companies. However, there are approximately 1.9 million close corporations registered in terms of the Close Corporations Act 69 of 1984. The 2008 Act recognises that existing close corporations should be free to retain their current status until such time as their members may determine that it is in their interests to convert to a company under the Act. The Act therefore provides for the indefinite continued existence of the Close Corporations Act. However, it provides that the Close Corporation Act will not be an avenue for the incorporation of new entities or for the conversion of companies incorporated under the 1973 Act into close corporations. In other words, close corporations that existed at the commencement of the 2008 Act will be allowed to continue, but the formation of a new close corporation after the date of commencement of the 2008 Act is not possible.

CONTEXTUAL ISSUE	**Future of close corporations**
	The Explanatory Memorandum to the Companies Bill, 2008 provides as follows:

> The DTI believes that the regime in the new Companies Act for forming and maintaining small companies, which has drawn on the characteristics of the Close Corporations Act, is sufficiently streamlined and simplified as to render it unnecessary to retain the application of that Act for the formation of new corporations. However, it is recognised that existing close corporations should be free to retain their current status until such time as their members may determine that it is in their interest to convert to a company. Therefore, the Bill provides for the indefinite continued existence of the Close Corporations Act, but provides for the closing of that Act as an avenue for incorporation of new entities, or for the conversion of companies into close corporations, as of the effective date of this Bill.

2.8   External companies

An **external company** is a foreign company that is carrying on business or non-profit activities within the Republic of South Africa. Section 23(2) explains the meaning of conducting business or non-profit activities.

In terms of this section, a foreign company is deemed to conduct business or non-profit activities within South Africa if it:

- is a party to one or more employment contracts within the Republic; or
- is engaging in a course of conduct, or has engaged in a course or pattern of activities within the Republic over a period of at least six months, such as would lead a person to reasonably conclude that the company intended to continually engage in business or non-profit activities within the Republic. When applying this test, a foreign company must not be regarded as conducting business activities, or non-profit activities, as the case may be, solely on the ground that the foreign company is or has engaged in one or more of the following activities:
  - holding a meeting or meetings within the Republic of the shareholders or board of the foreign company, or otherwise conducting any of the company's internal affairs within the Republic;
  - establishing or maintaining any bank or other financial accounts within the Republic;
  - establishing or maintaining offices or agencies within the Republic for the transfer, exchange, or registration of the foreign company's own securities;
  - creating or acquiring any debts within the Republic, or any mortgages or security interests in any property within the Republic;
  - securing or collecting any debt, or enforcing any mortgage or security interest within the Republic; or
  - acquiring any interest in any property within the Republic.

An external company is compelled to register with the Commission within 20 business days after it first begins to conduct activities within South Africa as an external non-profit company or as an external profit company. Each external company must maintain at least one office in South Africa and must then give details of itself on a prescribed form.[39] The information must include the name and address of any person who has undertaken to accept service of documents on behalf of the external company.

The Commission must then issue a registration certificate to each external company on the prescribed form.

The regulation of external companies requires a careful balance between encouraging foreign companies to do business in South Africa, free of unnecessary formalities, whilst at the same time ensuring that such companies carry on their activities in a responsible and accountable manner. Therefore, s 23 requires an external company to register and to furnish certain information, but most of the provisions of the Act do not apply to such a company. For example, external companies are not required to prepare annual financial statements, and even if they do so voluntarily, there is no requirement for such statements to be audited.

If an external company has failed to register within six months after commencing its activities in South Africa, the Commission may issue a compliance notice to that company requiring it to register as required, or if it fails to register within the required time, to cease carrying on its business or activities within South Africa.

---

39   Regulation 20, Companies Regulations Form CoR 20.

2.9 Domesticated companies

A **domesticated company** is a foreign company whose registration has been transferred to the Republic in terms of s 13(5) to (9) of the Companies Act, 2008. Section 13 provides that a foreign company may apply to transfer its registration to the Republic from the foreign jurisdiction in which it is registered. Such a company will then exist as a company in terms of the South African Companies Act as if it had been originally incorporated and registered in terms of that Act.

The requirements for such transfer are as follows:

- the law of the jurisdiction in which the company is registered must permit such a transfer, and the company must have complied with the requirements of that law in relation to the transfer;
- the transfer must be approved by the company's shareholders;
- the whole or a greater part of that company's assets and undertaking must be within the Republic, other than the assets and undertaking of any subsidiary that is incorporated outside the Republic;
- the majority of its shareholders must be resident in the Republic;
- the majority of its directors must be or become South African citizens; and
- immediately following the transfer of registration,
  - the company must satisfy the solvency and liquidity test,[40] and
  - the company must no longer be registered in another jurisdiction.

However, s 13(7) specifically provides that even if the requirements described above are satisfied, a foreign company may not transfer its registration to the Republic if:

- the foreign company is permitted to issue bearer shares, or has issued any bearer shares that remain issued;[41]
- the foreign company is in liquidation;
- a receiver or manager has been appointed, whether by a court or otherwise, in relation to the property of the foreign company;
- the foreign company is engaged in proceedings comparable to business rescue proceedings in terms of the South African Companies Act, or is subject to an approved plan, or a court order comparable to an approved business rescue plan, or has entered into a compromise or arrangement with a creditor, and the compromise or arrangement is in force; or
- an application has been made to a court in any jurisdiction, and not fully disposed of, to put the foreign company into liquidation, to wind it up or to have it declared insolvent.

2.10 Incorporation of a company

In the corporate law reform process in South Africa, five key objectives were agreed to at NEDLAC and these objectives were taken into account in the drafting of the Companies

---

40 See chapter 4 of this book for a detailed discussion of the solvency and liquidity test.
41 A bearer share is a share owned by whoever holds the physical share certificate. The issuing company does not register the owner of the share, nor does it track transfers of ownership. The company pays dividends to the shareholder when a physical coupon is presented to the company. Because a bearer share is not registered by any authority, transferring the ownership of the share simply involves delivering the physical share certificate. Bearer shares therefore lack the regulation and control of other shares because ownership is never recorded.

Bill.[42] The sections of the 2008 Act dealing with the **incorporation** of a company demonstrate most apparently the objectives of **flexibility** and **simplicity**.

The 2008 Act accordingly provides for a full range of corporate structures, from the simplest to the most sophisticated and complex of businesses.

CONTEXTUAL ISSUE

Incorporation is a right

The Explanatory Memorandum to the Companies Bill, 2008 clearly highlights the principle that incorporation of a company is a right, rather than a privilege bestowed by the State. The Memorandum states the following:

> The new law provides for incorporation as of right, places minimal requirements on the act of incorporation, allows for maximum flexibility in the design and structure of the company, and significantly restricts the ambit of regulatory oversight on matters relating to company formation and design.

2.10.1   The notice of incorporation and the Memorandum of Incorporation

The incorporation of a company involves the filing of a **notice of incorporation**. A notice of incorporation[43] is defined as the notice to be filed in terms of s 13(1), by which the incorporators of a company inform the Commission[44] of the incorporation of that company for the purpose of having it registered. The registration of a company is important because it allows for transparency and accountability, and the keeping of relevant information about the registered entity. For example, in terms of s 186 of the Act, one of the functions of the Commission is the maintenance of accurate, up-to-date and relevant information concerning companies, foreign companies and other juristic persons and the provision of that information to the public and to other organs of state. It is important for those dealing with a company to have information about the entity with which they are dealing.

In terms of s 13, the Notice must be filed together with the prescribed fee, and must be accompanied by a copy of the **Memorandum of Incorporation (MOI)**.

The MOI[45] is an important document that enables significant flexibility as to the relationship between a company and its stakeholders. It can accommodate very simple company structures or very detailed and complex provisions – for example, to protect minority shareholders and withhold certain powers from the board of directors.[46]

The MOI is defined in s 1 as the document, as amended from time to time, that sets out rights, duties and responsibilities of shareholders, directors and others within and in relation to a company, and other matters as contemplated in s 15.[47] The MOI can therefore determine the rights, powers and duties of all stakeholders, as well as the nature of the company – that is, whether it is a public or private company or another type of company.

---

42   See para. 1.3.2 above.
43   Section 1 of the Companies Act, 2008 defines 'Notice of Incorporation'.
44   See para. 1.6.8 above for provisions on the establishment of the Companies and Intellectual Property Commission.
45   Section 1 of the Companies Act, 2008 defines 'Memorandum of Incorporation'. In terms of the Companies Act, 1973, all companies were required to submit a memorandum and articles of association as the constitutive documents of a company formed under that Act. One could not incorporate a company unless both these documents were submitted to the office of the registrar of companies. In terms of the 2008 Act, the incorporators of a company now submit the MOI as the only founding document of the company.
46   See para. 1.5 above.
47   See para. 2.10.2 for a detailed discussion of the MOI.

2.10.2 Flexibility within the Memorandum of Incorporation

The Companies Act, 2008 allows a large degree of flexibility with regard to the content of the MOI. However, each provision of a company's MOI must be consistent with the provisions of the Act. Any provision that is inconsistent with the provisions of the Act will be regarded as void to the extent that it contravenes, or is inconsistent with, the Act. The incorporators of a company are free to include any provision in the MOI that is not covered by the Act.

The MOI is the founding document of a company, and determines the nature of the company, as well as the rights, powers and duties of stakeholders. In terms of the 2008 Act, there are certain:

- **unalterable provisions** (which an MOI cannot abolish);
- **alterable provisions** (which an MOI can change taking into account the specific needs and requirements of those wishing to make use of the company structure); and also
- **default provisions** (which will automatically apply if an MOI does not deal with that specific matter – that is, the default provisions will apply unless they are altered by a company's MOI).

Whilst the Act uses the word 'unalterable', this is not entirely correct because s 15(2)(*a*)(iii) provides that the MOI of a company may include any provision imposing on the company a higher standard, greater restriction, longer period of time or any similarly more onerous requirement than would otherwise apply to the company in terms of an unalterable provision of the Act. Therefore the unalterable provisions are not absolutely unalterable, in the sense that they can be altered by a provision in a company's MOI to provide for a higher standard, greater restriction, longer period or more onerous requirement. They are unalterable in the sense that they cannot be abolished or made more lenient by any provision in a company's MOI.

CASE STUDY	**MOI must be consistent with the Act**
	An example of a provision that would be inconsistent with the 2008 Act is found in the case of *Ben-Tovim v Ben-Tovim*,[48] where it was held that a clause in the articles that attempted to give the preference shareholders the right to approve of a transaction involving the disposal by the company of the greater part of its assets could not override s 228 of the 1973 Act. Section 228 gave the shareholders in general meeting the ultimate power to authorise or ratify the sale of the undertaking or assets of the company; the articles could not override this section of the Act.

The MOI may contain provisions:

- altering the effect of any alterable provision in the Companies Act, 2008;
- containing special conditions applicable to the company;
- containing requirements for the amendment of any special conditions applicable to the company in addition to any of the requirements set out in the Act; and/ or
- prohibiting the amendment of any particular provision contained in the MOI.

---

48 2001 (3) SA 1074 (C).

> **CONTEXTUAL**
> **ISSUE**
>
> **Flexibility and the Memorandum of Incorporation**
>
> The Explanatory Memorandum to the Companies Bill of 2008 describes the flexibility provided for in a company's MOI as follows:
>
>> The Bill imposes certain specific requirements on the content of a Memorandum of Incorporation, as necessary to protect the interests of shareholders in the company, and provides a number of default rules, which companies may accept or alter as they wish to meet their needs and serve their interests. In addition, the Bill allows for companies to add to the required or default provision to address matters not addressed in the Bill itself, but every provision of every Memorandum of Incorporation must be consistent with the Bill, except to the extent that it expressly contemplates otherwise. In other words, a company cannot fundamentally 'contract out' of the proposed Companies Act. This principle is re-enforced by s 6(1), which introduces a general 'anti-avoidance' regime to company law.

A company's MOI can deal with any number of different issues including the following:

- the objects and powers of the company;
- the authorised shares and types of shares;
- any restrictions or limitations on the powers of the company;
- what happens to the assets if the company is dissolved;
- the composition of the board of directors;
- the election and removal of directors;
- alternate directors;
- the frequency of board meetings;
- the committees of the board;
- the personal liability of directors;
- the indemnification of directors;
- powers of directors and powers of shareholders;
- restrictions on powers of directors or shareholders;
- types of shareholders' resolution;
- rights of shareholders, including voting rights;
- the disposal by shareholders of their shares;
- the ability to create rules of the company;[49]
- shareholders' meetings and the procedures involved;
- specific audit requirements; and
- the amendment of the MOI.

2.10.3   Rules made by the board of directors

Unless a company's MOI provides otherwise, the board of directors of a company may make,[50] amend or repeal any necessary or incidental rules relating to the governance of the company in respect of matters that are not addressed in the Act or in the MOI.

---

49   See para. 2.10.3 below.
50   Acting in terms of s 15(3) of the Companies Act, 2008.

The board must publish a copy of the rules in the manner required in terms of the MOI (or in the manner set out in the rules themselves). A copy of the rules must also be filed with the Commission if this is in accordance with the MOI or the rules themselves.

Any rules developed by the board must be consistent with the Act and with the company's MOI. Any rule that is inconsistent with the Act or with a company's MOI is void to the extent of the inconsistency.[51]

Any **rule made by the board of directors** takes effect 20 business days after the rule is published, or on the date, if any, specified in the rule, whichever date is the later.[52] The rule is binding on an interim basis from the time it takes effect until it is put to a vote at the next general shareholders' meeting of the company. The rule will become permanent once it is ratified by an ordinary resolution at the shareholders' meeting.[53] Where the rule is not accepted by the majority of the shareholders, the board of directors may not make a substantially similar rule within the ensuing 12 months, unless it has been approved in advance by ordinary resolution at a shareholders' meeting.[54]

2.10.4 Legal status of the Memorandum of Incorporation and the rules developed by the board of directors

A company's MOI and any rules of the company are binding[55] as follows:
- between a company and each shareholder;
- between or among the shareholders of the company;
- between the company and each director; and
- between the company and each prescribed officer of the company, or other person serving the company as a member of the audit committee or as a member of a committee of the board in the exercise of their respective functions within the company.

2.10.5 Ring-fenced companies

Section 11(3)*(b)* of the Companies Act, 2008 provides that a company's name must be immediately followed by the expression 'RF'(meaning **ring-fenced**), if a company's MOI contains:
- any restrictive conditions applicable to the company and any procedural requirement (in addition to the normal amendment requirements set out in s 16) that impedes the amendment of any particular provision of the MOI; or
- if a company's MOI contains any provision restricting or prohibiting the amendment of any particular provision of the MOI.

Therefore, if a company's name ends with the letters 'RF', outsiders dealing with that company are made aware that there are special provisions in that company's MOI. The Act specifically provides[56] that if a company's MOI includes any provision contemplated in s 15(2)*(b)* or *(c)*, the notice of incorporation filed by the company must include a prominent statement drawing attention to each such provision and its location in the MOI.

This is important for third parties dealing with an RF company because, usually, third parties dealing with a company are not affected by the provisions in a company's MOI.

---

51   Section 15(4)*(a)* of the Companies Act, 2008.
52   Section 15(4)*(b)* of the Companies Act, 2008.
53   Section 15(4)*(c)* of the Companies Act, 2008.
54   Section 15(5) of the Companies Act, 2008.
55   In terms of s 15(6) of the Companies Act, 2008.
56   Section 13(3) of the Companies Act, 2008.

Section 20 provides that a person dealing with a company in good faith, other than a director, prescribed officer or shareholder of the company, is entitled to presume that the company, in making any decision in the exercise of its powers, has complied with all the formal and procedural requirements in terms of the Act, its MOI and any rules of the company, unless, in the circumstances, the person knew or reasonably ought to have known of any failure by the company to comply with any such requirement. However, a third party dealing with an RF company can be presumed to have been made aware of certain special provisions in that company's MOI, and therefore ought reasonably to know that the company has to comply with such special provisions.

Section 19(5) specifically provides that a person must be regarded as having notice and knowledge of any provision of a company's MOI contemplated in s 15(2)(b) if the company's name includes the letters 'RF' and if the company's notice of incorporation or a notice of amendment has drawn attention to the provision, as contemplated in s 13(3). This means that, as far as RF companies are concerned, the doctrine of constructive notice is still applicable and third parties dealing with an RF company cannot rely on the Turquand Rule.[57]

2.10.6   Amending the Memorandum of Incorporation

A company's MOI may be amended in any of the following three ways:
1. in compliance with a court order;
2. in the manner contemplated in s 36(3) and (4); or
3. at any other time if a special resolution to amend it is proposed (a) by the board of the company, or (b) by shareholders who are entitled to exercise at least 10 per cent of the voting rights that may be exercised on such a resolution; and if (no matter who proposes such special resolution) that resolution is adopted at a shareholders' meeting, in the manner described below.

2.10.6.1   Amendment of MOI in compliance with a court order

Section 16(4) provides that an amendment to a company's MOI that is required by any court order must be effected by a resolution of the company's board. Such an amendment does not require a special resolution of shareholders.

2.10.6.2   Amendment of MOI when directors act in terms of s 36(3) and (4)

Section 36(3) provides that (except to the extent that a company's MOI provides otherwise),[58] the board of directors itself may:

(a)   **increase or decrease the number of authorised shares of any class of shares;**

(b)   **reclassify any classified shares that have been authorised but not issued;**

(c)   **classify any unclassified shares that have been authorised ... but are not issued; or**

(d)   **determine the preferences, rights, limitations or other terms of shares in a class contemplated in subsection (1)(d).**

Section 36(4) provides that if the board of a company acts pursuant to its authority in terms of s 36(3) as described above, the company must file a notice of amendment of its MOI, setting out the changes effected by the board.

---

57   See the discussion of the doctrine of constructive notice and the Turquand rule under para. 2.13.2 below.

58   This section is therefore an alterable provision.

2.10.6.3   Amendment by way of special resolution of shareholders

An amendment by way of special resolution may take the form of:

- a new MOI in substitution for the existing MOI; or
- one or more alterations to the existing MOI by
  - changing the name of the company;
  - deleting, altering or replacing any of its provisions;
  - inserting any new provisions into the MOI; or
  - making any combination of alterations as described above.

Clearly, there is much flexibility in the types of amendment that may be made by special resolution of shareholders. Where the amendment of the MOI of a profit company results in the company no longer meeting the criteria for its particular category of profit company, the company must also amend its name at the same time, by altering the ending expression to reflect the category of profit company into which it now falls. For example, if an amendment to a company's MOI has the effect that the company's shares become freely transferable, that company will no longer qualify as a private '(Pty) Ltd' company, and it will become a public 'Ltd' company.

2.10.6.4   Effective date of amendments to the MOI

In the case of an amendment to a company's MOI that changes the name of the company, the amendment takes effect on the date set out in the amended registration certificate issued by the Commission. In any other case, the amendment takes effect on the later of:

- the date on, and time at, which the notice of amendment is filed; or
- the date, if any, set out in the notice of amendment.

In terms of s 16(7), a company must file a notice of amendment together with the prescribed fee with the Commission, and the Commission may require the company to file a full copy of its amended MOI within a reasonable time.

2.10.6.5   Sections of the Act relevant to amendments

The following sections apply to an amendment of a company's MOI:

- section 13(3), which deals with any restrictive conditions in a company's MOI that would make it an 'RF' company;
- section 13(4)*(a)*, which provides that the Commission may reject an MOI if it is incomplete or improperly completed;
- section 14, which deals with the registration of a company and the name of a company;
- section 13(2)*(b)* (if the amendment to a company's MOI has substituted a new MOI), which provides that the notice of amendment must be accompanied by the new MOI – if an existing MOI has not been substituted but merely altered, the company must include a copy of the amendment with the notice of amendment; and
- section 14(2) and (3) (if a company's amendment to its MOI includes a change of the company's name), which deal with names of companies, and the requirements for and prohibitions of certain names.

2.10.6.6   Nature of and prohibition of amendments

Generally speaking, there is no restriction as to what can be changed in an MOI, unless of course the MOI contains some restrictive conditions (as provided for in s 15(2)*(b)* and (c)),[59] and provided that an amendment does not attempt to change an unalterable provision (except to the extent it imposes a greater burden, as explained earlier in this chapter).

Section 15 (which applies both to an original MOI and to any amendments thereto) provides that a company's MOI may include any provision dealing with any matter that the Act does not address, and can alter any alterable provision.

2.10.7 Alterations to correct errors in a Memorandum of Incorporation and rules

The board of a company, or an individual authorised by the board, may alter the company's rules or its MOI in order to correct a spelling error, punctuation, reference, grammar or similar defect on the face of the document.

This can be done simply by publishing a notice of the alteration, in any manner required or permitted by the MOI or the rules of the company, and filing a notice of the alteration.

2.10.8 Translations of a Memorandum of Incorporation

A company that has filed its MOI may file one or more translations of it in any official language or languages of the Republic. A translation of a company's MOI must be accompanied by a sworn statement, by the person who made the translation, stating that it is a true, accurate and complete translation of the MOI.

Should the provisions of the MOI of a company conflict with a translated provision, the provisions of the MOI will prevail.

2.10.9 Consolidation of a Memorandum of Incorporation

At any time after a company has filed its MOI and subsequently filed one or more alterations or amendments to it, the company may file a consolidated revision of its MOI as so altered or amended. The Commission may also require a company to file a consolidated revision of its MOI.

A consolidated revision of a company's MOI must be accompanied by a sworn statement by a director of the company, or by a statement by an attorney or notary public, stating that the consolidated revision is a true, accurate and complete representation of the company's MOI, as altered and amended up to the date of the statement.

2.10.10 Authenticity of versions of the Memorandum of Incorporation

Where there is a conflict between different versions of the MOI, the following rules apply for resolving the conflict:
- The MOI, as altered or amended, prevails in any case of a conflict between it and a translation filed in terms of s 18(1)(a).
- The MOI, as altered or amended, prevails in any case of a conflict between it and a consolidated revision filed in terms of s 18(1)(b), unless the consolidated revision has subsequently been ratified by a special resolution at a general shareholders' meeting of the company.
- The latest version of a company's MOI endorsed by the Commission prevails in the case of any conflict between it and any other purported version of the company's MOI in terms of s 18(2).

---

59   See para. 2.10.5 above. As far as prohibited amendments are concerned, s 15(2)(b) specifically provides that an MOI can contain any restrictive conditions applicable to the company, and any requirement for the amendment of any such condition in addition to the requirements set out in s 16, and can also prohibit the amendment of any particular provision of the MOI. Therefore any purported amendments must comply with any such restrictive or prohibitive clauses in an existing MOI.

2.10.11 Shareholders' agreement

The shareholders of a company may enter into any agreement with one another concerning any matter relating to the company. However, any such agreement must be consistent with the 2008 Act and with the company's MOI. Any provision of such an agreement that is inconsistent with the Act or with the company's MOI is void to the extent of the inconsistency. In terms of the 1973 Act, if there was an inconsistency between the contents of a shareholders' agreement and the articles of the company, the shareholders' agreement generally took preference. In terms of the 2008 Act this is no longer the case, and the provisions of a company's MOI will take preference if there is any inconsistency between such provisions and the contents of a shareholders' agreement.

2.10.12 Steps to incorporate a company

One or more persons may incorporate a profit company, whereas three or more persons may incorporate a non-profit company. The following are the necessary steps[60] that should be taken in order to incorporate a company:
- Each person should complete and sign the MOI.
- The notice of incorporation must be filed with the Commission[61] together with the prescribed fee and must be accompanied by a copy of the MOI, unless the company uses the MOI provided for in the 2008 Act. (The MOI can be in a form that is unique to the company or the company can use the MOI provided for in the 2008 Act.)

2.10.13 The Commission's role in the incorporation of a company

The Commission may reject a notice of incorporation if it is incomplete or improperly completed. However, a deviation from the design or content of the prescribed form does not invalidate the action taken by the person completing the form, unless the deviation negatively and materially affects the substance of the notice of incorporation, or where the deviation would reasonably mislead a person reading the notice.[62] In each instance, the particular completed form will determine whether the notice of incorporation is to be regarded as invalid.

The Commission is also compelled to reject a notice of incorporation if the number of initial directors of the company is fewer than the prescribed minimum number of members.[63] The Commission is also compelled to reject a notice of incorporation where one or more of the suggested directors is disqualified from becoming a director and the remaining directors are fewer than the required minimum.[64]

2.10.14 Registration of a company

The **registration** of a company is dealt with in s 14. Upon acceptance of the notice of incorporation, the Commission assigns a unique **registration number** to the company. The Commission must enter the prescribed information relating to the company into the companies register. This register is one that is opened by the Commission and does not refer to a register that is kept at the relevant company.

---

60 See s 13 of the Companies Act, 2008.
61 Section 185 of the Companies Act, 2008 deals with the establishment and nature of the Commission.
62 Section 6(8) of the Companies Act, 2008.
63 Section 13(4)(*b*)(i) of the Companies Act, 2008. In terms of s 66(2) of the Companies Act, 2008, a private company must have at least one director and a public or non-profit company must have at least three directors.
64 This provision allows the Commission to accept a notice of incorporation, even if one or more of the suggested directors are disqualified, as long as the remaining number of directors is not below the required statutory minimum.

If all formalities are in order,[65] a **registration certificate** will be issued and delivered to the company. Such a registration certificate is conclusive evidence that all the requirements for the incorporation of the company have been complied with and that the company is incorporated from the date stated in the certificate. The date of incorporation on the certificate is the date on which the company comes into existence as a separate legal entity.

PRACTICAL ISSUE	**Registration certificate**
	A registration certificate is defined in s 1 of the Companies Act, 2008 as follows:

When used with respect to a —

(a) company incorporated on or after the effective date, means the certificate, or amended certificate, issued by the Commission as evidence of the incorporation and registration of that company;

(b) pre-existing company registered in terms of —

(i) the Companies Act, 1973 (Act No. 61 of 1973), means the certificate of incorporation or registration issued to it in terms of that Act;

(ii) the Close Corporations Act, 1984 (Act No. 69 of 1984), and converted in terms of Schedule 2 of this Act, means the certificate of incorporation issued to the company in terms of that Schedule, read with section 14; or

(iii) any other law, means any document issued to the company in terms of that law as evidence of the company's incorporation; or

(c) registered external company, means the certificate of registration issued to it in terms of this Act or the Companies Act, 1973 (Act No. 61 of 1973).

2.11   Pre-incorporation contracts

Before incorporation, a company does not exist and it cannot perform juristic acts. In addition, no one can act as the company's agent, because an agent cannot act for a non-existent principal. This may present problems to a fledgling business. For example, the incorporators may wish to sign a lease for an appropriate property from which the business is to operate, but the formalities of incorporating the company may not yet have been completed. Section 21 of the 2008 Act ensures that a company will not lose a business opportunity that presents itself prior to incorporation of the company. The section allows pre-incorporation contracts to be entered into, provided certain requirements are complied with.

A **pre-incorporation contract** is a contract that is entered into by a person who is acting on behalf of a company that does not exist. The person entering into the agreement has the intention that once the company comes into existence, the company is to be bound by the provisions of the pre-incorporation contract.

The 2008 Act provides that the person who enters into a pre-incorporation contract on behalf of a yet-to-be-formed company will be jointly and severally liable if the company is not later incorporated, or where the company is incorporated and the company rejects any part of the agreement. However, such a person will not be liable if the company, after incorporation, enters into an agreement on the same terms as, or in substitution for, the agreement entered into prior to its incorporation.

---

65   See para. 2.12 below in respect of the formalities regarding the name of a company.

Once the company is incorporated, the board of directors may within three months after the date on which the company was incorporated, completely, partially or conditionally ratify or reject any pre-incorporation contract. Where the board has not ratified or rejected the pre-incorporation contract after three months of incorporation, the company will be deemed to have ratified that agreement or action.

Once the agreement has been either partly or completely ratified by the company, the company will be liable in terms of the agreement, as if it had been a party to the agreement when it was concluded. Should the company reject the agreement, the person who will incur liability in terms of the agreement will be allowed to recover from the company any benefit that it has received in terms of the agreement.

A further important matter should be noted: at first, the Companies Bill did not require the contract to be a written contract, and it seemed that the common-law methods of entering into a pre-incorporation contract would continue to apply as they would be unaffected by the Companies Act, 2008. However, as a result of criticisms of the Companies Bill, the Act now requires a written contract.

2.12　Registration of company names

The Companies Act, 2008 provides that the name of a company may not generally offend persons of a particular race, ethnicity, gender or religion.[66]

When choosing a name for the company, care must be taken to ensure compliance with the provisions of the Act, and also not to offend the common-law rule against passing off. Passing off occurs when one business adopts a distinguishing feature of a competitor – for example, the competitor's trade name. The harm this may pose to the competitor is that the offending business relies on a confusion of identity in the marketplace to attract business to itself, effectively using the goodwill of its competitor for its own benefit. Passing off is unlawful at common law.

CASE STUDY	**Company names**
	In *Peregrine Group (Pty) Ltd v Peregrine Holdings Ltd*,[67] the applicants sought an order directing the respondents to change their name by excluding the word 'Peregrine' from their name, and also restraining them from passing off their business as that of the applicants. The relief was claimed in terms of s 45(2A) of the Companies Act, 1973 and also on the ground of common-law passing off.
	The court held that in terms of the common law, a court could direct a company to change its name where the use of the name was 'calculated to cause damage to the objector'. To succeed, the objector would have to establish (a) that confusion or deception was likely to ensue and (b) that, if confusion or deception ensued, it would probably cause damage to the objector.
	The 1973 Act broadened the common-law rule, giving the courts a greater discretion to rule that a name was 'undesirable'.
	In this case, the court found that, on the evidence, none of the litigants had established the existence of a secondary meaning in the word 'Peregrine' that was associated

---

66　Section 11(2)(*d*) of the Companies Act, 2008.
67　2000 (1) SA 187 (W).

with their businesses. On that ground alone, given the generic nature of the word and the extent of its use by corporate entities, the court held that it would be inappropriate to allow either the applicants or the respondents a monopoly in the name.

The court also found that the clients of the respective businesses were unlikely to be confused by the use of similar names in these circumstances. The court also found that most of the applicants did not carry on business in the same field of endeavour as any of the respondents. The application was therefore dismissed.

However, in *Azisa (Pty) Ltd v Azisa Media CC*,[68] the applicant was Azisa (Pty) Ltd, which had been incorporated in 1993 and the name 'Azisa' had been used with regard to all company activities. Problems arose when the applicant attempted to register the name 'azisa.com' for use on the Internet. Another entity had already registered that name for its own website. As a result of its failure to secure the 'Azisa' name for its website, the applicant became aware for the first time of the existence of a close corporation, Azisa Media CC, the name of which was registered five years after the incorporation of the applicant in 1998. The corporation had started using the shortened version of its name, 'Azisa', in 2000.

The applicant argued that the registrar of companies had erred in registering the name of the respondent because it wholly incorporated the applicant's company name. As a result, so it was argued, there was a very real likelihood of confusion arising because of the similarity of names.

The court held that there are no hard-and-fast rules that can be applied in cases of this nature, and issues to be considered included the degree of similarity of the names, the likelihood of confusion, and the present and contemplated business activities of the parties. Both the company (the applicant) and the close corporation had built up successful businesses over the years. The court held that the registered names of the two entities shared the word 'Azisa', but were otherwise not identical or very similar, but the abbreviation 'Azisa' used by the close corporation was identical or at least very similar to the name of the applicant and would not have been capable of registration. The court concluded that the use of the abbreviated name would, in all likelihood, lead to confusion and inconvenience, and while the name as registered (Azisa Media CC) was not undesirable, the abbreviation 'Azisa' was undesirable. The court thus held that the corporation should not be allowed to use the abbreviation or any undesirable abbreviations of its registered name.

In addition to provisions relating to avoiding unlawful competition in terms of the common law when choosing a name, the 2008 Act contains specific provisions that have to be complied with when choosing a name for a company. These are discussed below.

2.12.1   Criteria for names of companies in terms of the Companies Act, 2008

It is clear from the provisions of the 2008 Act that there has been a fundamental shift in the approach taken to the regulation and registration of company names. Section 41 of the 1973 Act ('Names of companies not to be undesirable') provided that 'no memorandum

---

68   2002 (4) SA 377 (C).

containing a name for a company to be incorporated shall be registered if in the opinion of the Registrar the name is undesirable'. The 2008 Act does not contain a similar provision. Instead, the 2008 Act[69] provides that if the name of a company (as entered on the notice of incorporation) is a name that the company is prohibited[70] from using, or if it is reserved[71] for a person other than one of the incorporators, the Commission must use the company's registration number[72] as the interim name of the company in the companies register and on the registration certificate. The Commission must then invite the company to file an amended notice of incorporation using a satisfactory name.

Most importantly, the Commission cannot refuse the registration of a company on the grounds that the submitted name is undesirable. At worst then, even if the Commission has an objection to the submitted name, the company will still be registered, but with its registration number as its name rather than the submitted name.

Section 11(2) specifically provides that the name of a company may not be the same as (or confusingly similar to) the name of another company, registered external company, close corporation or cooperative. A name will be confusingly similar if the name has the ability to make a potential client think that the company is the same as, or is affiliated to, another company with either the same or a similar name. The name may also not be the same as:

- a name that has been registered as a business name in terms of the Business Names Act[73] (unless the registered user has transferred the registration in favour of the company); or
- a trade mark that has been filed for registration in terms of the Trade Marks Act[74] (unless the registered owner of that mark has consented in writing to the use of the mark as the name of the company).

The name of a company may also not falsely suggest that the company is part of or associated with any other person or entity, is an organ of state, is owned by a person having a particular educational designation or that is a regulated entity, is owned or operated by a foreign state, government or an international organisation.

In the case of a profit company, the name of the company could simply be the registration number of the company.[75] If such a name is adopted, the number must be followed by the expression 'South Africa'.[76] The name of a non-profit company may not be only a registration number.

A company name may comprise words in any language, even if the words are not commonly used. The name can be used together with any letters, numbers or punctuation marks. The following symbols can be used as part of a company name: +, &, #, @, %, = or any other prescribed symbol. Round brackets (...) may be used in pairs to isolate any part of the name. A combination of letters, numbers, symbols, punctuation marks and brackets may also be used in a name.

---

69   See s 14(2)(b) of the Companies Act, 2008.
70   In terms of s 11(2)(a) of the Companies Act, 2008.
71   In terms of s 12 of the Companies Act, 2008.
72   The registration number must be followed by 'Inc', 'Pty Ltd', 'Ltd', 'SOC' or 'NPC', depending on the type of company.
73   27 of 1960.
74   194 of 1993.
75   Section 11(1)(b) of the Companies Act, 2008.
76   Section 11(3)(a) of the Companies Act, 2008.

Table 2.1 *Different types of company and their names*

Type of company	Name must end in the manner described below
Personal liability company	'Incorporated' or 'Inc.'
Private company	'Proprietary Limited' or '(Pty) Ltd'
Public company	'Limited' or 'Ltd'
State-owned enterprise	'SOC Ltd'
Non-profit company	'NPC'
Ring-fenced	'RF'

2.12.2   Similar names

Where the Commission is of the opinion that the suggested name could be similar to that of another company, business entity or trade mark or that the name suggests that the applicant company is associated with another entity or an organ of state, the Commission can by written notice require the applicant to serve a copy of the application and name reservation on any particular person, or class of persons, named in the notice, on the grounds that the person or persons may have an interest in the use of the reserved name by the applicant. Any person with an interest in the company name may apply to the Companies Tribunal for a determination whether the name satisfies the requirements of the 2008 Act.

2.12.3   Use of name and registration number

In terms of s 32, a company must provide its full registered name or registration number to any person on demand and must not misstate its name or registration number in a manner likely to mislead or deceive any person. If the Commission has issued a registration certificate with an interim name, as contemplated in s 14(2)(*b*), the company must use its interim name, until its name has been amended.

PRACTICAL ISSUE	**Use of full name**
	The registered name of a company must be used at all times, and not a modified version. For example, in *Epstein v Bell*,[77] a company's name was 'South African Unlisted Securities Market Exchange (Pty) Ltd', whereas the company's cheques were printed 'SA Unlisted Sec Market Exchange (Pty) Ltd' and had been dishonoured on presentation. The court held that the name of the company had not been used properly, and an abbreviation such as 'SA' for 'South African' was not acceptable.

2.12.4   Reservation of a name for later use

A person may reserve one or more names for use at a later time. These **reserved names** may be used for newly incorporated companies or as an amendment to the name of an existing company.

---

77   1997 (1) SA 483 (D).

The Commission is compelled to reserve each name that the applicant applies for, unless the name applied for is the registered name of another company, close corporation or cooperative, external company or has already been reserved by someone else. The reservation continues for a period of six months from the date of the application for reservation.

A person for whom a name has been reserved may transfer the reservation to another person by filing a signed notice of transfer.

2.13 The impact of the Companies Act, 2008 on the *ultra vires* and constructive notice doctrines

The *ultra vires* and constructive notice doctrines are related to each other in that both are concerned with the effect of a company's constitution on the validity of actions taken by the company and its agents. Historically, the doctrines have been used to nullify certain unauthorised actions. However, the Companies Act, 2008 has now severely limited the impact of both these doctrines.

2.13.1 The *ultra vires* doctrine

The **ultra vires doctrine** has a long history and refers, in essence, to acts of a company that fall outside the scope of its powers, as determined in its memorandum of association, now referred to in the Companies Act, 2008 as the Memorandum of Incorporation. The doctrine follows upon the principle that when an act has been performed on behalf of another person and the act is beyond the authority of the actor, it is said that the latter acted *ultra vires*. When applied to a company, the doctrine involves the **legal capacity** of the company to perform. Thus, when the House of Lords was confronted with a company, the memorandum of association of which provided that its business was to make and sell railway coaches and wagons, and it entered into a finance agreement to assist in the construction of a railway, the court held that this contract was void and hence unenforceable.[78]

The doctrine arose primarily for two separate reasons: shareholders who invested in a company were entitled to be assured that their money was applied to the purposes for which such funds were invested; and, persons who advanced credit to a company wanted assurance that the company was creditworthy in that its risk profile could be calculated by way of recourse to its business as evidenced from its statement of objectives.

Companies responded to the doctrine by instructing their lawyers to draft extremely wide and lengthy clauses, seeking thereby to include within the ambit of the objects of the company all manner of conceivable business activity. In one case, the English Court of Appeal recognised as lawful a clause that provided that a company could carry on any other trade or business whatsoever that could, in the opinion of the board of directors, be carried on to the advantage of the company in connection with or as ancillary to any of the business activities stipulated earlier in the objects clause.[79]

The English courts further narrowed the scope of the doctrine. It was held that the use of an express power granted to a company in the memorandum, but which was then used by the directors to further an objective that was beyond the capacity of the company as defined in the memorandum, constituted an act done in abuse of the powers of the company rather than being *ultra vires*. That meant that the performed act was not void for being *ultra*

---

78 *Ashbury Railway Carriage and Iron Company Ltd v Riche* (1875) LR 7 (HL).
79 See *Bell Houses Ltd v City Wall Properties Ltd* [1966] 1 WLR 1323 (CA).

vires but was unenforceable only if the affected third party had notice that the company had performed within its capacity but for an improper purpose.

Of course, these moves did not mean that the doctrine had no consequences. If a company, pursuant to action of directors, concluded a contract that was *ultra vires* the powers of the company, the directors who had acted could be liable for a breach of their fiduciary duties and hence be liable for damages. Similarly, if shareholders gained knowledge of proposed *ultra vires* conduct, they could seek to obtain an interdict restraining the company from acting *ultra vires*.[80]

| CASE | **Application of the *ultra vires* doctrine** |
| STUDY | In *Quadrangle Investments (Pty) Ltd v Witind Holdings Ltd*,[81] the company's memorandum prohibited its capital reserves from being treated 'as revenue available for the payment of dividends'. Nevertheless, the company declared such a dividend. The court held that the declaration by the company of a dividend out of its capital reserve contravened the condition in the company's memorandum and was for that reason *ultra vires* and null and void. The court also held that such a dividend could not be validated by the unanimous assent of its shareholders. |

2.13.2   Constructive notice

The *ultra vires* doctrine is related to the principle of constructive notice. Briefly, the **doctrine of constructive notice** states that anyone dealing with a company is deemed to know the contents of the company's memorandum and articles of association as well as other internal documents filed with the registrar's office. The consequences could be extremely detrimental to a third party confronted with an argument that the contract into which it had entered with a company was null and void because the company had acted *ultra vires* its powers. In terms of the constructive notice doctrine, it would then be contended that the third party was deemed to have knowledge of the fact of the *ultra vires* action when it so contracted.

As a result, the English courts developed the so-called **Turquand rule**,[82] which mitigated the harsh effect of the doctrine of constructive notice. It ensured that if no act had taken place that was obviously contrary to the provisions of the documents of the company that were lodged with the registrar, the third party could assume that there was compliance with all the internal requirements of the company. This meant that the company was prevented from resiling from a contract on the grounds of non-compliance with an internal requirement contained in one or more of these documents.

This doctrine was accepted into South African law[83] and had the effect that a third party would not be affected by the doctrine of constructive notice unless this party knew that an

---

80   For the sake of history, it should be noted that s 36 of the Companies Act, 1973, which was enacted pursuant to recommendations of the Van Wyk de Vries Commission, provided that no act of a company was void by reason only of the fact that the company was without capacity or power to act because the directors had no authority to perform the act in question. The failure to so act *intra vires* could only be raised as between the company and its members or directors or between members and directors. There was some debate whether this wording justified the conclusion that the doctrine continued to apply in the case of transactions between the insiders (members/directors), but it was not the prevailing view. However, this section has now been replaced by s 20(1) of the 2008 Act.

81   1975 (1) SA 572 (A).

82   So-called because the rule was laid down in *Royal British Bank v Turquand* (1856) 6 E and B 327. The rule has also become known as the indoor management rule.

83   See *Mine Workers Union v Prinsloo* 1948 (3) SA 831 (A).

internal requirement or rule had not been followed or should reasonably have suspected this to be the case, and yet did not make enquiries.

2.13.3 *Ultra vires* and the Companies Act, 2008

Section 20(1) of the 2008 Act has made the doctrine of *ultra vires* inapplicable between a company and a third party. According to the section, no action of the company is void if the only reason therefor is that the action was prohibited by a limitation, restriction or qualification in the Memorandum of Incorporation (MOI) or that a consequence of this form of limitation was that the directors who purported to act on behalf of the company had no authority to authorise the company's action.

Section 20(2) provides for the shareholder, by way of special resolution, to ratify any action taken by the company that was inconsistent with or in breach of a specified limitation, restriction or qualification contained in the MOI.

If there is no ratification in terms of s 20(2), acts taken in breach of such limitations have legal consequences. Thus, in terms of s 20(4) read with sub-s (5), a shareholder, director or prescribed officer may institute proceedings to restrain a company from performing any action that is in breach of the Act or a specified limitation under the MOI. Such legal action is not, however, an obstacle to a third party that sues for damages on the basis of breach of contract pursuant to the unlawful action of the company, provided that the third party had acquired the alleged rights in good faith and had no actual knowledge of the limitation, qualification or restriction that has been shown to be applicable. The Act reduces the restriction on the right of the third party to claim in these circumstances by providing that only actual knowledge by the third party is an obstacle to a cause of action. Merely having reason to suspect a breach is not sufficient to bar a claim.

This position is qualified in s 20(7), in terms of which a person, other than a director, dealing with a company in good faith, is entitled to presume that the company, in making any decision in the exercise of its powers, has complied with all of the formal and procedural requirements of the Act, the MOI and any company rules, unless in the circumstances of the case the person knew or ought to have known of any failure by the company to comply. Thus, when these sections are read together, if an action is taken to restrain a company in terms of s 20(4) read with (5), this action may prejudice rights of a third party where the latter had actual knowledge as opposed to having ought reasonably to know of a failure to so comply with an internal restriction.[84]

2.13.4 The abolition of the doctrine of constructive knowledge

Section 19 of the Companies Act, 2008 dispenses with the obligation that was effectively imposed upon third parties to check the company's registered constitutional documents in order to ensure that the proposed transaction was in compliance with these constitutional documents. The only qualification to this abolition is to be found in s 19(5), which provides together with s 15(2)(b) and (c) that a person will be regarded as having knowledge of these restrictive provisions where the latter have been drawn to his or her attention in terms of s 13(3).

---

84 Section 1, the definition section of the Companies Act, 2008 provides that 'knowing' or 'knows' with respect to a person means actual knowledge, but also being in a position where the person reasonably *ought to have* actual knowledge, to have reasonably investigated the matter to the extent that this would have provided him or her with actual knowledge, or taken other measures which would reasonably be expected to have provided the person with actual knowledge. This definition, if applied to s 20(7), would extend the exclusion provided beyond that contained in the Turquand rule. The conclusion hereto depends upon whether, as appears to be the case, that the 2008 Act holds that only where a third party ought reasonably to have taken measures to gain actual knowledge can it be said that he or she acted in good faith sufficient to fall within the Turquand rule.

This means that where, in compliance with s 13(3), the notice of incorporation filed by the company includes a prominent statement that draws attention to each such restrictive provision and its location in the MOI and where the company's name includes the letters 'RF', a third party is deemed to have such knowledge of the applicable restriction.

These provisions impose an obligation on a company with restrictive provisions to incorporate the letters 'RF' into its name, and further provides that the notice of incorporation should warn parties as to exactly where the restrictive provisions are contained in the MOI.

THIS CHAPTER IN ESSENCE

1. A person wishing to open a business in order to trade has a choice of a number of different forms of business entity. Forming a company, of which there are a number of different types, in terms of the Companies Act, 2008 is not the only available or always the most appropriate vehicle for trading.
2. Which business entity will be the most appropriate for a particular business depends on a variety of factors, including: the number of persons involved in the business; the extent of their involvement; the capital required to commence business; the sources of that capital; the requirements of customers and clients; tax issues; and the strategic objectives of those involved.
3. A company is a separate **legal person** capable of acquiring rights and duties separate from its members.
4. Incorporation generally entails **limited liability** of shareholders, with the result that members are not liable for the debts of the company. However, the directors of a personal limited liability company are jointly and severally liable with the company for contractual debts and liabilities incurred during their period of office. Nonetheless, such a company has separate legal personality.
5. The Act distinguishes between **incorporation** (effected by the incorporators) and **registration** (effected by the Commission as soon as practicable after incorporation).
6. Although incorporation can provide for the limitation of liability of those persons behind the company, this principle may not be abused. At common law, courts have the power to **lift the corporate veil** and hold abusers personally liable for company debts:
   - where a company is used as a device to cover up or disguise fraudulent or illegal conduct;
   - where a director and/or a shareholder treats the company's assets as his or her own; or
   - when a statute empowers the court to ignore corporate legal personality.
7. Section 20(9) of the Companies Act, 2008 endorses the power of courts to lift the corporate veil and either:
   - ignore the separate legal existence of the company and treat its members as if they owned the assets and conducted the business in their personal capacities; or
   - attribute certain rights or obligations of the shareholders to the company.
8. A **branch** of a company is part of the company and does not have its own separate legal existence.
9. The 2008 Act provides for two principal types of company – namely, profit companies and non-profit companies. A company is a **profit company** if it is incorporated for the purpose of financial gain for its shareholders. The Act does not restrict the maximum number of shareholders in a profit company.
10. There are four types of for-profit company:
    10.1 a **public company**, which is any profit company that is not a state-owned enterprise, a private company or a personal liability company – shares in a public company may be offered to the public and are freely transferable, whether listed on a stock exchange or unlisted;
    10.2 a **state-owned enterprise** (SOC), which is a national government business enterprise falling either within the meaning of a state-owned enterprise under the Public Finance Management Act, or is owned by a municipality – an SOC provides goods or services in accordance with ordinary business principles and is financed mostly from sources other than tax or statutory money;

10.3 a **personal liability company**, which is a private (profit) company used mainly by professional associations to enjoy advantages of corporate personality such as perpetual succession – usually the directors will be jointly and severally liable together with the company for all contractual debts and liabilities incurred during their terms of office; and

10.4 a **private company**, which is a profit company whose MOI prohibits the offering of its shares to the public and restricts the transferability of its shares.

11. A **non-profit company** is a company that has, as at least one of its objectives, a public benefit object or an object relating to one or more cultural or social activities or communal or group interests. All assets and income of a non-profit company must be used to further the company's stated objective.

12. Schedule 5 to the Companies Act, 2008 contains **transitional provisions** designed to make the transition between the Companies Act, 1973 and the Companies Act, 2008 as seamless as possible. Close corporations that existed at the commencement of the 2008 Act will be allowed to continue, but no new close corporations will be formed after commencement of the 2008 Act.

13. An **external company** is a foreign company that is carrying on business or non-profit activities in the Republic of South Africa and is compelled to register with the Commission within 20 business days after it first begins to conduct activities in South Africa.

14. A **domesticated company** is a foreign company whose registration has been transferred to the Republic in terms of s 13(5) to (9) of the Companies Act, 2008.

15. The Companies Act, 2008 aims for **flexibility** and **simplicity** in the **incorporation** process and thus caters for a full range of corporate structures, from the simplest to the most sophisticated and complex of businesses.

16. The incorporation of a company involves the filing of a **notice of incorporation** with the Commission, together with the prescribed fee and a copy of the **Memorandum of Incorporation (MOI)**.

17. The MOI sets out rights, duties and responsibilities of shareholders, directors and others within and in relation to a company. The MOI therefore determines the rights, powers and duties of all stakeholders, as well as the nature of the company – that is, whether it is a public or private company or another type of company.

18. In terms of the 2008 Act, there are certain:
    • **unalterable provisions** (which an MOI cannot change);
    • **alterable provisions** (which an MOI can change taking into account the specific needs and requirements of those wishing to make use of the company structure); and also
    • **default provisions** (which will automatically apply if an MOI does not deal with that specific matter).

19. Unless a company's MOI provides otherwise, the **board of directors** of a company may make, amend or repeal any necessary or incidental **rules** relating to the governance of the company in respect of matters that are not addressed in the Act or in the MOI.

20. A company's name must be immediately followed by the expression '**RF**'(meaning **ring-fenced**) if a company's MOI contains restrictive conditions applicable to the company and any procedural requirements impeding the amendment of any particular provision of the MOI, or provisions restricting or prohibiting the amendment of any particular provision of the MOI. Outsiders dealing with that company are thus alerted to special provisions in that company's MOI. Accordingly, as far as RF companies are concerned, the doctrine of constructive notice is still applicable and third parties dealing with an RF company cannot rely on the Turquand Rule.

21. Amendments to a company's MOI must be approved by special resolution of shareholders or by order of court. If the board of directors acts in terms of s 36(3) or (4) to adjust the number, classification or character of any shares, it must also file a notice of amendment of its MOI, even though a special resolution is not necessary.

22. The shareholders of a company may enter into any agreement with one another concerning any matter relating to the company, provided it is consistent with the 2008 Act and with the company's MOI.

23. Upon acceptance of a notice of incorporation, the Commission assigns a unique **registration number** to the company. The Commission must enter the prescribed information relating to the company into the companies register. If all formalities are in order, a **registration certificate** will be issued and delivered to the company.

24. A **pre-incorporation contract** is a contract that is entered into by a person who is acting on behalf of a company that does not yet exist. The person entering into the agreement has the intention that once the company comes into existence, the company will be bound by the provisions of the pre-incorporation contract. In terms of the 2008 Act, pre-incorporation contracts may be entered into, in writing, but the person entering the agreement will be jointly and severally liable if the company is not later incorporated, or where the company is incorporated and the company rejects any part of the agreement.

25. **Company names** may not offend persons of a particular race, ethnicity, gender or religion, must comply with the Act and must not infringe the law against passing off. The name of a company may not be the same as (or confusingly similar to) the name of another company and it may also not make false suggestions about the company's associations, status or educational designation. The name of a company must indicate its type – for example, a public company's name must end with the designation 'Limited' or 'Ltd'. A person may **reserve a company name** for use at a later time.

26. At common law, for a contract between a company and a third party to be valid, the company must have had the **legal capacity** (defined with reference to the objects clause in the company's founding documents), and the directors must have had the authority, to enter into the contract.

27. The ***ultra vires* doctrine** at common law (which deems an act by a company that is beyond its legitimate powers – as defined in its founding documents – to be void) has been all but abolished by statute. The doctrine operated too harshly against third parties who unwittingly contracted with a company acting *ultra vires* and then found themselves unable to enforce their contract. Under the Companies Act, 2008, restrictions on a company's capacity may only be raised internally in legal proceedings between the company, its shareholders and directors. This is subject to the right to restrain an *ultra vires* contract in certain circumstances.

28. Directors who cause a company to act beyond its powers may incur liability for breach of fiduciary duty or face an action by the shareholders to restrain them from entering into the contract. Each shareholder has a claim for damages against any person who fraudulently or due to gross negligence causes the company to do anything inconsistent with the Act or the powers of the company as stated in its MOI, unless the latter is ratified by special resolution.

29. The **doctrine of constructive notice** stated that third parties contracting or dealing with a company were deemed to have had notice of the contents of the public documents of the company. The doctrine was designed to protect the company from the unauthorised acts of its directors or officers.

30. Prior to the Companies Act, 2008, the doctrine of constructive notice was coupled with the **Turquand rule**. Also known as the indoor management rule, the Turquand rule entitles a *bona fide* third party to assume that a company has complied with its internal formalities and procedures as specified in its constitution. Under the rule, a company cannot escape liability under an otherwise valid contract on the basis that internal procedures were not adhered to.

31. The Companies Act, 2008 abolishes the doctrine of constructive notice, but preserves the Turquand rule for the benefit of outsiders only. Corporate insiders, such as directors, company officers and shareholders, derive no protection from the statutory rule.

Chapter 3

Groups of companies

3.1   Introduction and definitions

Although a group of companies does not have separate legal personality, there are legal and practical consequences for companies that are associated with each other through related shareholdings and where one company is able to control another to a greater or lesser extent. The Companies Act, 2008 introduces some new definitions relevant to groups of companies. These are discussed below before a more detailed discussion of groups of companies in South African law.

3.1.1   Definition of group of companies

Section 1 of the Companies Act, 2008 defines a **group of companies** as a holding company and all of its subsidiaries.[1] A company (company H) is related to another company (company S) if:
- either company (company H or S) directly or indirectly controls[2] the other, or controls the business of the other; or
- either company (H or S) is a subsidiary of the other.[3]

3.1.2   Definition of control

Section 2(2)(*a*) of the Companies Act, 2008 provides that a company (company 'H') **controls** another company (company S), or its business, if:
- company S is a subsidiary of company H;[4] or
- company H, together with any related or inter-related person, is

---

1   Section 1 of the Companies Act, 2008.
2   As defined. See para. 3.1.2 below.
3   For the definition of subsidiary, see para. 3.1.4 below.
4   See para. 3.1.4 below.

- directly or indirectly able to exercise or control the exercise of a majority of the voting rights associated with the securities of company S, whether pursuant to a shareholder agreement or otherwise; or
- company H has the right to appoint or elect, or control the appointment or election of, directors of company S, who control a majority of the votes at a meeting of the board.

Section 2 also provides that a company (company H) controls another company (company S) if company H has the ability to materially influence the policy of company S. Significantly, the section therefore gives greater guidance as to the meaning of control than did the 1973 Act. It provides that if company H has the ability to materially influence the policy of company S in a manner comparable to a person who, in ordinary commercial practice, can exercise an element of control (such as is the case with a holding company), that company is considered to control company S.

3.1.3   Definition of holding company

A **holding company**, in relation to a subsidiary,[5] means a company that controls that subsidiary, as set out in s 2(2)(a) of the Companies Act, 2008[6] or as set out in s 3(1)(a).[7]

3.1.4   Definition of subsidiary company

Section 3(1)(a) provides that a company (company S) is a **subsidiary** of another company (company H) if company H, or one or more other subsidiaries of company H, or one or more nominees of company H or any of its subsidiaries, alone or in any combination:
- is or are directly or indirectly able to exercise, or control the exercise of, a majority of the general voting rights associated with issued securities of company S, whether pursuant to a shareholder agreement or otherwise; or
- has or have the right to appoint or elect, or control the appointment or election of, directors of company S who control a majority of the votes at a meeting of the board.

A company (company S) is a **wholly owned subsidiary** of another company (company H) if all of the general voting rights associated with issued securities of company S are held or controlled, alone or in any combination, by company H, one or more of its subsidiaries, or one or more nominees of company H or any of its subsidiaries.

The meaning of general voting rights is discussed below.[8]

PRACTICAL	**Examples of groups of companies**
ISSUE	Grindrod Limited is a holding company and its principal function is to hold (or own) shares in other companies. There are over 30 separate companies in the Grindrod group, as represented in Figure 3.1 below. Grindrod Limited itself is a listed company in the Marine Transportation sub-sector of the Industrial Transport sector of the Johannesburg Stock Exchange. Grindrod Limited's shareholding in each of its various subsidiary companies ranges from 40 per cent to 100 per cent. All the separate

---

5   See para. 3.1.4 below for a discussion of the meaning of subsidiary.
6   See para. 3.1.2 above.
7   See para. 3.1.4 below.
8   See para. 3.2 below.

companies together constitute a single group, and the financial results and financial position of the group as a whole are published together on an annual basis.

Another example of a group is Altron Limited together with its subsidiaries. The Altron group operates in the telecommunications, power electronics, multi-media and information technology industries. Altron Limited is listed on the Johannesburg Stock Exchange and its subsidiaries include Altech, Bytes Technology, and Powertech.

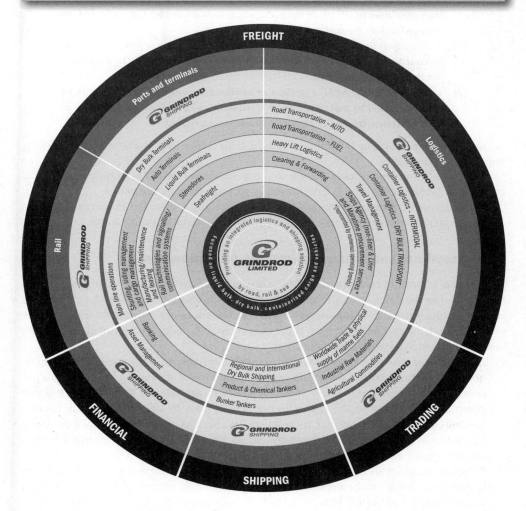

Figure 3.1 Structure of the Grindrod group[9]

---

9 This diagram appeared originally on the website *http://www.grindrod.co.za/About_GroupStructure.aspx*.

3.2 Determination of general voting rights

Section 3(2) provides that for the purpose of determining whether a person controls all (or a majority) of the **general voting rights** relating to a company's securities, the following rules will apply:

(*a*) voting rights that are exercisable only in certain circumstances are to be taken into account only (i) when those circumstances have arisen, and for so long as they continue; or (ii) when those circumstances are under the control of the person holding the voting rights;

(*b*) voting rights that are exercisable only on the instructions or with the consent or concurrence of another person are to be treated as being held by a nominee for that other person; and

(*c*) voting rights held by (i) a person as nominee for another person are to be treated as held by that other; or (ii) a person in a fiduciary capacity are to be treated as held by the beneficiary of those voting rights.

So, for example, if company H holds shares in trust for company B, the latter, as beneficiary, enjoys the voting rights.

Section 3(2) therefore makes it clear that the *number* of shares held is not the test for control of a company. Control is determined by an analysis of *voting power*.

A company's MOI can determine whether voting rights will attach to particular shares – for example, an MOI can determine when preference shares will carry a vote.

3.3 Legal consequences for groups of companies

A number of important consequences flow from the existence of a group of companies, even though the law does not recognise separate legal personality for the group. An act of, or in respect of, one particular company may have consequences not only for itself, but for the group of which the company is a part. These consequences, under the Companies Act, 2008, are summarised in six key points below.

1. *Acquisition of shares*: in terms of s 48(2), a subsidiary company may acquire shares in its holding company provided that the acquisition does not amount to more than 10 per cent in aggregate of the number of issued shares of any class of shares of the holding company. Furthermore, the cap of 10 per cent applies to all of the subsidiaries of a holding company taken together. No voting rights attached to the shares may be exercised for so long as the shares are held by the subsidiary company and for as long as the latter remains classified as a subsidiary of the holding company.

2. *Directors' conduct*: section 76 provides that a director of a company must not use his or her position as director, or any information obtained while acting in this capacity, to gain an advantage – either for him- or herself or for another person – other than for the company or the holding company or another subsidiary of that company. In addition, a director of a company is prohibited from using such information knowingly to cause harm to the company, and also to any subsidiary thereof.

3. *Public offerings*: the definition of employee scheme as it appears in s 95 of the Act refers to a scheme established by a company, whether by means of a trust or otherwise, for the purpose of offering participation solely to employees and officers of the company or of a subsidiary of the company. In this way, an employee of one company in the group is

treated as being an employee of the holding company or another subsidiary company; that is, as an employee of the group.

In similar fashion, a secondary offering of shares is regulated in s 101 of the Act as if the shares were those of a group of companies. A secondary offering of shares is defined to mean the offer for sale to the public of any securities of a company or of its subsidiary made by or on behalf of a person other than that company or its subsidiary.

4. *Disposal of all or the greater part of assets or undertaking*: section 115 provides that a company may not dispose or give effect to an agreement to dispose of the greater part of its assets or undertaking, unless such a disposal was approved by a special resolution adopted by persons who are entitled to exercise voting rights in such a matter, at a meeting called for that purpose and at which sufficient persons are present who exercise at least 25 per cent of all the voting rights that are entitled to be so exercised in respect of the disposal as contemplated.

   In reading s 115, reference must be made to s 112, which provides that, when the Act refers to the disposal of a greater part of the assets or of the undertaking of the company in terms of s 115, it does not cover a disposal between a wholly owned subsidiary and holding company, or between two or more subsidiaries of the same holding company or between a wholly owned subsidiary of a company on the one hand and one or more wholly owned subsidiaries of that company on the other.

5. *Financial assistance – purchase of shares:* section 44 provides that the board may authorise the company to provide financial assistance (by way of a loan, guarantee, the provision of security or otherwise) to any person for the purpose of, or in connection with, the subscription of any option, or any securities, issued or to be issued by the company or a related or inter-related company, or for the purchase of any securities of the company or a related or inter-related company. The exception to this provision is if the MOI of a company provides otherwise. Section 44 sets out certain requirements that must be complied with before the directors may authorise such assistance.

6. *Financial assistance, inter-company loans and assistance:* section 45 not only applies to directors but also to intra-group granting of financial assistance by way of loans and guarantees. Generally speaking, a special resolution of shareholders is required before a company can provide financial assistance to any other company in the same group.

3.4   Groups and annual financial statements

The Companies Act, 2008 does not specifically require a group of companies to prepare consolidated annual financial statements. However, the reference to International Financial Reporting Standards (IFRS) that apply to certain (but not all) companies[10] implies that consolidated financial statements must be prepared when IFRS are applicable to that company, and when IFRS require this to be done. Current IFRS require the preparation of consolidated financial statements. However, if IFRS do not apply to a company, no consolidated financial statements are required. Therefore private companies with a 'public interest score' below 100, whose financial statements are internally compiled, are not required to prepare consolidated financial statements.

---

10   See para. 7.10 below.

THIS CHAPTER IN ESSENCE

1. Although having no separate legal personality, groups of companies are recognised in law and practice for certain purposes and consequences.

2. A **group of companies** comprises a holding company and all of its subsidiaries.

3. A company **controls** another if the other is its subsidiary or if, together with a related or inter-related person, the company can control the exercise of a majority of the voting rights of the other company's securities, or if the company has the right to appoint or elect directors of the company who together control a majority of votes at a board meeting. A company also controls another company if it has the ability to materially influence the policy of the other company.

4. A **holding company** is a company that controls that subsidiary as set out in s 2(2)(a) or s 3(1)(a) of the Companies Act, 2008.

5. A company is a **subsidiary** of another company if the other company (together with any of its subsidiaries or nominees) can exercise or control the majority of the general voting rights associated with the company's issued securities, or if the other company can appoint or elect directors of the company who together control a majority of votes at a board meeting.

6. A company is a **wholly owned subsidiary** of another company if all of the general voting rights of the company's issued securities are held or controlled by the other company (together with any of its subsidiaries or nominees).

7. The rules for determining who controls the **general voting rights** are contained in s 3(2) of the Companies Act, 2008. It is clear that control is determined by voting power rather than the number of shares held.

8. Important consequences flow for groups of companies.

   8.1 A subsidiary company (together with all other subsidiaries of the same holding company) may acquire only a maximum of 10 per cent in aggregate of the number of issued shares of any class of shares of the holding company. No voting rights attached to these shares may be exercised while held by the subsidiary company or companies.

   8.2 A director's duty not to use information obtained for personal advantage (but to use it for company advantage and not to its detriment) applies also with respect to the holding company and subsidiaries of the company that the director serves.

   8.3 Employee schemes, in terms of which employees are offered shares, are defined so as to treat an employee of a company also as an employee of a holding or subsidiary company for the purposes of the scheme.

   8.4 Similarly, a secondary offer of shares (an offer of shares other than by the company whose shares they are) is treated as though the shares of one company in a group are those of any member of the group of companies.

   8.5 The regulation that is ordinarily applicable to the disposal of all or the greater part of the assets or undertaking of a company (approval by special resolution) does not apply to disposals concluded between companies in the same group of companies.

   8.6 Since holding companies are related to subsidiaries, the restrictions on companies providing financial assistance for the purchase of shares and loans to directors will apply also in relation to other companies in the group.

Chapter 4

Corporate finance: equity, debt instruments and distributions

4.1 Introduction to corporate finance

The term 'corporate finance' covers many areas. This chapter focuses predominantly on corporate finance in so far as it is relevant to company law. There is no doubt that the directors of a company have to make strategic, financing and investment decisions. In particular, the directors need to determine:

- what assets are to be acquired by the company and what assets should be retained;
- how assets under the control of the directors are to be financed; and
- how assets under the control of the directors are to be invested.

All these decisions are **corporate finance** decisions. Various provisions of the Companies Act, 2008 have an impact on directors when they make or implement these decisions. For example, the directors may decide that the company should expand its operations, and that the funding required for such expansion will be raised through an issue of shares. The Companies Act, 2008 sets out certain legal requirements and procedures that can or must be complied with before there is an issue of shares.

The nature and the number of assets that a company needs obviously depend on a number of factors, including the nature of the company's business, the type of assets required (such as cash or plant and equipment), whether or not the business is capital intensive, and the cash-flow needs of the company in conducting its business.

Once the asset needs of a company have been determined, a decision has to be made on how those assets will be financed. The Rand value of assets that a company has and needs in the future determines the level and type of financing (that is, funding) required by a company. Generally speaking, there are only two sources of funding available to the directors of a company, namely debt and/or equity. This chapter deals with those two sources of funding and with the provisions of the Companies Act, 2008 in so far as they are relevant to these two sources of funding of a company's assets.

Table 4.1 below gives examples of sections of the 2008 Act that refer to securities. When the Act refers to 'securities', it refers to both shares and debt instruments such as debentures and a company must comply with these provisions both as regards shares and as regards debt instruments.

Table 4.1 Sections of the 2008 Act dealing with securities

Section number	Topic concerning securities
42	Options for subscription of securities
43	Securities other than shares
44	Financial assistance for subscription of securities
49	Securities to be evidenced by certificates or uncertificated
50	Securities register and numbering
51	Registration and transfer of certificated securities
52	Registration of uncertificated securities
53	Transfer of uncertificated securities
54	Substitution of certificated or uncertificated securities
55	Liability relating to uncertificated securities
56	Beneficial interest in securities

4.1.1   Debt

Debt is money or assets obtained by a company when it does any of the following:

- issues debt instruments, such as (but not limited to) debentures;
- obtains long-term and/or short-term loans;
- enters into lease agreements;
- obtains credit terms from its suppliers, effectively allowing the company to pay in the future for goods or services already received; and
- obtains overdraft facilities from banks.

The Companies Act, 2008 specifically deals with 'debt instruments',[1] but the Act also indirectly deals with the incurrence of the other types of debt, for example by prohibiting reckless trading, and by imposing certain duties (and personal liability in certain circumstances) on directors.[2] Thus, for example, if the assets and operations of a company are largely financed by borrowings, and a company is unable to service the interest or repay any capital relating to those borrowings, the directors may very well fall foul of certain provisions of the Companies Act, such as the prohibition against reckless trading.[3]

The extent to which assets will be financed by debt and/or equity is therefore a very important part of corporate finance, company law and the provisions of the Companies Act, 2008.

---

1   These are discussed in para. 4.10 below.
2   See ss 76 and 77 of the Companies Act, 2008.
3   See s 22 of the Companies Act, 2008.

> **CASE STUDY**
>
> **When incurring debts is reckless**
>
> In *Ozinsky NO v Lloyd*,[4] the court held:
>
> > If a company continues to carry on business and to incur debts when, in the opinion of reasonable businessmen, standing in the shoes of the directors, there would be no reasonable prospect of the creditors receiving payment when due, it will in general be a proper inference that the business is being carried on recklessly.
>
> Similarly, in *Bellini v Paulsen*[5] the court concluded that the conduct of the defendant in this case constituted fraudulent and reckless management of the company's affairs because the defendant knew that the company would not be able to pay its debts as and when they fell due.
>
> > [T]he defendant, with reckless disregard of his duties, allowed this situation to continue when the plaintiff sought to exact payment from the company for the debt due to him ... well knowing that the company had no assets and no way of servicing the debt.

4.1.2   Equity

Equity consists of shares and retained income.

4.1.2.1   Shares

A company can therefore obtain funding for its business operations (that is, for its assets and expenses) by issuing **shares**.[6] The shares in issue can have the same or different rights. In other words, a company can have shares all of the same class, or it can have different classes of shares.[7] The number, nature and classes of shares are an important part of corporate finance (being a financing decision). Shares and share issues are also an important part of company law. The nature and types of shares, and share issues, are therefore dealt with in this chapter with specific reference to the provisions of the Companies Act, 2008.[8]

Company law, which now includes the Companies Act, 2008, has always made it very clear that the rights of shareholders are very different from the rights of creditors.[9] For example, creditors[10] have significant rights in business rescue proceedings, whereas shareholders do not; and the requirement to apply the solvency and liquidity test before certain transactions can take place is largely aimed at the protection of creditors.[11] Section 22(2), inter alia, provides that if the Commission has reasonable grounds to believe that a company is unable to pay its debts as they become due and payable in the normal course of business, the Commission may issue a notice to the company to show cause why the company should be permitted to continue carrying on its business, or to trade.

---

4   1992 (3) SA 396 (C) at 414G-H.
5   [2012] ZAWCHC 199.
6   The Act defines 'securities' as any shares, debentures or other instruments, irrespective of their form or title, issued or authorised to be issued by a profit company. The word 'securities', as used in the Act, therefore embraces both debt and shares. The Act defines 'share' as one of the units into which the proprietary interest in a profit company is divided.
7   See para. 4.6.1 below for greater detail.
8   See paras. 4.6 and 4.7 below.
9   Creditors are those who fund the company by way of debt instruments and other types of debt as discussed above.
10 Creditors also include unpaid employees in business rescue proceedings.
11 See paras. 4.2 to 4.4 below.

4.1.2.2   Retained income

Retained income is also an important part of the funding of a company. This is why the dividend policy of a company is an important corporate finance decision: instead of paying all profits to shareholders by way of dividends, directors can choose to retain all or some of those profits in the business (depending, of course, on the rights attaching to any specific shares)[12] in order to fund operations and expansions. However, directors need to be aware that in deciding upon a dividend policy (a financing decision) and in making investment decisions (determining how retained funds will be utilised), the company (through the decisions of the directors) needs to apply retained assets in a profitable manner, and possibly in a more effective manner than shareholders themselves would be able to do if those profits were paid to them as dividends. In this regard, directors should be mindful of the common-law and statutory duty[13] to be careful, diligent and skilful.

The provisions of the 2008 Act regarding the declaration and payment of dividends are discussed in this chapter, since retained profits form an important part of the equity funding of the assets of a company.[14] Moreover, the Act defines '**distribution**' as including not only dividends, but also share buybacks (s 48) and the payment of cash in lieu of issuing capitalisation shares (s 47). Since share buybacks and cash payments will have a direct bearing on equity and on the assets retained or paid out by a company, ss 47 and 48 are also discussed in this chapter.[15]

In summary, this chapter deals with debt and equity as sources of financing for a company's operations and assets, as indicated in Table 4.2 below:

Table 4.2 *Sources of funding: equity and debt instruments*

Topic	Paragraph where discussed in this book	Relevant section of the 2008 Act
Equity (shares and distributions)		
Shares as a source of finance: the nature of shares	Paragraph 4.5	Section 35
Authorised shares		
Useful disclosure?	Paragraph 4.6	
Content of MOI	Paragraph 4.6.1	Sections 36–37
Unalterable provisions	Paragraph 4.6.2	Section 37
Changing authorised shares	Paragraph 4.6.3	Section 36
Issued shares		
Introduction	Paragraph 4.7	Section 38
Consideration	Paragraph 4.7.1	Section 40
Future payments	Paragraph 4.7.2	Section 40(5)

---

12   For example, in the case of preference shares, a dividend often has to be declared on an annual (or more frequent) basis.
13   See s 76 of the Companies Act, 2008.
14   See para. 4.9 below.
15   See para. 4.9 below.

Topic	Paragraph where discussed in this book	Relevant section of the 2008 Act
Capitalisation shares	Paragraph 4.7.3	Section 47
When shareholder approval is required	Paragraph 4.7.4	Section 49
Pre-emptive rights	Paragraph 4.7.5	Section 39
Financial assistance for the subscription of a company's own shares	Paragraph 4.7.6	Section 41
Certificated and uncertificated shares	Paragraph 4.7.7	Sections 24 and 26
Records (securities register) and access thereto	Paragraph 4.7.8	Section 44
Unissued shares	Paragraph 4.8	
Distributions		
Introduction	Paragraph 4.9	
Requirements preceding distributions	Paragraph 4.9.1	Section 46
Acquisition by a company of its own shares (share buybacks)	Paragraph 4.9.2	Section 48
Payment of cash in lieu of the issue of capitalisation shares	Paragraph 4.9.3	Section 47
Debt instruments		
Securities other than shares (such as debt instruments)	Paragraph 4.10	Section 43

4.2 Sources of finance, nature of assets and the solvency and liquidity test

The Companies Act, 2008 introduces a **solvency and liquidity test**,[16] which must be applied and passed by a company prior to certain transactions taking place. For example, before the directors can declare a dividend they have to apply the solvency and liquidity test and confirm that the company passes this test. Similarly, the solvency and liquidity test must be applied and passed before a company repurchases any of its own shares.

The introduction of the solvency and liquidity test will influence directors when making the corporate finance decisions referred to earlier in this chapter. For example, in deciding how assets and ongoing operations should be financed (that is, whether by debt and/or equity), directors must be mindful of the fact that if assets and expenses are financed largely by debt, the company may fall foul of the solvency part of the solvency and liquidity

---

16   As defined in s 4 of the Companies Act, 2008.

test – because the company's debts may become greater than its assets. This may occur in particular when debt finance is used to fund expenses rather than assets. As mentioned earlier, if a company fails the test, it will not be able to do certain things, such as declare a dividend.

This test also has a direct influence on other corporate finance decisions (the strategic, financing and investing decisions referred to above). For example, the composition of the assets of a company is an important consideration (strategic decision): how much cash should a company have in order to satisfy the **liquidity** part of the solvency and liquidity test? A company may very well have an excess of assets over liabilities (that is, it may be **solvent**), but the assets could be illiquid (not easily turned into cash) resulting in a company being unable to pay its debts in the normal course of business and thereby offending the liquidity part of the test described above.[17]

The solvency and liquidity test is discussed in this chapter because it forms an important part of corporate finance decisions.

4.3   A new approach to capital regulation in the 2008 Act

One of the more significant changes brought about by the Companies Act, 2008 is a new approach to the regulation of the capital of a company. There are two important developments:

1. the virtual abolition of the capital maintenance concept; and
2. the extensive default[18] powers given to directors (rather than shareholders) to determine both the authorised and issued shares of a company, and to declare dividends.

4.3.1   Capital maintenance

The 1973 Act was originally based on the **capital maintenance** concept, which ensured that the contributed share capital of a company had to be maintained or preserved for a number of reasons, not least of which was the protection of creditors. The concept was based on the principle that the contributed share capital of a company was the fund, or reservoir, to which the creditors of a company could look for satisfaction of their claims. Accordingly, that fund had to be maintained.

Even though the Companies Amendment Act[19] 37 of 1999 relaxed many of the strict capital maintenance rules (such as on the strict prohibition on a company to repurchase its own shares), it was left to the 2008 Act to abolish the capital maintenance concept almost completely, and replace it with a company law regime based on the principles of liquidity and solvency. Thus, for example, before a company can buy back its own shares (s 48), or provide financial assistance in connection with the subscription of its securities (s 44), or before the directors can propose a distribution (s 46), the liquidity and solvency test has to be applied and satisfied. Not only does the 2008 Act abolish the capital maintenance rule, but it also does not use the word share 'capital' and simply refers to authorised and issued 'shares'. This may well mean that the traditional description of 'share capital' (both

---

17 If a company cannot pay its debts, it can offend other sections of the Act as well. For example, s 22(2) provides that if the Commission has reasonable grounds to believe that a company is engaging in reckless conduct, or is unable to pay its debts as they become due and payable in the normal course of business, the Commission may issue a notice to the company to show cause why the company should be permitted to continue carrying on its business, or to trade, as the case may be.

18 By 'default' is meant that the directors will automatically have these powers unless they are modified or abolished in terms of a company's Memorandum of Incorporation.

19 37 of 1999.

authorised and issued) in the financial statements of companies should be replaced by the description 'authorised and issued shares'.

An interesting observation regarding the abolition of the capital maintenance rule and its replacement by a liquidity and solvency test is that the 2008 Act probably protects the interests of creditors to a far greater extent than the capital maintenance rules did. Whilst capital had to be 'maintained' in terms of those rules (and could not, for example, be returned to shareholders), there was no minimum level of capital that had to be provided. In the result, many companies' assets were funded by a small nominal amount of share capital, and by very large shareholders' loans. All that was required was for that nominal capital to be maintained, which hardly afforded creditors any protection at all. In terms of the 2008 Act, companies that are funded by large shareholders' loans (which are obviously liabilities of the company) would mostly be insolvent in the sense that the value of their assets would be less than their liabilities, and such companies would not be able (under the 2008 Act) to declare dividends,[20] buy back shares,[21] or enter into other transactions that require a successful application of the solvency and liquidity test.[22]

4.3.2 Default powers of directors

Another significant change brought about by the 2008 Act in the corporate finance arena is the introduction of the so-called 'default' provisions of the Act (that is, the provisions that will automatically apply to a company unless altered in a company's Memorandum of Incorporation (MOI)). These empower the board of directors (and not the shareholders) to determine a company's authorised *and* issued shares, and to declare dividends. These default provisions suit 'owner-managed' private companies, but they will in most cases need to be altered or abolished in the MOI of a company that has a number of diverse and unrelated shareholders, especially if there are minority shareholders. Such shareholders would need to be protected, for example, from having their interests diluted as a result of the directors unilaterally deciding to increase authorised or issued shares. In terms of the 1973 Act, there had to be both authorisation in the articles, and a special resolution of shareholders, before there could be any change in a company's authorised shares. The 2008 Act therefore takes a significantly different view of this matter.

4.4 The application of the solvency and liquidity test

The solvency and liquidity test must be applied in each of the following circumstances:
- when a company wishes to provide financial assistance for subscription of its securities in terms of s 44;
- if a company grants loans or other financial assistance to directors and others as contemplated in s 45;
- before a company makes any distribution as provided for in s 46;
- if a company wishes to pay cash in lieu of issuing capitalisation shares in terms of s 47; and
- if a company wishes to acquire its own shares as provided for in s 48.

---

20 Section 46 of the Companies Act, 2008.
21 Section 48 of the Companies Act, 2008.
22 Such as ss 44, 45 and 47 of the Companies Act, 2008.

It is clear from the definition of the liquidity and solvency test[23] that a company satisfies the test if it is both 'solvent' (by reference to its assets and liabilities) and 'liquid' (by reference to its future cash flows).

Section 4 of the Companies Act, 2008 defines the requirements of the solvency and liquidity test as follows:

> [A] company satisfies the solvency and liquidity test at a particular time if, considering all reasonably foreseeable financial circumstances of the company at that time—
>
> (a) the assets of the company, as fairly valued, equal or exceed the liabilities of the company, as fairly valued; and
>
> (b) it appears that the company will be able to pay its debts as they become due in the ordinary course of business for a period of—
>
>   (i) 12 months after the date on which the test is considered; or
>
>   (ii) in the case of a distribution contemplated in paragraph (a) of the definition of 'distribution' in section 1, 12 months following that distribution.

4.4.1   Solvency

From a reading of the definition in s 4,[24] it is clear that the word 'valued' is used with reference to both assets and liabilities. The concept of 'value' is obviously very different from 'historic cost', or 'book value'. It may well be suggested that directors should have a separate record of all assets and liabilities indicating the respective values of those assets and liabilities. The value of an asset could of course be either higher or lower than its value as determined for financial reporting purposes, and the value of a liability could certainly be below its face value. Taking the latter as an example, if the liabilities of a company are greater than the fair value of its assets, it is submitted that the directors would be perfectly entitled, in applying the solvency and liquidity test to reduce the face value of liabilities to the recoverable amount.[25] By reducing the face value of liabilities (for example, a shareholders' loan) to its recoverable amount, the directors could in fact ensure that a company's liabilities are no longer greater than its assets, thereby satisfying the solvency and liquidity test, thus enabling the company to do certain things, such as declaring a dividend, which it would not otherwise be allowed to do in terms of the solvency and liquidity test.[26]

Under the 1973 company law regime, shareholders' loans were often subordinated or 'back-ranked'. In terms of the 2008 Act, any such subordination would not reduce the liabilities of a company, because a subordination merely back-ranks, but does not extinguish a debt. A subordination of shareholders' loans would therefore not restore a company's solvency in the manner here described. There is an additional reason not to subordinate shareholders' loans. In business rescue proceedings,[27] the voting interests of a secured or unsecured creditor are determined by giving a voting interest equal to the value of the amount owed to that creditor by the company. However, a concurrent creditor with a

---

23   See s 4 of the Companies Act, 2008.

24   See para. 4.4 above.

25   For example, if a company at a certain time has liabilities of R120 and assets of only R100, it is clear that the full amount owing of R120 (the face value of the debt) is not recoverable at that time. Therefore, the debt can be 'valued' at its net realisable value of R 100.

26   Re-valuing a liability, it is submitted, does not amount to a debt write-off. The latter could result in capital gains tax and other consequences. In re-valuing a liability, the directors are free to revalue it upwards, at some later stage to its original face value, once the assets of the company increase.

27   See Chapter 6 of the Companies Act, 2008, from s 128 onwards.

subordinated claim has a voting interest only equal to the amount, if any, that the creditor could reasonably expect to receive in such a liquidation of the company. In other words, any shareholder who subordinates a loan account could dilute any voting interest that is exercisable in considering a business rescue plan.

4.4.2 Liquidity

In applying the solvency and liquidity test, it is clear that the directors will have to prepare a cash flow statement indicating future inflows and outflows. Such a cash flow statement must contain an assessment of the future level of debt and the company's ability to settle its due debt commitments by cash as required by the section.

4.5 Shares as a source of finance and the nature of shares

Section 1 of the Companies Act, 2008 defines 'share' as one of the units into which the proprietary interest in a profit company is divided. This does not mean that a share entitles the holder thereof to the assets of the company. The company itself, being a separate legal entity, owns its assets. The number of shares held by a shareholder is therefore simply an indicator of the extent to which a holder has an interest in the company itself.

In *Cooper v Boyes NO*,[28] the court discussed the nature of a share, and held that a share represents an interest in a company, which interest consists of a complex of personal rights: a share is incorporeal movable property that gives rise to a bundle of personal rights. All the shares of the same class must have the same rights.[29] It follows then that if the rights attaching to the shares of a company differ, there are different classes of shares.

A share is part of the 'securities' of a company. The Act defines 'securities' as any shares, debentures or other instruments, irrespective of their form or title, issued or authorised to be issued by a profit company. This definition is important because when the Act refers to securities, it refers to both shares and debt instruments such as debentures.[30]

The question of what shares should be issued[31] focuses on the asset requirements of a company and the extent to which such assets will be funded by equity contributors (by way of issued shares and retained income), and the extent to which the assets are to be funded by lenders and creditors. In determining what shares should be issued, and at what price, it is important for the directors to avoid the dangers of over-capitalisation and under-capitalisation, by steering a middle course between the two.

Over-capitalisation arises when the amount received, or to be received,[32] by a company from the issue of its shares is in excess of its requirements, as measured by the earning capacity of its assets – it is then not possible for a satisfactory return to be earned on the equity invested. **Under-capitalisation**, on the other hand, occurs when a company finds itself short of funds, so that its expansion is curtailed, and it cannot seize appropriate business opportunities or extend credit to customers.

---

28 1994 (4) SA 521 (C).

29 Section 37(1) of the Companies Act, 2008 provides that all of the shares of any particular class authorised by a company must have preferences, rights, limitations and other terms that are identical to those of other shares of the same class.

30 Section 43 of the Companies Act, 2008 deals with debt instruments: see para. 4.10 below.

31 Obviously, not all authorised shares have to be issued: unissued shares are those shares that have been authorised but not yet issued.

32 See s 40(5) of the Companies Act, 2008, which allows shares to be issued for future benefits, services or payments.

A realistic assessment of the equity requirements of a company for the future is therefore necessary and highly desirable. The factors to be taken into account will include some or all of the following:

- the nature of the business and the assets required;
- the risk appetite of the company (the extent to which assets should be funded by equity or by debt and borrowings);
- the proposed outlay, if any, on capital infrastructure and expenditure;
- the amount of working capital required, such as the level and variety of inventories required, and the need for cash; and
- the availability of borrowings.

4.6   Authorised, issued and unissued shares

In terms of s 36 of the 2008 Act, a company's MOI must set out a company's authorised shares by specifying the classes of shares, and the number of shares in each class. Unlike the 1973 Act, where shares were either 'par value' or 'no par value' shares, under the 2008 Act, there are simply 'shares', which can comprise shares of different classes.

The classes and number of authorised shares as stated in a company's MOI are, however, not very meaningful because the amount (value) for which those shares have been or will be issued is not determined in the MOI. Moreover, the authorised shares, as disclosed in a company's MOI, can always be increased (or decreased) at a later stage.[33] And if a company issues shares that have not been authorised in a company's MOI, or which are in excess of the number of authorised shares of any particular class, the issue of those shares may be retroactively authorised by the board (s 36),[34] or by a special resolution of shareholders[35] within 60 business days after the date on which the shares were issued.

As opposed to authorised shares, the number of **issued shares**,[36] and the amount received or receivable[37] from their issue is indeed useful information, because these show not only the classes of shares, but also what the company has received, or will receive,[38] from such issue. Whether the company is over- or under-capitalised[39] can then be assessed and rectifying measures, if any, may be taken.

4.6.1   Authorised shares and the Memorandum of Incorporation

The MOI must set out,[40] with respect to each class of shares:
- a distinguishing designation for that class; and
- the preferences, rights, limitations and other terms associated with that class (unless these will be determined later by the board of directors).[41]

---

33   Section 36(3)(*a*) of the Companies Act, 2008.
34   Subject to the provisions of a company's MOI.
35   Section 16 of the Companies Act, 2008, which deals with the amendment of a company's MOI.
36   Section 38(1) of the Companies Act, 2008 provides that the board of a company may resolve to issue shares of the company at any time, but only within the classes, and to the extent, that the shares have been authorised by or in terms of the company's MOI, in accordance with s 36.
37   See s 40(5) of the Companies Act, 2008, which allows shares to be issued for future benefits, services or payments.
38   See s 40(5) of the Companies Act, 2008, which allows shares to be issued for future benefits, services or payments.
39   See para. 4.5 above.
40   Section 36 of the Companies Act, 2008.
41   See the discussion below.

All of the shares of any particular class must have the same rights and limitations.[42] Therefore, if there are different preferences, rights, limitations or other terms attaching to the shares of a company, that company has different classes of shares. Those with the same rights and limitations form part of the same class.

The authorised shares of a company may consist of one homogeneous type of share, or of several different classes of shares, each with different rights as regards voting, sharing in the profits, and participating in new issues of capital or in the distribution of assets in the event of the company being wound up. The following are the classes of authorised shares commonly encountered:

- **ordinary shares**;
- **preference shares**, which may be cumulative, non-cumulative, participating, redeemable, and/or convertible;
- **unclassified shares** (a stated number may be authorised in the MOI), which are subject to classification by the board of the company in accordance with s 36(3)(c) – this allows the board to re-classify shares into one or more existing classes of authorised shares or to increase the number of authorised shares of an existing class; and
- **'blank' shares**, which are a class of shares that does not specify the associated preferences, rights, limitations or other terms of that class, and for which the board of the company must determine the associated preferences, rights, limitations or other terms, and which must not be issued until the board of the company has determined the associated preferences, rights, limitations or other terms of those shares.[43]

Section 37(5) provides that a company's MOI may establish, for any particular class of shares, preferences, rights, limitations or other terms that:

- confer special, conditional or limited voting rights;
- provide for shares of that class to be redeemable or convertible;
- entitle the shareholders to distributions calculated in any manner, including dividends that may be cumulative, non-cumulative, or partially cumulative; or
- provide for shares of that class to have preference over any other class of shares with respect to distributions, or rights upon the final liquidation of the company.

Moreover, s 37(6) provides that a company's MOI may provide for preferences, rights, limitations or other terms of any class of shares of that company to vary in response to any objectively ascertainable external fact or facts.

4.6.2   Entrenched rights attaching to authorised shares

The Act allows for different classes of shares, which means that different rights can attach to different shares. However, the Act provides for a few 'unalterable' rights that attach to shares despite any terms to the contrary in the MOI. These are described below.

4.6.2.1   Right to vote on proposals to amend the rights attaching to shares

Section 37(3)(a) provides that despite anything to the contrary in a company's MOI, every share issued by that company has associated with it an irrevocable right of the shareholder to vote on any proposal to amend the preferences, rights, limitations and other terms associated with that share.

---

42   Section 37 of the Companies Act, 2008.
43   See C Stein *The New Companies Act Unlocked* (2011), chapter 30 and also pp 386–7.

4.6.2.2 Right to seek relief if the rights of a shareholder are materially and adversely altered

Section 37(8) provides that if a company's MOI has been amended to materially and adversely alter the preferences, rights, limitations or other terms of a class of shares, any holder of those shares is entitled to seek relief in terms of s 164 if that shareholder:

- notified the company in advance of the intention to oppose the resolution to amend the [MOI]; and
- was present at the meeting, and voted against that resolution.

Section 164 gives dissenting minority shareholders a so-called 'appraisal right' in terms of which a shareholder may demand that the company pay the shareholder the fair value for all of the shares of the company held by that person.

4.6.2.3 Rights when there is only one class of shares

Section 37(3)(b) provides that if a company has established only one class of shares:

- those shares have a right to be voted on every matter that may be decided by shareholders of the company; and
- the holders of that class of shares are entitled to receive the net assets of the company upon its liquidation.

4.6.3 Changes to authorised shares

Unless the MOI of a company provides differently, the directors of a company can increase (or decrease) a company's authorised shares, and make certain other changes.[44] If the MOI does not allow the directors to make changes, then the shareholders' approval will be necessary. The alteration of a company's MOI is discussed in detail in chapter 2 of this book.[45]

As far as changing the authorised shares of a company is concerned, s 36(3) provides that, except to the extent that a company's MOI provides otherwise, the board of directors itself may do any of the following:

- increase or decrease the number of authorised shares of any class of shares;
- reclassify any classified shares that have been authorised but not issued;
- classify any unclassified shares that have been authorised but not issued; or
- determine the preferences, rights, limitations or other terms of shares in a class contemplated in s 36(1)(d).

4.7 Issued shares

Issued shares are those that are actually issued – that is, they are allocated to a particular shareholder or shareholders and they cease to be merely potential shares in that sense. In terms of s 221 of the 1973 Act, before directors could make a further issue of shares, over and above the shares originally allotted, they had to secure the prior consent of the company in general meeting. This consent could have been specifically related to the new issue or could have been a general approval permitting the directors to issue further shares at their discretion.

Unlike the 1973 Act, the 2008 Act provides that the board itself may resolve to issue shares of the company at any time, but only within the classes, and to the extent, that the shares

---

44 In other words, this is a default position that can be changed by a company's MOI.
45 See para. 2.10.6 above.

have been authorised by or in terms of the company's MOI. In other words, the prior approval of shareholders is no longer required for the issue of shares (unless the company's MOI alters this power that is automatically given to directors in terms of the Act).

The issued shares may constitute a portion or the whole of the authorised shares but cannot exceed it, and, together with undistributed profits (or retained income), and other reserves, it constitutes the **equity** of the company for the operation of its undertaking.

However, if a company issues shares that have not been authorised, or shares that are in excess of the number of authorised shares of any particular class, the issue of those shares may be retroactively authorised in accordance with a company's MOI (s 36) or by shareholders' special resolution (s 16) within 60 business days after the date on which the shares were issued.

If they are not retroactively authorised, then the share issue is a nullity to the extent that it exceeds any authorisation, and the company must return to any person the fair value of the consideration received by the company in respect of that share issue to the extent that it is nullified, together with interest in accordance with the Prescribed Rate of Interest Act.[46]

4.7.1   Consideration for issued shares

Section 40(2) of the Companies Act, 2008 provides that before a company issues any particular shares, the board must determine the **consideration** for which, and the terms on which, those shares will be issued. In other words, the board must decide what value the company will receive in exchange for issuing shares to the holder of those shares.

In terms of s 40(1), the board of a company may issue authorised shares only:

* for adequate consideration to the company, as determined by the board;
* in terms of conversion rights associated with previously issued securities of the company; or
* as a capitalisation share (as contemplated in s 47).

In principle, there is no reason why shares cannot be issued for cash or for assets other than cash. The consideration for the shares can also be received in the future or in terms of an agreement for future services or benefits.[47] Where future benefits are not concerned, s 40(4) provides that when a company has received the consideration approved by its board for the issue of any share, the company must issue those shares and cause the name of the holder to be entered on the company's securities register.[48]

4.7.2   Issue of shares for future payments or services

As has already been mentioned in this chapter, many of the sections of the 1973 Act were based on the capital maintenance principle. For example, s 92 of that Act provided that only fully paid shares could be allotted or issued.[49] In terms of s 92, whatever was paid for the shares, in cash or in kind, had to be received by the company before or when it issued the shares. In *Etkind v Hicor Trading Ltd*,[50] the court held that an agreement that provides for a company to acquire assets by the issue of shares without or before receiving delivery of the assets, was void and unenforceable because it was in breach of s 92.

---

46   55 of 1975.
47   Section 40(5) of the Companies Act, 2008. See para. 4.7.2 below for a discussion of future benefits when shares are issued.
48   A company's securities register is discussed in para. 4.7.7 below.
49   Section 92(1) of the Companies Act, 1973.
50   1999 (1) SA 111 (W).

Section 40(5) of the 2008 Act takes a very different view, and provides that shares can be issued for future payments, future benefits or future services. Such shares are held in trust until that future event occurs. While the shares are held in trust, voting or appraisal rights are not exercisable (unless the trust deed provides differently).

An interesting question that arises when shares are issued for future benefits is whether or not any accounting entries could or should be passed at the time of the issue of the shares, and, if so, which accounting entries should be passed?

It is submitted that since there has to be a *consideration* before shares can be issued,[51] that consideration must be capable of being given a monetary value (even if it is present-valued), and that value must be recorded. Failure to do this could result in donations tax (except in the case of public companies, which are exempt from donations tax) because the company would then be issuing shares for no consideration. There is no doubt that a company that issues shares for future benefits acquires a right (in the form of a claim against the subscribing party), and the value of that right must be capable of determination.

The other interesting point is that if the shares are issued in exchange for labour, the person who has performed (or will perform) the labour, may have to include the value of the shares in his or her gross income for tax purposes.[52]

4.7.3   Issue of capitalisation shares

Section 47 of the Companies Act, 2008 provides that the board of directors may approve the issuing of any authorised shares of the company as **capitalisation shares**,[53] on a *pro rata* basis to the shareholders of one or more classes of shares. Capitalisation shares are 'bonus shares' issued in lieu of dividends and arise as a result of the capitalisation of the profits of the company rather than their distribution. The issue of shares by a company, even the issue of capitalisation shares, is *not regarded as a distribution* and is therefore not subject to the solvency and liquidity test or to the other provisions of s 46.[54] It is logical that a capitalisation issue is not regarded as a distribution because the company has not distributed or paid out any asset: there is merely a reclassification of equity (that is, a transfer of retained income to issued shares).

Subject to a company's MOI, the directors, when resolving to award a capitalisation share, may resolve to permit any shareholder who is entitled to receive such an award to elect instead to receive a cash payment at a value determined by the board. The payment of cash in lieu of a dividend is regarded as a distribution and must comply with the provisions of s 46,[55] which regulates the payment of distributions. This makes sense because if a shareholder chooses to receive cash instead of shares, the assets of the company are reduced by the payment made.

It is also important to note that s 47 allows the shares of one class to be issued as a capitalisation share in respect of shares of another class.

4.7.4   When shareholder approval is required to issue shares

Section 41 of the Companies Act, 2008 requires shareholder approval (by way of special resolution) for issuing shares in certain circumstances.

---

51   Section 40(2) of the Companies Act, 2008.
52   Section 1*(c)* of the 'gross income' definition in the Income Tax Act 58 of 1962 as amended.
53   The provisions of s 47 are alterable in that a company's MOI can abolish or modify this default position.
54   Section 1 defines 'distribution' as meaning a direct or indirect transfer by a company of money or other property of the company, other than its own shares, to or for the benefit of one more holders of any of the shares.
55   See para. 4.9.3 below.

4.7.4.1 Issue of shares to directors and related parties

Shareholder approval is required if the shares, securities, options or rights are issued to a director, future director, prescribed officer, or future prescribed officer of the company (or to a person related or inter-related to the company, or to a director or prescribed officer of the company; or to any nominee of such person).[56]

However, shareholder approval will not be required if the issue of shares is:[57]

- under an agreement underwriting the shares, securities or rights;
- in the exercise of a pre-emptive right to be offered and to subscribe shares as contemplated in s 39;
- in proportion to existing holdings, and on the same terms and conditions as have been offered to all the shareholders of the company or to all the shareholders of the class or classes of shares being issued;
- pursuant to an employee share scheme that satisfies the requirements of s 97; or
- pursuant to an offer to the public, as defined in s 95(1)(h), read with s 96.

4.7.4.2 Issue of shares when voting power of issue will be 30 per cent or more

Section 41(3) requires approval of the shareholders by special resolution if there is an issue of shares, securities convertible into shares, or rights exercisable for shares in a transaction (or a series of integrated transactions), and the voting power of the class of shares so issued will be equal to or exceed 30 per cent of the voting power of all the shares of that class held by shareholders immediately before the transaction or series of transactions.

4.7.5 Pre-emptive rights

Any company's MOI can provide that, if the company proposes to issue any shares, each shareholder has the right, before any other person who is not a shareholder of that company, to be offered and, within a reasonable time to subscribe for, a percentage of the shares to be issued equal to the voting power of that shareholder's general voting rights immediately before the offer was made. This is known as a **pre-emptive right**.

However, the Companies Act, 2008 makes a distinction between a public (including state-owned) company and a private company with regard to pre-emptive rights. In the case of a *private company*, s 39 makes the right of pre-emption a default position. In other words, shareholders in a private company automatically have this pre-emptive right unless it is changed or abolished by the company's MOI. The default position for *public and state-owned* companies is that the shareholders do not have this automatic right.

In the case of private companies, this right does not apply to shares issued:

- in terms of options or conversion rights;
- shares issued for future services or benefits;[58] or
- when there is a capitalisation issue.

In exercising the pre-emptive right, the default position is that a shareholder of a private company may subscribe for fewer shares than the shareholder would be entitled to subscribe for under that subsection. Shares that are not subscribed for by a shareholder may be offered to other persons to the extent permitted by the company's MOI.

---

56   Section 41(1) of the Companies Act, 2008.
57   Section 41(2) of the Companies Act, 2008.
58   See para. 4.7.2 above.

NB
4.7.6   Financial assistance

Section 44 of the Companies Act, 2008 sets out the requirements if a company provides **financial assistance** in connection with the issue of any of its securities.[59] Compliance with these requirements is not necessary if the company is a moneylender (as part of its ordinary and primary business). The default position[60] is that the board of directors may authorise the company to provide financial assistance[61] subject to the following three requirements:

1. the particular provision of financial assistance is
   - pursuant to an employee share scheme that satisfies the requirements of s 97; or
   - pursuant to a special resolution of the shareholders, adopted within the previous two years, that approved such assistance either for the specific recipient, or generally for a category of potential recipients, and the specific recipient falls within that category; and
2. the board is satisfied that
   - immediately after providing the financial assistance, the company would satisfy the solvency and liquidity test; and
   - the terms under which the financial assistance is proposed to be given are fair and reasonable to the company; and
3. any conditions or restrictions respecting the granting of financial assistance set out in the company's MOI have been satisfied.

4.7.7   Certificated and uncertificated securities

Any securities issued by a company must be either certificated or uncertificated.[62] A **certificated security** is one that is evidenced by a certificate, whereas uncertificated securities are defined as 'securities that are not evidenced by a certificate or written instrument and are transferable by entry without a written instrument',[63] and are therefore securities that are held and transferred electronically. Securities can only be traded on the JSE if they are uncertificated.[64]

Section 49(3)*(a)* of the Companies Act, 2008 makes it clear that except to the extent that the Act expressly provides otherwise, the rights and obligations of security holders are not different according to whether they are certificated or uncertificated. Certificated securities can be converted into uncertificated securities and vice versa.

If the company issues uncertificated securities, or where certificated shares are converted into uncertificated securities, a record of these securities must be kept in the prescribed form as the company's **uncertificated securities register** by a participant or central securities depository.[65] This register must contain the same information required in the case of certificated securities. This register forms part of the company's **securities register**.

---

59   A share is part of the securities of a company. The Act defines 'securities' as any shares, debentures or other instruments, irrespective of their form or title, issued or authorised to be issued by a profit company. This definition is important because when the Act refers to securities it refers to both shares and debt instruments such as debentures.
60   The default position may be altered by the provisions of a company's MOI.
61   Section 44(2) refers to 'financial assistance' as being extended by way of a loan, guarantee, the provision of security or otherwise.
62   Section 49(2) of the Companies Act, 2008.
63   Section 1 of the Companies Act, 2008.
64   See *www.strate.co.za/aboutstrate/overview/dematerialisation*.
65   Section 50(3) of the Companies Act, 2008.

A **central securities depository** is licensed[66] to operate the electronic system for the holding and transfer of uncertificated securities. The current licensee is Strate Ltd (the acronym 'Strate' is derived from Share TRAnsactions Totally Electronic). Only 'participants' can liaise with Strate directly. Persons trading in uncertificated securities and their brokers must therefore work through a participant.[67] A **participant** is a person who administers securities and who has been accepted as a participant by a central securities depository.[68] Currently, six CSD participants have been accepted by Strate. Five of them of them are banks and the other is Computershare. Of these, only Computershare currently offers investors the option of holding the securities in their own name. The others make all registrations in the name of their nominee companies.

4.7.8   Records of issued shares

Section 24 of the Companies Act, 2008 requires every company to maintain certain specific records. All of a company's accounting records must be kept at, or be accessible from, the registered office.[69] A company must notify the Commission of the location of, or any change in the location of, any company records that are not located at its registered office.

As far as issued shares are concerned, s 24(4) provides that every company must maintain a securities register or its equivalent, as required by s 50, in the case of a profit company, or a member's register in the case of a non-profit company that has members. The register reflects the names of the current holders of shares and other securities.

In practice, there is also extensive use of **nominees**, and this means that the registered holder is often not the beneficial holder of the rights pertaining to the securities. Therefore, where there is a nominee holding shares in a public company, details of the beneficial owner must also be disclosed by the nominee and given to the company. The total number of securities held in uncertificated form must also be entered in the securities register.[70] The securities register is proof of the facts recorded in it, in the absence of evidence to the contrary.

In terms of s 26, both shareholders and non-shareholders have the right to inspect the securities register in the manner provided for in that section.

CASE STUDY	**Entitlement to access securities registers**
	In *Basson v On-point Engineers (Pty) Ltd*,[71] the applicants were members of the media who had sought access to the respondents' registers to establish the shareholding of each of the respondents so that they could establish who benefitted from the state tenders that were awarded to the respondents. The court held that if there was any doubt as to whether the applicants were in terms of s 26(6) entitled to access the securities registers of the applicants then the court had to adopt an interpretation of s 26(6) which best promoted the spirit, purport and objects of the Bill of Rights as set out in s 39(2) of the Constitution. The court referred to previous cases where it has been held that s 113 of the 1973 Act did not oblige a person requesting information

---

66   Under s 29 of the Financial Markets Act 19 of 2012.
67   See *www.strate.co.za/aboutstrate/overview/dematerialisation*.
68   Section 1 of the Companies Act, 2008 provides that 'participant' has the meaning set out in s 1 of the Financial Markets Act 19 of 2012.
69   See a discussion of what is meant by 'registered office' in para. 7.6 below.
70   Section 50(2)(*a*) of the Companies Act, 2008.
71   2012 JDR 2126 (GNP); [2012] ZAGPPHC 251.

to provide motivation for doing so, and a person who seeks to inspect the register need not give reasons for doing so. The court referred to the case of *La Lucia Sands Share Block v Barkhan*[72] where the court states:

> In a constitutional state in which freedom of association and access to information are valued, courts should be slow to make orders that have a limiting effect. It bears repeating that in terms of s 113(3) of the Act a failure to comply with a legitimate request for access to the register of members renders a company, and every director or officer who knowingly is a party to the refusal, guilty of a criminal offence.

Similarly, the court held that in this case s 26(9) makes it an offence not to accommodate any reasonable request for access to any record in terms of s 26 or s 31. The court therefore concluded that all three respondents had to provide copies of the securities register or allow the inspection thereof.

Section 37(9) provides that a person acquires the rights associated with any particular securities of a company:
- when that person's name is entered in the company's certificated securities register; or
- as determined in accordance with the rules of the central securities depository, in the case of uncertificated securities.

A person ceases to have the rights associated with any particular securities of a company:
- when the transfer to another person, re-acquisition by the company, or surrender to the company has been entered in the company's certificated securities register; or
- as determined in accordance with the rules of the central securities depository, in the case of uncertificated securities.

4.8   Unissued shares

As the name implies, **unissued shares** are those shares that have been authorised but not yet issued. The default position (unless altered in a company's MOI) is that directors have the power to reclassify authorised yet unissued shares from shares of one class to shares of another, and to increase or to decrease such authorised shares.[73]

4.9   Distributions

The word '**distribution**' is very broadly defined and means the transfer of both cash and other assets by a company to its own shareholders or to the shareholders of any company within the same group. Such transfer can be in any of the following ways:
- by way of a dividend;
- as a payment in lieu of a capitalisation share;
- as payment for any share buyback (such shares can be the company's own shares, or those of a company within that group of companies);

---

72   2010 (6) SA 421 (SCA); [2010] ZASCA 132 at para. [13].
73   See para. 4.3.2 above.

- by the company incurring a debt or other obligation for the benefit of one or more of its shareholders, or shareholders of another company within the same group of companies; or
- by the forgiveness or waiver by a company of a debt or other obligation owed to the company by its own shareholders or shareholders of another company within the same group of companies.

Specifically excluded from the definition is any action taken upon the final liquidation of a company.

The definition of 'distribution' is also broadened by s 37(5)*(b)*, in terms of which a company's MOI can provide for **redeemable shares** of any class. However, any redeemable shares are also subject to the requirements of s 46 (on distributions), even though a share redemption is not regarded as a share buyback.[74] In summary, a share redemption is regarded as a distribution that must comply with the provisions of s 46. This means that, even though a redemption is pursuant to an obligation of the company, before the redemption can take place the solvency and liquidity test must be applied and passed in the same way that must happen for any other distribution. The difference between a redemption and a share buyback is that a company is not compelled to buy back its own shares, whereas in the case of a redemption there is an obligation on the company to buy back the shares in terms of the rights of shareholders attaching to the shares at the time of issue.

NB

4.9.1 Requirements preceding any distribution

Section 46 of the Companies Act, 2008 is headed, 'Distributions must be authorised by board'. It states that a company must not make any proposed distribution unless the following requirements have been complied with:

- the distribution is *either* pursuant to an existing legal obligation of the company, or a court order; *or* the board of the company, by resolution, has authorised the distribution; and
- it reasonably appears that the company will satisfy the solvency and liquidity test immediately after completing the proposed distribution; and
- the board has by resolution acknowledged that it has applied the solvency and liquidity test, and reasonably concluded that the company will satisfy the solvency and liquidity test immediately after completing the proposed distribution.

If a distribution takes the form of the incurrence of a debt or other obligation by the company, the requirements set out above:

- apply at the time that the board resolves that the company may incur that debt or obligation; and
- do not apply to any subsequent action of the company in satisfaction of that debt or obligation, except to the extent that the resolution, or the terms and conditions of the debt or obligation, provide otherwise.

It is clear that the solvency and liquidity test must be applied even if the distribution is pursuant to a court order. The section therefore provides that if the company fails to satisfy the solvency and liquidity test and accordingly cannot comply with a court order:

- the company may apply to a court for an order varying the original order; and

---

74   See s 48(1)*(b)* of the Companies Act, 2008.

- the court may make an order that
  - is just and equitable, having regard to the financial circumstances of the company; and
  - ensures that the person to whom the company is required to make a payment in terms of the original order is paid at the earliest possible date compatible with the company satisfying its other financial obligations as they fall due and payable.

4.9.2   Share buybacks NB

The definition of 'distribution' in s 1 makes it clear that a **share buyback** is regarded as a distribution to shareholders in the same way that a dividend is regarded as such.[75] A share buyback is the acquisition by a company of its own shares.

Section 48 of the Companies Act, 2008 provides that the board of a company may determine that the company will acquire a number of its own shares provided that certain requirements are complied with. The section also acknowledges that a share buyback can also be pursuant to an existing legal obligation of the company, or a court order.

The board must however acknowledge by resolution that it has applied the solvency and liquidity test,[76] and that it has reasonably concluded that the company will satisfy the solvency and liquidity test immediately after completing the proposed buyback. When a company's own shares are acquired by a company in terms of a dissenting shareholder's appraisal rights,[77] this is not regarded as a share buyback, and therefore the application of the solvency and liquidity test as provided for in s 48 does not apply to such acquisitions.

An unalterable provision of the Act is that a company may not acquire its own shares, and a subsidiary of a company may not acquire shares of that company, if, as a result of that acquisition, there would no longer be any shares of the company in issue other than:

- shares held by one or more subsidiaries of the company; or
- convertible or redeemable shares.

 In terms of s 48(8), if any shares are to be acquired by a company from a director or prescribed officer of the company, or a person related to a director or prescribed officer of the company, a decision by the board to buy back such shares must be approved by a *special resolution*.

Section 48(8) also provides that if the share buyback, either alone or together with other transactions in an integrated series of transactions, involves the acquisition by the company of more than 5 per cent of the issued shares of any particular class of the company's shares, the requirements of ss 114 and 115 must be complied with. These sections deal inter alia with schemes of arrangement, and, generally speaking, require a special resolution of shareholders as defined in those sections.

NB 4.9.3   Cash in lieu of capitalisation shares

The board of directors can decide to offer to award a **cash payment in lieu of a capitalisation share**,[78] but may only do so if:

- the board has considered the solvency and liquidity test, as required by s 46, on the assumption that every such shareholder would elect to receive cash; and

---

75   Section 37(5)(*b*) of the Companies Act, 2008 provides that a company's MOI can provide for redeemable shares of any class, but any redeemable shares must also be subject to the requirements of s 46 (distributions), even though share redemptions are not regarded as a share buyback.

76   As set out in s 4. See also paras 4.3 and 4.4 above.

77   As provided for in s 164.

78   See s 47 of Companies Act, 2008 and para. 4.7.3 above for a discussion of capitalisation shares.

- the board is satisfied that the company would satisfy the solvency and liquidity test immediately upon the completion of the distribution.

The taking of cash instead of shares does properly constitute a distribution, because if a shareholder chooses to receive cash instead of shares, the assets of the company are reduced by the payment made by the company to the shareholder.

It is also important to note that s 47 allows the shares of one class to be issued as a capitalisation share in respect of shares of another class.

4.10   Debt instruments

The 1973 Act[79] makes extensive reference to and provision for debentures, whereas the 2008 Act adopts a more modern approach when it comes to debt arrangements. The 2008 Act uses the term 'debentures' but does not define it. Instead it uses the expression 'debt instrument', which allows the company and a creditor to be flexible in contractually entering into a specific debt arrangement that suits each other's needs. A debenture is thus merely one form of debt instrument.

As already discussed,[80] a share is part of the securities of a company. The Act defines 'securities' as any shares, debentures or other instruments, irrespective of their form or title, issued or authorised to be issued by a profit company. This definition is important because when the Act refers to securities, it refers to both shares and debt instruments such as debentures.[81] A company must include its debt instruments in its register of issued securities.[82]

A **debt instrument** is defined[83] as including any securities other than the shares of a company, but does not include promissory notes and loans. Every security document must clearly indicate, on its first page, whether the relevant debt instrument is secured or unsecured.

Section 43(2) is an alterable provision and provides that the board of a company may (without consulting shareholders) authorise the company to issue a secured or unsecured debt instrument at any time. But the contents of a company's MOI might abolish or curtail this power or provide for other requirements.

Another default position, capable of being altered by the provisions of a company's MOI, is that any debt instrument issued by the company may grant special privileges regarding the following:
- attending and voting at general meetings;
- the appointment of directors; or
- the allotment of securities, redemption by the company, or substitution of the debt instrument for shares of the company, provided that the securities to be allotted or substituted in terms of any such privilege, are authorised by or in terms of the company's MOI.

A debt instrument may therefore have a number of rights attached to it. Although not a share, it may have any number of the rights that usually attach to shares, such as voting rights.

---

79   Sections 116 to 133 of the Companies Act, 1973.
80   In para. 4.5 above.
81   Section 43 of the Companies Act, 2008 deals with debt instruments.
82   Section 50(1) of the Companies Act, 2008.
83   In s 43 of the Companies Act, 2008.

Whilst the 2008 Act does not specifically deal with debentures, it has been pointed out[84] that the nature of a debenture, the various rights that might attach to a debenture, and the methods by which a debenture may be secured (for example, over property) are still governed by the common law and certain statutes such as the Deeds Registries Act.[85]

THIS CHAPTER IN ESSENCE

1. The Companies Act, 2008 has an impact on a company's **corporate finance** decisions – that is, what assets to acquire and retain, and how to finance and invest such assets.
2. The financing of a company's assets is generally sourced from debt and/or equity.
3. **Debt** may take the form of:
   - debt instruments (such as debentures);
   - loans
   - lease agreements;
   - credit terms; and
   - overdraft facilities.
4. **Equity** consists of shares and retained income.
5. A company may issue **shares** in return for assets with which to fund the company's operations. The shares of a company may have the same or different rights – that is, they may be of the same or different classes of share – but all entitle the holder to a defined interest in the company, as set out in the company's Memorandum of Incorporation (MOI).
6. **Retained income**, which implies a decision by the company to retain profits for future operations rather than to pay out a dividend, is a further form of funding for the company.
7. The 2008 Act gives the **directors** of a company certain **default powers** previously enjoyed by the shareholders – namely, the power to determine a company's authorised and issued shares and to declare dividends. Such powers may be altered in the company's MOI.
8. The 2008 Act abandons the priority given to the principle of **capital maintenance** in the 1973 Act and embraces the **solvency and liquidity test** in its place as a more flexible and better protection for creditors. A company is **solvent** if its assets equal or exceed its liabilities, and it is **liquid** if it is able to pay its debts.
9. The introduction of the solvency and liquidity test affects corporate finance decisions: too much debt finance could result in a failure to meet the solvency requirements of the test; too little cash in the asset make-up could negatively affect liquidity.
10. The solvency and liquidity test must be applied:
    - when a company wishes to provide financial assistance for subscription of its securities in terms of s 44;
    - if a company grants loans or other financial assistance to directors and others as contemplated in s 45;
    - before a company makes any distribution as provided for in s 46;
    - if a company wishes to pay cash in lieu of issuing capitalisation shares in terms of s 47; and
    - if a company wishes to acquire its own shares as provided for in s 48.
11. The **securities** of a company are made up of its shares and debt instruments.
12. A company's MOI must set out its **authorised shares** by specifying the classes and numbers of authorised shares. Unless the MOI provides otherwise, the directors may make changes to the company's authorised shares. However, it is more meaningful to note the number of **issued shares** and the value received or receivable from their issue in order to assess whether a company is **under-** or **over-capitalised**.

---

84   See C Stein *The New Companies Act Unlocked* at 169.
85   47 of 1937.

13. Classes of authorised shares include:
    - **ordinary shares**;
    - **preference shares**;
    - **unclassified shares**; and
    - **blank shares**.

14. A company's MOI may provide for any particular class of share to have particular preferences, rights or limitations. However, the 2008 Act provides that certain rights attaching to shares are unalterable by the MOI. These include rights:
    - to vote on proposals to amend the rights attaching to shares;
    - to seek relief if the shareholder's rights are materially and adversely altered; and
    - in the case when there is only one class of shares.

15. Before issuing shares, directors must determine the **consideration** to be received by the company in return for the issue of shares. Shares may be issued in return for **future payments, benefits or services** in terms of the 2008 Act.

16. Authorised shares may be issued as **capitalisation shares** – that is, in lieu of a payment of dividends.

17. The issue of shares generally requires shareholder approval in the following circumstances:
    - if issued to directors and prescribed officers of the company, or to persons related to or nominees of such persons; and
    - when the voting power of the issue will be 30 per cent or more of the total voting power of all the shares of that class.

18. A company's MOI may provide for shareholders to enjoy **pre-emptive rights** – that is, upon the issue of any new shares of the company, existing shareholders may have the right before any other person to subscribe for a percentage of the shares to be issued equal to the existing voting power of the shareholder's general voting rights. In the case of **private companies**, shareholders enjoy pre-emptive rights by default, whereas this is not the case for **public companies**.

19. A company may offer **financial assistance** to persons wishing to subscribe for its securities, provided:
    - the assistance is pursuant to an approved employee share scheme, or an approved special resolution of the shareholders; and
    - the board is satisfied that the requirements of the solvency and liquidity test are met, and that the terms of the assistance are fair and reasonable; and
    - any relevant conditions in the company's MOI are met.

20. Securities of a company may be **certificated** or **uncertificated** and may be converted from the one form to the other. Only uncertificated securities can be traded on the JSE.

21. Every company must keep a **securities register** reflecting the names of the current holders of shares and other securities and the number of shares held in uncertificated form. Shareholder and non-shareholders alike have the right to inspect the securities register.

22. **Unissued shares** are those that have been authorised but not yet issued.

23. A **distribution** is a transfer of cash or assets to shareholders and may take the form of:
    - a **dividend**;
    - a **payment in lieu of a capitalisation share**;
    - a **payment for a share buyback**;
    - a **debt** incurred for the benefit of one or more shareholders;
    - a **waiver of a debt** owed to a shareholder; or
    - a **share redemption**.

24. **Debt instruments** are securities other than shares of the company and include debentures. A debt instrument may have a number of rights attached to it, such as voting rights.

Chapter 5

Shareholders and company meetings

5.1 Introduction and definitions

A company is an artificial person and therefore has no physical existence. It acts through its shareholders in general meeting, its directors, its managers and/or its employees. Exactly who acts in respect of a particular matter is determined by a number of factors, not least of which are the provisions of the Companies Act, 2008 and a company's own Memorandum of Incorporation (MOI).

Certain provisions of the Act are 'unalterable' in the sense that a company's MOI cannot abolish those provisions. These unalterable provisions include ones impacting on who may act on behalf of a company. For example, the Act confers powers exclusively on shareholders in respect of certain decisions and transactions: s 71(1) is unalterable and enables shareholders to remove a director at any time by ordinary resolution. This section therefore entrenches the rights of shareholders in this matter.

It is essential to know which provisions of the Act are 'alterable' and which are not, because certain provisions of the Act will automatically apply unless they are abolished or altered by a company's MOI. An in-depth awareness of the provisions of both the Act and of a company's MOI is therefore essential in determining who can act in respect of a particular matter, and the requirements that must be met before certain transactions can be carried out.

The Companies Act, 2008 specifically provides that before certain transactions can take place, they must be approved by shareholders, either by way of special or ordinary resolution. Thus, for example, s 41 of the Act provides that an issue of shares to certain persons in certain circumstances can only take place if approved by special resolution of the shareholders of a company.[1] Another example is s 66(9), which provides that remuneration (directors' fees) can only be paid to directors in accordance with a special resolution of shareholders.[2]

However, the Act gives great flexibility when it comes to what is meant by an ordinary and a special resolution because it allows a company's MOI to change the default position. The MOI may provide that a 'greater' percentage than the default 50,1 per cent of the vote is required for an ordinary resolution, and the MOI may allow for a 'different' percentage from the default 75 per cent required for a special resolution.[3] Moreover, the Act allows an ordinary or special resolution to be defined differently for different transactions.

A company's own MOI can also restrict the powers of directors or others to act in respect of a particular matter, and an MOI can, for example, provide that certain transactions have to be pre-approved by shareholders, either by way of ordinary or special resolution. For example, s 46 requires a distribution to be authorised by the board of directors (not by shareholders) but a company's MOI can provide that before a dividend can be paid, it must also be approved by shareholders. Moreover, note that s 15(2)(*a*)(iii) provides that the MOI of a company may include any provision imposing on the company a higher standard, greater restriction, longer period of time or any similarly more onerous requirement, than would otherwise apply to the company in terms of an unalterable provision of the Act.[4]

A **shareholder** is defined in s 1 of the Act as the holder of a share issued by a company and who is entered as such in the certificated or uncertificated securities register of the company.[5] For the purposes of Part F of Chapter 2 of the Act,[6] 'shareholder' means a person

---

1 See paras. 5.15.2 and 4.7.4 of this book for further discussion.
2 See para. 5.15.2 below.
3 See para. 5.15 below for a more detailed discussion of resolutions.
4 As has been pointed out in para. 2.10.2 above, the unalterable provisions are not absolutely unalterable, in the sense that they can be altered by a provision in a company's MOI to provide for a higher standard, greater restriction, longer period or more onerous requirement. They are unalterable in the sense that they cannot be abolished or made more lenient by any provision in a company's MOI.
5 See chapter 4 of this book for an in-depth discussion of shareholders and the nature of shares. Section 50(2) of the Companies Act, 2008 provides that as soon as practicable after issuing any securities, a company must enter or cause to be entered in its securities register, in respect of every class of securities that it has issued (a) the total number of those securities that are held in uncertificated form; and (b) with respect to certificated securities certain specific details as required by s 50. See chapter 8 of this book for a more detailed discussion.
6 Part F of Chapter 2 is titled 'Governance of Companies' and comprises ss 57 to 78 of the Companies Act, 2008.

who is entitled to exercise any voting rights in relation to a company, irrespective of the form, title or nature of the securities to which those voting rights are attached. A share is part of the securities of a company. The Act defines securities as any shares, debentures or other instruments, irrespective of their form or title, issued or authorised to be issued by a profit company. This definition is important because when the Act refers to securities, it refers to both shares and debt instruments such as debentures.

This means that for the purposes of Part F, a shareholder could include the holder of a debt instrument who has been granted special privileges in the form of voting rights in terms of the rights attaching to that debt instrument.[7]

CONTEXTUAL ISSUE	**Structure of Part F of Chapter 2 of the Companies Act, 2008**
	As far as shareholders are concerned, Part F of the Companies Act deals with the governance of companies as follows:
	• section 58: shareholder right to be represented by proxy;
	• section 59: record date for determining shareholder rights;
	• section 60: shareholders acting other than at a meeting;
	• sections 61 to 64: shareholders' meetings, notice of meeting, quorum; and
	• section 65: shareholder resolutions.

In terms of s 1 of the Act, **share** means one of the units into which the proprietary interest in a profit company is divided. The phrase **'shareholders meeting'**, in relation to a particular matter concerning the company, is defined as a meeting of those holders of a company's issued securities[8] who are entitled to exercise voting rights in relation to that matter.

Shareholders, as shareholders, do not generally have any duties towards the company, but they may have duties or obligations towards each other in terms of a shareholders' agreement. Perhaps the one significant duty on a shareholder in terms of the 2008 Act is the duty to abide by the terms and provisions of a company's MOI.

CASE STUDY	**Relationship between shareholders**
	In *Hulett and Others v Hulett*,[9] three people created a small domestic company for a business purpose in which they were co-directors, with equal loan accounts, and in which they personally or in a representative capacity had equal shareholdings. The court stated:
	It is true that in some small domestic companies the association between the shareholders and directors may be purely commercial. However, in the case under consideration this was manifestly not the situation …. The evidence adduced on behalf of the appellants shows that the pre-existing personal bonds of mutual trust and confidence between the members … were imported into and sustained within the company. Apposite here is the reminder by Lord Wilberforce

---

7   See chapter 4 of this book, especially discussion of the definitions of shares and securities in para. 4.5, and also the discussion of debt instruments in para. 4.10.

8   As has been pointed out, when the Act refers to securities, it refers to both shares and debt instruments such as debentures.

9   1992 (4) SA 291 (A).

in *Ebrahim v Westbourne Galleries Ltd* [1973] AC H 360 (HL) at 379 b–c ([1972] 2 All ER 492 (HL) at 500 a–b) that a limited company is not merely a legal entity, and '... that there is room in company law for recognition of the fact that behind it, or amongst it, there are individuals, with rights, expectations and obligations inter se which are not necessarily submerged in the company structure.'

The court thus concluded that the relationship existing internally between the shareholders was one that could be loosely described as a 'quasi-partnership' and that 'in the present case nobody appreciated better than the defendant himself that during the continuance of a partnership one partner may not overreach his fellow-partners'.

5.2   General comments regarding meetings

The following important principles apply to shareholders' meetings:
- Before a meeting of shareholders[10] can be held, it has to be properly called and convened.
- A meeting is properly convened if the prescribed notice for convening the meeting was given by persons who have the relevant authority to convene the meeting.
- Notice convening a meeting must be given to all persons who are entitled to receive notice of the meeting.
- A meeting must be convened for a time, date and place that is accessible to the shareholders of the company.
- A meeting may commence only if a quorum is present.
- A **quorum** is the minimum number of members who have to be present at the meeting before the meeting can commence.

5.3   Record date

Section 1 of the Act defines the term '**record date**' as the date on which a company determines the identity of its shareholders and their shareholdings for the purposes of the Act.[11] The record date is therefore important because it is the date that determines shareholder rights – for example, the right to receive a notice of a meeting and the right to vote at a meeting.

5.3.1   Record date may be set by board of directors

As far as shareholders' meetings are concerned, the Act provides that the board of directors may set a record date for determining which shareholders are entitled to the following:[12]
- to receive notice of a shareholders' meeting;
- to participate in and vote at a shareholders' meeting; and
- to decide any matter by written consent or electronic communication.

Such a record date may not be earlier than the date on which the record date is determined or more than 10 business days before the date on which the event or action, for which the

---

10 In this chapter, a shareholder (in the context of meetings) is a person who is entitled to exercise any voting rights in relation to a company, irrespective of the form, title or nature of the securities to which those voting rights are attached.
11 Section 59 of the Companies Act, 2008.
12 *Ibid.*

record date is being set, is scheduled to occur and must be published to the shareholders in a manner that satisfies any prescribed requirements.

5.3.2   Where no record date is set by board of directors[13]

Where the board does not determine a record date for any action or event, unless the MOI or rules of the company provide otherwise, the record date is:

- in the case of a meeting, the latest date by which the company is required to give shareholders notice of that meeting; or
- the date of the action or event.

✳ 5.4   Calling of shareholders' meetings[14]

The board of directors, or any other person specified in the company's MOI or rules, may call a shareholders' meeting at any time. A shareholders' meeting *must* be called in the following circumstances:

- at any time that the board is required to convene a meeting and to refer a matter to decision by shareholders as provided for in the Companies Act or by the MOI – for example, to elect a director or to fill a vacancy; and
- when a meeting is demanded by shareholders, provided that the demand is signed by the holders of at least 10 per cent of the voting rights entitled to be exercised in relation to the matter proposed to be considered at the meeting. (A company's MOI may specify a lower percentage than 10 per cent.)

The following points are relevant when a demand is made:

- A demand to convene a meeting must specify the specific purpose for which the meeting is proposed.
- A company, or any shareholder of the company, may apply to a court for an order setting aside a demand for a meeting on the grounds that the demand is frivolous, or because it calls for a meeting for no other purpose than to reconsider a matter that has already been decided upon by the shareholders, or is vexatious.
- A shareholder who submitted a demand for a meeting may withdraw the demand before the start of the meeting.
- Where a demand for a meeting is withdrawn, the company must cancel the meeting if, as a result of one or more demands being withdrawn, the voting rights of any remaining shareholders continuing to demand the meeting, in aggregate, fall below the minimum percentage of voting rights required to call a meeting.

✳ 5.5   Notice of meetings[15]

The first step in convening a meeting is to send out a notice convening the meeting. The following issues relate to the giving of proper notice:

- A notice convening a shareholders' meeting must be in writing.
- The notice must include the date, time and place for the meeting.

---

13   Section 59(3) of the Companies Act, 2008.
14   Section 61 of the Companies Act, 2008.
15   Section 62 of the Companies Act, 2008.

- Where the company sets a record date for the meeting, the notice convening the meeting must include the record date.
- The notice should explain the general purpose of the meeting and any other specific purposes.
- With regard to a public company or a non-profit company that has voting members, notice of a shareholders' meeting should be given 15 business days before the date of the meeting. In the case of any other company, the notice convening the meeting must be sent 10 business days before the date of the meeting. The provisions of the MOI may prescribe longer minimum notice.
- A copy of any proposed resolution received by the company, and which is to be considered at the meeting, must accompany the notice convening the meeting.
- The notice should indicate the percentage of voting rights required for the resolution to be adopted.
- A notice convening the annual general meeting of a company must contain a summary of the financial statements that will be tabled at the meeting. The notice should also explain the procedure that a shareholder can follow to obtain a complete copy of the annual financial statements for the preceding financial year.
- A notice convening a meeting must contain a prominent statement that a shareholder is entitled to appoint a proxy[16] to attend, participate in, and vote at the meeting in the place of the shareholder.
- The notice should indicate that meeting participants will be required to provide satisfactory proof of identity at the meeting.

Where the company has failed to give notice of a meeting or where there has been a defect in the giving of the notice, the meeting may proceed if the persons who are entitled to vote in respect of each item on the agenda are present at the meeting, and acknowledge actual receipt of the notice, and agree to waive notice of the meeting, or, in the case of a material defect, ratify the defective notice. If a material defect in the notice relates only to one or more particular matters on the agenda for the meeting, any such matter may be taken off the agenda and the notice will remain valid with respect to any remaining matters on the agenda. Where the meeting ratifies a defective notice in respect to a matter taken off the agenda, the meeting may proceed to consider the matter. An immaterial defect or an accidental or inadvertent failure in the delivery of the notice to any particular shareholder does not invalidate any action taken at the meeting.

A shareholder who is present at a meeting is deemed to have received or waived notice of the meeting.

CASE STUDY	**Effects of an improperly constituted meeting**
	In *Thompson v ILIPS (Pty) Ltd*,[17] the court found that there was no doubt that the appointment of the fourth respondent as CEO as well as certain other decisions resulted from an improperly constituted meeting of the shareholders. In calling the meeting, no notice had been given to one of the shareholders. The court found that even though there had been a quorum, it was not a properly constituted meeting because of the lack of notice.

16 A proxy is someone chosen to represent or vote for the shareholder.
17 2012 JDR 1022 (GNP); [2012] ZAGPPHC 105.

The court held that item 7(5) of Schedule 5 (Transitional Arrangements) of the Companies Act, 2008 clearly stipulates that 'despite anything contrary in a company's Memorandum of Incorporation', the provisions of the Act about the meetings of shareholders and the adoption of resolutions apply from the effective date of the Act (1 May 2011) to every existing company. The court noted that s 62(1) of the Act stipulates that a company must deliver a notice to all of the shareholders; s 62(3) prescribes the contents of the notice; and s 62(4) stipulates that if a company fails to give the required notice of a shareholders' meeting, the meeting may proceed if all the persons who are entitled to exercise voting rights acknowledge actual receipt of the notice.

5.6   Postponement and adjournment of meetings[18]

A meeting may be postponed or adjourned for a week under the following conditions:
- within one hour after the appointed time for a meeting to begin, a quorum is not present;
- when a quorum is not present at the postponed or adjourned meeting, the members of the company present in person or by proxy will be deemed to constitute a quorum; and
- if there is other business on the agenda of the meeting, consideration of that matter may be postponed to a later time in the meeting without motion or vote.

The chairperson of the meeting where a quorum is not present within one hour of the scheduled starting time may extend the one-hour limit for a reasonable length of time, on the grounds that exceptional circumstances affecting weather, transportation or electronic communication have generally impeded the ability of shareholders to be present at the meeting, or that one or more shareholders, having been delayed, have communicated an intention to attend the meeting, and those shareholders, together with others in attendance, would constitute a quorum.

The one-hour-rule and the postponement of one week is an alterable provision, and members of a company can agree to different periods in the MOI. The company is required to give notice of the postponement only if the location of the postponed or adjourned meeting is different.

When a quorum is not present at the postponed or adjourned meeting, the members of the company present in person or by proxy will be deemed to constitute a quorum. Unless the company's MOI or rules provide otherwise, after a quorum has been established for a meeting, or for a matter to be considered at a meeting, the meeting may continue, or the matter may be considered, so long as at least one shareholder with voting rights entitled to be exercised at the meeting, or on that matter, is present at the meeting.

A shareholders' meeting may be adjourned without further notice on a motion supported by persons entitled to exercise, in aggregate, a majority of the voting rights held by all of the persons who are present at the meeting at the time. An adjournment of a meeting may be either to a fixed time and place or until further notice as agreed to at the meeting. Notice of adjournment must be given only where the meeting was postponed until further notice. A meeting may not be adjourned beyond the earlier of the date that is 120 business days after the record date or the date that is 60 business days after the date on which the adjournment

---

18   Section 64(4)–(13) of the Companies Act, 2008.

occurred. The latter is an alterable provision that can be altered by the provisions of a company's MOI.

5.7   Representation by proxy[19]

A **proxy** is a person who is appointed to represent a shareholder at a meeting. At common law, there was no right to appoint a person to attend, speak and vote on behalf of another.[20] The Companies Act, 2008, however, changes the common law and allows a shareholder to appoint any individual as his or her proxy. A person does not have to be a shareholder in the company to be appointed as a proxy. The provisions of the MOI may allow a shareholder to appoint two or more proxies.

PRACTICAL	**One person holding all the proxies**
ISSUE	Once appointed, a proxy will be allowed to attend, participate in, speak and vote at the shareholders' meeting. In *Ingre v Maxwell*,[21] the court held that there must be at least two persons present to constitute a meeting. No valid meeting is constituted where one person is in attendance and this person holds the proxies of all other persons who were entitled to attend the meeting.

The appointment of a proxy must be in writing and be signed by the shareholder appointing the person. The appointment remains valid for one year after it was signed. The shareholder may appoint a proxy for a specific period of time specified in the proxy appointment form. A shareholder of a company may appoint two or more persons concurrently as proxies for them to exercise voting rights attached to different shares held by the shareholder. A proxy may delegate authority to act on behalf of the shareholder to another person. A copy of the proxy appointment form must be delivered to the company prior to the proxy exercising any rights of the shareholder at a shareholders' meeting.

The company cannot compel the shareholder to make an irrevocable proxy appointment. The appointment of a proxy will be automatically suspended where the shareholder acts directly on a particular matter. The shareholder who appoints the proxy has the right to revoke the appointment by cancelling it in writing, or making a later inconsistent appointment of a proxy and delivering a copy of the revocation instrument to the proxy and to the company. The revocation of a proxy appointment constitutes a complete and final cancellation of the proxy's authority to act on behalf of the shareholder.

The shareholder can indicate on the proxy form whether the notice of meetings has to be delivered to the shareholder or the proxy. Where the shareholder instructs the company to deliver the notice convening a meeting to the proxy, the company may charge the shareholder a reasonable fee.

At the meeting, the proxy is entitled to vote as he or she thinks fit, unless the shareholder has indicated on the proxy appointment form whether the proxy should vote in favour of or against a particular resolution.

---

19   Section 58 of the Companies Act, 2008.
20   *Harben v Phillips* (1883) 23 Ch D.
21   (1964) 44 DLR 2d 764 British Columbia Supreme Court; JG Van der Merwe et al. *South African Corporate Business Administration* (2005) Revision Service 13, 2007 28–2.

The company could invite shareholders on the proxy appointment form to appoint a proxy from a list of names provided by the company. The company cannot compel the shareholders to choose one or more of the persons from the list. Should a shareholder wish to appoint someone who is not on the list, the appointment form should provide enough space for the shareholder to fill in the name of the person he or she wishes to appoint as proxy. The appointment form should also contain sufficient space so that the shareholder can indicate whether the appointed proxy should vote in favour or against resolutions to be taken at the meeting. The proxy appointment remains valid until the end of the meeting at which it was intended to be used.

CASE STUDY	**Proxy to be properly appointed**
	In *Getz v Spaarwater Goldmining Co Ltd*,[22] it was argued that certain proxies were invalid because the proxy forms were left undated by the proxy-giver and the proxy-holder and, therefore, did not comply with the articles of association of the company.
	The court held that the validity or otherwise of the appointment of a proxy must depend on the facts of each case. The court held that there can be little doubt that a material departure from the prescribed form could well invalidate the proxy form. In *Davey v Inyaminga Petroleum (1934) Ltd*,[23] the prescribed proxy form required the proxy-giver to set out the number of shares in respect of which he was authorising the proxy to vote. This was not done. It was held in that case that it was essential that the extent of the authority conferred upon the holder of the proxy should be disclosed, and that non-compliance with the prescribed form in this respect was a material omission that rendered the proxy incomplete and invalid. In *Getz's* case, however, the court found that the form of proxy complied in every respect with the prescribed form, save only that its date of execution was left blank. The court held that the proxy was valid and non-compliance in this single respect was not of a material nature.

5.8   Quorum[24]

Unless a company's MOI says otherwise, a shareholders' meeting may not begin until sufficient persons are present at the meeting to exercise, in aggregate, at least 25 per cent of all of the voting rights that are entitled to be exercised in respect of at least one matter to be decided at the meeting. A company's MOI may specify a lower or higher percentage in place of the Act's default quorum of 25 per cent.

If a company has more than two shareholders, a meeting may not begin, or a matter may not be debated, unless at least three shareholders are present at the meeting, and provided that the members present can exercise at least the required percentage of voting rights that they are entitled to exercise.

22   1971 (2) SA 423 (W).
23   1954 (3) SA 133 (W).
24   Section 64 of the Companies Act, 2008.

PRACTICAL	**Percentage required for resolution of shareholders**
ISSUE	Unless a company's MOI provides otherwise, it is possible to pass an ordinary shareholders' resolution (more than 50 per cent of voting rights) at a meeting where there is only a quorum (25 per cent). This is a very low percentage and it may be that a company's MOI should require a higher quorum, albeit for certain specific transactions.

5.9   Conduct of meetings[25]

Voting on any matter at a shareholders' meeting may be conducted by a show of hands or through a poll among those persons who are present at the meeting and entitled to exercise voting rights on that matter. Where voting is conducted by show of hands, any person present and entitled to exercise voting rights must have only one vote, irrespective of the number of shares held by that person. Where voting is by poll, any member (including his or her proxy) must be entitled to exercise all the voting rights attached to the shares held or represented by that person.

A company may provide for a shareholders' meeting to be conducted entirely by electronic communication or may allow one or more shareholders or proxies to participate by electronic communication in all or part of a shareholders' meeting that is being held in person. The electronic communication used must enable all persons participating in that meeting to communicate concurrently with each other without an intermediary and to participate reasonably effectively in the meeting. Where participation in a meeting by electronic communication is allowed, the notice convening the meeting should inform shareholders of the availability to participate electronically and provide any necessary information to enable shareholders or their proxies to access the available medium or means of electronic communication. The shareholder generally bears the cost of access to the medium or means of electronic communication.

Where a person abstains or fails to exercise his or her vote on a resolution, the person is deemed to have voted against the resolution.

PRACTICAL	**Company records**
ISSUE	Section 24(3)(*d*)(ii) specifically provides that a company is required to keep any document that was made available by the company to the holders of securities in relation to each shareholders' resolution.[26]
	Section 24(3)(*e*) provides that a company must keep copies of any written communications sent generally by the company to all holders of any class of the company's securities for a period of seven years after the date on which each such communication was issued.

---

25   Section 63 of the Companies Act, 2008.
26   These documents must be kept for at least seven years in terms of s 24(1) of the Companies Act, 2008.

5.10   Majority rule

When a person becomes a shareholder in a company, he or she agrees to be bound by the decisions of the majority.

CONTEXTUAL ISSUE	**Majority prevails**
	In *Sammel v President Brand Gold Mining Co Ltd*,[27] the court held:
	> By becoming a shareholder in a company a person undertakes to be bound by the decisions of the prescribed majority of shareholders, if those decisions on the affairs of the company are arrived at in accordance with the law, even where they adversely affect his own rights as a shareholder …. That principle of supremacy of the majority is essential in the proper functioning of the companies.
	In terms of the Companies Act, 2008, it is clear, however, that a shareholder is bound by the terms of a company's MOI. A company's MOI will determine the rights, including the voting rights of shareholders and others.[28]

5.11   Some exceptions to applicable rules and formalities[29]

The shareholder of a profit company, other than a state-owned company, with only *one shareholder* may exercise all of the voting rights pertaining to that company. The rules pertaining to setting a record date for the determination of shareholders' rights, proxies, notice of meetings and the like, as explained above, do not apply to a profit company with only one member.

Where a profit company, other than a state-owned enterprise, has only *one director*, the director may exercise any power or perform any function of the board at any time, without notice or compliance with any other internal formalities, except to the extent that the company's MOI provides otherwise.

Where *every shareholder is also a director* of a particular company, other than a state-owned enterprise, any matter that is required to be referred by the board to the shareholders for decision may be decided by the shareholders at any time after being referred by the board, without notice or compliance with any other internal formalities, except to the extent that the MOI provides otherwise. Every director must have been personally present at the board meeting when the matter was referred to them in their capacity as shareholders. A quorum must be present at the meeting and a resolution adopted by those persons in their capacity as shareholders must be accepted by enough shareholders for it to be either an ordinary or a special resolution.

The board of a *company that holds any securities of a second company* may authorise any person to act as its representative at any shareholders' meeting of that second company. A person authorised to act as a company's representative may exercise the same powers as the authorising company could have exercised if it were an individual holder of securities.

---

27   1969 (3) SA 629 (A).
28   See para. 5.15.3 below.
29   Section 57(2)-(6) of the Companies Act, 2008.

5.12 Shareholders acting other than at a meeting[30]

The Companies Act, 2008 provides that it is possible to take decisions without convening a meeting. If the company wishes to take an ordinary resolution in such a way, the company must submit a proposed resolution to every person who is entitled to vote on the resolution. The shareholders are then entitled to exercise their vote in writing within 20 days from receiving the proposed resolution and to return the written vote to the company.

Such a resolution is adopted if it is supported by persons entitled to exercise sufficient voting rights for it to be adopted as an ordinary or special resolution, as the case may be, at a properly constituted shareholders' meeting. If adopted, it has the same effect as if it had been approved by voting at a meeting.

An election of a director that could be conducted at a shareholders' meeting may instead be conducted by written polling of all of the shareholders entitled to exercise voting rights in relation to the election of that director.

Within 10 business days after adopting a resolution, the company must deliver a statement describing the results of the vote, consent process, or election to every shareholder who was entitled to vote on the resolution.

No business that is required to be conducted at the annual general meeting of the company may be conducted without convening a meeting.

5.13 Annual general meeting[31]

The first annual general meeting of a public company must occur no more than 18 months after the company's date of incorporation. The subsequent annual general meetings must occur no more than 15 months after the date of the previous annual general meeting. The Companies Tribunal may grant an extension if good cause is shown. The following matters must be discussed at a company's **annual general meeting**:

- presentation of the directors' report, the audited financial statements for the immediately preceding financial year and the audit committee report;
- election of directors;
- appointment of an auditor for the ensuing financial year and appointment of the audit committee; and
- any matters raised by shareholders, with or without advance notice to the company.

5.14 Convening meetings in special circumstances[32]

Where the company cannot convene a meeting because it has no directors, or because all of its directors are incapacitated, any other person authorised by the company's MOI may convene the meeting. In the event that no other person is authorised to convene a meeting, any shareholder may request the Companies Tribunal to issue an administrative order for a shareholders' meeting to be convened.

If a company fails to convene a meeting for any reason, a shareholder may apply to court for an order requiring the company to convene a meeting on a date, and subject to any terms, that the court considers appropriate in the circumstances. The company must compensate

---

30 Section 60 of the Companies Act, 2008.
31 Section 61(7)–(10) of the Companies Act, 2008.
32 Section 61(11)–(12) of the Companies Act, 2008.

a shareholder who applies to the Companies Tribunal or to a court for the costs of those proceedings. Failure to hold a required meeting does not affect the existence of a company or the validity of any action by the company.

5.15   Decisions of shareholders and others

The Companies Act, 2008 provides for two types of resolution that can be taken by shareholders – namely, an ordinary resolution and a special resolution. Shareholders can pass these resolutions either at a meeting of shareholders or by acting other than at a meeting in terms of s 60. It should also be noted that the holders of debt instruments may, in the case of certain companies, be allowed to vote at shareholders' meetings.[33]

5.15.1   Ordinary resolutions

An **ordinary resolution** means a resolution adopted with the support of more than 50 per cent of the voting rights exercised on the resolution (or a higher percentage as required by a company's MOI) either at a shareholders' meeting, or by holders of the company's securities acting other than at a meeting (as contemplated in s 60).

An important feature of the 2008 Act is that an ordinary resolution can be defined by a company's MOI differently for different transactions. In other words, for certain transactions, an ordinary resolution could be defined as requiring the support of more than 50 per cent of the voting rights exercised, whereas other transactions may require a greater support. It is therefore possible for a company's MOI to require a higher percentage of support for certain specified decisions.

However, the Act provides that there must at all times be a margin of at least 10 percentage points between the requirements for adoption of an ordinary resolution and that of a special resolution. Note that the required percentage is determined not in relation to shareholders as a whole, but in relation to those exercising their vote at a meeting where there is a quorum. What determines a quorum is discussed earlier in this chapter.[34]

There is an important exception to the rule that allows an MOI to require a percentage of more than 50 per cent of voting rights to approve an ordinary resolution, and that is in connection with the removal of a director. Section 65(8) provides that a resolution for the removal of a director cannot require a higher percentage – that is, the MOI cannot require a percentage greater than 50 per cent for such a resolution.

Whilst a company's MOI can require a higher percentage for an ordinary resolution, it cannot require a percentage *lower* than 50 per cent for any transaction. This contrasts with the definition of 'special resolution', which the Act defines as a resolution adopted with the support of at least 75 per cent of the voting rights, or a 'different' percentage (that is, including a lower percentage) as contemplated in s 65(10).

5.15.2   Special resolutions

A **special resolution** means a resolution adopted with the support of at least 75 per cent of the voting rights exercised on the resolution, or a 'different' (which could be higher or lower) percentage as specified in a company's MOI, either at a shareholders' meeting, or by holders of the company's securities acting other than at a meeting (as contemplated in s 60).

---

33   See para. 5.15.3 below.
34   See para. 5.8 above.

It should be noted that a company's MOI may permit a different percentage of voting rights to approve any special resolution. As is the case with ordinary resolutions, a special resolution can be defined by a company's MOI differently for different transactions. In other words, for certain transactions, a special resolution could be defined as requiring the support of 75 per cent of the voting rights exercised, whereas other transactions may require, say 60 per cent support. Once again, there must at all times be a margin of at least 10 percentage points between the requirements for adoption of an ordinary resolution and a special resolution on any matter.

The Act provides that a special resolution is required in a variety of different circumstances, as illustrated in Table 5.1 below:

Table 5.1 *The Companies Act, 2008 requires a special resolution in certain circumstances*

Nature of decision	Section of the Act
Amendment of a company's MOI: except no special resolution is required if the directors have altered the authorised shares as permitted in terms of s 36(3) and (4)	Section 16, read with s 36(3) and (4)
Ratification of a consolidated revision of a company's MOI: this ratification is filed in terms of s 17(5)	Section 18(1)(*b*), read with s 17(5)
Ratification of actions: if a company's MOI limits, restricts or qualifies the purposes, powers or activities of that company, or limits the authority of the directors to perform an act on behalf of the company, the shareholders, by special resolution, may ratify any action by the company or the directors that is inconsistent with any such limit, restriction or qualification	Section 20(2)
Issue of shares to directors: if shares, securities, options or rights are issued to a director, future director, prescribed officer, or future prescribed officer of the company (or to a person related or inter-related to the company, or to a director or prescribed officer of the company; or to any nominee of such person)	Section 41(1)
Issue of shares and the 30% rule: if there is an issue of shares, securities convertible into shares, or rights exercisable for shares in a transaction, or a series of integrated transactions, and the voting power of the class of shares that are issued or issuable as a result of the transaction, or series of integrated transactions, will be equal to or exceed 30% of the voting power of all the shares of that class held by shareholders immediately before the transaction or series of transactions	Section 41(3)
Financial assistance and issue of securities: if a company provides financial assistance in connection with the issue of any of its securities,[35] the particular provision of financial assistance must be either (i) pursuant to an employee share scheme that satisfies the requirements of s 97; or (ii) pursuant to a special resolution of the shareholders, adopted within the previous two years, which approved such assistance either for the specific recipient, or generally for a category of potential recipients, and the specific recipient falls within that category	Section 44

---

35 A share is part of the securities of a company. The Act defines 'securities' as any shares, debentures or other instruments, irrespective of their form or title, issued or authorised to be issued by a profit company. This definition is important because when the Act refers to securities, it refers to both shares and debt instruments such as debentures.

Nature of decision	Section of the Act
Loans and financial assistance to directors and to related companies: if a company provides loans or financial assistance to a director or to a related company, the particular provision of financial assistance must be either (i) pursuant to an employee share scheme that satisfies the requirements of s 97; or (ii) pursuant to a special resolution of the shareholders, adopted within the previous two years, which approved such assistance either for the specific recipient, or generally for a category of potential recipients, and the specific recipient falls within that category	
Share buybacks from directors: a decision by the board to buy back shares must be approved by a special resolution if any shares are to be acquired by the company from a director or prescribed officer of the company, or a person related to a director or prescribed officer of the company	Section 48(8)
Share buybacks and the 5% rule: if a share buyback, either alone or together with other transactions in an integrated series of transactions, involves the acquisition by the company of more than 5% of the issued shares of any particular class of the company's shares, the requirements of ss 114 and 115 apply. These sections deal inter alia with schemes of arrangement, and, generally speaking, require a special resolution of shareholders as defined in those sections.	Section 48(8)
Remuneration to directors: remuneration to directors, for services as directors, may only be paid in accordance with a special resolution approved by the shareholders within the previous two years	Section 66(9)
Voluntary winding-up of the company: a solvent company may be wound up voluntarily if the company has adopted a special resolution to do so – the resolution may provide for winding up by the company, or by its creditors	Section 80(1)
Winding-up by court order: a court may order a solvent company to be wound up if the company has (i) resolved, by special resolution, that it be wound up by the court; or (ii) applied to the court to have its voluntary winding-up continued by the court	Section 81(1)
Deregistration of company: A company may apply to be deregistered upon the transfer of its registration to a foreign jurisdiction, if the shareholders have adopted a special resolution approving such an application and transfer of registration	Section 82(5)
Fundamental transactions: generally speaking, a special resolution is required to approve any fundamental transaction as envisaged by ss 112 to 116	Sections 112 to 116
Dissenting shareholders' appraisal rights: a special resolution is required to revoke the special resolution that was adopted to change a company's MOI which gave rise to a dissenting minority shareholder's appraisal rights	Section 164(9)(c)
MOI extra requirements: a company's MOI may require a special resolution to approve any other matter not referred to above	Section 65(12)

PRACTICAL ISSUE

Company records

Section 24(3)(d) provides that a company must keep the notice and minutes of all shareholders' meetings.

Section 24(3)(d)(i) provides that a company must keep all resolutions adopted by shareholders for a period of seven years from the date on which each such resolution was adopted.

5.15.3 Voting rights of shareholders and others

Section 1 of the Act defines both the terms 'voting power' and 'voting rights'. The **voting power** with respect to any matter is determined by the voting rights that may be exercised in connection with a particular matter by a person as a percentage of all voting rights. **Voting rights** means, in the case of a profit company, the rights of any holder of the company's securities to vote in connection with a matter. It is clear from the definition of Memorandum of Incorporation (MOI) that it is a company's MOI that sets out, among other things, the voting rights of shareholders and of holders of other securities.

The 2008 Act provides for great flexibility in the matter of voting rights. There is no statutory provision requiring a shareholder to have voting rights or specifying that each share must carry at least one vote. Voting rights are left to the provisions of a company's MOI. Certain shareholders may well have no voting rights at all, or, for certain transactions, some shareholders may have greater votes than others. In other words, a company's MOI specifies the rights of shareholders, and it would be wrong to presume, for example, that all ordinary shareholders have similar voting or other rights. Similarly, voting rights may differ from transaction to transaction.

It is important to be aware that, in terms of s 43, the board of a company may authorise the company to issue a secured or unsecured debt instrument at any time, except to the extent provided by the company's MOI.[36] In terms of s 43, a **debt instrument** includes any securities other than the shares of a company, but does not include promissory notes and loans. In terms of the section, a debt instrument issued by the company may grant special privileges, including attending and voting at general meetings and the appointment of directors, except to the extent a company's MOI provides otherwise.

Therefore, in determining voting rights, regard must not only be had to the rights of shareholders, but the rights of any holders of any debt instrument must also be ascertained and be taken into account where necessary. The very flexible regime and environment created by the 2008 Act thus allows a company's MOI to be tailor-made to the needs and requirements of those who wish to make use of a company.

5.15.4 Proposal of resolutions

The board of directors can **propose** a resolution to shareholders[37] or shareholders can propose a resolution[38] to be considered by shareholders. A proposed resolution must be expressed with sufficient clarity and specificity and must be accompanied by sufficient information or explanatory material to enable a shareholder who is entitled to vote on the resolution to determine whether to participate in the meeting and to seek to influence the outcome of the vote on the resolution.[39]

Where a shareholder or director is of the opinion that a proposed resolution is not clear or is not accompanied by sufficient information, the shareholder or director may apply to court for an order restraining the company from putting the proposed resolution to a vote until the defect is remedied.[40] Once a resolution has been adopted, it may not be challenged or impugned by any person in any forum on the grounds that it was not clear or did not provide sufficient information.[41]

---

36   See chapter 4 of this book for a more detailed discussion of debt instruments.
37   Section 65(2) of the Companies Act, 2008.
38   Section 65(3) of the Companies Act, 2008.
39   Section 65(4) of the Companies Act, 2008.
40   Section 65(5) of the Companies Act, 2008.
41   Section 65(6) of the Companies Act, 2008.

5.15.4.1   Proposal of resolution by board of directors

When the board of directors proposes a resolution to the shareholders, the board may decide whether the decision will be taken at a meeting or by vote or by written consent votes.

5.15.4.2   Proposal of resolution by shareholders

Any two shareholders of a company may propose a resolution concerning any matter in respect of which they are each entitled to exercise voting rights. When proposing a resolution, they may require that the resolution be submitted to shareholders for consideration at a meeting demanded by the shareholders, or at the next shareholders' meeting or by written vote of the members.

THIS CHAPTER IN ESSENCE

1. A **shareholder** is the holder of a share issued by a company and is entered as such in the securities register of the company. A shareholder is entitled to exercise the voting rights attached to the shares held.
2. A **share** is essentially a collection of rights, and is one of the units into which the proprietary interest in a profit company is divided.
3. A **shareholders' meeting**, in relation to a particular matter, is a meeting of shareholders who are entitled to exercise voting rights in relation to that matter.
4. Shareholders have the duty to abide by the terms and provisions of a company's MOI.
5. A shareholders' meeting must be properly called and convened, with the prescribed notice being given by authorised persons to all persons entitled to receive notice.
6. A **quorum** is the minimum number of members who have to be present at the meeting before the meeting can commence. Unless a company's MOI says otherwise, a shareholders' meeting may not begin until sufficient persons are present to exercise, in aggregate, at least 25 per cent of all of the voting rights that are entitled to be exercised in respect of at least one matter to be decided at the meeting.
7. The **record date** is the date on which a company determines the identity of its shareholders and their shareholdings for the purposes of the Act. The record date determines shareholder rights.
8. A shareholders' meeting must be called if required in terms of the Companies Act, 2008 or the MOI, or when a meeting is demanded in writing by shareholders holding at least 10 per cent of exercisable voting rights. (A company's MOI may specify a lower percentage than 10 per cent.)
9. The notice of a meeting should explain the purpose of the meeting. A copy of any proposed resolution to be considered at the meeting must accompany the notice. A summary of the financial statements must accompany a notice convening an annual general meeting.
10. Conditions for the postponement and adjournment of meetings are set in the Companies Act, 2008.
11. A shareholder is entitled to appoint a **proxy** to attend, participate in, and vote at the meeting in the place of the shareholder. The appointment of a proxy must be in writing and is valid for one year after it was signed, but is not irrevocable. At the meeting, the proxy is entitled to vote as he or she thinks fit, unless the shareholder has indicated otherwise on the proxy appointment form.
12. Voting at a shareholders' meeting may be conducted by a show of hands or through a poll among those present and entitled to exercise voting rights. A company may provide for a shareholders' meeting to be conducted entirely by electronic communication or for participation of one or more shareholders or proxies by electronic communication.
13. Where a person abstains or fails to exercise his or her vote on a resolution, the person is deemed to have voted against the resolution.
14. A shareholder is bound by the decisions of the prescribed majority of shareholders.

15. It is possible for shareholders to take decisions without convening a meeting – by submitting a proposed resolution to every person entitled to vote on the resolution. The shareholders are then entitled to exercise their vote in writing within 20 days and to return the written vote to the company. No business required to be conducted at an annual general meeting may be conducted without convening a meeting.

16. The first annual general meeting of a public company must occur no more than 18 months after incorporation. Subsequent annual general meetings must occur no more than 15 months after the previous annual general meeting. The **annual general meeting** must discuss:
    - the directors' report, the audited financial statements for the immediately preceding financial year and the audit committee report;
    - election of directors;
    - appointment of an auditor and audit committee; and
    - any matters raised by shareholders.

17. Shareholders may pass both ordinary resolutions and special resolutions. Holders of debt instruments may, in the case of certain companies, also be allowed to vote at shareholders' meetings.

18. An **ordinary resolution** is a resolution adopted with the support of more than 50 per cent of the voting rights exercised at a quorate meeting on the resolution (or a different percentage as required by a company's MOI), except that a resolution for the removal of a director cannot require more than 51 per cent for such a resolution.

19. A **special resolution** is a resolution adopted with the support of at least 75 per cent of the voting rights exercised at a quorate meeting on the resolution (or a different percentage as specified in a company's MOI). A special resolution is required when:
    - amending the company's MOI;
    - approving the voluntary winding-up of the company;
    - approving a sale of assets, a merger, an amalgamation or a scheme of arrangement;
    - approving directors' remuneration; and
    - otherwise required by the MOI.

20. There must always be at least 10 percentage points between the requirements for adoption of an ordinary resolution and those for a special resolution.

21. A person's **voting power** with respect to any matter is determined by the voting rights that may be exercised in connection with the matter as a percentage of all voting rights. **Voting rights** are, in the case of a profit company, the rights of any holder of securities to vote in connection with a matter.

22. A company's MOI sets out the voting rights of shareholders and of holders of other securities. The Act allows for great flexibility in this area. There is no statutory provision requiring a shareholder to have voting rights or specifying that each share must carry at least one vote.

23. Resolutions may be **proposed** by either the board of directors or one or more shareholders.

24. The provisions of a company's MOI are very important in determining a number of issues, including:
    - the definition of ordinary and special resolution for certain transactions;
    - the voting rights and other rights of shareholders, holders of debt instruments and others;
    - the meaning of a quorum;
    - when a meeting must be called; and
    - the adjournment of meetings.

Chapter 6

Directors and board committees

6.1 Meaning of director, types of director and board composition

In terms of the definition in s 1 of the Companies Act, 2008, a **director** is a member of the **board** of a company as contemplated in s 66, or is an alternate director. The definition of a director also includes any person occupying the position of a director or alternate director, by whatever name designated. The definition of director therefore not only includes formally appointed directors, but also includes a *de facto* director – that is, someone who has not been officially appointed, but who acts as a director.

Section 66 recognises different types of director[1] and specifically provides that a person becomes a director only when that person has given his or her written consent to serve as a director after having been appointed or elected, or who holds office in accordance with the provisions of s 66.[2]

For the purposes of s 75 (director's personal financial interests) and s 76 (standards of directors' conduct),[3] the Companies Act, 2008 includes as a director all of the following:

- directors;
- alternate directors;
- prescribed officers;
- members of board committees (even if they are not board members); and
- members of the audit committee (who all have to be board members).

It is clear that the word 'directors' must be applied in a wider sense than is at first obvious when discussing the statutory duties of directors referred to in ss 75 and 76.

Section 66 provides that 'the business and affairs of a company must be managed by or under the direction of its board', which has the authority to exercise all of the powers and perform any of the functions of the company, except to the extent that the 2008 Act or the company's Memorandum of Incorporation (MOI) provides otherwise. It is therefore clear that both the 2008 Act and a company's MOI can curtail the powers of the board of directors.

---

1 The word 'director' specifically includes an alternate director of the company. For the types of director recognised by s 66, see Table 6.1 below.
2 See para. 6.4 below.
3 Section 76 of the Companies Act, 2008 is discussed in para. 6.3.2 below.

A company's MOI can therefore ensure that for certain transactions the directors cannot act alone and certain matters need to be referred to the shareholders of a company for consideration and approval.[4]

CASE STUDY	Directors act for a company
	In *R v Kritzinger*,[5] the point was made that a company is an artificial person that cannot read a written representation or hear a spoken representation. 'It reads or hears a representation through the eyes or ears of, *inter alios*, its directors acting in the course of their duty, and "board" is the collective term used to designate the directors when they act together in the course of their duty to the company.'

As to board composition, King 3 has a recommendation that there should ideally be a majority of non-executive independent directors, because this reduces the possibility of conflicts of interest. However, very little guidance is given as to what is meant by independence.

Some commentators take the view that if a director has been a director of a board for a lengthy period of time, length of service in itself can impair that director's independence. Others take the view that the continued appointment of a director who is experienced in the matter of a company's business is far more useful and will have a far greater positive impact on a company's sustainability than a newcomer who is appointed solely because he or she is independent and new. In *PPWAWU National Provident Fund v Chemical, Energy, Paper, Printing, Wood and Allied Workers' Union*,[6] the court made it clear that directors must act independently regardless of the views or decisions of those who appointed them. The court stated that a director is *not the servant or agent of* a shareholder who votes for or otherwise procures his appointment to the board and in carrying out his duties and functions as a director, he is in law obliged to serve the interests of the company to the exclusion of the interests of any such nominator, employer or principal.

The types of director recognised by the Companies Act, 2008 are described in Table 6.1 below.

Table 6.1 Types of director

Type of director	Characteristics
a An *ex officio* director[7]	An *ex officio director* is a person who holds office as a director of a company solely as a result of that person holding another office or title or status.[8] • *Ex officio* directors are not appointed by the shareholders. • An *ex officio* director of a company has all the powers and functions of any other director, except to the extent that the company's MOI restricts such powers and functions. • Such a director has all of the duties of, and is subject to the same liabilities as, any other director.

---

4   See chapter 5 of this book for a detailed discussion of shareholders' meetings and rights.
5   1971 (2) SA 57 (A).
6   2008 (2) SA 351 (W).
7   Section 1 and s 66(4)(*a*)(ii) of the Companies Act, 2008.
8   See Practical Issue below for further explanation.

Type of director		Characteristics
b	An **MOI-appointed director**[9]	• Such a director does not have to be appointed by the shareholders. A company's MOI may, for example, provide that debenture holders or other creditors of a company have the right to appoint a certain number of directors. • The MOI can specify how and/or by whom such a director is appointed.
c	An alternate director[10]	• The definition of director[11] specifically includes an alternate director of the company. • An alternate director may be appointed or elected depending on the contents of the MOI of a company. • An **alternate director**[12] is defined as a person elected or appointed to serve, as occasion requires, as a member of the board of a company in substitution for a particular elected or appointed director of that company. Section 66(4)(a)(iii) provides that the MOI can provide for the appointment or election of one or more persons as alternate directors. • In the case of a profit company, at least 50% of alternate directors must be elected by shareholders.
d	An **elected director**[13]	In the case of a profit company, at least 50% of directors must be elected by shareholders.
e	A **temporary director** who is appointed in order to fill a vacancy[14]	The MOI can provide for the appointment of a temporary director. Unless the MOI provides otherwise, the directors may appoint a temporary director.

PRACTICAL ISSUE	***Ex officio* directors** To illustrate what is meant by an *ex officio* director, the Mpumalanga Agricultural Development Corporation (MADC) 2006/7 Annual Report includes the following two persons as directors of the company: Mr. V.S. Mahlangu (Chief Executive Officer) *ex officio* Ms. M. Sithole (Head of Department) *ex officio*. This means that whoever is the CEO of MADC and whoever is the HOD will, by virtue of holding those respective offices, be directors of the MADC. These directors are, therefore, not elected by shareholders, but are appointed because they hold an office or position in the company.

The Companies Act, 2008 as well as King 3 endorses a unitary board structure. This means that a two-tier structure is not recommended, and that a company should have a single board of directors consisting of both executive and non-executive directors sitting and making

---

9   Section 1 and s 66(4)(a)(iii) of the Companies Act, 2008.
10 Section 66(4)(a)(i) of the Companies Act, 2008.
11 See the definition of director in s 1 of the Companies Act, 2008.
12 See the definition of alternate director in s 1 of the Companies Act, 2008.
13 Section 66(4)(b) and s 68 of the Companies Act, 2008.
14 Section 68(3) of the Companies Act, 2008.

decisions together at the same meeting. A director who is also an employee is referred to as an **executive director**. Other directors are **non-executive directors** and are not employees of the company.

CASE STUDY	**Types and duties of directors** In *Howard v Herrigel*,[15] the court held that:

> It is unhelpful and even misleading to classify company directors as 'executive' or 'non-executive' for purposes of ascertaining their duties to the company or when any specific or affirmative action is required of them. No such distinction is to be found in any statute. At common law, once a person accepts an appointment as a director, he becomes a fiduciary in relation to the company and is obliged to display the utmost good faith towards the company and in his dealings on its behalf. That is the general rule and its application to any particular incumbent of the office of director must necessarily depend on the facts and circumstances of each.

6.2   Directors and managers

There are many fundamental differences between being a director and a manager. A **manager** is an employee of a company, whereas a director does not have to be. King 3 recommends that there should be a majority of non-executive directors to ensure objective decision-making, and that a non-executive director should ideally be independent. The board should include a statement of its assessment of the independence of such non-executive directors in the integrated report.[16]

Table 6.2 below is adapted from the website of the London-based Institute of Directors,[17] which states that the difference between being a director and a manager is 'not simply a trivial matter of getting a new job title and a bigger office. The differences are numerous, substantial and quite onerous'. Table 6.2 gives a breakdown of some of the differences between directing and managing a business.

Table 6.2 The difference between directors and managers

	Directors	Managers
Leadership	It is the board of directors who must provide the intrinsic leadership and direction at the top of the organisation.	It is the role of managers to carry through the strategy on behalf of the directors.
Decision-making	Directors are required to determine the future of the organisation and to protect its assets and reputation. They also need to consider how their decisions relate to stakeholders and the regulatory framework. Stakeholders are generally seen to be the company's shareholders, creditors, employees and customers.	Managers are concerned with implementing the decisions and the policies made by the board.

---

15 1991 (2) SA 660 (A).
16 See paras. 2.18.1–2.18.10 and 2.18.9 of the King 3 Code.
17 See *www.iod.com/guidance/briefings/cgbis-differences-between-directors-and-managers*. South Africa has its own Institute of Directors (see *www.iodsa.co.za*), which is affiliated to the London-based IOD.

	Directors	Managers
Duties and responsibilities	Directors, not managers, have the ultimate responsibility for the long-term prosperity of the company. Directors are required by law to apply skill and care in exercising their duty to the company and are subject to fiduciary duties. If they are in breach of their duties or act improperly, directors may be made personally liable in both civil and criminal law. On occasion, directors can be held responsible for acts of the company. Directors also owe certain duties to the stakeholders of the company.	Managers have far fewer legal responsibilities, but they cannot act contrary to the interests of their employer.[18]
Relationship with shareholders	Directors are accountable to the shareholders for the company's performance and can be removed from office by them. Directors act as fiduciaries of the shareholders and should act in their best interests, but should also take into account the best interests of the company (as a separate legal entity) and the other stakeholders.	Managers are usually appointed and dismissed by directors or management and do not interact with shareholders.
Ethics and values	Directors have a key role in the determination of the values and ethical position of the company.	Managers must enact the company ethos, taking their direction from the board.
Company administration	Directors are responsible for the company's administration.	While the related duties associated with company administration can be delegated to managers, the ultimate responsibility for them resides with the directors.
Statutory provisions in general	There are many provisions of the Companies Act, 2008 that can create offences under which directors may face penalties if they act or fail to act in a particular way.	Generally, managers are not held responsible under the provisions of the Companies Act, 2008.
Disqualification	Directors can be disqualified as directors under the Companies Act, 2008 or in terms of a company's MOI.	The control over the employment of a manager rests with the board of directors and control is exercised in accordance with a manager's employment contract.

In terms of King 3, the functions of the board of directors include the following:
- to give strategic direction to the company;
- to ensure that management implements board plans and strategies;
- to be responsible for the performance and affairs of the company; and
- to retain full and effective control over the company.

---

18   See Case Study 'Employees and fiduciary duties' under para. 6.3.2.2 below.

It is therefore apparent that much is expected of the board.

Directors must also comply with the duties imposed in terms of statutes, including the Companies Act, 2008.

6.3   Duties and liabilities of directors

The Companies Act, 1973 did not contain clear rules regarding the duties and liabilities of directors. These matters were largely left to common law. However, in practice, directors need to know what their duties are and directors must be aware of what is expected of them, because the standard of a director's conduct can influence the profitability of a company, determine the extent of foreign and domestic investments and ultimately determine the success of a company.[19]

Perhaps in an attempt to create certainty, certain **duties of directors** have been **partially codified** in the 2008 Act. In other words, some of the duties of directors have been set out in a code – that is, they are set out in the Companies Act, rather than being left as common-law rules that have to be found in various sources, such as decided case law. A distinction should be drawn between complete codification and partial codification. Complete codification entails the creation of a finite body of rigid rules. Complete codification cannot accommodate an environment that keeps changing, because in a completely codified system, if a specific rule does not prohibit a particular action, that action is permissible simply because it is not specifically prohibited. In other words, in a completely codified system there is no room for the application of a legal principle, only the application of specific rules.[20] Partial codification, however, entails adopting the general principles of law, which allows some room for the development of the common law by the application of legal principles.

The provisions in the 2008 Act relating to directors' duties are a partial codification of the company law. The common-law principles remain, but only to the extent that they have not been narrowed by the 2008 Act. In fact, the statutory duties of directors as provided for in the 2008 Act do not really add anything to the law as it existed prior to the Act. These duties always existed at common law. If anything, the partial codification of directors' duties has indeed narrowed directors' duties, because there is now a statutory defence open to directors in the form of the so-called business judgement test.[21] Directors may use this test to prove that they have not acted in breach of their duties.

Section 76 of the Companies Act, 2008 introduces new statutory law, entitled 'Standards of directors' conduct', in the form of a partially codified regime of directors' duties, which includes a **fiduciary duty** and a **duty of reasonable care**. The provisions governing directors' duties are supplemented by other provisions addressing conflict of interest (s 75), directors' liability (s 77), and indemnities and insurance (s 78).

From the discussion above, it is clear that despite s 76 and the other provisions regarding the duties of directors in the Companies Act, the statutory provisions of the Act must still be read in the context of the common-law principles and these principles continue to apply in the absence of any contrary statutory provision and are not in substitution for any duties of a director under the common law. The courts must still have regard to the common law, including past case law, when interpreting the provisions of the Act.

---

19   J Kiggundu and M Havenga 'The regulation of directors' self-serving conduct: perspectives from Botswana and South Africa' (2004) 37 *CILSA* 272 at 290; BR Cheffins *Company Law: Theory, Structure and Operation* (1997) 133.

20   *Ibid.*

21   See para. 6.3.3 below.

CONTEXTUAL ISSUE	**The deficiencies in company law prior to the Companies Act, 2008**
	As part of the law reform process in South Africa, the dti issued a general notice entitled *South African Company Law for the 21st Century: Guidelines for Corporate Law Reform.* This document stated that there was no extensive statutory scheme covering the duties and obligations of directors and their accountability in cases of violations and it 'will be an important part of the review of company law to ensure that directors are made as accountable to shareholders as is practicable.'
	The document made it clear that perhaps the most significant deficiency in the law prior to the Companies Act, 2008 was that South African company law did not provide effective mechanisms for the enforcement of directors' duties prescribed under the old law: 'The result is that the directors and senior management of large companies are effectively immune from legal control, except perhaps in regard to the more outrageous criminal offences.'

Previously, the law regulating a director's fiduciary duties was found in the common law. At common law, a director was subject to the fiduciary duties to act in good faith to the benefit of the company as a whole and to avoid a situation where the director's personal interest conflicts with that of the company.[22] The Companies Act, 2008 re-emphasises this duty and also ensures harmonisation with other legislation, for example, the Financial Markets Act[23] and the Auditing Profession Act.[24]

6.3.1 Directors' personal financial interests

Section 75 of the Companies Act, 2008 deals specifically with a director's personal financial interests, and provides that if a director's personal interests conflict with those of the company, the director should disclose the **conflict of interest** in the manner described in that section.

6.3.1.1 Companies where there is more than one director

If a director of a company has a personal financial interest in respect of a matter to be considered at a meeting of the board, or knows that a **related person** has a personal financial interest in the matter, the director must disclose the interest and its general nature before the matter is considered at the meeting.

PRACTICAL ISSUE	**Related persons**
	An individual is related to another individual if they:
	• are married or live together in a relationship similar to a marriage; or
	• are separated by no more than two degrees of natural or adopted consanguinity or affinity.

---

22 HS Cilliers, ML Benade et al *Corporate Law* 3ed (2000) at 139; M Havenga 'Directors' fiduciary duties under our future company law regime' (1997) 9 *SA Merc LJ* 310; M Havenga 'Company directors – fiduciary duties, corporate opportunities and confidential information' (1989) 1 *SA Merc LJ* 122; MJ Blackman 'The Fiduciary Duty Doctrine and its Application to Directors of Companies' PhD thesis, University of Cape Town (1970).

23 19 of 2012. See, for example, ss 77 to 81, which deal with 'market abuse', including the offence of insider trading.

24 26 of 2005.

> An individual is related to a juristic person if the individual directly or indirectly 'controls' (as defined in the Act) the juristic person. A juristic person is related to another juristic person if:
> - either of them directly or indirectly controls the other or the business of the other; or
> - either is a subsidiary of the other; or
> - a person directly or indirectly controls each of them, or the business of each of them.

The director is compelled to disclose to the meeting any material information relating to the matter that is known to the director. The director may disclose any observations or pertinent insights relating to the matter, if requested to do so by the other directors and if present at the meeting, but must leave the meeting immediately after making any disclosure. The director is not allowed to take part in the consideration of the matter. During the director's absence, he or she will still be considered present for purposes of determination of the quorum. However, the director is not regarded as being present at the meeting for the purpose of determining whether a resolution has sufficient support to be adopted. The relevant director may not execute any document on behalf of the company in relation to the matter, unless specifically requested or directed to do so by the board.

If a director or a person related to the director acquires a personal financial interest in an agreement or other matter in which the company has a material interest, after the agreement or other matter was approved by the company, the director must promptly disclose to the board, or to the shareholders, the nature and extent of that interest, and the material circumstances relating to the director or related person's acquisition of that interest.

A decision by the board, or an agreement approved by the board, is valid despite any personal financial interest of a director, or person related to the director, if it was approved or has been ratified by an ordinary resolution of the shareholders.

Any interested person may apply to court for an order validating a transaction or agreement that was approved by the board or shareholders, despite the failure of the director to satisfy the disclosure requirements.

For purposes of the disclosure of a director's personal interests, the term 'director' has an extended meaning. It includes the following:
- an alternate director;
- a prescribed officer;
- a person who is a member of a board committee irrespective of whether the person is also a member of the company's board; and
- a member of the audit committee.

The disclosure and other requirements discussed above do not apply to a director of a company in respect of a decision that may generally affect all the directors of the company in their capacity as directors, or a class of persons of which a director is one, unless the only members of the class are the director or persons related to the director. These requirements also do not apply in respect of a proposal to remove that director from office, or to a company or its director, if one person holds all of the beneficial interests of all of the issued securities of the company and is the only director of that company.

6.3.1.2 Companies where there is a single director

Where a company has only one director, but the director does not hold all of the beneficial interests of all of the issued securities of the company, the director may not approve or enter into any agreement in which that director or a related person has a personal financial interest, unless the agreement is approved by an ordinary resolution of the shareholders, after the director has disclosed the nature and extent of that interest to the shareholders.

6.3.2 Standards of directors' conduct [25]

A director of a company must exercise the powers and perform the functions of director in good faith and in the best interests of the company, and must act with a certain degree of care, diligence and skill.

6.3.2.1 Position of director and information

A director must not use the position of director, or use information that is obtained as a director, for any personal benefit. Furthermore, a director must not in any way cause harm to the company or to a subsidiary of the company. It is interesting to note that in terms of the common law, a director has always had the duty to act in the best interests of a company of which he or she is a director. The 2008 Act goes a little further than this, by extending the duty to apply also in relation to a subsidiary.

A director must communicate to the board any information that comes to the director's attention,[26] unless the director reasonably believes that the information is:

- immaterial to the company;
- generally available to the public; or
- known to the other directors.

CASE STUDY	**Duty to disclose information to board despite strained relationships**
	The court in *Kukama v Lobelo*[27] held that s 76(2)*(b)* of the Companies Act, 2008 creates a duty on the part of a director to communicate to his board, at the earliest practicable opportunity, any information that comes to his attention. It was common cause that Mr L in this case failed to alert his co-director and co-shareholder in company A of a fraudulent transaction and the repayment by SARS of a certain sum of money into the account of another company that was not entitled to such repayment.
	The court commented that notwithstanding the strained relationship between the applicant and Mr L as both directors and shareholders, the legal obligations of a director bound Mr L to discharge his duties in the same manner as if the relationship between the two were normal.

A director is also not compelled to disclose information where a legal or ethical obligation of confidentiality prevents him or her from disclosing the information.

---

25   See s 76 of the Companies Act, 2008.
26   Section 76(2)*(b)* of the Companies Act, 2008.
27   JDR 0663 (GSJ); [2012] ZAGP JHC 60.

| PRACTICAL | **Misuse of information** |
| ISSUE | An example of misuse of information by a director would be where the director commits insider trading in terms of the Financial Markets Act.[28] However, note that the duty of directors not to misuse information as contained in the Companies Act, 2008 is not limited to a prohibition of insider trading. A director could be in breach of the statutory duty not to misuse information even where the misuse of the information does not constitute insider trading. |

In terms of s 78(1) of the Financial Markets Act, an 'insider' (the definition of which includes a director) who knows that he or she has inside information and who deals directly or indirectly or through an agent for his or her own account in the securities listed on a regulated market to which the inside information relates or which are likely to be affected by it, commits an offence.

In terms of s 82 of that Act, any person who contravenes s 78(1) (or 78(2) or (3)) will be liable to pay an administrative sanction not exceeding the following:

- the equivalent of the profit that the person, such other person or such insider, as the case may be, made or would have made if he or she had sold the securities at any stage; or the loss avoided, through such dealing;
- an amount of up to R1 million, to be adjusted by the registrar annually to reflect the Consumer Price Index, as published by Statistics South Africa, plus three times the amount referred to above;
- interest; and
- costs of any legal suit, including investigation costs, on such scale as determined by the Enforcement Committee.

The amount received under this administrative sanction will firstly be used to pay any expenses incurred by the Financial Services Board in respect of the matter, and any balance must be distributed to any claimants who are affected by the insider dealings and who submit claims and prove to the reasonable satisfaction of the claims officer that they were affected by the dealings referred to in s 78(1) to (5).

6.3.2.2   Fiduciary duty and duty of care, skill and diligence

The Companies Act, 2008 confirms that a director is under a fiduciary duty and that he or she must act with a certain degree of care, skill and diligence. Section 76(3) provides that a director must exercise the powers and perform the functions of a director:

(*a*)   in good faith and for a proper purpose;

(*b*)   in the best interests of the company; and

(*c*)   with the degree of care, skill and diligence that may reasonably be expected of a person–

(i)   carrying out the same functions in relation to the company as those carried out by that director; and

(ii)   having the general knowledge, skill and experience of that director.

Only directors (as defined) are subject to the duties discussed above.

---

28   19 of 2012. See ss 77 to 79.

CASE STUDY

Shareholders do not have fiduciary duties to the company

In *Bhagwandas v GMO Imaging (Pty) Ltd*,[29] in a case that involved a company carrying on a medical practice, the court made the following comments:

[I]n so far as it is alleged that (two doctors) have breached their fiduciary duties, I am of the view that they do not owe a fiduciary duty to the companies as neither of them are directors. As shareholders, they do not owe a fiduciary duty to the companies. As young professionals, it was not unreasonable or inappropriate, for that matter, for them to free themselves from the affairs of the companies, which were by that stage plagued by animosity, deadlock, and the lack of a cohesive, functional and effective administration and management. It was equally reasonable and appropriate for them to have sought to ensure their continued professional development and survival by setting up another practice.

It is clear that in determining whether or not a director has acted with the required degree of care, skill and diligence, a director must pass both an objective and a subjective test. An objective test is applied to determine what a reasonable director would have done in the same situation. In addition, a subjective test is also applied, taking into account the general knowledge, skill and experience of the particular director. It is therefore clear that much more is expected of a director who is qualified and experienced, than is the case if the director is new and inexperienced.

CASE STUDY

Breach of fiduciary duty

In *CyberScene Ltd v i-Kiosk Internet and Information (Pty) Ltd*,[30] it was held that a director clearly acts in breach of his fiduciary duty to the company where he sabotages the company's contractual opportunities for his own advantage, or where he uses confidential information to advance the interests of a rival concern or his own business to the prejudice of those of his company. The court also said that previous decisions, such as that in *Robinson v Randfontein Estates Gold Mining Co Ltd*,[31] have made it clear that a director has a duty not to misappropriate corporate opportunities, and a duty not to compete improperly with the company in the sense of becoming a director of or holding another office in a rival concern, thereby placing himself in a position in which his duties or interests conflict.

In the *CyberScene* case, while the respondents in this case were still directors of a company (CyberScene), they made a presentation to the City of Tygerberg for the marketing of a product that was exactly the same product as CyberScene's product. However, they had done this for their own account, and not on behalf of the company of which they were directors. The court held as follows:

This conduct was clearly unlawful as the respondents have placed themselves in a situation of conflict of interest and duty with CyberScene. The respondents have set up a business in direct competition with CyberScene and they have also

---

29   2011 JDR 1413 (GSJ); [2011] ZAGP JHC 138.
30   2000 (3) SA 806 (C).
31   1921 AD 168.

replicated the entire business of CyberScene using its assets, goodwill, trading name and proprietary information ... The respondents were under a duty not to interfere with existing contracts of CyberScene and the maturing business opportunities accruing to it. The presentation by the respondents to the City of Tygerberg ... constitutes clear proof that the respondents acted in breach of their fiduciary duties owed to CyberScene.

In *Robinson v Randfontein Estates Gold Mining Co Ltd*, a director of the plaintiff company had purchased property in circumstances where it was his duty to have acquired the property not for himself, but for the company. He thereafter re-sold the property to the company. The company was held to be entitled to claim from the director the profit he had made out of the transaction. The Appellate Division held that the action was one for neither breach of contract, nor for damages arising from a delict. It arose because the director breached his fiduciary duty to the company. The court held:[32]

> Where one man stands to another in a position of confidence involving a duty to protect the interests of that other, he is not allowed to make a secret profit at the other's expense or place himself in a position where his personal interests conflict with his duty.

There are, however, limits to the duties that a director owes to his or her company. In *Ghersi v Tiber Developments (Pty) Ltd*,[33] the provisional curator had recommended the institution of proceedings against the directors for a statement of account of all property developments and opportunities undertaken by them over the previous 23 years which were not offered to the company, for debatement of the account and for payment of all profits made by them. The court held that it does not follow that because a person is a director of a company that engages in property development, such a person is automatically, in the absence of an agreement to the contrary, obliged to offer all property developments of whatever nature to the company, on pain of being held to have breached his or her fiduciary duty to the company and being required in consequence to hand over profits made from the developments not so offered.

It is clear that the facts of each case are important in determining whether or not a person has acted in breach of the fiduciary duty owed to his or her company.

Directors are not the only ones owing duties to a company. Employees and managers also have certain fiduciary obligations or responsibilities towards their company.

CASE	**Employees and fiduciary duties**
STUDY	*Phillips v Fieldstone Africa (Pty) Ltd*[34] was a case that concerned the liability of an employee to account to his employer for secret profits made by the employee out of an opportunity arising in the course of his employment. The court confirmed the

---

32   1921 AD 168 at 177.
33   2007 (4) SA 536 (SCA).
34   [2004] 1 All SA 150 (SCA).

importance and validity of the principles set out in *Robinson v Randfontein Estates Gold Mining Co Ltd*[35] – namely that a person who has a duty to protect the interests of another is not allowed to make a secret profit at the other's expense or to allow his or her interests and duties to conflict.

The employee had argued that a distinction exists between the doctrine as applied to company directors and agents on the one hand, and employees on the other. It was argued that, as a mere employee, the employee should not be burdened with the strict and extensive application of the doctrine as described in the *Robinson* case above. In this case, the employee had acquired certain shares from a client, and he acquired these shares for himself, rather than on behalf of his employer. The court found that when the shares were offered to him, he was in a position of trust in relation to the business of his employers, which required him to place their interests above his own whenever a real possibility of conflict arose.

The court held that the defences open to a fiduciary that breaches his trust are very limited: only the free consent of the principal after full disclosure will suffice. The duty may even extend beyond the term of the employment. The court therefore found that it was clear that the employee had breached his duty: he had failed to inform his employer of the offer of shares to him and its terms and he took the shares for himself without their consent. The court concluded that the appellant must be deemed to have acquired the shares on behalf of his employers and was obliged to account to them in respect thereof.

In *Daewoo Heavy Industries (Pty) Ltd v Banks*,[36] the court confirmed that there is in most, if not in all, contracts of service, whether it is an employment contract or a contract of agency, an implied fiduciary duty.

CASE STUDY

A question of fiduciary relationship

In *Dorbyl Limited v Vorster*,[37] the plaintiff (the company) claimed for the disgorgement of secret profits (some R36 million) in breach of fiduciary duty on the part of the defendant (who was an executive director of the company at the time the profits were made).

In this case, it was common cause that the defendant, as a paid executive director of the plaintiff, received certain profits, in the form of joining fees, share allocation and proceeds of the re-sale of shares, without the knowledge of the plaintiff in breach of his duty of trust.

The defence was that the benefits were not and could never have been corporate opportunities for the plaintiff.

The court referred to *Phillips v Fieldstone Africa (Pty) Ltd*:[38]

> The fundamental question is not whether the appellant appropriated an opportunity belonging to the respondents, but whether he stood in a fiduciary relationship to them when the opportunity became available to him; if he did, it 'belonged to the respondents'.

---

35 Supra.
36 [2004] 2 All SA 530 (C).
37 2011 (5) SA 575 (GSJ).
38 Supra at para. [35].

In the present matter, it was expressly admitted that the defendant stood in a fiduciary relationship to the plaintiff when the so-called opportunity became available to him. The court found that he plainly breached his fiduciary duty to the plaintiff. He failed to inform the plaintiff of the offer to him or even its terms and he took it for himself without plaintiff's consent. The court ordered the defendant to pay the benefits that he had obtained to the plaintiff.

CASE
STUDY

Two strands of fiduciary duties

In *MMA Architects v LuyandaMpahlwa*,[39] the court referred to *Ultraframe (UK) Ltd v Fielding*,[40] where Lewison J considered that the general duties of directors included 'two strands of fiduciary duties', which were the 'no conflict rule' and 'no profit rule'. The first duty precludes a director from entering into a transaction where the director has an interest that conflicts with that of the company, and the second requires a director to account for any profit that he makes from his position unless there has been consent. Lewison J pointed out that:[41]

> (t)he rule does not preclude a fiduciary from retaining a benefit or gain which comes his way as a result of his fiduciary position, if those to whom he owes fiduciary duties have given informed consent to the benefit or gain. Perhaps a more felicitous way of formulating the no profit rule is that a director may not make 'an unauthorised profit'.

The court referred to the writings of Professor of Robert C. Clark who described the fundamental nature of the duty of loyalty as follows:

> The most general formulation of corporate law's attempted solution to the problem of managerial accountability is the fiduciary duty of loyalty: the corporation's directors ... owe a duty of undivided loyalty to their corporations, and they may not so use corporate assets or deal with the corporation, as to benefit themselves at the expense of the corporation and its shareholders. The overwhelming majority of particular rules, doctrines, and cases in corporate law are simply an explication of this duty or of the procedural rules and institutional arrangements involved in implementing it. The history of corporate law is largely the history of the development of operational content for the duty of loyalty. Even many cases that appear to be about dull formalities or rules of the road in fact involve disputes arising out of alleged managerial disloyalty ... Most importantly, this general fiduciary duty of loyalty is a residual concept that can include factual situations that no one has foreseen and categorised. The general duty permits, and in fact has led to, a continuous evolution in corporate law.

The court stated that it should, however, always be remembered that a director cannot abdicate his responsibilities or abandon his status without formally resigning.

---

39   [2011] ZAWCHC 259.
40   [2005] EWHC 1638 (Ch).
41   At para. 1318.

6.3.3 The business judgement test

Section 76(4) of the Companies Act, 2008 introduces the so-called **business judgement test** into South African law. Sub-paragraph *(a)* provides that a director satisfies his or her obligations if:

- he or she has taken reasonably diligent steps to become informed about a particular matter; and
- either the director had no material personal financial interest in the subject matter of the decision (and had no reasonable basis to know that any related person had a personal financial interest in the matter), or he or she disclosed the conflict of interest as required by s 75 of the Act; and
- the director had a rational basis for believing, and did believe, that the decision was in the best interests of the company.

This is known as the business judgement test and allows a director to show that he or she is not in contravention of his or her statutory duties. Carl Stein puts it this way:

> In short, if a director who has no personal financial interest in a matter takes reasonable steps to become informed of the matter but nevertheless, and in good faith, then makes an incorrect decision in relation to it, the director cannot be held liable for contravening ss 76(3)*(b)* or *(c)* if there was a rational basis for his decision .... The rationale for the business judgement test is that, since all businesses have to take some financial risk in order to grow and prosper, directors should be encouraged to take carefully considered, reasonable risks, and should not have to worry about being held personally liable for doing so.[42]

In terms of s 76(4)*(b)*, a director is entitled to rely on the performance of certain people or committees as follows:

- on one or more employees of the company whom the director reasonably believes to be reliable and competent in the functions performed;
- on the information, opinions, reports or statements provided by legal counsel, accountants, or other professional persons retained by the company; and
- on the board or a committee as to matters involving skills or expertise that the director reasonably believes are matters within the particular person's professional or expert competence or as to which the particular person merits confidence, or a committee of the board of which the director is not a member, unless the director has reason to believe that the actions of the committee do not merit confidence.

The business judgement rule entails that a director should not be held liable for decisions that lead to undesirable results, where such decisions were made in good faith, with care and on an informed basis and which the director believed were in the interest of the company.[43] The rule provides that a director can be excused from liability where the latter made a decision in circumstances based on adequate information and where the decision was arrived at in good faith and made in the interests of the company.[44]

---

42   Carl Stein with Geoff Everingham *The New Companies Act Unlocked* Cape Town: Siber Ink (2011) at 245.
43   L Coetzee and S Kennedy-Good 'The Business Judgment Rule' (2006) 27(2) *Obiter* 277.
44   *Ibid.*

Those supporting the business judgement rule argue that apart from creating an exemption from liability, the rule serves as motivation for capable persons to accept directorships, and that it encourages directors to engage safely in risk-taking activities.[45] Arguments against the introduction of the business judgement rule are:

- it could result in accepting a standard of conduct which is below an acceptable standard that ought to be required of directors;[46] and
- the exact content of the business judgement rule is difficult to define, and the difficulty in the codification thereof is evident in the various attempts undertaken in the United States of America.[47]

CASE STUDY	**Director's duty of skill and care**
	The court, in *Fisheries Development Corporation of SA Ltd v Jorgensen; Fisheries Development Corporation of SA Ltd v AWJ Investments (Pty) Ltd*,[48] held that the extent of a director's duty of skill and care largely depends on the nature of the company's business,[49] that the law does not require of a director to have special business acumen,[50] and that directors may assume that officials will perform their duties honestly.

6.3.4 Liability of directors

There are a number of sections in the Companies Act, 2008 that provide for the personal liability of directors. Two of the more significant sections are discussed in this chapter.

6.3.4.1 Section 77: liability of directors and prescribed officers

In terms of s 77 of the Companies Act, 2008, a company may recover loss, damages or costs sustained by the company from a director[51] under the following circumstances:

- in terms of the principles of common law relating to breach of a fiduciary duty;
- in accordance with the principles of the common law relating to delict for breach of the duty to act with the required degree of care, skill and diligence, or any provision of the Act not mentioned in s 77;
- where a director acted in the name of the company, or signed anything on behalf of the company, while the director knew that he or she lacked the necessary authority;
- where the director acquiesced in the carrying on of the business of the company knowing that it was being conducted recklessly or fraudulently, in contravention of s 22(1);
- where the director is a party to an act or omission by the company despite knowing that the act or omission was calculated to defraud a creditor, employee or shareholder of the company, or had another fraudulent purpose;

45 LCB Gower *The Principles of Modern Company Law* 3 ed (1969) at 640; LS Sealy 'Reforming the Law on Directors' Duties' (1991) 12(9) *The Company Lawyer* 175.
46 Coetzee & Kennedy-Good supra at 280; V Finch 'Company Directors: Who Cares about Skill and Care?' (1992) 55(2) *The Modern Law Review* 179; AL Mackenzie 'A Company Director's Obligations of Care and Skill' 1982 *Journal of Business Law* 460; Sealy supra at 176; M Trebilcock 'The Liability of Company Directors for Negligence' (1969) 32 *The Modern Law Review* 499 at 508.
47 Coetzee & Kennedy-Good supra at 291.
48 1980 (4) SA 156 (W); Cilliers & Benade supra at 147.
49 *Ibid* 165. JT Pretorius et al *Hahlo's Company Law through the Cases* 6 ed (1999) at 282; Cilliers & Benade supra at 147.
50 *Ibid.*
51 Defined to include alternate directors, prescribed officers and members of board and audit committees.

- where the director signed, consented to, or authorised, the publication of any financial statements that were false or misleading in a material respect;
- where the director signed, consented to or authorised the publication of a prospectus or a written statement that contained an untrue statement or a statement to the effect that a person had consented to be a director of the company, when no such consent had been given, despite knowing that the statement was false, misleading or untrue;
- where a director failed to vote against the issuing of any unauthorised shares, despite knowing that those shares were not authorised;
- where a director participated in the issuing of any authorised securities, despite knowing that the issue of those securities did not comply with the provisions of the 2008 Act;
- where a director participated in the granting of options to any person despite knowing that any shares for which the options could be exercised or into which any securities could be converted had not been authorised;
- where a director participated in the decision to grant financial assistance to any person for the acquisition of securities of the company, despite knowing that the provision of financial assistance was inconsistent with s 44 or the company's MOI;[52]
- where a director is provided with a loan or granted financial assistance despite the knowledge that the provision of financial assistance is inconsistent with s 45 of the 2008 Act or the company's MOI;[53]
- where the director participated in a resolution approving a distribution despite knowing that the distribution was contrary to the provisions of s 46;[54]
- where the company acquired any of its own shares, or the shares of its holding company, despite knowing that the acquisition was contrary to s 46 or s 48;[55] and
- where the company issues an allotment of shares contrary to any provision of Chapter 4 of the 2008 Act.

---

52 According to s 44, a company may provide financial assistance for the acquisition of shares, provided the company satisfies the solvency and liquidity test. The terms under which the financial assistance is proposed to be given must be fair and reasonable to the company. A company is allowed to provide financial assistance for the acquisition of shares pursuant to an employee share scheme or pursuant to a special resolution of the shareholders, adopted within the previous two years, which approved such assistance either for the specific recipient, or generally for a category of potential recipients.

53 This includes lending money, guaranteeing a loan or other obligation, and securing any debt or obligation. A company may provide a director with a loan or financial assistance, provided the particular provision of financial assistance is pursuant to an employee share scheme or is pursuant to a special resolution of the shareholders, adopted within the previous two years, which approved such assistance either for the specific recipient, or generally for a category of potential recipients, the specific recipient falls within that category, and the board is satisfied that immediately after providing the financial assistance, the company would be in compliance with the solvency and liquidity test, and the terms under which the financial assistance is proposed to be given are fair and reasonable to the company.

54 A company may make a distribution, provided the distribution is pursuant to an existing legal obligation of the company, or a court order; or the board of the company, by resolution, has authorised the distribution. The board should also be satisfied that it reasonably appears that the company will satisfy the solvency and liquidity test immediately after completing the proposed distribution. The board of the company must by resolution acknowledge that it has applied the solvency and liquidity test. The liability of a director who failed to vote against a distribution arises only if immediately after making the distribution the company does not satisfy the solvency and liquidity test and it was unreasonable at the time of the decision to conclude that the company would satisfy the solvency and liquidity test. The liability of a director does not exceed, in aggregate, the difference between the amount by which the value of the distribution exceeded the amount that could have been distributed without causing the company to fail to satisfy the solvency and liquidity test and the amount, if any, recovered by the company from persons to whom the distribution was made.

55 A company may acquire its own shares provided the company passes the solvency and liquidity test. Any subsidiary of a company may acquire shares of that company. Subsidiaries may not acquire more than 10%, in aggregate, of the number of issued shares of the holding company. No voting rights attached to shares are acquired by subsidiaries.

The director will be jointly and severally liable with any other person who is or may be held liable for the same act. Proceedings to recover any loss, damages or costs may not be commenced more than three years after the act or omission (giving rise to the liability) occurred.

Section 77 also gives a director a **statutory defence** to a director's liability in the form of the business judgement test referred to above.[56]

Section 77 (9) provides that in any proceedings against a director, other than for wilful misconduct or wilful breach of trust, the court may relieve the director, either wholly or partly, from any liability set out in this section, on any terms the court considers just if it appears to the court that:

- the director is or may be liable, but has acted honestly and reasonably; or
- having regard to all the circumstances of the case, including those connected with the appointment of the director, it would be fair to excuse the director.

Section 77(10) allows a director to anticipate any claims in terms of s 77. It provides that a director who has reason to apprehend that a claim may be made alleging that the director is liable, other than for wilful misconduct or wilful breach of trust, may apply to a court for relief, and the court may grant relief to the director on the same grounds as if the matter had come before the court in terms of sub-s (9).

6.3.4.2   Section 218: civil actions

Section 218(2) reads as follows:

> Any person who contravenes any provision of this Act is liable to any other person for any loss or damage suffered by that person as a result of that contravention.

Stein has stated that s 218(2) could have significant financial repercussions for directors:

> because it is wide enough to include a monetary claim by anyone against a director personally if that director contravened any provision of the Act and thereby caused that person to suffer monetary loss.[57]

It should also be noted that s 218(2) will not only apply to directors but to 'any person' who fails to comply with the provisions of the Act.

6.3.5   Indemnification and directors' insurance

Section 78 of the Companies Act, 2008, dealing with **indemnification** and **directors' insurance**, applies also to former directors of the company.

A company cannot undertake *not* to hold a director liable for breach of fiduciary duties. Any provision in an agreement, the MOI or rules of a company, or a resolution adopted by a company, whether express or implied, is void to the extent that it directly or indirectly purports to relieve a director of a duty. Except to the extent that a company's MOI provides otherwise, the company may advance expenses to a director to defend litigation in any proceedings arising out of the director's service to the company.

A company is entitled to take out indemnity insurance to protect a director against any liability or expenses for which the company is permitted to indemnify a director. The company may also take out indemnity insurance to insure itself against any expenses that

---

56   See para. 6.3.3 above.
57   See Carl Stein with Geoff Everingham *The New Companies Act Unlocked* Cape Town: Siber Ink (2011) at 407.

the company is permitted to advance to a director or for which the company is permitted to indemnify a director.

A company may not directly or indirectly pay any fine that may be imposed on the director of the company, or of a related company, who has been convicted of an offence in terms of any national legislation.

A company may also not indemnify a director in respect of any liability arising in the following circumstances:

- where a director acted in the name of the company or signed anything on behalf of the company or purported to bind the company or authorise the taking of any action on behalf of the company while knowing that he or she lacked the authority to do so;
- where the director acquiesced in the carrying on of the company's business in insolvent circumstances while knowing that it was being so conducted;
- where the director was a party to an act or omission by the company despite knowing that the act or omission was calculated to defraud a creditor, employee or shareholder of the company, or had another fraudulent purpose;
- where the company's loss or liability arose from wilful misconduct or wilful breach of trust on the part of the director; or
- where the director is liable to pay a fine for an offence in contravention of any national legislation.

Finally, s 78(8) entitles a company to claim restitution from a director of the company, or of a related company, for any money paid directly or indirectly by the company to or on behalf of that director in any manner inconsistent with the above restrictions.

6.4   Number of directors and consent

A private or personal liability company must have at least one director, while public and non-profit companies must have at least three directors.[58] A person becomes a director of a company when that person has been appointed or elected as a director in terms of the provisions of the Act or the MOI, or holds an office, title, designation or similar status entitling that person to be an *ex officio* director of the company. A person will only become a director if he or she delivers to the company a written consent accepting the position of director.

In spite of the requirement that certain types of company must have a minimum number of directors, s 66(11) of the Companies Act, 2008 specifically provides that where the company does not have the prescribed minimum number of directors (whether this be in terms of the 2008 Act or in terms of a company's MOI), this does not negate or limit the authority of the board, nor does it invalidate anything done by the board or by the company.

---

58   However, the MOI may specify a higher number of directors: see para. 6.5 below.

6.5   Memorandum of Incorporation may vary certain provisions of 2008 Act

Certain provisions concerning directors contained in the Companies Act, 2008 may be varied by the provisions of a company's MOI, whereas others may not be varied in that way. A summary of key issues is set out in Table 6.3 below.

Table 6.3 Scope for MOI to vary provisions on directors in Companies Act, 2008

	The 2008 Act	**The Memorandum of Incorporation**
Number of directors	• Private companies and personal liability companies must have at least one director (s 66(2)). • Public and non-profit companies must have at least three directors (s 66(2)). • Where the company does not have the prescribed minimum number of directors, any act done by the board will remain valid.	• The MOI can specify a higher number than the minimum number of directors required in terms of the 2008 Act. • It is not possible for the MOI to lower the number of directors prescribed by the Act. • The MOI cannot invalidate the acts of a board where it acts without the required number of directors.
Appointment of directors	Section 66(4)*(b)* provides that the MOI of a profit company must provide that the shareholders will be entitled to elect at least 50% of the directors and 50% of any alternate directors.	The MOI can provide that any person will have the power to appoint and remove one or more of the directors, but there must still be the minimum number of elected directors for a profit company.
Removal of directors[59]	Section 71 provides as follows: • despite the MOI or rules; and • despite any agreement between the company and a director; and • despite any agreement between any shareholders and a director, a director may be removed by an ordinary resolution adopted at a shareholders' meeting.	The MOI cannot entrench the position of any director and cannot override the will of ordinary shareholders as expressed in an ordinary resolution.
Ex officio directors	Section 66(4)*(a)*(ii) provides that the MOI may provide for a person to be an *ex officio* director. The 2008 Act does not insist on the appointment of such a director.	The MOI can provide that a person will be regarded as an *ex officio* director.
Alternate directors	The 2008 Act does not insist on the appointment of alternate directors.	The 2008 Act states that the MOI can provide[60] for the appointment or election of one or more persons as alternate directors of the company.

---

59   See para. 6.13 below.
60   Section 66(4)*(a)*(iii) of the Companies Act, 2008.

	The 2008 Act	The Memorandum of Incorporation
Remuneration of directors	• A director does not have an automatic right to remuneration in terms of the 2008 Act. • Section 66(9) provides that a company may pay remuneration to a director, unless prohibited in its MOI. • Remuneration payable (directors' fees), if not prohibited by the MOI, must be approved by a special resolution[61] within the previous two years (s 66(9)).	The MOI can provide for remuneration of directors but directors' fees still have to be approved by shareholders by way of special resolution.
Term of office	Each director of a company must be elected by the persons entitled to exercise voting rights in such an election to serve either for an indefinite term or for a fixed term as set out in the MOI.	The MOI can provide for the term of office of a director.
Ineligibility and disqualifications	See para. 6.6 below.	The MOI can provide for additional grounds of ineligibility or disqualification of directors, but an MOI cannot override the provisions of the Act.
Qualifications		The MOI can prescribe minimum qualifications to be met by directors of the company.

6.6 Ineligible and disqualified persons

Certain people are ineligible to be appointed as a director, while certain people are disqualified to be a director of a company. The provisions that make a person ineligible or disqualified apply not only to those wishing to be a director, but also to the following:

• an alternate director;
• a prescribed officer; and
• any person who is a member of a committee of a board of a company or of the audit committee of a company, irrespective of whether such person is also a member of the company's board.

If a person is **ineligible** for appointment as director, this means that such a person is absolutely prohibited from becoming a director of a company, and there are no exceptions to this prohibition. Persons ineligible to be appointed as a director are set out in Table 6.4 below.

---

61 It is interesting to note that the Act requires a special resolution of shareholders in approving directors' remuneration. Exactly what is meant by a special resolution is discussed in chapter 5 of this book. An ordinary resolution would arguably have been sufficient, but it seems that the Act wants to ensure that directors do not receive excessive or unauthorised benefits from a company.

Table 6.4 *Persons ineligible for appointment as director*

Person who is ineligible	Comment	Section of the 2008 Act
A juristic person	A company or close corporation cannot be appointed as a director because they are juristic persons. A trust cannot be appointed as a director because a trust is not a legal person.[62]	Section 69(7)*(a)*
An unemancipated minor or person under a similar legal disability[63]	A minor is any person under the age of 18 years.	Section 69(7)*(b)*
Any person who does not satisfy any requirement in a company's MOI		Section 69(7)*(c)*

PRACTICAL ISSUE	**Minors**
	If a person is ineligible to be a director, the prohibition is absolute, unlike other disqualifications discussed below. The 2008 Act expressly states that an unemancipated minor may not be a director, but in the case of *Ex parte Velkes*,[64] the court doubted that even an emancipated minor was eligible to be a company director.

Certain persons are **disqualified** from being appointed as a director. Except for persons who have been prohibited from being a director by a court of law, the other disqualifications provided for in the Act are not absolute, and a court has a discretion as to whether to allow such disqualified persons to be appointed as a director.[65] The following persons are disqualified from being appointed as a director:

Table 6.5 *Persons disqualified from appointment as director*

Person who is disqualified	Comment	Section of the 2008 Act
A person who has been prohibited by a court of law from becoming a director	See para. 6.7 below.	Section 69(8)*(a)*
A person who has been declared to be delinquent by a court of law in terms of s 162 of the Companies Act, 2008 or in terms of s 47 of the Close Corporations Act	See para. 6.7 below.	Section 69(8)*(a)*

---

62   See chapter 18 of this book for a discussion of trusts.
63   See Practical Issue below.
64   1963 (3) SA 584 (C).
65   Section 69(11) of the Companies Act, 2008 provides that a court may exempt a person from the disqualifications listed in s 69(8)*(b)*. See discussion and Case Study below.

Person who is disqualified	Comment	Section of the 2008 Act
An unrehabilitated insolvent	Although such a person is disqualified, s 69(11) confers a discretion on a court to allow such person to be appointed.[66]	s 69(8)(*b*)(i)
A person who is prohibited in terms of any public regulation from being a director	Although such a person is disqualified, s 69(11) confers a discretion on a court to allow such person to be appointed.[67]	s 69(8)(*b*)(ii)
A person who has been removed from an office of trust because of dishonesty	In spite of this disqualification, s 69(11) gives a court a discretion[68] to grant an exemption.	s 69(8)(*b*)(iii) A disqualification in terms of this section ends at the later of five years after the date of removal from office, or at the completion of the sentence imposed for the relevant offence, or at the end of one or more extensions, as determined by a court from time to time, on application by the Commission.[69]
A person who has been convicted and imprisoned without the option of a fine for theft, fraud, forgery, perjury or other offences as listed in s 69(8)(*b*)(iv)[70]	In spite of this disqualification, s 69(11) gives a court a discretion[71] to grant an exemption.	s 69(8)(*b*)(iv) The consequences are the same as those for s 69(8)(*b*)(iii) above.
A person disqualified in terms of a company's MOI		

Notes:

1. The disqualifications discussed above apply to all directors, including alternate directors, prescribed officers, or persons who are members of a committee of a board of a company, or of the audit committee of a company.
2. When a person is ineligible or disqualified, that person must not be appointed or elected as a director of a company or consent to be appointed or elected as a director or act as a director of a company.
3. A company must not knowingly permit an ineligible or disqualified person to serve or act as a director.
4. A person who becomes ineligible or disqualified while serving as a director of a company ceases to be a director and should immediately vacate office.

---

66   See para. 6.7 below.
67   See para. 6.7 below.
68   See para. 6.7 below.
69   At any time before the expiry of a person's disqualification, the Commission may apply to a court for an extension. The court may extend the disqualification for up to five years at a time, if the court is satisfied that an extension is necessary to protect the public, having regard to the conduct of the disqualified person up to the time of the application.
70   A person is disqualified if he or she has been convicted, in the Republic or elsewhere, and imprisoned without the option of a fine, or fined more than the prescribed amount, for theft, fraud, forgery, perjury, or an offence involving fraud, misrepresentation or dishonesty in connection with the promotion, formation or management of a company under this Act, the Close Corporations Act 69 of 1984, the Financial Intelligence Centre Act 38 of 2001, the Financial Markets Act 19 of 2012, the Prevention of Corruption Act 6 of 1958, or Chapter 2 of the Prevention and Combating of Corrupt Activities Act 12 of 2004.
71   See para. 6.7 below.

6.7   Exemptions to director disqualifications

Section 69(11) of the Companies Act, 2008 gives a court a discretion to grant an **exemption** from being disqualified from appointment as a director. The following persons may apply to court for such an exemption:

- an unrehabilitated insolvent;
- a person who was removed from an office of trust for dishonest misconduct; or
- a person who was convicted of a crime with an element of dishonesty.[72]

Section 69(11) implies that the relevant person will have to make an *ex parte* application to court for permission to act as a director despite the disqualification.

Where an applicant was removed from an office of trust for misconduct related to dishonesty or was convicted of a crime with an element of dishonesty, the applicant will have to prove to the court that he or she has been rehabilitated from his or her wrongful ways.[73] In an application for permission to accept the position of director despite the disqualification, the applicant will have to prove to the court that he or she has been rehabilitated from his or her wrongful ways and can be trusted with the responsibilities of directorship.

CASE **STUDY**	**Section 69(11): application to court** An example of an application by a disqualified person to court is to be found in *Ex Parte Tayob*.[74] The applicants had been convicted of bribery. One year after their conviction, they brought an application for permission to be allowed to act as directors despite their disqualification. The court held that bribery and corruption pose a serious threat to an open and honest community. The court therefore concluded that too little time had lapsed between the date of the conviction and the date of the application to prove that the applicants had been rehabilitated from their dishonest ways. The application was therefore refused.

CASE **STUDY**	**Authorising disqualified persons to act as director** In *Ex parte Barron*,[75] the applicant had been a director of several private companies of which he and his wife were the only shareholders. He had tried to circumvent certain regulations prohibiting the export of ostrich leather. He did this by calling the consignment of ostrich skins 'feathers', whereas it was in fact leather. That constituted fraud and he was tried and convicted on this charge. He was therefore a disqualified person under the 1973 Act. He subsequently applied to court for authorisation to act as a director. The court held that the factors that affect the discretion of the court are the following: • the type of offence; • whether or not it was a first conviction;

---

72   See Table 6.5 above.
73   *Ex Parte R* 1966 (1) SA 84 (SR).
74   1990 (3) SA 715 (T).
75   1977 (3) SA 1099 (C).

- the type of punishment imposed;
- whether it was a public company in regard to which the applicant wished to act as a director, or whether it was a private company; and
- the attitude of shareholders and whether all the shareholders supported the application.

The court held that it could be more lenient in a case where a private company is affected than where a public company is involved because, in the case of a public company, a director obviously deals with funds in which a vast number of people may have an interest.

6.8   Application to declare a person delinquent or under probation

In terms of s 162 of the Companies Act, 2008, a court can declare a person to be a **delinquent** or to be **under probation**. The following eight types of person can apply to court for such an order:

1. a company;
2. a shareholder;
3. a director;
4. a company secretary or prescribed officer of a company;
5. a registered trade union that represents employees of the company;
6. any other representative of the employees of a company;
7. the Commission; or
8. the Takeover Regulation Panel.

A person who has been declared to be a delinquent in terms of s 162 is disqualified from being a director in terms of s 69(8)*(a)*.

A summary of who can apply to court, the grounds for the application, the order sought and the effect of the order appears in Table 6.6 below.

Table 6.6 Applications for declarations of delinquency and probation orders

Applicant	Grounds for application	Order sought	Effect of order
Any of the persons from 1 to 6 inclusive listed above	The person consented to serve as a director, or acted in the capacity of a director or prescribed officer, while he or she was ineligible or disqualified.	Delinquency in terms of s 162(5)*(a)*[76]	A declaration is unconditional, and subsists for the lifetime of the person declared delinquent.
Any of the persons from 1 to 6 inclusive listed above	The person acted as a director while under probation and in contravention of such order under the Companies Act, 2008 or under s 47 of the Close Corporations Act.	Delinquency in terms of s 162(5)*(b)*	A declaration is unconditional, and subsists for the lifetime of the person declared delinquent.

---

76   The court will not grant the order if the person was acting under the protection of a court order or was a director in a private company where that person held all the issued shares.

Applicant	Grounds for application	Order sought	Effect of order
Any of the persons from 1 to 6 inclusive listed above	The person, while he was a director, grossly abused the position of director.	Delinquency in terms of s 162(5)*(c)*(i)	A declaration of delinquency in terms of s 169(5)*(c)* to *(f)* may be made subject to any conditions the court considers appropriate. A declaration subsists for seven years from the date of the order, or such longer period as determined by the court (s 162(6)). The 2008 Act does not in any way limit a court's powers, but provides that a court may order, as conditions applicable or ancillary to a declaration of delinquency or probation, that the person concerned: • undertake a designated programme of remedial education relevant to the nature of the person's conduct as director; • carry out a designated programme of community service; or • pay compensation to any person adversely affected by the person's conduct as a director, to the extent that such a victim does not otherwise have a legal basis to claim compensation.
Any of the persons from 1 to 6 inclusive listed above	The person took personal advantage of information or an opportunity contrary to s 76(2) *(a)*.	Delinquency in terms of s 162(5)*(c)*(ii)	Same as for s 162(5)*(c)*(i) delinquency: see above.
Any of the persons from 1 to 6 inclusive listed above	The person intentionally or by gross negligence inflicted harm upon the company or a subsidiary of the company contrary to s 76(2)*(a)*.	Delinquency in terms of s 162(5)*(c)*(iii)	Same as for s 162(5)*(c)*(i) delinquency: see above.
Any of the persons from 1 to 6 inclusive listed above	The person acted in a manner that amounted to gross negligence, wilful misconduct or breach of trust.	Delinquency in terms of s 162(5)*(c)* (iv)*(aa)*	Same as for s 162(5)*(c)*(i) delinquency: see above.

Applicant	Grounds for application	Order sought	Effect of order
Any of the persons from 1 to 6 inclusive listed above	The person acted in a manner contemplated in s 77(3)*(a)*, *(b)* or *(c)* – that is, various unauthorised, reckless or fraudulent activities by a director.	Delinquency in terms of s 162(5)*(c)* (iv)*(bb)*	Same as for s 162(5)*(c)*(i) delinquency: see above.
Any of the persons from 1 to 6 inclusive listed above	The director failed to vote against a resolution taken at a meeting in spite of the fact that the company did not satisfy the solvency and liquidity test.	Probation	A declaration placing a person under probation may be made subject to any conditions the court considers appropriate and subsists for a period not exceeding five years. Without limiting the powers of the court, a court may order, as conditions applicable or ancillary to a declaration of delinquency or probation, that the person concerned: • undertake a designated programme of remedial education relevant to the nature of the person's conduct as director; • carry out a designated programme of community service; • pay compensation to any person adversely affected by the person's conduct as a director, to the extent that such a victim does not otherwise have a legal basis to claim compensation; or • in the case of an order of probation, be supervised by a mentor in any future participation as a director while the order remains in force; or • be limited to serving as a director of a private company, or of a company of which that person is the sole shareholder.
Any of the persons from 1 to 6 inclusive listed above	The person acted in a manner materially inconsistent with the duties of a director.	Probation	As for the probation order referred to above.

Applicant	Grounds for application	Order sought	Effect of order
Any of the persons from 1 to 6 inclusive listed above	The person acted in, or supported a decision of the company to act in, a manner contemplated in s 163(1) (acted in an oppressive or unfairly prejudicial manner).	Probation[77]	As for the probation order referred to above.
The Commission or the Takeover Regulation Panel	Any of the grounds open to the persons from 1 to 6 listed above, and in addition, the grounds set out in s 162(5)(d) to (f). These grounds are discussed immediately below this table.	Delinquency	A declaration of delinquency in terms of s 162(5)(d) to (f) may be made subject to any conditions the court considers appropriate, including conditions limiting the application of the declaration to one or more particular category of company. Such declaration subsists for seven years from the date of the order, or such longer period as determined by the court at the time of making the declaration, subject to sub-ss (11) and (12).

The additional grounds on which the Commission or the Takeover Regulation Panel may rely on to apply for an order of delinquency are as follows:

- the person has repeatedly been personally subject to a compliance notice or similar enforcement mechanism, for substantially similar conduct, in terms of any legislation;[78] or
- the person has at least twice been personally convicted of an offence, or subjected to an administrative fine or similar penalty in terms of any legislation;[79] or
- the person was a director of one or more companies or a managing member of one or more close corporations or controlled or participated in the control of a juristic person, irrespective of whether concurrently, sequentially or at unrelated times, that were convicted of an offence or subjected to an administrative fine or similar penalty within a period of five years. (It has to be proved that the person was a director or a managing member or was responsible for the management of a juristic person at the time of the contravention that resulted in the conviction, administrative fine or other penalty. The court will grant a delinquency order only if it is satisfied that the declaration of delinquency is justified. The court will take into account the nature of the contraventions and the person's conduct in relation to the management, business or property of any company, close corporation or juristic person at the time prior to making its decision.)[80]

PTO

---

77   Section 162(8) of the Companies Act, 2008 provides that the court must be satisfied that the declaration is justified in taking into account certain factors including the person's conduct in relation to the management, business or property of the company or close corporation at the time.

78   Section 162(5)(d) of the Companies Act, 2008.

79   Section 162(5)(e) of the Companies Act, 2008.

80   Section 162(5)(f) of the Companies Act, 2008.

Wilful misconduct, breach of trust and gross abuse warrant order of delinquency

In *Kukama v Lobelo*,[81] the applicant launched an application to declare Mr L a delinquent director (in terms of s 162) and for his removal as a director of the second and third respondents (companies A and B). The court did declare Mr L to be a delinquent director for a number of reasons, including the following:

- He had allowed money destined for company A to be paid into an account of company B.
- He had failed to refund SARS a fraudulent claim of R39 million after the fraud was detected.
- He had failed to alert his co-director and co-shareholder (the applicant) of the fraudulent transaction and the payment into an account of company B in which the applicant held no directorship.

The court concluded that these failings demonstrated that the conduct of Mr L in his dealings with the affairs of company A, at the least, did not measure up to the standard required and expected of a director and was in breach of his fiduciary duties to company A.

The court held that s 76(2)*(b)* of the 2008 Act creates a duty on the part of a director to communicate to his board at the earliest practicable opportunity any relevant information that comes to his attention. It was common cause that Mr L did not communicate the above information to the applicant.

The court concluded that the effect of Mr L's failure to refund SARS the R39 million did not only cause irreparable harm upon company A as envisaged in s 162(5)*(c)*(iii), but also exposed company A and the applicant to criminal liability as envisaged in s 332(1) and (2) of the Criminal Procedure Act[82]. By utilising the funds destined for company A for the benefit of other companies that were not subsidiaries of company A, Mr L had also inflicted harm upon company A in terms of s 162(5)*(c)*(iii) and in breach of the fiduciary duties he owed to company A. By failing to detect the fraud of R39 million to SARS, the conduct of Mr L amounted to gross negligence, and by failing to pay it back to SARS and/or to the account that it should have been paid into, Mr L's conduct amounted to wilful misconduct or breach of trust as envisaged in s 162(5)*(c)*(iv)*(aa)* and *(bb)*.

The court therefore concluded that Mr L's conduct fell short of the standard expected of a director of company A to such an extent that it amounted to wilful misconduct, breach of trust and a gross abuse of his position as a director. An order of delinquency was accordingly made.

---

81 Supra. See also discussion of this case under para. 6.3.2.1 above.
82 51 of 1977, as amended.

6.9   Suspending and setting aside orders of delinquency

A person who has been declared delinquent, other than where the declaration is unconditional and applies for the lifetime of the person declared delinquent, may apply to a court as follows:[83]

- to suspend the order of delinquency, and substitute an order of probation, with or without conditions, at any time from three years after the order of delinquency was made; or
- to set aside an order of delinquency at any time from two years after it was suspended, as contemplated above.

On considering an application, the court may not grant the order applied for unless the applicant has satisfied any conditions that were attached to the order and may grant an order if, having regard to the circumstances leading to the original order, and the conduct of the applicant in the ensuing period, the court is satisfied that the applicant has demonstrated satisfactory progress towards rehabilitation, and that there is a reasonable prospect that the applicant would be able to serve successfully as a director of a company in the future.

6.10   First directors of a company

Every incorporator (person who forms a company) is deemed to be a director until sufficient directors have been appointed to meet the required minimum number of directors. If the number of incorporators of a company, together with any *ex officio* directors and appointed directors is fewer than the minimum number of directors required for that company, the board must call a shareholders' meeting within 40 business days after the date of incorporation for the purpose of electing sufficient directors to fill all vacancies on the board at the time of the election.

6.11   Vacancies on the board

A person ceases to be a director and a **vacancy** arises on the board of a company in any of the following circumstances:

- when the period for a director's fixed term contract expires as provided for in the MOI;
- the person resigns;
- the person dies;
- in the case of an *ex officio* director, the person ceases to hold the office or title that entitled the person to be a director;
- the person becomes incapacitated to the extent that the person is unable to perform the functions of a director and is unlikely to regain that capacity within a reasonable time;
- he or she is declared a delinquent;
- the person is placed on probation under conditions that are inconsistent with continuing to be a director of the company;
- he or she becomes ineligible or disqualified from being a director; or

---

83   Section 162(11) of the Companies Act, 2008.

- that person is removed from office by resolution of the shareholders, or by resolution of the board, or by order of the court. However, if the board removes a director, a vacancy in the board does not arise until the later of the expiry of the time for filing an application for review or the granting of an order by the court on such an application. The director is, however, suspended from office during that time.

6.12   Filling of vacancies[84]

If a vacancy arises on the board, other than as a result of an *ex officio* director ceasing to hold that office, it must be filled by a new appointment or by a new election conducted at the next annual general meeting of the company – if the company is required to hold such a meeting. In any other event, the vacancy must be filled within six months after the vacancy arose, at a shareholders' meeting called for the purpose of electing the director or by a poll of the persons entitled to exercise voting rights.

Where, as a result of a vacancy, there are no remaining directors or no remaining directors are resident within the Republic, any shareholder with voting rights may convene a meeting to elect directors.

A company must file a notice with the Commission within 10 business days after a person becomes or ceases to be a director of the company.

6.13   Removal of directors

A director may be removed by shareholders, and, in some circumstances, by the board of directors.

6.13.1   Removal by shareholders

A director may be removed by an ordinary resolution adopted at a shareholders' meeting. This is so, no matter what the terms of any agreement may provide.

CASE STUDY	Order of delinquency renders it unnecessary to remove director
	In *Kukama v Lobelo*,[85] the applicant launched an application to declare Mr L a delinquent director (in terms of s 162) and for his removal as a director of the second and third respondents (companies A and B). The court declared Mr L to be a delinquent director for a number of reasons.[86]
	However, the court held that, in view of the effect of an order declaring a director delinquent, it was not necessary also to order his removal as a director, owing to the automatic inherent effect of such a declaration. The effect of declaring Mr L a delinquent director also had the effect of reducing company A's directors to one.

In terms of s 71(2), the notice of a shareholders' meeting to remove a director, and the resolution, must be given to the director prior to considering the resolution to remove the

---

84   Section 70 of the Companies Act, 2008.
85   Supra.
86   This case is discussed in more detail under para. 6.8 above.

director. The period of notice that should be given is equivalent to that which a shareholder is entitled to receive when convening a meeting.

The director must be allowed the reasonable opportunity to make a presentation, in person or through a representative, to the meeting, before the resolution is put to a vote. The provisions of s 71(2) therefore mean that it is not possible to remove a director by round-robin resolution, because the director must be given the opportunity to address the meeting.

CONTEXTUAL ISSUE

Shareholders' agreements concerning retention of directors

Section 220 of the Companies Act, 1973 provided that a company may, 'notwithstanding anything in its memorandum or articles or in any agreement between it and any director', by resolution remove a director before the expiration of his or her period of office.

In *Amoils v Fuel Transport (Pty) Ltd*,[87] the court confirmed that s 220 afforded the company a statutory right to remove a director from its board notwithstanding an agreement between it and the directors to the contrary. The court, however, held that it:

> does not give those shareholders, who by contract have bound themselves to vote for the retention of the director in office, the right to breach their agreement. An agreement by shareholders regarding the exercise of their votes in general meeting of the company is valid and does not derogate from the company's right to elect or remove a director upon the requisite number of votes. It therefore seems to me that Stewart's case was correctly decided.

The court therefore found that the applicant in this case was entitled to restrain certain other shareholders from voting for his removal from office as a director of a company in breach of the shareholders' agreement.

The Companies Act, 2008, however, changes this position, because it specifically states that a director can be removed by an ordinary resolution adopted at a shareholders' meeting despite:

- anything to the contrary in a company's MOI or rules;
- any agreement between a company and a director; and
- any agreement between any shareholders and a director.

6.13.2   Removal by board of directors

If a company has more than two directors and it is alleged by a shareholder or by a director that the director of the company has become ineligible or disqualified, a director may be removed by a resolution of the board of directors if:

- a director has become incapacitated to the extent that the director is unable to perform the functions of a director and is unlikely to regain that capacity within a reasonable time; or
- the director has neglected or been derelict in the performance of the functions of director.

---

87   1978 (4) SA 343 (W).

Where the board has taken a resolution to remove the director, the director may apply to a court to review the determination of the board. An application for review must be brought within 20 business days from the date the decision is taken by the board. The court may confirm the determination of the board, or remove the director from office, if the court is satisfied that the director is ineligible or disqualified, incapacitated, or non-resident, or has been negligent or derelict.

The abovementioned rules do not apply to a company that has fewer than three directors. In the case of a company that has fewer than three directors, any director or shareholder may apply to the Companies Tribunal to determine any matter referred to above.[88]

CASE STUDY	One director applies for a determination of neglect and dereliction of duty against a fellow director
	In *Talisman Compressed Air (Pty) Ltd v Dykman*,[89] the court held that a scrutiny of s 71(8), read with sub-ss (3), (4), (5) and (6) of that section, shows that a shareholder or director of a company who alleges, inter alia, that another director of that company has neglected or been derelict in the performance of the functions of director, may apply (subject to certain requirements relating to notice and the *audi alteram partem* rule) to the Companies Tribunal for a determination on such directors' neglect and dereliction. Subsection (6) provides a right of any party to request a court of law to review such a determination.

The court therefore held that it was correct that the first respondent, being a director and shareholder of the first applicant who was of the view that the fourth applicant had neglected, or had been derelict in the performance of, his functions of director, could apply to the Companies Tribunal, for the removal of the fourth applicant as the director. |

6.13.3 Removal and breach of contract

Removal as a director in terms of the Companies Act, 2008 could constitute breach of contract and a person who is removed in this way could have a claim against the company arising from breach of contract. The particular director will retain the right to institute any claim that he or she has in terms of the common law for damages or other compensation for loss of office as a director or loss of any other office as a consequence of being removed as a director.

6.14 Board committees and the audit committee

Section 72 of the Companies Act, 2008 provides that, except to the extent that the MOI provides otherwise, the board of directors may appoint any number of **board committees**, and it may delegate any of the authority of the board to a committee. King 3, however, makes it clear that the board is the focal point of the corporate governance system, and although the board may delegate authority, there is an important distinction between a *delegation* and an *abdication* of powers. In other words, the board is responsible for carrying out its duties properly and a director cannot, for example, use the appointment of a committee as

---

88 Section 71(8) of the Companies Act, 2008.
89 2012 JDR 1310 (GNP); [2012] ZAGPPHC 151.

a shield against his or her own responsibility. Section 72(3) thus provides that the board of directors or the particular director will remain liable for the proper performance of a director's duty despite the delegation of the duty to a committee.

A committee may include persons who are not directors of the company, but s 72(2)(a) provides that such person cannot be a person who is ineligible or disqualified to be a director. Furthermore, a non-director appointed to a board committee will not have any voting rights on any matter to be decided upon by that committee. Any board committee may consult with or receive advice from any person, and a committee will have the full authority of the board in respect of a matter referred to it. Section 72(4) also entitles the Minister of Trade and Industry to prescribe that a company or a category of company must have a social and ethics committee, if it is desirable in the public interest, having regard to:

- its annual turnover;
- the size of its workforce; or
- the nature and extent of its activities.

Regulations 43(1) and 92 provide that every state-owned and every listed company must appoint a social and ethics committee. In addition, any other company that, in any two of the previous five years, has a 'public interest score' (as defined in regulation 26(2) and discussed further in chapter 7 of this book) of over 500 points, must also appoint such a committee.

There are some exceptions to the requirement for a social and ethics committee:

1. if a company (X) is a subsidiary of another company (Y), and Y has such a committee that will also perform the functions of that committee on behalf of X, then X does not need to appoint such a committee; or
2. if a company has been exempted by the Tribunal from appointing such a committee, (in terms of s 72(5) and (6)), then such company does not need to appoint a social and ethics committee.

A public company, state-owned company, and any other company that is required by its MOI to do so, must have an audit committee.

It is important to note that an audit committee is not a committee of the board of directors. Members of an **audit committee** are appointed by shareholders, not by the directors. The Companies Act itself regulates the composition and functions of the audit committee, and the members of this committee have to be directors of the company. The duties of an audit committee are extensive, and the committee has the power to report in the annual financial statements how the committee carried out its functions and comment on the annual financial statements in any way the committee considers appropriate.

Board committees could include a nomination committee, a remuneration committee and a risk committee, as more fully described in the paragraph below.

6.15   King 3 proposals on board committees

King 3 proposes that board committees should be established to assist the directors by giving detailed attention to important areas. It is likely that industry and company-specific issues will dictate what types of committee would be seen as relevant for a company.

The more important responsibilities of committees are summarised in Table 6.7 below.

Table 6.7 Responsibilities of board committees

Committee	Responsibilities
Remuneration committee	• To make recommendations to the board on specific remuneration packages for each of the executive directors • To make recommendations as to the fees to be paid to each non-executive director • To evaluate the performance of individuals in key areas contributing to the success of the company and the achievement of results
Nomination committee	• To assist the board in the formal and transparent procedures leading to board appointments • To assist the board in the formal and transparent procedures leading to the appointment of the company secretary • To review and evaluate the board's mix of skills and experience • To review and evaluate other qualities of the board such as its demographics and diversity • To review and evaluate all committees and the contribution of each director
Risk management committee	To assist the board in reviewing the risk management process and the significant risks facing the company

6.16 Board meetings

A director authorised by the board of a company may call a meeting of the board at any time. A directors' meeting must be called in certain circumstances:

- if required to do so by the number or percentage of directors specified in a company's MOI;
- if required to do so by at least 25 per cent of the directors, where the board has at least 12 members;[90] and
- where the board has fewer than 12 members, if a meeting is requested by at least two directors.[91]

6.16.1 Electronic communications

The 2008 Act makes it possible to conduct board meetings by electronic communication, such as by video conferencing. It is also possible for one or more directors to participate in the meeting by electronic communication, provided that the electronic communication facility used allows all persons participating in that meeting to communicate concurrently with each other without an intermediary and to participate effectively in the meeting.

6.16.2 Notice of board meetings

The form of the notice in which a meeting is called, and the notice periods, are determined by the board of directors. The only requirement is that what is determined should comply with the requirements set out in the MOI or rules of the company. No board meeting may be convened without notice to all of the directors. If all of the directors are present at a meeting and acknowledge actual receipt of the notice or waive notice of the meeting, the meeting may proceed, even if the company failed to give notice or where the notice given was defective.

---

90 The MOI may specify a higher or lower percentage or number.
91 See dti *South African Company Law for the 21st Century: Guidelines for Corporate Law Reform* (2004) 8.

6.16.3   Quorum at board meetings

A majority of the directors of the board must be present at a meeting before a vote may be called.

6.16.4   Voting at board meetings

Every director has one vote. The majority of the votes cast on a resolution is sufficient to approve that resolution. In the event of a tied vote, the chair may cast a deciding vote if the chair did not initially cast a vote; or if the chair does not cast such a vote, then the matter being voted on fails.[92]

6.16.5   Minutes and resolutions of board meetings

Minutes of all the board and committee meetings must be kept by the company. The minutes must include any declarations given by directors and resolutions adopted by the board. Resolutions must be dated and sequentially numbered and are effective as of the date of the resolution, unless the resolution states otherwise. Minutes of board and committee meetings and resolutions signed by the chair are evidence of the proceedings of that meeting or adoption of that resolution.

6.16.6   Directors acting other than at a meeting

A decision that could be voted on at a meeting of the board may instead be adopted by the written consent of a majority of the directors given in person or by electronic communication, provided that each director received notice of the matter to be decided. A decision taken in such a way has the same effect as if it had been approved by voting at a meeting.

THIS CHAPTER IN ESSENCE

1. A **director** is a member of the **board** of a company or is an alternate director or anyone who acts as a director, whether or not officially appointed. For certain purposes, a prescribed officer and members of a board committee or the audit committee will also be regarded as directors.
2. The business of a company must be managed by or under the direction of its board, which has the authority to exercise all of the powers and perform any of the functions of the company, except to the extent that the 2008 Act or the company's MOI provides otherwise.
3. A company may have a number of different types of director, including:
    3.1 **ex officio directors**, who hold office as a result of holding another office, title or status;
    3.2 **MOI-appointed directors**, who do not have to be appointed by the shareholders, but may, in terms of the MOI, be appointed by other stakeholders;
    3.3 **alternate directors**, who may be appointed or elected to serve in substitution for other elected or appointed directors of that company – at least 50% of alternate directors must be elected by shareholders;
    3.4 **elected directors** – in the case of a profit company, at least 50% of directors must be elected by shareholders;
    3.5 **temporary directors**, who are appointed in order to fill vacancies;
    3.6 **executive directors**, who are employees of the company; and
    3.7 **non-executive directors**, who are not employees of the company.

92   Section 73 of the Companies Act, 2008.

4. A **manager** is an employee of a company, whereas a director does not have to be. Directors are responsible for the strategic vision and decision-making of the company, whereas managers are responsible for the implementation of that strategy and those decisions. Directors are accountable to shareholders, whereas managers are accountable to the board of directors.

5. The common-law **duties of directors** have been **partially codified** in the 2008 Act. However, a statutory defence is now open to directors in the form of the business judgement test, which directors may use to prove that they have not acted in breach of their duties.

6. The **business judgement test** provides that a director satisfies his or her obligations if he or she has taken reasonably diligent steps to become informed about a particular matter, has no material personal financial interest in the subject matter and had a rational basis for believing that the decision was in the best interests of the company.

7. Directors' duties include a **fiduciary duty**, and a **duty of reasonable care**.

8. If a director's personal interests (or those of a **related person**) conflict with those of the company, the director should disclose the **conflict of interest** and may not participate in any decision affecting that interest.

9. If a company has only one director, but he or she does not hold all the issued securities of the company, the director may not approve or enter into any agreement in which he or she or a related person has a personal financial interest, unless the agreement is approved by an ordinary resolution of the shareholders after the director has disclosed the nature and extent of that interest to the shareholders.

10. A director must act in the best interests of the company and may not use information obtained as a director for personal benefit. A director must communicate to the board any relevant information that comes to his or her attention.

11. To determine whether a director has acted with the required degree of care, skill and diligence, he or she must pass both an objective and a subjective test – objective to test what a reasonable director would have done in the same situation, and subjective, taking into account the general knowledge, skill and experience of the particular director.

12. The Companies Act, 2008 provides that a company may recover damages from a director in various circumstances where the director has acted in breach of the Act, the MOI or his or her common-law duties.

13. A company is entitled to take out **indemnity insurance** to protect a director against certain liabilities or expenses, but this does not include a breach of a fiduciary duty or certain other breaches.

14. A private or personal liability company must have at least one director, while public and non-profit companies must have at least three directors. A person will only become a director if he or she delivers to the company a written consent accepting the position of director.

15. Certain provisions concerning directors in the 2008 Act may be varied by the provisions of a company's MOI, whereas others may not be varied.

16. Certain people are ineligible to be appointed as a director, while others may be disqualified.

17. If a person is **ineligible**, he or she is absolutely prohibited from becoming a director of a company. Ineligible persons include juristic persons, unemancipated minors or persons under a similar legal disability, and any person ineligible in terms of the company's MOI.

18. In contrast, a court has a discretion to allow a **disqualified person** to become a director. Disqualified persons include: a person prohibited by a court of law or by public regulation from being a director; a person declared to be delinquent; an unrehabilitated insolvent; a person removed from an office of trust because of dishonesty; a person who has been convicted and imprisoned without the option of a fine for theft, fraud, forgery, perjury or certain other offences; and a person disqualified in terms of the company's MOI.

19. A disqualified person may nevertheless act as a director of a private company if all the shares are held by that disqualified person alone, or if all the shares are held by the disqualified person and

persons related to such person and each such person has consented in writing to that person being a director of the company.

20. Upon application by various affected parties (and in some cases the Commission or the Takeover Regulation Panel), a court can declare a person to be a delinquent or to be under probation on grounds of various conduct specified in the Companies Act as being incompatible with being a director.

21. A person who has been declared to be a **delinquent** is disqualified from being a director. An order of delinquency may be unconditional and for life, or it may be made subject to conditions the court considers appropriate. A conditional order applies for a period of seven years or longer. Conditions may include participating in remedial education or community service, or the payment of compensation.

22. A declaration placing a person **under probation** may be made subject to any conditions the court considers appropriate and applies for not more than five years. Conditions may include remedial education, community service, payment of compensation or supervision by a mentor in any future participation as a director while the order remains in force, or being limited to serving as a director of a private company, or of a company of which that person is the sole shareholder.

23. Upon satisfactory proof of rehabilitation, a court may grant an order to suspend or set aside a conditional order of delinquency or to replace it with an order of probation.

24. Every incorporator is deemed to be a director until sufficient directors have been appointed to meet the required minimum number of directors.

25. If a **vacancy** arises on the board, other than as a result of an *ex officio* director ceasing to hold that office, it must be filled by a new appointment or by a new election conducted at the next annual general meeting of the company.

26. A director may be removed by shareholders, and, in some circumstances, by the board of directors. A director may be removed by an ordinary resolution adopted at a shareholders' meeting, or he or she may be removed by a resolution of the board of directors:
    - if a company has more than two directors and it is alleged by a shareholder or by a director that the director of the company has become ineligible or disqualified;
    - where a director has become incapacitated to the extent that the director is unable to perform the functions of a director and is unlikely to regain that capacity within a reasonable time; or
    - if the director has neglected or been derelict in the performance of the functions of a director.

27. Removal as a director in terms of the 2008 Act could constitute breach of contract and could found a claim against the company arising from breach of contract.

28. Except to the extent that the MOI provides otherwise, the board of directors may appoint any number of **board committees**, and it may delegate any of the authority of the board to a committee. A non-director appointed to a board committee will not have any voting rights on any matter to be decided upon by that committee. Examples of board committees include a remuneration committee, a nomination committee and a risk management committee.

29. Members of an **audit committee** are appointed by shareholders, and not by the directors. The Companies Act regulates the composition and functions of the audit committee, and the members of this committee have to be directors of the company. The duties of an audit committee are extensive. Some companies are obliged to appoint a social and ethics committee.

30. A director authorised by the board of a company may call a meeting of the board at any time. A directors' meeting must be called in certain circumstances specified in the Companies Act. A majority of the directors of the board must be present at a meeting before a vote may be called. Every director has one vote. The majority of votes cast on a resolution is sufficient to approve that resolution.

31. Minutes of all the board and committee meetings must be kept by the company.

Chapter 7

Company records and financial statements

7.1   The need for adequate financial regulation of companies

Companies fail for a number of different reasons. Causes of failure include adverse circumstances brought about by normal business risks, such as a decrease in the demand for goods and services in times of recession. Company collapses can also be due to a failure to keep pace with changing markets and technological innovations. An example of the latter is the failure of Eastman Kodak Company (Kodak) in the United States of America. During most of the twentieth century, Kodak held a dominant position in the photographic film market. In 1976, it had a 90 per cent market share of photographic film sales in the United States. Kodak began to struggle financially in the late 1990s as a result of the decline in sales of photographic film due to changes in technology. In January 2012, Kodak filed for Chapter 11 bankruptcy protection.

However, some companies fail because they pursue dubious business practices and fail to keep proper accounting records, and to adopt sound financial reporting practices.

The Companies Act, 2008 can do little to mitigate the adverse impact of normal business risks on companies and is unable to ensure that companies adapt appropriately to change, but the Act does attempt to ensure that companies do not engage in dubious business practices (such as reckless or fraudulent trading),[1] and it also provides that a company must keep proper records[2] and prepare financial statements that give a fair presentation of its activities.[3]

PRACTICAL ISSUE	Examples of corporate collapse due to dubious business practices and bad financial disclosures

There are a number of instances in South Africa of financial collapse arising from shortcomings in financial reporting:

- In February 2007, the Congress of South African Trade Unions issued a statement in which it expressed its anger over the reported disappearance of R689 million owed to 47 000 widows and orphans of mineworkers. The money had been invested in a trust owned and managed by Fidentia Asset Management. The Financial Services Board placed Fidentia under curatorship after its inspectors claimed that it had 'misappropriated client funds' and 'made numerous misrepresentations to clients'. The substantive part of the criminal trial of the former CEO of Fidentia started in January 2013, where the prosecutor accused him of using smoke-and-mirror tactics. The prosecutor alleged that the accused had orchestrated a huge exercise of inflated assets, back-dating of documents and asset-swap agreements, in an effort to defeat the attempts of the Financial Services Board to investigate and uncover the true picture.
- Another financial collapse occurred in September 1991 when the Masterbond Group of companies crashed and it emerged that R300 million had been raised from new investors, even though insiders had known that the business was in dire straits at the time the investments were made. When Masterbond collapsed, some

---

1   Section 22 provides that a company must not carry on its business recklessly, with gross negligence, with intent to defraud any person or for any fraudulent purpose.
2   Section 24 of the Companies Act, 2008.
3   Section 29 of the Companies Act, 2008. For a discussion of the audit and independent review of financial statements, see chapter 13 of this book.

22 000 investors had invested about R600 million. The auditors of Masterbond eventually agreed to pay R33 million to investors for negligence, accepting that they were party to the issuing of false information and misleading reports, and that they were party to the issuing of financial statements that departed so fundamentally from Generally Accepted Accounting Practice that no reliance could be placed on them.

Besides the issue of corporate failure, there are other good reasons for a company to disclose reliable information about itself and its activities. As this chapter will show, there are a number of stakeholders in a company – including actual or potential shareholders, analysts and stockbrokers, employees, trade unions, customers and suppliers. To some extent or another, all of these stakeholders require information about a company. Measures should therefore be in place to ensure that reliable and relevant information is available in respect of a company and its activities.[4]

To what extent is a company required to provide information and to whom must it be provided? Although some companies go well beyond statutory requirements as to the type of information they disclose in their annual financial statements, others fall well short of stakeholders' legitimate expectations.

The Companies Act, 2008 obliges a company to keep certain records and to provide certain financial information. This chapter will examine those sections of the Companies Act, 2008 that dictate what records and financial information must be maintained and provided by a company. The chapter will also identify other relevant Acts, Codes and business practices that encourage a company to adopt desirable financial reporting practices.

7.2   Factors affecting the documenting of a company's financial information

The nature, content and timing of the release of information in respect of a company's financial position, performance and activities, and the type of company and accounting records maintained by a company, are determined in practice by a number of factors, including:

- the provisions of the Companies Act, 2008;
- the JSE listing requirements in respect of companies whose shares are listed on the JSE;
- prescribed financial reporting standards;
- the extent to which a company embraces good business practice (as evidenced, for example, in the King 3 Code); and
- by the extent to which a company takes cognisance of the information needs of its various stakeholders.

Each of these factors will be discussed in this chapter.

---

4   For a discussion of the audit and independent review of financial statements, see chapter 13 of this book.

PRACTICAL ISSUE	**Good business practice**
	The 2012 annual report of Grindrod Limited provides an excellent example of good reporting practices that go beyond the bare minimum of what the law requires. Grindrod is a group that operates in a number of business divisions.
	In addition to a directors' report, balance sheet, income statement, statement of changes in equity and cash flow statement, Grindrod Limited also publishes a value-added statement, a share performance statement, a corporate governance report, a social performance report, a statement on corporate social investment, and an environmental performance report. These other reports and statements will be discussed in more detail later in this chapter, but they are indicative of the company's good communication policy and commitment to transparency. The Grindrod annual report provides comprehensive information about the company, its activities and its commitment to social and environmental issues, and embraces the information needs of a variety of stakeholders. Clearly, the company's annual report goes well beyond what is required in terms of the Companies Act.

7.3 The Companies Act, 2008 and financial information

Broadly speaking, the Companies Act, 2008 requires a company to do two main things with regard to its financial information:

1. keep certain **company records** (including accounting records); and
2. prepare annual **financial statements**.

7.3.1 Company records (including accounting records)

There is a difference between *company* records and *accounting* records. Section 24, which sets out what company records must be kept, makes it clear that accounting records are just one of the many company records that are required to be kept by a company.

The Companies Act, 2008 deals with the matter of company records as follows:

1. Section 1 defines 'records' as any information contemplated in s 24.
2. Section 24 deals with the *form and standards* of company records. In other words, s 24[5] sets out what company records must be kept. These include a copy of a company's MOI, a securities register and its accounting records.
3. Section 28 deals specifically with accounting records (as defined in s 1) and provides that a company must keep accounting records so as to comply with its financial reporting obligations, as well as with the requirements of the regulations. The expression 'accounting records' is defined in s 1 as the information in written or electronic form concerning the financial affairs of a company as required in terms of the Act, including but not limited to, purchase and sales records, general and subsidiary ledgers and other documents and books used in the preparation of financial statements. The Act also empowers the Minister of Trade and Industry to publish regulations concerning a number of matters, including regulations prescribing what accounting records must be kept by a company. The published regulations list a number of accounting records that must be kept by a company. These requirements are dealt with later in this chapter.

---

5 Discussed in para. 7.4 below.

4. Section 25 deals with the *location* of company records, in other words, the place where the company records have to be kept. All company records must be accessible at or from the registered office of the company.[6] A company must notify the Companies and Intellectual Property Commission (the Commission) of the location, or of any change in the location of, any company records that are not located at its registered office.[7]

5. Section 26 deals with the rights of *access* to the company records that are required to be kept in terms of s 24.

7.3.2   Financial statements (including annual financial statements)

The Companies Act, 2008 has various sections dealing with a company's financial statements. The Act deals with financial statements as follows:

1. Section 1 defines 'financial statement'. It is clear that this is a very broad definition and is not simply limited to annual financial statements. The definition is important because when a company issues a financial statement as defined, it has to comply with the requirements of the Companies Act, 2008.

2. Section 29 deals with the requirements relating to all the financial statements of a company, and its provisions ensure that every financial statement (as defined in s 1) measures up to certain standards, such as fair presentation and minimum content.[8]

3. Section 30 deals with the annual financial statements of a company.

4. Section 31 deals with the rights of access to a company's financial statements.

In terms of the 2008 Act, the nature of the financial statements that must be prepared by a company, depend on a number of factors, such as the type of company (for example, public or private), its purpose (for example, whether for profit or not for profit) and the nature and extent of its activities (for example, whether or not the company holds assets in a fiduciary capacity). Public companies have to comply fully with International Financial Reporting Standards (IFRS) whereas most private companies do not. Paragraph 7.11 below discusses the reporting requirements of different types of company.

Section 29 provides that financial statements must present the state of affairs and business of the company fairly and must explain the transactions and financial position of the business of the company. The financial statements must also show the company's assets, liabilities and equity, as well as its income and expenses and other prescribed information.[9] It is clear that the accounting records must be adequate in order to ensure fair presentation of the affairs and financial position of the company in a company's financial statements.

7.4   Company records required in terms of s 24

All companies are required to keep the following company records in terms of s 24:
- a copy of the Memorandum of Incorporation (MOI);
- any amendments or alterations to the MOI;
- a copy of any Rules made by the directors;
- a record of a company's directors;
- copies of all reports presented at an annual general meeting;

---

6   See discussion under para. 7.6 below as to what is meant by 'registered office'.

7   This is done by filing Form CoR 22, indicating the date as of which the records will be kept at the relevant location, which must be the date on which the notice is filed, or a later date.

8   For a discussion of the audit and independent review of financial statements, see chapter 13 of this book.

9   Section 29(1) of the Companies Act, 2008.

- copies of all annual financial statements;
- accounting records required by the 2008 Act;
- notice and minutes of all shareholders' meetings;
- all resolutions adopted by shareholders;
- any document made available to shareholders in relation to shareholders' resolutions;
- copies of any written communications sent to any class of shareholders;
- minutes of all meetings and resolutions of directors;
- minutes of directors' committee meetings including those of the audit committee; and
- for every profit company, a securities register.[10]

Table 7.1 below gives more detail about the company records that, in terms of s 24, must be maintained by a company.

PRACTICAL ISSUE	Company records and accounting records
	Company records (as required by s 24) set out important information about a company. For example, they provide answers to some significant questions about a company's key characteristics. Is the company a profit or non-profit company? If it is a profit company, is it a private, public or some other type of for-profit company? The type of company is determined by reference to the provisions of a company's MOI, which is one of the company records that is required in terms of s 24.
	Company records also indicate who is in control of a company (a record of directors must be kept), and who the holders of the company's securities are (a securities register must also be kept). Moreover, company records show if and how the directors have communicated with shareholders, whether there have been proper meetings of shareholders[11] and what was resolved at any meetings that have been held (minutes of both directors' and shareholders' meetings form part of the company records).
	The keeping of accounting records is also an important part of what constitutes company records in terms of s 24. Keeping accurate and up-to-date accounting records is vital to the success of any business. Many business owners invest a lot of time and effort in the running of their businesses and fail to realise the importance of maintaining good documentation. By analogy, it is important in a football match to keep the score so that a person can work out who is winning or whether no one is winning at all.[12] Keeping accounting records is like score-keeping. Many people do not know the 'current score' of their own business because they have failed to realise the importance of keeping good and adequate accounting records.
	Keeping clear and accurate records will contribute to the success of a business in many ways, including: (a) assisting in the preparation of financial statements timeously and accurately; (b) providing information on which to base business decisions; (c) assessing the financial situation of the business at any time; and (d) measuring the business performance against the projections that were originally set down in the business plan.[13]

---

10 Securities refer not only to shares, but include debt instruments as well: see chapter 4 of this book for a more detailed discussion of shares and debt instruments.
11 Shareholders and other securities holders.
12 This was well expressed in an article sourced at *http://www.ajml.com.au/downloads/resource-centre/references/ operational-management/The%20importance%20of%20record%20keeping.pdf.*
13 *Ibid.*

Table 7.1 Company records to be maintained in terms of s 24

Type of company record that must be maintained	Company Act reference and the length of time the records must be kept
• A copy of the company's **Memorandum of Incorporation (MOI)** • Any amendments or alterations to the MOI • Any **Rules** of the company made by the directors in terms of s 15(3) to (5) (Section 15(3) provides that the board of directors can make rules, and repeal or amend rules, relating to the governance of a company, provided such rules are consistent with the MOI)	Section 24(3)*(a)* The records must be kept indefinitely
A **record of directors** and details relating to every current director as well as details of any person who has served as a director of the company (and see the requirements of s 24(5) discussed below)	Section 24(3)*(b)* The records must be kept for a period of seven years after the person ceases to serve as a director
Copies of all **reports presented at an annual general meeting** of the company	Section 24(3)*(c)*(i) These records must be kept, for a period of seven years after the date of any such meeting
Copies of all **annual financial statements** required by this Act	Section 24(3)*(c)*(ii) These records must be kept for a period of seven years after the date on which each such statement was issued
Accounting records that are required to be kept in terms of the Act	Section 24(3)*(c)*(iii) These records must be kept for the current financial year and for the company's seven previous completed financial years
Notices and **minutes of all shareholders' meetings** and all resolutions adopted by shareholders	Section 24(3)*(d)*(i) These records must be kept for a period of seven years after the date on which each such resolution was adopted
Any document that was made available by the company to the holders of securities in relation to each shareholders' resolution	Section 24(3)*(d)*(ii) These records must be kept for a period of seven years after the date on which each such resolution was adopted

Type of company record that must be maintained	Company Act reference and the length of time the records must be kept
Copies of any **written communications** sent generally by the company to all holders of any class of the company's securities	Section 24(3)*(e)* These records must be kept for a period of seven years after the date on which each such communication was issued
Minutes of all meetings and resolutions of directors, or directors' **committees**, or the audit committee, if any	Section 24(3)*(f)* These records must be kept for a period of seven years
Every for-profit company must maintain a **securities register** or its equivalent, as required by s 50; and the records required by or in terms of s 85, if that section applies to the company (Section 85 provides for enhanced accountability and transparency requirements for certain companies such as for public companies. Section 85 provides for the maintenance of records giving details of the company secretary and auditor)	Section 24(4) refers to the securities register[14] A share is part of the securities of a company. The Act defines 'securities' as any shares, debentures or other instruments, irrespective of their form or title, issued or authorised to be issued by a profit company. This definition is important because when the Act refers to securities, it refers to both shares and debt instruments such as debentures

The Companies Act, 2008 prescribes further requirements regarding the records to be kept regarding directors. Section 24(5) provides that a company's record of directors must include, in respect of each director, that person's:

- full name, and any former names;
- identity number or, if the person does not have an identity number, the person's date of birth;
- nationality and passport number if the person is not a South African;
- occupation;
- date of their most recent election or appointment as director of the company;
- name and registration number of every other company or foreign company of which the person is a director, and
- in the case of a foreign company, the nationality of that company; and
- any other prescribed information.[15]

In addition to the information required by s 24(5), the regulations provide that a company's record of directors must include, with respect to each director of the company:

- the address for service on that director; and
- in the case of a company that is required to have an audit committee, any professional qualifications and experience of the director, to the extent necessary to enable the company to comply with s 94(5) and regulation 42.

---

14   See para. 4.7.8 above for further discussion of the securities register.
15   See below.

7.5   Accounting records required in terms of regulations

A company is required to keep such **accounting records** as are necessary to fulfil its reporting requirements in terms of the Act.[16]

The regulations also specifically provide that the requirements of the regulations in relation to the keeping of accounting records are in addition to any applicable requirements to keep accounting records set out in terms of any other law, or any agreement, to which the company is a party. This means, for example, that the requirements of statutes such as those of the Income Tax Act,[17] must also be taken into account by a company. In terms of the Income Tax Act, all books of prime entry (such as cash books, journals and ledgers) must be kept for a minimum of five years.[18]

The following types of accounting record are required to be kept by all companies in terms of the regulations:

- asset register;
- liabilities and obligations register;
- record of loans to directors, prescribed officers, shareholders, employees, and to any person related to any of them (including details of interest and repayment terms);
- a record of any property held by the company in a fiduciary capacity or in any manner contemplated by s 65(2) of the Consumer Protection Act;[19]
- register of revenues and expenditures;
- daily records of cash in and out;
- daily records of goods purchased and sold on credit;
- statements of every account maintained in a financial institution in the name of the company with vouchers;
- register of loans to the company from shareholders, directors, prescribed officers, employees, and any persons related to any of them;
- register of guarantees granted in respect of an obligation to a third party incurred by any of the above; and
- a register of contractual obligations due to be performed in the future.

All of a company's accounting records must be kept at, or be accessible from, the registered office of the company.

The regulations also provide that the accounting records must be kept so as to provide adequate precautions against theft, loss and falsification, as well as intentional and accidental damage or destruction, and must be kept to facilitate the discovery of any falsification. Furthermore, a company must provide adequate precautions against loss of the records as a result of damage to, or failure of, the media on which the records are kept. A company must also ensure that records are at all times capable of being retrieved in a readable and printable form.

---

16   Section 28 provides that a company must keep accurate and complete accounting records in one of the official languages of the Republic (a) as necessary to enable the company to satisfy its obligations in terms of the Act or any other law with respect to the preparation of financial statements; and (b) including any prescribed accounting records, which must be kept in the prescribed manner and form.

17   58 of 1962.

18   Section 73A of the Income Tax Act provides that records must be kept for the period of time prescribed by the Minister. It is currently five years in terms of the prescribed regulations.

19   68 of 2008.

The Commission may issue a compliance notice[20] in respect of any failure to comply with accounting record requirements. Such compliance notice can be issued to any person whom the Commission on reasonable grounds believes has contravened the Act.

7.6 Registered office

All companies are required to have a **registered office** in South Africa, and the records that they are obliged to maintain in terms of s 24 of the 2008 Act must be maintained at that office, or at another location, notice of which has to be given to the Commission. Section 28(2) of the Companies Act, 2008 provides that a company's other records (that is to say, the accounting records other than those required in terms of s 24) must also be kept at, or be accessible from, the registered office of the company. A company must initially give details of the location of its registered office on its Notice of Incorporation and any changes must thereafter be filed by way of a notice with the Commission. All of a company's records must be kept in a written form or in an electronic form or other form that allows that information to be converted into written form within a reasonable time.[21]

CASE STUDY	**What is meant by registered office?** In *Sibakhulu Construction (Pty) Ltd v Wedgewood Village Golf and Country Estate (Pty) Ltd*,[22] the court had to determine what was meant by 'registered office' (as used in s 23 of the Companies Act, 2008). Section 23(3) provides that every company must maintain at least one office in South Africa and it must register the address of its office with the Commission. The court acknowledged that, in practice, a company's registered office under the 1973 Act was often an address chosen for convenience rather than an office of the company itself in the ordinary sense; frequently the registered office of a company was, for example, that of the company's auditors. The court held that it would give effect to the purposes of the Act as set out in s 7(k) and (l) to interpret s 23 of the Act to the effect that a company can reside only at the place of its registered office (which must also be the place of its only or principal office). The court therefore found that a company can only reside in one place and a: material distinction between a 'registered office' under the 2008 Act and its predecessors … is that under the current Act the registered office must be the company's only office, alternatively, if it has more than one office, its '*principal office*'. The court therefore concluded that whilst the 1973 Act expressly acknowledged the possibility of a distinction between a company's registered office and its '*main place of business*', the 2008 Act requires the registered office and the principal place of business for jurisdictional purposes to be at one and the same address.

---

20 See s 171 of the Companies Act, 2008.
21 Section 24(1)(*a*) of the Companies Act, 2008.
22 2013 (1) SA 191 (WCC).

Since a company is obliged to keep its records at its registered office or at another location that has been disclosed to the Commission, it is also necessary to understand what is meant by the word 'records'. Section 1 of the 2008 Act defines records as any information contemplated in s 24(1) as summarised in Table 7.1 above.

7.7   Access to company records

The Companies Act, 2008 provides that persons have certain rights of access to a company's records but differentiates between holders of a company's securities and those who do not hold securities when determining which records may be accessed.

7.7.1   Access to company records by holders of securities

In terms of s 26, a person who holds or has a beneficial interest in any securities issued by a profit company,[23] or who is a member of a non-profit company, has a right to inspect and copy the information contained in the following company records:
- the company's MOI and any Rules;
- the records in respect of the company's directors;
- the reports to annual meetings, and annual financial statements;
- the notices and minutes of annual meetings, and communications; and
- the securities register of a profit company.

7.7.2   Access to company records by those who are not holders of securities

Any person is entitled to inspect a document that has been filed with the Commission. Therefore, a member of the public, for example, has access to a company's MOI. In addition, s 26(2) gives any person who does not hold securities in a company the following rights:
- a right to inspect the securities register of a profit company, or the members register of a non-profit company that has members; and
- a right to inspect the register of directors of a company.

CASE	**No reasons need be provided to inspect securities register**
STUDY	In *Basson v On-point Engineers (Pty) Ltd*,[24] the applicants were members of the media who had sought access to the respondents' registers to establish the shareholding of each of the respondents so that they could establish who benefitted from the state tenders that were awarded to the respondents.
	The court held that the applicants did indeed have the right of access to the securities register. The court held that a person who seeks to inspect the register need not give reasons for doing so. The court held that s 26(9) makes it an offence not to accommodate any reasonable request for access to any record in terms of s 26 or s 31. The court therefore concluded that all three respondents had to provide copies of the securities register or allow the inspection thereof.

---

23   Recall that securities refer to both shares and debt instruments: see chapter 4 of this book for more detail.
24   2012 JDR 2126 (GNP); [2012] ZAGPPHC 251.

7.8 Financial statements

The Companies Act, 2008 defines '**financial statement**' as including the following:
1. annual financial statements and provisional annual financial statements;
2. interim or preliminary reports;
3. group and consolidated financial statements in the case of a group of companies; and
4. financial information in a circular, prospectus or provisional announcement of results that an actual or prospective creditor or holder of the company's securities, or the Commission, Panel or other regulatory authority, may reasonably be expected to rely on.

The definition is not exhaustive (that is, it includes the above), and is widely couched. This is significant because s 29(1) provides that if a company provides any financial statements, including any annual financial statements, to any person for any reason, those statements must:
1. satisfy the financial reporting standards as to form and content, if any such standards are prescribed;
2. present fairly the state of affairs and business of the company, and explain the transactions and financial position of the business of the company;
3. show the company's assets, liabilities and equity, as well as its income and expenses, and any other prescribed information; and
4. set out the date on which the statements were published, and the accounting period to which the statements apply.

In addition to the fair presentation requirement, s 29(2) also provides that any financial statements prepared by a company, including any annual financial statements of a company, must not be false or misleading in any material respect or incomplete in any material particular.

The Companies Act, 2008, therefore, clearly seeks to ensure transparency and accountability when companies give financial information to any person or entity.[25]

CONTEXTUAL ISSUE	**Financial statements**
	The term 'financial statements' must not be confused with the term 'annual financial statements'. A financial statement is a much broader concept than what is referred to as 'annual financial statements'. It includes annual financial statements, but also reports, circulars, provisional announcements and the like. The policy paper that preceded the drafting of the Companies Bill specifically stated that public announcements, information and prospectuses should be subject to similar standards for truth and accuracy. That is why there is such a broad definition of financial statement.

Financial statements must be produced in a manner and form that satisfies any **prescribed financial reporting standards**. However, the prescribed standards may vary for different categories of company.[26] The important point is that the 2008 Act makes it a statutory

---

25 For a discussion of the audit and independent review of financial statements, see chapter 13 of this book.
26 Section 29(5)(c) of the Companies Act, 2008. The reporting requirements of different types of company are discussed in para. 7.11 below.

requirement for companies to comply with prescribed standards, and this is done to try to eliminate a multitude of choices when it comes to how assets, liabilities, revenues and expenses are reported. One of the characteristics of useful information is that it can be compared to other similar information. Thus, a company should be consistent not only in adopting accounting practices from year to year, but these practices should also make it possible for the financial position and performance of different companies to be compared. If companies are obliged to apply a common accounting standard, it is likely that accounting information will be more comparable, and hence more useful.

CONTEXTUAL ISSUE

Dubious accounting practices

In the United States of America, the adoption of misleading accounting techniques was one of the contributors to the collapse and bankruptcy of the Enron Corporation. Enron's use and misuse of the 'fair values' concept was not grounded upon actual market process, and although fair values allowed Enron to record substantial profits, these were unrelated to actual cash flows, and resulted in the overstatement of revenue and net income. Enron also adopted dubious accounting practices that resulted in the company omitting the disclosure of actual liabilities, while overstating asset values. The result was that the financial statements of Enron were not trustworthy and falsified the profit and financial position of the company.

In order to avoid an Enron-type situation, the South African Companies Act, 2008 gives statutory backing to the adoption of IFRS. By doing this, it is hoped that dubious accounting practices will be eliminated, and that a company will publish reliable, relevant, comparable and understandable information about its financial position and performance.

The Enron scandal must not be underestimated. Before its bankruptcy in 2001, the company employed about 22 000 people and was one of the world's leading electricity, natural gas, pulp and paper, and communications companies. *Fortune* magazine named the company 'America's most innovative company' for six consecutive years. It later emerged that the company's financial position and performance were sustained predominantly by creatively planned accounting fraud. The company's share price fell from a high of $90 per share to being worthless, causing huge investor losses. Other stakeholders, such as employees, also suffered. Moreover, the collapse of Enron caused the dissolution of Arthur Andersen, which at the time was one of the world's top five accounting and auditing firms.

Enron's collapse contributed to the creation of the United States's Sarbanes-Oxley Act, which became law in 2002. It is considered to be one of the most significant changes to federal securities laws since Franklin D Roosevelt's New Deal in the 1930s. The new law targets fraud, provides more severe penalties, requires more information to be provided to the public, and ensures that companies have stronger internal controls. Other countries, including South Africa, have also adopted new corporate governance legislation as a result of the Enron debacle.

7.8.1 Personal liability if financial statements are wrong or misleading

Section 77(3)*(b)* provides that a director of a company is liable for any loss, damages or costs sustained by the company as a direct or indirect consequence of the director having acquiesced in the carrying on of the company's business despite knowing that it was being conducted in a manner prohibited by s 22(1). Section 22 prohibits fraudulent and reckless trading. The courts have held that providing false or misleading information amounts to reckless and fraudulent trading.

Section 77(3)*(d)* is more specific, and it also provides for such personal liability if a director signed, consented to, or authorised, the publication of any financial statements that were false or misleading in a material respect. Section 424 of the 1973 Act also provides for personal liability if there is reckless or fraudulent trading.[27]

If misleading information is provided in the financial statements of a company, the persons responsible for providing that information can be made personally liable to third parties for losses caused. There are a number of sections of the Act that provide for such personal liability.[28]

CASE **STUDY**	**Furnishing misleading information amounts to reckless and fraudulent trading** In *Firstrand Bank v Fourie*,[29] the court found that the financial statements that had been furnished to the bank (the plaintiff in this case) by the defendant had consistently misrepresented the financial position of a company in material respects. The plaintiff had lent funds on the strength of those misleading financial statements. The bank now applied to court to declare the defendant to be personally liable in terms of s 424 of the 1973 Act for the amounts owing to it. The court held that the furnishing of misleading information amounted to reckless and fraudulent trading and therefore declared the defendant to be personally responsible for the indebtedness of the company to the plaintiff.

7.8.2 Summaries of financial statements

The Companies Act, 2008 provides that a company may provide a person with a summary of particular financial statements.[30] A summary is simply a short version of the full version. It does not mean that a prescribed part of a financial statement, such as a statement of financial position, can be omitted.

A **summary of financial statements** must comply with all the prescribed requirements, and the first page of the summary must clearly state that it is a summary of particular financial statements prepared by the company. It must set out the date of those statements. Furthermore, the steps to be taken to obtain a copy of the financial statements that it summarises must be stated. The Minister (after consulting the Financial Reporting Standards Council) can make regulations prescribing the form and content requirements for financial summaries.

---

27 Section 424 of the 1973 Act is still applicable to the winding up of both solvent and insolvent companies, and will continue to apply until a new insolvency law comes into operation in South Africa.

28 Sections 22, 77 and 218 of the 2008 Act, and s 424 of the 1973 Act are examples of such.

29 [2011] ZAGPPHC 94.

30 Section 29(3) of the Companies Act, 2008.

7.9   Annual financial statements

All companies are required in terms of the Companies Act, 2008 to produce **annual financial statements** and this must be done within six months of the end of their financial year. There are no exceptions to this requirement, and the requirement therefore constitutes one of the unalterable provisions relating to a company's MOI.

All companies must have a fixed **financial year**, which may be modified only within restrictions set out in s 27. The financial year of a company is its annual accounting period.[31]

A company's annual financial statements must fully comply with all requirements relating to a company's financial statements as described above. In addition to these, s 30 of the Act requires a company to make further disclosures in its annual financial statements. In terms of s 30(3), the annual financial statements of a company must:

- include an auditor's report, if the statements are audited;
- include a report by the directors with respect to the state of affairs, the business and profit or loss of the company, or of the group of companies, if the company is part of a group, including any matter material for the shareholders to appreciate the company's state of affairs, and any prescribed information;
- be approved by the board and signed by an authorised director; and
- be presented to the first shareholders' meeting after the statements have been approved by the board.

As already discussed in this chapter, financial statements, including annual financial statements, must fairly present the state of affairs of and business of a company, and must explain the transactions and financial position of the business of a company. In particular, such financial statements must also do the following:[32]

- state the date the statements were produced;
- specify the **accounting period**;
- show the company's assets, liabilities and equity – this will appear in the company's statement of financial position (**balance sheet**) and in the statement of changes in equity;
- show the company's income and expenses – this will appear in the company's **income statement**;
- show any other prescribed information – for example, specific disclosures in respect of annual financial statements required in terms of s 30(4) of the 2008 Act;[33]
- satisfy any relevant financial reporting standards as to form and content;
- include a **directors' report** with respect to the state of affairs, the business and profit or loss of the company; and
- bear a prominent notice on the first page of the statements, indicating whether the statements have been audited, or, if not audited, independently reviewed in compliance with the requirements of the 2008 Act, or have not been audited or independently reviewed. Where an audit is required, the annual financial statements must include the auditor's report.

Table 7.2 below summarises what the annual financial statements of a company must contain if the company is required by the 2008 Act to have its annual financial statements audited.[34]

---

31   Section 27(7) of the Companies Act, 2008.
32   Section 29(1) of the Companies Act, 2008.
33   See Table 7.2 below for a summary of these disclosure requirements.
34   For a discussion of the audit and independent review of financial statements, see chapter 13 of this book.

Table 7.2 *Specific disclosures required for companies whose annual financial statements must be audited*

Disclosure requirement	Companies Act reference	Notes
The remuneration and benefits received by each director, or by any person holding any prescribed office in the company	Sections 30(4)*(a)* and 30(6)*(a)* to *(g)*	Remuneration includes the following: • fees; • salary, bonuses and performance-related payments; • expense allowances, to the extent that the director is not required to account for the allowance; • contributions paid under any pension scheme not otherwise required to be disclosed in terms of sub-s (3)*(b)*; • the value of any option or right given to a director, past director or future director, or person related to any of them; • financial assistance to a director, past director or future director, or person related to any of them, for the subscription of shares, as contemplated in s 44; and • with respect to any loan or other financial assistance by the company to a director, past director or future director, or a person related to any of them, or any loan made by a third party to any such person, as contemplated in s 45, the value of the saving in interest charges.
The amount of any pensions paid by the company to or receivable by current or past directors or individuals who hold or have held any prescribed office in the company	Section 30(4)*(b)*(i)	
Any amount paid or payable by the company to a pension scheme with respect to current or past directors or individuals who hold or have held any prescribed office in the company	Section 30(4)*(b)*(ii)	
The amount of any compensation paid in respect of loss of office to current or past directors or individuals who hold or have held any prescribed office in the company	Section 30(4)*(c)*	

Disclosure requirement	Companies Act reference	Notes
The number and class of any securities issued to a director or person holding any prescribed office in the company, or to any person related to any of them, and the consideration received by the company for those securities	Section 30(4)(d)	
Details of service contracts of current directors and individuals who hold any prescribed office in the company	Section 30(4)(e)	

7.10   Financial reporting standards and the Financial Reporting Standards Council

With respect to any particular company's financial statements, financial reporting standards are the standards applicable to that company, as prescribed in terms of s 29(4) and (5) of the 2008 Act.

A **Financial Reporting Standards Council (FRSC)** is established in terms of Chapter 8D of the Act. The FRSC must advise the Minister on matters relating to financial reporting standards and consult with the Minister on the making of regulations establishing financial reporting accounting standards.[35] The FRSC will therefore be largely responsible for establishing financial reporting standards for both public and private companies. The Act specifically provides that the prescribed financial reporting standards must be consistent with the **International Financial Reporting Standards (IFRS)** of the **International Accounting Standards Board**.[36]

However, the prescribed standards do vary for different categories of company,[37] and certain private companies are subject to less stringent standards than those that apply to other companies. The stipulation that standards should be based on international standards ensures a tight correlation between the accounting practices of South Africa and the international investment community, thus making South African capital markets easily accessible and understandable to foreign investors.

PRACTICAL ISSUE	International Financial Reporting Standards (IFRS)
	Compliance with IFRS does eliminate some choices in how items may be treated from an accounting point of view, but there is still some leeway, because certain significant choices remain. For example, a company can choose whether or not to revalue buildings, or whether to disclose them at depreciated cost.

---

35   Section 204 of the Companies Act, 2008.
36   Section 29(5)(b) of the Companies Act, 2008.
37   Section 29(5)(c) of the Companies Act, 2008.

> From 1 January 2005, all companies that were listed on the Johannesburg Stock Exchange were obliged to comply with IFRS. The 2008 Act now requires all companies to be harmonious with IFRS, but these can be broken down into two broad categories – namely, IFRS for small and medium-sized entities, and full IFRS.

The FRSC takes over the function of the Accounting Practices Board (APB) that has been setting Statements of Generally Accepted Accounting Practice (Statements of GAAP) since 1975. The FRSC must advise the Minister on matters relating to financial reporting standards, and consult with the Minister on the making of regulations establishing financial reporting standards. The purpose of ensuring compliance with certain prescribed standards is to ensure conformity in the preparation of financial statements and to ensure, as far as possible, the preparation of information that is accurate and reliable.

CONTEXTUAL ISSUE

No departure from accounting standards

Under the Companies Act, 1973, item 5 of Schedule 4 allowed directors of a company to depart from any accounting concepts stated in GAAP Standards if particulars of the departure, the effects thereof and the reasons for such departure were given.

No similar paragraph exists in the 2008 Act and therefore no deviation from the prescribed standards is permitted. If a variety of accounting methods is possible, companies are able to select the mode of accounting that presents their financial position in the most favourable light. In recent decades, investors have lost significant amounts of money due to dubious accounting methods and a rank overstatement of profitability. The 2008 Act therefore seeks to protect investors and creditors by requiring companies to produce financial statements that cannot easily be manipulated by the adoption of favourable accounting procedures and policies.

Both public and private companies must therefore ensure that financial statements present their financial position and results of operations fairly, and must comply with the prescribed standards. Financial reporting standards are, in the first place, Statements of GAAP that have been developed by the APB, and secondly, any standards that are issued by the FRSC.

PRACTICAL ISSUE

GAAP for SMEs

In 2007, prior to the formation of the FRSC, the Accounting Practices Board approved a Statement of GAAP for Small and Medium-sized Entities (SMEs). The Statement of GAAP for SMEs puts into practice the policy of allowing private companies that do not have any real public accountability (as defined in s 1 of the GAAP Standard for SMEs) to adopt less stringent financial reporting standards than those that apply to public companies and to certain other private companies. Financial statements prepared in accordance with the GAAP Standard for SMEs must indicate that the financial statements have been prepared in accordance with that statement. Any audit report should do likewise.

7.11   Reporting requirements of different types of company

Reporting requirements vary according to the type of company involved. In Table 7.3 below, the audit requirements, independent review requirements and the prescribed standards that relate to a particular type of company are summarised.

Table 7.3 *Financial reporting standards for different categories of company*

Profit companies	Financial reporting standard
State-owned companies	IFRS, but in the case of any conflict with any requirement in terms of the Public Finance Management Act, the latter prevails
Public companies listed on an exchange	IFRS, but in the case of any conflict with the applicable listing requirements of the relevant exchange, the latter prevails provided the exchange's listings requirements require compliance with IFRS as issued by the International Accounting Standards Board
Public companies not listed on an exchange	One of (a) IFRS; or (b) IFRS for SMEs, provided that the company meets the scoping requirements outlined in the IFRS for SMEs
Private companies, whose public interest score for the particular financial year is at least 350. (The Minister has the power to change this public interest score at any time by regulation.)	One of (a) IFRS; or (b) IFRS for SMEs, provided that the company meets the scoping requirements outlined in the IFRS for SMEs
Private companies (a) whose public interest score for the particular financial year is at least 100, but less than 350; *or* (b) whose public interest score for the particular financial year is less than 100, and whose statements are independently compiled	One of (a) IFRS; or (b) IFRS for SMEs, provided that the company meets the scoping requirements outlined in the IFRS for SMEs; or (c) SA GAAP
Profit companies, other than state-owned or public companies, whose public interest score for the particular financial year is less than 100, and whose statements are internally compiled	No prescribed financial reporting standard
Non-profit companies	Financial reporting standard
Non-profit companies that are required in terms of Regulation 28(1)*(b)* to have their annual financial statements audited	IFRS, but in the case of any conflict with any requirements in terms of the Public Finance Management Act, the latter prevails
Non-profit companies, other than those contemplated in the first row above, whose public interest score for the particular financial year is at least 350	One of (a) IFRS; or (b) IFRS for SMEs, provided that the company meets the scoping requirements outlined in the IFRS for SMEs

Non-profit companies	Financial reporting standard
Non-profit companies, other than those contemplated in the first row above (a) whose public interest score for the particular financial year is at least 100, but less than 350; or (b) whose public interest score for the particular financial year is at less than 100, and whose financial statements are independently compiled	One of (a) IFRS; or (b) IFRS for SMEs, provided that the company meets the scoping requirements outlined in the IFRS for SMEs; or (c) SA GAAP
Non-profit companies, other than those contemplated in the first row above, whose public interest score for the particular financial year is less than 100, and whose financial statements are internally compiled	No prescribed financial reporting standard

The meaning of the phrase 'independently compiled and reported' is that the annual financial statements are prepared as follows:
- by an independent accounting professional;
- on the basis of financial records provided by the company; and
- in accordance with any relevant financial reporting standards.

7.12 Solvency and liquidity test and its effect on financial statements and records

The Act's shift away from a capital maintenance regime based on par value, and the adoption of the solvency and liquidity test in its place, may well influence the nature of financial information that companies disclose, and the way that accounting records are kept.

Section 4 of the Companies Act, 2008 provides that a company will satisfy the **solvency and liquidity test** if, considering all reasonably foreseeable financial circumstances at that time, the assets of the company, 'as fairly valued', equal or exceed the liabilities as 'fairly valued'. Section 4(2)(b) provides that in applying the solvency and liquidity test, the board or any other person must consider a 'fair valuation' of the company's assets and liabilities including any reasonably foreseeable contingent assets and liabilities, and may consider 'any other valuation' that is reasonable in the circumstances.[38]

Section 4(2) provides that any information to be considered must be based on accounting records that satisfy the requirements of s 28 and on financial statements that satisfy the requirements of s 29.

Section 28 states that accurate and complete records must be kept to enable a company to satisfy its obligations with regard to the preparation of its financial statements. Section 29 emphasises the need for 'fair presentation' of a company's affairs and the need to comply with IFRS.

It seems unlikely that financial information based predominantly or entirely on historic-cost accounting methods will meet the requirements of the Companies Act, 2008.

The solvency and liquidity test must be applied in each of the following circumstances:
- when a company wishes to provide financial assistance for subscription of its securities in terms of s 44;

---

38 Chapter 4 of this book deals with the solvency and liquidity test in detail.

- if a company grants loans or other financial assistance to directors as contemplated in s 45;
- before a company makes any distribution as provided for in s 46;
- if a company wishes to pay cash in lieu of issuing capitalisation shares in terms of s 47; and
- if a company wishes to acquire its own shares as provided for in s 48.

PRACTICAL ISSUE	**Will accountants need to abandon historic-cost accounting methods?**
	The adoption of the solvency and liquidity test in a variety of different circumstances may result in the need to apply current accounting concepts and for accountants to abandon historic-cost accounting methods, which were often favoured by them because of the reliability of the information prepared on that basis.
	Current accounting concepts include the disclosure of assets at market values. In terms of the solvency and liquidity test,[39] a company's assets must be fairly valued and all reasonably foreseeable financial circumstances of the company at that time must be considered. It seems unlikely that financial information based predominantly or entirely on historic-cost accounting methods will meet the requirements of the Companies Act, 2008.

7.13   Annual returns and financial accountability supplements

Every company and every external company conducting activities in South Africa must file an **annual return**[40] in the prescribed form with the Commission, and must include with it a copy of the company's annual financial statements (if it is required to have such financial statements audited in terms of the 2008 Act).

In addition to the annual return, a company that is required to have its annual financial statements audited must submit a copy of its financial statements. A company that is not audited must file a **financial accountability supplement** with its annual return. Companies that are voluntarily audited can choose either to file their financial statements, or to file a financial accountability supplement with their annual return.

CASE STUDY	**Failure to file annual return can result in deregistration**
	In *Absa Bank Ltd v Voigro Investments 19 CC*,[41] the court dealt with a company that had been deregistered. The court referred to s 82(3)*(a)* of the Companies Act, 2008, which inter alia provides that the Commission may remove a company from the companies register if the company has failed to file an annual return in terms of s 33 for two or more years in succession, and on demand by the Commission it has failed to give satisfactory reasons for the failure to file the required annual returns, or to show satisfactory cause for the company to remain registered.
	The court held that it is trite that there is a difference between dissolution and deregistration and referred to the case of *Ex Parte Jacobson: in re Alec Jacobson Holdings*

---

39   See s 4 of the Companies Act, 2008.
40   In terms of s 33 of the Companies Act, 2008.
41   [2012] ZAWCHC 182.

(Pty) Ltd,[42] where it was held that neither winding-up nor dissolution should be confused with deregistration, which is an act that does not affect the existence of the company, but deprives the company of its legal personality, so that it can continue to exist as an association whose members are personally liable for its debts. Should a deregistered 'company' nevertheless continue with its business, it is no longer a company doing so but an association without legal personality, in which event the members of the 'company' will during the time of deregistration be personally liable for the debts of the company.

7.14 Chapter 3 requirements: enhanced accountability and transparency

Chapter 3 of the 2008 Act imposes additional accountability and transparency requirements on certain types of company. In particular, these additional requirements apply to:
- a public company; and
- a state-owned company that has not been exempted from these provisions.

Chapter 3 deals essentially with the appointment of company secretaries, auditors, and audit committees. A public company and state-owned enterprise must make the following appointments:
- a company secretary in the manner provided for in ss 86 to 89;
- an auditor in the manner prescribed in ss 90 to 93; and
- an audit committee in the manner contemplated in s 94.

Every company that makes an appointment of a company secretary or auditor, irrespective of whether the company does so as required or voluntarily, must maintain a record of its secretaries and auditors, including, in respect of each such person, the following details:
- the name, including any former name, of each such person;
- the date of every such appointment;
- if a firm or juristic person is appointed, the name, registration number and registered office address of that firm or juristic person;
- if a firm is appointed, the name of any individual who is responsible for performing the functions of auditor as contemplated in s 90(3) of the 2008 Act; and
- any changes in the particulars of the secretary or auditor as they occur, with the date and nature of each such change.

7.15 Corporate governance, the King Code and implications for accounting records and financial reporting

The corporate governance concept was first introduced into South Africa in 1994 with the publication of the King Report on Corporate Governance in that year (the first King Report). Headed by former High Court Judge, Mervyn King, the first King report was aimed at promoting the highest standards of corporate governance in South Africa. Since then, the King Code has been revised and improved and the latest version of the code is the report

---

42   1984 (2) SA 372 WLD.

that is termed the **King 3 Code of Governance Principles (King 3)**. Although the King 3 Code has no statutory backing and is not law, listed companies are required to apply its provisions because the JSE listing requirements require such companies to do so. Companies that are not listed can voluntarily apply the Code, or such parts as they choose, if they believe that it is beneficial, relevant and cost-effective to do so.

Corporate governance can be described as the system by which an entity is directed and controlled with a view to ensuring the achievement of its objectives in a sustainable manner within an environment of accountability to its stakeholders. In other words, the whole purpose of adopting good corporate governance principles is to ensure that a company is successful in the long term. King 3 recommends standards of conduct for directors of companies and emphasises the need for responsible corporate activities, having due regard for the society and the environment in which companies operate. King 3 therefore seeks to set out the principles that constitute good corporate governance in South Africa.

King 3 has nine chapters as follows:
1. Ethical leadership and corporate governance
2. Boards and directors
3. Audit committees
4. The governance of risk
5. The governance of information technology
6. Compliance with laws, rules, codes and standards
7. Internal audit
8. Governing stakeholder relationships
9. Integrated reporting and disclosure.

As far as financial statements are concerned, King 3 emphasises that directors must address the issue of whether or not the company is a **going concern**. If there are any circumstances that exist that cast doubt on the future sustainability of the company, these should be carefully considered by directors. The financial statements must clearly highlight the issue if directors cannot conclude that a company is a going concern.

Chapter 4 of the Code is concerned with **risk management**. It is clear that the board must treat the issue of risk as a priority. The duty to recognise, evaluate and manage risks necessarily follows from the duty imposed on the board to address the going-concern status of the company, as well as the board's duty to be responsible for the performance and affairs of the company. Actual and potential risks should be identified, and each risk should be properly managed in the sense that the risk should be terminated, transferred, accepted or mitigated. It is interesting to note that the Code does not suggest that a company should avoid risks. The Code refers to the positive aspects of risk management.

In terms of King 3, there is also a recommendation to look at non-financial information in a company's annual financial statements and to address broader **stakeholder interests**.[43] Annual financial statements should therefore contain non-financial information, and report on social and environmental issues. King 3 thus recommends that a company should not simply report on profits but also on 'people' and 'planet'. The simple single-bottom-line approach should therefore give way to a **triple bottom-line** approach and the economic, social and environmental aspects of a company's activities should be reported on. In other words, emphasis should not only be on profits (economic reporting), but also on the non-financial aspects of a company's performance. The shift to this integrated or inclusive

---

43   Paras. 8.5.1–8.5.4 and paras. 9.1–9.3 of King 3.

method of reporting is based on the premise that to be successful in the long term – that is, for the business to be truly sustainable – the impact of a company's operations on the environment needs to be considered, as well as its commitment to its employees (health, training, empowerment and equity) and to society as a whole.

King 3 therefore seeks to ensure that a company does not simply report on financial matters to the providers of capital (the share owners). The interests of all stakeholders should be considered in an annual report. Non-financial information is regarded as equally important, and the economic, social and environmental activities of a company will all have a bearing on a company's future and success. Every company should therefore report annually on the nature and extent of its social, transformation, ethical, safety, health and environmental management policies and practices.

PRACTICAL	**Example of corporate governance statement**
ISSUE	The financial report of Grindrod Limited for the 2012 financial year has a corporate governance statement, which states the following:[44]

Grindrod is committed to the highest standards of ethical conduct and compliance, which is entrenched in Grindrod's core values of Respect, Integrity, Professionalism, Fairness and Accountability.

Grindrod applies the principles of good corporate governance recommended in the King Report on Governance and King Code of Governance for SA 2009 (King III), which is considered essential for the success of any governance framework. The group is committed to complying with the JSE Listings Requirements and all legislation, regulations and best practices relevant to its business in every country it conducts business.

The group has a comprehensive set of policies, regularly updated in line with changes in legislation and business governance requirements, with which all group companies and employees are obliged to comply. All divisions are required to provide assurances to the audit committee bi-annually, confirming they have complied with all applicable laws and consideration has been given to non-binding rules, codes and standards.

The report goes on to confirm that the group has complied with King 3 except for certain items that are specifically explained.

The company also adopts a triple-bottom-line reporting approach, as it reports on social performance issues, its corporate social investments and its environmental impact.

7.16   Stakeholder engagement and communication

The contents of a company's financial statements will also depend on the extent to which a company identifies various users of financial information and the information needs of its various stakeholders, and consequently furnishes these users and stakeholders with relevant information. A company has various stakeholders who would ordinarily want to have some

---

44   See *http://grindrod.investoreports.com/grindrod_iar_2012/sustainability/corporate-governance/*.

information about the company – such as information about the company's activities, financial performance and financial position. The extent and nature of a company's stakeholders and their various informational needs will depend on a number of issues including the nature, size and diversity of shareholding in that company.

Table 7.4 below identifies various users and stakeholders in a company and lists their various needs. In its financial statements, a company can provide any information that will assist in meeting the various information needs of shareholders.

Table 7.4 Stakeholders and their needs

User/stakeholder	Needs
Investors Actual investors Potential investors	• Knowledge about the certainty and amount of future dividends • Assess risk of losing capital • Assess probability of growth in capital • Determine an appropriate time to invest or increase shareholding • Determine a time to sell
Employees and their representatives (trade unions) Directors (executive, non-executive and independent) Managers Other employees	• Assess risk of liquidation • Determine ability of company to generate cash flows • Determine ability of company to pay salaries, retirement benefits and pensions, bonuses • Assess opportunities to benefit in terms of share option schemes
Lenders Long-term lenders Short-term creditors Secured creditors Unsecured creditors	• Assess certainty of being paid capital amount • Determine certainty of receiving interest • Assess risk of lending more • Assessment of need to insist on security
Suppliers and traders Cash suppliers Suppliers on credit	• Determine ability of company to generate cash flows • Certainty of being paid capital amount • Risk of supplying more • Possibility of trade discounts based on volumes
Customers	• Risk of no future supplies • Risk of liquidation
Government SARS Specific departments (e.g. dti) Local authorities Regulators Competition Board	• Need to regulate activities • Assess any state assistance • Assess tax liabilities • Formulate trade policies and incentives for industries
Public	• Environmental issues • Assessment of contribution to the economy
Analysts, stockbrokers and other agents	Performance and possibilities

THIS CHAPTER IN ESSENCE

1. There are a number of good reasons for a company to disclose reliable and relevant information about itself and its activities to a range of different stakeholders. This includes the need to avoid and control fraudulent activities.
2. The Companies Act, 2008 obliges a company to keep certain **company records** and to prepare certain **financial statements**. Other factors regulating and influencing such disclosures include prescribed financial reporting standards, the extent to which a company must (or does) embrace good business practice (as in the King 3 Code), and the information needs of various stakeholders.
3. In regulating disclosures by companies, the Companies Act, 2008 aims to strike a balance between adequate disclosure (in the interests of transparency) and over-regulation. This is achieved through differential reporting requirements. Thus, certain requirements apply to all companies, but additional more demanding disclosure and transparency requirements apply to public companies, state-owned companies and to some private companies. Some private companies are not subject to audit or independent review at all, and nor do they need to comply with International Financial Reporting Standards.
4. The Companies Act, 2008 requires certain records to be maintained by a company, including copies of all accounting records necessary to satisfy its statutory obligations to prepare financial statements. Thus the records required to be maintained will vary from company to company depending on its type, purpose, nature and extent of activities. The Act and regulations prescribe the period for which various records need to be maintained.
5. Financial statements must present the state of affairs and business of the company fairly and must show its assets, liabilities and equity, as well as its income and expenses and other prescribed information. They must not be false or misleading, or incomplete. They must state whether they have been subject to audit or independent review.
6. The Companies Act, 2008 requires every company to maintain **records** of its:
   - **Memorandum of Incorporation** (MOI);
   - **rules** made by the board of directors;
   - **directors** and their details;
   - **reports to annual general meetings**;
   - required **annual financial statements**;
   - required **accounting records**;
   - **notice** and **minutes of shareholders' meetings**;
   - **shareholder resolutions**;
   - any document made available to shareholders in relation to shareholders' resolutions;
   - **written communications** to any class of shareholder;
   - **minutes** of all **directors' meetings and resolutions**;
   - **minutes** of **directors' committee meetings**, including audit committee meetings; and
   - for every profit company, a **securities register**.
7. In addition, regulations in terms of the Companies Act, 2008 require all companies to keep the following **accounting records**:
   - asset register;
   - liabilities and obligations register;
   - record of loans to directors, prescribed officers, shareholders, employees and related persons;
   - any property held by the company in a fiduciary capacity or as contemplated by s 65(2) of the Consumer Protection Act;
   - register of revenues and expenditures;
   - daily records of cash in and out;

- daily records of goods purchased and sold on credit;
- bank account statements;
- register of loans to the company from shareholders, directors, prescribed officers, employees, and any related persons;
- register of guarantees granted in respect of an obligation to a third party incurred by any of the above; and
- register of contractual obligations due to be performed in the future.

8. A company's records must all be accessible from the **registered office** of the company.

9. All companies must have a fixed **financial year**. The financial year of a company is its annual accounting period.

10. Any **summary of financial statements** must comply with prescribed requirements, and must clearly state that it is a summary and give the date and manner of accessing the source document.

11. The Companies Act, 2008 defines financial statement broadly to include:
- annual financial statements;
- provisional annual financial statements;
- interim or preliminary reports;
- group and consolidated financial statements in the case of a group of companies; and
- financial information in a circular, prospectus or provisional announcement of results.

12. All companies must produce annual financial statements within six months of the end of their financial year. The annual financial statements of a company must be approved by the directors of the company, and must include a **directors' report**.

13. Companies' financial statements must satisfy **prescribed financial reporting standards**, which vary for different categories of company. A **Financial Reporting Standards Council (FRSC)** is established to advise the Minister on the making of regulations establishing financial reporting accounting standards, which must generally be harmonious with the **International Financial Reporting Standards (IFRS)** of the **International Accounting Standards Board**.

14. The Companies Act, 2008 adopts the **solvency and liquidity test** in preference to the former capital maintenance regime and this is likely to influence the nature of financial information that companies disclose, and the way that accounting records are kept. A company will satisfy the new test if the assets of the company, 'as fairly valued', equal or exceed liabilities 'fairly valued'. It seems unlikely that financial information based predominantly or entirely on historic-cost accounting methods will meet the new requirements.

15. Every company must file an **annual return** in the prescribed form with the Commission, and must include copies of the annual financial statements and other financial statements (if required to have such financial statements audited in terms of the 2008 Act). A company that is not audited must file a **financial accountability supplement** with its annual return.

16. **Chapter 3** of the 2008 Act imposes additional accountability and transparency requirements on public companies and state-owned companies. Chapter 3 deals with the appointment of company secretaries, auditors and audit committees.

17. **The King 3 Code of Governance Principles (King 3)** aims to promote the highest standards of **corporate governance** in South Africa. King 3 emphasises that directors must, in financial statements, address the issue of whether the company is a **going concern**. **Risk management** is also seen as a priority, as is the need to address broader **stakeholder interests**. Per King 3 therefore, annual financial statements should also report on social and environmental issues – that is, a **triple bottom-line** approach.

Chapter 8

Securities registration and transfer

8.1 Introduction and definitions

As part of its obligation to keep proper records, a profit company is required to maintain a **securities register**.[1] The register reflects the names of the current holders of shares and other securities. (Because of the extensive use of nominees, the registered holder is often not the real holder of the rights pertaining to the shares or securities. In the case of a nominee holding shares in a public company, details of the beneficial owner must also be disclosed by the nominee and given to the company.)

The word '**securities**' is defined in s 1 of the Companies Act, 2008 to mean: any shares, debentures or other instruments, irrespective of their form or title, issued or authorised to be issued by a profit company. The word 'securities' is therefore much broader than the word 'share'.

A share can be classified as a personal right or right of action.[2] A share has also been described as a bundle or conglomerate of personal rights entitling the holder to a certain interest in the company.[3]

---

1 Section 24(4)*(a)* of the Companies Act, 2008. See also para. 7.4 above on a company's obligations to keep records.
2 See *Smuts v Booyens; Markplaas (Edms) v Booyens* 2001 (4) SA 15 (SCA) at 17H. See also para. 4.1.1 above and see too para. 4.10 above regarding securities in the form of debt instruments or debentures.
3 *Standard Bank of SA Ltd v Ocean Commodities Inc* 1983 (1) SA 276 (A) at 288H.

CONTEXTUAL ISSUE	The need for efficiency in trading listed securities
	Securities can either be listed or not listed on an exchange. A securities exchange is a marketplace for buying and selling securities. In the case of listed securities, the public, being both local and foreign investors, are able to acquire and dispose of securities, and it is necessary to have a system that allows for transactions to be concluded and settled efficiently and effectively.
	Listed shares in South Africa used to be traded on an open-outcry trading floor, but some years ago, this gave way to an electronic system. Market activity increased dramatically as a result, and back-office support services were incapable of handling the increase in daily transactions efficiently in a paper-based environment.
	A transition to an efficient electronic trading system became necessary in the case of listed securities. Such a system allows for quick, efficient and instant trading of shares and therefore ensures market efficiency. The quick recording of the ownership of any security also ensures transparency and accuracy in market dealings. The electronic trading system has improved the international perception of the South African market by reducing settlement and operational risk in the market, increasing efficiency and ultimately reducing costs. By enhancing investor appeal, an electronic system of trading securities and settlement of trades has enabled South Africa to compete effectively with other international markets, and not just those of emerging markets.[4]

This chapter highlights the difference between a paper-based and a paperless system of ownership and transfer, and highlights the need for a securities register and accessible information relating to beneficial (as opposed to nominee) ownership of securities. It deals also with the procedures for the transfer of shares. The Act has different transfer procedures for certificated and uncertificated securities.

8.2　Certificated and uncertificated securities

A **certificated security** is one that is evidenced by a certificate – that is, a paper document that can be seen and held. **Uncertificated securities**, however, are defined as securities that are not evidenced by a certificate or written instrument, or certificated securities that are held in collective custody by a central securities depository, and are transferable by entry without a written instrument.[5] Uncertificated securities are therefore securities that are held and transferred electronically.[6]

Any securities issued by a company must be either certificated or uncertificated. In other words, there must either be a physical document or an electronic proof of ownership.[7] However, securities can only be traded on the JSE if they are uncertificated.[8] Except to the extent that the Act expressly provides otherwise, the rights and obligations of security holders

---

4　See Strate: South Africa's Central Securities Depository website *www.strate.co.za*.
5　See s 1 of the Financial Markets Act 19 of 2012.
6　During the transitional phase, the shares were dematerialised in that the paper share certificates were replaced with electronic records of ownership (see *www.strate.co.za/aboutstrate/overview/dematerialisation*; M Vermaas 'Dematerialisasie van die Genoteerde Aandeel in die Suid-Afrikaanse Reg (Deel 2)' (1997) 9 *SA Merc LJ* 171 at 176–87. See further para. 8.5.2 below.
7　Section 49(2) of the Companies Act, 2008 and see para 8.5.2 below.
8　See *www.strate.co.za/aboutstrate/overview/dematerialisation*.

are not different according to whether their securities are certificated or uncertificated.[9] It is possible for certificated securities to be converted into uncertificated securities and vice versa.[10]

As appears from paragraph 8.5 below, the transfer of certificated securities involves considerable paperwork. This ultimately made the system impractical for trading in listed securities on the JSE.[11] As a result, the Companies Act, 1973 was amended in 1998 to make provision for securities to be held and transferred electronically.[12] By January 2002,[13] all listed equities on the JSE were being traded, and the transactions concluded and settled, electronically. The Companies Act, 2008 thus also makes provision for uncertificated securities.

8.2.1   Nature of a certificate

A **certificate** is not a negotiable instrument and merely serves as evidence of ownership. It therefore has no inherent value itself and merely evidences a right. Accordingly, it is not necessary to deliver the certificate itself if the rights of ownership are transferred from one person to another. A new certificate will be issued when ownership passes reflecting the details of the new owner.[14] The certificate is proof that the named security holder owns the securities referred to in the certificate, in the absence of evidence to the contrary.[15] Thus, for example, it is open to the holder of the beneficial interest[16] to establish that the registered holder is actually the nominee of the owner.[17] The role of the certificate in the context of the transfer of securities is discussed later in this chapter.

8.2.2   Certificate requirements

A certificate evidencing certificated securities must state on its face:
- the name of the issuing company;
- the name of the person to whom the securities were issued or transferred;[18]
- the number and class of share or security; and
- any restriction on the transfer of securities evidenced by that certificate – for example, there could be a restriction imposed by a contract between shareholders or in terms of a company's MOI, such as a right of pre-emption in terms of which a shareholder in a private company must first offer his or her shares to other shareholders if he or she wishes to sell those shares.[19]

The certificate must be signed by two persons authorised by the company's board.[20]

---

9   Section 49(3)(*a*) of the Companies Act, 2008.
10   See s 49(5) and (6) and s 54 of the Companies Act, 2008.
11   The JSE is the JSE Ltd, or the Johannesburg Stock Exchange (formerly the Johannesburg Securities Exchange). See *http://www.strate.co.za/aboutstrate/overview/history%20of%20strate.aspx*. See also chapter 19 below.
12   Through the insertion of s 91A in the Companies Act, 1973 by s 1 of the Companies Second Amendment Act 60 of 1998.
13   See *http://www.strate.co.za/aboutstrate/overview/history%20of%20strate.aspx*.
14   *Botha v Fick* 1995 (2) SA 750 (A) at 778G-H; *Oakland Nominees (Pty) Ltd v Gelria Mining & Investment Co (Pty) Ltd* 1976 (1) SA 441(A) at 452H.
15   Section 51(1)(*c*) of the Companies Act, 2008.
16   See s 1 definition of beneficial interest and para. 8.4 below.
17   A nominee is a person who is approved to act as the holder of securities on behalf of another person or persons (see s 1 definition of nominee in the 2008 Act, as amended by the Financial Markets Act 19 of 2012 (FMA) and read with s 1 definition of nominee in FMA) and see para. 8.4 below.
18   As appears from the discussion above, this person could be the nominee of the owner.
19   Section 51(1)(*a*) of the Companies Act, 2008.
20   Section 51(1)(*b*) of the Companies Act, 2008. See further s 51(2) and, regarding the numbering of certificates, s 51(4).

8.2.3 Securities register

Every company must establish a securities register of its issued securities[21] in the prescribed form and maintain this register in accordance with prescribed standards.[22] As soon as practicable after issuing certificated securities, the names and addresses of the persons to whom the securities were issued,[23] and the number of securities issued to each of them must be entered in the securities register.[24] The total number of securities held in uncertificated form must also be entered in the securities register.[25] The securities register is proof of the facts recorded in it, in the absence of evidence to the contrary.[26]

If the company issues uncertificated securities, or where certificated shares are converted into uncertificated securities, a record of these securities, with the same information as required in the case of certificated securities, must be administered and maintained by a participant or central securities depository[27] in the prescribed form as the company's uncertificated securities register. This register forms part of the company's securities register.[28]

8.3 Central securities depository and participants[29]

A **central securities depository** is licensed[30] to operate the electronic system for the holding and transfer of uncertificated securities. The current licensee is Strate Ltd (**Strate**). A **participant** is a person who administers securities and who has been accepted as a participant by a central securities depository.[31] Only participants can liaise with Strate directly. Persons trading in uncertificated securities and their brokers must therefore work through a participant.[32]

PRACTICAL	**Strate and dematerialisation**
ISSUE	The following extract is from Strate's website (*www.strate.co.za*):
	What is dematerialisation?
	Dematerialisation is a technical term referring to the process whereby paper share certificates are replaced with electronic records of ownership.

---

21 See para. 8.1 above for the meaning of securities.

22 Section 50(1) of the Companies Act, 2008.

23 Unlike the 1973 Act (s 93), the 2008 Act makes no provision for a separate register of allotments of shares. The information regarding the identity of the persons to whom the shares were issued appears from the securities register and a record of the consideration received in the securities register is no longer necessary in view of the abolition of the doctrine of capital maintenance.

24 Section 50(2)(*b*) of the Companies Act, 2008, which imposes additional requirements for shares held in trust when they were issued as partly paid up and for securities other than shares.

25 Section 50(2)(*a*) of the Companies Act, 2008.

26 Section 50(4) of the Companies Act, 2008.

27 See the Practical Issue below for an explanation of these concepts.

28 Section 50(3)(*a*) of the Companies Act, 2008.

29 See also chapter 19 below.

30 Under s 29 of the Financial Markets Act 19 of 2012.

31 See s 1 of the Financial Markets Act 19 of 2012 for the definition of participant. The acronym 'Strate' is derived from Share TRAnsactions Totally Electronic. Currently six CSD participants have been accepted by Strate. Five of them them are banks and the other is Computershare. Of these, only Computershare currently offers investors the option of holding the securities in their own name. The others make all registrations in the name of their nominee companies. See *www.strate.co.za/aboutstrate/overview/dematerialisation*.

32 See *www.strate.co.za/aboutstrate/overview/dematerialisation.aspx*.

What is Strate and a Central Securities Depository (CSD) Participant?

Strate Ltd (Strate) is South Africa's Central Securities Depository (CSD) for equities, including a range of derivative products such as warrants, exchange-traded funds (ETFs), retail notes and tracker funds, Alt-X, bonds and money market securities.

Strate was introduced to the market to facilitate the dematerialisation and electronic settlement of the equities market.

'CSD Participant' stands for 'Central Securities Depository Participant'. The CSD Participants are the only market players who can liaise directly with Strate. Most of the current CSD Participants are banks. In order to qualify for CSD Participant status, they have to fulfill the entry criteria set out by Strate and approved by the Financial Services Board.

The authorised CSD Participants are:

1. ABSA Bank Ltd;
2. Citibank NA – South Africa;
3. Computershare Ltd;
4. Eskom Holdings SOC Ltd;
5. FirstRand Bank Ltd;
6. Link Investor Services (Pty) Ltd;
7. Nedbank Ltd;
8. South African Reserve Bank;
9. The Standard Bank of South Africa Ltd;
10. Standard Chartered Bank – Johannesburg Branch;
11. Société Générale – Johannesburg Branch

Controlled and non-controlled clients

Under the Strate system, there are essentially two types of clients: controlled and non-controlled. A controlled broker client is one who elects to keep his shares and cash in the custody of his broker and, therefore, indirectly with the broker's chosen CSD Participant. Because CSD Participants are the only market players who liaise directly with Strate, all brokers must have accounts with CSD Participants and communicate electronically with them using an international network called SWIFT (Society for Worldwide Inter-bank Financial Telecommunications). A controlled client deals directly and exclusively with his broker and his regular share statement comes from his broker.

Non-controlled broker clients appoint their own CSD Participant to act on their behalf. They surrender their certificates and open an account with their selected CSD Participant, while dealing with their broker only when they want to trade. They would have to provide their broker with the details of their share account at the CSD Participant when trading. Non-controlled clients receive their share statements directly from their CSD Participant.

A person wishing to inspect a company's uncertificated securities register may do so only through the relevant company and in accordance with the rules of the central securities depository.[33]

---

33 Section 52(2) of the Companies Act, 2008. See further s 52(1) regarding the company's right to obtain details of the company's securities reflected in the uncertificated securities register from the participant or central securities depository, and see s 52(4) regarding the right of the registered holder of the securities to regular statements of the uncertificated securities held.

8.4 Securities held by nominees

In practice, securities are not necessarily registered in the securities register in the name of the owner of the securities, but may be registered in the name of a nominee. In the case of listed securities issued by a public company, these securities are, in fact, usually registered in the name of a nominee.[34]

A **nominee** is defined as 'a person approved ... to act as the holder of securities or an interest in securities on behalf of other persons'.[35] The nominee is nominated by the owner of the securities to be the registered holder and holds the securities in name only.[36] The owner of securities that are held through a nominee is often referred to in commercial practice as the **beneficial owner** of the securities. From a legal perspective, the nominee is an agent with limited authority (or a trustee, in the wider sense) and must act on the instructions of the owner when, for example, exercising the voting rights of the securities. The nominee has no authority to dispose of the securities unless authorised by the owner.[37] Under the common law, the courts will accordingly usually allow the beneficial owner to vindicate (claim back) the securities from a *bona fide* purchaser to whom the nominee has sold the securities without authority.[38] For example, a nominee (N), without first obtaining authority from the beneficial owner (B), sells that owner's shares to a purchaser (P) who does not know that B has not authorised the sale. The courts will generally allow B to claim his shares from P, who will then only have a damages claim against N, but no right to the shares.

The term 'beneficial interest' is defined in s 1 of the Companies Act, 2008. The holder of the beneficial interest is the person, usually the owner, who is entitled to participate in any distribution; to exercise the rights attached to the securities (for example, the voting rights or rights regarding conversion); and to dispose of those securities.[39] As explained below, the company in practice recognises only the nominee as the registered holder of securities, with the result that the owner will usually have to exercise its rights against the company through the nominee.

The wording of the provision of the Companies Act, 1973 that permitted the use of nominee shareholders was rather obscure.[40] In practice, only the nominee was entered in the register and the register did not disclose the identity of the owner.[41] In effect, the 1973 Act permitted the company, even where it was aware that the shares were held by a nominee,

---

34 See *www.strate.co.za/aboutstrate/overview/dematerialisation.aspx*, from which it appears that five of the six participants administering securities on Strate are only prepared to register securities in the name of their nominee companies.

35 See s 1 of the Financial Markets Act 19 of 2012.

36 See too s 1 of the Companies Act, 2008 for the definition of shareholder, which generally refers to the person who is entered as such in the securities register. (For purposes of Chapter 2 Part F of the Act (Governance of Companies), 'shareholder' has a special meaning and refers to the (registered) holder of securities (including debt instruments) to which voting rights are attached (s 57(1)).)

37 See generally regarding nominees *Standard Bank of SA Ltd v Ocean Commodities Inc* supra at 288H–289B; *Sammel v President Brand Gold Mining Co Ltd* 1969 (3) SA 629 (A) at 666D–667A and HS Cilliers, ML Benade et al *Corporate Law* 3 ed (2000) paras. 15.09–15.13.

38 See *Oakland Nominees (Pty) Ltd v Gelria Mining & Investment Co (Pty) Ltd* supra. However, the position is different in the case of uncertificated securities (see para. 8.5.2 below regarding s 53(4) of the Companies Act, 2008).

39 See s 1 of the Companies Act, 2008 for the definition of beneficial interest. The holder of an interest in a unit trust or collective investment scheme is excluded.

40 Section 104 of the Companies Act 61 of 1973 read: '*Trust in respect of shares. – A company shall not be bound to see to the execution of any trust, whether express, implied or constructive, in respect of its shares.*'

41 The only indication that the shares were held by a nominee would be if the nominee was a company, and if its status as nominee appeared from its name, e.g. Standard Bank Nominees Ltd.

to recognise only the nominee,[42] and the company was under no obligation to investigate whether the nominee was acting within the scope of its mandate.

Section 56(1) of the 2008 Act provides as follows:

> **Except to the extent that a company's Memorandum of Incorporation provides otherwise, the company's issued securities may be held by, and registered in the name of, one person for the beneficial interest of another person.**

This provision clearly permits the use of nominee shareholders.[43]

A substantial portion of listed shares in South Africa is registered in the name of nominees. The following concerns regarding the large-scale use of nominees have been identified:[44]

- Insider trading becomes more difficult to detect.
- It is more difficult for minority shareholders to determine the identity of the owner of the controlling shareholder and to establish when there has been a change of control.
- The incumbent directors will not necessarily receive prior warning that a substantial shareholding is being accumulated with a view to a hostile takeover.
- Legislation to promote competition is difficult to enforce if the true owners of the company's shares are not known.
- The company only communicates with its registered shareholders, even if they are just nominees.

These concerns are addressed in s 56(2) to (10) of the 2008 Act. Thus, if the registered holder of securities in a public company is a nominee – that is, is not the holder of the beneficial interest of all the securities held by that person – that nominee is required by s 56(3) and (4) to provide the company with information regarding the identity of each person on whose behalf securities are held, together with the number and class of securities held, on a monthly basis. In short, the nominee is required on a regular basis to disclose to the company the identity of the owners on whose behalf it holds securities and the extent of those holdings.

A public company and certain private companies – that is, regulated companies[45] – must establish and maintain a register of the disclosures made by nominees, and, if they are required to have such statements audited in terms of s 30(2), the company must publish a list of the persons who hold beneficial interests equal to or in excess of 5 per cent of the total number of securities of that class issued by the company, together with the extent of those beneficial interests.

Section 56(9) of the Act provides that a person who holds a beneficial interest in any securities may vote in a matter at a meeting of shareholders, only to the extent that:

- the beneficial interest includes the right to vote on the matter; and
- the person's name is on the company's register of disclosures as the holder of a beneficial interest, or the person holds a proxy appointment in respect of that matter from the registered holder of those securities.

---

42 Dividends would be paid to the nominee, which would have to account to its principal. If the shares were certificated, the nominee would have to sign the instrument of transfer as transferor.

43 Although the word 'nominee' is not used in s 56(1), it is used elsewhere in the Act, e.g. in s 3(1)(a) in the context of the definition of a subsidiary company.

44 See the memorandum that accompanied the Bill that became the Companies Amendment Act 37 of 1999.

45 A regulated company is defined in s 117(2) of the Companies Act, 2008, read with s 118(1) and (2), to include not only public companies, but also certain private companies. As the duty of disclosure imposed on nominees by s 56(3) only applies to securities of a public company, it appears that a private company qualifying as a regulated company will have to use s 56(5) to obtain the necessary information.

The meaning of beneficial interest has been explained above. Section 56(2) gives an extended meaning to a person who is deemed to have a beneficial interest, so as to include, among other categories, the holding company of a subsidiary that holds the beneficial interest. The provision is problematic. A holding company is deemed to hold a beneficial interest if its subsidiary has a beneficial interest in such security.[46] Logically, the subsidiary and the holding company cannot simultaneously hold a beneficial interest in the same securities, unless the securities are held jointly, which is not the situation under consideration. The nominee will surely still continue to pay over the dividends it receives to the subsidiary. Is it the intention that the nominee must declare in the monthly returns that the holding company is the holder of the beneficial interest to the exclusion of the subsidiary? Section 56(2)[47] is on closer analysis an ill-considered attempt to prevent evasion, and it is unworkable in practice.

A company that knows or believes on reasonable grounds that its securities are held by a nominee, may require both the suspected nominee and the suspected beneficial owner to provide it with the prescribed information to enable it to verify the identity of the holder(s) of a beneficial interest and the extent of that interest.[48]

8.5 Transfer of shares

A share is movable property, transferable in any manner provided for in, or recognised by, the Companies Act, 2008.[49] A private company is required to restrict the transferability of its securities,[50] and this can be done by providing for a right of pre-emption, or by making transfer subject to the consent of the board.

It is important in this context to note that the term '**transfer**' in regard to shares and securities can be used in more than one sense:

> In regard to shares, the word 'transfer' in its full and technical sense, is not a single
> act but consists of a series of steps, namely an agreement to transfer, the execution
> of a deed of transfer and finally, the registration of transfer.[51]

Under the 1973 Act, it was decided that the restriction on transferability of a private company's shares referred to transfer in this full and extended sense – that is to say transfer relates to:

- the agreement to transfer the shares;
- the drawing up of a document showing that there is a transfer; and
- the actual registration of the change in ownership.[52]

In the case of certificated securities, registered transfer must be distinguished from the transfer of ownership, which takes place through cession under the common law. In this

---

46 Section 56(2)*(d)* of the Companies Act, 2008.
47 Like s 140A(2) of the 1973 Act on which it is based.
48 See s 56(5) of the Companies Act, 2008, but note that its wording is not restricted to public companies and could therefore apparently be used by a private company.
49 Section 35(1) of the Companies Act, 2008.
50 Section 8(2)*(b)*(ii)*(bb)* of the Companies Act, 2008.
51 *Inland Property Development Corporation (Pty) Ltd v Cilliers* 1973 (3) SA 245 (A) at 251C.
52 See *Smuts v Booyens; Markplaas (Edms) v Booyens* supra at 22A-B. The wording of s 8(2)*(b)*(ii)*(bb)* of the 2008 Act differs from that of the 1973 Act in that it is the 'transferability of its securities' that must be restricted under the 2008 Act, as opposed to '*the right to* transfer its *shares*' (our italics) in s 20*(a)* of the 1973 Act. This may affect the interpretation of transfer in the context.

context, mere consent is sufficient for a valid cession.[53] Where certificated securities have been sold, this informal cession will normally take place against payment of the purchase price, when the seller will normally deliver the certificate and a transfer form signed by the seller. The legal duty resting on a registered shareholder, who sells his or her shares, to deliver the share certificate and a transfer form signed by the seller to the purchaser flows from the agreement of sale.[54] Delivery of the share certificate by the seller, although not necessary to transfer ownership of the securities, may nevertheless facilitate proof that a cession (transfer of ownership in the securities) took place.[55] If certificated securities are stolen, and if the owner of the stolen shares, is able to trace them, he or she will be able to vindicate (claim back) those securities from a purchaser in good faith.[56]

Transfer of ownership of uncertificated securities is regulated by statute and, as explained below, the position differs radically from the position under the common law applying to certificated securities.

8.5.1   Registered transfer of certificated securities

Where certificated securities have been sold, the process for the transfer of ownership by cession has been described above. This will be followed by registration of transfer by the company. Traditionally, the transfer form is also signed by the purchaser and then submitted to the company by the purchaser together with the certificate evidencing the securities.[57] Unless the transfer is effected by operation of law,[58] the company may not register transfer unless the transfer is evidenced by a proper instrument of transfer delivered to the company.[59]

The company, after receiving the instrument of transfer, must enter in its security register the name and address of the transferee, the description of the securities transferred and the date of the transfer.[60] By implication, the company must then issue a new certificate evidencing the securities in the name of the transferee.

---

53 See *Botha v Fick* supra at 778F. Cession takes place by means of a transfer agreement that will coincide with or be preceded by a valid cause, usually in the form of an obligatory agreement. In the case of a cession pursuant to a sale, the obligatory agreement will be the agreement of sale (778G-H).

54 *Botha v Fick* supra at 778I-J.

55 *Botha v Fick* supra at 779B.

56 *Oakland Nominees Ltd v Gelria Mining & Investment Co Ltd* supra at 452A-C. The purchaser may be able to rely on estoppel, but this defence imposes a heavy burden on the purchaser, including the need to establish fault on the part of the owner.

57 The 1973 Act in ss 134-138 also had a special simplified paper-based system for the registered transfer of listed shares, which differed from the normal procedure in that the transfer form was not signed by or on behalf of the transferee. These provisions have been omitted from the 2008 Act, as listed securities must be uncertificated in order to be traded on the JSE.

58 This occurs, for example, where the executor of the estate of a deceased shareholder or the trustee of the estate of an insolvent shareholder requests in terms of the MOI or rules to be entered in the securities register as the registered holder of the company's securities in his or her official capacity, on presentation of proof of appointment and without an instrument of transfer. This is also traditionally referred to as the transmission of shares (see Cilliers & Benade supra at 287).

59 Section 51(6) of the Companies Act, 2008.

60 Section 51(5) of the Companies Act, 2008. Where the securities are shares held in trust under s 40(5)(*b*) as being partly paid up, the value of the consideration still to be received by the company must also be entered (s 50(5)(*d*)). Transfer of these shares requires the prior consent of the company (s 40(6)(*d*)(i)).

8.5.2 Transfer of uncertificated securities and liability[61]

The Companies Act, 2008 contains provisions for the transfer of uncertificated securities that apply only to uncertificated securities.[62] A transfer of uncertificated securities in an uncertificated securities register may be effected only by a participant or central securities depository, on receipt of either a properly authenticated instruction, or an order of court.[63] Transfer of ownership in any uncertificated securities is effected by the debiting and crediting of the relevant accounts in the uncertificated securities registers.[64] Unlike the position for certificated securities, the Act therefore imposes formalities for the transfer of ownership or cession of uncertificated securities and transfer of ownership takes place simultaneously with registered transfer.

Transfer of ownership takes place notwithstanding any fraud, illegality or insolvency affecting the securities or transfer, unless the transferee was a party to or had knowledge of the fraud or illegality or had knowledge of the insolvency.[65] The common-law right of the actual and true owner of stolen securities to vindicate (claim back) those shares is therefore removed. The court may also not order the removal of the transferee's name from the uncertificated securities register, unless that person was a party to or had knowledge of the fraud or illegality.[66]

The perpetrator of certain unlawful actions relating to uncertificated securities is liable to any person who has suffered any direct loss or damage arising out of that action,[67] including the former owner of the shares. Furthermore, the person giving an instruction to transfer uncertificated securities must warrant the legality and correctness of that instruction and must indemnify the company, participant and central securities depository against certain claims and losses.[68] A participant or central securities depository effecting transfer of uncertificated securities other than in terms of a properly authenticated instruction must indemnify the company against claims and any other person against direct loss or damage.[69]

THIS CHAPTER IN ESSENCE

1. The Companies Act, 2008 obliges a profit company to maintain a **securities register**, reflecting the names of the current holders of shares and other securities, even if the shares are held by nominees.
2. **Securities** are defined more widely than shares, and include debt instruments such as debentures.
3. A **certificated security** is one evidenced by a certificate. **Uncertificated securities** are not necessarily evidenced by a certificate or written instrument and are held and transferred electronically. In respect of any securities issued by a company, there must be either a physical document or electronic proof of ownership. Securities can only be traded on the JSE if they are uncertificated.

---

61 See also chapter 19 below.
62 Sections 52–55 of the Companies Act, 2008: see also s 49(4)(a). These provisions prevail should they conflict with any other provision of the Act, another law, the common law, a company's MOI or any agreement (s 49(4)(b)).
63 Section 53(1) of the Companies Act, 2008. There is an exception where the right to uncertificated securities has been transmitted by operation of law (s 53(6)).
64 Section 53(2) of the Companies Act, 2008. In practice, the transfer normally takes place between the accounts of the respective nominees of the transferor and the transferee of the securities.
65 Section 53(4) of the Companies Act, 2008.
66 Section 53(5) of the Companies Act, 2008.
67 Section 55(1) of the Companies Act, 2008.
68 Section 55(2) of the Companies Act, 2008.
69 Section 55(3) of the Companies Act, 2008.

4. A **certificate** evidencing certificated securities must state on its face the name of the issuing company, the name of the person to whom the securities were issued or transferred, the number and class of share or security, and any restrictions on transferability.

5. A **central securities depository** is licensed to operate the electronic system for the holding and transfer of uncertificated securities. The current licensee is Strate Ltd (**Strate**). A **participant** is a person who administers securities and who has been accepted as a participant by a central securities depository. Persons trading in uncertificated securities and their brokers must work through a participant.

6. A **nominee** is a person approved as a holder of securities on behalf of others. The nominee is nominated by the owner of the securities to be the registered holder and holds the securities in name only. The owner of securities that are held through a nominee is often referred to in commercial practice as the **beneficial owner** of the securities. A nominee is an agent with limited authority and must act on instructions.

7. The Companies Act, 2008 permits the use of nominee shareholders. However, owing to numerous problems with the widespread use of nominee shareholders, the Act requires a nominee to provide the company with information regarding the identity of each person on whose behalf securities are held, together with the number and class of securities held, on a monthly basis. Regulated companies maintain a register of the disclosures made by nominees.

8. A share is transferable property, but **transfer** is effected differently for certificated and uncertificated securities respectively.

9. The transfer of any certificated security requires: an agreement to transfer the securities; a document showing that there is a transfer; and registration of the change in ownership in a company's securities register. Transfer of ownership of certificated securities takes place by cession. Delivery of a security certificate by the seller is not necessary to transfer ownership of the securities, although it facilitates proof that a cession took place.

10. A transfer of uncertificated securities in an uncertificated securities register may be effected only by a participant or central securities depository, on receipt of either a properly authenticated instruction, or an order of court. Transfer of ownership takes place simultaneously with registered transfer, irrespective of any defect. A victim of any unlawful action relating to transfer of uncertificated securities will have a claim for damages, but not a right of vindication of stolen securities.

Chapter 9

Public offerings of company securities

9.1 Introduction to public offerings

A company often requires cash to keep operating, or to fund an expansion programme, or to enable it to undertake a special project. One way that a company obtains cash is by offering shares and other securities to the public. However, there is potential for abuse. Unscrupulous people behind a company might make false representations to the public in order to entice people to invest more readily in a company. Company law has therefore usually tried to protect the public by requiring open, honest and full disclosure of the affairs of a company that offers its shares to the public (potential investors). In principle, the offer of shares to the public must be accompanied by a prospectus, with the prescribed contents. A **prospectus**, simply put, is an invitation to the public inviting members of the public to invest in a company. A prospectus is intended to enable the prospective investor to take an informed decision. By registering the prospectus, the Commission does not indicate that the securities are a good investment – the investor must make his or her own decision on the basis of the information provided.

The possibility of being able to raise funds from the public provides entrepreneurs using public companies with the opportunity to gather the funds that are required for productive purposes and for the development of the South African economy. However, to further the aim of transparency, the prospectus and related announcements to the public regarding the marketing of securities must meet the required standards for truth and accuracy. This portion of company law needs to strike a careful balance between adequate disclosure (in the interests of transparency) and over-regulation.[1] Over-regulation on this point can deprive entrepreneurs from opportunities to raise required funds and discourage investment.

Although the relevant provisions of Chapter 4 in the 2008 Act present a simplified and modernised scheme compared to the 1973 Act,[2] this remains one of the more complex and technical parts of company law. This chapter therefore aims to provide an overview of the relevant principles and their practical implications in this area. The aim is to make this part of the 2008 Act accessible to those who need to use it in practice. The most important question is: what offers of securities require a prospectus or other form of prescribed public announcement in terms of the Act?

An overview of the main provisions of Chapter 4 of the 2008 Act and how they relate to each other appears from Table 9.1.

Table 9.1 *Overview of Chapter 4 – public offerings of company securities*

Subject	Section of the Companies Act, 2008
Special definitions	95
General restrictions on offers to the public	99
Offers that are not offers to the public	96
Secondary offerings to public	101
Advertisements relating to offers	98
Requirements concerning prospectus	100
Liability for untrue statements	104–106
Allotment of securities pursuant to prospectus	107–111

9.2 General restrictions on offers to the public

The Companies Act, 2008 imposes a number of restrictions on the offering of securities to the public. This paragraph gives an overview of those restrictions.

- Only securities of a company (including a foreign company)[3] may be offered to the public in terms of the Act.[4]
- No person may make an initial public offering[5] unless the offer is accompanied by a registered prospectus.[6]

1　See s 7*(b)*(iii) and *(d)*–*(f)* of the Companies Act, 2008; and also the Explanatory Memorandum at 466, paras. 4–5.
2　See the Explanatory Memorandum titled 'Company finance'.
3　See s 99(1)*(b)* of the Companies Act, 2008 regarding the additional requirements for foreign companies.
4　Section 99(1) of the Companies Act, 2008.
5　This concept is explained in para. 9.3.3 below.
6　Section 99(2) of the Companies Act, 2008.

- Regarding a primary offering of securities[7] that is not an initial public offering, the Act distinguishes between listed and unlisted securities.[8] A primary offering to the public of any listed securities must be in accordance with the requirements of the relevant exchange. A primary offering of any unlisted securities must be accompanied by a registered prospectus.
- A secondary offering to the public of unlisted securities must normally either be accompanied by a registered prospectus or by a written statement that complies with the requirements of s 101.[9]
- There are also restrictions on the distribution of application forms for securities unless those forms are accompanied by a registered prospectus.[10]

9.3   Important definitions

There are several definitions and concepts that are fundamental to understanding the provisions on public offerings of company securities in the Companies Act, 2008.

Basically, the 2008 Act distinguishes between three types of offer to the public:

1. primary offerings of securities;
2. secondary offerings; and
3. initial public offerings.

Differing statutory disclosure provisions apply to these types of offer to the public.

9.3.1   Primary offering

A **primary offering** is an offer to the public, made by or on behalf of a company, of securities to be issued by that company.[11] The purpose of the offer is the acquisition of funds by the company through the issue of securities.

9.3.2   Secondary offering

A **secondary offering** means an offer for sale to the public of any securities of a company or its subsidiary, made by or on behalf of a person other than that company or its subsidiary.[12] In essence, the maker of a secondary offering is selling the securities for his or her own account and not with a view to acquiring funds for the company or its subsidiary.

9.3.3   Initial public offering

An **initial public offering** relates to an offer to the public of any securities of a company, if no securities of that company have previously been offered to the public or if all the securities that had previously been the subject of an offer have subsequently been reacquired by the company. It is clear from the definition in s 95(1)(e), read with s 99(3), that an initial public offering could involve either a primary or a secondary offering.

---

7   This concept is explained in para. 9.3.1 below.
8   Section 99(3)(a) of the Companies Act, 2008.
9   Section 99(3)(b) of the Companies Act, 2008, read with s 101(1)(a).
10   Section 99(5) of the Companies Act, 2008, subject to the exceptions in sub-s (6).
11   Section 95(1)(i) of the Companies Act, 2008 defines a primary offering. The definition is extended to securities to be issued by another company in the same group as the company making the offer, or with which the offeror company proposes to merge or into which it is to be amalgamated.
12   Section 95(1)(m) of the Companies Act, 2008 defines a secondary offering.

The latter situation could arise where the controlling shareholder of a public company with unlisted shares offers some of those shares for sale to the public. However, if the shares are listed, the controlling shareholder may sell the shares through the JSE without having to comply with statutory requirements, as this is not regarded as an offer to the public.[13]

A primary offering is not restricted to an initial offering, because after securities have been issued by a company pursuant to an initial public offering, a further issue may be necessary to fund future operations of that company.

A fundamental difference between a primary and a secondary offering is that the former relates to fresh securities to be issued by the company, whereas a secondary offering relates to the sale of existing securities. A primary offering takes the form of an offer for subscription, in contrast to a secondary offering, which is an offer of securities for sale.

9.3.4   Application of the provisions of the Companies Act

From the definitions above, it is clear that a primary or secondary offering or an initial public offering only concerns offers made to the public. An offer, in relation to securities, means an offer made in any way by any person with respect to the acquisition of any securities in a company, for consideration.[14]

An **offer to the public**[15] includes an offer of securities issued by a company to any section of the public – however that section may be selected. An offer to a selected section of the public – for example, holders of the company's securities,[16] or clients of the person issuing the prospectus, or the holders of any particular class of property – is still one to the public. However, a secondary offer of listed securities made through an exchange is excluded from the definition of an offer to the public, as is an offer covered by one of the exceptions dealt with in paragraph 9.4.below.[17]

CASE	**Who is the public?**
STUDY	In *Gold Fields Ltd v Harmony Gold Mining Co Ltd*,[18] Goldfields contended that an offer by Harmony to the shareholders of Goldfields to issue shares in Harmony in exchange for their Gold Fields shares was an offer to the public.
	The court held that the term 'public' in the equivalent provisions of the 1973 Act was not used in any special sense. It referred to an offer made to and capable of being accepted by the public at large, including, in the case of a cash offer, a randomly selected section of the public, like the residents of Bloemfontein. The court, however, concluded that where the offer was aimed at acquiring specific private property, like the Gold Fields shares, it was not an offer to the public.
	It is submitted that the inclusion in the 2008 Act definition of 'offer to the public' of offers made to persons who are 'the holders of any particular class of property' was effected so as to overrule the *Gold Fields* decision.

---

13 See s 95(1)*(h)*(ii)*(bb)* of the Companies Act, 2008, which excludes a secondary offering 'effected through an exchange' from the definition of an offer to the public. In other words, when an existing shareholder sells its shares to a third party, this is not regarded as an offer to the public, and the JSE acts as the go-between between a seller and potential buyers.

14 See s 95(1)*(g)* of the Companies Act, 2008 for a definition of offer. For the meaning of consideration, see s 1 of the Companies Act (definitions).

15 Section 95(1)*(h)* of the Companies Act, 2008.

16 See too s 95(2) of the Companies Act, 2008, but compare s 96(1)*(c)* and *(d)*.

17 Section 95(1)*(h)*(ii) of the Companies Act, 2008, read with s 96.

18 2005 (2) SA 506 (SCA).

Because the term 'offer to the public' is so widely defined, the exceptions listed in s 96 regarding actions that do not constitute offers to the public are very important in practice.

Two of these exceptions relate to certain types of rights offer. A **rights offer** is widely defined as an offer for subscription of a company's securities, made to any existing holders of the company's securities. (A subscriber of shares indicates a willingness to acquire shares in a company from the company itself.) Offers with a right to renounce in favour of other persons (renounceable offers) and offers without such a right (non-renounceable offers) are both covered by the definition of rights offer.[19] A renounceable offer is an offer that gives existing shareholders the right either to acquire the shares themselves from the company, or to give up (renounce) this right in favour of another person. This other person will then have the right to subscribe for these shares if the existing shareholder gives up this right. A rights offer is made by way of a document known as a letter of allocation.[20]

9.4   Actions that are not offers to the public

In view of the wide definition of 'offer to the public' in s 95, the seven exceptions in s 96 (concerning offers that are not regarded as offers to the public) assume particular importance. They are important because the onerous provisions relating to the issue and contents of a prospectus will not apply if the issue is not an offer to the public. These exceptions are as follows:

1. an offer made only to specified share dealers or institutional investors like stockbrokers, authorised financial services providers, and financial institutions;[21]
2. the 'sophisticated investor' exception,[22] where the total acquisition cost of the securities for each investor[23] acting as principal is at least the prescribed amount (which may not be less than R100 000);
3. a non-renounceable offer[24] made only to existing holders of the company's securities or to persons related to such holders;
4. a rights offer in respect of listed securities;[25]
5. an offer made only to directors or prescribed officers of the company, or to persons related to them, unless the offer is renounceable in favour of a person outside that group;
6. an offer that pertains to an employee share scheme; or
7. the 'small issue' or 'seed capital' exception[26] – namely, an offer or series of offers for subscription, accepted by a maximum of 50 persons acting as principals, where the subscription price does not exceed the prescribed amount.[27]

---

19   Section 95(1)(*l*) of the Companies Act, 2008. The definition extends to offers for a subscription by a company of securities of any other company in the same group. In s 142 of the 1973 Act, a rights offer was more restrictively defined to cover only renounceable offers for subscription in respect of listed securities.
20   Section 95(1)(*f*) of the Companies Act, 2008.
21   The wholly owned subsidiary of a financial institution acting as manager of a pension fund or collective investment scheme is also covered by the exception.
22   HS Cilliers, ML Benade et al *Corporate Law* 3 ed (2000) at 260.
23   Section 96(1)(*b*) of the Companies Act, 2008 refers to 'any single *addressee*' (our italics).
24   Although the expression 'rights offer' is not used, this exception relates to a sub-category of rights offer as defined in s 95, but only if it is an offer for subscription.
25   The rights offer must satisfy the prescribed requirements, as well as any requirements of the relevant exchange (s 96(1) (*d*)).
26   Cilliers & Benade supra at 260.
27   The issue must be finalised within six months after the date on which the offer was first made. The company must also not have made a similar offer within the prescribed period, which may not be less than six months. See further s 96(1) (*g*) and (2).

Of these seven exceptions, three – namely, the rights offer in respect of listed securities, an employee share scheme, and the small issue or seed capital exception – are restricted to offers of securities for subscription. The other four apply to both offers for subscription and offers for sale.[28] As primary offerings and secondary offerings are both defined as offers to the public, the statutory requirements for such offerings, dealt with below, have no application to offers falling within the seven exceptions.

To fall under the exception regarding employee share schemes, the company must comply with s 97. (It is clear from the definition of an employee share scheme in s 95(1)*(c)*, read with s 42 on options to subscribe to shares, that an employee share scheme only applies to an offer of shares for subscription and not to an offer for sale.) Among other requirements, the company must appoint a compliance officer who will be responsible for administering the scheme as stipulated by the Act and who must provide employees receiving offers in terms of the scheme with the prescribed information.[29]

9.5 The prospectus

The Companies Act, 2008 requires a registered prospectus in the case of both an initial public offering[30] and a primary offering.[31] A prospectus is also required in the case of a secondary offering, unless the offer is accompanied by a written statement.[32] To prevent people from circumventing the procedural requirements relating to the issue of a prospectus, the Act imposes restrictions on advertisements relating to offers of securities to the public other than by way of a registered prospectus, as explained below.

9.5.1 Definition of prospectus

The 2008 Act does not define the term 'prospectus'.[33] However, s 95(1) does define the term 'registered prospectus' as a prospectus that complies with the Act and that has been filed[34] or, in the case of listed securities, has been approved, by the relevant exchange. In spite of the reference to filing, a prospectus will only be recognised as a registered prospectus for purposes of the Act if it has in fact been registered by the Commission and only for as long as the registration is current.[35] Under the 2008 Act, therefore, it is not any invitation or advertisement offering securities to the public that qualifies as a prospectus. To qualify as a prospectus, the document must be in the prescribed form and contain the prescribed contents and be registered by the Commission.

---

28 There are important differences between the wording of s 96 of the 2008 Act and s 144 of the 1973 Act in this regard. For example, under s 144*(b)* and *(d)* of the 1973 Act, both the sophisticated investor exception and the non-renounceable offer to existing shareholders were restricted to offers for subscription.

29 Section 97 of the Companies Act, 2008.

30 Section 99(2) of the Companies Act, 2008.

31 Section 99(3)*(a)* of the Companies Act, 2008.

32 Section 99(3)*(b)* of the Companies Act, 2008.

33 Compare s 1 of the 1973 Act, as amended in 2001, which defined a prospectus as 'any prospectus, notice, circular, advertisement or other invitation, irrespective of whether it is done in non-electronic or any electronic manner, offering any shares of a company to the public'. The omission of the definition from the 2008 Act would seem to allow for a broader interpretation.

34 The verb 'to file' is defined in s 1 of the Companies Act, 2008 as to deliver an acceptable document to the Commission in the manner and form prescribed for that document.

35 See s 99(8)-(11) of the Companies Act, 2008.

9.5.2   Form, content and supporting documentation

The form and content of a prospectus will be prescribed by regulation. As a general principle, the prospectus must contain all information that an investor may reasonably require to assess:

- the assets and liabilities, financial position, profits and losses, cash flow and prospects of the relevant company;[36] and
- the securities being offered.[37]

A copy of any material agreement as prescribed must be attached to the prospectus.[38]

The Commission, or an exchange in the case of listed securities, on application, may allow required information to be omitted from a prospectus if satisfied that the publication of the information would be unnecessarily burdensome for the applicant, seriously detrimental to the relevant company or against the public interest and that users will not be unduly prejudiced by the omission.[39]

As long as any initial public offering or a primary offering to the public of unlisted securities remains open, the 2008 Act imposes a duty on the person responsible for information in a prospectus to correct any error, to report on any new matter and to report on any changes, provided that the information is relevant and material.[40] This correction or report must be registered as a supplement to the prospectus and must be simultaneously published to known recipients of the prospectus and included in further distributions of the prospectus.[41]

9.5.3   Underwriting

Because of the considerable effort and expense involved for a company in offering its securities for subscription to the public, it is customary for the board of directors to arrange for the whole or at least a portion of the offer to be underwritten. If an offer is underwritten, it indicates to potential investors that the issue will be successful and will take place, thus eliminating any uncertainties regarding the success of the offer.

The company will enter into an agreement with an **underwriter** who guarantees the success of the company's issuing the securities to the public, by undertaking to subscribe to the securities that are not taken up by the public. In practice, the underwriting agreement will cover at least the minimum subscription, if not the whole issue.[42]

If the prospectus contains a statement to the effect that the whole or any portion of the issue has been underwritten, the underwriting agreement and an affidavit confirming the underwriter's ability to fulfil the undertaking must be filed before the prospectus can be registered.[43]

---

36   See s 100(2)(a)(i) of the Companies Act, 2008. This statement of general principle regarding the company is more specific than s 148(1)(a) of the 1973 Act, which merely required the prospectus to 'contain a fair presentation of the state of affairs of the company'.

37   See s 100(2)(a)(ii) of the Companies Act, 2008.

38   Section 100(4)(a) of the Companies Act, 2008.

39   Section 100(9) of the Companies Act, 2008.

40   Section 100(11) of the Companies Act, 2008 read with s 100(1).

41   Section 100(12) of the Companies Act, 2008. Section 100(13) gives a person who subscribed to shares as a result of an offer that pre-dates the publication of supplementary information a qualified right to withdraw the subscription under certain circumstances.

42   Compare JC De Wet & AH Van Wyk *Die Suid-Afrikaanse Kontraktereg en Handelsreg* 4 ed (1978) at 623–4. The minimum subscription is the minimum amount that, in the opinion of the directors, must be raised by the issue of securities.

43   Section 100(6)-(8) of the Companies Act, 2008.

9.5.4 Registration and publication

No person may issue to any person a prospectus unless that prospectus has been registered.[44] The prospectus may not be registered unless it complies with the provisions of the Act and it must be filed for registration within 10 business days after the date of the prospectus.[45] The Commission must notify the person who filed it as soon as the prospectus has been registered.[46] The prospectus may not be issued more than three months after the date of its registration.[47]

The function of a prospectus is to enable prospective investors from the public to make an informed investment decision, but this will be defeated if members of the public can acquire the shares without having had access to the registered prospectus. The Act therefore imposes restrictions on other advertisements relating to the offer. It also imposes certain restrictions on the allotment of shares pursuant to the offer. These provisions are discussed in the next two paragraphs.

9.5.5 Restrictions on advertisements

An **advertisement** is widely defined in the Act as any direct or indirect communication transmitted by any medium, by which a person seeks to bring any information to the attention of all or part of the public.[48] This definition is clearly wide enough to cover electronic means of communication. Advertisements relating to offers of securities to the public must either comply with all the requirements for a registered prospectus,[49] or must comply with the requirements of s 98(2), which deals with other advertisements.

In the latter event, the advertisement must include a statement clearly stating that it is not a prospectus and indicating where and how a person may obtain a copy of the full registered prospectus.[50] The advertisement will be deemed to be a prospectus if it does not include this statement.[51] The advertisement must not contain any untrue statements that would reasonably mislead the reader to believe either that the advertisement is a prospectus or as to any material matter addressed in the prospectus.[52] The advertisement is not required to be filed with the Commission or registered with an exchange.[53]

9.5.6 Provisions to ensure compliance, including restrictions on allotment

Certain restrictions apply to the **allotment** (issue) of securities by a company pursuant to an offer of those securities to the public. No allotment of those securities may be made more than four months after the filing of the prospectus.[54] This ensures that investors do not rely on stale information.

---

44 Section 99(8) of the Companies Act, 2008.
45 Section 99(9) of the Companies Act, 2008.
46 Section 99(10) of the Companies Act, 2008.
47 Section 99(11) of the Companies Act, 2008.
48 Section 1 of the Companies Act, 2008.
49 Section 98(1) of the Companies Act, 2008. In spite of the general wording of the introduction to s 98(1), it is unlikely that the legislature intended that a s 98(2) advertisement could be used as an alternative to the written statement required by s 101 for secondary offerings of unlisted securities to the public. See para. 9.7 below regarding s 101.
50 See s 98(2)(a) of the 2008 Act, which differs from s 157(1) of the 1973 Act in that it does not attempt to prescribe the maximum content of the advertisement.
51 Section 98(3) of the Companies Act, 2008.
52 Section 98(2)(b) of the Companies Act, 2008. The person responsible incurs the same statutory civil liability as applies to an untrue statement in a prospectus – see s 98(2)(c) read with ss 104–106, and para. 9.6 below.
53 Section 98(3)(a) of the Companies Act, 2008. The advertisement is nevertheless subject to the provisions of Chapter 4 of the Act regarding consent (s 102), variation of agreements referred to in a prospectus (s 103), untrue statements (ss 104–106) and restrictions on allotment (ss 107–111), with the changes required by the context.
54 Section 107 of the Companies Act, 2008.

Allotments may only be made if the subscription was made on an application form attached to or accompanied by a prospectus.[55] The company may not allot securities pursuant to the offer unless the minimum subscription has been received.[56] If the minimum subscription is not received within 40 business days after the issue of the prospectus, the amounts received from applicants must be refunded.[57] If the company makes an allotment before the minimum subscription has been received and the minimum subscription was not subsequently received, that allotment is voidable at the option of the applicant.[58]

No allotment of securities or acceptance of an offer in respect of securities may be made until the beginning of the third day after the prospectus has been issued.[59] This ensures that prospective investors have time to study the prospectus and to consider the reaction of the financial press. Non-compliance by the company does not affect the validity of an allotment or an acceptance.[60]

A prospectus containing a statement to the effect that application has been made for the relevant securities to be listed on an exchange must not be issued, unless the application to an exchange specified in the prospectus has in fact been made.[61] Any allotment pursuant to such a prospectus is conditional on the application being successful.[62]

9.6   Liability for untrue statements in a prospectus

To discourage those involved in issuing prospectuses from misleading investors, Chapter 4 of the Act on public offerings of company securities contains wide-ranging provisions relating to liability for untrue statements in a prospectus. The liability imposed by Chapter 4 is in addition to other remedies available under the Act[63] or under the common law.[64]

Under the common law, a subscriber or purchaser of shares wishing to recover damages for delictual liability on the basis of fraudulent or negligent misrepresentation would have to establish all the elements of delictual liability, including fault.[65] Under s 104(1) of the Act, a person who acquired securities on the basis of the prospectus is entitled to recover any loss or damage that that person may have sustained as a result of any untrue statement in the prospectus, without it being necessary to establish fault.[66]

Persons who can incur this liability include directors, promoters and persons who authorised the issue of the prospectus or who made the offer to the public.[67] These persons can also incur responsibility under the enforcement provisions of Chapter 7 (s 106(1)) and

---

55 Section 108(1)(a) of the Companies Act, 2008.
56 Section 108(2) of the Companies Act, 2008. The minimum subscription is the minimum amount that in the opinion of the directors must be raised by the issue of the securities in order to provide for the matters prescribed to be covered by the minimum subscription. This amount must be received in cash and deposited in a separate bank account (s 108(4) and (5)).
57 Section 108(6) of the Companies Act, 2008. See too s 108(7) for the potential personal liability of directors.
58 Section 109(1)(a) of the Companies Act, 2008. A director is liable for any resultant loss or damages suffered by the company if the director participated in an allotment of shares despite knowing that the allotment was contrary to Chapter 4 (see s 109(1)(b), read with s 77(3)(e)(viii)). Compare s 218(1), referred to in s 77(3)(e)(viii), which implies that the agreement is only voidable if declared so by the court.
59 Section 110(1) of the Companies Act, 2008. See s 110(2) as to how this date is determined.
60 Section 110(3) of the Companies Act, 2008.
61 Section 111(1) of the Companies Act, 2008.
62 Section 111(2) of the Companies Act, 2008.
63 See e.g. the company's remedy to recover damages from directors under s 77(3)(d)(ii) of the Companies Act, 2008 and the criminal liability imposed by s 214(1)(d)(ii).
64 Section 95(6) of the Companies Act, 2008.
65 See Cilliers & Benade supra at 275.
66 See De Wet & Van Wyk supra at 609.
67 Section 104(1) of the Companies Act, 2008.

could possibly therefore, for example, be the subject of a compliance notice under s 171. A dispute regarding liability for damages could also be referred to the Companies Tribunal under s 166.

An untrue statement is one that is misleading in the form and context in which it is made, and includes an omission that is calculated to mislead.[68] Liability is also imposed on the maker for any untrue statement purporting to be made by that person as an expert.[69]

Section 104(3) contains certain statutory defences to liability for untrue statements – for example, where a statement was made by a person reasonably believed to be an expert competent to make the statement.

9.7 Regulation of secondary offerings

Secondary offerings to the public must comply with the requirements for secondary offerings in s 101. These and the possible consequences of non-compliance are discussed briefly here.

As discussed above, a secondary offering is defined as an offer for sale to the public of any (issued) securities of a company or its subsidiary, made by or on behalf of a person other than the company or its subsidiary.[70] In essence, the seller is selling the securities for his or her own benefit and not with a view to obtaining funds for the company that issued the securities.

An important difference between the 2008 Act and its predecessor is that the 2008 Act uses basically the same criteria to determine when an offer of securities *for sale* is an offer to the public as in the case of an offer *for subscription*.[71] An offer for sale will not be one to the public when it falls within one of the four exceptions discussed above and therefore does not require a prospectus.[72]

Furthermore, the requirements of s 101 regarding secondary offerings do not apply to listed securities.[73] An offer for sale made by the executor of a deceased estate or by the trustee of an insolvent estate or by way of a sale in execution or by public auction is also exempted.[74]

In practice, the provisions on secondary offerings apply to offers for sale of unlisted shares[75] to the public by shareholders in a public company and to a lesser extent to such offers by shareholders in a private company. If the asking price is too low for the sophisticated investor exception to apply, the prospective seller not wishing to comply with the s 101 requirements could either make a non-renounceable offer to the other shareholders or could approach the directors with a view to the company acquiring the shares under s 48.

A person making a secondary offering to which none of the exemptions above apply must ensure that the offer is accompanied either by the registered prospectus that

---

68 Section 95(1)(*p*) read with s 95(3) and (4).

69 Section 105(2), subject to certain defences in s 105(2). An expert is defined in s 95(1)(*d*).

70 See para. 9.3.2 above and the definition in s 95(1) of secondary offering. It is not clear why the subsidiary of a public company that has acquired its holding company's unlisted shares under s 48 should be exempted from the requirements of a secondary offering where it offers those shares for sale to the public.

71 See paras. 9.3.4 and 9.4 above regarding the 2008 Act. Under the 1973 Act, the definition and exceptions regarding an offer to the public in ss 142 and 144 did not apply to an offer for sale under s 141. For this reason, case law regarding s 141 of the 1973 Act is no longer relevant.

72 See para. 9.4 above.

73 Section 101(1) of the Companies Act, 2008. See too s 95(1)(*h*)(ii)(*bb*) and para. 9.3.2 above regarding the definition of offers to the public.

74 Section 101(3) of the Companies Act, 2008.

75 Although the definition of secondary offering refers to securities, it is unlikely in practice that the holders of debt instruments (as defined in s 43(1)(*a*)) in the companies under discussion in the text will be offering them for sale to the public.

accompanied the primary offering of those securities,[76] or by a written statement complying with the requirements summarised below.[77]

The written statement must be signed and dated by the person making the offer.[78] It may not contain anything other than the particulars required by s 101(6) and must be accompanied by the last annual financial statements of the company. The particulars include certain information about the offeror, the company whose securities are the subject of the offer, details of the company's issued securities and dividend payments, the issue price of the securities subject to the offer, the price for which they were acquired by the offeror and the reasons for any difference between those prices and the prices at which the securities are being offered.[79]

Section 101 contains no provisions on the consequences of non-compliance and possible remedies for the person prejudiced by non-compliance. However, a person who is a party to the preparation, approval or publication of a written statement contemplated in s 101, and which contains an untrue statement, is guilty of an offence.[80] A director of a company who signs or authorises a written statement containing an untrue statement, despite knowing that the statement is false, is liable to compensate the company for any loss suffered by the company.[81] A person who is prejudiced by entering into a contract to purchase securities through the failure of the other party to comply properly with the statutory requirements for secondary offerings may be able to avoid the adverse consequences by applying to the Commission to issue a compliance notice.[82]

THIS CHAPTER IN ESSENCE

1. Companies may raise cash for their businesses by offering securities to the public. However, company law regulates this process closely to avoid abuse. An offer of securities to the public must be accompanied by a prospectus, the contents of which are prescribed.

2. A **prospectus** is an invitation to the public inviting members of the public to invest in a company and providing the prospective investor with information on which to take an informed decision.

3. The 2008 Act distinguishes between three types of offer to the public: primary offerings of securities; secondary offerings; and initial public offerings.

4. A **primary offering** is an offer by a company to the public of securities to be issued by that company to raise funds for the company.

5. A **secondary offering** is an offer for sale to the public of any securities of a company made by a person other than that company. The secondary offeror sells securities for his or her own account, not to raise funds for the company.

6. An **initial public offering** relates to an offer to the public of any securities of a company, if no securities of that company have previously been offered to the public or if all the securities that had previously been the subject of an offer have subsequently been reacquired by the company.

---

76 This option has no application to a shareholder in a private company, as the company is precluded by s 8(2)(b)(ii)(aa) from offering its securities to the public.

77 Section 101(2) of the Companies Act, 2008.

78 Section 101(5) of the Companies Act, 2008.

79 Section 101(6) of the Companies Act, 2008. The Act does not appear to impose an obligation on the company to provide assistance reasonably required by the offeror for purposes of compiling the statement.

80 See s 214(1)(d)(ii) of the Companies Act, 2008 and s 216(a) regarding the possible penalty. A person who contravenes s 101 of the Companies Act, 2008 is liable to compensate any other person who suffers any loss or damage as a result of the contravention (s 218(2)).

81 Section 77(3)(d)(ii) of the Companies Act, 2008, which is subject to s 104(3).

82 The Commission's powers under s 171(2)(a), (c) and (e) are wide enough to rectify the consequences of non-compliance and are not merely directed at causing the person in breach to comply with the Act.

7. An **offer to the public** includes an offer of securities issued by a company to any section of the public. However, a secondary offer of listed securities made through an exchange is excluded from the definition of an offer to the public, as are the offers listed in s 96. Offers excluded from the definition of an offer to the public do not require a prospectus.

8. The seven offers listed in s 96, which are excluded from the definition of an offer to the public, are:

    8.1 an offer made only to specified share dealers or institutional investors like stockbrokers, authorised financial services providers, and financial institutions;

    8.2 the 'sophisticated investor' exception;

    8.3 a non-renounceable offer made only to existing holders of the company's securities or to persons related to such holders;

    8.4 a **rights** offer in respect of listed securities;

    8.5 an offer made only to directors or prescribed officers of the company, or to persons related to them, unless the offer is renounceable in favour of a person outside that group;

    8.6 an offer that pertains to an employee share scheme; or

    8.7 the 'small issue' or 'seed capital' exception.

9. The Companies Act, 2008 requires a registered prospectus in the case of both an initial public offering and a primary offering. A prospectus is also required in the case of a secondary offering, unless the offer is accompanied by a written statement. The Act imposes restrictions on advertisements relating to offers of securities to the public other than by way of a registered prospectus.

10. A prospectus must be registered with the Commission to comply with the Act. Its form and content will be prescribed by regulation and must generally contain all information that an investor may reasonably require to assess assets and liabilities, financial position, profits and losses, cash flow and prospects of the relevant company, and the securities being offered.

11. If an offer is underwritten, an **underwriter** agrees to guarantee the success of the offer by undertaking to subscribe to the securities that are not taken up by the public.

12. The Companies Act, 2008 provides that a person who has acquired securities on the basis of a prospectus is entitled to recover any loss or damage sustained as a result of any untrue statement in the prospectus, without it being necessary to establish fault. Persons who can incur this liability include directors, promoters and persons who authorised the issue of the prospectus or who made the offer to the public. These persons could also be the subject of a compliance notice and a dispute regarding liability for damages may be referred to the Companies Tribunal.

13. In practice, the provisions on secondary offerings apply to offers for sale of unlisted shares to the public by shareholders in a public company and to a lesser extent to such offers by shareholders in a private company. A secondary offering that is not exempt must be accompanied by the registered prospectus that accompanied the primary offering of those securities, or by a **written statement** in the prescribed form. The written statement must be signed and dated by the person making the offer and must contain only the particulars required by the Act and be accompanied by the last annual financial statements of the company.

Chapter 10

Fundamental transactions and takeovers

10.1 Important transactions requiring additional regulation

Transactions that significantly affect the ownership of a company's assets or that signal a notable change in shareholding of a company attract additional regulation under the Companies Act, 2008 while some transactions are not permitted at all. Transactions that attract additional regulation are termed 'fundamental transactions' or 'affected transactions' in the Act and they are briefly discussed and considered in this chapter.

Fundamental transactions are transactions that will fundamentally alter a company, and the process for the approval of such transactions is set out in the Companies Act, 2008. The 2008 Act contemplates three kinds of fundamental transaction, namely:

1. disposals of the majority of a company's assets or undertaking;
2. mergers (also referred to as amalgamations); and
3. schemes of arrangement.

The rules relating to fundamental transactions are applicable to all companies, whether private or public. However, where a fundamental transaction also fits the description of an affected transaction, the Takeover Regulation Panel has jurisdiction over such a transaction and may exercise the necessary powers as stated in Chapter 5 of the 2008 Act.

A fundamental transaction will fit the description of an affected transaction only if the company to which it applies is a regulated company.

A company is a **regulated company** if it is:[1]

- a public company;
- a state-owned enterprise, except to the extent that any such company has been exempted in terms of s 9; or
- a private company, but only if:
  - the percentage of the issued securities of that company that have been transferred within the period of 24 months immediately before the date of a particular affected transaction or offer exceeds the prescribed percentage, being not less than 10 per cent; or
  - the Memorandum of Incorporation (MOI) of that company expressly provides that the company and its securities are subject to Parts B and C of Chapter 5 of the Companies Act, 2008 and the Takeover Regulations, irrespective of whether the company falls within the criteria set out above.

Section 117(1)(c) of the 2008 Act describes an affected transaction as:
- a transaction or series of transactions amounting to the disposal of all or the greater part of the assets or undertaking of a regulated company;
- a merger or amalgamation if it involves at least one regulated company; and
- a scheme of arrangement between a regulated company and its shareholders.

In addition to the above, an affected transaction also arises when there is:
- the acquisition of, or announced intention to acquire, a beneficial interest in any voting securities of a regulated company amounting to 5, 10, or 15 per cent, or any further whole multiple of 5 per cent;
- the announced intention to acquire a beneficial interest in the remaining voting securities of a regulated company not already held by a person or persons acting in concert;
- a mandatory offer; or
- a compulsory acquisition.[2]

In other words, **affected transactions** may be divided into two broad categories.
1. All fundamental transactions constitute affected transactions if a regulated company is involved.
2. The acquisition of prescribed percentages in voting securities invites the jurisdiction of the Takeover Regulation Panel and the application of certain special rules prescribed in Chapter 5 of the 2008 Act and the Takeover Regulations. The most common types of the second category of affected transaction are mandatory offers and compulsory acquisitions or so-called squeeze-out transactions.

---

1   Section 118(1) and (2) of the Companies Act, 2008.
2   Mandatory offers and compulsory acquisitions are discussed in more detail in paras. 10.5.1 and 10.5.2 below.

All affected transactions involve regulated companies and a transaction that does not involve a regulated company will not fall within the definition of an affected transaction.[3]

10.2   Identifying fundamental transactions

The term 'fundamental transaction' was introduced into South African law by the Companies Act, 2008 and did not appear in previous corporate legislative enactments.[4] It is a generic term used to refer to the following transactions collectively:

- proposals to dispose of all or a greater part of the company's assets or undertaking;[5]
- proposals for amalgamation or merger;[6] and
- proposals for a scheme of arrangement.[7]

These transactions, and their general approval requirements, will be discussed in turn.

10.2.1   Disposal of all or a greater part of the assets or undertaking

The first type of fundamental transaction is the **sale by a company of 'all or the greater part of the assets or undertaking'**, that is 'more than 50 per cent of [a company's] gross assets at fair market value, irrespective of its liabilities' or 'more than 50 per cent of the value of its entire undertaking, at fair market value'.

If the assets comprise over 50 per cent of the market value of the assets of the company, or are responsible for over 50 per cent of the profits generated by the company, the requirements of s 112 regulating these disposals will apply.

PRACTICAL ISSUE	**Disposal or sale of the greater part of a company's assets**
	Suppose that Alpha Co. Ltd, a public company, owns a warehouse in Midrand and stores earthmoving equipment in the warehouse. Suppose further that Alpha Co. Ltd has a total net asset value equalling R100 million. The consolidated value of the warehouse and the equipment is equal to R60 million or 60 per cent of the total net asset value of Alpha Co. Ltd. For commercial reasons, Alpha Co. Ltd then decides to dispose of or sell both the warehouse and the earthmoving equipment.
	Such a disposal or sale will constitute the disposal or sale of the greater part of the assets of the company as contemplated in the 2008 Act, will qualify as a fundamental transaction and will accordingly be subject to the rules of Chapter 5.

When a company intends to effect a transaction contemplated in the example given above, the requirements of s 112 of the Act, read with s 115, must be complied with, subject to exceptions stated in s 112(1).[8] The exceptions ensure that the section does not apply if the disposal is either part of a business rescue plan, or involves transfers within the same group of companies. Examples of transfers within a group of companies are given in the Practical Issue below.

---

3   See Figure 10.8 at the end of this chapter for a diagrammatic summary of fundamental and affected transactions and how they are regulated.

4   The two preceding statutes were the Companies Act, 1926, and the Companies Act, 1973.

5   Section 112 of the Companies Act, 2008.

6   Section 113 of the Companies Act, 2008.

7   Section 114 of the Companies Act, 2008.

8   For more on the regulation by the Companies Act, 2008 of significant disposals, see para. 10.3.1 below.

PRACTICAL
ISSUE

Examples of disposals of all or the greater part of the assets of a company within groups of companies that do *not* need to comply with s 112

1. *A disposal of all or the greater part of the assets of a company that arises from a transaction between a wholly owned subsidiary and its holding company*: suppose that Rand Merchant Bank Ltd (RMB) owns all of the securities with voting rights in First Rand Bank Ltd (FRB). It is clear that FRB is a wholly owned subsidiary of RMB. Assume that FRB owns all of the voting securities in First National Bank Ltd. The corporate structure is illustrated in Figure 10.1 below. In terms of s 112(1)*(b)*, if FRB sold all its securities in First National Bank to RMB, the provisions of s 112 and s 115 do not apply to such a transaction.

Figure 10.1 Corporate structure in example 1

2. *A disposal between two or more wholly owned subsidiaries of the same holding company*: suppose that RMB owns all of the securities with voting rights in FRB and in First National Bank. Refer to Figure 10.2 below for a diagrammatic representation of the corporate structure. A transaction for a disposal of the greater part of the assets of First National Bank to FRB is a transaction between two wholly owned subsidiaries of the same holding company. Such a transaction will also be exempted in terms of s 112(1)*(c)*(i).

Figure 10.2 Corporate structure in examples 2 and 3

3. *A disposal between or among a wholly owned subsidiary, on the one hand, and its holding company and one or more wholly owned subsidiaries of that holding company, on the other hand*: suppose that the facts in the second example stand (see Figure 10.2 above). If the disposal transaction involves a transaction between FRB (one of the wholly owned subsidiaries of RMB), on the one hand, and RMB (a holding company) and First National Bank (another wholly owned subsidiary of Rand Merchant Bank), on the other hand, then such a transaction would be exempted in terms of s 112(1)*(c)*(ii).

Subject to the exceptions discussed above, s 112 of the Companies Act, 2008 provides that no company may dispose of all (or the greater part) of its assets or undertaking, unless the following two requirements are met:

1. the disposal must be approved by a special resolution of shareholders; and,
2. the company must satisfy a number of other (largely procedural) requirements to the extent that they are applicable to the particular disposal.[9]

10.2.2   Amalgamation or merger

In a corporate context, **amalgamation** or **merger** means that the assets and liabilities of one company are amalgamated or merged with those of another, thus effectively merging their corporate identities. An amalgamation or merger occurs in terms of an agreement between two or more companies, and results in the survival of one or more of the merging or amalgamating companies, or the formation of one or more new companies. The surviving or new company or companies then together hold all of the assets and liabilities previously held by the several merging or amalgamating companies.[10]

In this business transaction, two or more companies combine their assets and liabilities, which are subsequently held by one or more surviving companies or by one or more newly formed companies, with the result that all the other merging or amalgamating companies cease to exist on completion of the transaction.

PRACTICAL	**Examples of amalgamations and mergers**
ISSUE	1. *Amalgamation or merger transaction leading to formation of new company*: the shareholders and directors of Alpha Co. Ltd, Bravo (Pty) Ltd, Charlie (Pty) Ltd, and Delta Co. Ltd resolve to merge or amalgamate their respective companies in order to take advantage of a potentially lucrative business adventure. They decide that a merger or amalgamation will constitute the best business transaction. Since the merger or amalgamation will result in all their companies ceasing to exist (which, they resolve, is appropriate under the circumstances), they resolve that all the assets and liabilities of their respective companies will be held by two newly formed companies to be called Elite Co. Ltd and Golf Co. Ltd. This is a clear example of a merger or amalgamation where all the merging or amalgamating companies cease to exist, and it would accordingly be regulated as a fundamental transaction under the Companies Act, 2008.
	2. *Amalgamation or merger transaction resulting in the survival of one or more of the merging companies and the formation of one or more new companies*: Golf Co. Ltd, Hyena (Pty) Ltd, India Co. Ltd and Jill Co. Ltd enter into a merger or amalgamation agreement in terms of which Hyena, India, and Jill will cease to exist and Golf Co. Ltd, together with King Stores Co. Ltd, a newly formed company, will subsequently hold all the assets and liabilities of all merging companies. This is another example of a merger or amalgamation as contemplated in s 1 of the Companies Act, 2008 and it will similarly be treated as a fundamental transaction.

9   These procedural requirements are contained largely in s 112(2)*(b)*, read with s 115(1) and (2)*(a)* of the Companies Act, 2008. Essentially, these requirements prescribe that relevant asset disposals must be approved by shareholders of the disposing company who together hold at least 75 per cent of the voting rights exercised on the resolution at a meeting at which sufficient persons are present to exercise, in aggregate, at least 25 per cent of the voting rights that are entitled to be exercised on the matter. See also para. 10.3.1 below.

10   See s 1 of the Companies Act, 2008.

The terms 'amalgamation' and 'merger' are not individually defined in the Act. Instead, the Act provides a composite definition of an amalgamation or merger, which essentially covers the following two broad categories of transaction that qualify as an amalgamation or merger:

1. The first category of transaction involves a situation where each of the merging companies is dissolved and the assets or liabilities of the merging companies are transferred to a newly formed company or companies.
2. In the second category of transaction, at least one of the merging companies survives, and the assets or liabilities of the non-surviving merging companies (which are subsequently dissolved by operation of law) are transferred to the surviving company or companies and, if applicable, a newly formed company or companies.

Davids, Norwitz and Yuill have aptly observed, '[t]he merger procedure provided for in the [2008] Act is both relatively straightforward and flexible, which is in keeping with the Act's intention of facilitating business combinations.'[11] These authors maintain that:

> [o]f particular importance in this regard is the fact that there is only recourse to the courts in limited circumstances, thus ensuring that the procedure is considerably quicker and possibly less expensive than would ordinarily be the case with a court-driven process. By comparison, the current scheme of arrangement procedure (which is generally the preferred method of implementing a recommended public M&A transaction), requires judicial sanction, and is both a costly and lengthy procedure. Although the limited involvement of the courts in the merger procedure increases the potential for prejudice to shareholders and other stakeholders, this is addressed (at least in theory) by the appraisal rights remedy which is available to dissenting shareholders in terms of s 164 of the Act (as well as the limited recourse which shareholders and creditors have to the courts) and the remedy provided for in s 163 of the Act (relief from unfair or prejudicial conduct).[12]

The regulation of amalgamations and mergers by the Companies Act, 2008 is discussed below.[13]

10.2.3 Schemes of arrangement

The third type of fundamental transaction is a scheme of arrangement. For the purposes of the Companies Act, 2008, a **scheme of arrangement** refers to any arrangement or agreement proposed by the board of directors and entered into between the company and holders of any class of its securities,[14] including a reorganisation of the share capital of the company by way of, among other things:

- a consolidation of securities of different classes;
- a division of securities into different classes;
- an expropriation of securities from the holders;[15]

---

11 See E Davids, T Norwitz and D Yuill 'A microscopic analysis of the new merger and amalgamation provision in the Companies Act 71 of 2008' in T Mongalo (ed.) *Modern Company Law for a Competitive South African Economy* (2010) 337 at 343. See also MF Cassim 'The introduction of the statutory merger in South African corporate law: majority rule offset by the appraisal right (Part I)' (2008) 20 *SA Merc LJ* 1 at 4 and 22.

12 See Davids, Norwitz and Yuill supra and Cassim supra at 1, 20 and 23. See also MF Cassim 'The introduction of the statutory merger in South African corporate law: majority rule offset by the appraisal right (Part II)' (2008) 20 *SA Merc LJ* 147 at 157 and 175.

13 See para. 10.3.2 below.

14 See s 114(1) of the Companies Act, 2008.

15 An expropriation takes place when shareholders are obliged to sell their shares to a third party. Obviously, an expropriation of shares involves an unwilling party who is forced to sell shares, and therefore certain proactive mechanisms need to be in place to ensure fairness.

- exchanging any of its securities for other securities;
- a re-acquisition by the company of its securities; or
- a combination of the above methods.

Schemes are often used as a compulsory takeover mechanism and the 2008 Act recognises this in permitting schemes to be utilised for the expropriation of shares.

PRACTICAL
ISSUE

Example of a scheme of arrangement

The issued shares of India Co. Ltd comprise 100 ordinary shares, 300 preference shares, 100 redeemable preference shares and 100 convertible preference shares.[16] India enters into an arrangement with its securities holders in terms of which its 100 convertible preference shares are to be immediately converted into 100 ordinary shares. The company and its securities holders further arrange and agree to divide existing preference shares into 100 ordinary shares and 100 redeemable preference shares and to expropriate the remaining 100 preference shares. As a result of this arrangement, India's share capital now comprises 300 ordinary shares and 200 redeemable preference shares.

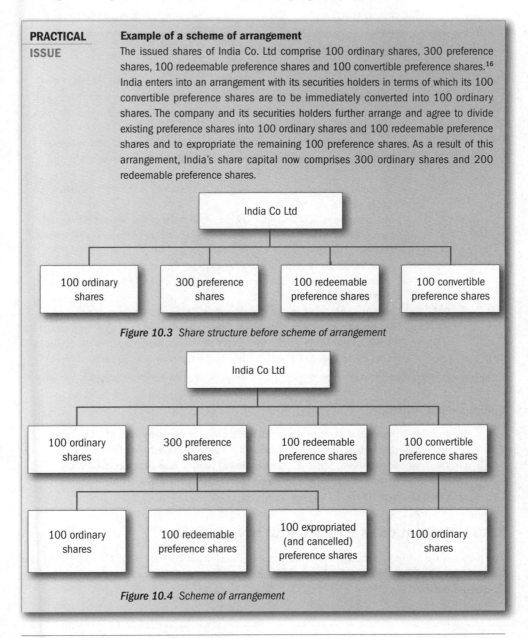

Figure 10.3 Share structure before scheme of arrangement

Figure 10.4 Scheme of arrangement

---

16   See para. 4.6 above for the different types of shares.

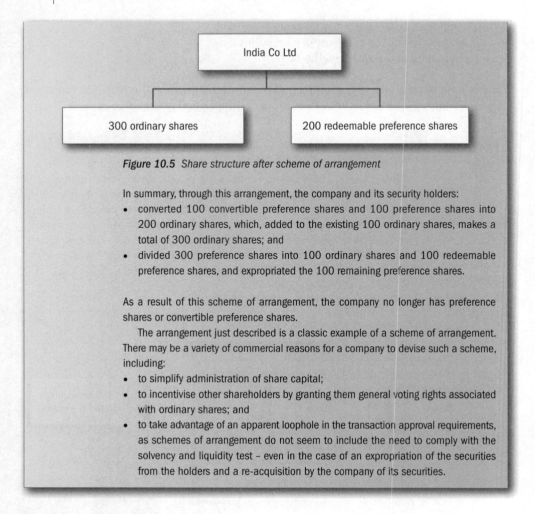

Figure 10.5 *Share structure after scheme of arrangement*

In summary, through this arrangement, the company and its security holders:
- converted 100 convertible preference shares and 100 preference shares into 200 ordinary shares, which, added to the existing 100 ordinary shares, makes a total of 300 ordinary shares; and
- divided 300 preference shares into 100 ordinary shares and 100 redeemable preference shares, and expropriated the 100 remaining preference shares.

As a result of this scheme of arrangement, the company no longer has preference shares or convertible preference shares.

The arrangement just described is a classic example of a scheme of arrangement. There may be a variety of commercial reasons for a company to devise such a scheme, including:
- to simplify administration of share capital;
- to incentivise other shareholders by granting them general voting rights associated with ordinary shares; and
- to take advantage of an apparent loophole in the transaction approval requirements, as schemes of arrangement do not seem to include the need to comply with the solvency and liquidity test – even in the case of an expropriation of the securities from the holders and a re-acquisition by the company of its securities.

Boardman has written:

> In practice, this means that a company can bring about almost any kind of takeover, merger, demerger or internal reorganisation through use of a scheme (provided, of course, that the requisite approvals are obtained) (which makes it a considerably more flexible means of effecting a takeover than either a business acquisition or a standard takeover offer).[17]

10.3 Regulation of fundamental transactions

The regulation of fundamental transactions is dealt with in Part A of Chapter 5 of the Companies Act, 2008. The legal rules applicable to each type of fundamental transaction are discussed below.

---

17 See N Boardman 'A critical analysis of the new South African takeover laws as proposed under the Companies Act 71 of 2008' in T Mongalo (ed.) *Modern Company Law for a Competitive South African Economy* (2010) 306 at 314.

10.3.1   Regulation of substantial disposals

If a company proposes to dispose of the greater part of its assets or undertaking, a number of requirements must be satisfied under the Companies Act, 2008.[18]

- A special resolution (not an ordinary resolution) of shareholders must approve the transaction. A special resolution is necessary in order to protect, in particular, minority shareholders by ensuring that a significant minority is still able to block large disposals – even if such disposals are thought to be in the best interests of, and have been approved by, the majority shareholders. The special resolution requirement for disposals is important because it prevents minority shareholders from becoming disenfranchised.
- Section 112(5) prevents a special resolution from being drafted widely to cover a broad category of generic business disposals. In fact, a resolution will only be effective to the extent that it authorises or ratifies a specific transaction. The effect of this provision is to remove the possibility of a company seeking a broad approval – for example, at an annual general meeting – and then carrying out substantial asset sales fairly soon thereafter.
- Another protective measure requires that any part of the undertaking or assets of the company that is being disposed of must be given its fair market value. What this means is that the price should be that which an interested seller would pay to an interested buyer in an open market. The fair market value must, in terms of s 112(4), be in accordance with the financial reporting standards (FRS)[19] at the time of the disposal.
- Yet another protective measure promotes fairness and minimises the risk of conflicts of interest. Section 115(4) requires that voting rights held by an acquiring party (or a party related to or acting in concert with the acquiring party) must be discounted from the quorum and must be excluded from the vote. In other words, a party that is buying a substantial shareholding in a company in which it already holds shares, cannot use its vote to support the disposal of the shares – it cannot act as both buyer and seller.
- If the business disposal involves a regulated company,[20] it will also be subject to certain takeover provisions in the Act (unless the disposal is part of a business rescue plan).[21]
- In terms of s 115(2)(b), a disposal will also require the approval of the shareholders of the selling company's holding company if the disposal substantially constitutes a disposal of all or the greater part of the assets or undertaking of that holding company.[22]

10.3.2   Regulation of mergers or amalgamations

The three key stages of the amalgamation or merger procedure are:

1. the merger agreement;
2. the shareholder approval process; and
3. the implementation of the merger.[23]

---

18   Sections 112(2) and 115 of the Companies Act, 2008.
19   See chapter 7 of this book for a discussion of financial reporting standards.
20   See para. 10.1 above for the definition of a regulated company.
21   Section 118(3) of the Companies Act, 2008.
22   This transaction would not be exempted from having to comply with the provisions of s 112, read with s 115, as it is not undertaken within the context of a group of companies. In other words, the person to whom the disposal is effected is neither the subsidiary nor the holding company of the disposing entity.
23   A detailed analysis of these three key stages is provided by Davids, Norwitz and Yuill supra at 343–55. See also MF Cassim (Part I) supra at 6–18.

10.3.2.1 The amalgamation or merger agreement

Section 113(2) of the Companies Act, 2008 states that two or more companies proposing to merge must enter into a written agreement setting out the terms and means of effecting the merger. The section further prescribes minimum particulars to be included in the agreement. These particulars include the following:

- the MOI of any new company that is to be formed during the merger process;
- the proposed directors of the merged entity or entities;
- to the extent that shares in the merging companies are to be converted into shares in the merged entity, the manner in which such conversion will be effected;
- to the extent that the shareholders in those of the merging companies that will not survive the merger will receive consideration other than shares in the new merged entity (or shares in another entity), the nature and manner of payment of such consideration;
- the manner in which the assets and liabilities of the merging companies will be allocated to the merged entities (if there is more than one);
- details of any arrangement or strategy necessary to complete the transaction and to provide for the subsequent management and operation of the proposed merged or amalgamated company; and
- the estimated cost of the transaction.

PRACTICAL ISSUE	**Structures and transactions in terms of the merger rules**
	The Companies Act, 2008 creates scope for a variety of mergers and amalgamations to take place. As observed by Davids, Norwitz and Yuill:

> [T]he new Act appears to place very little limitation on the substance of the agreement, and it is clear that companies will have considerable latitude to structure the merger transaction in a manner that best meets their requirements .... This would include the possibility of shareholders of the merging entities receiving shares in an entity other than the merged entity (such as, for example, the holding company of the merged entity) as consideration.[24] This would facilitate transactions structured in different ways to meet the parties' specific objectives. For example, the buyer (B) could acquire the target (T) through a 'reverse triangular merger' in which B creates a merger subsidiary (S) that merges into T, with T surviving the merger as a wholly owned subsidiary of B, and T's shareholders receiving shares in B. Benefits of this structure include the ability to interpose a corporate veil to shield B from liabilities at T, and the ability, because T survives the merger, to avoid triggering approval rights in T's contracts and franchises. For these reasons, the reverse triangular merger is by far the most common structure used in M&A in the United States and has recently been approved for cross-border mergers in Japan.[25]

---

24 Section 113(2)*(e)* of the Companies Act, 2008 states that the merger agreement should specify the manner of payment of any consideration instead of the issue of fractional securities of an amalgamated or merged company or of any other juristic person the securities of which are to be received in the amalgamation or merger; Although not particularly clearly worded, this would appear to contemplate that consideration could include shares in an entity other than the merged entity. See also MF Cassim (Part I) supra at 26–8 and (Part II) supra at 148.

25 Davids, Norwitz and Yuill supra at 344. See also MF Cassim (Part II) supra at 147–8.

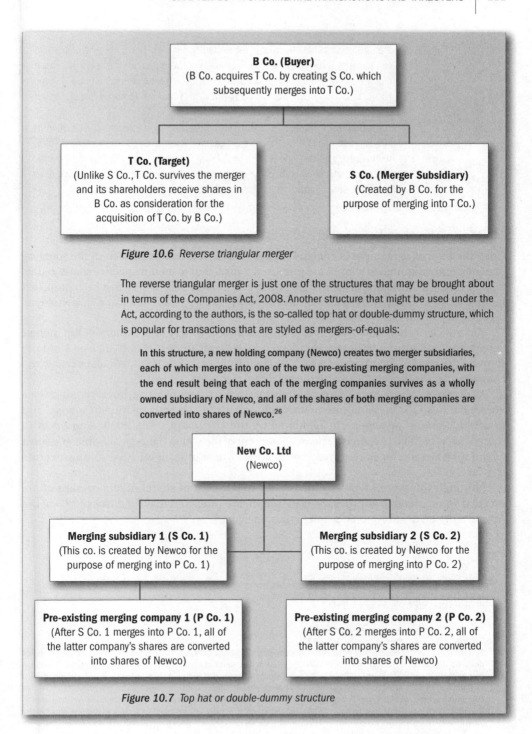

B Co. (Buyer)
(B Co. acquires T Co. by creating S Co. which subsequently merges into T Co.)

T Co. (Target)
(Unlike S Co., T Co. survives the merger and its shareholders receive shares in B Co. as consideration for the acquisition of T Co. by B Co.)

S Co. (Merger Subsidiary)
(Created by B Co. for the purpose of merging into T Co.)

Figure 10.6 Reverse triangular merger

The reverse triangular merger is just one of the structures that may be brought about in terms of the Companies Act, 2008. Another structure that might be used under the Act, according to the authors, is the so-called top hat or double-dummy structure, which is popular for transactions that are styled as mergers-of-equals:

> In this structure, a new holding company (Newco) creates two merger subsidiaries, each of which merges into one of the two pre-existing merging companies, with the end result being that each of the merging companies survives as a wholly owned subsidiary of Newco, and all of the shares of both merging companies are converted into shares of Newco.[26]

New Co. Ltd
(Newco)

Merging subsidiary 1 (S Co. 1)
(This co. is created by Newco for the purpose of merging into P Co. 1)

Merging subsidiary 2 (S Co. 2)
(This co. is created by Newco for the purpose of merging into P Co. 2)

Pre-existing merging company 1 (P Co. 1)
(After S Co. 1 merges into P Co. 1, all of the latter company's shares are converted into shares of Newco)

Pre-existing merging company 2 (P Co. 2)
(After S Co. 2 merges into P Co. 2, all of the latter company's shares are converted into shares of Newco)

Figure 10.7 Top hat or double-dummy structure

---

26   *Ibid* at 345.

Examples of the top-hat structure in the United States include the mergers of America Online, Inc. and Time Warner Inc. to form AOL Time Warner, and of Phillips Petroleum Company and Conoco, Inc. to form Conoco-Phillips. In that country, there are in some cases tax reasons to use this structure, but it also has the cosmetic benefit of not having one company appear to acquire the other.

The flexibility of the merger form is also illustrated by the recent combination of pharmaceutical companies Merck and Schering Plough, which was structured as a reverse merger, with the smaller Schering Plough technically buying the much larger Merck (and then changing its name to Merck) to address what might otherwise have been a significant contractual impediment.[27]

10.3.2.2 The shareholder approval process

Once the merger agreement is concluded, the boards of directors of each of the merging companies are required to submit the proposed transaction to their respective shareholders for approval.[28] If the boards of the merging companies reasonably believe that each proposed merged entity will satisfy the solvency and liquidity test, they can then call a shareholders' meeting to consider the transaction.

The notice of shareholders' meeting must include[29] a copy or summary of the merger agreement, and must advise shareholders of their rights under s 115 (which sets out the shareholder approval requirements and the circumstances when recourse can be had to the courts) and s 164 (which deals with the appraisal rights procedure).[30]

As discussed above in the context of disposals, the shareholder approval requirements are set out in s 115. These requirements apply equally to an amalgamation or merger, and to any scheme of arrangement regulated by the Companies Act, 2008. A quorum of shareholders entitled to exercise at least 25 per cent of the voting rights exercisable in respect of the relevant matter is required, and a special resolution is needed to approve the transaction.[31]

Although this would typically mean that 75 per cent of shareholders present at the meeting would need to approve the transaction, the threshold may, in terms of s 65 of the Act, be reduced to as low as 60 per cent plus one vote.[32]

---

27 See Davids, Norwitz and Yuill supra at 345 in footnote 11.
28 Section 115 of the Companies Act, 2008.
29 Section 113(5) of the Companies Act, 2008.
30 See para. 10.4 below for more on appraisal rights.
31 Section 115(2)(a) of the Companies Act, 2008.
32 Section 65(10) of the Companies Act, 2008. The company's MOI must make provision for this, however, and it seems doubtful that reduced thresholds will be common in practice, particularly in the case of listed companies. For listed companies, shareholders are unlikely to be particularly in favour of reduced thresholds (given the possibility of exploitation of the minority by controlling and/or large shareholders) and may therefore be less willing to invest in companies where such thresholds have been provided for in the MOI or to vote in favour of any such amendments to the MOI. Even if possible, given that retail shareholders are generally uninterested in technical matters such as the amendment of a company's constitutional documents, it may not be worth it for a significant shareholder to push such amendments through, as it could create an unintended embedded discount in the shares of the relevant company. Significant institutional investors may also put pressure on companies in this regard. In the context of a private company, a controlling shareholder would, to the extent that it is not already provided for in the MOI, need a 75 per cent majority to amend the MOI, in which case there would be little incentive for them to reduce the threshold.

10.3.2.3   The implementation of the amalgamation or merger

The final step the parties to a merger or amalgamation must take before implementation of the merger is to notify every known creditor of each of the merging companies of the merger.[33] Any creditor that believes it will be materially prejudiced by the merger is entitled to apply to court, within 15 business days of being notified, for a review of the transaction. The court must be satisfied: that the creditor is acting in good faith; that it would be materially prejudiced by the merger; and that there are no other remedies available to it.[34] The section is silent on when the merger or amalgamation will be set aside as a result of the creditor's objection in terms of s 116(1)(c). If no creditors object to the transaction within the requisite period, the parties may proceed with the implementation of the merger.

A notice of merger must be filed with the Companies Commission. The notice should confirm that the requirements of the Act have been satisfied and that any required regulatory approvals (such as competition approval) have been obtained, and should enclose the MOIs of any new merged entities that are to be incorporated.[35] On receipt of such a notice, the Commission will proceed to issue a registration certificate for each new company that is to be incorporated, and will deregister each of the merging companies that is not intended to survive the transaction.[36]

The amalgamation or merger then takes place in accordance with the terms and conditions of the agreement.[37]

To the extent that any shares in a merging entity are held by or on behalf of another merging entity, the Companies Act, 2008 provides that these must be cancelled upon the merger becoming effective without any repayment of capital. Such shares may also not be converted into shares in the merged entity.[38] This is to prevent the merged entity from, effectively, holding shares in itself, and to prevent an effective reduction of capital.[39]

Section 116(6)(b) provides that the merger will not affect any existing liability of any merging party or its directors to be prosecuted under any law, and provides that any legal proceedings against the merging entities may be continued against the merged entity or entities and any court order or judgment against the merging entities may be enforced against the merged entity or entities.

Most importantly, on the implementation of the merger, all of the assets and liabilities of the merging companies are transferred, by operation of law, to the merged company or companies. This is a key advantage of the merger procedure. Companies can avoid the costs and legal formalities normally required for the transfer of a business from one entity to another, as well as the length of time it takes to transfer things such as immovable and intellectual property.

Section 116(7)(a) provides that the property of each merging company becomes the property of the merged company or companies. In accordance with s 116(8), any property that is registered in a public registry[40] can automatically be registered in the name of the relevant merged entity upon presentation of the merger agreement and the filed notice of merger. Although property is not specifically defined, this would presumably include both corporeal and incorporeal property.

---

33   Section 116(1) of the Companies Act, 2008.
34   Section 116(1)(c) of the Companies Act, 2008.
35   Section 116(4) of the Companies Act, 2008.
36   Section 116(5) of the Companies Act, 2008.
37   Section 116(6)(a) of the Companies Act, 2008.
38   Section 113(3) of the Companies Act, 2008.
39   Davids, Norwitz and Yuill supra at 349. See also MF Cassim (Part I) supra at 25.
40   For example, immovable property registered in the deeds registry or motor vehicles listed in a public registry.

10.3.3 Regulation of schemes of arrangement

The regulation of schemes of arrangement is covered primarily in s 114, read with ss 115 and 164 of the Companies Act, 2008. Briefly, the Act provides that a company's board may propose and (subject to obtaining the requisite approvals) may implement any arrangement between the company and the holders of any class of its securities (provided that the company is neither in liquidation nor in the course of business rescue proceedings).[41] The arrangement can be about anything on which the company and its members can properly agree, including a share-for-share exchange or a share repurchase.

To effect a scheme of arrangement, the company (or in a takeover, the offeror) must employ the services of a qualified, impartial, independent expert to prepare a report about the proposed arrangement for the board. The report must be distributed to all holders of the company's securities.[42] The report must, among other things, identify the categories of shareholder that are affected by the proposed arrangement and must describe the material effects (and evaluate any material adverse effects).[43]

Schemes of arrangement between a regulated company and its shareholders will (unless it is pursuant to a business rescue plan) also be subject to certain takeover provisions of the Act.[44]

As with any other fundamental transaction regulated in Part A of Chapter 5 of the Companies Act, 2008, a scheme of arrangement must be approved by a special resolution of shareholders of the company proposing the scheme of arrangement at a meeting at which sufficient persons are present to exercise, in aggregate, at least 25 per cent of all of the voting rights that are entitled to be exercised on the matter.[45]

10.3.4 Opposition to fundamental transactions: dissenting shareholders

An entirely new concept is introduced in s 115 of the Companies Act, 2008, in terms of which **dissenting shareholders** are empowered to approach the courts to set aside a share-holders' resolution in favour of a fundamental transaction. Even where the resolution was passed by the requisite majority, the section provides that if at least 15 per cent of the voting rights that were exercised on that resolution were opposed to the resolution, any person who voted against the resolution may require the company to seek court approval for the transaction, in which event the resolution may not be implemented until such approval is obtained.[46]

Furthermore, even if less than 15 per cent of the shareholders voted against the resolution, any person may approach the court for leave to apply to court for a review of the transaction.

In order to minimise disruptions of corporate fundamental transactions and constant second-guessing of corporate decisions, s 115(6) provides that leave to apply may only be granted if the court is satisfied that the applicant is acting in good faith, appears prepared and able to sustain the proceedings and has a *prima facie* case. A company may not implement a transaction that is subject to a pending legal application.

---

41 See s 114(1) of the Companies Act, 2008.
42 Section 114(2)*(a)* of the Companies Act, 2008.
43 For the details of the minimum particulars of the report, see s 114(3) of the Companies Act, 2008.
44 See Parts A and B of Chapter 5 of the Companies Act, 2008.
45 See s 115(1) and (2)*(a)* of the Companies Act, 2008.
46 Section 115(3) of the Companies Act, 2008.

A court may set aside the resolution if:[47]

- the resolution is manifestly unfair to any class of shareholder; or
- the vote was materially tainted by a conflict of interest, inadequate disclosure, failure to comply with the Act, the MOI or any applicable rules of the company, or any other significant and material procedural irregularity.

It is important to note that the rights that shareholders have under s 115 to request a court review of the transaction in certain circumstances is in addition to their appraisal rights in terms of s 164.

10.4   Appraisal remedy[48]

The Companies Act, 2008 has introduced a new and fundamental concept into the regulation of mergers and acquisitions, and other fundamental transactions, in South Africa in the form of an **appraisal remedy**. The remedy was inspired by a similar protection provided in American corporate law[49] and effectively grants dissatisfied shareholders the right to tender or present their shares to the company in the event of certain transactions being undertaken by the company. If the shareholders disagree with these transactions, they are entitled to require the company to acquire their shares at fair value.

Appraisal rights essentially amount to a put option[50] by minority shareholders in respect of their shares against the company on the happening of certain events, including the passing of a resolution to approve a fundamental transaction.

The appraisal remedy applies not only in the context of a merger transaction, but also in a scheme of arrangement, a disposal of the greater part of the company's assets or undertaking and any change to the MOI that may materially affect the rights of the relevant shareholders.[51] The appraisal remedy in s 164 provides shareholders both with a means of exit, and, in the context of a scheme of arrangement or merger, with a means of challenging the adequacy of the consideration (payment) that they have received for their shares.

There are a number of procedural steps that a shareholder wishing to exercise its appraisal rights must follow. These are as follows:

- The shareholder must send a written notice of objection to the resolution proposing the merger at any time prior to the shareholders' meeting.[52]
- The shareholder must vote against the resolution at the shareholders' meeting.[53]
- If the resolution is passed, the company must advise dissenting shareholders accordingly, and they then have 20 days to demand, should they so wish, that the company pays them fair value for their shares.[54] Once such a demand is made, a dissenting shareholder has no further rights in respect of those shares other than the right to receive fair value for the shares.[55]

---

47   Section 115(7) of the Companies Act, 2008.
48   See also para. 14.3.2 below.
49   The American remedy has not been adopted wholesale, but has been tailored to the South African context. For example, the Act does not adopt the Delaware 'market out', which provides that appraisal rights are not available if target company shareholders are receiving only publicly traded stock in consideration for their shares.
50   A put option gives the holder of a share the right (but not the obligation) to sell that share.
51   See s 164(2) of the Companies Act, 2008.
52   Section 164(3) of the Companies Act, 2008.
53   Section 164(5)*(c)* of the Companies Act, 2008.
54   Section 164(7) of the Companies Act, 2008.
55   Section 164(9) of the Companies Act, 2008.

- The company is then required to make an offer to dissenting shareholders to acquire their shares at what the board deems is fair value.[56] If any shareholder accepts, they tender their shares, which are then acquired by the company, and that is the end of the matter.[57]
- If the company fails to make an offer or makes an offer that any shareholder does not believe is adequate, affected shareholders are entitled to apply to court to have the fair value determined by the court.[58] The time at which the fair value is required to be determined is the time immediately before the relevant resolution was adopted.[59]
- The court will then decide the matter and make an order as to what constitutes fair value for the shares.[60] The court is further required in terms of s 164(15)(c)(v) to make an order requiring the dissenting shareholders to either withdraw their respective demands, in which case the shareholder is reinstated to their full rights as a shareholder, or to comply with subsection 13(a) (and tender their shares to the company), in which case the company must pay the shareholder the fair value for its shares, as determined by the court.

Given the otherwise limited involvement of the courts in fundamental transactions, the appraisal rights mechanism provides an important potential safeguard for minority shareholders.

10.5 Affected transactions and the role of the Takeover Regulation Panel

A transaction is referred to as an affected transaction to signify that the Takeover Regulation Panel has jurisdiction over such a transaction.[61] As noted above, a fundamental transaction will fit the description of an affected transaction only if the company is a regulated company. The **Takeover Regulation Panel** is a regulatory institution established in terms of s 196(1) of the Companies Act, 2008. Its main purpose is to regulate affected transactions in the manner required by Chapter 5 of the 2008 Act and the Takeover Regulations. Briefly, the **Takeover Regulations** are rules that regulate affected transactions, and are issued by the Minister of Trade and Industry after consultation with the Takeover Regulation Panel.[62]

Under the Companies Act, 1973, these rules were referred to as the Takeover Rules and were issued by the Securities Regulations Panel (the predecessor of the Takeover Regulation Panel). Under the 1973 Act, the rules did not enjoy legislative status, as they did not constitute secondary legislation, which the Takeover Regulations now do in terms of the 2008 Act.

The promotion of the Takeover Rules under the 1973 Act to Takeover Regulations under the 2008 Act is a most important and fundamental change. The Takeover Regulations now

---

56 Section 164(11) of the Companies Act, 2008.
57 Section 164(13) of the Companies Act, 2008.
58 Section 164(14) of the Companies Act, 2008.
59 Section 164(16) of the Companies Act, 2008.
60 Section 164(15)(c)(ii) of the Companies Act, 2008. It is notable that in most US states, including Delaware, the appraised value is specified as the fair value of the shares on a going-concern basis without giving effect to the contemplated transaction (so that the shareholder asserting appraisal rights is not entitled to the control premium inherent in a takeover price, but may receive more or less than the deal price). Section 164 does not specify this, but the courts are likely at some point to have to respond to this question in determining what is meant by fair value.
61 See the explanation of an affected transaction in para. 10.1 above.
62 See s 120 of the Companies Act, 2008.

have statutory backing, but without the rigidity that would have resulted if all the Rules had been incorporated into the primary statute (the Companies Act, 2008). Regulations are a more flexible legislative instrument than statutes, as they are issued by the Minister of Trade and Industry, without requiring the cumbersome and time-consuming legislative procedure that would have been mandatory had the rules been enacted in a statute.

CONTEXTUAL ISSUE	**The significance of the Takeover Regulation Panel**
	The significance of the Takeover Regulation Panel (or its predecessor, the Securities Regulation Panel) cannot be disputed. In 2008:

> [T]he 58 affected transactions regulated by the Panel in that year ... had an aggregate value of approximately R55 billion compared with 64 affected transactions having an aggregate value in excess of R80 billion in the prior year.[63]

> Nevertheless, what needs to be clarified at the outset is that not all mergers and acquisitions regulated in Chapter 5 of the Act are subject to the regulation of the Takeover Regulation Panel. In fact, if a transaction does not involve a regulated company, as defined, it falls outside the jurisdiction of the Takeover Regulation Panel.[64]

The Takeover Regulation Panel must regulate any affected transaction or offer without regard to the commercial advantages or disadvantages of any transaction or proposed transaction. The purposes of the Panel's regulation are as follows:

- to ensure the integrity of the marketplace and fairness to the holders of the securities of regulated companies;
- to ensure the provision of necessary information to holders of securities of regulated companies, to the extent required to facilitate the making of fair and informed decisions;
- to ensure the provision of adequate time for regulated companies and holders of their securities to obtain and provide advice with respect to offers; and
- to prevent actions by a regulated company that are designed to impede, frustrate, or defeat an offer, or the making of fair and informed decisions by the holders of that company's securities.[65]

In carrying out its mandate, the Takeover Regulation Panel may:

- require the filing, for approval or otherwise, of any document with respect to an affected transaction or offer, if the document is required to be prepared in terms of Chapter 5 of the 2008 Act and the Takeover Regulations;
- issue clearance notices, if the Panel is satisfied that the offer or transaction satisfies the requirements of Chapter 5 and the Takeover Regulations; and
- initiate or receive complaints, conduct investigations, and issue compliance notices, with respect to any affected transaction or offer, in accordance with Chapter 7, and the Takeover Regulations.[66]

---

63   Annual Financial Statements of the Securities Regulation Panel dated 28 February 2009, at 7.
64   See para. 10.1 above.
65   Section 119(1) of the Companies Act, 2008.
66   Section 119(4) of the Companies Act, 2008.

A **compliance order** or notice issued by the Panel may, among other things:
- prohibit or require any action by a person; or
- order a person to
  - divest of an acquired asset; or
  - account for profits.[67]

The most common types of affected transaction (other than fundamental transactions involving regulated companies) are mandatory offers and compulsory acquisitions or squeeze-out transactions. These are discussed below.

10.5.1 Mandatory offers

A **mandatory offer** refers to a transaction where one or more persons who are related or inter-related or who are acting in concert attain a prescribed percentage of all voting securities in the company (currently being not less than 35 per cent). Upon attaining such a prescribed percentage, such person or persons will be required by law to make an offer to acquire any remaining securities on terms determined in accordance with the Companies Act, 2008 and the Takeover Regulations. One of the reasons for such a mandatory offer is to ensure that all shareholders are treated equally and that control of a company cannot simply occur by offers being made to controlling shareholders at a premium, while minority shareholders are ignored.

A mandatory offer is triggered if either:
- a regulated company re-acquires any of its voting securities (a buy-back of securities by the company); or
- a person acting alone has (or persons related, inter-related or acting in concert have) acquired a beneficial interest in any voting securities that enables them to exercise at least the prescribed percentage of all the voting rights attached to securities of that company.[68]

The need to make a mandatory offer happens automatically upon the trigger event, which is the attainment of the threshold (the prescribed percentage). Within one day after the date of a completed mandatory offer, the person or persons in whom the prescribed percentage (or more) of the voting securities beneficially vests must give notice in the prescribed manner to the holders of the remaining securities. The notice must include:
- a statement that they are in a position to exercise at least the prescribed percentage of all the voting rights attached to securities of that regulated company; and
- an offer to acquire any remaining such securities on terms determined in accordance with the Companies Act, 2008 and the Takeover Regulations.[69]

Within one month after giving notice, the issuers of the notice must deliver a written offer (this is the mandatory offer) in compliance with the Takeover Regulations, to the holders of the remaining securities of that company, to acquire those securities.[70]

---

67 Section 119(5) of the Companies Act, 2008.
68 Section 123(2) of the Companies Act, 2008.
69 Section 123(3) of the Companies Act, 2008.
70 Section 123(4) of the Companies Act, 2008.

10.5.2   Compulsory acquisitions and squeeze-out transactions

Another important affected transaction is commonly known as a **squeeze-out**. This is a transaction where a person or offeror attains 90 per cent of any class of securities in a company. If, within four months from the date of an offer for the acquisition of any class of securities of a regulated company, that offer has been accepted by the holders of at least 90 per cent of that class of securities, the offeror may notify the holders of the remaining securities of the class:

- that the offer has been accepted to that extent; and
- that the offeror desires to acquire all remaining securities of that class.[71]

After giving notice, the offeror is entitled, and bound, to acquire the securities concerned on the same terms that applied to securities whose holders accepted the original offer.[72] This ensures fairness to all shareholders.

Within 30 business days from receiving a notice, a holder of the remaining securities may apply to a court for an order:

- that the offeror is not entitled to acquire the applicant's securities of that class; or
- imposing conditions of acquisition different from those of the original offer.[73]

10.6   Impact of the 2008 Act on corporate restructuring in South Africa

The Companies Act, 2008 has consciously positioned itself to put South Africa and its regulation of corporate restructuring transactions on a par with those of the developed world.[74]

The introduction of a self-standing amalgamation or merger provision in s 113[75] is a clear acknowledgment that business combinations are appropriate for a healthy economy and should be encouraged beyond court-driven schemes of arrangement. Such schemes have, in the past, placed a large emphasis on share exchange rather than agreement-driven business combinations. In contrast, the new scheme for regulating fundamental transactions, takeovers and offers, as enacted in Chapter 5 of the Act, is underpinned by an acknowledgment that the existence of a market for corporate control should be the trigger for business combinations and takeovers.

Explained in simple terms, the market for corporate control refers to the availability of companies that may be targeted for change in management or control (because available corporate resources are not being optimally deployed to derive maximum benefits). In a jurisdiction where there is an active market for corporate control, corporate directors and managers are forced constantly to look over their shoulders, as the threat of a change in corporate control is too great to ignore. This potential threat, in turn, forces incumbent corporate directors and managers to be agile and ensures that available corporate resources are optimally used to benefit the company and its shareholders.

---

71   Section 124(1)*(a)* of the Companies Act, 2008.
72   Section 124(1)*(b)* of the Companies Act, 2008.
73   Section 124(2) of the Companies Act, 2008.
74   According to N Boardman, '...the practical effect of the new Act will be not altogether dissimilar to the laws in the UK, the USA and Australia ...'. Quoted in T Mongalo (ed.) supra at 319.
75   Read with ss 115 and 116 of the Companies Act, 2008.

The 2008 Act allows for an active market for corporate control by providing for a bouquet of measures to enable change of control. These measures are conveniently located in Chapter 5 of the Act, which is entitled 'Fundamental Transactions, Takeovers and Offers.'

PRACTICAL ISSUE	The market for corporate control
	In 2010, the financial press reported on the under-performance of Liberty Holdings Ltd in relation to its peers and this raised questions of whether a change of control of the company could be looming. In the Sunday Times report of 16 May 2010, Liberty Holdings was referred to as South Africa's worst-performing life insurance company, although it paid out R5.1 million in bonuses to three executives in a year in which earnings plummeted 91 per cent. The observation was made that Liberty did not fare well in comparison to rivals operating under the same difficult circumstances. The report observed that while Liberty's share price rose by 10 per cent during 2009, Old Mutual's shares gained 73 per cent in the same time, Sanlam's climbed 33 per cent, Discovery's rose 23 per cent and Metropolitan's gained 24 per cent.
	It is circumstances like these that may expose a company in Liberty's position to some form of change of control. A potential prospective controller may identify some value in the company that is not being optimally used by the current managers and controllers.[76]

THIS CHAPTER IN ESSENCE

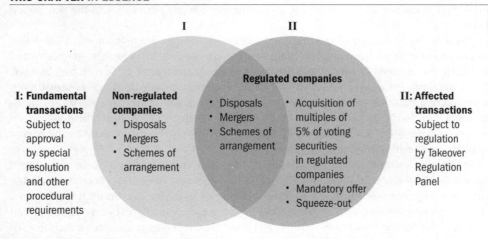

Figure 10.8 *Summary of the regulation of fundamental and affected transactions*

1. **Fundamental transactions** fundamentally alter a company and must comply with certain targeted provisions of the Companies Act, 2008. Fundamental transactions fall into three categories:
   • disposals of the majority of a company's assets or undertaking;
   • mergers or amalgamations; and
   • schemes of arrangement.

---

76   See Rob Rose 'Liberty bonuses queried' *Sunday Times Business Times*, 16 May 2010, at 4.

2. If a fundamental transaction is also an affected transaction, the Takeover Regulation Panel will have jurisdiction over the transaction as well. A fundamental transaction will fit the description of an affected transaction only if the company is a **regulated company**. A company is a regulated company if it is:
   - a public company;
   - a state-owned enterprise (unless exempted); or
   - a private company, but only if more than the prescribed percentage of its issued securities has been transferred in the previous 24 months, or the company's MOI expressly provides for it to be treated as a regulated company.

3. An **affected transaction** is either:
   - a fundamental transaction involving a regulated company;
   - an acquisition of multiples of five percentages in voting securities;
   - a mandatory offer; or
   - a compulsory acquisition (so-called squeeze-out transaction).

4. A **disposal of the majority of a company's assets or undertaking** is a fundamental transaction and must be approved by special resolution of the shareholders. It may also need to satisfy certain other procedural requirements, depending on the particular disposal. Disposals that form part of a business rescue plan, or that are transfers between companies in the same group of companies, do not need to comply with the requirements of the Companies Act, 2008 for significant disposals.

5. **Amalgamations** (or **mergers**) are fundamental transactions involving the merging, in terms of an agreement, of two or more companies into one or more. They either result in the survival of one or more of the merging or amalgamating companies, or the formation of one or more new companies, or a combination of the two. The surviving or new company or companies then together hold all of the assets and liabilities previously held by the several merging or amalgamating companies.

   The Companies Act, 2008 prescribes the minimum particulars to be included in a merger agreement, which must be in writing. The boards of directors of the respective companies must satisfy themselves that the proposed merged entity will pass the solvency and liquidity test and must then submit the proposed transaction to the shareholders for approval. A special resolution is required to approve the transaction. Every known creditor of each of the merging companies must be notified of the proposed merger and may review the transaction in court if it believes it will suffer material prejudice. A prescribed notice of merger must be filed with the Companies Commission.

6. Schemes of arrangement are also fundamental transactions and are a flexible tool often used for compulsory takeovers, and also to simplify administration of share capital or to incentivise shareholders in various ways. A **scheme of arrangement** is any arrangement or agreement proposed by the board of directors and entered into between the company and holders of any class of its securities, including a reorganisation of the share capital of the company, including:
   - a consolidation of securities of different classes;
   - a division of securities into different classes;
   - an expropriation of securities from the holders;
   - an exchange of any of its securities for other securities;
   - a re-acquisition by the company of its securities; or
   - a combination of the above methods.

The Companies Act, 2008 requires that a company's board may propose and implement a scheme of arrangement, provided that the company is neither in liquidation nor in the course of business rescue proceedings. The company (or in a takeover, the offeror) must commission a qualified, impartial, independent expert to prepare a report about the proposed arrangement for the board and this report must be distributed to all shareholders. As with other fundamental transactions, a scheme of arrangement must be approved by special resolution.

7. The Companies Act, 2008 empowers **dissenting shareholders** to approach the courts to set aside a shareholders' resolution in favour of a fundamental transaction. If at least 15 per cent of the exercised voting rights were opposed to the resolution, any person who voted against the resolution may require the company to seek court approval for the transaction. Even if less than 15 per cent of shareholders voted against the resolution, any person may approach the court for leave to apply to court for a review of the transaction. Leave to apply may only be granted if the court is satisfied that the applicant is acting in good faith, appears prepared and able to sustain the proceedings and has a *prima facie* case. A company may not implement a transaction that is subject to a pending legal application. A court may set aside the resolution if the resolution is manifestly unfair to any class of shareholder or if the vote was materially tainted by some significant and material procedural irregularity.

8. In addition to the dissenting shareholders' remedy, the Companies Act, 2008 provides for an **appraisal remedy**, which is the right of dissatisfied shareholders to tender their shares to the company in the event of certain transactions being undertaken by the company. If the shareholders voted against these transactions and indicated their intention to seek the appraisal remedy, they are entitled to require the company to acquire their shares at fair value. The appraisal remedy applies in the context of a merger transaction, a scheme of arrangement, a disposal of the greater part of the company's assets or undertaking and any change to the MOI that may materially affect the rights of the relevant shareholders.

9. The **Takeover Regulation Panel**'s main purpose is to regulate all affected transactions according to the Companies Act, 2008 and the **Takeover Regulations**. The aim is to ensure the integrity of the marketplace and generally to protect shareholders of regulated companies from unfair conduct.

10. A **mandatory offer** is an affected transaction and is a transaction where a regulated company buys back its own securities or where one or more persons who are related or inter-related or are acting in concert attain a prescribed percentage of all voting securities in the company (currently not less than 35 per cent). The company or such person/s are then required to make an offer to acquire any remaining securities on prescribed terms.

11. A **compulsory acquisition** (**squeeze-out**) is an affected transaction and occurs where a person or offeror attains 90 per cent of any class of securities in a company. The offeror may then notify the holders of the remaining securities of the class that it desires to acquire all remaining securities of that class and the offeror is then entitled and bound to acquire the securities concerned on the same terms that applied to securities whose holders accepted the original offer. A holder of remaining securities may apply to a court for relief.

Chapter 11

Insider trading

11.1 Introduction to insider trading

Insider trading is the trading of securities based on information that is not public. It is a form of market abuse and is illegal in many jurisdictions. It is therefore an offence to commit insider trading. Insider trading regulation is aimed at making markets transparent.

The basic hypothesis is that markets do not function efficiently when information concerning goods and services being traded in a particular market is subject to an asymmetry of information between participants in that market. Put differently, if such a state of affairs exists in relation to a market (on the assumption that all market participants have equal access to publicly available information), it is unfair to a market participant who does not have the same information as another market participant. Insider trading regulations are therefore intended to improve the efficiency, competitiveness, fairness and transparency of financial markets.

PRACTICAL ISSUE	**Examples of insider trading**
	1. Consider the case of a managing director (MD) of a public company that is listed on the Johannesburg Stock Exchange (JSE), and which is involved in mining activities. The MD receives a report from a consulting engineer that the new discovery of mineral deposits is of a disappointing quality. The MD knows that when this

information is made public the company's share price is likely to fall significantly. The MD therefore instructs his stockbroker to sell 50 per cent of his own personal shareholding in the company with immediate effect. By doing so, the MD avoids a massive loss because once the news is made public, the share price declined sharply.

The MD managed to avoid a loss because he made use of inside information that was not available to the public. This example is a typical case of insider trading.

2. In *S v Western Areas Ltd*,[1] the accused were jointly charged with the offence of insider trading. The accused had purchased shares in Randfontein Estates Ltd in the knowledge that an offer for the acquisition of the entire share capital of Randfontein Estates Ltd by Western Areas Ltd for a specific price was forthcoming. The accused therefore purchased the shares knowing that they would be able to sell them at a fixed profit.

The accused were found guilty of insider trading, and it was held that the defences under the now-repealed Securities Services Act[2] (SSA) were unavailable to them as they had committed fraudulent misrepresentation through failing to make certain disclosures required under the rules of the Securities Regulation Panel and the Companies Act.[3] Although this decision was made in relation to the SSA, it is nonetheless instructive.

South African legislation has for the past few decades provided a legal framework to prohibit insider trading. The Companies Act, 1973 originally dealt with the interests of and dealings by directors and others in the shares of the company.[4] These provisions proved to be ineffective and were repealed when the Securities Regulation Panel was established.[5] Section 440 of the 1973 Act also imposed criminal and civil actions for insider trading. The Insider Trading Act[6] was introduced in 1998 to deal with the regulation of insider trading. However, this Act was replaced six years later by the insider trading provisions in the SSA.

After 2004, the regulation of market abuses through insider trading was governed by the SSA, which came into operation on 1 February 2005. The SSA replaced the Stock Exchanges Control Act,[7] the Financial Markets Control Act,[8] the Custody and Administration of Securities Act,[9] and the Insider Trading Act.[10]

The Financial Markets Act[11] (FMA), which came into operation on 3 June 2012, repealed and replaced the SSA in its entirety. The FMA has amended, among other things, the offences of insider trading and the available defences.

---

1 [2006] JOL 16679 (W).
2 36 of 2004.
3 See R Itzkin & A Tregoning (Bell Dewar Inc) 'The insider trading regime in South Africa' *www.executiveview.com/ knowledge_centre.php?id=10499* 2 October 2009.
4 Sections 224 and 229–33 of the Companies Act, 1973.
5 These sections were repealed by s 6 of the Companies Amendment Act 78 of 1989.
6 135 of 1998.
7 1 of 1985.
8 55 of 1989.
9 85 of 1992.
10 135 of 1998.
11 19 of 2012.

11.2   Insider trading and the Financial Markets Act

The insider trading provisions of the FMA are contained in Chapter X (ss 77 to 88). Chapter X deals with both insider trading and market abuse. Market abuse is a prohibited practice in terms of which persons attempt to create a false or deceptive market in securities, and includes the manipulation of the price of the securities in question.

The responsible regulator for insider trading is the Directorate of Market Abuse,[12] a division of the Financial Services Board.[13]

The provisions of Chapter X are self-contained in so far as the chapter deals with almost all issues related to insider trading and market abuse, including defining the issues, defences and sanctions. Of course, Chapter X must be read within the context of the FMA as a whole as the general provisions of the FMA also apply to Chapter X.

Section 78 of the FMA provides that an insider who knows that he or she has inside information and, who deals, directly or indirectly or through an agent for his or her own account, or for any other person, in the securities listed on a regulated market to which the inside information relates, or which are likely to be affected by it, commits an offence.

11.2.1   The definition of an insider and of inside information

There is no definition of insider trading in s 1 of the FMA. However, the terms 'inside information' and 'insider' form the core of the insider trading provisions and these are defined in the provisions of Chapter X on market abuse.

The definition of an **insider** is crucial to establishing the rules regulating insider trading.[14] The FMA provides that an insider is a person who has inside information:

- through being a director, employee or shareholder of an issuer of securities listed on a **regulated market** to which the inside information relates; or
- through having access to such information by virtue of employment, office or profession; or
- where such person knows that the direct or indirect source of the information was a person contemplated above.

Insiders may include the directors of the company, employees of the company, shareholders of the company, professional persons and advisers (such as management consultants, bankers, auditors or legal advisers) who provide services to the company or are associated with the company, and also any person who receives inside information, knowing it is sourced from any of the abovementioned persons.

Chapter X of the FMA defines a person as including 'a partnership and any trust'.[15] 'Person' is not elsewhere defined but is historically understood to include companies.[16]

Inside information means specific or precise information that has not been made public and which:

- is obtained or learned as an insider; and
- if it were made public, would be likely to have a material effect on the price or value of any security listed on a regulated market.

---

12   See s 85 of the FMA.
13   See para. 11.2.2 below for more detail.
14   See s 77 of the FMA.
15   See s 77 of the FMA.
16   Including under the SSA.

The core of the insider-trading concept is the fiduciary relationship between the insider and the company.

PRACTICAL	**Who is an insider?**
ISSUE	The potential for persons to become insiders is great. For example, a legal adviser is asked for an opinion. In the brief provided to her, she gains access to significant confidential information. The legal adviser is therefore now an insider. Similarly, while working on the preparation of a company's financial statements, an accountant could become aware of confidential information that could affect the share price of a listed company's shares. The accountant is accordingly an insider in these circumstances.
	In both of these examples, the legal adviser and the accountant have inside information.

The Johannesburg Stock Exchange (JSE) requires companies listed on its exchange to issue cautionary announcements where an issuer – that is, the company – acquires knowledge of any material price-sensitive information and the confidentiality thereof cannot be maintained.[17] It has been suggested that prompt disclosure by listed companies of any price-sensitive information is one of the ways to limit the possibility of insider trading.[18]

PRACTICAL	**A cautionary announcement**
ISSUE	On 30 September 2010 reference[19] was made in the financial press to Nedbank's cautionary announcement as follows:
	Johannesburg – Nedbank [JSE:NED] issued a further cautionary on Thursday until a further announcement is made regarding a proposed offer by HSBC to acquire a controlling interest in the South African bank.
	Nedbank said it had indicated in August when the proposal was made that the making of a binding offer by HSBC is subject to a number of pre-conditions.
	'The process leading up to a potential offer is ongoing and accordingly, shareholders are advised to continue to exercise caution when dealing in Nedbank Group's securities until a further announcement is made,' it stated.

11.2.2   The regulation of insider trading

The Financial Services Board (FSB) is responsible for supervising compliance with Chapter X of the FMA.[20] The FSB is a creature of statute and is subject to the terms and provisions of the Financial Services Board Act.[21] The FMA creates broad additional powers for the FSB.

---

17   Paragraph 3.9 of the JSE Listing Requirements available at *http://www.jse.co.za/Libraries/JSE_-_Listings_Requirements_-_Service_Issues/Service_Issue_16.sflb.ashx*.

18   JSE Limited 'Insider trading and other market abuses (including the effective management of price sensitive information)' (2006) at 25 available on *http://www.jse.co.za/Libraries/JSE_-_Regulatory_Environment_-_Insider_Trading/Insider_Trading.sflb.ashx*.

19   See *http://www.fin24.com/Companies/Nedbank-issues-further-cautionary-20100930*.

20   Section 84 of the FMA.

21   97 of 1990.

The Directorate of Market Abuse (directorate) was established under the Insider Trading Act[22] and SSA, but continues to exist despite the aforementioned legislation having been repealed.

The directorate exists parallel to the FSB and can refer matters to it for investigation.

11.2.3   The insider-trading offences

Under the SSA, there were four insider-trading offences. An additional offence has been introduced by the FMA. The five insider-trading offences under s 78 are:

1. dealing in securities for one's own account, while in possession of inside information;
2. dealing in securities on behalf of another person, while in possession of inside information;
3. dealing in securities for an insider;
4. disclosing inside information to another person; and
5. encouraging or discouraging another person to deal.

Note that the definition of '**deal**' includes conveying or giving an instruction to deal.

The term 'securities' as defined in s 1 of the FMA includes listed and unlisted securities. However, the use of the term in the context of insider trading is restricted to listed securities in so far as this can clearly be inferred from the definition of 'inside information'. Inside information only relates to securities traded on a regulated market, which is itself defined in s 77. It means any market, domestic or foreign that is regulated in terms of the laws of the country in which the market conducts business as a market for dealing in securities listed on that market.

11.2.4   Defences to insider trading

An insider can escape liability under the FMA if he or she can prove that one of the defences in the Act applies.[23] These must be proved on a balance of probabilities.

The defences for each of the first four insider trading offence are discussed below. The Act does not provide a particular defence for encouraging or discouraging another person to deal.

11.2.4.1   Defences to dealing in securities for own account while having inside information

The defences for dealing in securities for one's own account, while in possession of inside information are:

*   that the person only became an insider *after* he or she had given the instruction to deal to an authorised user and the instruction was not changed in any manner after he or she became an insider; or
*   that the person was acting in pursuit of a transaction in respect of which
    *   all the parties to the transaction had the same inside information;
    *   trading was limited to the parties referred to above; and
    *   the transaction was not aimed at securing a benefit from exposure to movement in the price of the security, or a related security, resulting from the inside information.

---

22   135 of 1998.
23   See s 78 of the FMA.

11.2.4.2 Defences to dealing in securities for another while having inside information

The defences against dealing in securities on behalf of another person, while in possession of inside information are:

- that the person is an authorised user and was acting on specific instructions from a client, and did not know that the client was an insider at the time;
- that the person only became an insider after he or she had given the instruction to deal to an authorised user and the instruction was not changed in any manner after he or she became an insider; or
- that the person was acting in pursuit of a transaction in respect of which
  - all the parties to the transaction had possession of the same inside information;
  - trading was limited to the parties referred to above; and
  - the transaction was not aimed at securing a benefit from exposure to movement in the price of the security, or a related security, resulting from the inside information.

11.2.4.3 Defences to dealing in securities for an insider

The defences against dealing in securities for an insider are:

- that the person only became an insider *after* he or she had given the instruction to deal to an authorised user and the instruction was not changed in any manner after he or she became an insider; or
- that the person was acting in pursuit of a transaction in respect of which:
  - all the parties to the transaction had possession of the same inside information;
  - trading was limited to the parties referred to above; and
  - the transaction was not aimed at securing a benefit from exposure to movement in the price of the security, or a related security, resulting from the inside information.

11.2.4.4 Defence to disclosing inside information

The defence against disclosing inside information to another person is that he or she disclosed the inside information because it was necessary to do so for the purpose of the proper performance of the functions of his or her employment, office or profession in circumstances unrelated to dealing in any security listed on a regulated market, and that he or she at the same time disclosed that the information was inside information.

11.3 Insider trading and the Companies Act, 2008

The Companies Act, 2008 does not deal with insider trading. However, the provisions of the Companies Act, 2008 dealing with the fiduciary duties of directors indirectly speaks to the issues which are the subject matter of the insider trading provisions of the FMA. The core concept of insider trading is the fiduciary relationship that the insider has with the company. Under common law, a director may not use confidential information entrusted to him or her in his or her position as director for personal purposes. Use of this information would be a breach of a fiduciary duty.

The Companies Act, 2008 codifies certain provisions of the common law dealing with directors' fiduciary duties.[24] Should a director breach a fiduciary duty, he or she may be held personally liable in terms of the Act[25] and in accordance with the principles of common law.

---

24 See s 76 of the Companies Act, 2008.
25 See s 77 of the Companies Act, 2008.

In terms of s 76(2) of the Companies Act, 2008, a director must:

(a) not use the position of director, or any information obtained while acting in the capacity of a director –

   (i) to gain an advantage for the director, or for another person other than the company or a wholly owned subsidiary of the company; or

   (ii) to knowingly cause harm to the company or a subsidiary of the company; and

(b) communicate to the board at the earliest practicable opportunity any information that comes to the director's attention, unless the director –

   (i) reasonably believes that the information is –

      (aa) immaterial to the company; or

      (bb) generally available to the public, or known to the other directors; or

   (ii) is bound not to disclose that information by a legal or ethical obligation of confidentiality.

PRACTICAL **ISSUE**	**Wide definition of director** A director in this context includes a prescribed officer, an alternate director or a person who is a member of a committee of a board of a company, or of the audit committee of a company, irrespective of whether the person is also a member of the company's board. An auditor sitting on the audit committee, who gains access to information that is considered to be inside information, is prevented in terms of the Companies Act, 2008 from using that information for personal or another person's advantage. The auditor is also under a duty to disclose that information to the board of a company, or he or she may be held to be liable under s 77 of the Companies Act, 2008.

Section 69 of the Companies Act, 2008 sets out the circumstances in which a person will be disqualified from acting as a director. A person will be disqualified from acting as a director of a company if, inter alia, he or she has been convicted, in South Africa or elsewhere, and imprisoned without the option of a fine, or fined more than the prescribed amount, for theft, fraud, forgery, perjury or an offence in connection with the promotion, formation or management of a company, or under the Companies Act, 2008 or the FMA.[26]

A director will therefore be disqualified from acting as a director if he or she is convicted of insider trading under the FMA.

11.4   Insider trading and King 3

The third King code (King 3)[27] on corporate governance became necessary because of the enactment of a new Companies Act in 2008 and other international changes to corporate governance.

King 3 does not change the position on insider trading and nor does it deal with it directly. However, there are references to the concept. King 3 sets out guidelines for boards

---

26   See s 69 of the Companies Act, 2008.
27   See chapter 7 of this book and para. 7.15 for more information on the King codes.

of directors at Chapter 2, for the governance of risk at Chapter 4, and for compliance with laws, rules, codes and standards at Chapter 6. Among these guidelines are the following:

- directors' personal interests or those of the people closely associated with them should not take precedence over the interests of the company[28] – in other words, directors or associated persons should not use price-sensitive information for their own benefit to the detriment of the company;
- the board should ensure that the company complies with applicable laws[29] – this would include the FMA; and
- every listed company should have a policy of prohibiting dealing in its securities by directors, officers and other selected employees for a specified period before the announcement of its financial results, or in any other period considered sensitive.[30]

PRACTICAL	Illustration of insider trading
ISSUE	Consider the following scenario: Mr Jones is an independent information technology consultant who is called out to remove a virus from the computer system at Gold Co Limited, a listed gold mining company. While Mr Jones is removing the virus from the computer of Mr Smith, a director of the company, he gets bored and reads some of the director's emails. One of the emails contains information about a merger between Gold Co Limited and an Australian gold mining company, Aus Gold. The merger is to be finalised in the next week. Mr Jones immediately decides to buy shares in Gold Co Limited. Subsequently, the two companies merge and the share price increases.
	It should be clear from discussion in this chapter that Mr Jones is an insider with inside information, and that he has engaged in insider trading.

THIS CHAPTER IN ESSENCE

1. Insider trading is prohibited in many jurisdictions as a form of market abuse that is unfair to other market participants.
2. The Financial Markets Act (FMA) regulates insider trading in South Africa. Insider trading is an offence and potential offenders include juristic persons, partnerships and trusts.
3. An **insider** is a person who has inside information owing to his or her role as director, employee or shareholder of an issuer of securities listed on a **regulated market**, or who has access to such information by virtue of employment, office or profession, or where such person knows that the source of the information was an insider.
4. **Inside information** means specific or precise information that has not been made public and which is obtained or learned as an insider, and if it were made public would be likely to have a material effect on the price or value of any security listed on a regulated market.
5. Prompt public disclosure by listed companies of any price-sensitive information is one way to limit insider trading.
6. The FMA provides for five insider-trading offences:
   6.1 dealing in securities for one's own account, while in possession of inside information;
   6.2 dealing in securities on behalf of another person, while in possession of inside information;

---

28 Paras. 2.14 and 2.14.4 of the King 3 Code.
29 Chapter 6 of the King 3 Code.
30 Para. 2.14.5 of the King 3 Code.

6.3 dealing in securities for an insider;

6.4 disclosing inside information to another person; and

6.5 encouraging or discouraging another person to **deal**.

7. An insider can escape liability under the FMA if able to prove one of the defences provided for in the Act.

8. The Companies Act, 2008 does not regulate insider trading directly, but its provisions on the fiduciary duties of directors are relevant. A director may not use confidential information of a company for personal purposes. A director here includes a prescribed officer, an alternate director or a person who is a board committee member, or an audit committee member. A director will be disqualified from acting as a director if convicted of insider trading under the FMA.

9. Although the third King code (King 3) on corporate governance does not deal directly with insider trading, certain of its guidelines are relevant:

9.1 Personal interests of directors or those closely associated with them should not take precedence over the interests of the company.

9.2 The board should ensure that the company complies with applicable laws.

9.3 Every listed company should have a policy prohibiting directors, officers and other selected employees from dealing in its securities for a specified period before the announcement of its financial results, or in any other period considered sensitive.

Chapter 12

Business rescue proceedings and compromises

12.1   Options for financially distressed companies: a new approach

A natural consequence of any market-based economy is that some companies will fail. This is not necessarily a bad thing, and most industrialised nations recognise that failed companies are part and parcel of a healthy economy. If companies cannot be competitive in the marketplace, then it is a satisfactory result that those companies are either taken over by other, stronger companies, or wound up (liquidated).

Various factors may give rise to the failure of a company – for example, factors in the company's sphere of operation, national or international demand for a particular product, poor marketing strategies, or poor management of the company by its office bearers. There is no single factor that can be attributed to the failure of companies.

While it is quite healthy and normal for some companies to fail, the downside is that it may have a major impact on the economy and on the employees who are employed by that company. Winding up a company means that the revenue previously generated by that company will be lost to the economy, and job losses will have an extremely negative impact on the communities in which the business operated.

It is fair to state that a liquidation culture is prevalent in South Africa when dealing with failed companies. If a failed company is not the subject of a takeover or a compromise and arrangement, the only real alternative before the enactment of the Companies Act, 2008 was the winding-up[1] or liquidation of the company in terms of the provisions of the Companies Act, 1973. Liquidation of a company entails the appointment of a liquidator, who then sells off the assets of the company and distributes the proceeds in terms of a prescribed set of rules. This is also the process that would precede the dissolution of a failed company.

Since the late 1990s, there has been a shift in approach in most industrialised nations towards rescuing companies instead of liquidating them. Corporate rescue is the new international buzzword, and the straightforward liquidation of companies has become rather unfashionable. Although the term 'corporate rescue' is used to describe this relatively new phenomenon, the terms 'business rescue', 'restructuring' and 'reorganisation' are all terms that are used to describe essentially the same thing. It needs to be emphasised that the term '**business rescue**' (which is the term used to describe the new procedure introduced by Chapter 6 of the Companies Act, 2008) or 'corporate rescue' is not meant to denote or imply that the company or the business will necessarily be saved by the prescribed procedure. While the new procedure obviously does strive to save failing businesses, this will not always be the eventual outcome. For example, the business of the company may ultimately be sold as a going concern in cases where the company cannot be saved; but if the sale of a business as a going concern means that employees' jobs can be saved and a better return be obtained for the creditors of the company, then this would fall within the parameters of a corporate rescue.

Note that the notion of rescuing a company is not entirely novel under South African company law. The **judicial management** procedure was introduced into South African company law in 1926, and although its provisions were largely ineffective, it was nonetheless an early attempt by government to assist businesses that were in financial decline owing to mismanagement or other reasons.

The liquidation or winding-up of a company prior to its dissolution does not always indicate the failure of a company. Any company (even a solvent one) that wishes to be

---

1   In this context, note that the terms 'winding-up' and 'liquidation' will be used interchangeably to denote the same concept. The term 'winding-up' is used in the Companies Act, 1973, and since these provisions will apply until such time as a unified Insolvency Act is promulgated in South Africa, the term 'winding-up' will be used as far as possible in this chapter.

dissolved will have to go through a process of dissolution. The Companies Act, 2008 makes provision for solvent companies to go through a procedure of winding-up (voluntarily or by court order), but companies that have failed, and which cannot or have not been saved by the business rescue procedure, will have to go through the traditional process of liquidation in terms of the Companies Act, 1973.

This chapter examines the concept of business rescue, but deals also with another option for financially distressed companies – namely, a compromise with the company's creditors with regard to the company's financial obligations. Essentially, a **compromise** with creditors involves an agreement with creditors for them to receive less than is otherwise owing to them. This chapter examines a new procedure for a compromise between a company and its creditors. The new procedure was introduced in a late addition to the Companies Act, 2008 after it had already been decided that compromises would form part of the liquidation provisions in a new Insolvency Act.

PART A – BUSINESS RESCUE PROCEEDINGS

12.2 The concept of business rescue

The failure of a company affects not only its shareholders and creditors, but also its employees, suppliers, distributors and customers: whole communities could experience serious socio-economic problems when a large company in their area collapses. It is therefore important that at least some attempt be made to rescue a company or business that is suffering a temporary setback, but which nevertheless has the potential to survive if it is given some breathing space to overcome its financial woes. South Africa was one of the very first countries to introduce a formal corporate rescue procedure – namely, judicial management – into its legal system. Judicial management appeared for the first time in the Companies Act, 1926 and was then, although in a slightly amended form, retained in the Companies Act, 1973.

The Companies Act, 2008 in s 128(1)*(b)* defines **business rescue proceedings** as:

> proceedings to facilitate the rehabilitation of a company that is financially distressed by providing for—
>
> (i)   the temporary supervision of the company, and of the management of its affairs, business and property;
>
> (ii) a temporary moratorium on the rights of claimants against the company or in respect of property in its possession; and
>
> (iii) the development and implementation, if approved, of a plan to rescue the company by restructuring its affairs, business, property, debt and other liabilities, and equity in a manner that maximises the likelihood of the company continuing in existence on a solvent basis or, if it is not possible for the company to so continue in existence, results in a better return for the company's creditors or shareholders than would result from the immediate liquidation of the company.

Rescuing a company is defined with reference to the above definition by describing it as 'achieving the goals set out in the definition of business rescue'.[2] These goals are found in the last part of the definition – namely to maximise the likelihood of the company continuing

---

2   Section 128(1)*(h)* of the Companies Act, 2008.

in existence on a solvent basis or, if that is not possible, to result in a better return for creditors or shareholders of the company than would result from the immediate liquidation of the company.

A company will, according to s 128(1)(f), be **financially distressed** in the following circumstances:

- if it appears to be reasonably unlikely that the company will be able to pay all of its debts as they become due and payable within the immediately ensuing six months (often referred to as commercial insolvency); or
- if it appears to be reasonably likely that the company will become insolvent (in other words, its debts are likely to be more than its assets) within the immediately ensuing six months (actual or factual insolvency).[3]

Although the 2008 Act uses the term 'business rescue', this is strictly speaking a corporate rescue procedure. Its primary aim is not just to rescue a company's business or potentially successful parts of the business; the procedure aims to rescue the whole company or corporate entity, which could be more difficult. In fact, the definition does not even mention the rescue of the business or part of it as one of the aims of the procedure. In this respect, the new procedure is similar to judicial management, its predecessor in the Companies Act, 1973.[4] However, the courts have emphasised that there are substantial differences between business rescue and judicial management, including the fact that business rescue proceedings are not an exceptional procedure as judicial management was and that the test for granting a business rescue order is not as onerous as it was for judicial management.[5] Section 7(k) of the Act specifically refers to 'the efficient rescue and recovery of financially distressed companies in a manner that balances the rights and interests of all relevant stakeholders' as one of the purposes of the Act.

There are two ways in which business rescue proceedings may be commenced:

1. through a resolution by the board of directors of the company; or
2. by court order.

The following are the important questions regarding business rescue:
- Who can apply for business rescue proceedings to commence?
- What is the effect of business rescue proceedings on:
  - the control (board of directors) of the company?
  - creditors of the company?
  - employees of the company?
  - shareholders of the company?
  - agreements entered into by the company with outsiders?
- What are the qualifications, rights, powers and duties of a business rescue practitioner?
- Who is an affected person and what rights does such a person have?

All of these questions are answered in this chapter.

---

3 See the discussion in para. 12.4.2 below on the interpretation of this definition by some courts.
4 See *Le Roux Hotel Management (Pty) Ltd v E Rand (Pty) Ltd* [2001] 1 All SA 223 (C) for a discussion of the history and weaknesses of judicial management.
5 See, for example, *Employees of Solar Spectrum Trading 83 (Pty) Ltd v Afgri Operations Limited* (unreported case no 6418/2011 (GNP)) and *Nedbank Limited v Bestvest 153 (Pty) Ltd* (unreported case no 21857/2011 (WCC)).

12.3 Resolution by board of directors to begin business rescue

Business rescue proceedings may be commenced by resolution of the board of directors of the company. The Companies Act, 2008 provides for the procedure that the board must use to commence proceedings, as well as the circumstances under which such proceedings are permitted and how the proceedings may be stopped or set aside.

12.3.1 Procedure to commence business rescue by resolution

The procedure to commence business rescue proceedings by resolution of the board of directors involves the passing of a resolution by the board, followed by filing of the resolution with the Commission, notification to all affected parties and the appointment of a business rescue practitioner.

12.3.1.1 Business rescue resolution by board of directors

The board of directors of a company may take a formal decision (by majority vote) to begin business rescue proceedings in respect of the company[6] under certain specified circumstances.[7] However, a **business rescue resolution** may not be adopted[8] if liquidation proceedings by or against the company have already been initiated.[9] Unfortunately, the 2008 Act uses the word 'initiated' (which is not defined) instead of the word 'commenced' (which is clearly defined in the Companies Act, 1973).[10] As a result, there was some uncertainty whether 'initiated' was intended to have the same meaning as 'commenced'. In *Firstrand Bank Ltd v Imperial Crown Trading 143 (Pty) Ltd*[11] the court held that it would have to be assumed to mean the same because it would otherwise cause unnecessary uncertainty. Once the directors have taken the resolution to commence business rescue proceedings, and for as long as it is valid, the company may not resolve to commence liquidation proceedings.[12]

The business rescue resolution will become effective only when it is filed with (that is, delivered to) the Companies and Intellectual Property Commission (the Commission).[13] The rescue proceedings officially commence on the date of filing.[14]

---

6   Section 129(1) of the Companies Act, 2008.
7   See para. 12.3.2 below.
8   It is interesting to note that although the resolution is of no force and effect until it has been filed with the Commission, the Act does not even allow the adoption of such a resolution.
9   Section 129(2)(*a*) of the Companies Act, 2008.
10 In ss 348 and 352 of the Companies Act, 1973 respectively. These provisions are contained in Chapter 14 of the Companies Act, 1973, which will continue to apply to the winding-up of insolvent companies until alternative legislation is promulgated. A voluntary winding-up commences at the time the applicable special resolution is registered with the Commission (s 352). A winding-up by the court commences at the time of the presentation of the application to court (s 348), which is when the application is filed with the registrar of the court (*Nel and Others NNO v The Master and Others* 2002 (3) SA 354 (SCA)).
11 2012 (4) SA 266 (KZD).
12 Section 129(6) of the Companies Act, 2008.
13 Section 129(2)(*b*) of the Companies Act, 2008. This must be done by filing Form CoR123.1 with a copy of the resolution and affidavit attached.
14 Section 132(1)(*a*)(i) of the Companies Act, 2008.

12.3.1.2   Notification of affected parties

Within five business days (or more, if permission has been granted by the Commission)[15] after filing the resolution, the company must notify, in the prescribed manner,[16] every affected person of:

- the resolution;
- the date on which it became effective; and
- the grounds, set out in a sworn statement, on which the resolution was taken.[17]

According to the definition of an **affected person** in s 128(1)*(a)*, this means that the company must notify every shareholder and creditor, as well as any registered trade union representing the company's employees and those employees (or their representatives) who are not represented by a registered trade union. The 2008 Act allows notification to be given by way of electronic communication if the recipient can print it in a reasonable time and at a reasonable cost, or by providing the intended recipient with a summary of the contents and instructions on how to obtain the full document.[18]

If the company does not notify the affected persons as prescribed, the business rescue resolution 'lapses and is a nullity'.[19] This seems an unduly harsh consequence for what could be a minor oversight, such as notifying some affected persons one day too late or not notifying only one affected person. However, in *Advanced Technologies and Engineering Company (Pty) Ltd*,[20] the court held that s 129(5) required full compliance with the prescribed procedural requirements in sub-ss (3) and (4) and did not provide for the possibility of mere substantial compliance being sufficient or for condonation of non-compliance. If the procedural requirements of s 129(3) and (4) were not fully complied with, the resolution automatically lapsed and became a nullity. The matter is still far from settled because in *Ex parte Van den Steen NO and South Gold Exploration (Pty) Ltd*,[21] the court held that substantial compliance with the notification requirements is allowed by s 6(9) of the Act. The court thus issued a declaratory order that the company had substantially complied with the requirements of s 129(3)*(a)* and the business rescue resolution was therefore valid in spite of the fact that a group of creditors had mistakenly not been notified of the filing of the resolution. It is important to note, however, that the creditors were aware of the filing because of notices published by the company in local newspapers and on the website of its holding company.

In addition to the lapsing of the resolution, s 129(5) further provides that the company will not be allowed to file another business rescue resolution within three months after the date of adopting the one that has lapsed unless a court, on good cause shown, approves the filing of a further resolution by the company. The application to court for permission to file a new resolution before the expiry of the period of three months is brought by way of an *ex parte* application, which means that the company need not notify affected persons of the application.

The business rescue proceedings will then be regarded as having commenced when the company applied to court for its consent.[22]

---

15 In *Advanced Technologies and Engineering Company (Pty) Ltd (in business rescue) v Aeronautique et Technologies Embarquées SAS* (unreported case no 72522/20110 (GNP)) the court made it clear that the Commission cannot grant this extension after the period, of five days has expired because by then the resolution has already lapsed and cannot be revived.
16 Prescribed in regulation 123(2).
17 Section 129(3)*(a)* of the Companies Act, 2008.
18 Section 6(11) of the Companies Act, 2008.
19 Section 129(5) of the Companies Act, 2008.
20 Supra.
21 Unreported case no 3624/2013 (WCC).
22 Section 132(1)*(a)*(ii) of the Companies Act, 2008.

12.3.1.3 Appointment of business rescue practitioner

The company must also, within the same period of five business days (or the longer period previously granted by the Commission), appoint a **business rescue practitioner** to oversee the company and its rescue proceedings. This person (or persons, if more than one is appointed) must meet the requirements of s 138[23] and must provide his or her written consent to be appointed.[24] Within two business days after the business rescue practitioner has been appointed, the company must file a notice of his or her appointment with the Commission (in Form CoR 123.2) and, within five business days after filing this notice, the company must make a copy of the notice of appointment available to every affected person.[25]

If the company fails to comply fully with any of these requirements within the prescribed periods, it will have the same effects as those described in paragraph 12.3.1.2 above – namely, that the resolution will automatically lapse and become a nullity and no further such resolution may be filed within three months after adoption of the lapsed one without the court's approval.[26] The Act does not provide for any extension that may be granted by the Commission to file the notice of appointment or notify affected persons and the time periods must therefore be strictly adhered to.

In *Madodza (Pty) Ltd (in business rescue) v ABSA Bank Ltd*,[27] the business rescue resolution was held to be void because the business rescue practitioner had not been appointed within five days after filing of the resolution. In the *Advanced Technologies and Engineering Company* case,[28] the resolution was found to have lapsed for the same reason.

12.3.2 Circumstances under which business rescue resolution may be taken

The directors of a company may pass a resolution to begin business rescue proceedings only if the board has reasonable grounds to believe that the company is financially distressed and that there appears to be a reasonable prospect of rescuing the company.[29] Once the board has reasonable grounds to believe that the company is financially distressed, it must either pass a business rescue resolution, or deliver a written notice to each affected person explaining on which of the two possible grounds[30] the company is believed to be financially distressed and why they have decided not to adopt a business rescue resolution.[31] This notice must be in Form CoR123.3 (Notice of Decision Not to Begin Business Rescue) and each affected person must either receive a copy delivered in accordance with regulation 7 or be informed of the availability of a copy of the Notice.[32] Although neither the Act nor the Regulations prescribe any period within which this Notice must be published to the affected persons, Form 123.3 itself contains a note to the effect that the Notice must be published to affected persons within five business days after the board has considered the matter. It is

---

23 See para. 12.6.1 below.

24 Section 129(3)(*b*) of the Companies Act, 2008.

25 Section 129(4) of the Companies Act, 2008.

26 Section 129(5) of the Companies Act, 2008. In terms of regulation 123(3), this must be done by either delivering a copy of the Notice of Appointment of a Business Rescue Practitioner (Form 123.2) to each affected person in accordance with regulation 7, or by informing each affected person of the availability of a copy of the Notice.

27 [2012] ZAGPPHC 165

28 Supra.

29 Section 129(1)(*a*) and (*b*) of the Companies Act, 2008. In terms of the definition of 'rescuing the company', there must therefore be a reasonable prospect of achieving either the continued existence of the company in a solvent state or a better return for creditors or shareholders of the company.

30 See s 128(1)(*f*) of the Companies Act, 2008 and para. 12.2 above.

31 Section 129(7) of the Companies Act, 2008.

32 Regulation 123(5).

questionable whether this period is binding on any board since it is not based on any provision of the Act or Regulations.

There is no reference to the second requirement for a business rescue resolution, namely a reasonable prospect of rescuing the company, which means that the board must send the notice even though their reason for not taking the resolution is that liquidation seems to be the only option. Whatever the reason may be for the board not taking a business rescue resolution, the consequences of delivering such a notice to affected persons will have dire consequences for the company and it must be expected that creditors of the company will immediately demand payment of their claims, refuse any further credit or delivery of supplies to the company and possibly apply for the winding-up of the company. Since there is no direct sanction for non-compliance found in s 129(7) itself, it is not clear whether failure to notify affected persons will constitute a contravention of the Act or merely attract possible civil liability for reckless or fraudulent trading[33] or breach of the duty of care, skill and diligence.[34]

12.3.3   Setting aside business rescue resolution or appointment of business rescue practitioner

Once started, the business rescue process is not irreversible. Provision is made in the 2008 Act for a court to set aside both the resolution and the appointment of the business rescue practitioner in certain circumstances. The procedure to be followed and the circumstances under which this can happen are discussed below.

12.3.3.1   Application to court

After the directors of a company have taken a resolution to commence business rescue proceedings, and until such time as a business rescue plan has been formally adopted, any affected person may apply to court to set aside the resolution on any of the following grounds:

- there is no reasonable basis to believe that the company is financially distressed; or
- there is no reasonable prospect that the company will be rescued; or
- the company has failed to comply with the procedures set out in s 129.[35] (Since s 129(5) already stipulates that the resolution automatically 'lapses and is a nullity' if the company fails to comply with the provisions of s 129(3) and (4) in which the prescribed procedures are set out, it is unclear what the purpose of this provision is. The only reasonable explanation would be that this applies to the situation where the company disputes the allegation of non-compliance and a court has to decide whether there has been non-compliance resulting in the resolution lapsing and becoming void, although the court would not in such a case actually set aside the resolution but merely issue a declaratory order confirming that it has already lapsed.)

An affected person may also apply to court to set aside the appointment of the business rescue practitioner on the grounds that the business rescue practitioner:

- does not meet the requirements set for a business rescue practitioner in s 138; or
- is not independent of the company or its management; or

---

33 In terms of s 77(2)(*b*) of the Companies Act, 2008.
34 In terms of s 76(3)(*c*) of the Companies Act, 2008.
35 Discussed in para 12.3.1 above and see s 130(1)(*a*) of the Companies Act, 2008.

- lacks the skills that are necessary to supervise the rescue of the particular company.[36] (Since a lack of such skills can be used as grounds for a practitioner's removal, the question that arises is why s 138(1) does not include in the requirements for appointment as a business rescue practitioner that the person must have the necessary skills required by the particular company's circumstances.)

An affected person may also apply to court for an order that the business rescue practitioner must provide security to protect the interests of the company and any affected persons.[37]

CRITICAL ISSUE	No default requirement for business rescue practitioner to provide security
	By implication, the Act does not require a business rescue practitioner to provide security before being appointed, although it has previously been a requirement for the appointment of liquidators and judicial managers.[38] This is an unfortunate omission, since a company could suffer serious harm as a result of the actions of a dishonest or fraudulent, or merely incompetent or negligent practitioner.

A director of the company who voted in favour of the resolution to start business rescue proceedings may not bring an application in his or her capacity as an affected person for either the resolution or the appointment of the business rescue practitioner to be set aside, unless the director can satisfy the court that he or she supported the resolution in good faith based on information that he or she later found to be false or misleading.[39]

12.3.3.2 Procedure to set aside business rescue or appointment of business rescue practitioner

A person who brings any of these applications must serve a copy of the application on the company and the Commission and notify each affected person of the application.[40] Each affected person also has the right to take part in the hearing of the application by the court.[41]

12.3.3.3 Powers of court to set aside business rescue resolution or appointment of business rescue practitioner

The court may set aside the business rescue resolution on any of the stipulated grounds on which such an application may be based, or simply because the court regards it as just and equitable to do so.[42] Before the court decides whether or not to set aside the resolution it may, after giving the business rescue practitioner sufficient time to form an opinion on the matter, ask the business rescue practitioner to report to the court whether, in his or her opinion, the company appears to be financially distressed, or whether there is a reasonable prospect of rescuing the company.[43]

---

36 Section 130(1)(b) of the Companies Act, 2008.
37 Section 130(1)(c) of the Companies Act, 2008.
38 See ss 368, 375, 429 and 431(4) respectively of the Companies Act, 1973.
39 Section 130(2) of the Companies Act, 2008.
40 Section 130(3) of the Companies Act, 2008.
41 Section 130(4) of the Companies Act, 2008.
42 Section 130(5)(a) of the Companies Act, 2008.
43 Section 130(5)(b) of the Companies Act, 2008.

If the court sets aside the resolution, it may make any further order that may be necessary, including an order that the company be placed under liquidation. If the court finds that there were no reasonable grounds for believing that the company would be unable to pay all its debts as they became due and payable, an order of costs may be made against any director who voted in favour of the business rescue resolution. However, the court will not make an order for costs against a director who can satisfy the court that he or she acted in good faith and on the basis of information that he or she was entitled to rely on in terms of s 76(4) and (5).[44]

If the court sets aside the appointment of the business rescue practitioner, it must appoint another business rescue practitioner who meets the requirements of s 138, and is recommended by or is acceptable to the majority (in value)[45] of recognised independent creditors of the company who were represented in court.[46] (Note that, although the original business rescue practitioner was appointed by the board, the directors do not have the power to nominate the new practitioner.) **Independent creditors** are those creditors, including employees, who are not related to the company, not directors of the company and not the business rescue practitioner.[47] An employee of a company is not related to that company solely as a result of being a member of a trade union that holds shares in that company. A person is related to the company if he or she has the ability to influence materially the policy of the company and can exercise an element of control. He or she is also related to a director or business rescue practitioner if they are married, live together in a relationship similar to marriage, or are relatives separated by no more than three degrees.[48]

A business rescue practitioner appointed by the court in this way may also be asked by the court to report on his or her opinion regarding the company's financial distress, or reasonable prospects of being rescued.[49] This implies that if the practitioner's report indicates that one of the requirements for taking the resolution to commence business rescue proceedings is not present, the court may set aside the resolution and even place the company under liquidation. This is despite the fact that the application was merely one for replacing the practitioner.

12.4   Court order to commence business rescue proceedings

If the board of directors does not resolve to commence business rescue proceedings, an affected person may apply to court to order business rescue proceedings to commence. However, liquidation of the company always remains a possibility if the court decides that business rescue is not appropriate or if such proceedings end.

12.4.1   Application by affected person

If the directors of a company have not adopted a resolution to commence business rescue proceedings, an affected person may apply to court for an order placing the company under supervision and commencing business rescue proceedings.[50] The applicant must serve a copy of the application on the company and the Commission, and notify each affected

44 Section 130(5)(c) of the Companies Act, 2008.
45 See para. 12.5.8.2 below on the voting interests of creditors.
46 Section 130(6)(a) of the Companies Act, 2008.
47 Section 128(1)(g) of the Companies Act, 2008.
48 Section 2(1)(a)–(c) of the Companies Act, 2008.
49 Section 130(6)(b) of the Companies Act, 2008.
50 Section 131(1) of the Companies Act, 2008.

person of the application in the prescribed manner.[51] Each affected person has the right to take part in the hearing of such an application.[52]

CASE STUDY	**Requirement in regulation 124 for delivery of whole application to all affected persons is onerous**
	In *Cape Point Vineyards (Pty) Ltd v Pinnacle Point Group Ltd*,[53] Rogers AJ remarked that the requirement in regulation 124 that a copy of the whole application and not just a notification of the application (as required by s 131(2)*(b)*) must be delivered to affected persons was 'problematic' since a company could have thousands of shareholders and neither physical delivery nor sending such a data-heavy file by email may be feasible. The court expressed the view that regulation 124 probably went further than what could lawfully be prescribed. Future applicants were advised to seek permission in advance from the court in terms of regulation 7(3) for substituted service by way of publication on SENS and in a national newspaper, or permission to email only a notification and not the whole application.
	However, in *Kalahari Resources (Pty) Ltd v Arcelor Mittal SA*,[54] it was held that although regulation 124 probably went too far it could not just be ignored and until declared invalid, its requirements had to be complied with. The court pointed out that s 6(11)*(b)*(ii) could be used to solve the problem because it allowed the company merely to notify the recipients of the availability of the document with instructions on how to obtain the document rather than providing the full document.

The application for a business rescue order may also be made if 'liquidation proceedings have already been commenced by or against the company'.[55] The courts have therefore in a number of cases refused to postpone the issuing of (mostly provisional) liquidation orders to give affected persons an opportunity to apply for a business rescue order since these applications could still be brought later.[56]

The application for a business rescue order in respect of a company where liquidation proceedings have already been commenced will have the effect of suspending the liquidation proceedings until the court has refused the application for business rescue or, if the application is granted, until the business rescue proceedings have ended.[57] Although the Act is far from clear on this aspect, it must be assumed that the suspension will take effect as soon as the application is filed with the court.

Unfortunately, this provision in the Act is badly worded and incomplete and it is not clear whether 'liquidation proceedings' refer only to the legal proceedings until a final liquidation order is issued, or to the whole process of winding-up until a final liquidation and distribution account has been approved. In *Van Staden v Angel Ozone Products CC (in liquidation)*,[58] the court rejected the argument that only legal proceedings were meant and held that

---

51 Section 131(2) of the Companies Act, 2008.
52 Section 131(3) of the Companies Act, 2008.
53 2011 (5) SA 600 (WCC).
54 [2012] ZAGPJHC 130 (GSJ).
55 Section 131(6) of the Companies Act, 2008.
56 See *Firstrand Bank Limited v Imperial Crown Trading 143 (Pty) Ltd* (unreported case no 12910/2011 (KZD)); *AG Petzetakis International Holdings Limited v Petzetakis Africa (Pty) Ltd* (unreported case no 35891/2011 (GSJ)).
57 Section 131(6) of the Companies Act, 2008.
58 [2012] ZAGPPHC 328 (NGP).

'proceedings' here refer to the whole winding-up process until it ends with the approval of a final liquidation and distribution account. This means that even after a final liquidation order has been issued and the winding-up has progressed quite far, as in this case, an affected person can still apply for a business rescue order. This is an extremely unsatisfactory situation, since an almost completed winding-up may now be summarily halted by simply filing a spurious and baseless application for commencement of business rescue proceedings. A far more sensible approach would have been for the legislature to limit an application for business rescue to the period before a final liquidation order is issued or at least to provide that the liquidation proceedings will only be suspended from the moment when (and if) the court grants an order for commencement of business rescue proceedings.

In terms of s 132(1)(b), the business rescue proceedings formally begin when 'an affected person applies to the court for an order' placing the company in business rescue. Again the Act does not explain at what moment this will be but it probably also refers to the time of filing the application. In *Investec Bank Ltd v Bruyns*,[59] the court acknowledged that the time of commencement was uncertain and a problem that the courts would have to decide in due course, but decided that in this particular case it was unnecessary to do so.

The court may also, at any time 'during the course of any liquidation proceedings or proceedings to enforce any security against the company' make an order for the company to be placed under supervision and for business rescue proceedings to commence.[60] This means that the court may issue such an order of its own accord (*mero motu)* and without an application for a business rescue order having been made by an affected person. In this instance, the words 'liquidation proceedings' must be taken to refer only to the court proceedings since the company would not otherwise be before court and the business rescue proceedings formally commence when the court makes the actual order for business rescue.[61]

12.4.2 Grounds on which a court may order commencement of business rescue proceedings

The grounds on which an affected person may base such an application are much broader than the grounds on which a resolution by directors to commence business rescue may be based.

The court may make an order placing a company under supervision and commencing business rescue proceedings if it is satisfied that:

- the company is financially distressed;[62] or
- the company has failed to pay over any amount in terms of an obligation in respect of its employees under a public regulation (such as contributions to the Unemployment Insurance Fund, Workmen's Compensation Fund or SARS), or in terms of a contract (for example, salary to an employee, or a contribution to a medical aid fund). Apparently only one missed payment, irrespective of the reasons for missing it, will suffice; or
- it is otherwise just and equitable to do so for financial reasons; *and*
- there is a reasonable prospect of rescuing the company.[63]

---

59   [2011] ZAWCHC 423 (WCC).
60   Section 131(7) of the Companies Act, 2008.
61   Section 132(1)(c) of the Companies Act, 2008.
62   To assist registered trade unions in obtaining the necessary information to determine whether a company is in financial distress, s 31(3) provides that they must be given access to company financial statements for purposes of initiating a business rescue process. This must be done through the Commission and under conditions as determined by the Commission.
63   Section 131(4)(a) of the Companies Act, 2008.

The requirements for a business rescue order have already enjoyed a lot of attention from our courts. In *Gormley v West City Precinct Properties (Pty) Ltd (Anglo Irish Bank Corporation Ltd intervening); Anglo Irish Bank Corporation Ltd v West City Precinct Properties (Pty) Ltd*,[64] it was held that the second part of the definition of 'financially distressed' used the words 'will become insolvent' and thus referred to the future insolvency of the company. A company that was already insolvent therefore did not meet the requirements of the definition and could not be placed in business rescue. In *Firstrand Bank Ltd v Lodhi 5 Properties Investment CC*,[65] the court also expressed the view, although only obiter, that the definition of 'financially distressed' did not refer to present commercial or factual insolvency and in such a case a court would probably issue a winding-up order. However, in many other cases where the company was already insolvent or unable to pay its debts, the courts did not mention this as a reason in itself to dismiss an application for the commencement of business rescue proceedings but rather as one of the factors to be taken into account when determining whether there was a reasonable prospect that the company could be rescued.[66] This, with respect, seems to be the better approach to follow.

The requirement that there should be a reasonable prospect of rescuing the company has also presented some problems because the Act gives no indication of what could be regarded as a reasonable prospect.[67] In *Southern Palace Investments 265 (Pty) Ltd v Midnight Storm Investments 386 Ltd*,[68] the court stated that a rescue plan had to be disclosed to the court that addressed the reasons for the company's failure and offered a remedy that had a reasonable chance of being successful. If the intended aim of the business rescue proceedings was to rescue the company, some concrete and objectively ascertainable details had to be provided on:

- the likely costs of commencing or resuming the company's business;
- the likely availability and source of capital enabling the company to meet its running expenses;
- the availability of any other necessary resources such as materials and human resources; and
- why the proposed business rescue plan would have a reasonable prospect of success.

If, on the other hand, the application was based on the alternative aim of procuring a better return for creditors or shareholders, the applicant was expected to provide concrete factual details of the source, nature and extent of resources that were likely to be available, as well as the basis and terms on which they would be available.[69] The court emphasised that 'vague and undetailed information' and mere speculation would not suffice. Similar views were expressed in other judgments and this raised fears that every application for a business rescue order would have to disclose a detailed business rescue plan that would

---

64 Unreported case nos 19075/11 and 15584/11 (WCC).

65 Unreported case no 38326/2011 (GNP).

66 See, for example, *Swart v Beagles Run Investments 25 (Pty) Ltd (four creditors intervening)* 2011 (5) SA 422 (GNP); *Southern Palace Investments 265 (Pty) Ltd v Midnight Storm Investments 386 Ltd* 2012 (2) SA 423 (WCC).

67 As already explained in para. 12.2 above, the Act does indicate the two possibilities included in the meaning of 'rescuing the company' namely restoring the company to solvency or alternatively, resulting in a better return for creditors or shareholders than in a winding-up of the company.

68 2012 (2) SA 423 (WCC).

69 See also *Oakdene Square Properties(Pty) Ltd v Farm Bothasfontein (Kyalami) (Pty) Ltd* 2012 (3) SA 273 (GSJ), where the court refused to issue a business rescue order where there was no business or employees but merely an immovable property to be sold and there was no evidence that a better price would be achieved in business rescue than through a sale in liquidation.

not always be possible at this early stage and was really the main task of the business rescue practitioner.[70]

However, in *Employees of Solar Spectrum Trading 83 (Pty) Ltd v Afgri Operations Limited*,[71] Kollapen J stated that the requirements stipulated in the *Southern Palace* case[72] were not applicable in every instance but would depend on the circumstances of each case and the information available to the applicant. Requiring the applicant to produce a business rescue plan in every case would be importing a requirement not envisaged by the Act. This was also the view of the court in *Nedbank Limited v Bestvest 153 (Pty) Ltd*,[73] although the court stressed that an application could not be based on flimsy grounds.

12.4.3   The order commencing business rescue proceedings

As in the case of a business rescue resolution, a company may not adopt a resolution placing itself in liquidation until a court-ordered business rescue has ended.[74]

If the court makes an order for business rescue proceedings to commence, it may also appoint an interim business rescue practitioner nominated by the applicant, if the business rescue practitioner meets the requirements of s 138. In such a case, the appointment will be subject to approval by the majority-in-value of the independent creditors at the first meeting of creditors.[75] Although the Act states that the court 'may' appoint an interim business rescue practitioner, it must be clear that the court will have to do so, because it is the practitioner who has to convene the meeting of creditors to approve his or her appointment or to appoint another practitioner. If the court makes no appointment, nobody will have the required authority to convene a meeting of creditors and the proceedings will not progress any further.

If the court grants the application, the company must notify each affected person within five business days after the date of the order placing it under supervision.[76] If the court does not grant an order for business rescue, it may dismiss the application and make any further order that may be necessary, including one placing the company under liquidation.[77]

12.5   Legal consequences of business rescue proceedings

With a view to protecting a company while it tries to return to a viable position, the commencement of business or corporate rescue proceedings has profound legal consequences for a number of a company's activities and stakeholders. In particular:

- most civil legal proceedings are stayed (paused) until the end of the business rescue process;
- disposal of the company's property is restricted;
- re-financing the company is facilitated by allowing for company assets to be used to secure loans, but obligations to employees are also regarded as post-commencement finance and as such, are similarly preferential claims;
- employment contracts are protected;
- other contracts may be suspended or cancelled in certain circumstances;

---

70   *Koen v Wedgewood Village Golf & Country Estate (Pty) Lt*d 2012 (2) SA 378 (WCC).
71   Unreported case no 6418/2011 (GNP).
72   Supra.
73   [2012] 4 All SA 103 (WCC).
74   Section 131(8)(*a*) of the Companies Act, 2008.
75   Section 131(5) of the Companies Act, 2008.
76   Section 131(8)(*b*) of the Companies Act, 2008.
77   Section 131(4)(*b*) of the Companies Act, 2008.

- the status of issued shares may not be altered, and shareholders may only participate in decisions about business rescue if their interests will be affected; and
- directors must cooperate with the business rescue practitioner.

Each of these consequences of commencing business rescue is discussed in more detail below.

12.5.1 General moratorium on civil legal proceedings

One of the most important results of the start of business rescue proceedings is that, subject to some specific exceptions, there is an automatic stay (hold or pause) on legal proceedings, including enforcement action, against the company or in relation to any property belonging to the company or lawfully in its possession for as long as the business rescue continues.[78] Such legal proceedings may not be started or continued in any forum except:

- with the written consent of the business rescue practitioner; or
- with the court's permission, subject to any condition the court may impose; or
- as a set-off against a claim instituted by the company in legal proceedings commenced before or after business rescue proceedings started; or
- in the form of criminal proceedings against the company or any of its directors or officers; or
- in the case of proceedings regarding any property or right over which the company exercised powers as a trustee; or
- in the case of proceedings by a regulatory authority in the execution of its duties after giving the practitioner written notice. This exception must not be understood to mean that a regulatory authority has any preferential claim against the company: it merely refers to the exercise of regulatory actions by professional bodies or entities such as the Financial Services Board, SARS and the Unemployment Insurance Fund.[79]

A guarantee or surety provided by the company in favour of any other person may also not be enforced against the company except with the leave of the court subject to any conditions the court considers just and equitable.[80]

If any right or claim against the company must be enforced within a specified time, the period during which the company is in business rescue proceedings will not be counted.[81] This means that prescription will also not run on a claim against the company during its business rescue proceedings.

12.5.2 Protection of property interests

The power of the company to deal with its property is restricted during business rescue. The company may only dispose of property if it takes place:

- in the ordinary course of its business; or
- in a transaction in good faith to which the business rescue practitioner has given his or her prior written consent; or
- as part of the approved rescue plan of the company.[82]

---

78 In *Madodza (Pty) Ltd (in business rescue) v ABSA Bank Limited* (unreported case no 38906/2012 (GNP)), the court held that the moratorium did not apply to leased vehicles in possession of the company because the court had ordered the return of the vehicles before commencement of business rescue and they were thus not in lawful possession of the company when the business rescue proceedings commenced.

79 Section 133(1) and (2) of the Companies Act, 2008.

80 Section 133(2) of the Companies Act, 2008.

81 Section 133(3) of the Companies Act, 2008.

82 Section 134(1) of the Companies Act, 2008.

The requirements contained in ss 112 and 115 for a disposal by the company of all or a greater part of its assets or undertaking, will thus have to be met unless the disposal is part of an approved business rescue plan.[83]

Any person who is in lawful possession of property of the company in terms of an agreement made in the ordinary course of the company's business before business rescue proceedings began, may continue to exercise the rights contemplated in the agreement, but subject to s 136.[84]

Furthermore, irrespective of any agreement to the contrary, no person may exercise any right in connection with any property that is in the lawful possession of the company – even if the company is not the owner – unless the business rescue practitioner has given his or her written consent.[85] The practitioner may not unreasonably withhold consent taking into consideration the purposes of business rescue proceedings, the circumstances of the company, the nature of the property and the rights claimed in respect of it.[86]

If the company wants to sell any property over which a creditor holds security rights, such as a mortgage bond, the company does not have to ask the creditor's permission if the proceeds of the sale will be enough to pay him or her in full.[87] The company must promptly pay over proceeds of such a sale to meet its debt, or must provide security.

12.5.3   Post-commencement finance

It can be very difficult for a company to obtain capital once business rescue proceedings have commenced, as creditors will be concerned that they may not be paid. In order to solve this problem, s 135(2) allows the company to use its assets as security for post-commencement loans in so far as these assets are unencumbered. Claims by these lenders, whether secured or unsecured, will enjoy preference in the order in which the debts were incurred and also over all unsecured claims against the company.

However, any employment-related payments that become due during business rescue proceedings to employees of the company are also regarded as post-commencement finance and must be paid even before the providers of post-commencement loans are paid, including those whose claims are secured.[88] Only the practitioner's remuneration and expenses, and other costs of the business rescue proceedings may be paid before these claims of the employees. If liquidation proceedings later replace the business rescue proceedings, these post-commencement lenders and employees will retain their preferential rights.[89]

PRACTICAL ISSUE	**Liquidation proceedings**
	If liquidation proceedings later replace the business rescue proceedings, then the creditors that have obtained preferential rights under the business rescue provisions will retain these under the liquidation proceedings that follow. This effectively means that a new order of preference for the payment of creditors can be created by using

---

83   Section 112(1)(*a*) of the Companies Act, 2008 and see para.10.2.1 above.
84   Section 136 of the Companies Act, 2008 authorises the practitioner to suspend any of the company's contractual obligations or apply to court to cancel any obligation: see para. 12.5.5 below.
85   Section 134(1)(*c*) of the Companies Act, 2008.
86   Section 134(2) of the Companies Act, 2008.
87   Section 134(3) of the Companies Act, 2008.
88   Section 135(1)-(3) of the Companies Act, 2008.
89   Section 135(4) of the Companies Act, 2008.

the business rescue proceedings, overriding even the statutory order of preference set out in the Insolvency Act.[90] This may mean that stronger rights may be created under the business rescue procedure for certain categories of creditor that may not have had such strong rights under traditional liquidation procedures.

12.5.4 Employment contracts and employees

The aim of the Companies Act, 2008 is to protect the rights of employees as much as possible during business rescue proceedings.

12.5.4.1 Employment contracts

Business rescue proceedings have no effect on the company's contracts with its employees: they continue to be employed by the company on the same terms and conditions as before. However, the employees and the company may, in accordance with applicable labour legislation, agree to different terms and conditions.[91] Any retrenchment of employees, even if it forms part of a company's business rescue plan, is subject to all the relevant labour legislation.[92]

CRITICAL ISSUE

New business rescue procedure compared to insolvency laws

The new business rescue procedure introduced by the Companies Act, 2008 is not aligned with the insolvency laws that apply to a company that is being wound up.

Consider the example of the ABC Company Limited, a company with 200 employees and which is experiencing financial difficulties. An application is brought in the High Court for the winding-up of the company based on its inability to pay its debts. If the company is placed in liquidation, all contracts of employment will be suspended, subject to the provisions of s 38 of the Insolvency Act[93] (which applies to companies in liquidation). During such suspension, the employees are not required to work, but will also not be paid. After a statutory period (currently 45 days from the appointment of a final liquidator), the contracts of employment may be terminated. The only time that the contracts of employment will not be terminated is if the contracts pass to the purchaser of the business in the context of a sale, out of the insolvent estate, of the business as a going concern.

However, if the company is on the verge of being wound up by an order of the High Court, it is possible for the employees to intervene (as an affected party) in the liquidation proceedings by applying for a business rescue order. If such an order is granted, the business rescue provisions in the Companies Act, 2008 provide for the maintenance of all employment contracts on the same terms and conditions as existed prior to the granting of the business rescue order.

It should be clear that it is far more beneficial for employees if the company is placed under business rescue than if the company is liquidated. It will be interesting to see to what extent this difference in approach will be used or abused in practice.

---

90 24 of 1936.
91 Section 136(1)(*a*) of the Companies Act, 2008.
92 Section 136(1)(*b*) of the Companies Act, 2008.
93 24 of 1936.

12.5.4.2   Unpaid remuneration before business rescue proceedings

In respect of any unpaid salary and other employment-related payments already due to an employee when business rescue proceedings commenced, the employee becomes a preferred unsecured creditor of the company.[94] A medical scheme, pension fund or provident scheme to which the company owes money at the commencement of business rescue is an unsecured creditor of the company.[95]

12.5.4.3   Employees' committee

Apart from their rights as affected persons to be notified and consulted and to participate in all stages of the business rescue proceedings through their registered trade union or in person, employees may also form a committee of employees' representatives.[96] The business rescue practitioner must convene a meeting of the employees or their representatives within 10 business days after his or her appointment to inform them about the company's future. It is at this meeting that they will decide whether or not to appoint an employees' committee.[97] This committee may consult with the business rescue practitioner and must ensure that the employees' interests are properly represented, but its members may not give instructions to the business rescue practitioner.[98]

12.5.5   Other contracts and agreements

In its original version, s 136(2) of the Companies Act, 2008 provided that the business rescue practitioner could entirely, partially or conditionally cancel or suspend any provision of an agreement to which a company is a party at the commencement of business rescue proceedings – even if the agreement provides that this may not be done. The only exception was for contracts that were subject to ss 35A and 35B of the Insolvency Act.[99]

This would have meant that a practitioner could simply cancel a provision requiring a company to pay interest or give security for a debt it owes, or suspend payment of a debt for an indefinite period. As a result of serious objections to this provision, the original provision was amended to provide that a business rescue practitioner may entirely, partially or conditionally suspend (not cancel) for the duration of the business rescue proceedings, any contractual obligation of the company that arises under an agreement entered into before commencement of the business rescue proceedings and that would otherwise become due during business rescue proceedings.[100] This will not apply to an employment contract or an agreement to which ss 35A or 35B of the Insolvency Act would have applied had the company been liquidated.[101]

The practitioner will not have the power to cancel any provision of a contract, but may apply to court to cancel entirely, partially or conditionally any obligation described above, on terms that are just and reasonable in the circumstances (except an employment contract or one to which ss 35A or 35B of the Insolvency Act would have applied in a winding-up).[102] Unfortunately, there is no indication of the grounds on which the court may grant such an

---

94   Section 144(2) of the Companies Act, 2008.
95   Section 144(4) of the Companies Act, 2008.
96   Section 144(3) of the Companies Act, 2008.
97   Section 148 of the Companies Act, 2008.
98   Section 149 of the Companies Act, 2008.
99   24 of 1936. These sections provide for the protection of participants in the South African financial markets in the event of insolvency and allow contracts with financially distressed companies to be terminated.
100   Proposed s 136(2)(*a*) of the Companies Act, 2008.
101   See proposed s 136(2A)(*a*) of the Companies Act, 2008.
102   Proposed s 136(2)(*b*) of the Companies Act, 2008.

order or what a court should take into consideration when deciding whether to grant such an order.

The other party to a contract that has been partially or entirely suspended or cancelled may claim only damages from the company and not, for example, specific performance of the contract.[103]

12.5.6 Shareholders

Shareholders are not too affected by a business rescue, but certain restrictions apply.

12.5.6.1 No change in rights

No alteration in the classification or status of any issued securities of the company is allowed during business rescue proceedings, unless authorised by the court or contained in an approved business rescue plan.[104]

12.5.6.2 Participation

Since shareholders of the company are also affected persons, they have the right to be notified of important events and to participate in court proceedings and business rescue proceedings to the extent allowed by the Companies Act, 2008.

However, shareholders do not have the right to attend the meeting held to consider the business rescue plan or to vote on the business rescue plan, except for any shareholder whose rights will be altered by the plan. If a business rescue plan is rejected, a shareholder who was present at the meeting (because his or her rights would be altered by the plan) may propose that a new plan be developed, and any shareholder – even one without the right to attend the meeting and vote – may make an offer to take over the voting interests of some or all creditors or shareholders who opposed adoption of the business rescue plan.[105]

12.5.7 Directors

The directors of a company must cooperate with the business rescue practitioner and they will be excused from certain of their duties and liabilities while operating under the instructions of the business rescue practitioner. Failure to cooperate could lead to the removal of a director during business rescue.[106]

12.5.7.1 Duties and liabilities of directors

Directors must continue to perform their functions during the business rescue procedure, but must do so under the authority and according to all reasonable instructions of the business rescue practitioner.[107] Directors must cooperate with the business rescue practitioner, deliver books and records of the company to him or her, and within five business days after the beginning of business rescue proceedings provide him or her with a statement of the company's affairs containing the prescribed information.[108]

A director is relieved from the duties contained in s 76 and from most of the liabilities set out in s 77, if he or she follows the express instructions of the business rescue practitioner to the extent that it is reasonable to do so. However, a director remains bound by the duty

---

103 Section 136(3) of the Companies Act, 2008.
104 Section 137(1) of the Companies Act, 2008.
105 Section 146 of the Companies Act, 2008. See para. 12.7.5 below.
106 See para. 12.5.7.2 below.
107 Section 137(2)(a) and (b) of the Companies Act, 2008.
108 Section 142 of the Companies Act, 2008.

contained in s 75 concerning the disclosure of personal financial interests. A director also remains personally liable to the company for loss or damages sustained as a consequence of the director:

- acting on behalf of the company knowing that he or she has no authority to do so;
- acquiescing in the carrying on of the company's business despite knowing that it was being conducted in a manner prohibited by s 22(1) – that is, recklessly, with gross negligence, with intent to defraud any person or for any fraudulent purpose; or
- being a party to an act or omission by the company despite knowing that it was intended to defraud a creditor, employee or shareholder of the company or had another fraudulent purpose.[109]

Acts for which the approval of the business rescue practitioner is required will be void if performed by a director or the board without the necessary approval.[110]

12.5.7.2   Removal of a director

The business rescue practitioner may apply to court for the removal of a director if the director fails to comply with any provisions of the Companies Act, 2008 regulating a director's conduct during business rescue or hinders the business rescue practitioner in the performance of his or her duties or in carrying out a business rescue plan.[111] It must be assumed that just as in the case of the removal of a director by the shareholders or the board,[112] a director who is also an employee of the company (that is, an executive director) will merely be removed from office by the court order and not dismissed as an employee.[113] The right of certain persons to apply to court for an order declaring a director delinquent or under probation[114] also exists during the business rescue procedure.[115]

12.5.8   Creditors

As affected persons, the creditors (including those employees who have become creditors because of their unpaid remuneration due before the business rescue proceedings commenced) have the right to be notified of, and formally and informally participate in, all stages of the proceedings. They play a particularly important role in voting on the amendment, approval or rejection of the business rescue plan.[116]

12.5.8.1   Creditors' committee

Within 10 days after his or her appointment, the business rescue practitioner must convene a meeting of creditors to inform them of the company's future, and to allow them to prove their claims against the company.[117] The creditors have the right to form a creditors' committee to represent their interests. The business rescue practitioner is then obliged to

---

109   Section 137(2)(d) of the Companies Act, 2008.
110   Section 137(4) of the Companies Act, 2008.
111   Section 137(5) of the Companies Act, 2008.
112   In terms of s 71 of the Companies Act, 2008. The Act is silent on whether shareholders and the board retain this power during business rescue proceedings.
113   An executive director will be entitled to the same protection as any other employee during business rescue proceedings since s 136(1) does not exclude any employees: see para. 12.5.4.1 above.
114   Section 162 of the Companies Act, 2008.
115   Section 137(6) of the Companies Act, 2008.
116   Section 145(1) and (2) of the Companies Act, 2008.
117   Section 147 of the Companies Act, 2008.

consult this committee during the development of the business rescue plan,[118] although the committee may not direct or instruct the business rescue practitioner in any way.[119]

12.5.8.2 Voting rights

Whenever creditors have to vote on any decision regarding business rescue proceedings, each creditor has a voting interest[120] equal to the full value of his or her claim against the company – irrespective of whether the claim is secured or unsecured.[121] However, a concurrent creditor whose claim would be subordinated in liquidation will have a vote based only on the amount, if any, that he or she could reasonably expect to receive in the case of liquidation.[122] In *Commissioner for the South African Revenue Service v Beginsel NO*,[123] the court made it clear that this subsection did not refer to all concurrent creditors, but only to those who had subordinated their claims in terms of an existing agreement.

Apart from the special provisions regarding the approval of a business rescue plan, a decision needs only the support of the holders of a majority of the voting interests of the independent creditors to be a valid and binding decision by creditors.[124]

12.6 The business rescue practitioner

The Companies Act, 2008 regulates the appointment and activities of a business rescue practitioner in a number of areas. These include the qualifications a person should have to be appointed as a practitioner, how he or she may be removed and replaced, his or her powers and duties and the remuneration that a practitioner may receive.

12.6.1 Qualifications of business rescue practitioner

The original version of s 138 envisaged the creation of a dedicated profession of business rescue practitioners who would have been regulated by a regulatory authority that functioned 'predominantly to promote sound principles and good practice of business turnaround or rescue'. This plan has now been abandoned. The qualifications for appointment as a business rescue practitioner are now fivefold. The person must:[125]

1. *be a member in good standing of a legal, accounting or business management profession that is subject to regulation by a regulatory authority,*[126] *or be licensed by the Commission to practise as a business rescue practitioner*: s 138(2) authorises the Commission to license any 'qualified' person to practise as a practitioner and to suspend or withdraw such licence. Section 138(3) authorises the Minister to make regulations prescribing standards and procedures to be followed by the Commission in carrying out its licensing functions and powers in terms of this section, and prescribing minimum qualifications for a person to practise as a business rescue practitioner;

---

118   Section 145(3) of the Companies Act, 2008.
119   Section 149 of the Companies Act, 2008.
120   A 'voting interest' refers to the votes of a creditor based on the creditor's claim against the company as determined in terms of s 145(4)-(6) of the Companies Act, 2008 (see s 128(1)(j)), while the votes of shareholders are referred to as 'voting rights' as determined in s 1 of the Act.
121   Section 145(4)(a) of the Companies Act, 2008.
122   Section 145(4)(b) of the Companies Act, 2008.
123   [2012] ZAWCHC 194 (WCC).
124   Section 147(3) of the Companies Act, 2008.
125   Section 138 of the Companies Act, 2008.
126   To date, no professions have been accredited.

2. *not be subject to an order of probation in terms of s 162(7)*: since an order of probation may only be issued against a director, who must always be an individual, it is unclear how this requirement can be applied to a juristic person although it may apparently be appointed as a practitioner because the definition of the term 'person' in s 1 includes a juristic person;

3. *not be disqualified from acting as a director of the company in terms of s 69(8)*: as with the last-mentioned requirement, s 69(8) applies only to natural persons and cannot be applied to a juristic person;

4. *not have any other relationship with the company that would lead a reasonable and informed third party to conclude that his or her integrity, impartiality or objectivity is compromised by that relationship*; and

5. *not be related to a person who has such a relationship.*

12.6.2   Removal and replacement of business rescue practitioner

The only way in which a business rescue practitioner can be removed from office is by an order of court – either in terms of s 130[127] or in terms of s 139. The order in terms of s 139 may be made on application by an affected person or on the court's own initiative, based on any of the grounds stipulated in s 139(2). These grounds are:

- incompetence or failure of the person to perform his or her duties as practitioner of the particular company;
- failure to exercise the proper degree of care in the performance of the practitioner's functions;
- engaging in illegal acts or conduct;
- no longer meeting the requirements for appointment as a business rescue practitioner as set out in s 138;
- having a conflict of interests or lack of independence; or
- becoming incapacitated and unable to perform the functions of a practitioner and being unlikely to regain that capacity within a reasonable time.

Strangely enough, although incompetence constitutes grounds for removal of a business rescue practitioner, the ability or competence of a person to act as a business rescue practitioner for that particular company is not stipulated as a requirement for appointment in the first place. The only requirement that is linked to the practitioner's competence and experience is found in regulation 127(2)*(c)* in terms of which practitioners are classified as senior, experienced or junior based on their years of experience in business turnarounds. A junior practitioner may only be appointed as the sole business rescue practitioner for a small company, while an experienced practitioner may be appointed as sole practitioner for a small or medium company. Only a senior practitioner may be appointed as sole business rescue practitioner for a state-owned company or any other company.[128]

If a business rescue practitioner dies, resigns or is removed from office, a new business rescue practitioner must be appointed by the company or, if applicable, by the creditor who nominated the previous one.[129]

---

127   Discussed in para. 12.3.3.3 above.
128   Classification of companies as small, medium or large is based on their public interest score calculated in terms of regulation 28.
129   Section 139(3) of the Companies Act, 2008.

12.6.3 Powers, duties and liability of business rescue practitioner

The powers and duties of a business rescue practitioner are provided for in the Companies Act, 2008. These include taking full responsibility for the management of the company, investigating and monitoring the company's affairs with a view to ending business rescue proceedings when no longer appropriate, developing and implementing a rescue plan and accepting liability for a breach of duties. The business rescue practitioner may not be appointed as the liquidator of the company if the company is liquidated when the business rescue ends.[130]

12.6.3.1 Management responsibilities of business rescue practitioner

The business rescue practitioner takes over the full management of the company from the board and other managers, but may delegate any of his or her powers or functions to a director or other member of management.[131] The practitioner may remove from office any person who forms part of the pre-existing management of the company[132] and may also appoint a new member of management. If the practitioner wishes to appoint a person as part of the company's management or as an adviser to the company or to the practitioner and such a person has any other relationship with the company that might cast doubt on his or her integrity, impartiality or objectivity, or is related to such a person, the court must approve this appointment on application by the business rescue practitioner.[133]

As soon as possible after his or her appointment, the business rescue practitioner must inform all regulatory authorities with authority in respect of the company's activities that the company has been placed under business rescue proceedings and that he or she has been appointed as the company's business rescue practitioner.[134]

12.6.3.2 Investigation by business rescue practitioner

The business rescue practitioner must investigate the affairs of the company as soon as possible after his or her appointment and decide whether the company has a reasonable chance of being rescued. If the business rescue practitioner then or at any other time during business rescue proceedings finds that it does not, he or she must inform the court, the company and all affected persons and apply to court for the business rescue proceedings to end and for the company to be placed in liquidation.[135] Strangely enough, s 81(1)(*b*) specifically provides for a winding-up order to be issued on application by the practitioner in this situation although the court only has the power to order the winding-up of a *solvent* company in terms of s 81 and the company would almost certainly be insolvent at this stage.

If the business rescue practitioner discovers that the company is no longer financially distressed, he or she must likewise inform the abovementioned parties and take steps to terminate the business rescue proceedings. If an order of court commenced the business

---

130 Section 140(4) of the Companies Act, 2008. However, the Act does not specifically prohibit the appointment of the liquidator as the business rescue practitioner, although it may be argued that the liquidator's 'other relationship with the company' would compromise his or her objectivity and impartiality and thus disqualify the liquidator from appointment as the company's practitioner (see para. 12.6.1 above).

131 Section 140(1) of the Companies Act, 2008.

132 Section 140(1)(*c*) of the Companies Act of 2008. It is not clear whether this provision refers only to members of management who are not directors, since the removal of a director requires an order of court and is specifically regulated by s 137(5): see para. 12.5.7.2 above.

133 Section 140(2) of the Companies Act, 2008.

134 Section 140(1A) of the Companies Act, 2008. Apparently, entities such as SARS, the Financial Services Board and the UIF as well as possibly bodies regulating certain professions (like auditors and engineers) are included although this is not very clear from the definition of a 'regulatory authority' in s 1.

135 Section 141(2)(*a*) of the Companies Act, 2008.

rescue proceedings or confirmed them after an application had been heard to set them aside, the business rescue practitioner must apply to court for termination. Otherwise, a notice of termination must be filed with the Commission.[136]

If the investigation of the company's affairs reveals evidence of 'voidable transactions'[137] or failure by the company or any director to perform a material obligation relating to the company in dealings of the company before business rescue proceedings started, the practitioner must take steps to rectify the matter and may direct the management to do so. Any evidence of reckless trading, fraud or other contravention of any law must be forwarded to the appropriate authority for further investigation and possible prosecution and the management must be directed to rectify the matter and recover any misappropriated assets of the company.[138]

12.6.3.3 Development of rescue plan

Probably the most important duty of the business rescue practitioner is to develop a rescue plan for the company and, if the plan is adopted, to see to its implementation.[139]

12.6.3.4 Duties and liability of business rescue practitioner

The business rescue practitioner has all the duties and responsibilities of a director, and is liable for a breach of these duties in the same way as a director (in terms of ss 75 to 77). Apart from liability on these grounds, the practitioner is not otherwise liable for any act or omission in good faith while exercising the powers and performance of the function of a business rescue practitioner – unless he or she was grossly negligent.[140] The practitioner is an officer of the court and must therefore report to the court as required by any court order.[141]

12.6.4 Remuneration of business rescue practitioner

The business rescue practitioner is entitled to payment by the company in accordance with a tariff prescribed by the Minister.[142]

However, he or she may also enter into an agreement with the company to be paid an additional fee if a rescue plan is adopted or any specified result is achieved in the business rescue proceedings.[143] Such an agreement will be binding on the company only if approved by the majority-in-value of creditors who attend the relevant meeting, and the majority of shareholders who are entitled to a portion of the residual value of the company on liquidation.[144] A creditor or shareholder who voted against approval of the agreement may apply to court, within 10 business days after the date of voting, to have the agreement cancelled on the grounds that it is not just and equitable, or that it is highly unreasonable in light of the company's financial circumstances.[145]

---

136 Section 141(2)(b) of the Companies Act, 2008.
137 It is highly unlikely that these refer to the voidable transactions found in the Insolvency Act, 1936 because no provisions of the Insolvency Act have been made applicable to business rescue proceedings. It probably refers to transactions that are voidable in terms of the Companies Act, 2008 because the requirements of the Act were not met, such as the company acquiring its own shares contrary to ss 46 and 48.
138 Section 141(2)(c)(ii) of the Companies Act, 2008.
139 Section 140(1)(d) of the Companies Act, 2008.
140 Section 140(3)(c) of the Companies Act, 2008.
141 Section 140(3)(a) of the Companies Act, 2008.
142 The tariff is prescribed in regulation 128 and is based on whether the company is classified as a small, medium or large company based on the public interest score of the company as calculated in terms of regulation 28.
143 Section 143(1)-(2) of the Companies Act, 2008.
144 Section 143(3) of the Companies Act, 2008.
145 Section 143(4) of the Companies Act, 2008.

12.7 The business rescue plan

It is the duty of the business rescue practitioner to prepare a **business rescue plan** for the company, but he or she must consult the creditors, other affected persons and the management of the company when doing so.[146]

12.7.1 Prescribed contents

A rescue plan must contain all the information that affected persons may need to decide whether they should accept or reject the plan. Section 150(2) provides that the plan must be divided into three parts and must conclude with a certificate. It also prescribes the minimum details that each part must contain, but in *Commissioner for the South African Revenue Service v Beginsel NO*,[147] the court held that substantial compliance with s 150(2) will suffice because not all the details required by s 150(2) will apply in every case. The emphasis should thus be on the first part of the subsection, which requires that all the information reasonably required to assist affected persons in deciding whether or not to accept or reject the plan should be provided.

The plan must contain the prescribed parts and contents described below.

12.7.1.1 Part A – Background[148]

This part of the plan mainly supplies details about the financial situation in which the company finds itself. It must therefore contain the following information:

- a complete list of the material assets of the company, indicating which assets were held as security by creditors at the start of business rescue proceedings – although the Act does not require that the value of each asset must be reflected, it can be assumed that this is indeed required;
- a list of the creditors of the company when business rescue proceedings began, indicating the classification of each one in terms of insolvency law as secured, statutory preferent or concurrent, and indicating which creditors have proved their claims – again, it must be assumed that the legislature intended that the amount of each claim must be reflected although it is not specifically required;
- the dividend that each specific class of creditors would probably receive should the company be placed in liquidation;
- a complete list of holders of issued securities of the company;
- a copy of the written agreement regarding the business rescue practitioner's remuneration (it is not clear whether this requirement refers only to an agreement for additional remuneration in terms of s 143(3) or also to the basic remuneration to which the practitioner is entitled in terms of the prescribed tariff of fees[149] since s 143 does not require either of the two kinds of remuneration to be reflected in a written agreement. It would obviously be preferable for the practitioner and the company's board to enter into an agreement at the start of business rescue proceedings regarding any fees that the practitioner may charge and to do so in writing); and
- a statement whether the plan includes any proposal made informally by a creditor of the company. (Since the practitioner is specifically instructed to consult the creditors and they have been given the express right to make proposals informally for the business

---

146   Section 150(1) of the Companies Act, 2008.
147   Supra.
148   Section 150(2)*(a)* of the Companies Act, 2008.
149   The prescribed tariff of fees is found in regulation 128.

rescue plan to the practitioner,[150] the purpose of this requirement, which creates the impression that such a proposal is somehow suspect, is not clear.)

12.7.1.2   Part B – Proposals[151]

In this part of the plan, all the proposed measures to assist the company in overcoming its problems and managing its debts are explained. It must therefore contain details of the following aspects (in so far as they may be applicable):

- the nature and duration of any moratorium for which the plan provides – this does not refer to the automatic stay that results from the commencement of business rescue proceedings, but is a further moratorium on the payment of its debts by the company that will apply after the business rescue proceedings have ended if the plan is approved;
- any release of the company from payment of its debts, and the conversion of any debts into equity (in other words, shares) in the company or another company;
- the ongoing role of the company and the treatment of existing contracts – the first part of this requirement presumably refers to whether, how and to what extent the company is expected to survive during and after the business rescue proceedings; in the second part, the practitioner has to indicate which contractual obligations have been or will be suspended or cancelled with the permission of the court[152] – the practitioner may suspend obligations of the company only for the duration of the business rescue proceedings and will have to indicate how existing contracts will be dealt with after the business rescue has ended;
- which assets of the company will be available to pay creditors in terms of the business rescue plan;
- the order of preference in which creditors will be paid – this provision appears to indicate that the plan may provide for any order of preference to which the affected persons (and the creditors in particular) will be prepared to agree; for example, it could provide that a small but important supplier whose claim is unsecured will be paid before secured creditors to ensure the supplier's continued existence and ability to deliver;
- a comparison of the benefits creditors will receive if the plan is adopted with what they would receive if the company were placed in liquidation – this will enable creditors to weigh their options and to decide whether it is worthwhile to approve the plan; and
- the effect that the plan will have on the holders of each class of the company's securities – as indicated before,[153] any alteration in the classification or status of any issued securities during business rescue proceedings is invalid unless it is in terms of a court order or an approved business rescue plan. If the plan provides for such an alteration, the holders of these securities will have the right to vote on the plan in terms of s 152(3)(c).[154]

12.7.1.3   Part C – Assumptions and conditions[155]

This part of the plan must indicate the following:

- any conditions that must be fulfilled before the plan can come into operation or before it can be fully implemented;

---

150   See s 145(1)(d) of the Companies Act, 2008.
151   Section 150(2)(b) of the Companies Act, 2008.
152   In terms of s 136 of the Companies Act, 2008.
153   See para. 12.5.6.1 above.
154   See para. 12.7.3 below.
155   Section 150(2)(c) of the Companies Act, 2008.

- the effect, if any, that the business rescue plan will have on the number of employees and their conditions of employment – for example, the proposed retrenchment of any employees must be disclosed in this part of the plan, although even if the plan is approved, this does not mean that the intended retrenchments will be any easier than usual as the company will still have to comply with all the requirements and procedures prescribed by the Labour Relations Act[156] in the same way as a solvent company has to do;
- the circumstances under which the business rescue plan will come to an end – although not specifically required by the Act, it is important to set out exactly at what point the rescue plan will be regarded as substantially implemented because the business rescue proceedings will end and the practitioner relieved from office as soon as he or she files a notice of substantial implementation;[157] and
- a projected balance sheet and statement of income and expenses for the next three years based on the assumption that the plan will be adopted (this will clearly not apply if the rescue plan entails selling the business or all the assets of the business) – if these documents are included, there must also be a notice of any material assumptions on which the projections are made and they may also include alternative projections based on varying assumptions and contingencies.

12.7.1.4 Certificate

The business rescue plan must conclude with a certificate by the business rescue practitioner in which he or she states that the information provided in the plan appears to be correct and up to date, and that the projections were made in good faith on the basis of factual information and assumptions set out in the statement.[158]

12.7.2 Publication of the plan

The business rescue plan must be published within 25 business days after the appointment of the business rescue practitioner, unless a longer period is allowed either by the court on application by the company, or the holders of the majority of creditors' voting rights agree to allow additional time.[159]

12.7.3 Meeting to consider business rescue plan

The business rescue practitioner must first convene a meeting of the company's creditors to consider the rescue plan. This meeting must take place within 10 business days after publication of the plan.[160] All affected persons, including those who do not have the right to attend or vote at the meeting, must be notified of the meeting at least five business days before it is due to take place.[161]

The business rescue practitioner must explain the plan to the meeting and inform the meeting as to whether he or she still believes that there is a reasonable prospect of the company being rescued. The 2008 Act specifically provides that the representatives of the employees must be given an opportunity to address the meeting.[162] The meeting may discuss and propose amendments to the plan before voting on its approval. If the plan is supported

---

156   66 of 1995.
157   See para. 12.8 below.
158   Section 150(4) of the Companies Act, 2008.
159   Section 150(5) of the Companies Act, 2008.
160   Section 151(1) of the Companies Act, 2008.
161   Section 151(2) of the Companies Act, 2008.
162   Section 152(1)(c) of the Companies Act, 2008.

by more than 75 per cent in value of all the creditors who voted, and at least 50 per cent in value of independent creditors[163] who voted, and if no rights of shareholders[164] of any class are altered, the plan is regarded as finally approved.

However, if the rights of any shareholders are altered by the plan, the approval by creditors is only a preliminary approval, and the plan must also be approved by the majority of the relevant shareholders at a meeting convened for this purpose.[165]

12.7.4   Effect of approval

Approval of the rescue plan makes the plan binding on the company and all its creditors (including, apparently, the secured creditors) and holders of its securities, irrespective of whether such a person voted for or against the plan or even attended the meeting where the plan was considered.[166] A creditor may therefore enforce a debt that was owed by the company immediately before the business rescue started only in accordance with the rescue plan that was approved and implemented in terms of Chapter 6 of the Act.[167]

The business rescue practitioner must now take all the necessary steps to fulfil any conditions to which implementation of the plan may be subject, and to implement the plan itself. As soon as the rescue plan has been substantially implemented, the business rescue practitioner must file a notice to this effect with the Commission.[168]

12.7.5   Effect of rejection

If the plan is rejected by the creditors or, where applicable, by the shareholders, the business rescue practitioner may either seek approval from the holders of voting interests (in other words, the creditors) to prepare and publish a revised plan, or inform the meeting that the company will apply to court to have the result of their votes set aside on the grounds that the majority decision was inappropriate.[169] The Act does not contain any criteria to determine whether the result of a vote was inappropriate but in *Advanced Technologies and Engineering Company (Pty) Ltd (in business rescue) v Aeronautique et Technologies Embarquées SAS*,[170] Tuchten J remarked *obiter* that a court could not declare the vote itself inappropriate since it was based on the voter's personal opinion of what would be in his or her own best interests and the court could not substitute its own view for that of the person who voted. The court could merely determine whether the *result* of the vote was inappropriate at the time of voting and if so, whether it was reasonable and just to set it aside at the time of the application. Section 153(7) provides that in deciding whether it is just and reasonable to set aside a vote the court has to consider the interests of the person or persons who voted against the plan, the provision made in the plan with regard to those interests and a fair and reasonable estimate of the return to those persons should the company be liquidated.

---

163 Section 128(1)(*g*) of the Companies Act, 2008 provides that an independent creditor is a person who (i) is a creditor of the company, including an employee who has not been paid prior to the commencement of business rescue proceedings; and (ii) is not related to the company, a director, or the practitioner.

164 The Act refers to the holders of the company's securities and not to shareholders, but since debenture holders (who are also holders of securities according to the definition of 'securities' in s 1) are creditors of the company and would be entitled to vote as such, it is possible that the legislature intended to include only shareholders in this provision.

165 Section 152(3) of the Companies Act, 2008.

166 Section 152(4) of the Companies Act, 2008.

167 Section 154 of the Companies Act, 2008.

168 Section 152(8) of the Companies Act, 2008.

169 Section 153(1)(*a*) of the Companies Act, 2008. Note that even where the shareholders have rejected the plan, the creditors must approve the preparation of a new plan.

170 Supra.

If the business rescue practitioner fails to do either of the above (that is, seek approval for a revised plan or set aside a negative vote), any affected person present at the meeting may either ask for approval from the creditors for a proposal that the business rescue practitioner must prepare a revised plan, or may apply to court for an order setting aside the result of the voting on the same grounds as above.[171]

A third alternative is that one or more affected persons may make an offer to purchase the voting interests of any of the persons who opposed the plan, thereby obtaining enough votes for approval of the plan at the next meeting that must be held within five business days.[172] The use of the words 'voting interests' appears to limit the application of this option to the purchase of creditors' votes but this is not correct since s 146(e)(ii) specifically allows a holder of the company's securities to acquire the interests of creditors or other holders of the company's securities. The drafters of the Act appear to have drafted this provision without considering that the definition of 'voting interests' only refers to the votes of creditors.

In cases where the business rescue practitioner has to prepare and publish a new plan, he or she must do so within 10 business days after the meeting, and then go through the process for approval all over again.[173]

If nobody takes any of the above actions, the business rescue practitioner must file a notice of termination of the business rescue proceedings with the Commission.[174]

12.8 Termination of rescue proceedings

It is generally believed that the rescue of a business has the best chance of succeeding if it begins as soon as possible after problems arise and is then completed within the shortest possible period. As a result, the business rescue proceedings in the 2008 Act are intended to take no more than three months in total (which in practice has proved to be completely unrealistic: a period of between six and 18 months is more likely to be realistic). If the proceedings cannot be completed within three months after being commenced, the business rescue practitioner may apply to court for more time. The practitioner is not compelled to make such an application but may choose the alternative option which is to deliver a monthly report on the progress of the business rescue proceedings to each affected person and to the court (if the proceedings were started by a court order) or otherwise to the Commission, until the termination of the business rescue proceedings.[175]

In terms of s 132(2), business rescue proceedings are terminated in any of the following ways:

- by an order of court setting aside the resolution or order that commenced the proceedings; or
- by the court converting[176] the rescue into liquidation proceedings;
- by the practitioner filing a notice of termination of business rescue proceedings with the Commission in terms of s 153(5) or s 141(2)(b)(ii);

---

171 Section 153(1)(b)(i) of the Companies Act, 2008.
172 Section 153(1)(b)(ii) of the Companies Act, 2008.
173 Section 153(3) of the Companies Act, 2008.
174 Section 153(5) of the Companies Act, 2008. See para. 12.8 below.
175 Section 132(3) of the Companies Act, 2008.
176 Strictly speaking, the Act does not provide for any conversion of business rescue proceedings to liquidation proceedings but clearly states in s 141(2)(a)(ii) that if the practitioner concludes that there is no reasonable prospect for the company to be rescued, the practitioner must apply to court for an order *discontinuing* the business rescue proceedings and placing the company into liquidation.

- by a business rescue plan being adopted and substantially implemented, as confirmed by the business rescue practitioner in a filed notice; or
- by a business rescue plan being rejected without any further steps being taken by an affected person to extend the proceedings, as described in paragraph 12.7.5 above. Although s 132(2)(c)(i) creates the impression that the mere fact that no steps have been taken by an affected person after rejection of the rescue plan will automatically end the business rescue proceedings, this is not correct. Section 153(5) clearly stipulates that the practitioner must file a notice of termination if no person takes any action as contemplated in s 153(1).

PART B – COMPROMISES

12.9   Compromises: introduction

Prior to the introduction of the Companies Act, 2008, the Companies Act, 1973 made provision for a company to enter into a compromise with its creditors and/or an arrangement with its shareholders.[177]

The compromise procedure was dealt with under ss 311 to 313 of the 1973 Act, and was a court-driven procedure from the time the procedure commenced, right up to the time the court sanctioned the compromise and arrangement. Essentially, a **compromise** is an agreement between a company and its creditors in terms of which the creditors agree to accept less than their full claims against the company, for example accepting 50 cents in the rand in full settlement of what is due to them.

It should be clear that the purpose of a court-monitored process is to protect the parties that may be affected by any compromise and arrangement, in order to ensure that none of the parties is prejudiced by its terms. Since the concept of a court-driven compromise has been part of South Africa's company law for decades, building up a substantial body of case law over this period of time, it was surprising to see the introduction of a new compromise procedure that requires the court to sanction the compromise only once one has been reached by all the parties involved.

In essence, the new procedure does away with court involvement in commencing the procedure and in reaching a compromise. This is quite a deviation from the earlier, entrenched procedure, and it will be interesting to see how this works – especially as the court's power to decline the sanctioning of the compromise has been retained. It is clear that the legislature has opted to simplify the procedure in order to allow a company to enter into a compromise with its creditors.[178]

According to s 155(1) of the Companies Act, 2008, the provisions relating to a compromise can apply to a company even if the company is not financially distressed,[179] but they do not apply to a company that is 'engaged in business rescue proceedings' or is a company contemplated in s 128(1) of the 2008 Act.

Table 12.1 below sets out who may propose a compromise, to whom and in what manner, as provided for in s 155(2).

---

177   A scheme of arrangement between a company and the holders of any class of its securities is now one of the fundamental (or affected) transactions regulated by Chapter 5 of the Act. See para. 10.3.3 above.

178   Section 155(1) of the Companies Act, 2008.

179   For the meaning of the term 'financially distressed', see s 128(1)(f) of the Companies Act, 2008.

Table 12.1 Proposals of compromise

Who may propose a compromise?	To whom?	How?	To whom?
• A company's board of directors, or • The liquidator of the company (if the company is being wound up)	• All the company's creditors, or • All the members of any class of the company's creditors	By delivering a copy of the proposal and notice of a meeting to consider the proposal	• Every creditor of the company,[180] or • Every member of the relevant class of creditors whose name and address is known to or can reasonably be obtained by the company,[181] and • The Commission[182]

PRACTICAL ISSUE

Compromise

If the liquidator of a company in liquidation intends to propose a compromise, it makes sense and is good business practice for a notice to be given to the shareholders who are the major stakeholders in the company. A meeting of shareholders should ideally be held in order to consider the compromise.

12.10 Information to accompany a proposal of compromise

A proposal for a compromise must contain all information reasonably required to assist creditors in deciding whether or not to accept or reject the proposal.[183] In order to achieve this, s 155(3) states that the proposal must be divided into three parts, namely:

1. Part A – Background;
2. Part B – Proposals; and
3. Part C – Assumptions and conditions.

You will notice that the required information is almost identical to that required for a business rescue plan, which is unfortunate since a compromise is intended to be an informal and flexible process that can easily be adapted to fit a particular situation. Requiring all the prescribed information – some of which will not always be applicable – could result in a rigid and expensive procedure. However, it is hoped that the courts will adopt the same approach as in *Commissioner for the South African Revenue Service v Beginsel NO*,[184] where substantial (rather than complete) compliance with the applicable requirements was accepted as sufficient in a business rescue plan.

---

180 Section 155(2)*(a)* of the Companies Act, 2008.
181 *Ibid.*
182 Section 155(2)*(b)* of the Companies Act, 2008.
183 Section 155(3) of the Companies Act, 2008.
184 Supra.

12.10.1   Part A – Background to the proposal

In terms of s 155(3)*(a)*, Part A of the proposal must contain at least the following information:

- a complete list of all the material assets of the company, including an indication as to which of these assets are held as security by creditors on the date of the proposal;[185]
- a complete list of the creditors of the company as on the date of the proposal, including an indication as to which creditors qualify as secured, statutory preferent and concurrent creditors under the laws of insolvency, and an indication as to which of the creditors have proved their claims;[186]
- the probable dividend that would be paid to creditors (in their specific class) if the company was placed in liquidation;[187]
- a complete list of the holders of the securities issued by the company, and the effect the proposal will have on them (if any);[188] and
- whether the proposal includes a proposal made informally by a creditor of the company.[189]

CRITICAL ISSUE	**List of material assets**
	Although a complete list of the material assets needs to be provided to creditors, it seems strange that the list does not need to be provided with a recent valuation of such assets. If the purpose of the additional information is to allow creditors to make an informed decision, then a list of assets without stating the value of the assets does not seem to be of much assistance.
	The reference to creditors having proved their claims will be relevant only where the company is in liquidation. There will be no other circumstances in which there will be an opportunity for creditors to formally prove their claims.

12.10.2   Part B – Details of proposal

In terms of s 155(3)*(b)*, Part B must contain details of the proposals, and must include at least the following:

- the nature and duration of any proposed debt moratorium;[190]
- the extent to which the company will be released from the payment of its debts, and the extent to which any debt is proposed to be converted to equity in the company (or another company);[191]
- the treatment of contracts and the ongoing role of the company (in those contracts);[192]
- the property of the company that will be made available for the payment of creditors' claims;[193]

---

185   Section 155(3)*(a)*(i) of the Companies Act, 2008.
186   Section 155(3)*(a)*(ii) of the Companies Act, 2008.
187   Section 155(3)*(a)*(iii) of the Companies Act, 2008.
188   Section 155(3)*(a)*(iv) of the Companies Act, 2008.
189   Section 155(3)*(a)*(v) of the Companies Act, 2008.
190   Section 155(3)*(b)*(i) of the Companies Act, 2008.
191   Section 155(3)*(b)*(ii) of the Companies Act, 2008.
192   Section 155(3)*(b)*(iii) of the Companies Act, 2008.
193   Section 155(3)*(b)*(iv) of the Companies Act, 2008.

- the order of preference in terms of which the proceeds of property will be applied to pay creditors once the proposal is adopted;[194] and
- the benefits of adopting the proposal as opposed to the benefits that would be received by creditors if the company was placed in liquidation.[195]

12.10.3 Part C – Assumptions and conditions of the proposal

In terms of s 155(3)*(c)*, Part C must contain the assumptions and conditions contained in the proposals, and must include at least the following:
- a statement of the conditions that must be satisfied (if any)
  - for the proposal to come into operation;[196] and
  - for the proposal to be fully implemented;[197]
- the effect (if any) that the plan will have on the number of employees, as well as on their terms and conditions of employment;[198] and
- a projected
  - balance sheet for the company;[199] and
  - statement of income and expenses for the three ensuing years.[200]

12.11 Other requirements

There are various other requirements that must be met with regard to the proposal in which the compromise is embodied.

12.11.1 Projected balance sheet and statement

The projected balance sheet and statement required by s 155(3)*(c)*(iii) must include a notice 'of any significant assumptions on which the projections are based',[201] and 'may include alternative projections based on varying assumptions and contingencies'.[202]

CRITICAL ISSUE	Compromise
	If a company is no longer trading, it will be difficult to comply with the strict requirements of providing a balance sheet and a statement of income and expenses. Since these are set as an absolute requirement by the 2008 Act, this may mean that a compromise may not be entered into in such cases. In addition, the question arises whether this information is important if the compromise provides for creditors to be paid in full, or to receive an immediate cash payment.

---

194 Section 155(3)*(b)*(v) of the Companies Act, 2008.
195 Section 155(3)*(b)*(vi) of the Companies Act, 2008.
196 Section 155(3)*(c)*(i)*(aa)* of the Companies Act, 2008.
197 Section 155(3)*(c)*(i)*(bb)* of the Companies Act, 2008.
198 Section 155(3)*(c)*(ii) of the Companies Act, 2008.
199 Section 155(3)*(c)*(iii)*(aa)* of the Companies Act, 2008.
200 Section 155(3)*(c)*(iii)*(bb)* of the Companies Act, 2008.
201 Section 155(4)*(a)* of the Companies Act, 2008.
202 Section 155(4)*(b)* of the Companies Act, 2008.

12.11.2   Certificate by authorised director or prescribed officer of company

A proposal for a compromise must conclude with a certificate by an authorised director or prescribed officer of that company,[203] stating that:

- any factual information provided in the proposal appears to be accurate, complete and up to date;[204] and
- any projections provided are estimates made in good faith on the basis of factual information and assumptions as detailed in the statement.[205]

12.11.3   Majority required for adoption of proposal

In terms of s 155(6), a proposal for a compromise will be regarded as adopted by the creditors of the company (or by the members of a relevant class of creditors) if it is supported by a majority in number, representing at least 75 per cent in value of the creditors or class, as the case may be, present and voting in person or by proxy, at the meeting called for that purpose. It is noticeable that the Act does not specify a quorum for this meeting and the proposal could thus be adopted even if only a small number of the affected creditors attend the meeting. However, this is one of the factors that a court must take into consideration when exercising its discretion whether to sanction the compromise.[206]

12.11.4   Adopted proposal to be sanctioned by court

In terms of s 155(7)(a), the company may apply to the High Court for an order approving (sanctioning) the proposal, if it has been adopted by the creditors in accordance with s 155(6). Although the 2008 Act uses the word 'may', it is clear that the proposal will not be enforceable until such time as the court has sanctioned it.

In terms of s 155(7)(b), the court may sanction the compromise as embodied in the adopted proposal if it considers it just and equitable to do so. In determining whether it would, in fact, be just and equitable to sanction the proposal for a compromise, the court must have regard to:

- the number of creditors of any affected class of creditors who were present or represented at the meeting and who voted in favour of the proposal;[207] and
- in the case of a compromise in respect of a company that is in liquidation, a report by the Master.[208]

In contrast to the situation under the 1973 Act where the court scrutinised the proposal at the time it was approached for permission to convene a meeting of the affected creditors (or shareholders), the company will now have no prior indication whether the court will find the terms and conditions of the proposal acceptable until after the creditors concerned have adopted it. Much time and money could be wasted if a court refuses to sanction the proposal because it is not considered just and equitable to do so.

203   Section 155(5) of the Companies Act, 2008.
204   Section 155(5)(a) of the Companies Act, 2008.
205   Section 155(5)(b) of the Companies Act, 2008.
206   Section 155(7)(b)(i) of the Companies Act, 2008.
207   Section 155(7)(b)(i) of the Companies Act, 2008.
208   Section 155(7)(b)(ii) of the Companies Act, 2008.

12.11.5 Filing requirements and effect of sanctioned compromise

In terms of s 155(8), a copy of the court order sanctioning a compromise must be filed by the company within five business days, and must be attached to each copy of the company's MOI.

Once a compromise has been sanctioned by the court, it is final and binding on all the company's creditors or all members of the relevant class of creditors, as the case may be, as from the date on which the copy of the order is filed.[209] A major weakness of the procedure is that there is no moratorium protecting the company against enforcement action by creditors in the period between delivering a copy of the proposal and filing of the order sanctioning the compromise. Creditors who are opposed to the compromise or even ones who are not part of the affected class of creditors could thus start legal proceedings against the company to enforce payment of their claims.

A compromise sanctioned in terms of s 155 does not affect the liability of any person who is a surety of the company.[210] A creditor who receives less than the total amount of a debt in terms of a compromise may thus claim the difference from the surety.

THIS CHAPTER IN ESSENCE

1. In market-based economies, some companies will inevitably fail. However, owing to the negative impact of failed businesses, efforts to avoid the liquidation of companies are warranted where possible.
2. The Companies Act, 2008 introduces a new procedure for financially distressed companies termed **business rescue** in the place of the **judicial management** procedure of the 1973 Act, which had similar aims. Another option for financially distressed companies is to enter into a **compromise** with creditors, in terms of which creditors agree to receive less than is otherwise owing to them.
3. **Business rescue proceedings** under the 2008 Act comprise the temporary supervision of the company and management of its affairs, a temporary moratorium on the rights of claimants against the company, and the development and implementation of a plan to rescue the company or achieve a better return for the company's creditors than liquidation would.
4. A company is **financially distressed** if it is reasonably unlikely to be able to pay all its debts as they become due in the next six months; or if the company is reasonably likely to become insolvent within the next six months.
5. Business rescue proceedings may be commenced through a resolution by the board of directors of the company or by court order.
6. The board of directors of a company can commence business rescue proceedings by passing a **business rescue resolution** by majority vote. Such a resolution may not be adopted if liquidation proceedings have already been initiated. The resolution takes effect upon filing with the Commission.
7. Within five business days, notice of the business rescue resolution must be given to all **affected persons** – that is, to every shareholder, creditor, registered trade union and every other unrepresented employee. Within this same period, the company must appoint a **business rescue practitioner**, which appointment must be filed with the Commission and communicated by notice to all affected persons.
8. The board may only pass a business rescue resolution if it has reasonable grounds to believe the company is financially distressed and that there appears to be a reasonable prospect of rescuing the company. If it believes the company to be financially distressed, it must either pass a business rescue resolution or notify every affected person of the reason not to adopt such a resolution.

---

209 Section 155(8)(c) of the Companies Act, 2008.
210 Section 155(9) of the Companies Act, 2008.

9. Any affected person may apply to court to set aside a business rescue resolution and/or an appointment of a business rescue practitioner, at any time before a formal business rescue plan has been adopted.

10. If the board of directors does not pass a business rescue resolution, an affected party may apply to court for an order commencing business rescue proceedings. All other affected parties must be notified of the application.

11. If the court does not grant an order for business rescue, it may dismiss the application and make any further order that may be necessary, including one placing the company under liquidation.

12. The commencement of business or corporate rescue proceedings has, among others, the following legal consequences:

    12.1 most civil legal proceedings are stayed (paused) until the end of the business rescue process;

    12.2 disposal of the company's property is restricted;

    12.3 re-financing the company is facilitated by allowing the company to use its assets to secure loans and by giving new creditors preferential claims, but debts to employees are payable first;

    12.4 employment contracts are protected and employees are preferential claimants;

    12.5 other contracts may be suspended or cancelled in certain circumstances;

    12.6 the status of issued shares may not be altered, and shareholders may only participate in decisions about business rescue if their interests will be affected; and

    12.7 directors must cooperate with the business rescue practitioner.

13. A business rescue practitioner must:

    13.1 be a member in good standing of a legal, accounting or business management profession, or be licensed by the Commission to practise as a business rescue practitioner;

    13.2 not be subject to an order of probation;

    13.3 not be disqualified from acting as director of a company;

    13.4 not have any relationships with the company leading to conflicts of interest; and

    13.5 not be related to a person with such a relationship.

14. A business rescue practitioner can be removed from office by an order of court, either on application by an affected person or on the court's own initiative.

15. A business rescue practitioner takes full responsibility for the management of the company, investigates and monitors the company's affairs with a view to ending business rescue proceedings when no longer appropriate, develops and implements a rescue plan and accepts liability for a breach of duties. The business rescue practitioner is entitled to payment by the company per prescribed tariff.

16. The business rescue practitioner must prepare a **business rescue plan** for the company in consultation with creditors, other affected persons and management. The plan must contain all information necessary for affected persons to decide whether to accept or reject the plan. The plan must be divided into:

    16.1 Part A – Background to the business rescue plan, which must include, inter alia, lists of assets, liabilities and secured creditors;

    16.2 Part B – Proposals to assist the company in overcoming its problems;

    16.3 Part C – Assumptions and conditions to be fulfilled before implementation of the plan; and

    16.4 a certificate by the business rescue practitioner stating that the information appears correct and projections are made in good faith.

17. The business rescue plan must be published within 25 business days after the business rescue practitioner's appointment, and he or she must convene a meeting of creditors within 10 business days of such publication. All affected persons must be notified.

18. If the plan is supported by more than 75 per cent in value of all voting creditors, and at least 50 per cent in value of voting **independent creditors**, and no rights of shareholders of any class are altered, the plan is regarded as finally approved. If the rights of any shareholders are altered, the plan must also be approved by the majority of relevant shareholders at a further meeting.

19. Approval of the rescue plan makes the plan binding on the company, its creditors and its shareholders. The business rescue practitioner must take all necessary steps to implement the plan and must file a notice with the Commission after implementation.

20. If the plan is rejected by creditors or shareholders, the business rescue practitioner may either prepare a revised plan, or apply to court to set aside the majority decision as irrational or inappropriate.

21. Business rescue proceedings are intended to take no more than three months, but a court may grant more time.

22. Business rescue proceedings are terminated by:

    22.1 an order of court setting aside the resolution or order that commenced the proceedings; or

    22.2 the court converting the rescue into liquidation proceedings;

    22.3 the practitioner filing a notice of termination of business rescue proceedings with the Commission;

    22.4 a business rescue plan being adopted and substantially implemented, as confirmed by the business rescue practitioner in a filed notice; or

    22.5 a business rescue plan being rejected without any further steps being taken by an affected person.

23. The other option for companies, irrespective of whether they are financially distressed or not, is to agree a compromise with creditors. The 2008 Act introduces a new compromise procedure, apparently to simplify the old s 311 procedure, which required continuous court involvement. The court's sanction will now be required only after a compromise has been agreed to.

24. A company's board of directors or a liquidator may propose a compromise to all creditors (or all members of any class of creditor). Such a proposal must contain all information reasonably required to decide whether or not to accept or reject the proposal. This information is similar to that required for a business rescue plan.

25. A proposal for a compromise will be regarded as adopted, if it is supported by a majority in number, representing at least 75 per cent in value of the relevant voting creditors. A compromise will not be enforceable until it has been made an order of court.

Chapter 13

Audit, independent review, audit committees and the company secretary

13.1 Audit and the Auditing Profession Act

Subjecting the financial statements of companies to an audit or to an independent review is a key tool used by the legislature to attempt to protect stakeholders from potential harm caused by unreliable, inaccurate, unfair, misleading or dishonest information that could be contained in financial statements. However, in terms of the Companies Act, 2008, not all companies need to have their financial statements audited or independently reviewed. It is therefore necessary to stipulate on any financial statements or summary of any financial statements whether the statements have been audited or independently reviewed, or whether they are unaudited or not reviewed.[1]

---

1 Section 29(1)(e) of the Companies Act, 2008.

Section 1 of the Companies Act, 2008 provides that the words 'auditor' and 'audit' have the meaning as set out in the Auditing Profession Act (AP Act).[2] The latter defines a **registered auditor** as an individual or firm registered as an auditor with the Independent Regulatory Board for Auditors (IRBA). This Board is established in terms of the AP Act.[3] In the context of financial statements, an **audit** is defined as the examination of financial statements, in accordance with prescribed or applicable auditing standards, with the objective of expressing an opinion as to their fairness or compliance with an identified financial reporting framework and applicable statutory requirements. An auditor is obliged to give an opinion on the annual financial statements.

An independent review is a less onerous process than an audit, and is discussed in paragraph 13.3 below.

---

2   26 of 2005.
3   Section 3 of the AP Act. See para. 13.8 below for more details on this Board.
4   Supra.

regulated under the Public Accountants' and Auditors' Act.[5] That Act has now been repealed and replaced by the Auditing Profession Act, 2005.

The purpose of the Auditing Profession Act is to improve the integrity of South Africa's financial sector and financial reporting by introducing a more comprehensive and modern legislative framework for overseeing and regulating the auditing profession. The Independent Regulatory Board for Auditors is formed in terms of that Act. In terms of s 20, the Board must appoint several permanent committees, including a committee for auditing standards in accordance with s 22. This committee will, inter alia, assist the Regulatory Board to maintain, adopt, issue or prescribe auditing pronouncements and consider relevant international changes by monitoring developments by other auditing standard-setting bodies and sharing information where requested.

The Act specifically provides that only a registered auditor can perform an audit as defined. This means, for example, that members of the South African Institute of Professional Accountants (SAIPA) cannot perform an audit and express an audit opinion. However, members of SAIPA would be able to conduct an independent review, in the same way that they are empowered to issue a report of an accounting officer of a close corporation.

In a comprehensive article[6] on the reasons for the introduction of the AP Act, the authors, Professors Odendaal and De Jager, state the following in their introduction to the article:

> As a result of the worldwide spate of financial scandals, society has lost much of its confidence in the auditing profession because of a growing perception that the profession does not act in the public interest. Ineffective regulation is one of the key factors detracting from the value of the audit function, thereby undermining public confidence in the profession as a whole. The opportunity has been grasped in South Africa, as in some other countries, to make changes to the regulatory mechanisms of the auditing profession in an effort to restore trust in the profession. In this article the regulation of the auditing profession in South Africa, according to the Auditing Profession Act, 2005, (implemented in April 2006), is evaluated against the factors that are of importance to an effective and creditable regulatory system with reference to the regulation of the profession in some other English speaking countries with which the South African auditing profession has historical and professional ties. It appears that those factors that are important to a regulatory system are to a large degree addressed by the regulation of the auditing profession in South Africa. This should contribute to restore the trust in the auditing profession.

The Companies Act, 2008 seeks to ensure that the auditor of a company is independent of the company that is being audited.[7] Section 90(2) therefore disqualifies certain people from being appointed as auditor of a company. Thus, for example, the auditor cannot be a director or an employee of the company. An auditor is not an officer of the company. Nevertheless, details of the auditor must be included in the company's records.[8]

---

5   80 of 1991.
6   EM Odendaal and H De Jager 'Regulation of the auditing profession in South Africa' (2008) 8 *The Southern African Journal of Accountability and Auditing Research* 1.
7   Discussed in para. 13.4 below.
8   See para. 13.4 below for more detail.

The Auditing Profession Act[9] makes provisions for who may practise as an auditor and restricts unregistered persons from certain auditing activities.

PRACTICAL ISSUE	Auditor's engagement letter
	When appointing an auditor, generally accepted auditing standards require the preparation of an engagement letter. The letter should give details of the terms of appointment of the auditor of a company. The letter will also include the objective of the audit, while ensuring that management is responsible for the financial statements.
	The engagement letter is also likely to include a variety of other matters – including making arrangements regarding the planning of the audit, as well as the description of any other letters or reports that the auditor expects to issue to the client.

CASE STUDY	Appointment of an auditor
	An auditor is appointed by a company in terms of a contract that obliges the auditor to perform certain services for the client. Failure to perform the obligations properly in terms of this contract can lead to the auditor being personally liable to its client for any loss suffered by that client as a result of inadequate performance.
	This principle was clearly illustrated in the case of *Thoroughbred Breeders' Association v Price Waterhouse*.[10] In this case, during the course of investigations into the affairs of a business, it became apparent that an employee had stolen considerable sums of money from the business. It was common cause in this case that the auditors were contractually bound to exercise reasonable care in the execution of the audit and not to do the work negligently. The allegation in this case was that the auditors had failed in that respect, and that had the audit work been done properly, the employee's theft would have been uncovered fairly early on, and that all the direct losses suffered by the business due to the employee's subsequent thefts and his inability to repay were accordingly for the auditor's account.
	The auditors, however, denied that they were negligent and argued that they had not committed a breach of contract vis-à-vis their client. In the alternative, the auditors argued that the true cause of the loss was the business's own negligence: first, in employing the thief; second, in retaining him as its financial officer after discovering that he had a criminal record; third, in failing to inform the auditors of such a record; and, fourth, in failing, through inadequate and lax internal controls, to supervise and control the employee's activities properly.
	The court held that had the auditors probed further in the course of their audit, as they should have done when certain accounting records were found to be missing, the employee's past thefts would have been uncovered and his future ones avoided. The court concluded that a competent auditor would have known that the failure to recognise, identify and engage a problem of this kind could lead to a prospective loss of the kind suffered. The auditors were therefore found to be negligent and liable for the losses suffered by their client.

---

9   26 of 2005.
10 2001 (4) SA 551 (SCA).

Chapter 3 of the Companies Act, 2008[11] is entitled 'Enhanced accountability and transparency'. It deals specifically with the appointment, duties and other matters pertaining to the company secretary, auditors and audit committees. Generally speaking, the enhanced accountability and transparency provisions apply to public companies and to state-owned companies, and not to private companies.

However, certain private companies must comply with the sections relating to the appointment of auditors if they are required by the Companies Act or by the company's MOI to have their financial statements audited.[12] However, even those private companies that are required to appoint an auditor are not required by the Companies Act to appoint a company secretary or an audit committee, but of course a company's MOI might require any private company to appoint a company secretary and/or audit committee.

13.2   Which companies' financial statements are subject to an audit?

Public companies, both listed and unlisted, as well as state-owned companies are obliged by the Companies Act to have their annual financial statements audited. Moreover, these companies must appoint an audit committee,[13] which has certain statutory functions.[14]

A private company may also be required to have its annual financial statements audited in terms of the regulations made in terms of s 30(7) of the 2008 Act. In determining which companies will be required to appoint an auditor, the Minister may, in terms of s 30(2)*(b)* of the Act, take into account whether an audit of the financial statements is desirable in the public interest, having regard to the economic or social significance of the company, as indicated by its annual turnover, the size of its workforce, or the nature and extent of its activities. All other private companies, with the exception of owner-managed private companies,[15] require an **independent review** of their financial statements.[16]

13.2.1   Private companies: activity criteria for appointment of auditor

Any private company[17] must appoint an auditor if, in the ordinary course of its *primary* activities:

- it holds assets in a fiduciary capacity;
- for persons who are not related to the company; and
- the aggregate value of such assets held at any time during the financial year exceeds R5 million.

This activity test relates to the *primary* activities of the company, not incidental or resulting activities, and specifically states 'in a fiduciary capacity'.

The South African Institute of Chartered Accountants (SAICA) gives the example of a company that operates as an estate agency: the holding of funds in trust is incidental to the company's primary business and is not in a fiduciary capacity. The Companies Act would

---

11   Sections 84 to 94 of the Companies Act, 2008.
12   See paras. 13.2 below to determine which private companies are required to have their financial statements audited.
13   These companies must also appoint a company secretary.
14   See para. 13.9 below for further discussion of audit committees.
15   See para. 13.2.3 below for the exemption applicable to owner-managed private companies.
16   Independent review is discussed in para. 13.3 below.
17   Including an owner-managed private company. See para. 13.2.3 below.

thus not require an audit on this basis, but laws applicable to estate agents might well require an audit.[18]

13.2.2 Private companies: size criteria for appointment of auditor and meaning of public interest score

A private company[19] would also be required by the regulations to appoint an auditor if its public interest score in a financial year is:

- 350 or more; or
- at least 100, but less than 350, if its annual financial statements for that year were *internally* compiled.

As SAICA points out, the inclusion of size criteria will inevitably mean that a large number of private companies will be required to have their financial statements audited. Private companies with a score below 350 but above 100, who wish to avoid having to appoint an auditor, would therefore be well advised to have their financial statements *externally* compiled.

The concept of a **public interest score** appears to be an attempt to satisfy the requirement in the Act[20] that the audit requirement should take into consideration the turnover, size of workforce and the nature and extent of the company's activities. The public interest score must be calculated by a company for each financial year as the sum of the following:

1. one point each for the average number of employees of the company at any one time during the financial year;
2. one point for every R1 million (or portion thereof) in third party debt of the company at the financial year end;
3. one point for every R1 million (or portion thereof) in turnover during the financial year; and
4. one point for every individual who, at the end of the financial year, is known by the company in the case of a profit company, directly or indirectly to have a beneficial interest in any of the company's issued securities; or in the case of a non-profit company, to be a member of the company, or a member of an association that is a member of the company.

Whereas a company would have to be quite sizeable to score the 350 points required for an audit, a private company with as low a score as 100 points (up to 349 points) would nevertheless require an audit if its annual financial statements are compiled internally. This is presumably an attempt to ensure that the compilation of financial statements is performed by an independent external professional.

13.2.3 Private companies: exemption from audit and independent review

If a private company does not require an audit in terms of the regulations (due to their activities or size criteria as discussed above), *and* if all holders of beneficial interests are also directors of the company, then the requirement for an independent review is also not

---

18 See *www.saica.co.za.*
19 Including an owner-managed private company. See para. 13.2.3 below.
20 Section 30(2)*(b)*(i) of the Companies Act, 2008.

applicable to such 'owner-managed' private companies.[21] In other words, such 'owner-managed' private companies require neither an audit nor an independent review of their financial statements.

However, all owner-managed private companies that meet the requirement to be audited in terms of the activity or size tests do require an audit.

In practice, this exemption means that owner-managed private companies that are required by the regulations to appoint an auditor do not benefit from this exemption, and the exemption then only really applies to certain owner-managed private companies in respect of the need for an independent review.

13.2.4   Summary of which companies should appoint an auditor

It is clear that not all companies are required to have their annual financial statements audited. A public company, a state-owned company and certain private companies[22] must appoint an auditor every year at the annual general meeting.[23] Other companies may voluntarily appoint an auditor, even though they are not obliged to do so. A company could also be required to appoint an auditor in terms of its MOI.

In summary, the following companies are required to appoint an auditor:

- public companies;
- state-owned companies;
- any private company[24] that, as its primary activity, holds assets in a fiduciary capacity for persons not related to the company, where the aggregate value of the assets exceeds R5 million at any time during the financial year;
- any private company with a public interest score[25] in that financial year, of 350 points or more;
- any private company with a 'public interest score' in that financial year, of between 100 and 349 points, if its annual financial statements were *internally* compiled;
- a company whose MOI requires it to be audited;
- a company that voluntarily has its annual financial statements audited either as a result of a directors' or shareholders' resolution; and
- any non-profit company that was incorporated by the State, an organ of state, a state-owned company, an international entity, a foreign state entity or a company; or was incorporated primarily to perform a statutory or regulatory function.

All other companies, with the exception of owner-managed private companies that are not required by the regulations to be audited, require an independent review of their financial statements.[26]

Table 13.1 summarises the audit and independent review requirements.

---

21 Section 30(2A) of the Companies Act essentially provides that if every person who is a holder of, or has a beneficial interest in, any securities issued by a private company is also a director of the company, that company is exempt from the requirements to have its annual financial statements audited or independently reviewed, unless it falls into a class of company that is required to have its annual financial statement audited in terms of the regulations.

22 Generally speaking, private companies that hold assets in a fiduciary capacity on behalf of third parties, or private companies with a certain level of public interest score, are required to have their financial statements audited.

23 The Companies Act refers to the appointment of an auditor at a company's 'annual general meeting'. Although a private company is not obliged to hold an annual general meeting, the company's auditor must nevertheless be appointed at a shareholders' meeting on an annual basis.

24 The activity and size criteria apply to both private companies and to close corporations.

25 Note that the Minister has power to change the qualifying score, and the number of points required for audit can change at any time by regulation. It is advisable to confirm the most recent qualifying score determined by the Minister.

26 Independent review is discussed in para. 13.3 below.

Table 13.1 Summary of audit and independent review requirements

Profit companies	Audit or independent review
State-owned companies	Audit by a registered auditor
Public companies listed on an exchange	Audit by a registered auditor
Public companies not listed on an exchange	Audit by a registered auditor
Private companies (a) whose public interest score for the particular financial year is at least 350[27] *or* (b) who hold assets in excess of R5 million in a fiduciary capacity	Audit by a registered auditor
Private companies whose public interest score for the particular financial year is at least 100, but less than 350	(a) Independent review by a registered auditor or CA (SA), provided the financial statements are *independently* compiled. Owner-managed private companies would not have to have an independent review (b) Audit by a registered auditor if the financial statements are *internally* compiled. The owner-managed exemption will not apply to these companies
Private companies whose public interest score for the particular financial year is less than 100, and whose statements are *internally* or *independently* compiled	Independent review by (a) a registered auditor, or (b) by a CA (SA) or (c) by any person who qualifies to be an accounting officer of a close corporation. Owner-managed private companies would not have to have an independent review

---

CONTEXTUAL ISSUE

Audit requirement for companies holding assets in fiduciary capacity

If any private company holds assets in a fiduciary capacity as part of its primary activity for persons not related to the company (where the aggregate value of the assets exceeds R5 million), it is required to have an audit done of its financial statements. A company holds assets in a fiduciary capacity if, for example, it receives money from people to invest on their behalf. The audit requirement in these circumstances makes sense.

There have been so many cases of fraud and theft involving companies taking deposits from investors, with a subsequent theft or misappropriation of such funds leading to huge losses for investors. There is a real need to protect people who invest funds with companies. An audit of the financial statements of such companies is one of the measures put in place to try to prevent theft, fraud and losses for the investing public.

---

27 The Minister has the power to change this public interest score at any time by regulation.

13.3   Independent review and the role of the independent accounting professional

The regulations provide that certain companies, although not required to have their financial statements audited, need their statements to be independently reviewed – unless the company is exempt from such review. Generally speaking, a private company's financial statements are subject to independent review.[28] Any company that has voluntarily opted to have its financial statements audited does not have to be subject to an independent review. An independent review must comply with published International Review Standards.

In terms of the latest draft regulations, the independent review must be performed by an auditor or other approved professional in terms of the Auditing Profession Act[29] if the company's public interest score for a particular financial year is 100 points and above. If the company's public interest score is less than 100 points, the review may be performed by any person defined as an independent accounting professional.

An **independent accounting professional** is defined in the Regulations as a person who is:

- a registered auditor in terms of the Auditing Profession Act; or
- a member in good standing of a professional body that has been accredited in terms of s 33 of the Auditing Profession Act; or
- qualified to be appointed as an accounting officer of a close corporation in terms of s 60(1), (2) and (4) of the Close Corporations Act 69 of 1984;

and who:

- does not have a personal financial interest in the company or a related or inter-related company;
- is not involved in the day-to-day management of the company's business, nor has been so involved at any time during the previous three financial years;
- is not a prescribed officer, or full-time executive employee, of the company or another related or inter-related company, nor has been such an officer or employee at any time during the previous three financial years;
- is not related to any of the above persons; and
- was not involved in the preparation of the relevant annual financial statements.

The effect of the regulations is therefore that only registered auditors and CAs (SA) may do an independent review of companies with a public interest score of more than 100. An independent review may also not be carried out by a person who is not independent of the company nor by an independent accounting professional (IAP) who was involved in the preparation of the financial statements. This latter prohibition is interpreted to apply only to the individual concerned and not the firm. Where one partner prepares the financial statements and another performs the review, the firm will need to consider whether there is an impairment of independence before accepting the appointment as IAP.

---

28   As discussed earlier in this chapter, the exception is a private company where all shareholders are also directors of the company. This type of company requires neither an audit nor an independent review.

29   In other words, such person has to be a member of the South African Institute of Chartered Accountants (SAICA).

13.4 Appointment and independence of an auditor

A public company, a state-owned company and certain private companies[30] must appoint an auditor every year at the annual general meeting.

Section 90 of the Companies Act, 2008 states who can and who cannot be appointed as an auditor. To be appointed as an auditor of a company, a person or firm:

- must be a registered auditor;
- must not be a director, company secretary or prescribed officer of the company, or an employee or consultant of the company who was or has been engaged for more than one year in either the maintenance of any of the company's financial records, or the preparation of any of its financial statements;
- cannot be a person who, alone or with a partner or employees, habitually or regularly performs the duties of accountant or bookkeeper, or performs related secretarial work, for the company;
- must not be a person who, at any time during the five financial years immediately preceding the date of appointment, was acting in a capacity that would have precluded that person from being appointed as the auditor of the company; and
- must be acceptable to the company's audit committee as being independent of the company.[31]

A retiring auditor may be automatically re-appointed at an annual general meeting without any resolution being passed, unless any of the following circumstances apply:

- the retiring auditor is no longer qualified for appointment;
- the retiring auditor is no longer willing to accept the appointment;
- the retiring auditor is required to cease serving as auditor in terms of s 92;[32]
- the company's audit committee objects to the reappointment; or
- the company has notice of an intended resolution to appoint some other person or persons in place of the retiring auditor.

If an annual general meeting of a company does not appoint or re-appoint an auditor, the directors must fill the vacancy in the office within 40 business days after the date of the meeting.

13.5 Resignation of auditors and vacancies

The resignation of an auditor is effective when the notice of resignation is filed. If a vacancy arises in the office of auditor of a company, the board of the company must appoint a new auditor within 40 business days, if there was only one incumbent auditor of the company. That deadline does not apply if there was more than one incumbent, although while any

---

30 Generally speaking, private companies that hold assets in a fiduciary capacity on behalf of third parties, or private companies with a certain level of public interest score, as discussed above, are required to have their financial statements audited. Although a private company is not obliged to hold an annual general meeting, the company's auditor must nevertheless be appointed at a shareholders' meeting on an annual basis.

31 This reference to the audit committee would obviously only apply to a company that has such a committee. Private companies, even if they are required by the regulations to appoint an auditor, are not required by the Act to have an audit committee. But any company that is required by the Act to have, or who voluntarily (by virtue of its MOI or otherwise) has an audit committee, must comply with this requirement.

32 See discussion on rotation of auditors in para. 13.6 below.

such vacancy continues, the surviving or continuing auditor must act as auditor of the company.

Before making an appointment to fill a vacancy, the board must propose to the company's audit committee, within 15 business days after the vacancy occurs, the name of at least one registered auditor to be considered for appointment as the new auditor. The board can make an appointment of the person proposed to the audit committee if, within five business days after delivering the proposal, the audit committee does not give notice in writing to the board rejecting the proposed auditor.

If a company appoints a firm as its auditor, any change in the composition of the members of that firm does not, ordinarily, by itself create a vacancy in the office for that year. However, if, by comparison with the membership of a firm at the time of its latest appointment, fewer than one half of the members remain after any change in the composition of the firm, that change will constitute the resignation of the firm as auditor of the company, giving rise to a vacancy.

13.6   Rotation of auditors

Section 92 of the Companies Act, 2008 provides that the same individual may not serve as the auditor or designated auditor of a company for more than five consecutive financial years.[33] This does not mean that the same firm cannot be appointed for longer than five years. The five-year restriction applies to any individual person within a firm. The purpose of this five-year rule is to ensure that the auditor of a company remains independent of the board of directors, so that he or she is able to express an objective opinion on a company's annual financial statements.

If an individual has served as the auditor or designated auditor of a company for two or more consecutive financial years and then ceases to be the auditor or designated auditor, the individual may not be appointed again as the auditor or designated auditor of that company until after the expiry of at least two further financial years.

If a company has appointed two or more persons as joint auditors, the company must manage the rotation required by this section in such a manner that all of the joint auditors do not relinquish office in the same year.

13.7   Rights and restricted functions of auditors

Section 93 of the Companies Act, 2008 sets out the rights of auditors and also places certain restrictions on auditors.

1. The auditor of a company has the right of access at all times to the accounting records and all books and documents of the company, and is entitled to require from the directors or prescribed officers of the company any information and explanations necessary for the performance of the auditor's duties.[34]

2. In the case of the auditor of a holding company, the auditor has the right of access to all current and former financial statements of any subsidiary of that holding company and is entitled to require from the directors or officers of the holding company or subsidiary, any information and explanations in connection with any such statements and in

---

33   The period of five years commences from 1 May 2011, and the time prior to that date is ignored in applying the five-year rule.

34   Section 93(1)(a) of the Companies Act, 2008.

connection with the accounting records, books and documents of the subsidiary as necessary for the performance of the auditor's duties.[35]

3. The auditor of a company is also entitled to attend any general shareholders' meeting, and to receive all notices of and other communications relating to any general shareholders' meeting, and to be heard at any general shareholders' meeting on any part of the business of the meeting that concerns the auditor's duties or functions.[36]

4. An auditor may apply to a court for an appropriate order to enforce its rights as auditor. A court may make any order that is just and reasonable to prevent frustration of the auditor's duties by the company or any of its directors, prescribed officers or employees.[37]

5. An auditor appointed by a company may not perform any services for that company that would place the auditor in a conflict of interest as prescribed or determined by the IRBA in terms of s 44(6) of the AP Act, or as may be determined by the company's audit committee in terms of s 94(7)(d) of the Companies Act, 2008.[38]

Section 41 of the AP Act states that only a registered auditor may:
- engage in public practice;
- hold him- or herself out as a registered auditor in public practice; or
- use the description 'public accountant', 'certified public accountant', 'registered accountant and auditor', 'accountant and auditor in public practice' or any other desig- nation or description likely to create the impression of being a registered auditor in public practice.

A person not registered may not:
- perform any auditing services;
- pretend to be, or in any manner hold or allow him- or herself to be held out as, a person registered in terms of the AP Act;
- use the name of any registered auditor or any name or title referred to above; or
- perform any act indicating or calculated to lead persons to believe that he or she is registered in terms of the AP Act.

Section 41 of the AP Act does not prohibit:
- a person employed exclusively by an entity for a salary, and not carrying on business on his or her own account, from using the description 'internal auditor' or 'accountant' in relation to that entity;
- any member of a not-for-profit club, institution or association from acting as auditor for that club, institution or association, if he or she receives no fee or other consideration for such auditing services; or
- the Auditor-General from appointing any person who is not a registered auditor to carry out on his on her behalf any auditing services which he or she is in terms of the Public Audit Act[39] required to undertake.

Section 44(1) of the AP Act provides that the registered auditor may not, without such qualifications as may be appropriate in the circumstances, express an opinion to the effect

---

35 Section 93(1)(b) of the Companies Act, 2008.
36 Section 93(1)(c) of the Companies Act, 2008.
37 Section 93(2) of the Companies Act, 2008.
38 See s 93(3) of the Companies Act, 2008.
39 25 of 2004.

that any financial statement, including any annexure thereto, which relates to the entity, fairly represents in all material respects the financial position of the entity and the results of its operations and cash flow, unless a registered auditor who is conducting the auditing services of an entity has met certain criteria, including:

- the registered auditor has carried out the auditing services free from any restrictions whatsoever and in compliance, so far as applicable, with auditing pronouncements relating to the conduct of the audit;
- the registered auditor has by means of such methods as are reasonably appropriate having regard to the nature of the entity satisfied him- or herself of the existence of all assets and liabilities shown on the financial statements;
- proper accounting records have been kept in connection with the entity in question so as to reflect and explain all its transactions and record all its assets and liabilities correctly and adequately;
- the registered auditor has obtained all information, vouchers and other documents which in the registered auditor's opinion were necessary for the proper performance of the registered auditor's duties;
- the registered auditor has not had occasion, in the course of the auditing services or otherwise during the period to which the auditing services relate, to send a report to the IRBA under s 45 relating to a reportable irregularity or that, if such a report was so sent, the registered auditor has been able, prior to expressing the opinion referred to above, to send to the IRBA a notification under s 45 that the registered auditor has become satisfied that no reportable irregularity has taken place or is taking place;
- the registered auditor has complied with all laws relating to the auditing services of that entity; and
- the registered auditor is satisfied, as far as is reasonably practicable having regard to the nature of the entity and of the auditing services carried out, as to the fairness or the truth or the correctness, as the case may be, of the financial statements.

Whilst the Act sets out the rights of an auditor, it is silent on the duties of an auditor. The duties of an auditor are to be found in s 44 of the AP Act.

13.8   Independent Regulatory Board for Auditors (IRBA)[40]

The AP Act establishes the **Independent Regulatory Board for Auditors (IRBA)**, which is established to do the following:

- promote the integrity of the auditing profession, including investigating alleged improper conduct, conducting disciplinary hearings, and imposing sanctions for improper conduct;
- protect the public in their dealings with registered auditors;
- prescribe standards of professional qualifications, competence, ethics and conduct of registered auditors;
- participate in the activities of international bodies whose main purpose is to develop and set auditing standards and to promote the auditing profession;
- publish a journal or any other publication, and issue newsletters and circulars containing information and guidelines relating to the auditing profession; and

---

40   General acknowledgement for extracts on this topic: see the *Contemporary Gazette www.gazette.co.za*, editor Pieter Stassen.

- encourage education in connection with, and research into, any matter affecting the auditing profession;
- accredit professional bodies;
- be in charge of the requirements for the registration of an auditor; and
- be the final authority on education, training and professional development.

PRACTICAL	**The IRBA**
ISSUE	The following is taken from the IRBA's website:[41]

Corporate Mission

To protect the financial interest of the South African public and international investors in South Africa through the effective regulation of audits conducted by registered auditors, in accordance with internationally recognised standards and processes.

Vision

To be an internationally recognised and respected regulator of the auditing profession in South Africa.

Objectives

- Develop and maintain auditing standards which are internationally comparable;
- Develop and maintain ethical standards which are internationally comparable;
- Provide an appropriate framework for the education and training of properly qualified auditors as well as their ongoing competence;
- Inspect and review the work of registered auditors and their practices to monitor their compliance with the professional standards;
- Investigate and take appropriate action against registered auditors in respect of non-compliance with standards and improper conduct;
- Conduct our business in an economically efficient and effective manner, in accordance with the relevant regulatory frameworks.

In doing so, we support and protect registered auditors who carry out their duties competently, fearlessly and in good faith.

Values

Our core values are:

- Independence
- Integrity
- Objectivity
- Commitment
- Accountability
- Transparency

In terms of s 20 of the AP Act, the IRBA must appoint the following permanent committees:
- a committee for auditor ethics in accordance with s 21;
- a committee for auditing standards in accordance with s 22;

---

41 See *www.irba.co.za.*

- an education, training and professional development committee;
- an investigating committee; and
- a disciplinary committee.

13.9   Audit committees[42]

At each annual general meeting, a public company, a state-owned enterprise, or any other company that has voluntarily determined to have an audit committee,[43] must elect an **audit committee** comprising at least three members. However, no audit committee need be elected if the company is a subsidiary of another company that has an audit committee, and if the audit committee of that other company will perform the functions required in terms of the Act.

Each member of the audit committee of a company must be a director of the company, but must not be involved in the day-to-day management of the company's business or have been so involved at any time during the previous three financial years. Nor can a member of the committee be a prescribed officer, or full-time executive employee, of the company or of another related or inter-related company, or have been such an officer or employee at any time during the previous three financial years. A member of an audit committee should therefore be a non-executive independent director of the company.

There are further restrictions on audit committees, in that a member also cannot be a material supplier or customer of the company, such that a reasonable and informed third party would conclude in the circumstances that the integrity, impartiality or objectivity of that director is compromised by that relationship.

Finally, a member of an audit committee also cannot hold or control more than five per cent of the general voting rights associated with the securities issued by the company or its holding company. It is therefore obvious that a member of an audit committee should be an independent person who is able to act objectively and without bias.

If the board of a company, taking into account the education, skills and experience of the company's directors who are members of the audit committee, reasonably determines that it is necessary to enhance the financial knowledge and experience of the audit committee, the board may appoint, as an additional member of the audit committee, a person who is not a director, but who has, in the opinion of the directors, the requisite knowledge and experience in financial matters to better equip the audit committee to carry out its functions. Such a person, however, must not be ineligible or disqualified in terms of the Act, as just described.

An audit committee of a company has a number of duties.[44] It must:

- nominate, for appointment as auditor of the company under s 90, a registered auditor who, in the opinion of the audit committee, is independent of the company;
- determine the fees to be paid to the auditor and the auditor's terms of engagement;
- ensure that the appointment of the auditor complies with the provisions of the Act and any other legislation relating to the appointment of auditors;
- determine, taking into account the provisions of the Act, the nature and extent of any non-audit services that the auditor may provide to the company, or that the auditor must not provide to the company, or a related company;

---

42   Section 94 of the Companies Act, 2008.
43   Or is required in terms of its MOI to appoint an MOI.
44   Section 94(7) of the Companies Act, 2008.

- pre-approve any proposed agreement with the auditor for the provision of non-audit services to the company;
- prepare a report to be included in the annual financial statements for that financial year describing how the audit committee carried out its functions, stating whether the audit committee is satisfied that the auditor was independent of the company, and commenting in any way the committee considers appropriate on the financial statements, the accounting practices and internal financial control of the company;
- receive and deal appropriately with any concerns or complaints, whether from within or outside the company, or on its own initiative, relating to the following:
  - the accounting practices and internal audit of the company;
  - the content or auditing of the company's financial statements;
  - the internal financial controls of the company; or
  - any related matter;
- make submissions to the board on any matter concerning the company's accounting policies, financial control, records and reporting; and
- perform other functions determined by the board including the development and implementation of a policy and plan for a systematic, disciplined approach to evaluate and improve the effectiveness of risk management, control, and governance processes within the company.

In considering whether a registered auditor is independent of a company,[45] an audit committee must, in relation to the company, and if the company is a member of a group of companies, any other company within that group:

- ascertain that the auditor does not receive any direct or indirect remuneration or other benefit from the company, except as auditor, or for rendering other services to the company, to the extent permitted in terms of the Act;
- consider whether the auditor's independence may have been prejudiced as a result of:
  - any previous appointment as auditor; or
  - having regard to the extent of any consultancy, advisory or other work undertaken by the auditor for the company; and
- consider compliance with other criteria relating to independence or conflict of interest as prescribed by the Independent Regulatory Board for Auditors established by the AP Act.

It is important to note that nothing prevents a public company from appointing a different auditor at its annual general meeting from the one nominated by the audit committee, but if such an auditor is appointed, the appointment is valid only if the audit committee is satisfied that the proposed auditor is independent of the company.

13.10 Mandatory appointment of company secretary[46]

A public company and a state-owned enterprise must appoint a company secretary. Other companies will appoint a company secretary if they are required to do so in terms of their MOI. The **company secretary** is the chief administrative officer of a company. When the directors appoint a person as a company secretary, they must be satisfied that the person is suitably qualified with the necessary experience to perform the duties of company secretary.

---

45   Section 94(8) of the Companies Act, 2008.
46   Sections 86–89 of the Companies Act, 2008.

A company secretary is accountable to the company's board, and his or her duties include, but are not restricted to, the following:[47]

- providing the directors of the company collectively and individually with guidance as to their duties, responsibilities and powers;
- making the directors aware of any law relevant to or affecting the company;
- reporting to the company's board any failure on the part of the company or a director to comply with the Act;
- ensuring that minutes of all shareholders' meetings, board meetings and the meetings of any committees of the directors, or of the company's audit committee, are properly recorded in accordance with the Act;
- certifying in the company's annual financial statements whether the company has filed required returns and notices in terms of the Act, and whether all such returns and notices appear to be true, correct and up to date;
- ensuring that a copy of the company's annual financial statements is sent, in accordance with the Act, to every person who is entitled to it; and
- carrying out the functions of a person designated in terms of s 33(3) of the Companies Act, 2008.[48]

A juristic person or partnership may be appointed secretary, provided that every employee of that juristic person or partner and employee of that partnership is not disqualified from being appointed company secretary. A person will be disqualified from appointment as company secretary if:[49]

- a court has prohibited that person from being a director, or declared the person to be delinquent;
- he or she is an unrehabilitated insolvent;
- he or she is prohibited in terms of any public regulation from being a director of the company;
- the person has been removed from an office of trust on the grounds of misconduct involving dishonesty; or
- he or she has been convicted, in South Africa or elsewhere, and imprisoned without the option of a fine, or fined more than the prescribed amount, for theft, fraud, forgery, perjury, or an offence:
  - involving fraud, misrepresentation or dishonesty;
  - in connection with the promotion, formation or management of a company, or in connection with any act contemplated in s 69(2) or (5) of the Companies Act, 2008; or
  - under the Companies Act, 2008, the Close Corporations Act,[50] the Financial Intelligence Centre Act,[51] the Financial Markets Act,[52] the Prevention of Corruption Act,[53] or Chapter 2 of the Prevention and Combating of Corrupt Activities Act.[54]

---

47   Section 88 of the Companies Act, 2008.
48   That is, a person designated to be responsible for ensuring the company complies with the various record-keeping and disclosure requirements of the Act.
49   See s 87(1)(a) of the Companies Act, 2008, read with ss 84(5) and 69(8).
50   69 of 1984.
51   38 of 2001.
52   19 of 2012.
53   6 of 1958.
54   12 of 2004.

The disqualifications on the grounds of removal from an office of trust and of criminal conviction terminates five years after the date of removal from office or the completion of the sentence imposed for the relevant offence.

Where a juristic person or partnership is appointed company secretary, at least one employee of that juristic person or one partner or employee of that partnership must be permanently resident in South Africa and must have the required knowledge and experience to perform the duties of company secretary. A change in the membership of a juristic person or partnership that holds office as company secretary does not constitute a casual vacancy in the office of company secretary, provided that the juristic person or partnership continues to have at least one person that meets the requirements for being a company secretary.

If a juristic person or partnership no longer meets the requirements for being a company secretary, it must immediately notify the directors of the company. It will be deemed to have resigned as company secretary on giving notice to the company. Any action taken by the juristic person or partnership in performance of its functions as company secretary is not invalidated merely because the juristic person or partnership became disqualified from being the company secretary.

The board of directors of a company can take a resolution to remove a company secretary. Where the company secretary is removed by the company, the secretary may insist that a statement be included in the annual financial statements relating to that financial year, not exceeding a reasonable length, setting out the secretary's contention as to the circumstances that resulted in the removal. The secretary must give written notice to the company by not later than the end of the financial year in which the removal took place, and that notice must include the statement to be included in the annual financial statements. The statement of the company secretary must be included in the directors' report in the company's annual financial statements. The fact that a company secretary has the opportunity to make a statement in the manner described above no doubt ensures that there is full transparency, and will discourage an arbitrary or secretive removal of a company secretary that could occur in order to conceal some wrongdoing or statutory contravention.

13.11 Registration of secretaries and auditors[55]

Every company that appoints a company secretary or auditor, even if the appointment is voluntary and not required by the Act, is required to maintain a record of its secretaries and auditors, including, in respect of each person appointed as secretary or auditor of the company, the name, including any former name, of each such person, and the date of every such appointment.

If a firm or juristic person is appointed, the following information must be disclosed:
- the name, registration number and registered office address of that firm or juristic person;
- the name of any individual contemplated in s 90(3) if that section is applicable; and
- any changes in the particulars referred to above as they occur, with the date and nature of each such change.

---

55 Section 85 of the Companies Act, 2008.

THIS CHAPTER IN ESSENCE

1. Subjecting financial statements of companies to an audit or independent review aims to protect stakeholders from unreliable or dishonest information in financial statements.

2. In the context of financial statements, an **audit** is the examination of financial statements, in accordance with prescribed or auditing standards, with the objective of expressing an opinion as to their fairness or compliance with an identified financial reporting framework and applicable statutory requirements. An auditor must be independent of the company that is being audited.

3. Not all companies are required to have their annual financial statements audited, but all public companies, state-owned companies and certain private companies must do so.

4. An **independent review** is a less onerous process than an audit and is required to be applied to most private companies in accordance with International Review Standards.

5. Owner-managed private companies – where every shareholder is also a director of the company – need neither an audit nor an independent review of their annual financial statements, unless they hold assets in a fiduciary capacity or they have a certain **public interest score**, as described in this chapter.

6. The Companies Act, 2008 provides for the appointment, duties and other matters pertaining to the company secretary, auditors and audit committees. Generally, these requirements apply only to public companies and state-owned companies, but certain private companies are affected too.

7. Auditors, where applicable, must be appointed every year at the annual general meeting of a company. To be appointed, the person or firm must be a registered auditor, must be independent of the company and must not fill various other defined roles at the company (or have done so in the previous five years).

8. A **registered auditor** is defined in the Auditing Profession Act 26 of 2005 (AP Act), as an individual or firm registered as an auditor with the Independent Regulatory Board for Auditors (IRBA).

9. The same individual may not serve as auditor of a company for more than five consecutive financial years, but this restriction does not apply to a firm of auditors if individuals responsible for an account within the firm are rotated.

10. The auditor has the right to access all accounting records, books and documents of the company (and its subsidiaries), and is entitled to require from the directors or prescribed officers of the company (and subsidiaries) any information and explanations necessary for the performance of the auditor's duties. The auditor is entitled to attend, and be heard at, any general shareholders' meeting.

11. An auditor may not place him- or herself in a position of conflict of interest.

12. A person who is not a registered auditor may not perform auditing services, pretend to be a registered auditor, use the name of a registered auditor or lead others to believe that he or she is a registered auditor.

13. Registered auditors are appointed to express their expert opinion on whether a company's financial statements fairly represent in all material respects the financial position of the entity and the results of its operations and cash flow. The auditor may not express a positive opinion in this regard unless he or she is satisfied that the conditions set out in the Companies Act, 2008 have been met.

14. The AP Act was enacted in 2005 to restore faith in the auditing profession after numerous firms were implicated in corporate failures worldwide. The AP Act establishes the **Independent Regulatory Board for Auditors (IRBA)**, which must promote the integrity of the auditing profession, investigate and sanction improper conduct, protect the public in their dealings with registered auditors and prescribe professional standards (among other roles).

15. At each annual general meeting, a company must elect an **audit committee** (where applicable) comprising at least three members. A member of an audit committee must be a non-executive independent director of the company. The board of directors may appoint as an additional member of an audit committee a person who is not a director, but whose financial knowledge and experience will enhance the capacity of the committee.

16. An audit committee of a company has a number of duties, including nominating a registered auditor for appointment, determining the fees and terms of engagement of the auditor and making submissions to the board on the company's accounting policies, financial control, records and reporting.

17. A public company and a state-owned enterprise must appoint a **company secretary**. The company secretary is the chief administrative officer of a company and is accountable to the company's board. His or her duties include (among others) providing the directors with guidance on their duties, responsibilities and powers; making the directors aware of relevant laws; reporting any compliance failures to the board; and ensuring that minutes of all meetings of shareholders, directors and committees are properly recorded.

18. A juristic person or partnership may be appointed secretary, provided that every employee of that juristic person or partner and employee of that partnership is not disqualified from being appointed company secretary.

19. Every company that appoints a company secretary or auditor is required to maintain a record of its secretaries and auditors.

Chapter 14

Remedies, enforcement agencies and alternative dispute resolution

14.1 Decriminalising company law

The Companies Act, 1973 relied extensively on criminal sanctions as a means of ensuring compliance with its provisions. However, criminal sanctions are an inadequate deterrent if they are not enforced, and indeed this was usually what happened in the case of South African companies and company law.

The Companies Act, 2008 aims to decriminalise company law, where possible, and instead of criminal sanctions, the Act largely provides effective private-law remedies that seek to discourage gross mismanagement and abuse of power, and to uphold the enforcement of stakeholders' rights. The 2008 Act therefore reduces the use of criminal law, and provides for other non-criminal law tools to ensure compliance with the law and the protection of stakeholders' rights.

The 2008 Act gives many remedies and rights to stakeholders who never enjoyed such rights under the 1973 Act. These include employees, trade unions representing employees, minority shareholders, and directors and shareholders who feel that they are oppressed.[1]

There is also a fundamental shift in holding directors and others statutorily responsible and accountable. Apart from the fact that the common-law duties of directors (the fiduciary duty and the duty of care, diligence and skill)[2] are now specifically provided for in the Act, there are many provisions that ensure compliance with the provisions of the Act through making directors and others personally liable for losses, damages and costs of the company under a variety of circumstances.[3] For example, s 218(2) provides that any person who contravenes any provision of the Act is liable to any other person for any loss or damage suffered by that person as a result of that contravention.

Criminal sanctions still exist for certain matters, however. Thus, for example, in terms of s 26 of the 2008 Act, it is an offence to fail to provide access to any record that a person has a right to inspect or copy. Similarly, in terms of s 214, if any financial statement of a company is false or misleading, any person who is a party to the preparation, approval or publication of that statement is guilty of an offence.

The non-criminal measures that seek to ensure compliance with the provisions of the Act, or that aim to protect the rights of shareholders include the following:

- The Commission can issue compliance notices to companies or to other persons in certain situations – for example, if the Commission believes that such company or person has contravened the Act.
- The Commission can levy an administrative fine in certain circumstances.
- Application can be made for a court order to ensure compliance in certain circumstances.
- Application can be made to declare a director delinquent or under probation.
- Defaulting directors and certain other persons may be personally liable in certain circumstances.
- A number of provisions give rights to shareholders and other stakeholders.

Some of these more important non-criminal law alternatives are discussed in this chapter.

Various sections of the 2008 Act, including Part B of Chapter 7 contain a number of important remedies available to stakeholders. Some of these remedies are highlighted in Table 14.1 below.

Table 14.1 Part B Chapter 7: Rights of stakeholders to seek specific remedies

Section of the Companies Act, 2008	Subject
20	Relief from abuse of the separate juristic personality of a company
77	Personal liability of directors and prescribed officers[4]

---

1   See C Stein *The New Companies Act Unlocked* (2011) at chapter 30, and see also pp 386–7.
2   See s 76 of the Companies Act, 2008 (discussed in chapter 6 of this book – see para. 6.3.2 above).
3   In this regard, see s 77 (discussed in chapter 6 of this book – see para. 6.3.4.1 above).
4   This is discussed in para. 6.3.4 above.

Section of the Companies Act, 2008	Subject
160	Disputes concerning reservation or registration of company names
161	Application to protect rights of securities holders
162	Application to declare director delinquent or under probation[5]
163	Relief from oppressive or prejudicial conduct
164	Dissenting shareholders' appraisal rights
165	Derivative actions
218	Any person who contravenes any provision of the Act is liable to any other person for any resulting loss or damage suffered by that person

Other remedies are found elsewhere in the Act. For example, in terms of s 171, compliance notices can be issued by the Commission to ensure compliance with the provisions of the Act. It is suggested that non-criminal (civil) remedies fall, generally speaking, under three broad categories:

1. remedies where there has been an abuse of the position of director or prescribed officer;
2. remedies given to shareholders to protect their own rights; and
3. remedies where there has been an abuse of the separate juristic personality of a company.

14.1.1   Abuse of position of director or prescribed officer

The first category of non-criminal remedies concerns directors who have blatantly abused their position. Thus, in terms of s 162, an application can be made to declare a director delinquent or under probation. A court is empowered to disqualify a delinquent director from serving as a director or can place a director under probation. Another remedy against directors who have abused their position is given in terms of s 165. In terms of that section, a shareholder is given a statutory right to bring proceedings on behalf of a company where the company has been prejudiced by acts of its controlling directors and where the company has failed to take the necessary action to call these directors to account. Section 77 also provides for the personal liability of directors and prescribed officers under a variety of different circumstances.[6] Section 218 also provides for personal liability of those people who contravene the provisions of the Act resulting in loss or damages to others.[7]

14.1.2   Remedies available to shareholders to protect their own rights

The second category concerns remedies available to shareholders to protect their own rights – for example, where they are the victims of oppressive or prejudicial conduct by the company or a related person. Section 163 offers relief from oppressive or prejudicial conduct, s 161 allows for an application to protect the rights of securities holders, and s 164 provides for dissenting shareholders' appraisal rights.

---

5   This is discussed in this chapter, and also see para. 6.8 above for a detailed discussion of delinquency and probation.
6   See para. 6.3.4 above for a detailed discussion of s 77.
7   Section 218(2) of the Companies Act, 2008 reads as follows: 'Any person who contravenes any provision of this Act is liable to any other person for any loss or damage suffered by that person as a result of that contravention.'

14.1.3 Abuse of the separate juristic personality of a company

The third category concerns the remedy that effectively allows for the lifting of the corporate veil and the imposition of personal liability in instances where there has been abuse of the separate juristic personality of a company. This remedy always existed at common law in South Africa, and the 2008 Act specifically provides for this remedy in s 20.

These remedies are discussed in more detail below.

14.2 Remedies against directors who have abused their position

The remedies against directors who have abused their position include the right to apply for an order of delinquency or probation[8] as well as giving certain persons the right to institute an action on behalf of the company.[9] It is interesting to note that in terms of s 165, a variety of stakeholders (not just shareholders) can bring an action: a director, a representative of employees (a registered trade union), or any other person with leave of the court can bring such an action. The remedies provided by ss 162 and 165 are discussed below.

14.2.1 Application to declare director delinquent or under probation in terms of s 162[10]

A court may, on application, declare a director to be a delinquent director or place a director under probation.[11] A director in this context includes a person who was a director of the company within two years prior to the application. The persons who may bring the application include the company, a shareholder, a director, a representative of the employees of the company, or the Commission.

An order by the court under s 162 has serious consequences for the director concerned. A person who has been placed **under probation** by the court must not serve as a director except to the extent permitted by the order of probation.[12] A person who has been declared a **delinquent** is disqualified from being a director of any company. This disqualification can, for certain offences, be for life, or for minimum periods of seven years in other cases.[13]

The Commission must establish and maintain a public register of persons who are subject to an order declaring them to be delinquent or under probation.[14]

14.2.1.1 Delinquency

The court is obliged to make an order declaring a person to be a delinquent director if one of the statutory grounds[15] is established. These grounds include, among others:

- consenting to act as director while ineligible or disqualified;[16]
- while under probation, acting as a director in a manner that contravenes the relevant order; or
- while a director, acting in a manner that amounts to gross negligence, wilful misconduct or breach of trust.

---

8 Section 162 of the Companies Act, 2008.
9 Section 165 of the Companies Act, 2008.
10 See para. 6.8 above for a detailed discussion of delinquency and probation.
11 Section 162 of the Companies Act, 2008.
12 Section 69(5) of the Companies Act, 2008.
13 Sections 162(6) and 69(8)(*a*) of the Companies Act, 2008.
14 Section 69(13) of the Companies Act, 2008.
15 Section 162(5) of the Companies Act, 2008.
16 Section 162(5)(*a*) read with s 69 of the Companies Act, 2008.

A declaration of delinquency may be unconditional and for life,[17] or it may be made subject to any conditions the court considers appropriate, including limiting the declaration to apply to only one or more particular category of company. A conditional declaration of delinquency subsists for a period of seven years or a longer period determined by the court.[18]

14.2.1.2   Probation[19]

A court may place a director under probation on the grounds set out in s 162(7). These include the following:

- acting in a manner materially inconsistent with the duties of a director; or
- being present at a meeting and failing to vote against a resolution despite the inability of the company to satisfy the solvency and liquidity test in circumstances where this is required by the Companies Act, 2008.[20]

A declaration placing a person under probation may be made subject to any conditions the court considers appropriate and subsists for a period determined by the court not exceeding five years.[21] The court may also order that the director under probation must be supervised by a mentor during the period of probation, or be limited to serving as a director of a private company or of a company of which that person is the sole shareholder.[22]

14.2.1.3   Conditions of order of delinquency or probation

Examples of conditions that a court may impose when declaring a director delinquent or on probation include a requirement that the person undergo remedial education or perform community service.[23] Certain delinquent directors or directors under probation may, after the stipulated period, apply to court to modify or set aside the order.[24]

14.2.2   The derivative action in terms of s 165

Under the common law, it was accepted that the company itself must act to have a wrong committed against it redressed.

This was decided in *Foss v Harbottle*.[25] In that case, two minority shareholders alleged that property of the company had been misapplied and wasted by the directors and that various mortgages were given improperly over the company's property. The minority shareholders, acting as the plaintiffs in this case, asked that the guilty parties (the directors of the company) be held accountable to the company and that a receiver be appointed.

The court dismissed the claim and held that when a company is wronged by its directors, it is only the company that has standing to sue – not shareholders of the company. In effect, the court established the **proper plaintiff rule**, which states that a wrong done to the company may be vindicated by the company alone. The company itself must be the plaintiff, and not shareholders of that company.

However, it is clear that a company is unlikely to act where the wrongdoers control the company, because those in control are unlikely to act against themselves. The common law,

---

17   If in terms of s 162(5)(*a*) or (*b*). See s 162(6)(*a*) of the Companies Act, 2008.
18   Section 162(6)(*b*) of the Companies Act, 2008.
19   See para. 6.8 above for a detailed discussion of delinquency and probation.
20   See further s 162(7) of the Companies Act, 2008.
21   Section 162(9) of the Companies Act, 2008.
22   Section 162(10)(*d*) of the Companies Act, 2008.
23   Section 162(10) of the Companies Act, 2008.
24   See s 162(11) and (12) of the Companies Act, 2008.
25   1843 2 Hare 461.

therefore, accepted that in certain circumstances the shareholders of a company could institute court proceedings on behalf of the company. The action was referred to as a **derivative action** because the member derived the right to bring the action from the right of the company. The same facts may also give rise to a personal remedy to enforce the member's individual rights against the company or fellow shareholders.[26]

CASE STUDY	**The derivative action**
	Usually only a company may institute legal proceedings in relation to wrongdoings committed against it, and that is why the derivative action departs from this usual practice in the circumstances envisaged in s 165. The action is referred to as 'a derivative action' because a person who initiates it derives the right of action in law from the company whose legal interests is sought to be protected.
	It is often used when the person allegedly committing the wrongdoing against the interests of the company is the person (such as a director) who controls the company. Such person would naturally be reluctant to take action against him- or herself. A derivative action is a court action initiated by any of the persons described in s 165, on behalf of a company, in order to protect a company's legal interests. The word 'interests' is used in s 165 rather than the word 'rights'. The concept of 'interests' is a far wider concept than 'rights'.
	In the case of *TWK Agriculture Ltd v NCT Forestry Co-operative Ltd*,[27] the court examined the nature of the derivative action and held that, as a general rule, where a wrong is alleged to have been committed against a company, it is the company that must seek redress. This is the proper plaintiff rule referred to above.
	This proper plaintiff rule is subject to the exception that a shareholder will be allowed to enforce the company's rights where those who control the company, wrongfully or in breach of duty, benefit themselves and, by use of their control, ensure that no action is brought by the company to obtain redress. This exception is generally described as the 'fraud on the minority' exception. The court held that the terminology used is somewhat misleading, as it is clear from the authorities that 'fraud' is not used in the technical sense, but in the sense of any misuse or abuse of power by those who control the company.

The common-law derivative action was unsatisfactory for a number of reasons:
* The shareholder could personally incur substantial legal costs while attempting to obtain a remedy for the company.
* The plaintiff shareholder often had to launch the proceedings while the required information was in the hands of the company and the wrongdoers.
* It was unclear as to precisely what conduct could or could not be ratified by a simple majority, so the scope of the remedy was unclear. As stated in *Foss v Harbottle*, the **majority rule principle** states that if the alleged wrong can be confirmed or ratified by a simple majority of members in a general meeting, then the court will not interfere with that transaction. In other words, it was unclear that a plaintiff shareholder would succeed if a simple majority of other shareholders had ratified the actions of the directors.

---

26   See further HS Cilliers, ML Benade et al *Corporate Law* 3 ed (2000) at 296–300.
27   2006 (6) SA 20 (N).

- Reported cases also failed to distinguish clearly between the derivative action and a member instituting proceedings to enforce the member's individual rights (as opposed to the company's rights).[28]

In light of these problems, a statutory derivative action as provided for in s 165 is a more certain alternative to the common-law remedy. Section 165 provides that the persons who may use the statutory derivative action are a shareholder, a director (including a prescribed officer), a representative of employees (normally a registered trade union), or any other person with the leave (permission) of the court.[29] The remedy is typically available against an alleged wrongdoer who is in control of the company.[30]

The following five steps need to be taken to use the s 165 derivative action:

1. The first step is for the person wishing to pursue the derivative action to serve a demand on the company requiring it to commence or continue legal proceedings to protect the interests of the company.[31]
2. Unless the company successfully applies to court to set aside the demand on the grounds that it is frivolous, vexatious or without merit,[32] the company must appoint an independent and impartial person or committee to investigate the demand and to report to the board especially on whether or not it appears to be in the best interests of the company to institute or continue with legal proceedings.[33]
3. Within 60 business days of receiving the demand, the company must either initiate or continue legal proceedings, or must serve on the person who made the demand a notice refusing to comply with the demand.[34]
4. If a notice refusing to comply is served on the person who made the demand, that person may then apply to court for leave to bring or continue proceedings on the company's behalf.
5. To grant such leave, the court must be satisfied that the company (in dealing with the demand and the report) has failed to comply with the statutory requirements and that the applicant for leave is acting in good faith, that the proceedings will involve the trial of a matter of material consequence to the company and that it is in the best interests of the company that leave be granted.[35] If the shareholders of a company have ratified or approved any particular conduct of the company, this does not prevent a person from making a demand or applying for leave under s 165, but the court may take the ratification or approval into account in making any judgment or order.[36]

---

28   See Cilliers & Benade supra at 305–6.
29   See further s 165(2), read with s 157(3) and s 165(16) of the Companies Act, 2008.
30   See the comment in note 35 below regarding the requirement that the court must be satisfied that the use of the remedy is in the best interests of the company.
31   Section 165(2) of the Companies Act, 2008. The court may in exceptional circumstances allow a person to apply to court for leave to bring proceedings on behalf of the company without first making a demand to the company. See further s 165(6).
32   Section 165(3) of the Companies Act, 2008.
33   Section 165(4)*(a)* of the Companies Act, 2008.
34   Section 165(4)*(b)* of the Companies Act, 2008.
35   Section 165(5). Section 165(7) basically creates a rebuttable presumption that leave is not in the best interests of the company if the proceedings will be between the company and a 'third party', subject to certain other conditions. A person is a third party if the company and that person are not related or inter-related (as defined in s 2). It therefore appears that the court will not easily grant leave to proceed against a director of the company, unless that director directly or indirectly controls the company.
36   Section 165(14) of the Companies Act, 2008.

Derivative action should not abuse court process

In *Mouritzen v Greystones Enterprises (Pty) Ltd*,[37] one of the directors of a company submitted that the expenses charged to the company by another director for the use of his personal credit card had escalated out of all proportion to what might be regarded as reasonable expenditure for a director and had reached a point where they were having an impact on the financial results of the company, a situation that was prejudicial to the company and to the company's shareholders. The alleged wrongdoer disputed any suggestion that he was cheating the company and alleged that he had been paying legitimate company expenses using the credit card.

The court held that it is important that there must be a demonstration of good conscience and sincere belief on the existence of reasonable prospects of success in the proposed litigation and, therefore, there must be an absence of ulterior motive on the part of an applicant who brings an action in terms of s 165. The court held that if a court was not satisfied that an applicant actually holds the requisite belief, that fact alone would be sufficient to lead to the conclusion that the application must be made for a collateral purpose, as to be an abuse of process. An applicant may, however, believe that the company has a good cause of action with a reasonable prospect of success but nevertheless be intent on bringing the derivative action, not to prosecute it to a conclusion, but to use it as a means for obtaining some advantage for which the action is not designed or for some collateral advantage beyond what the law offers. If that is shown, the application and the derivative suit itself would be an abuse of the court's process.

In the court's view:

> [F]actual proof of any pre-existing personal animosity between the parties, such as in the present instance, does not *per se* serve as conclusive proof that any person referred to in section 165(2) of the Act is not acting in good faith in serving a demand under that subsection, or instituting an application under section 165(5). However, personal animosity between the opposed parties is an important factor which the Court will always take into account together with other relevant evidentiary material presented before the Court in a given situation, in determining whether or not an applicant has, on a balance of probabilities, satisfied the 'good faith' requirement.

The court commented that indeed there is no requirement in law that the directors of a company need to be friends or even to be on talking terms. What is of utmost fundamental importance, amongst others, is the fiduciary duty that they individually owe to the company of which they are the directors. This aspect of a director's responsibility vis-à-vis his or her company is equally relevantly important in relation to this application, in that such fiduciary duty entails, on the part of every director, the same duty as required of an applicant under s 165(5)(*b*), namely, to 'act in good faith' and 'in the best interests of the company'. The court referred to *Da Silva v CH Chemicals*,[38] which stated that '[i]t is a well-established rule of company law that directors have a fiduciary duty to exercise their powers in good faith and in the best interests of the company'.

---

37   2012 (5) SA 74 (KZD).
38   2008 (6) SA 620 (SCA).

The court found it important that the director in this case that had alleged wrongdoing by the other director had himself offered to have his own credit card account examined:

> ... on this basis, the applicant is demonstrating that he has nothing to hide. Generally, such conduct would be consistent to a person who is acting in good faith. Accordingly, I find that the applicant has succeeded to demonstrate on a preponderance of probabilities that he is acting in good faith.

The court confirmed that the Act requires the court to be satisfied that granting leave to commence the proposed proceedings 'is in the best interests of the company'. In most, but not all, instances this requirement will overlap with the requirement of good faith. An instance where a person does not act in good faith but is driven by an ulterior motive, such as personal vendetta, will generally not be in the best interests of the company.

In this case, the director that had alleged wrongdoing was given leave, in terms of s 165(5), to institute action in the name of the company against the alleged wrongdoer, and the latter was ordered to render a full account of his expenditure on his credit card for a period of three years prior to the date of the order.

14.3   Statutory remedies for shareholders

The statutory remedies available to shareholders to protect their own rights include:
- relief from oppressive or prejudicial conduct in terms of s 163;
- dissenting shareholders' appraisal rights in terms of s 164, which are the rights of dissenting shareholders to require a company to pay fair value in exchange for their shares in certain circumstances; and
- additional relief to protect rights of securities holders in terms of s 161 in the form of declaratory orders or other appropriate relief.

14.3.1   Relief from oppressive or prejudicial conduct in terms of s 163

Section 252 of the Companies Act, 1973 aimed at providing a statutory remedy to minority shareholders who were the victims of oppressive conduct by the majority in their control of the company.[39] This remedy was in addition to the personal or private action that minority shareholders could bring against the company under the common law. The s 252 remedy involved allowing an aggrieved shareholder to apply to court for relief in certain circumstances.

Section 163 of the 2008 Act brings a number of important refinements to the remedy. These are clearly aimed at making it more effective and include the following seven important refinements:
1. Section 163 of the 2008 Act applies to both shareholders and directors,[40] whereas s 252 of the 1973 Act provided a remedy only for shareholders.

---

39   Section 252 of the 1973 Act was based, with substantial amendments, on s 111*bis* of the 1926 Act, introduced in 1952. See further on s 252, Cilliers & Benade supra at 313-9.

40   Section 163(1). 'Director' in s 1 is defined to include an alternate director.

2. The circumstances in which the remedy for **oppressive or unfairly prejudicial conduct** is available have been more clearly and broadly defined in the 2008 Act.[41] The applicant must establish that an act or omission of the|company (*or a related person*)| has had a result that is oppressive or unfairly prejudicial'to, or that unfairly disregards the interests of the applicant.[42] Alternatively, the applicant must establish that the business of the company or a related person is being or has been conducted in a manner that is oppressive or unfairly prejudicial to, or that unfairly disregards, the interests of the applicant.[43] It is clear that the remedy is available as a result of a single act or omission, or as a result of a course of dealing. A related person in this context is one who directly or indirectly controls the company.[44] Therefore, the applicant does not need to show that the oppressive conduct was that of the company – for example, through a resolution of a general meeting or of the board of directors. An act, omission or course of dealing by the person controlling the company may also provide the basis of the oppressive conduct complained of.

3. A new ground for relief is contained in s 163(1)*(c)* – namely, where the powers of a director, prescribed officer or person related to the company are being or have been exercised in a manner that is oppressive or unfairly prejudicial to, or that unfairly disregards, the interests of the applicant. This ground is likely to be used particularly in the event of the abuse of powers by the managing director, or by an executive director, or a person controlling the company, where it would be difficult or superfluous to show that the director's act constituted an act of the company.

4. A court appears to have a less restricted discretion under the 2008 Act. The court could intervene under s 252(3) of the 1973 Act only if one of the grounds was established, *and* the court considered it just and equitable to intervene with a view to bringing to an end the matters complained of. Under s 163 of the 2008 Act, the court may make an order if one of the grounds is proved, without it being necessary to establish specifically that the latter factors are present, although in practice it is likely that they will be.

5. Under the 1973 Act, the court, for the purpose of putting an end to the matters complained of, could 'make such order as it thinks fit', whether for regulating the future conduct of the company's affairs or for the purchase of shares, typically those of the minority. Section 163(2) gives a much more comprehensive and detailed description of the type of relief that the court may give, whether in the form of interim or final relief, including an order restraining the conduct complained of. An order regulating the company's affairs can direct the company to amend its memorandum or create or amend a shareholders' agreement.[45] The court may appoint replacement or additional directors or declare any person delinquent or under probation.[46] The court may also order the varying or setting aside of a transaction to which the company is a party and compensation for the company or any other party to the transaction or agreement. The court may also direct the rectification of the registers or records of the company. Clearly,

---

41 Section 163(1) of the Companies Act, 2008.
42 Section 163(1)*(a)* of the Companies Act, 2008. The italicised portions indicate the additions in the 2008 Act. A related person would, for example, include a company's holding company or a subsidiary. The remedy is also available to a director, whereas in terms of the 1973 Act it was only available to a shareholder.
43 Section 163(1)*(b)* of the Companies Act, 2008. Again, the italicised portions indicate the additions in the 2008 Act.
44 Section 2(1) of the Companies Act, 2008.
45 Where the order directs the company to amend its MOI, the directors must file the necessary notice of amendment (under s 16(4) of the Companies Act, 2008) and no further amendment limiting or negating the effect of the court order may be made, until a court orders otherwise (s 163(3) of the Companies Act, 2008).
46 See para 14.2.1 above regarding delinquent directors and directors under probation.

the grounds for court intervention will be easier to establish and the court will also be able to intervene more effectively to put an end to the conduct complained of and to regulate the company's future conduct to prevent a recurrence. Because of the wide range of relief that the court may grant, the applicant should carefully motivate the relief that the applicant regards as appropriate in the circumstances.

6.   Under s 252 of the 1973 Act, it was possible for the same circumstances to justify both a court intervention to end oppressive conduct, and an order for the winding-up of the company. Where it is apparent that some shareholders wish a company to continue, and the interest of dissatisfied shareholders can be equitably and effectively addressed under s 252, the court in *Robson v Wax Works (Pty) Ltd*[47] held that it would generally be inappropriate for a court to grant an order to wind up a company against the wishes of shareholders who want the company to continue. In the *Robson* case, those shareholders who wanted the company to continue were prepared to purchase the shares of the dissatisfied shareholder. Section 163(2)*(b)* takes account of the *Robson* decision by providing that one of the alternative forms of relief that a court may grant is an order appointing a liquidator 'if the company appears to be insolvent'. Where the company is not insolvent, the court's discretion under s 163 is restricted to relief that will enable the company to continue in existence. It could on facts equivalent to *Robson's* case, order the company or another person to pay the dissatisfied shareholder for its shares.[48]

7.   With a view to the court providing relief under s 163 expeditiously, s 163(1) provides for the shareholder or director to approach the court by way of application proceedings (which is suitable where there are no material disputes of fact). In application proceedings, evidence is provided on affidavit, rather than being led in time-consuming oral evidence. Where an application is opposed, there could easily be conflicting evidence on affidavit, which the court will be unable to resolve without oral evidence. It is therefore logical that s 163(2)*(l)* expressly empowers the court to make an order for the trial of any issue as determined by the court, where it cannot be decided by way of application proceedings. A trial involves the leading and cross-examination of oral evidence.

CASE STUDY	**Dissatisfied shareholder under s 252 of the 1973 Act**
	In *Robson v Wax Works (Pty) Ltd*,[49] the applicant held 30 per cent of the issued share capital of a company. The agreement in terms of which the applicant acquired his shareholding in the company did not, however, provide for his appointment as a director of the company. The applicant was, in fact, effectively a so-called 'sleeping partner'.
	At the time that the applicant acquired his interest in the company, he lived in Gauteng, but he then moved to Cape Town, where the business of the company was carried on, and he developed a more direct interest in the business of the company.
	In his application for winding-up in terms of s 344*(h)* of the Companies Act, 1973 (on the grounds that it was just and equitable to do so), the applicant alleged that he had been effectively excluded from the decision-making process by the other shareholders. He also alleged that no proper shareholders' meetings had taken place, and he alleged a lack of probity on the part of the other shareholders in the management of the company.

---

47   2001 (3) SA 1117 (C) at 1130H–J.
48   See the Practical Issue below.
49   Supra.

The court held that as a dissatisfied minority shareholder, the applicant was not entitled, without more, to achieve his escape from an unhappy investment in the company by winding up the company. The court had no difficulty in appreciating the frustration and dissatisfaction that the applicant experienced as a shareholder. The court held, however, that many cases had emphasised that justice and equity required consideration not only of the position of the applicant for winding up, but also the need to take into account the situation and interests of all the other affected, legally interested parties.

The court found that the other shareholders recognised that the applicant should be able to withdraw from the company, but they argued that winding up the company on just and equitable grounds was not the appropriate means of achieving the objective. The other shareholders wished to continue with the company's business. The court held that the provisions of s 252(1) of the Companies Act, 1973 plainly afford an alternative remedy to winding up a company, and was suitable in the present case.

The court held that since it was apparent that the other shareholders desired the company to continue and the interests of the dissatisfied shareholder could be equitably, justly and effectively addressed under s 252, it seemed that it would be inappropriate to wind up the company against the wishes of the members who wanted it to continue. The majority shareholders in this case were willing to buy the applicant's shares at fair value as determined by an independent and appropriately qualified third party, and the court was of the view that the applicant was likely to recoup a greater sum in respect of a sale of his shares to one or both of his fellow shareholders than he would have done upon a liquidation of the company. The court was also of the view that there was no reason why a court making an order in terms of s 252(3) could not, in framing its order, give appropriate directions that the applicant's shareholding had to be valued on a basis or formula that would address any potential or alleged prejudice.

The court therefore concluded that the majority shareholders had sufficiently established that it was unreasonable of the applicant not to have commenced proceedings in terms of s 252, and that appropriate relief under that section would more justly and equitably address the exigencies of the disintegration of the relationship between the shareholders than would a winding-up order.

The court's findings under the 1973 Act have been accommodated under the 2008 Act.[50]

CASE STUDY

Court has broad powers in terms of s 163

In *Kudumane Investment Holding Ltd v Northern Cape Manganese Company (Pty) Ltd & others*,[51] the applicant (company K) was the minority (49 per cent) shareholder and the second respondent (company N) was the majority (51 per cent) shareholder in the first respondent (NCMC), which was a joint venture company constituted for the purpose of exploiting certain prospecting rights. Company K relied on s 163 to obtain relief from certain alleged 'oppressive and prejudicial conduct' of company N.

---

50 See the discussion above in this para. 14.3.1 under the paragraph numbered 6.
51 [2012] 4 All SA 203 (GSJ).

The relief was sought by reason of alleged acrimonious infighting within company N, which resulted in pending High Court litigation between disputed 'shareholders' and disputed 'directors' of company N. Company K claimed that the infighting and litigation hampered the ability of NCMC to conduct the affairs for which it was constituted, thereby prejudicing the commercial rationale for its existence. Company K asserted that while the litigation was unresolved, there remained continued uncertainty both as to the shareholding of company N and also of the identity of company N's directors authorised to sit on the NCMC board. Accordingly, NCMC had no assurance that the persons who purported to represent company N at any board meetings were in fact and in law authorised to do so. NCMC therefore had no guarantee that any resolutions passed at any meeting of the board of NCMC would be valid because they could subsequently be challenged by the successful party in the pending litigation. The prospecting right held by NCMC was 'results driven' in that if NCMC did not comply with the terms of the right, the Minister was empowered in terms of the Mineral and Petroleum Resources Development Act[52] to either cancel or suspend the right granted to NCMC.

The court held that s 163(1) provides that a shareholder of a company may apply to court for relief if any act or omission of a person related to the company has had a result that is oppressive or unfairly prejudicial to or unfairly disregards the interests of the applicant. The court held that the conduct complained of must not be an act or omission which may or will occur in the future. It must be 'something which had already been done or performed' at the time of bringing the application. However it stated that it could see no reason why there cannot be a continuing state of affairs that constitutes the complaint: 'after all an act may be repeated; an omission may be enduring; the current state of affairs will certainly have commenced in the past and may continue indefinitely.'

The court held that there was uncertainty as to the identity of the directors of company N and there was doubt which directors were authorised to sit on the NCMC board: 'no meeting can be held or resolution passed in the complete confidence that such meeting or resolution will be secure from challenge. It is the lack of confidence and uncertainty which is the result'.

The court held that the powers of a court to grant appropriate relief in such circumstances are framed in the broadest of terms in s 163. A court is empowered to make any order 'it considers fit'. The court concluded that the actions of company N in the litigation had a result that the affairs of NCMC, and hence of company K were being oppressed and unfairly prejudiced and unfairly disregarded. The relief that the court granted was an order declaring who the directors of NCMC would be, and they would validly hold office until the infighting within company N had been resolved by the pending litigation.

14.3.2   Dissenting shareholders' appraisal rights in terms of s 164[53]

Under the 1973 Act, if a company had different classes of shares and it decided to vary class rights attaching to these shares, s 102 permitted dissenting shareholders who were aggrieved by the decision, to apply to court for relief under s 252, which could include the purchase by

---

52   28 of 2002.
53   This remedy is also discussed in para. 10.4 above.

the company of their shares. Although little success was achieved with this remedy in reported cases, its existence discouraged abuse of power by controlling shareholders in the context of the variation of class rights.[54]

Although, as discussed above, the 2008 Act in s 163 retains a more effective equivalent to s 252 of the 1973 Act, it also introduces in s 164 an independent remedy for dissenting shareholders. The new statutory remedy is referred to as a **dissenting shareholder's appraisal right**[55] – that is, the right of a dissenting shareholder to require the company to pay it the fair value of its shares in exchange for the shares.

The purpose of s 164 is to provide minority shareholders with a means of protection against certain actions of majority shareholders, rather than against actions of the directors. There are four situations covered by s 164.

The remedy is firstly available to shareholders who consider themselves aggrieved through the company adopting a special resolution to amend its Memorandum of Incorporation (MOI) by altering the preferences, rights or other terms of any class of its shares in a manner that is materially adverse to the rights or interests of the holders of that class of shares.[56] The resolution must adversely affect the rights or interests of the shareholders against the company or relative to other shareholders before the remedy is available. A resolution to amend the MOI in a way that affects the commercial value of the shares without altering the rights of the shareholders or the terms on which the shares are held is not subject to the protection provided by the section.[57] In the case of listed shares, if the market price of the relevant shares increases as a result of the passing of the resolution to alter the class rights or preference, it will be extremely difficult for the objectors to establish that the resolution altered their rights in a way that is materially adverse to their rights or interests.[58]

Section 164 also applies to resolutions concerning three other situations – namely, where a company is considering adopting a resolution concerning the disposal of the greater part of the undertaking, or an amalgamation or merger, or a scheme of arrangement.[59] However, s 164 does not apply to a transaction, agreement or offer pursuant to a business rescue plan.[60]

Exercising the dissenting shareholders' appraisal rights in terms of s 164 requires the following five-step procedure:

1. A dissenting shareholder who wishes to have the option of exercising the appraisal rights conferred by s 164 must notify the company in writing of that shareholder's opposition before the relevant resolution is put to the vote.
2. If the resolution is passed, the shareholder, in order to exercise the appraisal rights, must demand payment of the fair value of the shares from the company.
3. The fair value must, in the first instance, be determined by the company, because all dissenting shareholders of the same class are entitled to the same amount per share.

54 Compare the protracted litigation that culminated in *Donaldson Investments (Pty) Ltd v Anglo-Transvaal Collieries Ltd* 1983 (3) SA 96 (A).
55 See the heading to s 164.
56 See s 164(2)(a) of the Companies Act, 2008. Section 36(2) envisages that class rights set out in the MOI may only be altered by a special resolution or by the board. However, the board may only exercise this power in respect of unissued shares unless the MOI provides otherwise.
57 Compare Cilliers & Benade supra at 233 para. 14.31 regarding the concept 'variation of class rights' for purposes of the 1973 Act.
58 See *Donaldson Investments (Pty) Ltd v Anglo-Transvaal Collieries Ltd* supra.
59 See s 164(2)(b) read with ss 112, 113 and 114. Where the resolution results in the company whose shares are subject to the appraisal rights under s 164 ceasing to exist, its obligations pass to its successor resulting from the acquisition or merger (see s 164(18)).
60 See s 164(1) regarding the approval of a business rescue plan under s 152.

4. Dissenting shareholders who do not accept the company's offer can either allow the offer to lapse, in which case they will be reinstated to full rights as shareholders (as now changed), or they can apply to court for the court to determine the fair value.

5. Once again, the shareholders can choose between surrendering their shares for the amount determined by the court, or withdrawing their respective demands, if they regard the fair value determined by the court as unacceptable. In other words, shareholders either surrender their shares or they accept the changes that have been made. The value determined by the court does not apply to dissenting shareholders who accepted the company's original determination of the fair value.[61]

Under the procedure in s 164, the following points are pertinent:

- The dissenting shareholder has the right to require the company to acquire the shareholder's shares at their fair value at the time immediately before the company adopted the resolution.[62] In practice, the share value may have been influenced by publicity surrounding the proposed resolution – the market price of the shares could have increased or decreased. If the amount of compensation offered by the company is not acceptable to the shareholder, the fair value must be determined by the court.[63]

- When the company gives notice of a meeting being convened to consider a resolution regarding one of the four situations covered by s 164, the notice must include a statement informing the shareholders of their appraisal rights under the section.[64]

- A shareholder wishing to exercise the appraisal rights must give written notice to the company of the objection at any time *before* the resolution is put to the vote.[65] The shareholder must also attend the meeting and vote against the resolution and comply with the procedural requirements of s 164.[66]

- If the resolution is adopted, the company must notify all shareholders who informed it of their objection within the prescribed period that the company has adopted the resolution, unless they have withdrawn their objection or voted in support of the resolution.[67]

- However, if shareholders failed to vote against the resolution, they apparently forfeit their appraisal rights.[68]

- The shareholder wishing to exercise the appraisal rights must notify the company accordingly within 20 business days of receipt of the company's notification that the resolution was passed.[69]

- The company must respond to the demand by offering each of the shareholders who sent a demand an amount considered by the directors to be the fair value of the shares,[70] accompanied by a statement showing how the value was determined.[71]

---

61 Section 164(15)(*a*) of the Companies Act, 2008.
62 Section 164(16) of the Companies Act, 2008.
63 Section 164(14) and (15) of the Companies Act, 2008.
64 Section 164(14) and (15) of the Companies Act, 2008.
65 Compare s 164(3) with s 37(8) and s 164(5), read with s 164(6) of the Companies Act, 2008.
66 See ss 164(5) and 37(8).
67 Section 164(4) of the Companies Act, 2008.
68 Section 164(5) of the Companies Act, 2008.
69 Section 164(7). The shareholder's notice to the company containing the demand must comply with s 164(8). Subject to certain exceptions, the shareholder who sends a demand forfeits all further rights in respect of the shares other than to be paid their fair value (s 164(9) and (10)).
70 Having regard to s 164(16).
71 Section 164(11) of the Companies Act, 2008.

- Every offer in respect of the same class or series of shares must be on the same terms. The offer lapses if not accepted within 30 business days.[72]
- If the company fails to make an offer, or if the shareholder regards the offer as inadequate, the shareholder may approach the court to determine the fair value of the shares.
- All dissenting shareholders who have not accepted the offer must be joined as parties and are bound by the decision of the court.[73]
- The court may appoint one or more appraisers to assist it to determine the fair value.[74]
- The court must make its order in a form that gives the dissenting shareholders the choice of either withdrawing their respective demands and being reinstated to their full rights as shareholders or of complying with the formalities regarding the surrender of their shares[75] and being paid by the company the fair value determined by the court.[76]

The tendering of shares by a shareholder under s 164 and the payment by the company does not qualify as an acquisition of shares under s 48 or as a distribution, with the result that the solvency and liquidity test in s 4 does not apply.[77] Nevertheless, if there are reasonable grounds for believing that payment by the company of the fair value would result in the company being unable to pay its debts as they fall due in the ensuing 12 months, the company may apply to court for an order varying the company's obligations. The court may make an order that is just and equitable to ensure that the dissenting shareholders receive payment at the earliest possible date compatible with the company satisfying its other financial obligations.[78]

14.3.3 Additional remedy to protect rights of securities holders in terms of s 161

Section 161 of the Companies Act, 2008 provides a remedy to protect the rights of the holders of issued securities in addition to other remedies under the 2008 Act or other remedies that they may have in terms of the common law.[79] The holder of issued securities may apply to court for a **declaratory order** regarding the rights that the person may have in terms of any of the following:[80]

- the 2008 Act;
- the company's MOI;
- any rules of the company; or
- any applicable debt instrument.

Alternatively, the holder of the securities can apply for an appropriate order to protect those rights or to rectify any harm done to the securities holder by the company or by any of its directors.[81]

---

72 Section 164(12) of the Companies Act, 2008. The shareholder would then be reinstated to his or her rights as shareholder, as modified by the resolution (see s 164(9)(a) and compare s 164(15)(c)(v)(aa)).
73 Section 164(15)(a) of the Companies Act, 2008.
74 Section 164(15)(c)(iii)(aa) of the Companies Act, 2008.
75 See s 164(13)(a) for these formalities.
76 Section 164(15)(c)(v)(aa) of the Companies Act, 2008.
77 Section 164(19) of the Companies Act, 2008.
78 Section 164(17) of the Companies Act, 2008.
79 Section 161(2)(b) of the Companies Act, 2008.
80 Section 161(1)(a) of the Companies Act, 2008.
81 Section 161(1)(b). The provision applies to harm done by the directors only to the extent that they may be held liable under s 77.

14.4   Liability for abuse of separate juristic personality of company

The exceptional circumstances in which a court may **lift** or **pierce the corporate veil** to impose personal liability on its shareholders or directors has been discussed in chapter 2 of this book.[82] This power was originally developed in terms of the common law. The Companies Act, 2008 includes a new statutory power for this purpose.

In terms of s 20(9) of the 2008 Act, whenever a court finds that the incorporation of, or any act by or on behalf of, or any use of, a company constitutes an **'unconscionable abuse'**[83] **of juristic personality** of the company as a separate entity, the court may declare that the company is deemed not to be a juristic person in respect of any right, obligation or liability of the company, or of a shareholder or member of the company, or of another person as specified in the declaration. Consequently, the court may give any further order it considers appropriate in order to give effect to such declaration.

The declaration can be made by the court on application by an interested person, or in any proceedings in which a company is involved.

14.5   Enforcement of rights and ensuring compliance with the Act

It is all very well for shareholders and other stakeholders to be offered remedies in terms of the Companies Act, 2008, but if there is no way to exercise the remedies, there would be no point in having them. Moreover, the decriminalisation of company law requires alternative methods to ensure compliance with the Act. All of these matters are discussed in the following paragraphs.

The 2008 Act envisages four basic alternatives for addressing complaints regarding alleged contraventions of the Act or for the enforcement of rights – whether in terms of the Act or under a company's MOI or rules.[84] The aggrieved party can:

1.   attempt to resolve the dispute using alternative dispute resolution (ADR)[85] procedures; or
2.   apply to the Companies Tribunal for adjudication, but only in respect of any matter for which such an application is permitted in the Act; or
3.   apply to the High Court; or
4.   file a complaint with the Companies and Intellectual Property Commission, which could result in the Commission, after investigating the complaint, issuing a compliance notice.

The Companies Act, 2008 therefore generally uses a system of administrative enforcement. The body normally responsible for the enforcement of the Act is the **Companies and Intellectual Property Commission** (the **Commission**), except as regards matters within the jurisdiction of the Takeover Regulation Panel.[86] The 2008 Act also establishes a Companies Tribunal, whose functions include the review of certain decisions of the Commission.

---

82   See para. 2.3 above.
83   Section 65 of the Close Corporations Act 69 of 1984 refers to a 'gross' abuse, which is arguably a less stringent test than an 'unconscionable' abuse.
84   Section 156 of the Companies Act, 2008.
85   ADR is the acronym for alternative dispute resolution. See further para. 14.5.3 below.
86   Section 187(2) of the Companies Act, 2008 and see para. 10.5 above for a discussion of the role of the Takeover Regulation Panel.

The discussion below deals briefly with the Commission and the Companies Tribunal and their respective functions, as well as the provisions of the Companies Act on ADR procedures.

However, the High Court remains the primary forum for resolving disputes regarding the interpretation and enforcement of the Companies Act.[87] In specifying three alternatives to litigation, the legislature is clearly encouraging disputants to consider more expeditious, informal and cheaper alternatives, before resorting to court proceedings. Parties who approach the court directly, except where the 2008 Act clearly indicates that the court is the only avenue, run the risk that the court will decline to hear the matter until other alternatives have been attempted. Alternatively, the court may consider penalising a party in its order, for not first making use of alternative procedures, in so far as liability between the parties for the legal costs of court proceedings is concerned.

14.5.1 The Companies and Intellectual Property Commission

The Commission takes the place of the registrar of companies under the 1973 Act.[88] In practice, even before the commencement of the 2008 Act, many of the functions of the registrar had been taken over by the Companies and Intellectual Property Registration Office (CIPRO) within the Department of Trade and Industry.[89] The Commission is an organ of state within the public administration.[90] The Commission has jurisdiction throughout the Republic.[91] It is independent and must perform its functions impartially and in the most cost-efficient and effective manner.[92]

The Commission is headed by a Commissioner appointed by the Minister, who must also appoint a Deputy Commissioner.[93]

14.5.1.1 Objectives and functions of the Commission

As its name indicates, the primary objectives of the Commission are the efficient and effective registration of companies and external companies under the 2008 Act, and of intellectual property rights in terms of relevant legislation.[94]

The following are among the functions of the Commission:[95]

- monitoring proper compliance with the Act;
- receiving and promptly investigating complaints concerning contraventions of the Act;
- promoting the use of ADR by companies for resolving internal disputes;
- issuing and enforcing compliance notices;[96]
- promoting the reliability of financial statements and making recommendations to the Financial Reporting Standards Council[97] for improving financial reporting standards;[98]

---

87 See the Explanatory Memorandum accompanying the 2008 Bill at 189 and 193.
88 See s 7 of the Companies Act, 1973 for the appointment and functions of the registrar.
89 See the Explanatory Memorandum accompanying the 2008 Bill at 188.
90 Section 185(1) of the Companies Act, 2008. The establishment and functions of the Commission are dealt with in Chapter 8 Part A of the Act. Although it is outside the public service, it must exercise its functions in accordance with the basic values and principles governing public administration under the Constitution. See s 185(1) and s 185(2)(d)(ii), read with s 195 of the Constitution.
91 Section 185(2)(a) of the Companies Act, 2008.
92 Section 185(2)(b) to (d) of the Companies Act, 2008.
93 Section 189(1). See further s 189(3)–(4) regarding the functions and powers of the Commissioner.
94 Section 186(1)(a) of the Companies Act, 2008. See further s 186 on the other objectives of the Commission.
95 Section 187 of the Companies Act, 2008.
96 Section 187(2) of the Companies Act, 2008.
97 The Council is established under s 203 of the Companies Act, 2008.
98 Section 187(3) of the Companies Act, 2008.

- establishing a companies' register and any other register contemplated by the 2008 Act and making the information in those registers available to the public;[99]
- advising the Minister on changes to the law and administration of the 2008 Act in line with international best practice;[100]
- providing guidance to the public by issuing explanatory notices on procedures and non-binding opinions on the interpretation of the Act;[101] and
- conducting research relating to its mandate and activities and publishing the results of that research.[102]

14.5.1.2   Compliance notices[103]

The Commission may issue a **compliance notice** to any person whom the Commission on reasonable grounds[104] believes has either:

- contravened the Companies Act, 2008; or
- assented to, been implicated in, or directly or indirectly benefited from, a contravention of the Act, unless the alleged contravention could otherwise be addressed in terms of the Act by an application to a court or to the Companies Tribunal.

Any person issued with a compliance notice can apply to the Tribunal for a review of that notice if such person is dissatisfied with the notice.

The formalities concerning compliance notices are contained in s 171 of the Companies Act, 2008 and are summarised below.

1. *What a person must do on receiving a compliance notice:* a compliance notice may require the person to whom it is addressed to do any of the following:
   - cease, correct or reverse any action in contravention of the Act;
   - take any action required by the Act;
   - restore assets or their value to a company or any other person;
   - provide a community service; or
   - take any other steps reasonably related to the contravention and designed to rectify its effect.
2. *Contents of compliance notice:* the notice must set out the following:
   - the person or an association to whom the notice applies;
   - the provision of the Act that has been contravened;
   - details of the nature and extent of the non-compliance;
   - any steps that are required to be taken and the period within which those steps must be taken; and
   - any penalty that may be imposed in terms of the Act if those steps are not taken.
3. *Duration of compliance notice:* a compliance notice remains in force until any of the following occur:
   - it is set aside by the Tribunal, or by a court on a review of the notice; or
   - the Commission issues a compliance certificate – such a certificate will be issued if the requirements of the compliance notice have been satisfied.

---

99   Section 187(4). See further s 187(5)-(7) regarding public access to registers maintained by the Commission.
100 Section 188(1)*(a)* of the Companies Act, 2008.
101 Section 188(2)*(b)* of the Companies Act, 2008.
102 Section 188(2)*(c)* of the Companies Act, 2008.
103 Section 171 of the Companies Act, 2008.
104 The Commission could believe that reasonable grounds exist for issuing a compliance notice as a result of its investigation of a complaint. See para. 14.5.1.3 below and s 170(1)*(g)* of the Companies Act, 2008.

4. *Failure to comply with a compliance notice:* if a person to whom a compliance notice has been issued fails to comply with the notice, the Commission may either:
   - apply to a court for the imposition of an administrative fine; or
   - refer the matter to the National Prosecuting Authority for prosecution as an offence in terms of s 214(3) of the Companies Act, 2008.

14.5.1.3   Investigation of complaints by the Commission

The Commission plays a central role in the enforcement of the Companies Act, 2008. Parts D and E of Chapter 7 of the Act regulate the investigation of complaints by the Commission in detail.

Any person may file a written complaint with the Commission alleging that another person has acted in a manner inconsistent with the Act or alleging that the complainant's rights under the Act or under a company's MOI or rules have been infringed.[105] The Commission may also initiate complaints directly on its own motion or at the request of another regulatory authority.[106] The Commission may respond to a complaint in one of three basic ways:

1. it may notify the complainant that it will not investigate a complaint that appears to be frivolous, vexatious or without sufficient grounds;
2. it may recommend that the complainant resort to ADR; or
3. it may direct an inspector or investigator to investigate the complaint.[107]

An inspector is an employee of the Commission (or another suitable employee of the State) who has been appointed by the Commissioner. The Commissioner must furnish the inspector with a certificate of appointment.[108] An investigator may be appointed by the Commissioner to assist the Commission in carrying out an investigation, but such a person is not an inspector within the meaning of the 2008 Act.[109]

The Commission may issue a summons to a person, who is believed to be able to furnish information or documents relevant to an investigation, to appear before the Commission or before an inspector or independent investigator.[110] A judge of the High Court or a magistrate may issue a warrant for an inspector or police officer to enter and search premises if, from information furnished on oath or affirmation, there are reasonable grounds to believe that a contravention of the Act is taking place on those premises or that anything connected with an investigation is in the possession or control of a person at those premises.[111]

On receipt of the report of an inspector or independent investigator, the Commission has several options:

- it may refer the complainant to the Companies Tribunal if the matter falls within its jurisdiction;
- it may propose that the complainant and any affected party meet with the Commission or the Tribunal, with a view to resolving the matter by consent order;

---

105 Section 168(1) of the Companies Act, 2008.
106 Section 168(2) of the Companies Act, 2008. The Minister may also direct the Commission to investigate an alleged contravention (see s 168(3)).
107 Section 169(1). See further s 169(2)*(b)* regarding the possibility of investigating a company's internal disputes by an independent investigator at the company's expense.
108 Section 209(1) of the Companies Act, 2008.
109 Section 209(3) of the Companies Act, 2008.
110 Section 176(1) of the Companies Act, 2008. The powers of the inspector or investigator to examine the person summoned to appear are contained in s 176(3).
111 Section 177(1) and (2)*(b)*. See further s 177(3)-(6) as to how the warrant may be executed; s 178 on the powers of the inspector, who may be accompanied and assisted by a police officer, to enter and search premises; and s 179 on the duties of the person conducting the search.

- it may commence court proceedings in the name of the complainant;
- it may refer the matter to the National Prosecuting Authority or other regulatory authority;
- it may issue a compliance notice;[112] or
- it may in effect decide to take no action, by issuing the complainant with a notice of non-referral, while simultaneously advising the complainant of any rights that it may have to seek a remedy in court.[113] In this event, the complainant may apply to court for leave to refer the matter directly to court.[114] The court may grant leave only if it appears that the applicant has no other remedy under the Act.[115] If leave is granted, the court after hearing the matter may direct the Commission to issue an appropriate compliance notice.[116]

The Commission may in its sole discretion publish the report of the inspector or independent investigator. Irrespective of whether it publishes the report, it must deliver a copy to the complainant and to any person who was the subject of the investigation.[117]

14.5.2   The Companies Tribunal

The provisions of the Companies Act, 2008 regarding the establishment and functions of the **Companies Tribunal** are to some extent based on the corresponding provisions of the Competition Act relating to the Competition Tribunal.[118] The three main tasks of the Tribunal[119] are:

1. to adjudicate in relation to any application that may be made to it in terms of the Act;[120]
2. to assist in the resolution of disputes as contemplated in the ADR provisions of the Act, discussed below; and
3. to perform any other function that may be assigned to it in terms of the Act.[121]

The Companies Tribunal is a juristic person and has jurisdiction throughout the Republic. It is independent and must perform its functions impartially.[122]

The Tribunal consists of a chairperson and at least 10 other full-time or part-time members appointed by the Minister.[123] The Act imposes certain restrictions on membership – for example, a person who is disqualified from serving as a director of a company or who is an office-bearer of a political party or body of a partisan political nature is disqualified from being a member of the Companies Tribunal.[124] There are also statutory provisions aimed at ensuring that members avoid a conflict of interest when serving as a member and

---

112 See para. 14.5.1.2 above.
113 Section 170(1)*(c)* of the Companies Act, 2008.
114 Section 174(1) of the Companies Act, 2008.
115 Section 174(2)*(a)* of the Companies Act, 2008.
116 Section 174(2)*(b)* of the Companies Act, 2008.
117 Section 170(2) of the Companies Act, 2008. A holder of securities or creditor of a company that was the subject of the report is entitled to a copy against payment of the prescribed fee. The Commission must also furnish a copy of the report to any court at the request of the court.
118 See ss 26 and 27 of the Competition Act 89 of 1998.
119 See the long title of the Act and the Explanatory Memorandum which accompanied the Bill, p. 189.
120 See s 156*(b)* of the Companies Act, 2008 and the text below.
121 Examples include resolving disputes concerning company names (s 160 and s 17(2) of the Companies Act, 2008); issuing an administrative order convening a company meeting as contemplated by s 61(11); the removal of a director from office under s 71(3) read with s 71(8); and the review of a compliance notice issued by the Commissioner (s 172).
122 Section 193(1) of the Companies Act, 2008.
123 Section 193(4) of the Companies Act, 2008.
124 Sections 194(2)*(a)* and 205 of the Companies Act, 2008.

a prohibition on the private use or disclosure of confidential information acquired in that capacity.[125]

In terms of s 156*(b)* of the Companies Act, 2008, a person seeking to address an alleged contravention of the Act or to enforce rights under the Act or under a company's MOI or rules has the option of applying to the Tribunal for adjudication.[126] The provisions of the Act regarding adjudication by the Tribunal are also clearly modelled on the corresponding provisions of the Competition Act relating to hearings before the Competition Tribunal.[127]

The Tribunal must conduct its adjudication proceedings expeditiously and in accordance with natural justice and may conduct the proceedings informally.[128] Parties may participate in adjudication proceedings in person or through a representative.[129] At the conclusion of the hearing, the presiding member must issue a decision together with written reasons for that decision.[130]

Under s 195(7), a decision by the Tribunal regarding a decision, notice or order by the Commission is binding on the Commission, subject to any review by the court.[131] The effect of this provision appears to be that the Commission can only take the Tribunal's decision on review, and that it has no right of appeal. Conversely, if the Tribunal as adjudicator finds in favour of the Commission, the other party can have the matter considered afresh by the court.

14.5.3 Voluntary resolution of disputes

As an alternative to applying to court or filing a complaint with the Commission, an applicant or complainant may refer a matter to the Companies Tribunal or to an accredited entity for resolution by mediation, conciliation or arbitration.[132] It is clear that when the 2008 Act refers to **alternative dispute resolution (ADR)**,[133] the expression is restricted to the following three alternatives to court proceedings:

1. mediation;
2. conciliation; and
3. arbitration.[134]

---

125 Section 194(6) read with s 206. The Act empowers the Minister to remove a member who acts in breach of these restrictions (s 207(3)). A member of the Tribunal is also expressly prohibited from representing any person before the Tribunal (s 195(9)).

126 See further footnote 120 above regarding s 156. Although s 156 refers to an application for adjudication 'in respect of any matter for which such an application is permitted in this Act', the 2008 Act is further unclear as to precisely which matters may be subjected to adjudication, as opposed to a review by the Tribunal of the Commissioner's administrative decisions.

127 Compare ss 180–184 of the Companies Act, 2008 with ss 52–56 of the Competition Act 89 of 1998.

128 See s 180(1) of the Companies Act, 2008. When acting as an adjudicator, the Tribunal is required to determine a dispute between parties by deciding between the conflicting submissions and evidence submitted by the parties. Although the procedure is similar to arbitration, in that the Tribunal must conduct the proceedings in accordance with the principles of natural justice, the Arbitration Act 42 of 1965 and the court's powers under that Act have no application to adjudication.

129 Section 181 of the Companies Act, 2008.

130 Section 180(3) of the Companies Act, 2008.

131 When performing its function as adjudicator, the Companies Tribunal is an organ of state exercising public power. The Constitution therefore requires its actions to be lawful, procedurally fair and reasonable, and they are subject to court review to ensure that these standards are achieved. See *Sidumo v Rustenburg Platinum Mines Ltd* 2008 (2) SA 24 (CC) paras. 138 and 139 regarding s 33 of the Constitution. In terms of paras. 88, 89, 110, 112 and 124 of the judgment, it appears that s 34 of the Constitution also applies to the Companies Tribunal when exercising its adjudication function. This should present no difficulties in view of the procedural safeguards in s 180(1) and the requirements of s 193(1)*(b)* and *(d)*, which require the Tribunal to be independent and to perform its functions impartially.

132 Section 166(1) of the Companies Act, 2008. An accredited entity is either a juristic person or association of persons that meets the prescribed criteria and has been accredited by the Commission or an appropriate organ of state designated by the Minister, after consulting with the Commission (see s 166(3), (4) and (5)).

133 See, for example, s 156*(a)* of the Companies Act, 2008.

134 See s 166(1) and (2) of the Companies Act, 2008.

Conciliation and **mediation** are processes whereby the parties to a dispute involve a third party to facilitate discussions between the disputants with a view to the parties arriving at a negotiated settlement of their dispute. The conciliator or mediator cannot impose a solution on the parties: any proposed solution recommended by the conciliator or mediator will only bind the disputants if they accept it.

With **arbitration**, the parties make submissions and present evidence to the arbitrator and agree in advance to accept the arbitrator's award as final and binding. There is no appeal to the court against an arbitrator's award, but the court may review the award on limited grounds, especially where there has been a serious procedural irregularity or an excess of jurisdiction.[135]

Use of the ADR process by the complainant or applicant is voluntary. It appears that the other party must also agree to the use of the process[136] and that neither the Tribunal nor the accredited entity has compulsory jurisdiction under s 166.[137] If the Tribunal or accredited entity to whom a matter has been referred for ADR concludes that either party to the conciliation, mediation or arbitration is not participating in good faith or there is no reasonable probability of the parties resolving their dispute through that process, it must issue a certificate in the prescribed form stating that the process has failed.[138]

The Tribunal or accredited entity that (through a voluntary ADR process) has resolved a dispute, or helped the parties to resolve a dispute, may record the resolution in the form of an order. If the parties consent to the order, the Tribunal or entity may submit it to the court to be confirmed as a consent order in terms of the court's rules.[139]

THIS CHAPTER IN ESSENCE

1. The Companies Act, 2008 aims to decriminalise company law, where possible, by providing for effective private-law remedies that discourage mismanagement and abuse of power in companies. Certain criminal sanctions remain.

2. Non-criminal (civil) remedies may generally be categorised into: remedies where there has been an abuse of the position of director; remedies given to shareholders to protect their own rights; and remedies where there has been an abuse of the separate juristic personality of a company.

   2.1 If directors blatantly abuse their position, an application can be made in terms of s 162 to declare a director delinquent or under probation. Alternatively, a shareholder may bring a derivative action against directors in terms of s 165 on behalf of the company.

   2.2 Shareholders can protect their own rights in terms of: s 163 (if they are the victims of oppressive or prejudicial conduct); s 161 (to protect their rights as holders of securities); and s 164 (to exercise the dissenting shareholder's appraisal right).

---

135   See DW Butler 'Arbitration' in WA Joubert et al (eds) (2003) *LAWSA* vol. 1 (2), 2 ed at para. 542.

136   The board of a company subject to the King 3 report is nevertheless required to ensure that disputes are resolved as effectively, efficiently and expeditiously as possible and should adopt appropriate ADR procedures for both internal and external disputes (see the King Code of Governance Principles (2009) principle 8.6). A Practice Note to the Code contains a recommended ADR clause, which provides first for mediation and if this is unsuccessful, the dispute must be referred to arbitration. The Institute of Directors, which issued the Practice Note, recommends that AFSA (the Arbitration Foundation of Southern Africa) and its expedited arbitration rules should be used for this purpose.

137   It is not entirely clear whether s 34 of the Constitution ('Access to courts') applies to a voluntary arbitration conducted by the Tribunal. In *Lufuno Mphaphuli (Pty) Ltd v Andrews* 2009 (6) BCLR 527 (CC), the majority of the Constitutional Court decided that the section does not apply directly to private arbitration. However, a voluntary arbitration conducted by the Tribunal meets only one of the two main criteria for private arbitration identified in para. 198 of the judgment. The arbitration is consensual in that it takes place by agreement. It is not, however, 'private' in the sense of a 'non-state process' – see ss 193 and 194 of the Companies Act, 2008.

138   Section 166(2) of the Companies Act, 2008.

139   Section 167(1) of the Companies Act, 2008.

2.3 The corporate veil may be lifted (that is, the separate legal personality of a company may be ignored) where such legal personality has been abused.

3. A person who has been placed **under probation** by the court must not serve as a director except to the extent permitted by the order of probation. A person who has been declared a **delinquent** is disqualified from being a director of any company for between seven years and life.

3.1 A court must declare a person to be delinquent if he or she has consented to act as director while ineligible or disqualified, has acted as director in a manner contrary to an order of probation, or has acted as a director in a manner amounting to gross negligence, wilful misconduct or breach of trust.

3.2 A court may place a director under probation if he or she has acted materially inconsistently with the duties of a director or if, in voting at a meeting, he or she has failed to comply with the solvency and liquidity requirements of the 2008 Act.

4. The **proper plaintiff rule** indicates that when a company is wronged by its directors, it is only the company that has standing to sue – not the shareholders. However, where wrongdoers control a company, the common law recognises a **derivative action** for a shareholder to sue on behalf of a company. Section 165 of the Companies Act, 2008 provides for a statutory derivative action.

5. Section 163 of the Companies Act, 2008 allows shareholders and directors who are victims of **oppressive or unfairly prejudicial conduct** to apply to court for an appropriate order to end the conduct complained of. This could include an order appointing a liquidator if the company appears to be insolvent.

6. Section 164 of the 2008 Act introduces an independent remedy for **dissenting shareholders** – that is an **appraisal right** entitling a shareholder to require the company to pay it the fair value of its shares in exchange for the shares. This remedy provides minority shareholders with some protection against actions of majority shareholders.

7. Section 161 of the 2008 Act allows the holder of issued securities to apply to court for a **declaratory order** or another appropriate order regarding his or her rights in terms of the 2008 Act, the company's MOI, any rules of the company, or any applicable debt instrument.

8. If a court finds that a company's incorporation, acts, or use constitutes an **unconscionable abuse of the juristic personality** of the company as a separate entity, the court may declare that the company is deemed not to be a juristic person for certain purposes – that is, a court may **lift the corporate veil**.

9. The 2008 Act envisages four basic alternatives for addressing complaints:

9.1 alternative dispute resolution (ADR) procedures;

9.2 adjudication by the Companies Tribunal;

9.3 application to the High Court; and

9.4 filing a complaint with the Companies and Intellectual Property Commission.

10. The primary objectives of the **Companies and Intellectual Property Commission** (the **Commission**) are the efficient and effective registration of companies and external companies under the 2008 Act, and of intellectual property rights. Its functions include monitoring compliance with the 2008 Act, investigating complaints, promoting ADR, and issuing and enforcing compliance notices. The Commission may issue a **compliance notice** to any person whom the Commission, on reasonable grounds, believes has contravened the Act or been implicated in a contravention.

11. The three main tasks of the **Companies Tribunal** are: to adjudicate applications made to it in terms of the Act; to assist in the resolution of disputes as contemplated in the ADR provisions of the Act; and to perform any other function assigned to it in the Act.

12. As an alternative to applying to court or filing a complaint with the Commission, a complainant may refer a matter to the Companies Tribunal or to another entity accredited for **alternative dispute resolution (ADR)** – that is, **conciliation**, **mediation** and **arbitration**.

Chapter 15

The winding-up and deregistration of companies

15.1 Introduction to the winding-up and deregistration of companies under the Companies Act, 2008

Item 9 of Schedule 5 of the Companies Act, 2008 provides that the Companies Act, 1973 will continue to apply to the winding-up and liquidation of companies (ss 337 to 426 of the 1973 Act) except that:

- certain sections of the 2008 Act will apply to the winding-up of a *solvent* company; and
- sections 343, 344, 346, and 348 to 353 of the 1973 Act will not apply to the winding-up of a *solvent* company.

What this effectively means is that the winding-up of **insolvent companies** is dealt with in terms of the 1973 Act, while the winding-up of **solvent companies** is dealt with in terms of both the 2008 and 1973 Acts, except that certain sections of the latter are specifically made inapplicable to the winding-up of solvent companies. Thus, for example, ss 354 to 366 of the 1973 Act ('General provisions affecting all windings-up') apply to the winding-up of both solvent and insolvent companies, as do ss 367 to 411, which deal with all aspects of a liquidator including appointment, removal, remuneration and powers and duties.

The reason for the continuation of certain provisions of the 1973 Act is that new uniform insolvency legislation will soon be developed and implemented, and then the provisions of the 1973 Act will cease to apply.

Section 79(1) of the 2008 Act provides that a solvent company may be dissolved either by **voluntary winding-up** initiated by the company as contemplated in s 80, or winding-up and **liquidation by court order**, as contemplated in s 81.

In terms of s 82, the Master must file a certificate of winding-up of a company in the prescribed form when the affairs of the company have been completely wound up, and upon receiving that certificate the Companies and Intellectual Property Commission (the Commission) must:

- record the dissolution of the company; and
- remove the company's name from the companies register.

In terms of the 1973 Act, the circumstances in which a company can be wound up by a court (as set out in s 344) included the ground that the company was deemed to be unable to pay its debts as described by s 345. This ground is not a ground for the winding-up of a solvent company by a court in terms of the 2008 Act, and the latter specifically provides that s 344 will not apply to the winding-up of a solvent company.

It is therefore necessary to know what is meant by the term 'insolvent company'. In this regard, there appear to be two different schools of thought:

1. Some court judgments take the view that a company is insolvent if either its liabilities exceed its assets (so-called **factual** or **balance sheet insolvency**) or it cannot pay its debts in the normal course of business (so-called **commercial insolvency**).
2. Others are of the view that a company is only insolvent if it is factually insolvent, and that it is therefore solvent if its assets are greater than its liabilities even though it may be illiquid.

The grounds upon which a court may order the winding-up of a solvent company are clearly set out in s 81 of the 2008 Act. In terms of that section, it is not possible for a court to order a company to be wound up on the grounds that it is unable to pay its debts.

In *Knipe v Kameelhoek (Pty) Ltd*,[1] the court stated that, in its view, a company is solvent, even though illiquid, if its assets, fairly valued, exceed its actual liabilities. It was clear in this case that the company was solvent, based on this view, and the application was brought in terms of s 81(1)(*d*)(iii) of the 2008 Act.

However in *Firstrand Bank Ltd v Lodhi 5 Properties Investment CC*,[2] the court held that there is, in the absence of an express provision, no indication in the 2008 Act that the legislature intended to do away with the principle that a company may be liquidated on the grounds of its 'commercial insolvency'. This was particularly so as it left s 345 of the 1973 Act intact. The court held that the expression 'solvent company' in item 9(2) of Schedule 5 to the 2008 Act relates to solvent companies, being companies that are either not 'actually (or factually) insolvent' or 'commercially insolvent', as envisaged in Part G of Chapter 2 of the 2008 Act, in contrast to companies that are insolvent, being companies that are either 'commercially insolvent' or 'actually (or factually) insolvent', which are to be dealt with in terms of Chapter XIV of the 1973 Act.

Another issue that arises is whether or not a creditor as applicant must allege and show that a company is insolvent before being able to proceed under the 1973 Act, or whether there is no such obligation on a creditor to do this, but the risk in that case would be that the defendant would merely have to show that it was solvent, and that the creditor was therefore not entitled to proceed in terms of the 1973 Act.

In *Scania Finance Southern Africa (Pty) Ltd v Thomi-Gee Road Carriers CC / Absa Bank Ltd v Fernofire Bethlehem CC*,[3] the court held that in order to rely on the grounds in Chapter XIV

---

1 [2012] ZAFSHC 160.
2 2012 JDR 2561 (GNP); 2012 ZAGPPHC 263.
3 2012 JDR 1385 (FB); [2012] ZAFSHC 148.

of the 1973 Act, the applicant must first (and as a *sine qua non*) prove insolvency. The court held that should an applicant be unable to prove insolvency, such applicant must then make out a case for winding-up in terms of s 81.

15.2   The winding-up of solvent companies

As described above, a solvent company is wound up mainly in terms of the provisions of the 2008 Act, but certain sections of the 1973 Act, other than those specifically excluded in terms of item 9 of Schedule 5, will also apply. The sections that are specifically excluded are set out in the table below.

Table 15.1 Sections of the 1973 Act not applying to the winding-up of a solvent company

Section of the 1973 Act	Subject matter
343	Modes of winding up
344	Circumstances in which company may be wound up by court
346	Application for winding-up of company
348	Commencement of winding-up by court
349	Circumstances under which company may be wound up voluntarily
350	Members' voluntary winding-up and security
351	Creditors' voluntary winding-up
352	Commencement of voluntary winding-up
353	Effect of voluntary winding-up on status of company and on directors

15.2.1   Voluntary winding-up of a solvent company initiated by the company

A solvent company may be wound up voluntarily if the company has adopted a special resolution to do so. Such a resolution may provide for the winding-up to be by the company, or by its creditors.

Before the resolution and notice are filed, the company must:
- arrange for security, satisfactory to the Master, for the payment of the company's debts within no more than 12 months after the start of the winding-up of the company;[4] or
- obtain the consent of the Master to dispense with security, which the Master may do only if the company has submitted to the Master,
  - a sworn statement by a director stating that the company has no debts; and
  - a certificate by the company's auditor, or if it does not have an auditor, a person who meets the requirements for appointment as an auditor, and who is appointed for the purpose, stating that to the best of the auditor's knowledge and belief and according to the financial records of the company, the company appears to have no debts.

---

4   Arranging security means that there is a written unconditional promise or undertaking to pay a certain amount (evidenced in a document issued by a financially secure and reputable person or institution) or a specific sum of money is lodged. Security is arranged to safeguard the interests of a company's creditors.

Section 80(5) provides that a liquidator appointed in a voluntary winding-up may exercise all powers given by the 2008 Act, or 1973 Act, to a liquidator in a winding-up by the court without requiring specific order or sanction of the court; and subject to any directions given by:
- the shareholders of the company in a general meeting, in the case of a winding-up by the company; or
- the creditors, in the case of a winding-up by creditors.

Section 20(8) provides that despite any provision to the contrary in a company's Memorandum of Incorporation the company remains a juristic person and retains all of its powers as such while it is being wound up voluntarily, but from the beginning of the company's winding-up:
- it must stop carrying on its business except to the extent required for the beneficial winding-up of the company; and
- all of the powers of the company's directors cease, except to the extent specifically authorised
  - in the case of a winding-up by the company, by the liquidator or the shareholders in a general meeting; or
  - in the case of a winding-up by creditors, the liquidator or the creditors.

15.2.2   The winding-up of a solvent company by court order

In terms of s 81, a court may order a solvent company to be wound up if:
- the company has *either* resolved, by **special resolution**, that it be wound up by the court; *or* it has applied to the court to have its voluntary winding-up continued by the court;
- the practitioner of a company appointed during business rescue proceedings has applied for liquidation in terms of s 141(2)*(a)*, on the grounds that there is no reasonable prospect of the company being rescued;
- one or more of the company's creditors have applied to the court for an order to wind up the company on the grounds that *either* the company's business rescue proceedings have ended in the manner contemplated in s 132(2)*(b)* or *(c)*(i) and it appears to the court that it is **just and equitable** in the circumstances for the company to be wound up, *or* it is otherwise just and equitable for the company to be wound up;
- the company, one or more directors or one or more shareholders have applied to the court for an order to wind up the company on the grounds that
  - the directors are **deadlocked** in the management of the company, and the shareholders are unable to break the deadlock, and *either* irreparable injury to the company is resulting, or may result, from the deadlock; *or* the company's business cannot be conducted to the advantage of shareholders generally, as a result of the deadlock;
  - the shareholders are deadlocked in voting power, and have failed for a period that includes at least two consecutive annual general meeting dates to elect successors to directors whose terms have expired; or
  - it is otherwise just and equitable for the company to be wound up;
- a shareholder has applied, with leave of the court, for an order to wind up the company on the grounds that
  - the directors, prescribed officers or other persons in control of the company are acting in a manner that is **fraudulent** or otherwise illegal; or
  - the company's **assets** are being **misapplied** or wasted; or

- the Commission or Panel has applied to the court for an order to wind up the company on the grounds that
    - the company, its directors or prescribed officers or other persons in control of the company are acting or have acted in a manner that is fraudulent or otherwise illegal, the Commission or Panel, as the case may be, has issued a compliance notice in respect of that conduct, and the company has failed to comply with that compliance notice; and
    - within the previous five years, enforcement procedures in terms of the Act or the Close Corporations Act,[5] were taken against the company, its directors or prescribed officers, or other persons in control of the company for substantially the same conduct, resulting in an administrative fine, or conviction for an offence.

CASE STUDY

Interpretation of s 81(1)(d)

In *Budge NNO v Midnight Storm Investments 256 (Pty) Ltd*,[6] the applicants sought the winding-up of two companies in terms of s 81(1)(d)(iii) of the 2008 Act. Section 81(1)(d) reads as follows:

> (1) A court may order a solvent company to be wound up if
>
> ...
>
> (d) the company [or others] have applied to the court for an order to wind up the company on the grounds that
>
> (i)   the directors are deadlocked in the management of the company ... ;
>
> (ii) the shareholders are deadlocked in voting power ... ; or
>
> (iii) it is otherwise just and equitable for the company to be wound up.

The respondents argued that the just and equitable ground for winding-up referred to in s 81(1)(d)(iii) should be restrictively interpreted and limited to the circumstances referred to in the preceding ss 81(1)(c) and 81(1)(d) thereof, which circumstances did not include the circumstances upon which the applicants relied in seeking the winding-up of the companies. The court therefore had to deal with an interpretation of s 81(1)(d) of the 2008 Act.

The court held that the 'just and equitable' basis for the winding-up of a solvent company in terms of s 81(1)(d)(iii) should not be interpreted so as to include only matters *ejusdem generis* the other grounds enumerated in s 81.[7] The *ejusdem generis* rule, in the court's view, was inapplicable to s 81(1)(d)(iii).

The court stated that in enacting s 81(1)(d)(i), which applies to a situation where the directors are deadlocked in the management of a company, and s 81(1)(d)(ii),

---

5   69 of 1984.

6   2012 (2) SA 28 (GSJ).

7   *Ejusdem generis* is Latin for 'of the same kind'. In the interpretation of legislation, when general words follow a list of specific and particular persons or things, the *ejusdem generis* rule says that such general words should not be given a wide meaning but should be regarded as applicable only to persons or things of the same kind or class as those specifically mentioned. For example if a law refers to automobiles, trucks, tractors, motorcycles and other vehicles, then the term 'vehicles' would not include airplanes, since the list was of land-based transportation. Similarly in a statute forbidding the concealment on one's person of 'pistols, revolvers, derringers, or other dangerous weapons', the term 'dangerous weapons' may be construed to comprehend only dangerous weapons of the kind enumerated, i.e., firearms, or perhaps even more narrowly, handguns.

which applies to a situation where the shareholders are deadlocked in voting power, the legislature modified the judicially developed deadlock category that forms part of the just and equitable ground for winding-up of a company and made its application subject to certain new requirements.

The court held that the application of s 81(1)(*d*)(iii) to deadlock categories and to the circumstances referred to in s 81(1)(*c*) would render the provisions of s 81(1)(*d*)(i) and of s 81(1)(*d*)(ii) of no effect, since an applicant who is unable to meet the requirements of those sections would nevertheless be able to invoke the judicially developed deadlock category that forms part of the just and equitable ground for winding-up in terms of s 81(1)(*d*)(iii). The court was also of the view that the *ejusdem generis* rule is excluded, because the specific words of s 81(1)(*d*)(i) and of s 81(1)(*d*)(ii) exhaust the 'deadlock' genus – that is, there can be no other types of deadlock in the specific circumstances and therefore the application of the rule would be unfruitful.[8]

The court therefore held that instances of deadlock are dealt with in sub-paragraphs (i) and (ii) of paragraph *(d)* and this had the effect of excluding consideration of deadlock in applications brought in terms of s 81(1)(*d*)(iii).

CASE STUDY	**Applying the partnership principle, does the just and equitable ground for winding up apply similarly to dissolution of private companies?** In *Muller v Lilly Valley (Pty) Ltd*,[9] the court held that the 'just and equitable' basis for winding up a company 'postulates not facts but only a broad conclusion of law, justice and equity as a ground for winding-up'. The 'justice and equity' is that between the competing interests of all concerned. In this case, the applicant relied upon this principle on the basis that the breakdown in the relationship between the shareholders of the respondent provided grounds analogous to those for the dissolution of partnership. The argument was that where (as in this case) there is, in substance, a partnership in the form of a private company, circumstances which would justify the dissolution of a partnership would also justify the winding-up of the company under the just and equitable provision. The court held that the applicant had two hurdles to overcome: 1. to show that the breakdown is as a result of the other shareholders' conduct and not his own conduct; and 2. to show that even if the other shareholders acted contrary to his wishes, that this is not simply a matter of the majority binding the minority. The court held, in relation to the second hurdle, that when evaluating the conduct of shareholders within the company, the guiding principle is that by becoming a shareholder in a company a person undertakes by his contract to be bound by the decisions of the prescribed majority of the shareholders, if those decisions on the affairs of the company are arrived at in accordance with the law, even where they adversely affect his own rights as a shareholder.

---

8 See *Carlis v Oldfield* (1887) 4 HCG 379 at 383.
9 [2012] 1 All SA 187 (GSJ).

In this case, the court concluded that the applicant had failed to establish:

- that the misconduct complained of was that of the other shareholders as opposed to his;
- that he resigned as an employee and director from the respondent on justifiable grounds;
- that the conduct upon which he relied was such that it destroyed the relationship between the parties and created a 'justifiable lack of confidence' in the conduct and management of the respondent's affairs (in so far as he relied on the partnership principle);
- that, even though he was a minority shareholder (and not an equal shareholder), he did not undertake to be bound by the decisions of the prescribed majority of the shareholders;
- that his position (if the respondent was not wound up) outweighed the prejudice to the other shareholders as well as the 50 permanent staff members and their families who enjoyed cost-free accommodation on the premises and the 50 temporary employees, whose livelihood would be affected; and
- that it would be just and equitable that the respondent be wound up.

The court concluded that even if the applicant had established that it was just and equitable to wind up the respondent based upon the partnership principle under s 81(1)(*d*)(iii), before a court will grant a winding-up of a solvent company, it must be satisfied that all alternative means have been investigated and have failed.

15.3   The winding-up of insolvent companies

A detailed discussion of the winding-up of insolvent companies is beyond the scope of this book. As has been mentioned above, in terms of the 2008 Act, the winding-up of insolvent companies continues to be dealt with in terms of the 1973 Act. The table below sets out the various sections of the 1973 Act in Chapter XIV (ss 337–426) that deal with the winding-up of companies, including the appointment, powers and duties of liquidators.

Table 15.2 Sections of the Companies Act, 1973 applicable to a winding-up

Heading	Section/s	Subject matter
General	337–343	
Winding-up by the court	344–348	
	344	Circumstances in which company may be wound up by court
	345	When company deemed unable to pay its debts
	346	Application for winding-up of company
	346A	Service of winding-up order
	347	Power of court in hearing application
	348	Commencement of winding-up by court

Heading	Section/s	Subject matter
Voluntary winding-up	349–353	
	349	Circumstances under which company may be wound up voluntarily
	350	Members' voluntary winding-up and security
	351	Creditors' voluntary winding-up
	352	Commencement of voluntary winding-up
	353	Effect of voluntary winding-up on status of company and on directors
General provisions affecting all windings-up	354–366	
	354	Court may stay or set aside winding-up
	355	Notice to creditors or members in review by court in winding-up, and no re-opening of confirmed account
	356	Notice of winding-up of company
	357	Notice of winding-up to certain officials and their duties
	358	Stay of legal proceedings before winding-up order granted
	359	Legal proceedings suspended and attachments void
	360	Inspection of records of company being wound up
	361	Custody of or control over, and vesting of property of, company
	362	Court may order directors, officers and others to deliver property to liquidator or to pay into bank
	363	Directors and others to submit statement of affairs
	363A	Change of address by directors and secretaries and certain former directors and secretaries
	364	Master to summon first meetings of creditors and members and purpose thereof
	365	Offences in securing nomination as liquidator and restriction on voting at meetings
	366	Claims and proof of claims
Liquidators	367–385	
	367	Appointment of liquidator
	368	Appointment of provisional liquidator
	369	Determination of person to be appointed liquidator
	370	Master may decline to appoint nominated person as liquidator
	371	Remedy of aggrieved persons
	372	Persons disqualified from appointment as liquidator

Heading	Section/s	Subject matter
Liquidators	373	Persons disqualified by court from being appointed or acting as liquidators
	374	Master may appoint co-liquidator at any time
	375	Appointment, commencement of office and validity of acts of liquidator
	376	Title of liquidator
	377	Filling of vacancies
	378	Leave of absence or resignation of liquidator
	379	Removal of liquidator by Master and by the court
	380	Notice of removal of liquidator
	381	Control of Master over liquidators
	382	Plurality of liquidators, liability and disagreement
	383	Cost and reduction of security by liquidator
	384	Remuneration of liquidator
	385	Certificate of completion of duties by liquidator and cancellation of security
Powers of liquidators	386–390	
Duties of liquidators	391–411	
Provisions as to meetings in winding-up	412–416	
Examination of persons in winding-up	417–418	
Dissolution of companies and other bodies corporate	419–422	
Personal liability of delinquent directors and others and offences	423–426	

15.4 The deregistration of companies

In terms of s 14 of the 2008 Act (dealing with the registration of companies), as soon as practicable after accepting a Notice of Incorporation in terms of s 13(1), the Commission must:

- assign to the company a unique registration number; and
- enter the prescribed information concerning the company in the companies register.

The Commission must then endorse the Notice of Incorporation, and issue and deliver to the company a registration certificate in the prescribed manner and form. Section 19 provides that from the date and time that the incorporation of a company is registered, as stated in its registration certificate, the company is a juristic person, which exists continuously until its name is removed from the companies register in accordance with the Act.

In terms of s 83(1), a company is **dissolved** from the date its name is removed from the companies register.[10] However, note that s 83(2) specifically provides that the **removal of a company's name from the companies register** does not affect the liability of any former director or shareholder of the company or any other person in respect of any act or omission that took place before the company was removed from the register.[11]

15.4.1 Procedures for the deregistration of a company

Section 82 provides that a company will be **deregistered** when the following procedures are completed:

- The Master must file a certificate of winding-up of a company in the prescribed form when the affairs of the company have been completely wound up.[12] Upon receiving such a certificate, the Commission must
  - record the dissolution of the company in the prescribed manner; and
  - remove the company's name from the companies register.[13]
- The Commission may also remove a company from the companies register if the company has transferred its registration to a foreign jurisdiction in terms of s 82(5).[14]
- The Commission may also remove a company from the companies register if it has failed to file an annual return in terms of s 33 for two or more years in succession, and on demand by the Commission, it has either failed to give satisfactory reasons for the failure to file the required annual returns; or it has shown satisfactory cause for the company to remain registered.[15]
- The Commission may also remove a company from the companies register if the Commission
  - has determined in the prescribed manner that the company appears to have been inactive for at least seven years, and no person has demonstrated a reasonable interest in, or reason for, its continued existence; or

---

10 Unless the reason for the removal is that the company's registration has been transferred to a foreign jurisdiction, as contemplated in s 82(5).
11 In terms of s 83(3), any liability contemplated in sub-s (2) continues and may be enforced as if the company had not been removed from the register.
12 Section 82(1).
13 Section 82(2).
14 Section 82(3).
15 Section 82(3).

♦   has received a request in the prescribed manner and form and has determined that
the company has ceased to carry on business, and has no assets or, because of the
inadequacy of its assets, there is no reasonable probability of the company being
liquidated.[16]

CASE STUDY	**Company's assets pass to the State upon deregistration**
	In *Valley View Homeowners' Association v Universal Pulse Trading 27 (Pty) Ltd*,[17] the court made it clear that ss 82 and 83 of the 2008 Act deal with deregistration, and that s 83(1) goes further than s 73 of the 1973 Act, by expressly stating that 'a company is dissolved as of the date its name is removed from the companies register'. Thus a company's existence as a corporate persona ends on deregistration, and it becomes incapable of retaining ownership of any of its assets, all of which pass into the ownership of the State.
	On deregistration, there remains neither a corporate entity capable of being placed in the hands of a liquidator, nor any assets to be realised by a liquidator for the purpose of distributing the proceeds to creditors. Self-evidently there cannot be a winding-up and subsequent liquidation of assets of a company which has simultaneously ceased to exist and transferred ownership of all its assets to the State.
	The court referred to 4 (Part 3) *LAWSA* 98 where Blackman defines winding-up or liquidation as:
	the process by which, prior to its dissolution, the management of a company's affairs is taken out of its directors' hands, its assets are ascertained, realised and applied in payment of its creditors according to their order of preference, and any residue distributed amongst its members according to their rights. The company's corporate existence is then put to an end by the formal process of dissolution.[18]
	Referring to the 1973 Act, Blackman points out that deregistration in terms of s 73 is to be distinguished from dissolution in terms of s 419 of a company following its winding-up, although each leads to the cessation of the existence of the company as a legal persona, as held in *Ex parte Jacobson: in re Alec Jacobson Holdings (Pty) Ltd*.[19]

15.4.2   Reinstatement and application to declare dissolution void

Section 82(4) provides that if the Commission deregisters a company in terms of s 82(3),[20]
any interested person may apply in the prescribed manner and form to the *Commission*, to
reinstate the registration of the company. However the regulations[21] provide that the
Commission may re-instate a deregistered company only after it has filed the outstanding
annual returns and paid the outstanding prescribed fee in respect thereof.

Section 83(4) provides a similar but different remedy and states that at any time after a
company has been dissolved:

---

16   Section 82(3).
17   2011 JDR 0652 (GNP); [2011] ZAGPPHC 154.
18   MS Blackman 'Companies' in Joubert WA et al (eds), *The Law of South Africa* vol. 4(3) 1st reissue.
19   1984 (2) SA 372 (W) at 376-7.
20   For example, if it has failed to file an annual return, or it is inactive as described above.
21   Regulation 40(6).

- the liquidator of the company, or other person with an interest in the company, may apply to a *court* for an order **declaring the dissolution void**, or any other order that is just and equitable in the circumstances; and
- if the court declares the dissolution to have been void, any proceedings may be taken against the company as might have been taken if the company had not been dissolved.

It is clear that the Commission (not a court) has power to 'reinstate' the registration of a company in terms of s 82(4), whereas a court has the power in terms of s 83(4) to declare a dissolution to be void in the circumstances set out in that section.

CASE STUDY

Reinstatement necessary before winding-up can be ordered

In *Valley View Homeowners' Association v Universal Pulse Trading 27 (Pty) Ltd*,[22] the court referred to the case of *Suid-Afrikaanse Nasionale Lewensassuransie-Maatskappy v Rainbow Diamonds (Edms) Bpk*,[23] where it was confirmed that on deregistration all a company's property, whether movable or immovable, corporeal or incorporeal, automatically becomes property owned by the State as *bona vacantia*.

The court therefore held that ss 82(4) and 83(4) of the 2008 Act provide procedures for the restoration or reinstatement of a deregistered company's registration. Accordingly, the applicant would only be able to apply for the winding-up of the respondent after successfully using the procedures for reinstating the registration of the respondent. For these reasons, the provisional winding-up order was discharged.

CASE STUDY

No difference between deregistration and dissolution in a court's power to declare dissolution void

In *Absa Bank Ltd v Companies and Intellectual Property Commission of South Africa, Absa Bank Ltd v Voigro Investments 19 CC*,[24] (being a successful appeal from the judgment of the court *a quo*), a close corporation was deregistered because of its failure to lodge annual returns. The court *a quo* had been of the view that s 83(4) only applied to a company that had been deregistered as a result of its liquidation and held that s 83(4)*(a)* of the 2008 Act does not empower a court to revive a company that has been deregistered for a failure to lodge annual returns. A close corporation (or company) that has been deregistered because of its failure to lodge annual returns could not, so the court held, be either revived by a court in terms of s 83(4) or 'reinstated' by a court in terms of s 82(4) – that power lay exclusively in the hands of the Commission.

On appeal, the decision of the court *a quo* was set aside. The court held that s 83(4) applies to any company that has been dissolved, whether as a result of a failure to lodge annual returns (or pursuant to any other administrative deregistration as envisaged by s 82(3)) or as a result of its liquidation. The court held that in terms of s 83(4) a court is not confined to declaring a dissolution void: it can make any other order that is just and equitable in the circumstances. Therefore s 83(4) applies in all

---

22 Supra.
23 1984 (3) SA 1 (A) at 10–12.
24 [2012] ZAWCHC 182.

cases where a company or close corporation's name has been removed from the register and where, as a result, it has been dissolved. This includes deregistration on any of the grounds set out in s 82(3).

In practice, this means that where a company or close corporation is deregistered by the Commission in terms of s 82(3), rather than in terms of s 82(2)(b), an interested party can apply either to the Commission for restoration in terms of s 82(4) or to the court in terms of s 83(4).

An interested party therefore has a choice, and will approach a court where the prescribed requirements under s 82(4) cannot or have not been met. (In terms of the regulations,[25] the Commission may only re-instate a deregistered company after it has filed the outstanding annual returns and paid the outstanding prescribed fee in respect thereof.) These requirements do not have to be met if an interested party applies to court in terms of s 83(4).

The court also confirmed that if the dissolution is declared void, then the company's assets are no longer *bona vacantia* (that is, they are no longer owned by the State) and the company is re-vested with its assets.

As an aside, the court also stated that because it has the power to make any order that is just and equitable, this power may perhaps include the power to validate things that happened during its period of dissolution.

15.4.3   Legal effect of a company's actions when it has been deregistered

The case of *Fintech (Pty) Ltd v Awake Solutions (Pty) Ltd*[26] concerned the validity and effect of certain actions taken by or against a company during the period of its deregistration. The company was deregistered in terms of the 1973 Act by the then Registrar of Companies because it failed to file annual returns. In April 2012, the company's deregistration was 'cancelled' by the Commission under the provisions of the 2008 Act.

The issue was the determination of the status of the company in the period from its deregistration to the cancellation thereof.

The pertinent section of the 2008 Act (s 82(4) read with regulation 40(6)) provides for *reinstatement* of registration by the Commission. In this case, however, the deregistration of the company was *cancelled*. The question that therefore arose was whether there is any difference in meaning between the two concepts.

The court held that there was this difference: the cancellation of the process connotes an elimination of the entire process, including the initial deregistration, as if it had never occurred, whereas reinstatement implies putting it back in its former position, prior to deregistration. On this construction, the court concluded that by the cancellation of the deregistration process the company, at all times, remained a corporate entity.

The court therefore declared that all acts done by or against the company from the date of its deregistration until the date of the cancellation were validly done and that those acts were of full force and effect.

The court went further and also decided the issue on the assumption that the company was reinstated as provided for in the 2008 Act.

---

25   Regulation 40 (6).
26   2013 (1) SA 570 (GSJ).

In the current case, the company was deregistered in terms of the 1973 Act, as a consequence of its failure to file an annual return, as required in terms of s 173 of that Act. The court held that it is now settled law that deregistration puts an end to the existence of the company.[27]

The court confirmed that reinstatement of registration of a deregistered company in terms of the 2008 Act follows upon an application for this in terms of s 82(4). The court stated, however, that the 2008 Act does not expressly provide for retrospectivity in regard to reinstatement.

The court referred to the case of *Peninsula Eye Clinic (Pty) Ltd v Newlands Surgical Clinic (Pty) Ltd*,[28] and agreed with the *prima facie* view expressed there that the word 'reinstate' as used in s 82(4), implies that the restoration to the register is meant to be with retrospective effect. The court in *Absa Bank Ltd v Companies and Intellectual Property Commission of South Africa*[29] did however comment that, while it was making an order declaring the dissolution of the company to be void, 'nothing done by the company and no action taken against the company during the period of dissolution is of any effect and no validity or life is breathed into such conduct or action by the making of the order'.

THIS CHAPTER IN ESSENCE

1. The Companies Act, 2008 provides that certain provisions of the **1973 Act** will continue to apply to the winding-up and liquidation of companies.
2. In particular, the winding-up of **insolvent companies** is dealt with in terms of the 1973 Act, while the winding-up of **solvent companies** is dealt with in terms of both the 2008 and 1973 Acts, except that certain sections of the latter are specifically made inapplicable to the winding-up of solvent companies.
3. A solvent company may be dissolved either by **voluntary winding-up** initiated by the company, or winding-up and **liquidation by court order**.
4. Although the 1973 Act provided that a company could be wound up on the ground that it was deemed to be unable to pay its debts (**commercial insolvency**), this is not a ground for the winding-up of a solvent company by a court under the 2008 Act.
5. A solvent company may be wound up voluntarily if the company has adopted a **special resolution** to do so. The company remains a juristic person and retains all its powers while being wound up voluntarily, but it must stop carrying on its business except to the extent required for the beneficial winding-up of the company. All of the powers of the company's directors cease, except if they are specifically authorised by the liquidator, shareholders or creditors.
6. A court may order a solvent company to be wound up in any of the following (summarised) circumstances:
   6.1 The company has resolved, by special resolution, that it be wound up by the court; or it has applied to the court to have its voluntary winding-up continued by the court.
   6.2 The practitioner of a company appointed during business rescue proceedings has applied for liquidation on the grounds that there is no reasonable prospect of the company being rescued.
   6.3 The company's creditors have applied for an order to wind up the company on the grounds that *either* the company's business rescue proceedings have ended and it appears to be **just and equitable** for the company to be wound up, *or* it is otherwise just and equitable for the company to be wound up.

---

27 See *Miller v Nafcoc Investment Holding Co Ltd* 2010 (6) SA 390 (SCA) at para [11]; *Silver Sands Transport (Pty) Ltd v SA Linde (Pty) Ltd* 1973 (3) SA 548 (W) at 549.
28 2012 (4) SA 484 (WCC).
29 Supra.

6.4 The company, directors or shareholders have applied to the court for an order to wind up the company on the grounds that either the directors are **deadlocked** in the management of the company, the shareholders are deadlocked in voting power, or it is otherwise just and equitable for the company to be wound up.

6.5 A shareholder has applied for an order to wind up the company on the grounds that the company or persons in control of the company are acting in a manner that is **fraudulent** or otherwise illegal, or that the company's **assets** are being **misapplied** or wasted.

6.6 The Commission or Panel has applied to court for an order to wind up the company on the grounds that the company or persons in control of the company have acted **fraudulently** or illegally, that the company has failed to comply with a compliance notice issued in respect of the conduct and that within the previous five years, the company or the persons in control of the company were fined or convicted for substantially the same conduct.

7. The 2008 Act provides that a company is **dissolved** from the date its **name is removed from the companies register**.

7.1 The Commission must record the dissolution of a company and remove its name from the register upon receiving from the Master a certificate of the winding-up of a company.

7.2 The Commission may also remove a company from the companies register if the company has transferred its registration to a foreign jurisdiction or if it has failed to file an annual return for two or more years in succession without showing satisfactory cause for it to remain registered.

7.3 The Commission may also remove a company from the companies register if the company appears to have been inactive for at least seven years and has no reason for continued existence. It may also, on request, deregister the company if it is determined that the company has ceased to carry on business and has no or inadequate assets for liquidation.

8. If the Commission **deregisters** a company, any interested person may apply to the *Commission* to **reinstate the registration** of the company. An interested person may also apply to a *court* for an order **declaring the dissolution void**, or any other order that is just and equitable in the circumstances.

PART TWO

Close corporations

Chapter 16

Close corporations

16.1   The nature of a close corporation and its members

The Close Corporations Act[1] (referred to in this chapter as the Act) provides for the formation of **close corporations**, which are simple, deregulated, and flexible, limited liability entities, suitable for small businesses. They have their own legal personality and enjoy the benefits

---

1   69 of 1984.

of perpetual succession.[2] The founding statement (Form CK1) is the document that establishes a close corporation and sets out certain details about the corporation, including the name of the corporation, its financial year, details of members, details of the accounting officer, and the principal business of the corporation. Members of a close corporation can also voluntarily draw up an association agreement, which is a contract that principally sets out the rights and duties of, and relationship between, members.

Even though a close corporation is a juristic person, it has the capacity and all the powers of a natural person in so far as a juristic person is capable of having such capacity or exercising such powers.[3] Therefore, the *ultra vires* doctrine has no application in respect of close corporations, and the statement of the principal business of the corporation in the **founding statement** does not affect the corporation's capacity and powers.[4] As far as third parties dealing with a close corporation are concerned, there is no constructive notice of any particulars stated in a founding statement, and therefore third parties will not be adversely affected by any limitations in a close corporation's founding statement.[5] Consequently, all contracts entered into by a close corporation with outsiders will be valid, even if the transaction goes beyond the stated business of the corporation (as expressed in the founding statement).

A close corporation does not have shareholders, but has **members**. A close corporation is a separate legal person and is distinct and apart from its members. In spite of the principle that a close corporation is a separate legal entity, members can be liable for its debts in certain circumstances. The issue of the personal liability of members is discussed later in this chapter.[6]

A close corporation can have from one to 10 members. The restriction on the number of members emphasises the legislature's intention that the close corporation is meant for smaller businesses, with the relationship between the members themselves being similar to that of partners.[7] In essence, therefore, there is no separation between ownership and control. A close corporation is thus ideally suited for those entrepreneurs who wish to own and manage their own businesses. The Act therefore allows every member to participate in the business and to make legally binding decisions on behalf of the corporation.[8]

Subject to the exceptions referred to below, only natural persons may be members of a close corporation and no juristic person may hold a member's interest in a close corporation.[9] Therefore, a company or close corporation cannot be a member of a close corporation and any contravention of this prohibition can result in the juristic person incurring liability for certain debts of the close corporation.[10] Conversely, however, a close corporation itself may be a shareholder and a close corporation can even become the controlling shareholder of a company.[11]

---

2   Section 2(2) of the Close Corporations Act, and see WD Geach and T Schoeman *Guide to the Close Corporations Act and Regulations* (loose-leaf service).
3   Section 2(4) of the Close Corporations Act.
4   See para. 2.13.1 above for a discussion on corporate capacity and the *ultra vires* doctrine.
5   See para. 2.13.2 above for a discussion on constructive notice.
6   See para. 16.13 below.
7   See Geach & Schoeman supra; Henning et al 'Close Corporations' in WA Joubert et al (eds) (1996) *LAWSA* 4 (3), 1st reissue at para. 437.
8   Section 54 of the Close Corporations Act.
9   Section 29(1) of the Close Corporations Act.
10 See s 63(*d*) of the Close Corporations Act.
11 HS Cilliers, ML Benade et al *Corporate Law* (2000) 3ed at para. 35.03. Section 55 of the Close Corporations Act (which applies certain provisions of the former Companies Act, 1973 to such close corporation as if it were a holding company) has been repealed by the Companies Act, 2008 (see Schedule 3, item 5) of the 2008 Act).

A trustee of either an *inter vivos* trust or of a testamentary trust can be a member of a close corporation in the capacity of trustee.[12] There are, however, certain restrictions on allowing a trustee of an *inter vivos* trust to be a member, such as the requirement that no juristic person can be a beneficiary of that trust. Furthermore, based on the underlying principle that close corporations are really meant for small businesses (and hence the number of members is restricted to 10), if at any time the number of beneficiaries of the trust who are entitled to receive any benefit from the trust, when added to the number of members of the corporation, is greater than 10, the membership of the trustee will cease. Once membership ceases in terms of this condition, no trustee of that trust will ever again be eligible for membership of the trust even if the number becomes 10 or fewer.[13]

Although there is a restriction as to the number of members of a close corporation, there is no restriction on the number of its employees, or on the corporation's turnover, value of assets or type of business. A close corporation will therefore not necessarily outgrow its legal form.

16.2   Close corporations and the Companies Act, 2008

The Companies Act, 2008 has important implications for close corporations. In particular, no new close corporations will be incorporated under the Close Corporations Act after the commencement of the 2008 Act (1 May 2011), and no company can be converted into a close corporation after that date. Close corporations that existed on 1 May 2011 (the effective date) are allowed to continue indefinitely, but no new close corporations can be formed. Smaller businesses may now incorporate as private companies under the Companies Act, 2008.

The 2008 Act contains some sections that are similar to those of the Close Corporations Act. In particular, the concept of capital maintenance is abandoned in both Acts, and the solvency and liquidity test has to be applied before certain transactions can take place – such as the declaration of a dividend (distribution to members in the case of a close corporation) and share buybacks (corporation acquiring its own interests).

The Companies Act, 2008 also contains special provisions affecting close corporations:
1. All close corporations that existed when the Companies Act, 2008 became effective can continue indefinitely, and do not have to be converted into companies. The Close Corporations Act will continue to govern existing close corporations. However, no new close corporations can be formed[14] and no companies can be converted into close corporations.
2. Schedule 2 of the Companies Act, 2008 provides for the steps to be taken when close corporations are converted to companies; and
3. Schedule 3 of the Companies Act, 2008 makes certain amendments to the Close Corporations Act, including the following:
   • annual financial statements of a close corporation must comply with International Financial Reporting Standards (IFRS) and must be audited if the close corporation falls within any of the categories of private company that are required to have their financial statements audited;[15]
   • the members of a close corporation can voluntarily decide that the corporation must comply with the extended accountability provisions of the 2008 Act and to appoint

---

12   See chapter 18 of this book to see what is meant by an *inter vivos* trust and a testamentary trust.
13   Section 29(1A) of the Close Corporations Act refers.
14   Section 2(1) of the Close Corporations Act, as amended by the Companies Act, 2008.
15   See para. 13.2 above for a discussion of this topic.

an audit committee or a company secretary – in such a case, the close corporation must comply with Chapter 3 of the Companies Act, 2008; and[16]

- the business rescue provisions of the 2008 Act will also apply to close corporations.[17]

Although no new close corporations can be formed under the 2008 Act and companies cannot be converted into close corporations, any close corporation can be converted into a company at any time. There must be a notice of **conversion** and this notice must be accompanied by the following:[18]

- a written statement of consent approving the conversion of the close corporation, signed by members of the corporation holding, in aggregate, at least 75 per cent of the members' interest in the corporation;
- a Memorandum of Incorporation (MOI) consistent with the requirements of the Companies Act, 2008; and
- the prescribed filing fee.

Every member of a close corporation that has been converted is entitled to (but does not have to) become a shareholder of the company resulting from that conversion, and furthermore the shares to be held in the company by the shareholders individually need not necessarily be in proportion to the members' interests as stated in the founding statement of the close corporation.

On the registration of the new company, the juristic person that existed as a close corporation before the conversion continues to exist as a juristic person, but in the form of a company, and all the assets, liabilities, rights and obligations of the close corporation vest in the company.

In addition to the above, the following should be noted:

- any legal proceedings instituted by or against the corporation may be continued by or against the newly formed company; and
- any liability of a member of the corporation for the corporation's debts that had arisen in terms of the Close Corporations Act survives the conversion and continues as a liability of that person, as if the conversion had not occurred.[19]

16.3   Contributions by members and nature of members' interests

On the formation of a close corporation, each person who became a member on its incorporation was required to make a contribution of either money or other assets or services relating to the formation of the corporation.[20] Particulars of these contributions have to be included in the founding statement. By agreement between the members, these contributions can subsequently be increased or reduced, and details of the change must be reflected in an amended founding statement.[21] The size of a member's interest need not necessarily be in proportion to this contribution.[22]

---

16   Chapter 3 of the Companies Act, 2008 deals with auditors, audit committees and the company secretary.
17   Chapter 12 of this book deals with business rescue provisions.
18   Schedule 2 of the Companies Act, 2008 deals with the conversion of a close corporation to a company.
19   See para. 16.13 below as to the personal liability of members.
20   Section 24(1) of the Close Corporations Act.
21   Sections 24(2) and 15(1). These contributions had to be or must be made, as the case may be, within 90 days of the registration of the corporation or the registration of the amended founding statement (s 24(4)). The member who fails to do so within the time stipulated by the Act becomes personally liable for certain debts of the corporation (s 63(b)).
22   See Cilliers & Benade supra at para. 35.15.

Each member of a close corporation has a member's interest in the corporation. The member's interest is a single interest expressed as a percentage.[23] This implies that a member may not hold more than one interest. The aggregate of the members' interests in the corporation expressed as a percentage must be 100 per cent.[24] A member's interest may not be held jointly;[25] this is to ensure that the member number restriction (a maximum of 10 members) is not evaded through joint holding of members' interests.

A person became a member of a close corporation when the founding statement reflecting that person's membership was registered.[26] Each member of the corporation is entitled to be issued with a certificate of member's interest, signed by or on behalf of the members of the corporation, stating the current percentage of that member's interest in the corporation.[27] This certificate has a dual function, reflecting both membership and the member's interest. There is no securities register as in the case of a company. There is no need for such a register, as the particulars of the current members and their respective interests appear in the founding statement[28] or amended founding statement,[29] as the case may be. Such statement and any amended founding statement is filed with and kept by the Commission.[30]

A member ceases to be a member after disposing of his or her member's interest and after the registration of an amended founding statement reflecting the loss of membership.[31] Disposal of members' interests and cessation of membership can also occur by order of court under s 36 of the Close Corporations Act.[32]

As to the legal nature of a member's interest, the Act states only that it is movable property transferable in the manner provided by the Act.[33] The member's interest is clearly also incorporeal. It is helpful to regard a member's interest in a close corporation as analogous in some respects to a share in a company. A **member's interest** may therefore be described as a personal right against the corporation, entitling the member to a proportionate share in the aggregate members' interests, to participate in a distribution of profits, and to share in a distribution of the assets on liquidation once all the creditors have been paid.[34]

Unless otherwise provided in an **association agreement** (a written agreement between members regulating internal relationships and other lawful matters),[35] members' voting rights and their right to participate in distributions of profits and other payments by the corporation to its members will be in proportion to their members' interests.[36]

---

23 Section 30(1) of the Close Corporations Act.
24 Section 38 of the Close Corporations Act.
25 Section 30(2) of the Close Corporations Act.
26 Although the opening portion of s 15(1) of the Close Corporations Act might create the impression that membership could be acquired earlier, the concluding portion is quite clear that the new member only becomes a member on the registration of the amended founding statement. The reliance in *Geaney v Portion 117 Kalkheuwel Properties CC* 1998 (1) SA 622 (T) at 624J on s 15(2) is misplaced. Changes of membership are regulated by s 15(1), which refers to s 12*(d)*; s 15(2) has no application. See Cilliers & Benade supra at para. 35.09.
27 Section 31 of the Close Corporations Act.
28 Section 12*(d)* and *(e)* of the Close Corporations Act.
29 Section 15(1) of the Close Corporations Act.
30 It will no longer be necessary for the names of all the members to be on all business letters, once the repeal of s 41 of the Close Corporations Act by the Companies Act, 2008 comes into operation (Schedule 5, item 6(4)*(b)*).
31 See *Geaney v Portion 117 Kalkheuwel Properties CC* supra at 624B and form CK2. The person who ceases to be a member is required to sign this form personally, as a way of protecting that person against improper attempts by other members to deprive him or her of membership.
32 See para. 16.6 below.
33 Section 30 of the Close Corporations Act.
34 Cilliers & Benade supra at para 35.19.
35 For more on association agreements, see para. 16.8 below.
36 Section 46*(d)* and *(f)* of the Close Corporations Act.

16.4 Acquisition and disposal of a member's interest

New members who join after the registration of the corporation must acquire their members' interests either from an existing member,[37] or by making a contribution in the form of money or other assets to the corporation.[38] In the latter event, the percentage of the member's interest of the new member is agreed between him or her and the existing members, and the interests of the existing members must be reduced proportionately, or as agreed.[39]

The Act makes specific provision for the **disposal of a member's interest** in the event of the death or insolvency of a member, and where a member's interest is attached and sold by way of a sale in execution. It also provides for the termination of membership pursuant to a court order, which must also direct the disposal of the member's interest. These provisions are dealt with below.

Every other disposition[40] of a member's interest, whether in whole or in part, must be made either in accordance with the association agreement (if any), or with the consent of every other member. The disposition can either be to another person qualifying for membership or to the corporation.[41] In the latter event, the corporation must have one or more other members.[42] It is advisable to provide for the disposal of a member's interest in the association agreement – for example, by making it subject to a right of pre-emption in favour of the other members of the corporation. Otherwise, the consent of all the other members to the disposal is required, which means that any member objecting to the disposal has in effect a right of veto. This may necessitate a court application to resolve the matter.[43]

In the case of an insolvent member, s 34(1) of the Act contains a mandatory procedure for the disposal of the insolvent member's interest. This procedure is aimed at striking a balance between the interests of the other members in controlling who can become a member of the corporation on the one hand, and the creditors of the insolvent member on the other. The member's interest may be sold to the corporation, to the other members or to an outsider who qualifies for membership. In the latter event, the sale to an outsider is subject to a **right of pre-emption** in favour of the corporation and the other members.[44] The same procedure applies to the sale in execution of a member's interest pursuant to its attachment to satisfy a judgment debt.[45]

---

37 Or from the estate of a deceased or insolvent member. See further below.

38 Section 33(1) and (2) of the Close Corporations Act.

39 See s 33(1)*(b)* read with s 38*(b)* of the Close Corporations Act. A new member who fails to pay this contribution within the time stipulated by the Act also becomes liable for certain debts of the company (s 63*(b)* read with s 24(2)*(a)* and 33(1)*(b)*).

40 It is suggested that the term 'disposition' in this context does not just refer to the transfer of the member's interest by cession, but includes the obligatory agreement, e.g. a sale or donation. The use of the member's interest as security by way of an out-and-out cession is almost certainly a disposition to which the restrictions on disposition in the text below apply. If the member's interest is pledged, the realisation of the pledge would be a disposition. Moreover, the member's interest cannot be sold to or held by a juristic person, even by using a nominee. See s 29(1) of the Close Corporations Act and para. 16.1 above. These statutory obstacles make the use of a member's interest as security impractical, particularly if the creditor requiring security is a juristic person. See further, on the use of member's interests as security, Cilliers & Benade supra at paras. 35.32–35.37.

41 See para. 16.7 below for a discussion on the acquisition by a corporation of an interest in itself.

42 Section 37 of the Close Corporations Act, and see para 16.8 below for a discussion of association agreements.

43 See s 36 of the Close Corporations Act (discussed in para. 16.6.1 below), unless the members have agreed to some alternative form of dispute resolution.

44 See s 34 of the Close Corporations Act for the detailed provisions.

45 See s 34A of the Close Corporations Act, which was introduced to overturn the decision in *Jones v Trust Bank of Africa Ltd* 1993 (4) SA 415 (C) to the effect that a member's interest was not included under the limited concept of movables for purposes of attachment and sales in execution in the magistrates' courts in terms of s 68(1) of the Magistrates' Courts Act 32 of 1944 (see Cilliers & Benade supra at para. 35.14).

In the case of a disposal of the member's interest of a deceased member, the statutory provision applies in the absence of any other arrangement in an association agreement.[46] In terms of the Act, transfer of the interest to the legatee or heir of the deceased member requires the consent of the other members. If that consent is not forthcoming within the prescribed period, the executor may sell the member's interest, subject to the same restrictions that apply in the case of an insolvent member, discussed above.[47]

CASE

STUDY

Factors affecting sale of deceased member's interest

The court in *Livanos v Oates*[48] had to interpret and apply s 35 of the Close Corporations Act in respect of the sale of a member's interest of a deceased member.

In this case the executors of an estate sold a 50 per cent interest in a close corporation to the son of the deceased. The person who held the other 50 per cent in the corporation sought to have this sale set aside. The corporation's association agreement did not deal with what happened to a member's interest on death. Accordingly the matter had to be dealt with in terms of s 35*(b)*(iii) as read with s 34(2) of the Close Corporations Act.

The court stated that an executor must first seek a transfer of a deceased member's interest to the legatee or heir and that such transfer can only be effected if the remaining member(s) of the corporation consent to the transfer.

In this case it was common cause that there was a sole heir (the deceased's daughter), and that the executors requested the remaining member, to consent to the transfer of the deceased member's interest to that heir. The remaining member declined to consent to the transfer of the member's interest to the heir in terms of s 35*(a)*. Accordingly, the executors were entitled to proceed to sell the deceased member's interest in terms of s 35*(b)*, which they did, to the deceased's son.

The remaining member of the close corporation was then requested by the executors to consent to the transfer of the deceased's 50 per cent member's interest in the close corporation to the son as buyer of that interest in terms of a sale agreement. The request was made in terms of s 35 as read with s 34(2) of the Close Corporations Act.

The remaining member did not consent to the transfer within 28 days as provided for in s 34(2). The court held that a failure to transfer the deceased member's interest pursuant to s 35*(a)* results in the executor's obligation to act pursuant to s 35*(b)*. The court held that the section does not oblige the executor to sell the member's interest to the corporation or the remaining members:

> The intention of the legislature is clearly that in the event of s 35*(a)* not being applicable, that the executors can dispose of the member's interest in one of the three manners provided for in s 35*(b)*.

The remaining member had the opportunity to acquire the member's interest but he failed to do so within the time period as provided for in the section. The court held that the executors were therefore free to employ the options contained in s 35*(b)* and, in particular, the option contained in s 35*(b)*(iii). Having entered into a sale with a person who qualified as a member, the executors also had to comply with the provisions of

---

46   Section 35 of the Close Corporations Act.

47   See s 35*(a)* and *(b)*, read with s 34 of the Close Corporations Act.

48   [2012] ZAGPJHC 30.

s 34(2): the corporation or the remaining member is entitled, in terms of s 34(2)*(b)*, to exercise what is effectively a pre-emptive right, within 28 days of receipt of the applicable written statement, to be substituted as purchaser for the member's interest at the price and on the terms set out in the written statement and that if they fail to do so, then the sale to the purchaser would become effective and be implemented.

The remaining member indicated that he wished to acquire the member's interest but at a price considerably lower than what the sale agreement provided for. The court held that the price that the remaining member or the corporation had to match in order to be substituted as purchasers was that which was contained in the sale agreement. The remaining member had failed to exercise his pre-emptive right in terms of s 35*(b)* (iii) as read with s 34(2) of the Close Corporations Act to match the offer, and the sale to the deceased's son therefore became effective.

16.5   The duties members owe to the close corporation

The Act imposes two specific duties on members towards the corporation as follows:
1. a fiduciary duty;[49] and
2. a duty of care and skill.[50]

These statutory provisions are based on the common-law duties traditionally owed by company directors to the company. These have now been essentially incorporated into the Companies Act, 2008 by ss 75 and 76 of that Act.[51]

16.5.1   Fiduciary duty

The Close Corporations Act states several specific instances where the fiduciary relationship applies, but these are not intended to be exhaustive. A member has a **fiduciary duty** to do all of the following:
- act honestly and in good faith;
- exercise his or her powers in the interests of and for the benefit of the corporation;[52]
- not exceed his or her powers;
- avoid a material conflict of interest;
- not compete in any way with the corporation in its business activities; and
- notify the other members as soon as practicable of the nature and extent of any material interest that he or she has in any contract of the corporation.[53] Where the member fails to do so, the contract is voidable at the option of the corporation upon the interest becoming known to the corporation. The court may nevertheless, if it considers it fair, order that the contract be binding.[54] The court must therefore balance the interests of the corporation in voiding the contract against those of other affected parties.

---

49   Section 42(1) of the Close Corporations Act provides that each member stands in a fiduciary relationship to the corporation.
50   Section 43 of the Close Corporations Act provides for personal liability of a member in respect of that person's negligence.
51   See Cilliers & Benade supra at para. 36.14 and see chapter 6 of this book for a discussion of directors' duties in terms of the Companies Act, 2008.
52   Section 42(2)*(a)*(i) of the Close Corporations Act. A breach of the duty to act for the benefit for the corporation cannot afterwards be ratified by the members. See s 42(4).
53   Section 42(2)*(b)*(ii) of the Close Corporations Act.
54   Section 42(3)*(b)* of the Close Corporations Act.

A member who breaches a duty arising from his or her fiduciary relationship is personally liable to the corporation for any loss suffered by the corporation or for any economic benefit derived by the member.[55] A member who breaches a fiduciary duty must also repay any benefit obtained as a result of breaching that duty. Conduct will not constitute a breach of the fiduciary relationship if the conduct has the written approval of all the members and if they were aware of all the material facts.[56] Even though the Act does not provide that members owe any specific duties to each other, an association agreement[57] can impose any such duty, and, in any event, it may well be the case that the common law imposes such a duty between members.

CASE STUDY	**Fiduciary duties**
	In *Geaney v Portion 117 Kalkheuwel Properties CC*,[58] the court found that a close corporation, in this case, was for practical purposes a partnership between two people in a small domestic close corporation, and held that the affairs of the close corporation 'require a personal relationship of confidence and trust normally existing between partners'.
	The court referred to the case of *Moosa NO v Mavjee Bhawan (Pty) Ltd*,[59] in which the court stated:[60]
	Usually that relationship is such that it requires the members to act reasonably and honestly towards one another and with friendly co-operation in running the company's affairs. If by conduct which is either wrongful or not as contemplated by the arrangement, one or more of the members destroys that relationship, the other member or members are entitled to claim that it is just and equitable that the company should be wound up, in the same way as, if they were partners, they could claim dissolution of the partnership.

16.5.2   Duty of care and skill

As far as the **duty of care and skill** is concerned, a member will be liable for a breach of the duty of care and skill in carrying on the business of the corporation, only if this has resulted in a loss for the corporation. The standard of care is that which may reasonably be expected from a person with that member's knowledge and experience. This introduces a subjective element into the test. Liability will not be incurred if the conduct has the written approval of all the members and they were aware of all the material facts.[61]

16.5.3   Legal proceedings for breach of duty

A member instituting court proceedings in the name of the corporation usually requires the authorisation of a members' resolution, passed by members holding at least 51 per cent of the members' interests. However, it can happen that a loss has been caused to the

---

55   Section 42(3) of the Close Corporations Act.
56   Section 42(4) of the Close Corporations Act, which, as mentioned above, does not apply where the member has exercised his or her powers other than in the interest of and for the benefit of the corporation.
57   See Practical Issue below.
58   1998 (1) SA 622 (T).
59   1967 (3) SA 131 (T).
60   At 137.
61   Section 43 of the Close Corporations Act, and see Cilliers & Benade supra at paras. 36.19–36.21.

corporation by members in control of the corporation. In certain circumstances, s 50 of the Close Corporations Act accordingly authorises any other member to institute proceedings on behalf of the corporation, irrespective of the size of that person's member's interest.[62]

The proceedings may be brought against a member or former member who is in default regarding the making of an initial or additional contribution,[63] or who is liable to the corporation through the breach of his or her fiduciary duty or duty of care and skill.[64] Section 50 therefore provides a statutory derivative action,[65] with the corporation being the plaintiff. Once instituted, the proceedings cannot be settled or withdrawn without the consent of the court.[66] This is a safeguard for the other members and the corporation against the abuse of this remedy on frivolous or vexatious grounds, because the costs of unsuccessful proceedings would normally be for the account of the corporation as the plaintiff in the proceedings.[67]

16.6 Cessation of membership by order of court

The Close Corporations Act provides two main remedies for members against other members, namely:
1. the termination of the offending member's membership by an order of court in terms of s 36; and
2. assistance from the court where a member or members have been guilty of unfairly prejudicial conduct in terms of s 49.

An order of court may have the effect of amending or adding to an existing founding statement or association agreement.[68]

The applicant may be unable to establish grounds for relief under either s 36 or s 49 in circumstances where it is clear that the corporation is in serious financial difficulties or where the members are deadlocked. This leaves the court little alternative but to order the winding-up of the corporation if there is an application for winding-up before it in addition to an application under either s 36 or s 49.[69]

16.6.1 Section 36: order of court

Section 36 allows any member of a close corporation to apply for a court order to the effect that any member, including the applicant him- or herself, will cease to be a member of the corporation. This section has numerous uses, including ending a deadlock between members.

---

62   See s 50(1) of the Close Corporations Act; and see *Cuyler v Shiers; Cuyler v C & S Marketing* 1999 (3) SA 118 (W), which concerned a situation where each of the only two members held a 50 per cent member's interest in the close corporation. Section 50(1) applies only to the institution of proceedings in the specified circumstances and does not authorise a member to defend proceedings on behalf of the corporation. See *De Franca v Exhaust Pro CC (De Franca Intervening)* 1997 (3) SA 878 (SE) at 891A–C.

63   In terms of s 24 of the Close Corporations Act. See para. 16.3 above.

64   See s 50(1) of the Close Corporations Act, which requires the member bringing the proceedings first to notify the other members of this intention. Members holding a majority interest cannot defeat a claim arising from breach of duty by condoning the breach as ss 42(4) and 43(2) permit condonation only with the approval of all the members.

65   The procedure was designed to avoid the pitfalls of the statutory derivative action in s 266 of the Companies Act, 1973, which has been replaced by a vastly improved procedure under s 165 of the Companies Act, 2008.

66   Section 50(2) of the Close Corporations Act.

67   The court may order the member personally to pay the costs of the corporation and the defendant if the court finds that the proceedings were instituted on grounds that were patently inadequate (s 50(3) of the Close Corporations Act).

68   See s 49(3) and also s 49(4) of the Close Corporations Act regarding the prescribed formalities. Failure to comply with the formalities will no longer be a criminal offence, following the repeal of s 49(5) by Schedule 3, item 8 of the Companies Act, 2008.

69   See *De Franca v Exhaust Pro CC (De Franca Intervening)* supra at 897–8.

In cases where the applicant uses s 36 in order to oppose an application for winding-up, the applicant bears the onus of providing sufficient evidence in respect of all the requirements to enable the court to grant the relief.[70] The applicant[71] under s 36 must first establish one or more of the following grounds against the member whose membership is to be terminated:

- the permanent inability of the member to perform his or her part in carrying on the business;
- conduct on the part of the member that is likely to have a prejudicial effect on the carrying on of the business;
- conduct making it reasonably impossible for the other members to associate with him or her in the carrying on of the business; and
- that there are circumstances making it just and equitable that he or she should cease to be a member.

The cessation of membership necessarily affects the relevant member's interest in the corporation. The applicant must therefore provide sufficient evidence so that the court can carry out its functions under s 36(2). To grant the application, the court must decide that the member's interest of the member concerned is to be acquired either by the corporation or by the other members, and what other financial adjustments are to be made.[72]

16.6.2   Section 49: unfairly prejudicial conduct

The remedy under s 49 of the Close Corporations Act is available to a person who is being unfairly prejudiced as a result of a single act or omission by the corporation or one or more of the members. It is also available with reference to the way in which the affairs of the corporation are being or have been conducted. In both cases, the member or members applying for relief from such unfair conduct will have to establish that there is **unfairly prejudicial conduct** on the part of the corporation or by another member or members.[73]

The court must first be satisfied that unfairly prejudicial conduct took place, or is taking place, and that it would be just and equitable for the court to intervene. The court may then make such order as it deems fit with a view to settling the dispute – whether for regulating the future conduct of the affairs of the corporation, or for the purchase of the member's interest of any member by other members or by the corporation.[74] The court will not consider it just and equitable that one member's interest be acquired by the close corporation, where it is unclear how the corporation will be able to pay its major trade

---

70   See *Kanakia v Ritzshelf 1004 CC t/a Passage to India* 2003 (2) SA 39 (D) at 48E (discussed in the Case Study below).

71   The applicant must be a member. In the case of the first and fourth grounds, the applicant may be the member whose membership will be terminated if the application succeeds (s 36(1) of the Close Corporations Act).

72   See s 36(2) of the Close Corporations Act and *Geaney v Portion 117 Kalkheuwel Properties CC* supra at 631H. If one member is to acquire the interest of another, the former must satisfy the court that he or she can pay for it. It has been held that the court cannot order that the close corporation acquire the interest, unless it can be shown that the solvency and liquidity requirements imposed by s 39 of the Close Corporations Act will be met (see *De Franca v Exhaust Pro CC (De Franca Intervening)* 1997 (3) SA 878 (SE) at 895B). However, s 36 is not expressly subject to s 39 and the application will usually be brought because the other requirement of s 39 (namely, the prior written consent of all the members) cannot be met. Nevertheless, the court should logically take the interest of creditors into account before granting the relief.

73   Section 49 of the Close Corporations Act is based on s 252 of the Companies Act, 1973, which can be compared to s 163 of the Companies Act, 2008. Among other important differences, s 163 spells out the alternative forms of possible relief in detail.

74   Section 49(2) of the Close Corporations Act.

creditors.[75] The courts have interpreted the expression 'regulating the future conduct of the affairs of the corporation' widely and have not restricted it to the day-to-day running of the ordinary business of the corporation. Thus the court may direct that the corporation accept an offer for the purchase of its major asset where the acceptance of the offer would be the best option having regard to the corporation's serious financial difficulties.[76]

CASE STUDY	Winding up on just and equitable grounds

In *Kanakia v Ritzshelf 1004 CC t/a Passage to India*,[77] the applicant and second respondent were equal members of a close corporation. The close corporation carried on a restaurant business. There had been a complete breakdown in the relationship between the two members.

The applicant sought an order for the liquidation of the corporation in terms of s 68*(d)* of the Close Corporations Act on the ground that the deadlock between the members made it just and equitable that the close corporation be wound up. The second respondent brought a counter-application in terms of ss 36 and 49 of the Act for an order that the applicant cease to be a member of the corporation and that his member's interest be transferred to the second respondent, and alternatively, that the second respondent purchase the applicant's member's interest in and claims against the close corporation standing to the credit of his loan account for a sum to be determined by the court.

The court approved the principle that the mere existence of a deadlock does not per se entitle an applicant to a winding-up order under the just and equitable provision of s 68*(d)*. The court emphasised that a court is concerned with what is 'just and equitable', not with whether or not there is a deadlock. 'The existence of a deadlock is one example of what might be regarded in a proper case as just and equitable, but a court must always have regard to all the circumstances of the case.'

The court held that an approach that accepted that a close corporation must be wound up if there was a deadlock would lead to unjust and unfair results: 'It would in fact be an abdication by the court of its responsibility or an abuse of the discretionary power which is bestowed upon the court to decide whether or not to wind up a close corporation.'

Before launching into the issue of the liquidation of the close corporation, the court found it appropriate to consider whether the counter-application provided an alternative to the winding-up. It would be just and equitable to do so, because the court found that the liquidation of the close corporation would have some grave consequences for the members.

The court held that a member who makes an application under s 36(1) bears the onus of proving that he is entitled to the relief that he seeks and it is incumbent upon him to place before the court the necessary evidence – not only to enable the court to

---

75   See *De Franca v Exhaust Pro CC (De Franca Intervening)* supra at 895G–896D. This finding was completely separate from its finding (at 895B–C) that the solvency and liquidity requirements of s 39(1) of the Close Corporations Act must be met before the court will order the corporation to require a member's interest under s 49 of the Close Corporations Act.

76   See *Gatenby v Gatenby* 1996 (3) SA 118 (E) at 123G and 125I–126B. Moreover, this would enable the member with the heaviest financial exposure in the corporation to terminate his membership, instead of remaining locked into the corporation against his will. The other members had no reasonable prospects of buying his member's interest and paying his credit loan account.

77   2003 (2) SA 39 (D).

decide whether it should grant an order in terms of s 36(1)*(a)*, *(b)*, *(c)* or *(d)*, but also to make any further order envisaged in s 36(2):[78]

> It is apparent that the enactment of the aforesaid provision was to empower the court to dissolve the association between members without winding up the corporation on the grounds that such would be just and equitable, as envisaged by s 68*(d)*, in circumstances which, in the context of a partnership, would warrant its dissolution.

The court found that it could not make an order under s 36 of the Act. The court stated that just because the restaurant was making a gross profit did not mean that it was a viable business. The court found that it was apparent that the financial position of the close corporation was not even clear to the second respondent, notwithstanding that he was the one who was currently operating the corporation's business. The court concluded that in the absence of properly audited financial statements, the court was not in a position to place a value on the close corporation or its business, and therefore it could not be in a position to grant the order sought by the second respondent.

The court found that there was a clear deadlock between the members and that attempts at resolving the impasse failed. The applicant member who had applied for the liquidation of the corporation was also still bound as surety to some of the corporation's creditors. Thus the court held that it was just and equitable for the corporation to be wound up. The counter-application in terms of s 36 was therefore dismissed:

> It is apparent that the second respondent has made certain undertakings which he has not honoured previously. In the circumstances, and in the absence of tangible evidence that the applicant will be released from the suretyships at the time of the granting of this order, it would be a fruitless exercise for this court to grant an order in accordance with the order prayed in the counter-application. In actual fact, it would not be just and equitable for the court to terminate the applicant's membership in the first respondent or transfer the applicant's member's interest to the second respondent in terms of s 36(2) or s 49(2) and to leave the applicant with a contingent liability towards the creditors in favour of whom he had signed suretyships. In light of all the aforegoing reasons, this court will not be inclined to exercise its discretion in favour of granting the order sought in the counter-application.

16.7   Acquisition of member's interests by corporation and financial assistance

Special requirements in the form of the application of the solvency and liquidity test (as more fully described hereunder) apply when a member's interest is acquired by the close corporation itself. These requirements are very similar to the requirements when a company wishes to buy back its own shares. They primarily seek to ensure that creditors of the corporation are not prejudiced by the buyback.[79]

---

78   At 48.
79   See chapter 4 of this book, which deals with shares, including share buybacks.

In the case of a close corporation, the corporation must have at least one other member at the time of the acquisition.[80] The member's interest acquired by the corporation must be added to the respective interests of the other members as agreed or in proportion to their existing interests in order to keep the aggregate at 100 per cent.[81]

The corporation may pay for the interest, only if it has the previously obtained written consent of the other members to the specific payment and if it complies with the statutory solvency and liquidity requirements.[82] The solvency and liquidity requirements are primarily intended to protect creditors. These requirements are that:

- after the payment has been made, the corporation's assets, fairly valued, must exceed its liabilities;
- the corporation must be able to pay its debts as they become due in the ordinary course of business; and
- the payment in the particular circumstances must not render the corporation unable to pay its debts in the ordinary course of business.[83]

Special requirements also apply where the corporation gives **financial assistance** to any other person to enable that person to acquire a member's interest in the corporation. The close corporation requires the previously obtained written consent of every member of the corporation to the specific assistance and compliance with the solvency and liquidity requirements.[84] The requirements apply to financial assistance by the corporation given directly or indirectly for the purpose of, or in connection with, the acquisition of a member's interest. It is suggested that the words 'in connection with' in the context should be given their usual meaning of a clear causal link. Where, for example, financial assistance is given by the corporation by repaying the seller's loan account when the loan account had been sold together with the member's interest, thereby reducing the total amount that the purchaser will have to pay to the seller, the statutory requirements should be complied with.[85]

---

80 Section 37 of the Close Corporations Act.

81 Section 38(c) of the Close Corporations Act.

82 Failure to comply with these requirements regarding payments results in the members who were aware of the payment becoming personally liable for certain debts of the company (see s 63(e) and para. 16.13 below).

83 See s 39(1) of the Close Corporations Act. A similarly worded test is imposed for financial assistance for the acquisition of a member's interest (s 40) and for payments by the corporation to members in that capacity (s 51).

84 Section 40 of the Close Corporations Act. Failure to comply with these requirements results in the members who were aware of the financial assistance, as well as the recipient, being held personally liable for certain debts of the close corporation. See s 63(f) and para. 16.13 below.

85 In cases like *Lipschitz NO v UDC Bank Ltd* 1979 (1) SA 789 (A) at 804 and *Zentland Holdings (Pty) Ltd v Saambou Nasionale Bouvereniging* 1979 (4) SA 574 (C) at 580G–581B, the words 'in connection with' were given a deliberately narrow interpretation in the context of the prohibition on financial assistance by a company for the purchase of its shares in s 86bis(2) of the Companies Act, 1926, the predecessor of the virtually identical s 38 of the Companies Act, 1973 (prior to its amendment in 2006). A contravention of the prohibition resulted in the transaction being void. The courts deliberately adopted a restrictive interpretation to prevent normal business transactions being struck down as void for contravening the prohibition. However, in the context of s 40 of the Close Corporations Act, this consideration does not apply. Non-compliance with the requirements by itself does not result in the transaction being void. (However, if the financial assistance took the form of a loan to a member made without the prior consent of all the members, it will be void in terms of s 52 – see para. 16.11 below.) A wider interpretation of 'in connection with' provides better protection for the interests of creditors and makes it more difficult for corporations to avoid having to comply with the requirements of s 40. Although s 51(3)(a)(ii) of the Close Corporations Act specifically excludes repayments of loans from the solvency and liquidity requirements in the context of payments under s 51, s 40 is a specific provision that arguably takes precedence over the general provision in s 51.

16.8 Internal relations and association agreements

The Close Corporations Act makes no formal distinction between the providers of capital and its managers. All members are in principle entitled to participate in management. The close corporation was intended to be equally suitable for the needs of sophisticated entrepreneurs and the informal sector. Therefore, the Act does not make it obligatory for members to enter into an association agreement to regulate the corporation's management.

Although such agreements are optional, the Act contains rules that apply to close corporations, unless they are excluded or modified in an association agreement. It will nevertheless appear from the discussion below that it is highly desirable for the members of a close corporation with more than one member to conclude an association agreement. However, care is needed in the drafting of such agreements, as they bind new members and can be varied only with the agreement of all the members.

PRACTICAL ISSUE	Default rules between members
	The following rules in respect of internal relations apply unless an association agreement provides differently:
	• Every member is entitled to participate in the carrying on of the business of the corporation.
	• Members have equal rights with regard to the management of the business of the corporation and with regard to the power to represent the corporation in the carrying on of its business. However, the consent in writing of members holding at least 75 per cent of the members' interests is required for:
	♦ a change in the principal business carried on by the corporation;
	♦ a disposal of the whole, or substantially the whole, undertaking of the corporation;
	♦ a disposal of all, or the greater portion of, the assets of the corporation; and
	♦ any acquisition or disposal of immovable property by the corporation.
	• Differences between members as to matters connected with a corporation's business are decided by majority vote at a meeting of members of the corporation.
	• At any meeting of members of a corporation, each member has the number of votes that corresponds with the percentage of his or her interest in the corporation.
	• A corporation must indemnify every member in respect of expenditure incurred or to be incurred by him or her:
	♦ in the ordinary and proper conduct of the business of the corporation; and
	♦ with regard to anything done or to be done for the preservation of the business or property of the corporation.
	• Payments by a corporation to its members by reason only of their membership in terms of s 51(1) are agreed by members, and such payments are made to members in proportion to their respective interests in the corporation.

An **association agreement** is defined as an agreement entered into by the members in terms of s 44.[86] It is a written agreement signed by or on behalf of each member[87] and regulates

---

86 Section 1 of the Close Corporations Act defines association agreement. An association agreement also includes one that has been altered by a court order pursuant to s 49(3) to rectify the results of unfairly prejudicial conduct.

87 The Act does not require the agreement to be signed by or on behalf of the corporation.

any matter that may be regulated in such agreement under the Act and any other matter relating to internal relationships, in a manner not inconsistent with the Act.[88]

A new member is bound by an existing association agreement, as if he or she had signed it as a party.[89] Any amendment to or the dissolution of the association agreement must be in writing and signed by or on behalf of each member at the time of such amendment or dissolution.[90]

A corporation must keep any association agreement at its registered office, where any member may inspect or copy it.[91] Non-members are not entitled to inspect it, except by virtue of a provision of the Act.[92] No person dealing with the corporation is deemed to have constructive knowledge of that agreement.[93] The association agreement is also not lodged with the Commission.

It is advisable to provide expressly that the association agreement is an association agreement, to distinguish it clearly from other written agreements that may be entered into by the members. The Act provides that other agreements (express or implied) may be entered into by all the members.[94] Such other agreements may validly deal with any matter that may be regulated by an association agreement, provided that they are not inconsistent with the association agreement. However, any such other agreement ceases to have effect when any party to it ceases to be a member of the corporation.

The association agreement, or an agreement referred to in s 44(3), binds the corporation to every member in that capacity, and every member in that capacity to the corporation and to every other member.[95]

Certain matters cannot be changed or altered by an association agreement. These are the following:

- the manner in which an insolvent member's interest is disposed of;[96]
- section 47 disqualifies certain members from taking part in the management of a corporation and an association agreement cannot override this section; and
- every member has an unalterable right to call a meeting.

Certain rules apply automatically,[97] unless they are varied by the terms of an association agreement. Some of the variable rules are as follows:

- every member of a corporation is entitled to participate in the carrying on of the business and management of the corporation (unless, of course, disqualified from doing so in terms of the Act);
- decisions of members will be by majority vote; and
- payments to members by reason of membership will be in proportion to their interest in the corporation.

---

88 Section 44(1) of the Close Corporations Act.
89 Section 44(5) of the Close Corporations Act.
90 Section 44(6) of the Close Corporations Act. As a result, a provision in an association agreement to the effect that it may be amended with the written consent of members holding a member's interest of at least 75 per cent is inconsistent with s 44(6) and therefore invalid.
91 Section 44(2) of the Close Corporations Act.
92 Section 45 of the Close Corporations Act provides that third parties (i.e. outsiders) are not affected by the contents of an association agreement and are not deemed to be aware of its contents.
93 Sections 45 and 17 of the Close Corporations Act.
94 Section 44(3) of the Close Corporations Act.
95 Section 44(4) of the Close Corporations Act.
96 Section 34 of the Close Corporations Act deals with such a disposal.
97 Section 46 of the Act contains the variable rules.

16.9   Power of members to contract on behalf of close corporation

The purpose of s 54 of the Act is to ensure that every member of a close corporation qualifies as an **agent of the corporation** for all purposes – including even a purpose that has nothing whatsoever to do with the carrying on of the actual business of the corporation – in relation to a person who is a non-member and who is dealing with the corporation. Section 54 provides as follows:

(1)   Subject to the provisions of this section, any member of a corporation shall in relation to a person who is not a member and is dealing with the corporation, be an agent of the corporation.

(2)   Any act of a member shall bind a corporation, whether or not such act is performed for the carrying on of business of the corporation, unless the member so acting has in fact no power to act for the corporation in the particular matter and the person with whom the member deals has, or ought reasonably to have, knowledge of the fact that the member has no such power.

CASE STUDY

Any member can bind a corporation in contract

In *J & K Timbers (Pty) Ltd t/a Tegs Timbers v G L & S Furniture Enterprises CC*,[98] the court held that a member is an agent, even though no authority, express or implied, has been conferred upon him by the corporation, and the corporation is bound by the related act, unless the third party knew, or ought reasonably to have known, of the absence of such power.

It is therefore apparent from this case that the existence of a resolution or unanimous consent of all members is not a prerequisite to a close corporation being bound to a third party by one of its members. Section 54 is specifically aimed at avoiding the application of the *ultra vires* doctrine and the doctrine of constructive notice so far as the dealings by third parties with a corporation are concerned.

The court confirmed that that there is no doubt that s 54 would not assist a third party who contracts with a close corporation represented by an employee (as opposed to a member). The issue would then be whether the non-member who purports to bind the corporation is authorised by the corporation to represent the corporation and whether what he or she purports to do falls within the scope of his or her authority. However, the court stressed that the reference to 'any act' of a member binding a corporation would also include the appointment of an agent on behalf of the close corporation. Therefore, if a member appoints an outsider (such as an attorney) to represent the corporation, that outsider will have the authority to conclude a contract and finalise a settlement on behalf of the corporation, even though the other members neither approved nor authorised such appointment.

16.10   Payments by corporation to members

Section 51 of the Close Corporations Act provides that any payment by a corporation to any member by reason only of his or her membership may be made only if the corporation meets the solvency and liquidity requirements[99] after the payment is made. For purposes of s 51, a payment includes a distribution or a repayment of the whole or part of any contribution to a member. However, payments made to the member in his or her capacity as creditor or employee are specifically excluded in terms of s 51(3)*(a)*(ii). Payments include not only cash payments, but also the delivery or transfer of any property. It is submitted that a distribution by way of a transfer to a member's credit loan account also constitutes a payment for this purpose.[100]

Additional formalities for such payments depend on the nature of the payment. The repayment of the whole or part of a contribution requires the lodging of an amended founding statement.[101] A distribution of income requires approval by way of a formal resolution of members holding at least 51 per cent of the members' interests.[102]

In terms of s 51(2), a member is liable to the corporation for any payment received contrary to any of the solvency and liquidity requirements,[103] with the onus being on the corporation to show that the requirements were not met. However, if the corporation is being wound up because the corporation cannot pay its debts, the onus is reversed. The member is liable to repay a payment made by reason only of membership within a period of two years before the commencement of winding-up, unless the member can prove that the corporation complied with the solvency and liquidity requirements after the payment was made.[104] The question as to which party bears the onus is of great practical importance if the financial records of the corporation for the relevant period are inadequate.

16.11 Prohibition on loans to and security on behalf of members

In terms of s 52 of the Close Corporations Act, without the express prior consent of all its members in writing, a corporation may not make a loan directly or indirectly:

- to any of its members;
- to any other corporation in which one or more of its members together hold more than a 50 per cent interest; or
- to a company or other type of juristic person controlled by one or more of the corporation's members.

The same restriction applies to the provision of security by the corporation on behalf of those persons.[105] A loan or security in breach of the restriction is invalid and cannot subsequently be ratified.[106]

---

99 See para. 16.12 below for a further discussion.
100 To hold otherwise would mean that corporations could distribute profits to members by way of a two-stage procedure, first crediting the loan account and then repaying the loan, without having to comply with solvency and liquidity requirements. The second stage, the repayment of the loan account, is clearly not a payment subject to s 51. Under the Companies Act, 2008 it is clear from the definition of 'distribution' in s 1 that a transfer by a company to a shareholder's loan account is regarded as a distribution to which the solvency and liquidity requirements apply.
101 Section 15(1) of the Close Corporations Act.
102 See Cilliers & Benade supra at para. 39.08. Alternatively, approval can be given by the same majority of members approving annual financial statements in which the distribution of income is proposed.
103 See para. 16.13 below.
104 Section 70(2) of the Close Corporations Act.
105 Section 52(1) and (2) of the Close Corporations Act. See s 52(4) for the meaning of the word 'loan' in this context.
106 See s 52(3) of the Close Corporations Act and Cilliers & Benade supra at para. 36.32. See also s 52(3) regarding the remedy against members who permitted the transaction.

CASE STUDY

Section 52 of the Close Corporations Act

In *Hanekom v Builders Market Klerksdorp (Pty) Ltd*,[107] a member of a close corporation signed surety on behalf of that close corporation for a debt of another company of which he was the sole director and shareholder. In these circumstances, it was clear that s 52 applied, which requires that the member must have the 'express previously obtained consent in writing of all the members' of the close corporation for such a transaction. In this case, however, the close corporation that had provided the surety had only one member. On the strength of the suretyship, a third party afforded further credit to the company, but the company subsequently failed to discharge its debt and was placed in liquidation.

Relying on the suretyship executed on behalf of the close corporation, the third party applied for the corporation's liquidation. At a creditors' meeting, objection was taken to the third party's claim on the ground that the suretyship executed on behalf of the close corporation was invalid for want of compliance with s 52 of the Act. The member's contention was that the suretyship executed on behalf of the corporation purported to secure a debt of a company that he controlled and was invalid for the reason that, when he executed it, he did not have 'the previously obtained consent in writing of all the members of the corporation' as contemplated in s 52(2). In other words, he, as the sole member of the close corporation, had not previously consented in writing to the suretyship that he himself executed. The court made certain general observations regarding s 52 as follows:

1. Although s 52(1) provides for a general prohibition, and s 52(2) an exemption from that prohibition, the court held that the object of s 52, read as a whole, is undoubtedly to protect non-consenting members – that is, to prevent a member from using the resources of a close corporation for his or her own benefit to the detriment of other members. The section seeks to achieve this by requiring not only that the other members consent to the loan or security, but also that they do so in writing so as to provide written proof of that consent.
2. The consent that is contemplated is not consent on behalf of the close corporation in question, but consent of the members in their personal capacities as members of that corporation. The court held that it is noteworthy that s 54 provides that 'any member' is an agent of the corporation and, subject to certain exceptions, is able to bind the corporation.
3. Although not expressly stated in s 52, the court held that it is clear from s 52(3) that any loan or security falling within s 52(1) and not exempted in terms of s 52(2) is void and not capable of ratification (as per *Neugarten v Standard Bank of South Africa Ltd*[108] in relation to s 226 of the Companies Act, 1973). Section 52(3) not only renders the member who authorises an invalid loan or security liable to an innocent third party for loss, but also makes such member guilty of an offence.

The court therefore concluded that, based on the above, it was apparent that where a close corporation has only one member, the section really serves no purpose. The court held that where there is only one member, not only are there no other members who

107 2007 (3) SA 95 (SCA).
108 1989 (1) SA 797 (A) at 808F.

require protection, but the member signing the suretyship on behalf of the close corporation is notionally incapable of doing so, unless he had previously in his personal capacity given himself permission to do so.

Counsel for the appellant had, however, referred to the unambiguous language of s 52(2) and argued that there was nothing in the section to indicate that it did not apply to the case of a sole member of a corporation and that from an ordinary reading of its provisions, it was clear that in the absence of 'the express previously obtained consent in writing' of that sole member, a suretyship securing the debt of a company controlled by him would not be exempted from the prohibition contained in s 52(1). The question that therefore arose in this case was whether a court would be justified in departing from the clear and unambiguous meaning of the section to avoid 'a manifest absurdity'. The court held as follows:

1. To give effect to the unambiguous language of s 52 where the close corporation has only one member leads to an absurdity.
2. Nothing could possibly be achieved by requiring the sole member of a close corporation, before signing a suretyship on behalf of the corporation and in his personal capacity, to give himself permission in writing to do so.
3. The member's signature on the suretyship demonstrated unequivocally his consent.
4. The object of the section is to protect non-consenting members.
5. In circumstances such as those in the case before it, a literal interpretation does not achieve the object of the section, and a literal interpretation does no more than provide a sole member of a corporation with a defence that could never have been intended by the legislature.
6. When construing s 52(2) in the context of a sole member of a close corporation who has signed a loan agreement or a suretyship on behalf of a corporation, the words 'previously obtained' must be disregarded.
7. The suretyship was therefore held to be valid.

16.12 Accounting officer, accounting records and annual financial statements[109]

The Close Corporations Act provides[110] that the annual financial statements of a corporation must consist of a statement of financial position, an income statement, and a report of the accounting officer. As discussed later in this paragraph, the annual financial statements of certain corporations are required by the Companies Act, 2008 to be audited.[111]

The reference to 'generally accepted accounting practice' in s 58(2)*(a)* and the need to make specific disclosures in terms of s 58(2)*(c)* require that annual financial statements of a close corporation should probably consist of the following:

- a statement of financial position together with appropriate notes thereto;
- an income statement together with appropriate notes thereto;
- a statement of changes in equity;
- a cash flow statement;

---

109 A general acknowledgement is given for this section: see Geach & Schoeman supra.
110 Section 58(2)*(a)*.
111 See also para. 13.2.4 above and note 24 in chapter 13 of this book.

- the accounting officer's report (or audit report if the corporation is required by the Companies Act, 2008 to be audited, or if members have voluntarily decided that an audit is required);
- a statement of members' net investment in the corporation and movements therein; and
- a schedule of transactions with members.

There must be an approval of the annual financial statements by or on behalf of the member(s) who hold at least 51 per cent of the interest in the corporation.[112]

In terms of the Companies Act, 2008, a close corporation's annual financial statements have to be audited if the close corporation falls within any of the categories of private company that are required to have their financial statements audited.[113]

CASE STUDY	Accounting officer's report forms part of the financial statements
	In *Maccelari v Help U Build Project Management CC*,[114] the court held that by signing the set of financial statements it must have been clear to members that they had accepted not only the veracity of the accounts, but the accounting officer's report in terms of which the accounts had been predicated. The accounting officer had thought it prudent for the members to subordinate their loan accounts in order for the corporation not to be in an insolvent position. He therefore had subordinated the members' loan accounts in his report. The members, however, unsuccessfully argued that no such back-ranking or subordination agreement had been entered into between the members and the corporation. The accountant admitted that he had not even entered into discussions with the members regarding the subordination of their loan accounts.
	The court held that such an agreement does not have to be reduced to a separate written agreement and that by signing the financial statements, the members had accepted their content, and even the content of the accounting officer's report.
	Effect therefore had to be given to the subordination by the liquidator, and the court held that the liquidator's account had been correctly framed.
	The annual financial statements must fairly present the state of affairs of the corporation as at the end of the financial year, and the results of its operations for that year, in conformity with generally accepted accounting practice appropriate to the business of the corporation.

The Close Corporations Act contains a number of sections that refer to '**fair value**' of assets and to 'assets exceeding liabilities', all of which suggest that assets should be disclosed on a revalued or current market basis, rather than on the basis of historic costs. The following sections are worth noting:

1. Section 39: *payment by corporation for members' interests acquired* – payment by a corporation in respect of its acquisition of a member's interest shall be made only if, after such payment, the corporation's assets, fairly valued, exceed all its liabilities.

---

112   Section 58(3) of the Close Corporations Act.
113   See para. 13.2.4 above for a discussion of this topic.
114   2001 (4) SA 1282 (C).

2. Section 40: *financial assistance by the corporation in respect of the acquisition of a member's interest* – a corporation may give financial assistance in respect of the acquisition of a member's interest provided that after such assistance has been given, the corporation's assets, fairly valued, exceed all its liabilities.

3. Section 51: *payments by a close corporation to members by reason of membership* – any payment by a corporation to a member shall be made only if, after such payment, the corporation's assets, fairly valued, exceed all its liabilities.

4. Section 62: *duties of accounting officers* – if the accounting officer finds that the annual financial statements incorrectly indicate that, as at the end of the financial year, the assets of the corporation exceed its liabilities, or has reason to believe that such an incorrect indication is given, he or she must issue a report to the Commission.

Failure to comply with the requirement of determining the fair value of assets in the circumstances referred to can have adverse consequences for members and others. For example, in terms of s 51, a member will be liable to a close corporation for any payment contrary to the provisions of s 51(1). This effectively means that any distributions made to members in any year can be reclaimed by or on behalf of a close corporation, if the fair value of assets, after such payment, does not exceed the liabilities of the close corporation.

In terms of s 58(2)*(e)*, the annual financial statements of a close corporation must contain the report of the accounting officer referred to in s 62(1)*(c)*. The accounting officer must determine whether or not the financial statements are in agreement with a corporation's accounting records. The accounting officer must also review the appropriateness of the accounting policies that have been applied in the preparation of the annual financial statements, and must issue a statement in his or her report that he or she has done so. The accounting officer must report in respect of these matters to the close corporation.[115] The accounting officer must report to the Commission if:

- he or she finds that the annual financial statements indicate that the corporation's liabilities exceed its assets;
- he or she finds that the financial statements incorrectly indicate that the assets exceed its liabilities; or
- he or she has reason to believe that such an incorrect indication is given.

An example of an accounting officer's report appears below.

PRACTICAL ISSUE	**Sample report of the accounting officer to the ABC Close Corporation**
	We have performed the duties of the accounting officer as required by s 62 of the Close Corporations Act 69 of 1984 to ABC Close Corporation for the year ended 31 December 2008.
	The annual financial statements are the responsibility of the members of the close corporation, and are set out on pages xx–xx. These annual financial statements have been approved by members in accordance with the requirements of s 58(3) of the Close Corporations Act.
	In terms of the Close Corporations Act, no audit is required of the annual financial statements and we have not audited these financial statements.

---

115 Section 62(1)*(c)* of the Close Corporations Act.

In accordance with our statutory duties, we have determined that the annual financial statements are in agreement with the accounting records of the close corporation. We have determined this by adopting such procedures and conducting enquiries in relation to the accounting records as were considered necessary having regard to the circumstances and the business carried on by the close corporation. We have also reviewed the appropriateness of the accounting policies which have been represented to us as having been applied in the preparation of the annual financial statements, and in our opinion these accounting policies are appropriate having regard to the business carried on by the close corporation.

Dated _____ 20 _____ Signed _____

It is apparent that in terms of the Close Corporations Act there are certain duties imposed on the corporation, as well as its members and its accounting officer, in respect of accounting records, financial statements and similar matters. These duties are summarised in the tables below.

Table **16.1** *Duties of the corporation in relation to accounting records and financial statements*

Section of the Close Corporations Act	Duty of the corporation	Liability for non-compliance
Section 56	Keep such accounting records as 'are necessary'. Definition of accounting records (s 1) includes: accounts, deeds, writings and such other documents as may be prescribed	The corporation and every member who was party to such failure will be guilty of an offence
Section 57	Fix a year-end	
Section 59	• Appoint an accounting officer • Appoint an accounting officer if there is a vacancy within 28 days • Notify the accounting officer if he or she is removed from office	

Table **16.2** *Duties of members in relation to accounting records and financial statements*

Section of the Close Corporations Act	Duty of members	Liability for non-compliance
Section 58	• Cause annual financial statements to be made out within six months of the year-end • Members holding at least 51% of the members' interests must approve and sign the annual financial statements	Members who fail to comply will be guilty of an offence

Table 16.3 Duties of the accounting officer in relation to accounting records and financial statements

Section of the Close Corporations Act	Duty
Section 59(5)	• Inform every member in writing on his or her resignation or removal • Send copy of letter to corporation's registered office • Inform the Commission of certain information
Section 59(5)*(b)*	Inform the Commission and every member if he or she believes he or she was removed for improper reasons
Section 60	Ensure that he or she is properly qualified
Section 62	• Determine whether the financial statements are in agreement with the accounting records and report in respect thereof to the corporation • Review the appropriateness of the accounting policies represented to him or her as having been applied in the preparation of the financial statements • Report in respect of the above two duties to the corporation • Describe in his or her report the nature of any contraventions of the provisions of the Close Corporations Act of which he or she becomes aware • Disclose in his or her report if he or she is a member or employee of the corporation or it is a firm of which a partner or employee is a member or employee • Report to the Commission if he or she knows or has reason to believe that the corporation is not carrying on business and has no intention of resuming operations • Report to the Commission if he or she finds that changes of particulars in a founding statement have not been registered • Report to the Commission if the financial statements indicate that the liabilities exceed the assets at the end of the year • Report to the Commission if he or she finds that the financial statements incorrectly indicate that the assets exceed liabilities at end of year or has reason to believe that such an incorrect indication is given

16.13   Personal liability for a corporation's debts

A member of a close corporation, and, in some cases, other persons, can be **personally liable** for the debts of a close corporation.[116] The Close Corporations Act contains a number of sections that provide that members can be personally liable for a corporation's debts under a variety of different circumstances. Essentially, these sections aim to ensure compliance with the provisions of the Close Corporations Act, by providing for personal liability when there has been abuse of the separate juristic personality of the corporation or when certain requirements of the Act have not been complied with.

The position of members of a close corporation therefore stands in sharp contrast with the position of shareholders of a company. Shareholders of a company, as shareholders, can never be personally liable for the debts of their company, and this is one reason that entrepreneurs may have preferred to use the company form rather than form a close corporation.

---

116 See Geach & Schoeman supra.

16.13.1   Section 65: abuse of separate juristic personality of corporation

Section 65 of the Act provides that a court has extensive powers to ignore the existence of a close corporation in cases where there is an abuse of a corporation as a juristic person. Although this is not really different from the common-law position in which a court can 'lift the corporate veil' of a company,[117] it is interesting to note that s 20 of the Companies Act, 2008 also provides that if, on application by an interested person or in any proceedings in which a company is involved, a court finds that the incorporation of the company, any use of the company, or any act by or on behalf of the company, constitutes an unconscionable abuse of the juristic personality of the company as a separate entity, the court may:

- declare that the company is to be deemed not to be a juristic person; and
- make any further order the court considers appropriate.

CASE STUDY	Application of section 65
	In *Airport Cold Storage (Pty) Ltd v Ebrahim*,[118] the court held that if the requirements of the Close Corporations Act are ignored, this can amount to the abuse of the separate juristic personality of the corporation as envisaged by s 65. In this case, the court found that the business conducted through the corporation was 'conducted in a very loose and informal manner with little or no regard for the requirements of the Act'. It kept no conventional books of account and the business was conducted largely on a cash basis. The court also found that the corporation had not kept the accounting records as required by s 56. The court found that the defendants had operated the business of the corporation as if it were their own, and without due regard for, or compliance with, the statutory and bookkeeping requirements associated with the conduct of the corporation's business. The court noted that when it suited them, the defendants chose to ignore the separate juristic identity of the corporation and held: 'In these circumstances, the defendants cannot now choose to take refuge behind the corporate veil' of the corporation in order to evade liability for its debts. The court concluded that the plaintiff was entitled to a declaratory order in terms of s 65 to the effect that the corporation was deemed not to be a juristic person, but a venture of the defendants personally. The defendants were therefore held to be jointly and severally liable to the plaintiff for the amounts owed to the plaintiffs at the time of liquidation.

16.13.2   Personal liability of members in other circumstances

Other sections of the Act also make members personally liable for the debts of a corporation in certain circumstances – including:

- section 23 (which requires the name and registration number of a corporation to appear on certain documents, cheques and orders issued by the corporation);
- section 52 (which prohibits the making of certain loans); and
- section 64 (which imposes personal liability on those who have acted recklessly or fraudulently).

---

117 See para. 2.3 above for a discussion of lifting the corporate veil.
118 2008 (2) SA 303 (C).

The Close Corporations Act therefore seeks to ensure legal compliance by making offenders personally liable for the debts of a corporation in a variety of different circumstances.[119]

CASE STUDY	**Personal liability of members**
	In *Haygro Catering BK v Van der Merwe*,[120] the applicant applied for an order declaring that members of a close corporation were, together with the corporation, jointly and severally liable for a debt owed to the applicant for meat it had supplied. The applicant had supplied meat to a business that had been conducted under the name of 'Mr Meat Man'.
	The applicant was under the impression that he had been dealing with partners in a business called 'Mr Meat Man', and had issued summons in that name. No appearance to defend had been entered and judgment had therefore been granted against 'Mr Meat Man'. Because no such business existed, the writ could not be executed. The applicant subsequently became aware of the fact that the 'partners' were actually members of a close corporation, Toitbert Vleismark CC. This name had not appeared anywhere on the business premises of the business, nor on any of its documents or correspondence. Neither was the fact that it was a close corporation mentioned anywhere.
	The court held that s 65 (gross abuse) could apply. Section 65 makes provision for a more all-embracing manner of conduct. The court came to the conclusion that the failure to display the name of the corporation constituted a gross abuse, and that the court was justified in making an order in terms of the wide discretion conferred on it by s 65. The application for an order that the members be held jointly and severally liable for payment of the amount owing was accordingly granted.

CASE STUDY	**Ambit of liability under s 23**
	Section 23 of the Close Corporation Act provides that any member of, or any other person on behalf of, a corporation commits an offence if he or she:
	• issues (or authorises the issue of) any notice or official publication of the corporation; or
	• signs (or authorises to be signed) on behalf of the corporation any bill of exchange, promissory note, endorsement, cheque or order for money, goods or services; or
	• issues or authorises the issue of any letter, delivery note, invoice, receipt or letter of credit of the corporation,
	without the name of the corporation, and its registration number being mentioned therein.
	The section also makes the offender liable to the holder of the bill of exchange, promissory note, cheque or order for money, goods or services for the amount thereof, unless the amount is duly paid by the corporation.
	The application of s 23 was considered in *Byway Projects 10 CC v Masingita Autobody CC*.[121] The issue in this case was whether the members of a close corporation

---

119   Paras. 16.13.1 and 16.13.2 summarise the circumstances in which members and others can be personally liable for the debts of a corporation.
120   1996 (4) SA 1063 (C).
121   [2011] ZAGPJHC 54.

were personally liable for the obligations of their close corporation in terms of a lease agreement. The lease was signed in the name of the close corporation but neither the letters 'CC' nor its registration number appeared on the lease. The court held that there was no doubt that if there was a contravention of s 23, then there would be both criminal and civil consequences as provided for in s 23. The sole issue was therefore whether a 'lease agreement' was one of the documents listed in s 23.

The court held that s 23 envisages only four types of document: (1) a bill of exchange, (2) a promissory note, (3) a cheque or (4) order for money or goods and services. The document has to fall under one of these categories before there is the imposition of personal liability to the holder of such document. On behalf of the landlord it was argued that a lease agreement is an order 'for services'. This argument was based on the contention that regard should be had to the purpose of s 23, which is to protect the public by ensuring that it is not exposed to the risk of being misinformed or misled, by requiring objective compliance in the document itself. So, the argument went, the word 'order' should include any contract.

The court however held that the word 'order' was simply an instruction or direction, and should be interpreted in this ordinary and restrictive way by reason of the penalties imposed in s 23(2) and the existence of a remedy under s 63(a) of the Close Corporations Act that is capable of application to contracts generally. Accordingly, the court found that the lease agreement did not fall under the documents contemplated in s 23, and therefore the members of the corporation were not personally liable for the corporation's debts under s 23.

Table 16.4 below summarises some of the other more important sections of the Close Corporations Act that provide for personal liability.

Table 16.4 *Personal liability under the Close Corporations Act*

Section of the Close Corporations Act	Issue	Wrongdoing	Who is liable
Section 65	Abuse of separate juristic personality of the corporation	Gross abuse of the incorporation of a close corporation	A court can make any order it sees fit including declaring the corporation not to be a juristic person, which could include making members personally liable for a corporation's debts
Section 52	Prohibition of certain loans	Certain loans made without the consent of all members	Any member who authorised the loan or was party to the making of such loan must make good any loss to the corporation or loss to any other person who incurred loss

Section of the Close Corporations Act	Issue	Wrongdoing	Who is liable
Section 63	Joint liability for all a corporation's debts incurred from date of registration to date of payment or delivery	Failure to contribute the agreed contribution (s 24)	The person who fails to contribute
Section 63	Joint liability for a corporation's debts: liability for every debt incurred during the contravention	Failure to qualify as a member of the corporation in terms of the Act	A member, as further described in s 63
Section 63	Joint liability for a corporation's debts: every debt of the corporation prior to the giving of financial assistance	Failure to comply with the rules relating to the giving of financial assistance by a corporation to acquire a member's interest (s 39)	• Every member who was aware of the giving of the financial assistance • Any member who receives such assistance • Any former member who receives such payment
Section 63	Joint liability for a corporation's debts: every debt incurred during the existence of the vacancy	Failure to appoint an accounting officer (s 59) and vacancy lasts for a period exceeding six months	Every member who was aware of the vacancy
Sections 42(3) and 50	Fiduciary position of members – duty towards the corporation: liability to repay any benefit he or she has obtained	Breach of this duty either by an act or omission	A member who has breached that duty
Section 43	Liability for negligence: liability for loss caused by his or her actions	Failure to act with the degree of skill that may reasonably be expected from a person of his or her knowledge and experience	A member who fails to act in this manner
Section 64	Liability for reckless or fraudulent trading: liability for the debts of the corporation	• Acting recklessly • Acting with gross negligence • Acting with intent to defraud • Acting for any fraudulent purpose	Any person who was knowingly a party to that conduct (including non-members, such as the accounting officer)

CASE **STUDY**	**Factual enquiry into what constitutes gross negligence or recklessness** Whether or not conduct falls within the conduct contemplated under s 64 (acting recklessly, or with gross negligence or fraudulently) is essentially a factual enquiry. In the unreported case of *Raflatac SA (Pty) Ltd v Bell and another*,[122] the plaintiff alleged that the defendants were jointly and severally liable, together with their close corporation, for amounts due to the plaintiff because they knowingly carried on the business of the close corporation, recklessly, alternatively in a grossly negligent fashion in that (a) no adequate accounting records were kept; (b) the defendants permitted the close corporation to trade in insolvent circumstances; and (c) they permitted the close corporation to incur credit with the plaintiff with little or no reasonable prospect of the close corporation being in a position to repay such debt. There is no doubt that any of these allegations, if substantiated, would lead to the conclusion that there was recklessness or gross negligence. On the facts, however, the court concluded that the plaintiff had failed to prove recklessness or gross negligence. The member of the close corporation had raised a bond on her home and had injected these funds into the corporation, the member had relied on the opinion of the corporation's financial officer that the business was viable, and the defendants had at all times been frank and open with their dealings with the plaintiff, to the extent that 'nothing was hidden from the plaintiff'. The plaintiff had been told of the corporation's financial problems and this had not deterred the plaintiff from trading with the corporation. As the court stated: despite the fact that the close corporation was well over its credit limit and despite plaintiff not having seen financial statements, plaintiff made a calculated business decision to continue supplying the close corporation with product in circumstances where the defendants had disclosed their difficulties to them. For all these reasons, the claim against the defendants personally for the amount owed by the close corporation was dismissed by the court.

THIS CHAPTER IN ESSENCE

1. The Close Corporations Act 69 of 1984 provides for the formation of **close corporations**, which are simple, deregulated, and flexible, limited liability entities, suitable for small businesses. They have their own legal personality and enjoy perpetual succession.
2. A close corporation has **members**, rather than shareholders. Although a close corporation is a separate legal entity, members can be liable for its debts in certain circumstances.
3. A close corporation can have between one and 10 members and there is no separation between ownership and control. The Act allows every member to participate in the business and to make legally binding decisions on behalf of the corporation.
4. Only natural persons may be members of a close corporation and no juristic person may hold a member's interest in a close corporation. However, a close corporation may be a shareholder.
5. A trustee of an *inter vivos* or testamentary trust can be a member of a close corporation as trustee, subject to certain restrictions. No juristic person can be a beneficiary of such an *inter vivos* trust and

if the number of beneficiaries of the trust, added to the number of members of the corporation, is greater than 10, the membership of the trustee will cease.

6. The *ultra vires* doctrine does not apply to close corporations, as they have the same capacity and powers as a natural person (to the extent possible). There is also no constructive notice of particulars in the founding statement, and therefore third parties are not adversely affected by limitations in a founding statement.

7. In terms of the Companies Act, 2008, no new close corporations may be incorporated under the Close Corporations Act. Existing close corporations will continue indefinitely or may **convert** to companies (with the written consent of at least 75 per cent of the members' interest in the corporation).

8. Under the Companies Act, 2008, annual financial statements of a close corporation must comply with International Financial Reporting Standards (IFRS) and must be audited if the close corporation holds assets in a fiduciary capacity.

9. The business rescue provisions of the Companies Act, 2008 also apply to close corporations.

10. On formation, each member of a close corporation was required to make a contribution of money, assets or services. The size of a member's interest (expressed as a percentage) need not necessarily be in proportion to this contribution.

11. A **member's interest** is a personal right against the corporation, entitling the member to a proportionate share in the aggregate members' interests, to participate in a distribution of profits, and to share in a distribution of the assets on liquidation, once all the creditors have been paid.

12. Unless otherwise provided in an **association agreement**, members' voting rights and their right to participate in distributions of profits and other payments by the corporation to its members will be in proportion to their respective member's interests.

13. New members acquire their members' interests either from an existing member, or by making a contribution, in the form of money or other assets, to the corporation. In the latter event, the percentage of the member's interest of the new member is agreed with existing members and the interests of existing members are reduced proportionately.

14. **Disposals of a member's interest** may be to another person qualifying for membership or to the corporation itself, in accordance with the association agreement or with the consent of all existing members.

15. The Close Corporations Act contains a mandatory procedure for the disposal of an insolvent member's interest. The member's interest may be sold to the corporation, to other members or to an outsider who qualifies for membership. A sale to an outsider is subject to a **right of pre-emption** in favour of the corporation and the other members. The same procedure applies to the sale in execution of a member's interest pursuant to its attachment to satisfy a judgment debt.

16. The Close Corporations Act provides for the disposal of a deceased member's interest in the absence of any other arrangement in an association agreement. A transfer of the interest to the legatee or heir of the deceased member requires the consent of the other members.

17. The Close Corporations Act has included in the duties imposed on members **fiduciary duties** and a **duty of care and skill** towards the corporation. These are based on the common-law duties traditionally owed by company directors to companies.

18. Proceedings may be brought against a member or former member who is in default regarding the making of an initial or additional contribution, or who is liable to the corporation through a breach of fiduciary duty or duty of care and skill.

19. The Close Corporations Act provides two main remedies for members against other members – namely, the termination of the offending member's membership by an order of court in terms of s 36, and assistance from the court where a member has been guilty of **unfairly prejudicial conduct** in terms of s 49. Where the corporation is in serious financial difficulties or members are deadlocked, the court may order the winding-up of the corporation.

20. A corporation must meet the solvency and liquidity test if it acquires a member's interest itself or if it gives financial assistance to any person to acquire a member's interest.

21. An **association agreement** is not required, but is desirable between members of a corporation. It regulates the internal relationships of the corporation. The association agreement binds the corporation to every member in that capacity, and every member in that capacity to the corporation and to every other member. Certain matters cannot be changed or altered by an association agreement.

22. Every member of a close corporation is an **agent of the corporation** for all purposes in relation to a non-member dealing with the corporation.

23. Any payment or **financial assistance** by a corporation to a member may be made only if the corporation meets the solvency and liquidity requirements after the payment is made. Without the prior written consent of all members, a corporation may not make a loan or provide security to any of its members, or to another juristic person controlled by one or more of its members.

24. The annual financial statements of a corporation must consist of a statement of financial position, an income statement, and a report of the accounting officer. Certain close corporations (as with certain private companies) must prepare annual financial statements in accordance with International Financial Reporting Standards (IFRS) and have them audited.

25. A member of a close corporation can be **personally liable** for the debts of a close corporation in a variety of different circumstances, especially where there has been an abuse of the corporation's juristic personality.

Partnerships

Chapter 17

Partnerships

17.1   Definition of partnership

A **partnership** may be defined as a legal relationship created by way of a contract between two or more persons, in terms of which each of the partners agrees to make some contribution to the partnership business, which is carried on for the joint benefit of the parties and the object of which is to make a profit.[1]

---

1 *Pezzutto v Dreyer* 1992 (3) SA 379 (A) at 390.

17.2 Partnerships and the Companies Act, 2008

The Companies Act, 2008 does not define or deal with partnerships, but does allow for the formation of a personal liability company. If a company is a **personal liability company**, the directors and past directors are jointly and severally liable, together with the company, for any debts and liabilities of the company that are or were contracted during their respective periods of office.

The name of a personal liability company must end with the word 'Incorporated' or its abbreviation 'Inc.' A personal liability company would usually be formed by those persons who would normally form a partnership, such as attorneys or other professionals, but who wish to obtain the benefits of incorporation, such as the benefits of perpetual succession. However, such a company's Memorandum of Incorporation (MOI) must expressly provide that the directors and past directors will be personally liable for the contractual (not delictual) obligations and liabilities of the company, if the company does not meet those obligations and liabilities.

A personal liability company could perhaps be described as an incorporated partnership.

17.3 Types of partnership

There are two significant ways of categorising a partnership:
1. a universal partnership may be distinguished from a particular partnership; and
2. an ordinary partnership may be distinguished from an extraordinary partnership.

17.3.1 Universal and particular partnerships

A **universal partnership** involves partners contributing all their property or all their profits to the partnership, usually for an open-ended period and for wide-ranging purposes, with a commensurate sharing of the profits of their enterprises. In contrast, a **particular partnership** will usually be a more temporary and focused arrangement, in terms of which partners contribute their resources for a particular defined purpose only and share only in profits from that particular project together.

In *Bester v Van Niekerk*,[2] Holmes AJA cited with approval the following passage from Lindley on partnership:

> It is customary for writers of partnership law to divide partnerships into universal (general) and particular (special or limited) according to the extent of the contract entered into by the members ... If persons who are not partners in other business share the profits and loss, or the profits, of one particular transaction or adventure, they become partners as to that transaction or adventure but not as to anything else. For example, if two solicitors who are not partners are jointly retained to conduct litigation in some particular case, and they agree to share the profits accruing therefrom, they become partners so far as the business connected with that particular case is concerned, but no further. So a partnership may be limited through the purchase and sale of particular jewels, or to the working of some particular patent, or to the working of it in some particular place or district. In all such cases as these, the rights and liabilities of the partners are governed by the same principles

---

2   1960 (2) SA 779 (A) at 784.

as those that apply to ordinary partnership; but such rights and liabilities are necessarily less extensive than those of persons who have entered into less limited contracts.

There are two types of universal partnership. The first type, a partnership *universorum bonorum*, generally takes place within the context of marriage, mostly within a context of a marriage in community of property, but it can also be entered into, whether expressly or implicitly, by spouses married out of community. In *Isaacs v Isaacs*,[3] the court described such a partnership as one 'by which the contracting parties agree to put in common all their property, both present and future. It covers all their acquisitions whether from commercial undertakings or otherwise'. It is clear that such a partnership *universorum bonorum* is part of South African law.[4] A partnership *universorum bonorum* can also take place outside of marriage.

CASE STUDY	**Universal partnership**
	In the case of *Schrepfer v Ponelat*,[5] the court was called on to determine whether a universal partnership existed between the parties. In this case, the plaintiff (who had never married the defendant but who had lived with him over many years) relied on a tacit and/or implied agreement of universal partnership brought about by the conduct of the parties. Accordingly, when the parties ceased to live together, she successfully relied on the existence of such a partnership to claim a share of the assets owned by the defendant.
	The court accepted that a universal partnership, also known as domestic partnership, can come into existence between spouses and co-habitees where they agree to pool their resources. The court stated that the '... partnership *universorum bonorum* is that by which the contracting parties agree to put in common all their property, both present and future.' The court accepted that a universal or domestic partnership is similar to a marriage in community of property even though the parties may not even be married at all. The court referred to HR Hahlo: *The South African Law of Husband and Wife*,[6] where marriage in community of property is described as follows:
	Community of property is a universal economic partnership of the spouses. All their assets and liabilities are merged in a joint estate, in which both spouses, irrespective of the value of their financial contributions, hold equal shares.

The second form of universal partnership occurs within the context of commercial undertakings. In such partnerships, the parties agree that all that they may acquire during the relationship from whatever form of commercial activity shall be treated as part of the property of the partnership.[7]

---

3   1949 (1) SA 952 (C) at 955.
4   *Ally v Dinath* 1984 (2) SA 451 (T) 453; JJ Henning 'Partnership' in WA Joubert et al (Eds) *LAWSA* (2006) vol 19 2ed at para. 257.
5   [2010] ZAWCHC 193.
6   (1985) 5 ed at 157–8.
7   *V (aka L) v De Wet NO* 1953 (1) SA 612 (O) at 614.

17.3.2 Ordinary and extraordinary partnerships

In an **ordinary partnership**, partners are jointly and severally liable for all of the debts of the partnership. An ordinary partnership must therefore be contrasted with an **extraordinary partnership** in which the liability of certain partners is limited in some way. There are three forms of extraordinary partnership in which the liability of certain of the partners to third parties may be limited. These are the following:

1. an anonymous partnership;
2. a partnership *en commandite*; and
3. a special partnership registered under the now-repealed Special Partnerships Limited Liability Acts of the Cape Province and Natal.[8]

17.3.2.1 Anonymous partnership

An **anonymous partnership** is one 'in which two or more persons agree to share in some business which will be conducted by one of them in his own name' and not in the name of the partnership or in the name of any of the anonymous partners.[9] For as long as the anonymous partner is not disclosed to the public, he or she is not liable to third parties for the debts of the partnership, but is liable only to his or her partners to the extent agreed between the partners.

17.3.2.2 Partnership *en commandite*

A **partnership *en commandite*** bears a similarity to an anonymous partnership, but should not be equated thereto. This form of partnership exists only in a case where the business of the partnership is carried on in the name of one or more of the partners, and every partner whose name is not disclosed (the undisclosed partner is called a partner *en commandite*) makes a contribution in the form of *a fixed sum* of money on condition that he or she receives a certain share of the profits. If there are no profits but a loss, he or she is liable to the other parties to the extent of the fixed amount of the agreed capital contribution made by him or her.[10]

The distinction between the anonymous and *en commandite* partnerships is therefore that, whereas in an anonymous partnership, the silent or anonymous partner may well be liable to the other partners for a *pro rata* share of all the partnership debts (or to the extent that was expressly agreed), the liability of the *en commandite* partner is always limited to the amount of his or her agreed capital contribution.

17.3.2.3 Special partnership

The third category of extraordinary partnership was a **special partnership** registered in terms of pre-Union statutes that have now been repealed by the Pre-Union Statute Law Revision Act.[11] The repeal of this legislation does not affect any action undertaken under the repealed law nor rights acquired or liabilities incurred under such law. A brief mention of these partnerships is therefore necessary.

Special partnerships consist of:

- one or more persons, so-called general partners, (who are jointly and severally liable for the debts of the partnership) and who are the only persons authorised to transact the business of the partnership, and

---

8   Act 24 of 1861 (Cape Province) and Law 1 of 1864 (Natal) were repealed by the Pre-Union Statute Law Revision Act 36 of 1976.

9   Van Der Linden 4.1.12.

10   *Eaton & Louw v Arcade Properties (Pty) Ltd* 1961 (4) SA 233 (T) at 240.

11   36 of 1976.

- one or more special partners, who make a contribution of a specific sum in actual cash payment, and who are not personally liable for any debts of the partnership beyond the amount so paid in by them.

In terms of these partnerships, the limited liability of a special partner depends on the fact that the name of the partner is not disclosed and such a partner does personally enter into a transaction with a third party regarding the business of the partnership.

17.4   Essentials of partnership

The four essentials of a partnership were set out definitively a long time ago in *Joubert v Tarry and Company*:[12]

1. Each of the partners brings something into the partnership, or binds him- or herself to bring something into it, whether it be money, labour or skill.
2. The business should be carried on for the joint benefit of the partners.
3. The object should be to make a profit.
4. The contract between the parties should be a legitimate contract.

Where all these four essentials are present, in the absence of something showing that the contract between the parties is not an agreement of partnership, the court must come to the conclusion that it is a partnership. It makes no difference what the parties have chosen to call it – for example, they may call it a joint venture, or letting and hiring.[13]

Certain additional legal formalities are also required for a valid partnership. The respective requirements are discussed below in turn.

17.4.1   Contribution by partners

Each partner must make an appreciable **contribution** to the partnership – that is, something that has commercial value – although the contribution need not be capable of precise pecuniary assessment. A case in point would be that of a partner who contributes labour or skill to the partnership.[14] A partner may contribute money, other property, such as shares or immovable property, skill, knowledge, contacts, experience, expertise, or the equivalent thereof.

17.4.2   Business should be carried on for joint benefit of the parties

Business in this context is defined as 'anything which occupies the time and attention and the labour of a person for the purpose of profit'.[15] It is clear from the forms of partnership analysed that a partnership can exist if it is formed to complete a particular, single project. The business activity does not have to be of an indefinitely continuous nature; a venture that constitutes a single transaction could well be implemented by a partnership, provided that the other requirements as outlined above are met.[16]

The concept of **joint benefit** means that a partnership cannot exist where each party can claim individual benefit from the business as he or she deems fit. The very idea of a partnership is that the venture is designed to benefit all of the parties to the contract of

---

12   1915 TPD 277 at 280–1.
13   See, for the more recent exposition of the law, *Purdon v Muller* 1961 (2) SA 211 (A) at 217–8.
14   *Pezzutto v Dreyer* supra at 390.
15   *Standard General Insurance Co v Hennop* 1954 (4) SA 560 (A) at 565.
16   *Bester v Van Niekerk* supra at 784–5.

partnership. Accordingly, each partner must share in the losses and profits of the partnership business. South African law does not recognise a partnership where one partner is entitled to all the benefits and another (or all the others) is obliged to incur all the losses.[17]

17.4.3 Business should be carried on to make profit

In *Ally v Dinath*,[18] Eloff J (as he then was) said:

> It is at once necessary to state what is meant by the requirement that the object of the enterprise was to make a profit .... What is required is not a pure pecuniary profit motive; the achievement of another material gain, such as a joint exercise for the purpose of saving costs, will suffice .... And in Isaacs's case ... an object 'to provide for the livelihood and comfort of the parties, and their children, including the proper education and upbringing of the latter' was held to be equivalent to making a profit and thus sufficient for partnership purposes. In the present case the objective of the accumulation of an appreciating joint estate is alleged and, at least for pleading purposes, that is in my estimation sufficient.

That Eloff J appears to have softened the requirement that there should be a **profit objective** does not detract from the foundation of the requirement – to make gain or profit. Thus, sports clubs and welfare or charitable institutions cannot be considered to be partnerships.

17.4.4 Legitimate contract

A partnership is established by means of a valid agreement or **legitimate contract**. That agreement must embody the basic essentials of a partnership and must be entered into with the clear intention of creating a partnership. Before it can be said that a partnership exists, the requirements of the essentials have to be met. In addition, the contracting parties must have the intention of establishing a partnership.

In this regard, the dictum of Smalberger JA in *Pezzutto v Dreyer*[19] is relevant:

> In determining whether or not an agreement creates a partnership, a court will have regard, inter alia, to the substance of the agreement, the circumstances in which it was made and the subsequent conduct of the parties. The fact that parties regard themselves as partners, or referred to themselves as such, is an important though not necessarily decisive consideration. What is necessary to create a partnership agreement is that the essentialia of a partnership should be present.

The conduct of the parties may well, in the absence of clarity concerning the nature of the agreement, provide guidance as to the real intention of the parties. For example, if the parties by their conduct share profits in the joint business for their mutual benefit, and if they have all made a contribution to the business, that would constitute powerful evidence to prove the presence of the essence of a partnership.[20]

The person alleging the existence of partnership must provide proof. Like most legal disputes, an examination of the facts is necessary in addition to consideration of the legal principles.

---

17 Henning 'Partnership' in *LAWSA* supra at para. 261.
18 1984 (2) SA 451 (T) at 455.
19 Supra at 389.
20 Henning 'Partnership' in *LAWSA* supra at para. 265.

<table>
<tr><td>CASE
STUDY</td><td>

The existence of a partnership: examples from the cases

In *Harrington v Fester*,[21] the applicant claimed the existence of a partnership. However, there was no written agreement. The court found that, at best, the correspondence between the parties revealed no more than a possible intention to enter into partnership. Certain other correspondence indicated that the applicant had treated the respondent as an employee, which would be totally inconsistent with the existence of a partnership. In this case, it also could not be shown that there was ever a partnership banking account.

In *Pezzutto v Dreyer*,[22] the appellant had alleged that a 'handshake agreement' of partnership between himself and three others had come into existence. The court stated that for a partnership to come about, there must be an agreement to that effect between the contracting parties.

On his evidence, which the court found to have been uncontradicted, unchallenged and plausible, the appellant was held to have proved the *essentialia* necessary for the creation of a partnership agreement. The court found that there had been clarity among the parties in regard to the nature of each party's contribution, and the fact that the exact extent of such contribution and the precise role of each party had not been spelled out had not made the agreement void for vagueness.

</td></tr>
</table>

17.4.5   Other legal formalities

Certain additional legal formalities may apply to partnerships:

- A partnership must comply with the law. It cannot conduct business that is prohibited by law or public policy.
- There are no formalities per se required for the conclusion of a partnership agreement. A partnership contract may therefore be concluded, either in writing or orally, and may, in certain instances, be implied by conduct.
- The parties may agree on certain formalities between themselves and, if they so agree, the partnership only becomes established on compliance with the agreed formalities. The most obvious example is a case where the parties agree that a partnership must be established pursuant to a written contract; in that event, only after a written partnership contract has been concluded and signed will the partnership come into legal existence.

17.5   Legal nature of partnership

Most common-law jurisdictions do not regard a partnership as a legal person standing apart from its members. A partnership is thus clearly different from a company and its shareholders.

South African law appears to have adopted the aggregate theory of partnership as opposed to the entity theory. In brief, the **entity theory of partnership** views a partnership as an entity separate from its members, so that it becomes the holder of rights and obligations and can continue existence, notwithstanding a change of the members of the

---

21   1980 (4) SA 424 (C).
22   Supra.

partnership.[23] In contrast, the **aggregate theory** treats a partnership as an aggregate or collection of individual parties, being the partners. It is these partners who are the owners of the partnership property, and the rights and liabilities of the partnership are considered to be their rights and liabilities. Viewed in this way, a change of partner destroys the identity of the partnership.

The aggregate theory therefore entrenches a dramatic difference in law between a partnership and an incorporated company, in that only the latter enjoys legal personality. Similarly, the aggregate theory dictates that since the partnership is not a legal person, a partnership as such cannot own property. Thus, the general rule is that the assets of the partnership are held by the partners as co-owners – that is, they own the property in undivided shares.

The problem with declaring allegiance to the aggregate theory is that our courts have not always been clear in this regard. Even early in the development of our law, our courts were ambivalent as to the nature of a partnership. For example, in *Potchefstroom Dairies v Standard Fresh Milk Supply Co*,[24] Bristowe J said:

> I do not think, however, it makes much difference whether we regard a partnership as a persona or whether we regard it as a contractual compound of several personae .... And the distinction between the two seems more academic than substantial. I am, however, prepared to go to the extent of holding that a partnership, though not a corporate individual, is so far analogous to a persona that it may be called quasi-persona. This indeed seems to me to be an accurate statement of the law deducible from recent cases. For many purposes it has, or is treated as having a persona of its own; and particularly in relation to commercial transactions is this a convenient and succinct way of regarding its position.[25]

CASE STUDY	**Partnerships and tax law**
	In *Sacks v Commissioner for Inland Revenue*,[26] the court held that in a case of a partnership, unless the partnership agreement provided to the contrary, receipts and accruals of income of a partnership were so received or accrued by the partners in common. Only when the time arose to bring partnership income to account (at the end of an accounting period as fixed by the partnership agreement) would a partner become entitled to claim a separate determinable share of the partnership profits. Only then would that determinable share of income accrue to him or her as gross income to which there would be liability for tax. This position has now been altered. Section 24H of the Income Tax Act[27] ensures that each partner is regarded as carrying on the business of the partnership. The South African Revenue Services were therefore concerned that income could be held as if by a separate entity, with tax not being paid until a later distribution to individual partners.

23 See JJ Henning and E Snyman 'Die regsaard van die vennootskap: die entiteitsteorie seëvier in Verenigde State' 1993 *TSAR* 306. See also J Henning & E Snyman 'Revision of the law of partnership in the United States of America: a commendable precedent?' 1997 (114) *SALJ* 684. In this article, the authors analyse the most recent US legislation, the Revised Uniform Partnership Act of 1997, in which the law has moved to embrace the entity theory of partnership. Correctly, it is noted that South African law has virtually ignored these modern developments.
24 1913 TPD 506 at 513.
25 See also the comments of De Villiers JP at 511–2.
26 1946 AD 31.
27 58 of 1962.

Although, at common law, a partnership is not considered to be a legal person, legislation has created exceptions to this position in two areas – namely, insolvency and litigation.

17.5.1   Insolvency exception to partnership lack of legal personality

Section 13(1) of the Insolvency Act[28] provides that sequestration of a partnership estate is to be treated as distinct from the estates of the individual members of the partnership. The section provides that '[i]f the court sequestrates the estate of a partnership ... it shall simultaneously sequestrate the estate of every member of that partnership.'

While the estate of the partnership and the personal estates of the individual partners are simultaneously sequestrated, the creditors of the partnership can prove claims against the partnership estates only, and the creditors of the partners can prove claims against the personal estate of the partners only. Any balance that is left over from a partner's personal estate will be available to the trustees of the partnership estate for distributions amongst the creditors of the partnership, but only where needed and only after all the private creditors of the partner have been paid in full. Likewise, any balance in the partnership estate will pass to the trustee of the individual partner's estate in so far as that partner would have been entitled to the balance had his or her estate not been sequestrated.[29]

CASE STUDY	**The exception on insolvency**
	In *Michalow NO v Premier Milling Co Ltd*,[30] the court held as follows:

> It is at this stage that the Insolvency Act departs from the common law by retaining the 'partnership estate' as a separate estate from the estate of the individuals and by precluding 'partnership creditors' from preferring their claims against individual estates; they have to look for payment to the partnership estate only, in the initial stages at least ... . To justify such a drastic departure from legal principle one would have to adopt the hypothesis that those who deal with and grant credit to a partnership, do so in reliance on the partnership assets only; they must be taken to have looked, throughout their dealings with it, on the partnership as a separate entity. It is, of course, a fiction but a fiction that is indispensable in justifying the provisions operating against partnership creditors.

However, the courts have been careful to emphasise the limited extent of this exception, and that it should not be construed as recognising a quasi personality in partnerships beyond the purposes of the Insolvency Act.

17.5.2   Litigation exception to partnership lack of legal personality

Another exception exists when a claim is made either by or against the partnership. Such claims must be instituted by or against all the partners at the time that the cause of action arises. For example, prior to the introduction of Rule 14 of the Uniform Rules of the High Court, litigation by (or against) a partnership in the High Court presented difficulties because

---

28   24 of 1936.
29   See s 49 of the Insolvency Act. Whether all partners had to be sequestrated in the event of their partnership being sequestrated was controversial, but the matter has been settled by the Supreme Court of Appeal in *CSARS v Hawker Air Services (Pty) Ltd* [2006] 2 All SA 565 (SCA), where it was held that it was sufficient where only those partners who were capable of being sequestrated were so sequestrated.
30   1960 (2) SA 59 (W).

the partnership was not considered to be a separate legal person. It could not generally therefore be sued; nor could it sue in its own name apart from the individual members, whose names and addresses had to be alleged in the summons, being the document that launches the legal action.

Rule 14 now provides that a partnership may be sued in its own name. A similar provision is to be found in Rule 54 of the Magistrates' Courts Act.[31]

17.6 Relationship between partners

At common law, a partnership is considered to be a contract *uberrimae fidei* – that is, a contract of the **utmost good faith**.[32] This means that the relationship between the partners must be based on mutual trust and the utmost confidence. Each partner is in a fiduciary relationship to the others. However, this rule needs qualification, because, in our modern law, there is no such thing as a contract *uberrimae fidei*. All contracts require good faith and, as with honesty, good faith does not admit of degrees or increments.[33] The reason that certain contracts attract a greater duty of disclosure, however, is that there exists crucially in these contracts a fiduciary relationship between the parties and hence a form of involuntary reliance.[34]

The relationship between partners is governed in essence by way of the partnership agreement. However, the principle of utmost good faith must be employed as a means to give content to the interpretation of the agreed relationship.

The rights of partners between themselves have been summarised as constituting a right to share in the profits of the partnership, a right to participate in the management of the business, the right to compensation, the right to inspect the partnership books and the right to distribution of assets on dissolution. The correlative duties to the partnership include the duty to make a contribution towards the partnership, a duty to share in the losses, a duty of care and skill, and a duty of full disclosure or a duty to account.[35]

The value of utmost good faith can be employed to give content to four separate duties as described below.

1. *Duty to accept and fulfil the obligations of the partnership agreement*: as Ogilvie Thompson JA, following English law, said in *Purdon v Miller*,[36] 'If one partner repudiates the contract of partnership and will not perform his duty towards his co-partners, he cannot justly complain if they in return decline to treat him on a footing of equality with themselves.'

2. *Duty to acquire benefits for partnership*: since partners owe a fiduciary duty to their fellow partners, they may not acquire or retain any benefit or advantage that falls within the scope of the business of the partnership. It is the duty of that partner to acquire such benefits or advantage for the partnership. Colman J set out the scope of this principle in *Mattson v Yiannakis*:[37]

> In order that the gain (made by a partner) may become a partnership asset, the profit-making transaction must, in my view, be within the scope of the partnership objects. If, for example, a partner in a firm of plumbers or stock brokers uses the

---

31 32 of 1944. See in general Cilliers et al *Herbstein and Van Winsen: Civil Practice of the Supreme Court of South Africa* (2009) 5ed at 150–4.
32 *Purdon v Muller* 1961 (2) SA 211 (A) at 231.
33 See the finding in *Mutual and Federal Insurance Co Ltd v Oudtshoorn Municipality* 1985 (1) SA 419 (A) at 433.
34 Dale Hutchison in *Wille's Principles of South African Law* 9 ed (2007) at 779–80.
35 Henning 'Partnership' in *LAWSA* supra at para. 289.
36 Supra.
37 1976 (4) SA 154 (W) at 159.

firm's typewriter for the purpose of typing a prize-winning novel or epic poem, the prize does not, I think, become the property of the partnership merely because an asset of the partnership was used in creating the prize-winning entry. Whatever other remedy the partnership may have in such a case for the unauthorised use of the asset, it is, to my mind, inconceivable that the prize, so far outside the scope of its objects and activities, can be said to have been acquired for it.

What is even clearer is that a partner may not compete with the partnership by carrying on a business of the same nature as that of a partnership – that is, a business that has clearly been competing with that of the partnership. In the event of such a conflict, all the profits so earned must be shared with and thus accounted to the partnership.

3. *Duty to guard against a conflict of interest*: a partner should not place him- or herself in a position where a prime interest of the partner may conflict with the duties that the partner holds towards the partnership. Where A is a debtor of the partnership, as well as a debtor of a partner in terms of an obligation incurred by A in the partner's private capacity, that partner cannot obtain payment of his debt from A in preference to that of a debt owed by A to the partnership. If A pays the debt to the partner, but fails to pay his debt to the partnership, the partner must account to the partnership for that which he has received and to him- or herself *pro rata* to the amount of the respective debts.

CASE STUDY

Conflict of interest

A leading illustration of the duty of a partner to prevent a conflict of interest between himself and the partnership is to be found in *De Jager v Olifants Tin 'B' Syndicate*.[38] In this case, a syndicate, which in law was recognised as a partnership, prospected on a farm for tin. The syndicate had been granted the right to prospect on the farming property for a period of two months. One of the partners discovered tin just outside the boundary of the land within which the syndicate had been negotiating for an option, but which had not been concluded at the time of the individual partner's discovery. That partner, without notice to fellow partners of his discovery, succeeded in obtaining for himself an option in respect of the farm, the possession of which was essential for the mining operation on the adjoining property, as well as further rights on the property where discovery had been made. Innes ACJ (as he then was) set out the principles of law that have been recognised ever since:

> The relationship between the members of a partnership is one of mutual trust and confidence and the principles of law bearing upon the present controversy are not seriously in dispute. No partner may acquire and retain for himself any benefit or advantage which was in the scope of the partnership business, and which it was his duty to acquire for the partnership. All such benefits must be shared with and accounted for to his fellow members.[39]

The partner argued that he had acquired a so-called discoverer's right over the land on which the tin had been found and the syndicate had, as its purpose, the acquisition of options over farms, which constituted a different form of right. The court was not

---

38   1912 AD 505.
39   At 509.

prepared to accept such a narrow, formalistic distinction between the business of the partnership and the business of the partner. It held that the acquisition by the partnership of options over the farm 'was only a means to an end, which was a discovery of tin and the acquisition of rights in regard to it'. For this reason, it could not be said that the essence of the syndicate's business was not the discovery of tin and, when the partner made his discovery of tin, as a member of a partnership, he owed a duty to his partners to avoid a conflict of interest. Accordingly, he could not retain the resulting benefits of the discovery for himself, as he was obliged in law to transfer them to the syndicate.

4. *Duty of disclosure*: a partner has a duty to disclose to all co-partners all information in his or her possession that affects the partnership. For example, if there is a prospect of profit to the partnership by virtue of the participation of a partner in a particular venture, any such prospect should be brought to the attention of the other partners, who should then be placed in a position to consider what approach should be adopted with regard to this proposed venture. A partner may not conceal facts from his or her partners if knowledge of such facts may have an influence on the remaining partners' decision regarding the partnership. This rule flows directly from the principle that partners must act in accordance with the utmost good faith towards each other in all business transactions.

17.7 Authority of partners to contract with third parties

If the law adopted an entity approach to partnership, then a partner who contracts on behalf of the partnership would act as an agent on behalf of the partnership. However, South African law adopts the aggregate theory of partnership. On this basis, when a partner contracts on behalf of the partnership, that partner acts as a **principal** in relation to him- or herself, and as a representative of the other partners – in that he or she acts as an **agent** and binds all remaining partners, provided that he or she acts within the scope of his or her authority.

CASE STUDY	Agency
	Jessel MR said the following more than a century ago in *Pooley v Driver*:[40]

You cannot grasp the notion of agency properly speaking unless you grasp the notion of the existence of the firm as a separate entity from the existence of the partners ... If you cannot grasp the notion of a separate entity for the firm (partnership), then you are reduced to this, that in as much as he (partner) acts partly for himself and partly for the others, to the extent that he acts for the others he must be an agent and in that way you get him to be an agent for the other partners but only in that way because you insist upon ignoring the existence of the firm as a separate entity.

---

40   (1876) 5 Ch 458.

Unfortunately, the position is rather more complicated than a simple application of the rules relating to agency. As a principal, the partner is bound by his or her authorised actions and by the actions of the other partners when they also act on behalf of the partnership, provided again that each partner acts within the limits of his or her authority. Accordingly, a partner plays a double role, being that of agent to the partnership and a principal, in one and the same transaction.[41]

17.8   Authority of partner to bind partnership

The authority of a partner to bind his or her partners may be based either on actual or ostensible authority. **Actual authority** to enter into a contract on behalf of the partnership may be expressly granted to a partner or may be implied in the manner in which the partner customarily deals with third parties. If a partner has been granted express authority to enter into a legal relationship on behalf of the partnership, then provided the partner acts in terms of the mandate granted to him or her, the partnership is bound – even if that transaction falls outside the scope of the usual business conducted by that partnership. It may be that a partner has been given a general authority to bind the partnership in relation to its ordinary business – for example, where a partner is granted power of management of the partnership business. This is a general authority and, unlike an express authority granted to a partner in relation to a particular (and possibly extraordinary) transaction, will extend only to transactions that fall within the scope of the partnership business.

Unless there is an express provision in the partnership agreement to the contrary, each partner will have the authority to perform all acts that are necessary for, or are incidental to, the proper conduct of the business of the partnership. Such acts bind the partnership and fall within the scope of implied authority of each partner.

A problem arises when there is a dispute as to whether a particular transaction has fallen within the scope of the business of the partnership. The legal test is easily stated: if it can be shown that the transaction falls outside the scope of the partnership business, then the contracting partner has exceeded his or her implied authority to bind the partnership. However, the application of this test will, as always, depend on the particular facts and the determination as to whether a partner has bound the partnership is a factual question. The onus of proving that the contracting partner did not exceed his or her implied authority to bind the partnership lies with the third party who seeks to hold the partnership to the agreement.

CASE STUDY	Implied authority to bind partnership
	In *Goodricke's v Hall*,[42] a partnership existed between A and B for the purpose of carrying on a restaurant business. B appointed an attorney to make an application for the grant of a liquor licence for their restaurant. The question was raised as to whether B had the authority to bind the partnership when he so instructed the attorney. The court accepted that whatever B's actual agreement may have been with A, in the absence of an express agreement specifically limiting B's authority to act on behalf of the partnership, his act of instructing the attorney to apply for a liquor licence for the restaurant was one that was clearly done in furtherance of the business of the partnership. Thus, it fell within the scope of his implied authority to bind the partnership.

---

41   Henning 'Partnership' in *LAWSA* supra at para. 304.
42   1978 (4) SA 208 (N).

In accordance with the underlying notion that a partnership is an agreement, the implied authority of a partner to act on behalf of the partnership in the conduct of its business may be varied, limited or excluded by express agreement between the partners.[43]

When partner B has this form of express (but limited) power, and exceeds this express authority by concluding a contract with a third party, who is unaware of an express limitation on partner B's power, if it can be shown that partner B acted within his implied or ostensible authority, the partnership has no defence on the basis of any private instruction that might have been given to the partner. It is accordingly bound by the contract into which the partner entered with the third party.[44]

The rule is, therefore, that the third party in our example will be entitled to assume that partner B with whom she contracted had implied authority to act on behalf of the partnership in transactions that fell within the scope of the partnership business. Thus, if the third party can show that the act of partner B fell within the scope of the business of the partnership, she will be entitled to rely on the contract. The situation would be different if the partnership was able to prove that the third party was aware of the arrangement limiting the authority of partner B when they contracted.

If a partner has **ostensible authority**, he or she appears to the outside world to be authorised to act on behalf of the partnership in the way he or she does. The estoppel defence is then inescapable – partners may be estopped from denying that one of their group had authority to bind the group. Thus in *Levin v Barclays Bank DCO*,[45] the court drew an inference that two persons were trading in a partnership where they had both opened and operated as a partnership a bank account, and had given no explanation for their conduct. In this case, the court accepted the rule that a partnership may be liable to a *bona fide* third party if it represents a non-partner to be a partner, or with knowledge allows the non-partner to represent himself as a partner.

Strictly speaking, ostensible authority is a misnomer for such a situation. No authority actually exists; the point is that it is the appearance rather than the reality of authority that will bind the partnership where the appearance has been created by the principal (in this case, the partnership).[46]

17.9 Personal liability of a partner

In general terms, each of the partners is **jointly and severally liable** for partnership debts. Thus in *Geldenhuys v East and West Investments (Pty) Ltd*,[47] the appellant, an attorney, was ordered by the court to pay his erstwhile landlord the sum of R36 761,10 in respect of unpaid arrear rental. As the attorney's partner had settled a larger sum with the landlord, the question arose as to the liability of the partner who was the appellant. The court held that the landlord was entitled to sue both partners, jointly and severally, for the full amount of the disputed debt. Judgment had to be given against both partners.

It therefore follows that, during the existence of the partnership, creditors of the partnership cannot sue some of the individual partners, but must sue all of them. Only on the dissolution of the partnership does this rule no longer apply. Until then, the partners are co-debtors and hence joint and several liability arises.

---

43 See in general MJ Oosthuizen 'Die Turquand-reël as reël van die verenigingsreg' 1977 *TSAR* 210 at 218.
44 See Coaker JF & Zeffert (eds) *Wille and Millin's Mercantile Law of South Africa* 18 ed (1984) at 547.
45 1968 (2) SA 45 (A).
46 See Henning 'Partnership' in *LAWSA* supra at 210.
47 2005 (2) SA 74 (SCA).

As already noted, if a partnership becomes insolvent, the creditors of the partnership look to the partnership assets to satisfy their claims before seeking satisfaction from the assets of the individual partners – and then only after the claims of the individual partners' creditors have been satisfied from those assets.

17.10   Dissolution of partnerships

A partnership may be dissolved or terminated in a number of different ways, the most important of which are the following:

- *Effluxion of a period of time*: it has been agreed that the partnership will exist for a certain period only.
- *The end of an undertaking*: if a partnership has been set up to conduct a particular undertaking or business, once that business or undertaking is completed, the partnership will terminate.
- *Mutual agreement between the partners.*
- *Change in the membership of a partnership*: the retirement or death of a partner or the admission of a new partner terminates the existing partnership. If a partner retires or dies, the remaining partners may agree to continue the business of the partnership, so that a new partnership is created. This, of course, follows from a principle that has been discussed – namely, that a partnership does not enjoy a separate legal personality. When this new partnership is created, the creditors are not duty-bound to accept the incoming partners as debtors in substitution for the members of the old partnership with whom they had previously contracted. Debtors, however, cannot generally object to the transfer by the old firm to the new of the claims that the old partnership had against them. Movable property will pass by law. This is another illustration of the outdated nature of the aggregate theory of partnership.

    On the death of one of the partners, the partnership terminates unless the partnership agreement provides that on the death of a partner, the partnership is to continue and that the remaining partners shall purchase the share of the deceased partner. A partnership can carry on between the surviving partners and the estate of the deceased partner where the latter has duly authorised such action by way of his or her will. In the absence of any such authorisation, the partnership cannot be carried on with the deceased estate.
- *Insolvency of the partnership or any of its members.*
- *Notice of dissolution given by one of the members*: the notice must be given in good faith and in reasonable time. If, for example, a partner seeks to dissolve the partnership in order to take a benefit that would otherwise flow to the partnership, that would be considered to be an act in bad faith.
- *Where the partners become alien enemies on or after the outbreak of war*: the dissolution of a partnership in these circumstances reflects the ancient nature of the law of partnerships.
- *Order of court granted on application of one or more of the partners for good cause*: what constitutes good cause is a factual question that will need to be determined in each individual case. Illustrations of what courts have held to be good cause include the prolonged absence of a partner; continued incapacity of a partner by reason of illness to perform substantially his or her duties in terms of the partnership agreement; an inability to continue the partnership business because of an irretrievable breakdown in the relationship of the partners where the situation is generally not due in large measure to the applicant for the order for dissolution; or persistent negligence on the part of a partner.

On the dissolution of the partnership and in the absence of any provision in the agreement to the contrary, a proper rendering of an account must be completed before amounts owed to the individual partners can be claimed, unless such amounts can be easily ascertained.

On termination, any creditor of the partnership can sue the members of the firm as individuals, jointly and severally, for the debt.

After termination, no partner has the implied authority to bind the partnership, although it is possible that one partner may have the implied authority to bind his co-partners for the purposes of liquidating the partnership business.

Each partner may, once the partnership is terminated, demand an account from his or her co-partners.[48]

THIS CHAPTER IN ESSENCE

1. A **partnership** is a contract between two or more persons, in terms of which each partner agrees to contribute to the partnership business, which is carried on for joint benefit of the parties and with the object of making a profit.
2. If a company is a **personal liability company** under the Companies Act, 2008, the directors and past directors are jointly and severally liable, together with the company, for any debts and liabilities of the company contracted during their respective periods of office. A personal liability company is usually formed as an alternative to a partnership to reap some benefits of incorporation (such as perpetual succession).
3. Partnerships may be universal partnerships (as opposed to particular partnerships) or ordinary partnerships (as opposed to extraordinary partnerships).
4. A **universal partnership** involves partners contributing all their property or all their profits to the partnership, usually for an open-ended period and for wide-ranging purposes, with a commensurate sharing of the profits of their enterprises. Marriage in community of property (or a similar relationship) is a partnership *universorum bonorum*, but universal partnerships also occur in commercial undertakings. A **particular partnership** will usually be a more temporary and focused arrangement, in terms of which partners contribute their resources for a particular defined purpose only and share only in profits from that particular project together.
5. In an **ordinary partnership**, partners are jointly and severally liable for all of the debts of the partnership. The liability of partners in an **extraordinary partnership** is limited in some way. There are three forms of extraordinary partnership:
    5.1 An **anonymous partnership** has at least one partner whose name is not disclosed to the public and who is not liable to third parties for the debts of the partnership, but is liable to the other partners to the extent agreed between the partners.
    5.2 A **partnership en commandite** has undisclosed partners who make a fixed contribution and who are not liable to other parties beyond that fixed commitment.
    5.3 A **special partnership** (a form of partnership registered under a now-repealed Act) has general partners (who are jointly and severally liable for the debts of the partnership and are the only persons authorised to transact the business of the partnership) and special partners (whose names are not disclosed and who are not liable beyond an agreed specific contribution).
6. The four essential elements of partnership are that:
    6.1 each party makes an appreciable **contribution** to the partnership;
    6.2 the business is carried on for the **joint benefit** of the partners;
    6.3 there should be a **profit objective**; and

---

48   *Carr v Hinson* 1966 (3) SA 303 (W) at 304.

6.4 the contract between the parties should be a **legitimate contract** made with the intention of establishing a partnership.

7. South African law adopts the **aggregate theory of partnership**, which does not regard the partnership as having separate legal personality from its members. The partners own the partnership property as co-owners and the rights and liabilities of the partnership are also the individual partners' rights and liabilities. Thus, a change of partner destroys the identity of the partnership.

8. There are two exceptions to a partnership's lack of legal personality:

    8.1 In the area of **insolvency**, the sequestration of a partnership estate is, to some extent, treated as distinct from the estates of the individual members of the partnership.

    8.2 In **litigation**, a partnership may be sued and may sue in its own name, rather than the names of all individual partners.

9. At common law, a partnership is a contract *uberrimae fidei* (**utmost good faith**). In modern law, all contracts require good faith, but the fiduciary nature of the relationship between partners means that it attracts a greater duty of disclosure.

10. Partners have the following rights between themselves:

    10.1 to share in the profits of the partnership;

    10.2 to participate in the management of the business;

    10.3 to compensation;

    10.4 to inspect partnership books; and

    10.5 to a distribution of assets on dissolution.

11. Partners have the following duties:

    11.1 to make a contribution towards the partnership;

    11.2 to share in losses;

    11.3 to exercise care and skill;

    11.4 to make full disclosures of information relevant to the partnership;

    11.5 to account to the partnership;

    11.6 to accept and fulfil the obligations of the partnership agreement;

    11.7 to acquire benefits for the partnership; and

    11.8 to guard against a conflict of interest.

12. When a partner contracts on behalf of the partnership, he or she acts both as **principal** in relation to him- or herself, and as a representative (**agent**) of the other partners (provided that he or she acts within the scope of their authority).

13. The authority of a partner to bind the other partners may be based on either actual or ostensible authority. **Actual authority** to enter into a contract on behalf of the partnership may be expressly granted to a partner or may be implied in the manner in which the partner customarily deals with third parties. If a partner has **ostensible authority**, he or she appears to the outside world to be authorised to act on behalf of the partnership, and partners may be estopped from denying that one of their group had authority to bind the group.

14. In general terms, each partner is jointly and severally liable for partnership debts.

15. A partnership may be dissolved or terminated by:

    15.1 effluxion of time;

    15.2 the end of the undertaking;

    15.3 mutual agreement between the partners;

    15.4 change in the membership of a partnership (a new partnership may be agreed to);

    15.5 insolvency of the partnership or any of its members;

    15.6 notice of dissolution given by one of the partners;

    15.7 partners becoming alien enemies on or after the outbreak of war; or

    15.8 order of court granted upon application of one or more of the partners for good cause.

Business trusts

Chapter 18

Business trusts

18.1   Meaning and uses of a trust

A trust can be a very useful device. Apart from its place in estate and financial planning, a trust can be used to protect assets, and can also be used as a structure for business or trading purposes in place of a company or close corporation structure. One of the great advantages of a trust remains its flexibility and relative lack of formality in its creation and operation.

A **trust** is a legal relationship that has been created in a trust *deed* (otherwise known as a trust instrument). A trust has the following four key characteristics:

1. The relationship is created by a person who is known as the founder, donor or settlor.
2. The founder places assets under the control of another person (or persons), who is known as the trustee *(or trustees)*.
3. This can be done either during the founder's lifetime (an *inter vivos* trust) or on the founder's death (a testamentary trust – also known as a will trust).
4. The purpose of the exercise is to benefit third persons (the beneficiaries).

It is therefore apparent that there are three main parties to a trust:

1. the founder;
2. the trustees; and
3. the beneficiaries.

Many 'family trusts' and many 'trading trusts' consist of persons who occupy all three positions. This, in itself, might be sufficient for a trust to be regarded as a sham that may be legally disregarded.

In *Land and Agricultural Bank of South Africa v Parker*,[1] the court stated that trusts were designed essentially to protect the weak – that is, to protect beneficiaries – and to safeguard the interests of those who are absent or dead (the founder). Thus, the essence of a trust is that a trustee, or trustees, is or are appointed, and the trustee accepts office, which is to exercise fiduciary responsibility over certain property (held in trust) on behalf of and in the interests of a beneficiary or beneficiaries. The rights and interests of a beneficiary or beneficiaries in the trust property are determined by what is written in the trust deed.

There is one statute that applies specifically to trusts, and that is the Trust Property Control Act.[2] This Act deals largely with administrative aspects relating to trusts, and is not nearly as comprehensive as the Companies Act, 2008 is in regulating companies, or the Close Corporations Act[3] is in regulating close corporations. To illustrate this point, the Trust Property Control Act consists of only 27 sections, whereas the Companies Act, 2008 consists of 225 sections and five schedules. Although the provisions of the Trust Property Control Act do not regulate the formation or administration of trusts in the way that the Companies Act and Close Corporations Act regulate companies and close corporations, they do have a direct bearing on trusts, particularly on the authorisation and duties of trustees.[4]

The Trust Property Control Act defines a trust[5] as:

- an arrangement
- through which the ownership in property of one person
- is by virtue of a trust instrument made over or bequeathed
    - to another person, the trustee, to be administered or disposed of according to the provisions of the trust instrument for the benefit of the beneficiary or beneficiaries as designated in the trust instrument, or for the achievement of the object stated in the trust instrument; or

---

1 2005 (2) SA 77 (SCA).
2 57 of 1988.
3 69 of 1984.
4 See paras. 18.11 and 18.12 below.
5 Section 1 of the Trust Property Control Act.

- to the beneficiaries designated in the trust instrument, which property is placed under the control of another person, the trustee, to be administered or disposed of according to the provisions of the trust instrument for the benefit of the beneficiary or beneficiaries as designated in the trust instrument, or for the achievement of the object stated in the trust instrument.

This definition envisages two types of trust:
1. where ownership[6] and control of trust assets lies with the trustees (an **ordinary trust**); and
2. where the beneficiary or beneficiaries have ownership of trust assets, but these are under the control of the trustees (a **_bewind_ trust**).[7]

PRACTICAL	**A _bewind_ trust**
ISSUE	A _bewind_ trust may, for example, involve someone bequeathing assets to his or her minor child, but these assets are placed under the control of trustees until the child reaches majority. In such a trust, the child has ownership of trust assets, but the assets are controlled by the trustees.
	Another example of a _bewind_ trust is as follows: Paul dies and leaves his farm to his sister but the last will and testament provides that the trustees will manage the farm in whatever way they choose, by farming or leasing the farm. It is clear that the sister has ownership of the farm, but it is controlled by trustees.

Trusts that are formed for estate-planning purposes, or for asset-protection purposes, or for business purposes, fall under the first type of trust – that is, they are ordinary trusts. In such a trust, the trustees have non-beneficial ownership in the trust assets and they are obliged to control and administer these assets on behalf of the beneficiaries of the trust. This is the type of trust discussed in this chapter.

In an ordinary trust, although trustees may be the owners and controllers of trust property, it is nevertheless non-beneficial ownership. In other words, they have only bare ownership, because they do not own the property for their own benefit, but in a representative capacity on behalf of beneficiaries in accordance with the provisions of the trust deed. Section 12 of the Trust Property Control Act specifically provides that trust property does not form part of the personal estate of the trustee, except in so far as the trustee is him- or herself a beneficiary of the trust and, as such, entitled to the enjoyment of the trust property as provided for in terms of the trust deed.

An ordinary trust has many uses. As mentioned above, apart from its role in estate-planning, a trust can be used to protect assets from a beneficiary's personal creditors and misfortunes. A trust can also be used for business or for trading purposes as an alternative to using a company, close corporation or partnership. One of the great advantages of a trust is its flexibility and lack of statutory formality in its creation, administration and operation. The complete law of trusts is not found in a single statute and is not codified. The basis of the law of trusts is neither statute nor a code, but is the common law and decided case law.

---

6   Trustees do not have beneficial ownership but only 'bare' ownership.
7   See Practical Issue below. _Bewind_ trusts are not otherwise dealt with in this book.

18.2 Trusts and the Companies Act, 2008

It is clear from the definitions of 'person' and 'juristic person' (as set out in s 1 of the Companies Act, 2008) that a trust is a juristic person for the purposes of the Act. This is quite important, because a trust is really a relationship or arrangement[8] and, as such, is not (ordinarily) a person in law. A trust is only regarded as a separate legal person if it is recognised as such by legislation. Some statutes do regard a trust as a legal person, such as the Income Tax Act,[9] the Value Added Tax Act,[10] and most recently, the Companies Act, 2008.

The fact that a trust is a person for the purposes of the Companies Act is significant for a number of reasons.

One section of the Companies Act, 2008 that is interesting with respect to trusts is s 40, which deals with the issue of shares and the consideration, if any, received by the company for such share issue. Section 40(5) of the Companies Act, 2008 provides that:

- if the consideration for any shares that are issued or to be issued is in the form of an instrument such that the value of the consideration cannot be realised by the company until a date after the time the shares are to be issued, or
- if the consideration for any shares is in the form of an agreement for future services, future benefits or future payment by the subscribing party,

then the company must upon receiving the instrument or entering into the agreement,

- issue the shares immediately; and
- cause the issued shares to be transferred to a third party, to be held in trust and later transferred to the subscribing party in accordance with a trust agreement.

Thus, for example, if a company has agreed to issue shares for services to be rendered in the future, the shares relating to such agreement must be held in trust until such time as those services have, in fact, been rendered.

| CASE STUDY | **Correctly reflecting a trust as a shareholder**

In *Blue Square Advisory Services (Pty) Ltd v Pogiso*,[11] the issue was whether or not certain persons were lawfully removed as directors of a company by a valid share-holders' resolution at a general meeting of shareholders in terms of the provisions of s 220 of the Companies Act, 1973. The difficulty in this case was that for the resolution of the company to be valid it had to be passed by or on behalf of 'a shareholder'. Whether or not that was done had to be determined with recourse to the register of shareholders. However, the name in the register was the name of a family trust, which under the 1973 Act was neither a person nor a body corporate.

The court (it is submitted, quite correctly) described a trust as a legal relationship, and accordingly found that the share register did not disclose the name of a person. The court confirmed that a trust is a legal relationship incapable of owning anything,[12] and cannot be the shareholder as it is not 'a person'. The names of the trustees should |

---

8   See discussion in para. 18.1 above.
9   58 of 1962, as amended.
10   89 of 1991, as amended.
11   [2011] ZAGPJHC 53.
12   The trustees have non-beneficial ownership of trust assets.

> have been disclosed in the register because they were the (non-beneficial) owners of the shares:
>
> > To the extent that the shares were trust assets, one or more of the trustees' names ought to have been reflected on the register in order to exercise the voting rights attaching to the status of a shareholder.
>
> The court concluded that the resolution removing the directors was passed by a trustee whose name was not reflected on the register as a shareholder. The resolution to remove the directors was not the resolution of 'a shareholder' and was thus invalid and ineffective.

Section 50(2) of the 2008 Act provides inter alia that as soon as practicable after issuing any securities a company must enter or cause to be entered in its securities register, in respect of every class of securities that it has issued: the names and addresses of the persons to whom the securities were issued; and the number of securities issued to each of them. It is therefore submitted that since a trust is regarded as a person in terms of the 2008 Act, the company must reflect the name (and possibly the Master's reference number) of the trust in its securities register as the person to whom the securities have been issued in respect of any certificated shares.

18.3   Trusts and close corporations

Generally speaking, membership of a close corporation is limited to natural persons,[13] and a juristic person cannot directly or indirectly be a member of a close corporation. In other words, a company or another close corporation cannot hold a member's interest in a corporation.

As a result of a 2005 amendment to the Close Corporations Act, a trustee of a trust can be a member of a close corporation in the capacity of trustee. This is so whether the trust is a testamentary or an *inter vivos* trust. However, there are certain restrictions on allowing a trustee to be a member, such as the requirement that no juristic person can be a beneficiary of that trust. The Close Corporations Act provides that a natural or juristic person in the capacity of a trustee of an *inter vivos* trust may be a member of a corporation, provided certain conditions are met. A *trustee* of the trust will be the member of the close corporation, not the trust itself. The following requirements and conditions apply:

- A juristic person cannot (directly or indirectly) be a beneficiary of the trust.
- The corporation is not obliged to observe any clauses in the trust deed – that is, a corporation is not in any way concerned with the provisions of a trust deed and merely looks to the registered trustee (as per the CK 1) in so far as rights and obligations are concerned. Beneficiaries can only look to trustees for their rights, not to the corporation itself.
- If at any time the number of beneficiaries of the trust who are *entitled* to receive any benefit from the trust, when added to the number of members of the corporation, is greater than 10, the membership of the trustee shall cease. Once membership ceases in terms of this condition, no trustee of that trust will ever again be eligible for membership of the trust even though the number (as described in this paragraph) becomes 10 or less.

---

13   Section 29(1) of the Close Corporations Act.

18.4 Business trusts

A **business trust** is quite simply an ordinary trust in which the trustees have been given the power to carry on business and to trade. There is no fundamental difference between a family trust and a business trust, except that in a business trust:

- the trustees have the power to take business risks and to trade with the assets that are held in trust; and
- beneficiaries usually have the right to sell their interest in the trust when they choose to do so.

Ordinarily, a trustee may not expose trust assets to business or other risks, because this would be in breach of a trustee's fiduciary duties,[14] but the trust deed of a business trust specifically gives trustees the power to trade or to carry on a business. Thus, for example, if entrepreneurs want to develop a property for commercial purposes, rather than form a company or close corporation, they can cause a trust to be formed and the trust can acquire the property to be developed. The development of the property will therefore take place under the direction of the trustees of the trust, and the proceeds from the development will accrue to the trust itself.

In *Land and Agricultural Bank of South Africa v Parker*,[15] the court stated that there was nothing inherently wrong with using as flexible an instrument as a trust for business purposes, but the court stressed that the separation between, on the one hand, control and ownership (by trustees), and on the other hand, enjoyment of trust assets (by beneficiaries), is at the very core of trust law and the basis on which it has developed. This principle (that is to say, the distinction between control and enjoyment) is discussed in greater detail later in this chapter.

As stated in *Essack Family Trust v Soni*,[16] it is interesting to note that '... at common law a trustee has no power to carry on business with the assets of a trust estate since he is not allowed to expose them to business risks'. However, a trust deed can expressly give trustees powers to carry on business, which means that a trust deed can allow trustees to expose trust assets to the ordinary risks associated with an authorised type of business. A trading or business trust is therefore very different from a more passive trust that is formed as part of an estate duty plan, or is formed in order to protect assets by ensuring that such assets are beyond the reach of a beneficiary's creditors or other claimants.

The terms of a business trust deed can also be such as to allow beneficiaries to sell, cede or otherwise deal with their interests in the trust, in the same way that a shareholder can deal with shares. A trust can therefore be structured so as to ensure that it resembles a company or close corporation: trustees can be given most of the powers of a director or member, and beneficiaries can be given rights that are similar to those of a shareholder, including the right to sell or otherwise dispose of his or her interest in the trust. In a business trust, beneficiaries are often issued with a certificate of interest in the trust, giving details of the rights of beneficiaries and certain other details such as the reference number of the trust.

Beneficiaries of a trust, as beneficiaries, enjoy limited liability and are not exposed to business risks and failures. However, the same cannot be said of trustees, because they are

---

14 See para. 18.12 below.
15 Supra.
16 1973 (3) SA 625 (D) at 627.

not immune from personal liability if they are reckless or fail to exercise the required duty of care and skill.[17]

A trust can, through its trustee, borrow money, and creditors can look to the trust property alone for the satisfaction of their claims. A great advantage of a trading trust is that it offers the possibility of a limited-liability form of trading without the complexities or expense inherent in trading through a company or close corporation.

However, the danger of a trading trust is that it could be regarded as a partnership, because all the elements of a partnership are often present in such a structure. In order to avoid a trust being regarded as a partnership, the trustees, or at least some of them, should be persons independent of, and different persons from, the beneficiaries.[18] Care must also be taken in the case of a trading trust to ensure that beneficiaries are not seen as the owners of the property subject to the trust. If the terms of the trust deed are interpreted to indicate that the beneficiaries have ownership, it could then be open for a third party to treat the trust either as a *bewind* trust[19] or as a partnership.

What is clear is that a trust is not a body corporate, but a trust can be sequestrated.[20]

CASE STUDY	**Trust treated as partnership**
	In *Khabolan NO v Ralitabo*,[21] a 'trust' was formed for the purpose of acquiring agricultural land on which farming activities were to be conducted. A loan was taken out and the trustees were each to contribute a monthly amount towards the repayment of the loan. No beneficiaries were appointed in the trust instrument. No trustee meetings were held. The court held that it seemed that the parties intended to form a partnership and the alleged trust seemed simulated. The parties to the so-called trust were therefore treated as partners by the court, even though the parties thought that they had formed a valid trust.

18.5   Parties to a trust

The three main parties to any type of trust are the following:

1. *The **founder** of the trust*: the founder is the person who forms or establishes the trust. The founder is also known as the **donor** or **settlor**.

2. *The **trustees***: a trust must have at least one trustee, but can have more than one trustee. Generally speaking, the trustees are responsible for the administration and control of the trust property. The trustees must act within the law and must comply with the provisions of the trust deed. If, for whatever reason, there is no trustee, the Master of the High Court will appoint a trustee.

3. *The **beneficiaries***: these are the persons who benefit in terms of the trust deed. They derive their rights from the terms of the trust deed. There cannot be a valid trust if there is not at least one beneficiary.

---

17 See para. 18.12 below.
18 See *Land and Agricultural Bank of South Africa v Parker* supra, where the court stressed that there was nothing inherently wrong with using as flexible an instrument as a trust for business purposes, but that the separation between control and enjoyment is at the very core of trust law and the basis on which it has developed.
19 See para. 18.1 above.
20 *Magnum Financial Holdings (Pty) Ltd (in liquidation) v Summerly NNO* 1984 (1) SA 160 (W).
21 [2011] ZAFSHC 62.

18.6 The trust deed, deed of trust or trust instrument

A trust has been described as a creation of document – as opposed to a company or close corporation, which are creations of statute. A trust is created by a document (the document is called the **trust deed**, deed of trust or trust instrument) because, generally speaking, a trust is created either by a contract (an *inter vivos* trust) or by the will of a testator (a testamentary trust). As the court stated in *Land and Agricultural Bank of South Africa v Parker*,[22] a trust deed is a trust's 'constitutive charter'.

18.7 Types of trust

Trusts can be classified in a number of different ways, including:
- according to whether the founder is living or dead;
- according to the powers of trustees and the rights of beneficiaries; and
- using other criteria.

These classifications are discussed below.

18.7.1 *Inter vivos* trusts compared with testamentary trusts

Trusts can be formed either during the lifetime of the founder or on the death of a founder. **Testamentary trusts** (also known as will trusts) are trusts that are formed (established) on the death of the founder of the trust. They are formed in terms of the last will and testament of the founder. **Trusts *inter vivos***, however, are trusts formed during the lifetime of the founder. A business or trading trust is likely to fall into this category, as are trusts that are established as part of an estate plan to avoid estate duty and capital gains tax that can arise on a person's death.

18.7.2 Family trusts compared with business trusts

Some trust deeds give trustees extensive powers to carry on trade or business, and also give the beneficiaries the right to sell their interests in the trust to a third party. These are known as business or trading trusts, and can be either public or private. The trust deeds of family trusts, however, are likely to give trustees more limited powers and the rights of beneficiaries are unlikely to be transferable.

In a public trading trust, members of the general public are invited to become income beneficiaries of the trust upon payment of money or assets. In return for the contribution, the member of the public will receive proof of his or her share in the trust in the form of a certificate. Private trading trusts are formed by entrepreneurs whose intention it is to contribute funds towards a business, and to use the trust as a vehicle to carry on that business. The rights of beneficiaries are such that they can be transferred to other beneficiaries upon the payment of an amount of money. In other words, a beneficiary of a business trust usually has the right to sell his or her interest in the trust. These so-called trading or business trusts are used by business people as an alternative to other business entities, such as a company or close corporation.

Family trusts are formed primarily to protect and preserve assets for future generations. Although trustees in this type of trust are usually given powers of investment, investment

---

22 Supra.

decisions by such trustees are primarily aimed at long-term growth, rather than short-term speculation or trading.

18.7.3   Other trusts

Other types of trust include statutory trusts (formed in terms of a specific statute for a particular purpose, such as a trust established to own and run a game reserve), court-order trusts (these trusts are formed in terms of an order of court – for example, to settle a divorce action), charitable trusts (formed to serve some cause or charity), and international trusts or offshore trusts. An international or offshore trust is one that is formed outside South Africa and is not subject to the jurisdiction of the Master of the High Court in South Africa.

18.8   Legal nature of trusts

As mentioned in paragraph 18.6 above, a trust is a creation of document – unlike companies or close corporations, which are creations of statute. Generally speaking, a trust is either created by a contract (an *inter vivos* trust) or by the last will and testament of a testator (a testamentary trust).

It has been seen from the definition of a trust that a trust must be reduced to writing. There must therefore be a document, either a written contract (creating an *inter vivos* trust) or a will (creating a testamentary trust).

The case of *Crookes NO v Watson*,[23] one of the leading cases dealing with *inter vivos* trusts, makes it clear that an *inter vivos* trust is really a contract. The contract is entered into between the founder and the trustees, who accept the office of trustee subject to the terms of the trust deed. A testamentary trust, on the other hand, is a legal institution in its own right. It is not a contract, but comes into being on the death of the founder. It is thus created by the last will and testament of a deceased.

It also follows logically that if the trust is created by a will, the formalities prescribed in the Wills Act[24] must be followed. If, however, the trust is created *inter vivos*, the formalities prescribed for a valid contract must be followed.

18.9   Consequences of forming a valid trust

Once a valid trust has been formed, certain legal consequences follow.

On the one hand, the trustees will have certain obligations, duties and powers. The obligations and duties of trustees are set out in the Trust Property Control Act.[25] They are also found in the common law, and in the trust deed itself. The powers of trustees are found in the provisions of the trust deed.

On the other hand, the beneficiaries will have certain rights. The rights of beneficiaries are ascertained by the contents of the trust deed, and certain protections of those rights are to be found in certain sections of the Trust Property Control Act. A beneficiary could have **vested rights** or **discretionary rights** (or even a combination of the two – for example, a vested right to income, but only a discretionary right to the capital of the trust).

---

23   1956 (1) SA 277 (A).
24   7 of 1953.
25   Supra.

18.10   How to form a valid trust

The following are the essential elements for the creation of a valid trust:
- There must be the intention by the founder to create a trust and this intention must be expressed in a way that creates an obligation. The obligation must be imposed on the trustees to manage and control the assets under their care for the benefit of the beneficiaries of the trust.
- The object of the trust must be lawful.
- The trust property must be defined with certainty.
- The trust object must be sufficiently certain.
- The beneficiaries must be ascertained or ascertainable or the impersonal object must be clearly defined. A trust without a beneficiary is a nullity.
- There must be at least one beneficiary. If there is no identified or identifiable beneficiary, no trust has been created.
- The trust should be reduced to writing in a trust deed or deed of trust.
- At least one trustee should be appointed either in terms of the trust deed or, if no appointment is made or is possible in terms of the trust deed, the appointment must be made by the Master. A trustee must have the capacity to act as trustee and the person must not be disqualified from acting as trustee. Furthermore, the person appointed must obtain written authorisation by the Master to act as trustee.

CASE STUDY	**Trustees must be under an obligation**
	In *Estate Price v Baker and Price*,[26] a will gave the surviving spouse a usufruct 'in order that she may be better enabled to maintain our children until they become of age or they marry'. It was held that no 'trust' was created in favour of the children (that is, they were not 'beneficiaries'), since the words merely expressed a desire. The surviving spouse was 'enabled' but not 'compelled' to use the income for the children. In other words, she was not under 'an obligation' to maintain the children. It is therefore clear that a trust must ensure that a trustee or the trustees are under a legal obligation to manage the assets on behalf of others.

18.11   Authorisation of trustees

The Trust Property Control Act defines a trustee[27] as any person who acts as trustee by virtue of an authorisation under s 6 of the Trust Property Control Act. Section 6(1) of the Trust Property Control Act provides that any person can only act as a trustee once they have been authorised by the Master to act as such.

CASE STUDY	**No legal consequences if trustee is unauthorised**
	In the case of *Simplex (Pty) Ltd v van der Merwe NNO*,[28] the court had to decide exactly what was meant by s 6 of the Trust Property Control Act.

26   (1905) 22 SC 321 (C).
27   Section 1 of the Trust Property Control Act 57 of 1988, and see W Geach *Trusts: Law and Practice* (2007).
28   1996 (1) SA 111 (W).

The court held that this section was not enacted purely for the benefit of the beneficiaries, but that it was in the public interest to provide written proof to outsiders of the incumbency of the office of trustees. The court concluded that an act by a person acting with no authority from the Master has no legal consequences. In other words, before a trustee can act as a trustee, that person must obtain the prior written consent of the Master to act as a trustee as required by s 6.

In this case, there had been an application to eject certain persons from a property that had been 'purchased' by trustees who had not been authorised by the Master to act as such. The application was granted by the court because the purchase agreement was held to be null and void because it had been signed by a person who had not yet been authorised by the Master to act as a trustee.

The other question raised in this case was whether the purchase agreement could be resuscitated by subsequent ratification, either by the Master or by the trustees once the trustees had been authorised by the Master to act as such. The court upheld the following legal principle: 'There can be no ratification of an agreement which a statutory prohibition has rendered *ab initio* void in the sense that it is to be regarded as never having been concluded.'

Similarly, in *Watt v Sea Plant Products Bpk*,[29] s 6(1) was interpreted to mean that a trustee could not, prior to authorisation, acquire rights for, or contractually incur liabilities on behalf of, a trust.

It should therefore be noted that it is highly problematic for a person to act as a trustee on behalf of a trust that is still to be formed. Such a person cannot act as a trustee, because he or she has not yet been authorised to act in that capacity by the Master. By comparison, the Companies Act, 2008 allows for so-called pre-incorporation contracts in terms of s 21 of the Act, but the Trust Property Control Act does not have any similar section.

The trustee of a trust can be a beneficiary of that trust, but the roles of trustee and beneficiary must not be confused or merged. Only a trustee can control and manage a trust acting as a trustee. If there is more than one trustee, the trustees must act together. A beneficiary, acting as a beneficiary, cannot manage or control trust assets.

CASE STUDY	**Trustee should be independent**
	The court, in *Land and Agricultural Bank of South Africa v Parker*,[30] made it clear that the core idea of the trust concept is the separation of ownership (or control) from enjoyment. Although a trustee can also be a beneficiary, the central notion is that the person entrusted with control exercises it on behalf of and in the interests of another. The court held as follows: 'This is why a sole trustee cannot also be the sole beneficiary: such a situation would embody an identity of interests that is inimical to the trust idea, and no trust would come into existence.'

---

29   [1998] 4 All SA 109 (C).
30   Supra.

18.12   Duties of trustees

The Trust Property Control Act[31] imposes onerous duties on a trustee. In addition to the duties imposed in terms of the provisions of the Act, certain duties also arise in terms of the common law because of the fiduciary nature of the trustee's position.

The statutory and common-law duties of a trustee include the following:

- A trustee must act with the care, diligence and skill that can reasonably be expected of a person who manages the affairs of another.[32] Section 9(2) of the Trust Property Control Act specifically provides that any provision contained in a trust instrument shall be void – that is, be of no force and effect – in so far as it would have the effect of exempting a trustee from, or indemnifying him or her against, liability for breach of trust where he or she fails to show the degree of care, diligence and skill required in terms of s 9(1).
- A trustee must open a separate **trust account** at a banking institution.[33] This means that there must be a separate bank account for each trust and that the funds of one trust cannot be mixed with those of another.
- A trustee must keep records indicating the property that is held by the trustee in trust.[34]
- A trustee must make any account or investment at a financial institution identifiable as a trust account or trust investment.[35]
- A trustee must, at the written request of the Master, account to the Master in accordance with the Master's requirements, for the trustee's administration and disposal of trust property.[36]
- A trustee may not destroy any document that serves as proof of the investment, safe custody, administration, alienation or distribution of trust property before the expiry of a period of five years from the termination of the trust, without the written consent of the Master.[37]
- A trustee must give effect to the terms of the trust deed or trust instrument.
- A trustee must act with the utmost good faith.
- A trustee must exercise an independent discretion at all times with respect to trust matters.
- A trustee must not expose the assets of a trust to undue risk.[38] Thus, an unsecured loan or one at less than the market rate of interest is not a good investment.[39] However, in a business or trading trust, trustees are specifically given powers to carry on business or to trade.[40] By implication, the granting of these powers allows a trustee to assume normal business risks associated with the carrying on of a business or trade.
- A trustee must invest the trust property productively. In *Administrators Estate Richards v Nichol*,[41] it was stated that if the trust is to endure for a long period, the trustees are obliged to invest the assets of the trust in a manner that provides adequate income as well as capital growth.

---

31   57 of 1988.
32   Section 9(1) of the Trust Property Control Act.
33   Section 10 of the Trust Property Control Act.
34   Section 11 of the Trust Property Control Act.
35   Section 11 of the Trust Property Control Act.
36   Section 16 of the Trust Property Control Act.
37   Section 17 of the Trust Property Control Act.
38   *Sackville West v Nourse* 1925 AD 516.
39   *Ex Parte Bennett NO* 1969 (3) SA 598 (N).
40   See para. 18.13 below.
41   1999 (1) SA 551 (A).

- A trustee must account to the beneficiaries. In *Doyle v Board of Executors*,[42] the court held that there was a duty on those who occupied a fiduciary position to keep proper accounts. In this case, a beneficiary alleged that the accounts presented to him were not sufficient. The court held that in cases where an account had been rendered, but it was alleged that it was insufficient, the court might enquire into and determine the issue of sufficiency. The court made it clear that it enjoyed a discretion to deal with that matter with such flexibility as practical justice required.
- A trustee must act within the powers granted in terms of the trust deed. If a power is not stipulated, it will not be inferred. The power to sell a property does not grant the power to mortgage the property.

It is evident that the duties of a trustee are onerous and a person should never accept appointment as a trustee unless he or she is familiar with these duties and is confident in his or her capabilities to carry out such duties. A person should never accept appointment as a trustee and then leave all future actions and decisions to the other trustee(s). This would amount to extreme negligence and could cause that person to become subject to legal claims for compensation, if trust assets are badly managed or lost.

CASE STUDY	**Trustees ordered to account**

Trustees ordered to account

In *Thabantsho Beneficiaries Association v Rammupudu II NO*,[43] a trust was established to hold land on behalf of the beneficiaries of the trust. The beneficiaries demanded that the trustees account for the monies accrued and accruing to the trust on behalf of the beneficiaries, from the time that a certain lease was entered into.

The beneficiaries had lodged a complaint with the Master about the manner in which the funds meant for the benefit of the beneficiaries were allegedly handled and the apparent lack of accountability to the beneficiaries by the trustees. The Master sent letters to the trustees requesting delivery to the Master of copies of all books, records, accounts, or documents relating to the administration or disposal of the trust properties within 30 days. The request was made in terms of s 16(1) of the Trust Property Control Act.

When a response was not forthcoming from the trustees, a second letter was sent, requesting a response within 14 days. When there was still no response, the Master threatened to remove them as trustees, and the beneficiaries applied to court. The court held that the beneficiaries had a right in terms of s 19 to bring the application to court. Section 19 provides as follows:

> If any trustee fails to comply with a request by the Master in terms of section 16 or to perform any duty imposed upon him by the trust instrument or by law, the Master or any person having an interest in the trust property may apply to the court for an order directing the trustee to comply with such request or to perform such duty.

The court ordered the trustees to submit to the Master all books, records, accounts or documents relating to the administration of the trust, and the court interdicted the trustees from continuing to use the trust monies of the trust until the order was complied with and the books, records and accounts had been audited by a legally recognised auditor.

18.13 Powers of trustees

A trustee derives his or her powers from the trust deed. If a trust deed makes no provision for a particular power, it is to be inferred that the founder intended that the trustee should not have that power. The reason for this is that the trustee should really preserve and protect trust assets, and this should be done, as far as possible, free from risk. Nevertheless, it is now fashionable for trust deeds to give trustees extensive powers. This is particularly the case if the trust is going to be trading or carrying on some business.

18.14 Rights of beneficiaries

A trust must have a beneficiary, or it fails. In other words, a trust without a beneficiary is a nullity. The purpose of a trust is usually for trustees to manage and control trust assets on behalf of a beneficiary or beneficiaries. A beneficiary should be identified or identifiable. In other words, a trust can provide for beneficiaries who exist or for a beneficiary who has yet to be born. The founder of the trust can be a beneficiary. A trustee can also be a beneficiary. Any rights of a beneficiary (even discretionary rights) can be ceded, provided, of course, that this is not prohibited by the trust deed itself. In a so-called business trust, the trust deed will usually be specific and allow a beneficiary to cede or otherwise dispose of his or her rights in the trust.

THIS CHAPTER IN ESSENCE

1. A **trust** is a legal relationship created in a trust deed (otherwise known as a trust instrument). The relationship is created by the **founder** (**donor** or **settlor**), who intentionally places assets under the control of another (the **trustee**) for the benefit of third persons (the **beneficiaries**).
2. The Trust Property Control Act 57 of 1988 regulates trusts on a mainly administrative level. The basis of the law of trusts is the common law and decided case law.
3. The Trust Property Control Act envisages two types of trust: one where the ownership and control of trust assets lies with the trustees (an **ordinary trust**), and the other where the beneficiary or beneficiaries have ownership of trust assets, but these are under the control of the trustees (a *bewind* **trust**).
4. Ordinary trusts are formed for estate-planning purposes, asset-protection purposes, and for business purposes. The trustees' ownership of trust assets is non-beneficial ownership.
5. For the purposes of the Companies Act, 2008, a trust is a juristic person.
6. A **business trust** is an ordinary trust in which the trustees have been given the power to carry on business and to trade. The terms of a business trust deed can structure the trust to resemble a company or close corporation, with trustees being given the powers of a director or member, and beneficiaries similar rights to shareholders, including the right to sell or otherwise dispose of their interests in the trust.
7. A trust is created by a document (called the **trust deed**, deed of trust or trust instrument) because a trust is created either by a contract (an *inter vivos* **trust**) or by the will of a testator (a **testamentary trust**). If the trust is created by a will, the formalities prescribed in the Wills Act 7 of 1953 must be followed. The formalities prescribed for a valid contract must be followed for an *inter vivos* trust.

8. The difference between a family trust and a business trust is evident in the difference in the powers given to the trustees and the rights that beneficiaries have. Business trust deeds generally give trustees extensive powers to carry on trade or business, and also give beneficiaries the right to sell their interests in the trust to a third party. The trust deeds of **family trusts** (formed primarily to protect and preserve assets for future generations) are likely to give trustees more limited powers and the rights of beneficiaries are unlikely to be transferable.

9. Business trusts may be public or private. In a public trading trust, members of the general public are invited to become income beneficiaries of the trust upon payment of money or assets. Private trading trusts are formed by entrepreneurs whose intention it is to contribute funds towards a business, and to use the trust as a vehicle to carry on that business.

10. Trustees must be authorised under the Trust Property Control Act to act as trustees. They then have many onerous duties in terms of the Act and at common law, and certain powers in terms of the trust deed. Many of a trustee's duties arise owing to the fiduciary nature of the trustee's position. Among other duties, a trustee must act with the care, diligence and skill expected of a person who manages the affairs of another; open a **trust bank account** and keep scrupulous records of trust property; account to the Master and to beneficiaries; act with utmost good faith; exercise independent discretion; invest assets productively; and act in terms of the trust deed.

11. Beneficiaries (who must be identified or identifiable) have rights as granted in the trust deed, and certain protections of those rights are found in the Trust Property Control Act. A beneficiary could have **vested rights** or **discretionary rights**. If the trust deed allows, the rights of a beneficiary may be ceded or transferred.

12. A trustee of a trust can also be a beneficiary of the trust, but the roles of trustee and beneficiary must not be confused or merged.

Chapter 19

Financial markets

19.1 Introduction

A **stock exchange** is an organised and regulated financial market where securities (bonds, notes, shares, derivatives) are bought and sold. Stock exchanges typically provide a primary market where corporations, governments and municipalities can raise capital from investors, and a secondary market where investors can sell their securities to other investors.

As of July 2009, there is a single licensed exchange in South Africa – namely, the **Johannesburg Stock Exchange (JSE)**. Exchanges in South Africa are licensed in terms of the **Financial Markets Act (FMA)**,[1] which is the legislation that creates the framework for their operation and regulation. The exchange operates under the auspices of the registrar and deputy registrar of securities services, who have the responsibility for ensuring compliance of regulated persons in terms of the FMA.

---

1   19 of 2012.

19.2 The Johannesburg Stock Exchange (JSE)

The JSE was established in 1887 and has evolved dramatically since that time. Over time, through a combination of organic growth and acquisition, the JSE has become a 'vertically and horizontally integrated exchange'. This means that the JSE not only connects buyers and sellers in a variety of different financial markets – namely equities, financial derivatives, commodity derivatives and interest rate instruments (horizontal integration), but also provides listing, trading, clearing, and settlement services for these markets (vertical integration). The JSE, as a self-regulatory organisation, is also responsible for regulating both the members that trade in its markets, and the companies listed on its equities market.

Understanding the JSE and its current role in the South African financial landscape requires some understanding of its history.

19.2.1 History of the JSE

A brief history of the JSE is set out in Table 19.1 below.

Table 19.1 History of the JSE

Date	Event
1887	The JSE is established as a stock exchange in response to the discovery of gold on the Witwatersrand and the consequent need to raise capital to finance mining and exploration activity.
1947	The first legislation applicable to the operation of exchanges is the Stock Exchanges Control Act.[2]
1963	JSE becomes a member of the World Federation of Exchanges.
1979	Krugerrands are officially listed.
1995	Substantial amendments are made to the legislation applicable to stock exchanges, which result in the deregulation of the JSE through the introduction of limited liability corporate and foreign membership. The South African Institute of Stockbrokers is formed to represent, train and set standards for the qualification of stockbrokers.
1996	The open-outcry trading floor is closed on 7 June and replaced by an order-driven, centralised, automated trading system known as the Johannesburg Equities Trading (JET) system. Dual trading capacity and negotiated brokerage is introduced.
1997	A real-time news service, SENS (Securities Exchange News Service and then known as Stock Exchange News Service), for the dissemination of company announcements and price-sensitive information is introduced. SENS ensures early and wide dissemination of all information that may have an effect on the prices of securities that trade on the JSE.
1999	In January, the new Insider Trading Act[3] is introduced based on recommendations made by the King Task Group on Corporate Governance, which included representatives from the JSE. The JSE establishes, in collaboration with South Africa's four largest commercial banks, the electronic settlement system, Strate, and the process to dematerialise (the process of converting paper securities to electronic records) and electronically settle securities listed on the JSE on a rolling, contractual and guaranteed basis is initiated.

---

2 7 of 1947.
3 135 of 1998.

Date	Event
2000	The JSE successfully lists Satrix 40, the JSE's first exchange-traded fund aimed at individual and first time investors and which tracks the top 40 companies listed on the JSE's Main Board.
2001	The JSE acquires SAFEX, the South African Futures Exchange, and becomes the leader in both equities and equity and agricultural derivatives trading in the South African market.
2002	All listed securities are successfully dematerialised and migrated to the Strate electronic settlement environment, with rolling, contractual and guaranteed settlement for equities taking place five days after trade (T+5). Since the completion of this process, the JSE has had a near-zero failed trade record, contributing to market integrity and representing a major milestone in winning both local and international investor confidence.
	The JET equities trading system is replaced by the London Stock Exchange's (LSE) SETS system, hosted by the LSE in London. The JSE also introduces the LSE's LMIL system to provide an enhanced information dissemination system and substantially improve the distribution of real-time equities market information. The introduction of JSE SETS also represented the forging of a strategic alliance with the LSE and improved the international visibility of the JSE.
	The JSE takes another important step forward in its campaign to modernise its operations with the launch of a new free float indexing system in conjunction with FTSE, namely the FTSE/JSE African Index Series to replace the then existing indices. The FTSE/JSE African Index Series enhances the investability of South African stocks by providing foreign investors with an indexing system with which they are familiar.
	Two new exchange-traded funds are launched, namely Satrix Fini, which tracks the top 15 financial counters and Satrix Indi, which tracks the top 25 industrial counters, on the Main Board of the JSE.
2003	The JSE launches AltX, a parallel equities market developed in partnership with the Department of Trade and Industry and focused on good quality small and medium-sized high growth companies.
2004	The JSE launches the Socially Responsible Investment (SRI) Index, which measures compliance by companies with triple bottom-line criteria for economic, environmental and social sustainability, as well as corporate governance practice.
2005	The JSE launches Yield-X, its market for a wide range of interest rate products.
	The JSE (until this point, owned by its members) demutualises and incorporates in South Africa as JSE Limited, a public unlisted company on 1 July. Existing rights holders of the JSE become its first shareholders and for the first time in the JSE's history, a person who is not an authorised user of the JSE or a stockbroker can own a share in the JSE itself. Over-the-counter trading in JSE shares commences with settlement of the trades occurring through Strate.
2006	In June, the JSE Ltd lists on the Main Board of the exchange. Unlike other listed companies, the JSE's listing is regulated not by the JSE's Issuer Regulation department, but by the Financial Services Board.
2007	In April, the JSE migrates its equities trading to the new LSE trading platform. The JSE also receives exchange control dispensation to launch a market for the trading of currency derivatives.

Date	Event
2009	The JSE launches its Africa Board aimed at attracting African companies.
	In June, the JSE acquires the Bond Exchange of Africa (BESA) and begins the process of merging BESA and the JSE's interest rate markets. The JSE also wins the Future and Options World award for 'Top Contract of the Year' (Can Do Options).
2010	The World Economic Forum's annual competitiveness report ranks South Africa first in the world for securities market regulation.
2012	The JSE again replaces its equities trading platform, this time with a solution provided by the London Stock Exchange's Millennium IT. The new trading platform is now hosted in Johannesburg.
	The JSE relooks its Africa strategy and effectively incorporates the Africa Board into the JSE's Main Board.
	The JSE – as part of its alliance with the BRICS exchanges (the Bombay Stock Exchange, BM&F Bovespa in Brazil, the Hong Kong Exchanges, and Micex-RTS in Russia) – lists derivatives on the benchmark equity indices of the partner exchanges. The JSE's benchmark Top 40 futures contract is likewise listed on the other exchanges.
	The JSE responds to regulatory changes after the global financial crisis by ensuring that its clearing house for derivatives (SAFCOM) is CPSS-IOSCO compliant. Under new banking regulations, banks that are exposed to non-CPSS-IOSCO compliant clearing houses would face much higher capital charges. In this way, the JSE limits the capital exposure of its banking participants.
	For the third year running, South Africa is ranked first in the world for securities market regulation.
	The JSE receives regulatory permission to list a dollar-denominated Zambian grain contract on its commodity derivatives market. This is done in collaboration with the Zambian Grain Traders Association who will use the derivative contract for purposes of managing price risk.
	The Namibian government lists its first rand-denominated sovereign bond on the JSE.

19.2.2   Some facts and figures about the JSE

As at February 2013, the JSE had 397 listed companies, of which 61 were listed on its market for small and medium capitalisation companies.[4] Of the 397 listed companies, 52 were foreign companies. The JSE's market capitalisation at that point was R8.6 trillion.

The main indicator of the equity market's performance is the FTSE/JSE All Share Index (sometimes known as the Alsi). Other commonly referenced indices are the FTSE/JSE Top 40 Index, the FTSE/JSE Industrial 25 and FTSE/JSE Financial 15. A **share** (or **stock**) **index** is a statistical indicator used to measure changes in the market value of a group of underlying stocks. For example, as can be deduced from the name, the FTSE/JSE Top 40 Index measures the change in value, as represented by share price, of the top 40 (or 40 largest by market capitalisation) companies listed on the JSE.[5] It is precisely because indices serve to aggregate

---

4   The market capitalisation of a company is determined by multiplying the number of issued shares in the company by the price at which the shares are trading.

5   This is a slightly simplified definition. There are a number of factors that go into the calculation of an index and the determination of how and at what value companies are included in an index. In addition, it is not the absolute value of the index that matters, but rather the relative changes in the value of the index.

the changes in the share prices of the underlying companies that they by and large serve as shorthand for the overall well-being of the economy. The indices also form the basis of exchange-traded products such as Exchange Traded Funds, aimed at individual investors who wish for uncomplicated access to the JSE's equities.

The JSE's commodity derivatives market is currently the only functioning commodity derivatives market on the continent (although this is set to change with a number of parties looking to establish a commodity market in the east African region). This market had its origins in agricultural derivatives and these instruments still play a vital role in price determination and transparency in the local agricultural market, while providing an efficient price risk management facility.

The JSE is one of only four African exchanges that is a member of the World Federation of Exchanges (the other three are Egypt, Morocco and Mauritius). It is by far the largest and most diversified exchange on the continent and still accounts for approximately 70 per cent of the market capitalisation of the exchanges on the continent (of which there are over 20).

19.2.3   Becoming a public listed company

There are a number of potential benefits associated with a listing on the JSE. These include:

- *Accessing capital for growth*: listing gives companies the opportunity to raise capital from the public to fund acquisitions as well as growth.
- *Boosting company profile*: listing generally raises a company's public profile with customers, suppliers, the media and investors. As a result of this enhanced public profile, more business opportunities may become available (although there is obviously also greater scrutiny associated with a listing).
- *Creating value and liquidity for shareholders*: because a listed company's value is independently assessed by the marketplace, shareholders can realise their investment, liquidity is stimulated and the shareholder base may be broadened.
- *Facilitating broad-based black economic empowerment (BEE) deals*: a listing allows companies to facilitate broad-based black economic empowerment (BEE) deals, a prerequisite to effective corporate citizenship in South Africa.
- *Facilitating share incentive schemes*: a listed company is more easily able to offer share incentive schemes to employees to encourage commitment and improve the quality of recruits.

That said, not all companies are eligible for a listing. All listed companies are bound to comply on an initial and ongoing basis with the **listings requirement**s of the JSE. These impose requirements on the company beyond those required under the Companies Act, 2008. Complying with these can be expensive in terms of cost and management time. Listed companies may also be sanctioned (penalised) by the JSE, if they breach the listings requirements.

Some of the key requirements for listing on one of the JSE's equity boards are set out in Table 19.2 below.

As part of the process of applying for a listing, a company must produce a pre-listing statement containing certain prescribed information concerning the company, its business and its prospects. While the pre-listing statement may promote investment in the company's shares, it is not an invitation to the public to subscribe for shares. Rather, it is aimed at enabling potential investors to make an informed investment decision regarding the company's shares. If the pre-listing statement contains a public offer, it will also have to comply with the prospectus provisions contained in s 100 of the Companies Act, 2008.

Table 19.2 JSE listing requirements

Requirement	Main Board	AltX
Share capital	R25m	R2m
Profit history	3 years	n/a
Pre-tax profit	R8m	n/a
Shareholder spread[6]	20%	10%
Minimum number of shareholders	500	100
Sponsor/designated adviser[7]	Sponsor	Designated Adviser
Educational requirements	n/a	All directors to attend the Directors Induction Programme (DIP)

19.3 The Financial Markets Act 19 of 2012 (FMA)

The FMA repeals and replaces the Securities Services Act.[8] It also amends certain incidental provisions in other statutes. The FMA came into operation on 3 June 2013.

The Securities Services Act at the time of its commencement consolidated the regulatory framework in South Africa dealing with financial markets. According to the Explanatory Memorandum to the Financial Markets Bill, the Securities Services Act aligned the supervision of South African financial markets with then-prevailing international developments and standards.

Effective securities regulation is an ongoing challenge. It requires the regular review and assessment of established legislative and regulatory frameworks. According to the National Treasury, recent developments in local and international financial markets and the global financial crisis necessitated amendments to the South African legislative and regulatory framework.

19.3.1 Overview of the FMA

The most important conceptual innovation contained in the FMA deals with the regulatory approach to systemic risk. The principal object in this regard is to reduce such risk. **Systemic risk** is defined as the danger of a failure or disruption of the whole or a significant part of the South African financial system.

The registrar of securities services (the registrar), who is the regulator under the FMA, is required under the FMA to report any matter that may pose a systemic risk to the financial system to the Minister of Finance (the Minister) and the Governor of the South African Reserve Bank (the governor). The FMA therefore creates an important new role for the Reserve Bank. The governor is, for the first time, included within the ambit of legislation of

---

6   Shareholder spread means that of the shares being listed, a certain percentage must be held by the public – i.e. must not be held or owned by persons associated with the company such as a director of the company.

7   A sponsor (or designated adviser (DA) in the case of an Alt-X company) is an entity approved by the JSE to act as such. The company is required to appoint an approved sponsor when it decides to seek a listing, and the sponsor is responsible for ensuring that the company complies with the JSE's Listings Requirements on an ongoing basis. The sponsor is also the conduit between the listed company and the JSE.

8   36 of 2004.

this nature and plays a role, not only in areas of systemic risk, but also in the case of the oversight of trade repositories and clearing houses. The registrar is likewise required to cooperate with other regulators and the governor in relation to systemic risk and related matters.

In summary, the provisions dealing with systemic risk fall into two categories:

1. The first simply imposes a reporting responsibility on the registrar in the event that the registrar perceives circumstances to be indicative of systemic risk.
2. The second simply requires that market infrastructures not do anything that could result in or cause systemic risk.

The FMA introduces important innovations in relation to the regulation of capital markets in South Africa in comparison with its predecessor. The architecture of the FMA is premised upon the so-called twin-peak approach now being applied in South Africa in relation to prudential and market-conduct regulation. The first of the two peaks deals with the prudential requirements applicable to those active in capital markets, particularly banks and insurance companies. In this instance, the Reserve Bank is the lead regulator on macro-prudential, micro-prudential and financial stability issues. The second of the two peaks deals with market conduct. In this case, the Financial Services Board is the lead regulator on market conduct for financial services. It regulates market conduct of all aspects of financial services, including, banking, insurance, advisory and other related services.

The FMA has much the same subject matter as its predecessor. The key differences are:
- the introduction of measures to deal with financial crisis;
- increased regulation in respect of over-the-counter derivative financial instruments;
- the creation of a new type of clearing house;
- the creation of a so-called trade repository;
- an increase in the duties and powers of the registrar; and
- the resolution of certain inefficiencies in relation to insider trading regulation.

19.3.2   Purpose and functions of the FMA

The purpose of the FMA (as was the case with its predecessor) is to balance investor protection and enhance the international competitiveness of securities services in South Africa. The FMA promotes confidence in the South African securities market, locally as well as internationally, by regulating and supervising all aspects of securities markets in line with international developments and regulatory standards. The functions of the FMA thus include:
- the custody and administration of securities;
- the provision of clearing house services to an exchange;
- regulating exchanges on which securities may be traded; and
- the introduction of trade repositories.

19.3.3   Application of the FMA

The FMA principally regulates those participating in the financial markets from a service-provider supply-side perspective, both in respect of the supply of services and the provision of the infrastructure that provides the practical structure to the composition of what is loosely referred to as the financial market. Such regulation requires the definition of:

1. regulated person; and
2. market infrastructure.

'**Regulated person**' means a person involved in financial markets for purposes of the FMA. These include:

- licensed central securities depositories;
- clearing houses;
- exchanges;
- trade repositories;
- authorised users;
- clearing members;
- nominees;
- participants;
- issuers (in certain cases); and
- any other persons designated as such by the Minister.

The FMA makes use of this definition, for example, by providing that codes of conduct apply commonly to regulated persons, depending on their specific activities.

According to s 1 of the FMA, '**market infrastructure**' means each of the following:

- a licensed central securities depository;
- a licensed clearing house;
- a licensed exchange; and
- a licensed trade repository.

These persons, for example, are all required to inform the registrar of events that may pose systemic risk to the financial markets. The latter term is unfortunately not itself defined and is to be inferred from the activities conducted by those regulated under the FMA.

19.3.4 Regulation of trading securities

The FMA governs all things related to the buying and selling of securities, both listed and unlisted, and market abuse. In the case of the former, the FMA divides the value chain relating to the buying and the selling of listed shares into discrete steps. In the case of the latter, the FMA deals with market abuse manifested in the forms of insider trading and market manipulation.

The discrete steps in the buying and selling of securities on an exchange are:

1. The securities in question must be listed on the exchange.
2. The securities are held in safekeeping – detailed rules deal with the holding and transfer of securities.
3. The transfer of securities must be cleared and settled.

In the case of the first of these discrete steps, the FMA regulates and governs exchanges. This step also regulates the requirements applicable to issuers of securities who wish to list their securities on the exchange in question.

'Exchange' is defined in the FMA as a person who constitutes, maintains and provides an infrastructure:

- for bringing together buyers and sellers of securities;
- for matching bids and offers for securities of multiple buyers and sellers; and
- whereby a matched bid and offer for securities constitutes a transaction.

An exchange functions via intermediaries, generally known as brokers or stockbrokers. In other words, those who trade in listed securities employ the services of brokers to trade on their behalf. These brokers are defined as authorised users.

19.3.4.1   Authorised users

The gatekeepers between those who buy and sell securities, and the exchange on which such securities are traded, are the authorised users. The FMA governs authorised users in two ways. Firstly, authorised users must comply with the rules of the exchange applicable to authorised users. Secondly, the FMA directly regulates authorised users by providing for the formulation of a code of conduct by the registrar with which authorised users are required to comply.

The FMA prescribes a **code of conduct** for authorised users, their officers, employees and clients. The FMA prescribes the basic principles for the code, while the code deals with general duties of authorised users, furnishing of advice, disclosure to clients, record-keeping, inducements, advertisements, and client statements.

19.3.4.2   Custody and administration of securities

The second discrete step is the one relating to the **custody and administration of securities**. Generally, those buying and selling securities do not want to be burdened by the responsibility of taking physical delivery of the underlying certificates of securities acquired, nor for the subsequent safekeeping of such certificates, or for the arrangements for transfer of such certificates on disposal. It is convenient to use service providers for this purpose. The FMA therefore regulates persons providing custody and administration services to the holders of securities. This ensures that transactions taking place on an exchange are efficiently discharged.

However, the provision of a custody and administration service is not only about the provision of the service itself. It is also about the convenience of a single custody and administration platform where transactions between market participants using the services of different custody and administration service providers can be recorded, and where arrangements regarding the transfer of securities between these service providers are carried out in accordance with acceptable standards and protocols.

The FMA then also regulates the provision of such a common platform. The person providing the common custody-and-administration platform is defined as the **central securities depository**. Those persons providing general custody and administration services to market participants and who use the common platform for the reasons referred to are defined as **participants**. Put differently, the gatekeepers between those who buy and sell securities and the central securities depository are the participants.

Furthermore, certificates of listed securities issued under the Companies Act, 2008 are now issued and traded in **dematerialised** form – that is, these securities are not evidenced by physical certificates. A system had to be devised whereby the issue and subsequent transfer of such dematerialised certificates could be reliably recorded in accordance with practices accepted by all market participants.

In the case of material certificates or physical certificates, such certificates are evidence of the security in question (and of the owner or the person holding it on behalf of the owner). However, upon the issue or subsequent disposal of securities by one person (the owner thereof) to another, the person disposing of the securities delivers the certificate/s to the person acquiring the securities as evidence of the transaction.

In the case of dematerialised certificates, these same requirements can of course not be met in the same way. Rather, requirements for evidence of a transfer of securities are met by simply recording these acts (that is, of the initial issue of the security in question, and subsequent transfers) as entries in a central registry designed for that purpose.

When these provisions were first formulated, it was decided that a central securities depository (also licensed for that purpose under the FMA) would be well suited to administer the central record-keeping required in order to ensure the efficient and reliable administration of the issuing and trading of dematerialised certificates.

Where holders of securities request physical certificates from the issuer of the securities in question, and wish to place such certificates in the custody of another for the reasons mentioned, the central securities depository plays the same role as in the case of dematerialised certificates. However, in order to transact securities on an exchange, disposers of securities may only do so in relation to dematerialised certificates. The issuer in question will thereafter record in its records or securities' registers that the securities in question have been transferred. This obviously prevents fraud.

The process of the dematerialisation of securities in the South African equities market was started in March 2001 and completed in 2003, replacing manual settlement of share transactions with electronic settlement. Only dematerialised securities, as noted already, are good for settlement on the JSE. At present, the only licensed central securities depository in South Africa is Share Transactions Totally Electronic Limited, better known by its acronym, STRATE.

Any person who wishes to deposit securities in STRATE must first open an uncertificated securities account with a central securities depository participant or CSD participant (defined in the FMA simply as a participant). To date, the following institutions qualify as CSD participants: ABSA Bank Limited, First Rand Bank Limited, Nedbank Group Limited, Computershare, Société Générale (Johannesburg) and the Standard Bank of South Africa Limited.

At an investor level, there are broadly two types of client from a custody and administration perspective:

1. The first type elects to keep their shares and cash in the custody of their brokers. All brokers are required to maintain accounts with a CSD participant. In as much as only CSD participants are permitted to deal directly with STRATE, it follows that the securities in question will be in the custody and administration of the CSD participant with whom the client's broker maintains an account for custody and administration purposes.
2. The second type elects to appoint their own CSD participant to act on their behalf.

19.3.4.3 Nominees

Related to the custody and administration of securities are those provisions dealing with the use of nominees. The owner of a security may not necessarily want securities registered in its name. It may, for a host of reasons, be more convenient for securities to be registered in the name of a person other than the owner of the securities in question. Such persons are called **nominees** and are also regulated under the FMA. Because nominees are so often used, reference is made in this chapter not to an owner of securities disposing of its securities, but simply to the disposer. The latter could include a nominee, the executor of a deceased estate disposing of securities owned by the deceased, or a trustee disposing of the securities owned by an insolvent.

The FMA provides for the approval of nominees to act as the registered holders of securities or an interest in securities on behalf of others. A nominee of an authorised user that is a member of an exchange must be approved by the exchange in terms of the rules of the exchange. The nominee of a participant must be approved by the central securities depository in terms of its rules. Nominees that are not approved by an exchange or the central securities depository must be approved by the registrar.

19.3.4 4   Clearing and settling transactions

The third discrete step in the analysis above involves market participants clearing and settling transactions taking place on an exchange – that is, the payment and associated transfer of such securities from the disposing party to the acquiring party. Firstly, the exact number of securities to be transferred and the payment required to achieve this must be calculated and determined. Secondly, an act is required to settle or discharge the obligations arising from a transaction in listed securities.

The person who is appointed by an exchange to provide the services of the clearing and settling of transactions is for purposes of the FMA defined as a **clearing house**, which is also required to be licensed under the FMA.

Clearing houses, when this function is not performed in-house by an exchange, must be licensed separately. Also, their licences need to be renewed by the registrar annually. The FMA enables two or more clearing houses to amalgamate or merge with each other or with any self-regulatory organisation. It also provides for any of the assets and liabilities of a clearing house to be transferred to or taken over by any other clearing house with the registrar's approval.

The FMA also introduces a new type of clearing house. These are independent clearing houses created for the clearing of unlisted securities through a central counter party.

19.3.4.5   Trade repositories

The FMA also creates a new type of market participant, namely a **trade repository**. The function of a trade repository is to maintain a central electronic database of transaction data. The FMA requires that all transactions, dealing with or in relation to unlisted securities, including, for example, trading in derivative instruments, be disclosed to the trade repository. These provisions are aimed at achieving or improving market transparency. The data collected by trade repositories may be used for purposes of surveillance and financial stability policy objectives identified by the FMA.

19.3.4.6   Segregation of securities

According to the Explanatory Memorandum to the Financial Markets Bill, the FMA incorporates the International Organisation of Securities Commissions and Bank of International Settlement's recommendations that securities regulation framework should support the **segregation of securities**. Under the FMA, authorised users are required to deposit their securities and the securities of their clients in separate securities accounts. Securities must be identifiable as belonging to a specific person. These provisions address custody risk in the event of the demise of an authorised user. Similar provisions apply to the requirement to segregate the funds of the clients of authorised users.

19.3.5   Definitions in the FMA

To achieve the regulation of exchanges and authorised users, the FMA defines a number of key terms, including:
- central securities depositories;
- participants;
- clearing houses;

- trade repositories; and
- market abuse.

The central definition contained in the FMA is that for **securities services**, which refers, among other things, to the buying and selling of securities, the custody and the administration of securities, the management of securities (this term is itself defined), and the clearing and settling of transactions in listed securities.

This definition is relevant to the extent that the FMA applies to regulated persons who provide securities services. This then answers the two questions that are asked with respect to legislation – that is, who is regulated, and which activities are regulated? Others who are also regulated are of course the issuers of securities, and the clients of authorised users and participants.

Other key definitions include those defining the market participants already referred to, their activities (which are regulated under the FMA), and securities. Securities are widely defined and, among other things, include shares, stocks and depository receipts in public companies and other equivalent equities, notes, derivative instruments, bonds, debentures, participatory interests in a collective investment scheme and instruments based on an index. The definition of securities specifically excludes money market instruments (except as regards the custody and administration of securities).

19.3.6 Prohibitions in the FMA

The FMA contains certain prohibitions. These provide, for example, that no person may operate as an exchange, a central securities depository, a clearing house or a trade repository unless licensed for that purpose under the FMA.

It also prohibits persons from acting as authorised users and participants unless authorised or accepted for that purpose. In the case of authorised users, such persons may not conduct business with a person providing services in relation to the management of securities and funds, where the latter does not hold the necessary approvals to do so. This is a reference to investment managers and those persons regulated under the Financial Advisory and Intermediary Services Act.[9] Lastly, no person may carry on the business of buying or selling listed securities unless such person also complies with the FMA; and likewise, no person may carry on the buying and selling of unlisted securities unless such person complies with the regulations and the conditions imposed respectively by the Minister and the registrar for the buying and selling of unlisted securities.

The policy objective behind the powers of the Minister and the registrar to regulate and impose conditions in the case of unlisted securities is principally aimed at better regulation of over-the-counter derivative instruments. These instruments are otherwise not regulated. Globally, the concern has arisen that the unregulated nature of these instruments played a key role in the origins of the financial crisis of 2008.

In the case of the buying and selling of listed securities, except in certain prescribed circumstances, a person may not carry on the business of buying or selling listed securities (that is, securities listed on a South African exchange), unless that person:

- is an authorised user of the relevant exchange;
- effects such buying or selling through an authorised user; or
- is a financial institution transacting as principal with another financial institution also transacting as principal.

---

9   37 of 2002.

Financial institutions or parties to a corporate transaction (bringing about a change of control, amongst other things) resulting in a change of beneficial ownership of listed securities outside of an exchange, are required to report the transaction to the registrar. The latter must disclose this information to the exchange on which the securities are listed, if doing so will enhance regulatory effectiveness or transparency. All transactions placed via an authorised user require disclosure on the trading system of the exchange in question; hence, in the case of executing a transaction via an authorised user, such a transaction may not take place off the market.

19.3.7   Regulators appointed under the FMA

The FMA provides that the executive officer of the Financial Services Board and his or her deputy are *ex officio* appointed as the **registrar** and the deputy registrar of securities services respectively. These persons are the regulators under the FMA in relation to those matters specifically delegated to each of them.

According to the Explanatory Memorandum on the Financial Markets Bill, the powers and functions of the registrar under the FMA have been clarified to be consistent with international norms and standards. Importantly, the FMA specifies that the registrar shall be subject to the Promotion of Administrative Justice Act.[10]

19.3.8   Self-regulatory organisations

The Securities Services Act conferred the status of a **self-regulatory organisation** on exchanges and central securities depositories. The FMA now extends this dispensation to independent clearing houses. The JSE Securities Exchange South Africa and STRATE operate as self-regulatory organisations. They are expected to regulate their activities and those of authorised users (members of exchanges) and participants (members of central securities depositories) by making and enforcing rules that comply with the FMA's requirements. The FMA reviews the self-regulatory organisation model. It establishes a clearer separation between securities services and infrastructure, and it strengthens the engagement and adjudication process. The FMA furthermore introduces fit and proper requirements for directors and senior management of self-regulatory organisations.

The FMA confers significant powers on an exchange in relation to the listing of securities. For example, an exchange is required to make listing requirements that prescribe the steps that the exchange must take for the investigation and discipline of an issuer, director, officer or employee of an issuer who contravenes or fails to comply with the listing requirements. The penalties that may be imposed by the exchange for any failure to comply with the listing requirements include a reprimand, imposing fines, disqualification from holding the office of a director or officer of a listed company for any period of time, or the payment of compensation to any person prejudiced by the contravention or failure.

19.3.9   Regulation of a market infrastructure

No person may be appointed as a member of the controlling body of a market infrastructure if that person may not be appointed as a director in terms of the Companies Act, or has been penalised in disciplinary proceedings for a contravention of the rules of any professional organisation (including a market infrastructure) for dishonesty, or does not meet the fit and proper requirements prescribed by the registrar.

---

10   3 of 2000.

The FMA limits the control of and shareholding in a market infrastructure. The FMA requires the registrar's approval for acquiring shares in a market infrastructure if the nominal value of those shares will amount to more than 15 per cent of the total nominal value of all the issued shares of that market infrastructure. The purpose of this provision is to prevent disreputable people from controlling a market infrastructure and thereby introducing systemic risks into securities markets.

19.3.10 Regulation of market abuse

The Financial Services Board is given powers under the Act for the purposes of the regulation of market abuse, in addition to its powers under the Financial Services Board Act.

The FMA maintains the appointment of the Directorate of Market Abuse (the directorate), formerly known as the Insider Trading Directorate, and which was established under the former Insider Trading Act.[11] This directorate is tasked with the supervision and regulation of market abuse and insider trading.

Market abuse covers a wide range of issues. These include manipulative, improper, false or deceptive practices of trading (including, artificial market prices) as well as false, misleading or deceptive statements, promises, and forecasts.

Price-stabilising mechanisms, regulated by the rules or listing requirements of an exchange are expressly excluded from these provisions. The purpose of such mechanisms is to promote an orderly secondary market for a limited period following a new issue of shares.

The directorate has wide investigative powers to carry out its duties, including rights of attachment, removal of documents, interrogation and interdict, and access to surveillance information. The directorate may sue for the amount by which the individual profited or the loss which he or she avoided as a result of dealing. It may also sue for a penalty for compensatory and punitive purposes for an amount not exceeding three times the amount of the profit gained or loss avoided as a result of dealing.

The amount recovered by the directorate, less certain deductions, may then be claimed by those who were affected by the dealings in question. The directorate may also prosecute for offences under the FMA where the State declines to prosecute. In terms of the FMA, an individual convicted of **insider trading** is liable to a fine or to imprisonment, or to both.

Criminal and civil liability for insider trading is limited to individuals. However, a corporate body may still incur civil liability because the FMA provides that an employer or principal may be vicariously liable.

Any individual who knows that he or she has inside information and who deals for his or her own account in the securities or financial instruments to which the information relates or may be affected, commits an offence. The inside information must be likely to have had a material effect on the price or value of any securities or financial instruments, be specific or precise, and not have been made public.

It is also an offence for someone with inside information to encourage or discourage another person to trade. For both criminal and civil liability, it is required that the individual knows that he or she has inside information, the onus of proof being on the prosecution or plaintiff. It is not necessary to prove that the individual dealt on the basis of the information, only that he or she had it.

---

11   135 of 1998.

THIS CHAPTER IN ESSENCE

1. A **stock exchange** is an organised and regulated financial market where securities (bonds, notes, shares, derivatives) are bought and sold. Stock exchanges provide a primary market for corporations, governments and municipalities to raise capital from investors, and a secondary market for investors to sell their securities to other investors.

2. Exchanges must be licensed in terms of the **Financial Markets Act (FMA)**. The **Johannesburg Stock Exchange (JSE)** is the only licensed exchange in South Africa. The JSE was established in 1887 and is now a full-service electronic securities exchange, where equities, financial derivatives, commodity derivatives and interest rate instruments (both cash and derivative) are traded.

3. As at February 2013, the JSE had 397 listed companies and market capitalisation was R8.6 trillion. The main indicator of the equity market's performance is the FTSE/JSE All Share Index (sometimes known as the Alsi). A **share** (or **stock**) **index** is a statistical indicator used to measure changes in the market value of a group of underlying stocks and it is a good indicator of the overall well-being of the economy.

4. Becoming a public listed company holds the following potential benefits for companies:
   - access to capital for growth;
   - boost to company profile;
   - creation of value and liquidity for shareholders;
   - facilitation of broad-based black economic empowerment (BEE) deals; and
   - facilitation of share incentives schemes.

5. Not all companies are eligible to list on the JSE. The JSE creates its own **listing requirements** beyond the requirements of the Companies Act, 2008.

6. The FMA governs trading in all kinds of securities services and financial instruments in the financial market. It replaced the Securities Services Act 36 of 2004, which previously regulated this area. The FMA also regulates market abuse.

7. The FMA was introduced to improve regulation and reduce **systemic risk** in the wake of the global financial crisis.

8. It regulates certain defined regulated persons as well as the market infrastructures.

9. **Regulated persons** are all those involved in financial markets for purposes of the FMA, including licensed central securities depositories; clearing houses; exchanges; trade repositories; authorised users; clearing members; nominees; participants; issuers (in certain cases); and any other persons designated as such by the Minister.

10. A **market infrastructure** means a licensed central securities depository; a licensed clearing house; a licensed exchange; and a licensed trade repository.

11. The FMA governs all things related to the buying and selling of securities. In so far as this happens on an exchange, three discrete steps may be identified, namely: securities are listed on the exchange; they are held in safekeeping; and when subsequently transferred to a new owner, they are cleared and settled in compliance with the FMA's provisions and the requirements of the market infrastructure.

12. The FMA prescribes a **code of conduct** for authorised users, their officers, employees and clients. Authorised users (generally known as stockbrokers) are the intermediaries used by investors to buy and sell securities.

13. The **custody and administration of securities** refers generally to the safekeeping and transfer of securities. These services are provided by a single, common platform in the form of a **central securities depository** (CSD). The CSD holds securities in safe custody and records and arranges transactions between market participants in accordance with acceptable standards and protocols. The only licensed CSD in South Africa is Strate Limited.

14. A **participant** is a person that holds in custody and administers securities and that has been accepted by a central securities depository as a participant in that central securities depository.

15. Certificates of listed securities have been **dematerialised** – that is, securities are no longer evidenced by physical certificates and only dematerialised securities are good for settlement on the JSE. The CSD provides the system that records the issue and transfer of dematerialised certificates.

16. The FMA provides for the approval of **nominees** to act as the registered holders of securities on behalf of others.

17. The clearing and settling of a transfer of securities is effected by a **clearing house**. This process involves the payment and associated transfer of securities from the disposing party to the acquiring party. A clearing house is required to be licensed under the FMA.

18. The FMA creates a new type of market participant in the form of a **trade repository**, whose function it is to maintain a central electronic database of transaction data. All transactions in relation to unlisted securities must be disclosed to the trade repository.

19. The FMA also requires authorised users to deposit securities in separate securities accounts so as to be identifiable as belonging to a specific person.

20. The FMA provides that the executive officer of the Financial Services Board and his or her deputy are *ex officio* appointed as the **registrar** and deputy registrar of securities services respectively. These persons are responsible for implementing the regulatory framework of the FMA.

21. The FMA confers the status of a **self-regulatory organisation** on exchanges, central securities depositories and independent clearing houses. Thus, the JSE and Strate Limited operate as self-regulatory organisations and must determine their listing requirements and rules, subject to the requirements of the FMA.

22. The FMA regulates who may be a member of the controlling body of a market infrastructure and limits the control and shareholding in a market infrastructure.

23. The FMA controls **market abuse** by providing for penalties for the offences of **insider trading** (using information likely to have a material effect on the price of securities and not publicly available) and market manipulation (using manipulative, improper, false or deceptive trading practices and statements).

24. The FMA provides for both criminal and civil actions to be brought against individual persons contravening the FMA, but corporate bodes may incur civil liability vicariously.

Bibliography

Books

Blackman MS 'Companies' in Joubert WA et al (eds), *The Law of South Africa* vol. 4(3) 1st reissue, Durban: LexisNexis Butterworths

Butler DW 'Arbitration' in Joubert WA et al (eds), *The Law of South Africa* vol. 1, 2 ed, Durban: LexisNexis Butterworths 2003

Cheffins BR, *Company Law: Theory, Structure and Operation*, Oxford: Clarendon Press 1997

Cilliers AC, Loots C and Nel HC, *Herbstein and Van Winsen: The Civil Practice of the High Courts & Supreme Court of Appeal of South Africa*, 5 ed, Cape Town: Juta & Co 2009

Cilliers HS, Benade Ml, Henning JJ, Du Plessis JJ, Delport PA, De Koker L and Pretorius JT, *Corporate Law*, 3 ed, Durban: Lexis Nexis Butterworths 2000

Coaker JF and Zeffert (eds), *Wille and Millin's Mercantile Law of South Africa*, 18 ed, Johannesburg: Hortors 1984

De Wet JC and Van Wyk AH, *Die Suid-Afrikaanse Kontraktereg en Handelsreg*, 5 ed, Durban: Butterworths 1992

Farrar JH and Hannigan BM, *Farrar's Company Law*, 4 ed, Durban: LexisNexis Butterworths 1998

Geach WD and Schoeman T, *Guide to Close Corporations Act and Regulations*, Cape Town: Juta & Co 1984 (looseleaf service)

Geach WD with Yeats J, *Trusts: Law and Practice*, Cape Town: Juta & Co Ltd 2007

Gower LCB, *The Principles of Modern Company Law*, 3 ed, London: Stephens 1969

Hahlo HR, *The South African Law of Husband and Wife*, 5 ed, Cape Town: Juta & Co 1985

Henning JJ 'Partnership' in Joubert WA et al (eds) *The Law of South Africa* vol. 19, 2 ed, Durban: LexisNexis Butterworths 2006

Henning JJ, Cilliers HS, Benade ML and Du Plessis JJ 'Close Corporations' in Joubert WA et al (eds), *The Law of South Africa* vol. 4(3) 1st reissue, Durban: LexisNexis Butterworths

Hutchison D, Van Heerden B, Visser DP and Van Der Merwe CG, *Wille's Principles of South African Law*, 9 ed, Cape Town: Juta & Co 2007

Mongalo T (ed), *Modern Company Law for a Competitive South African Economy*, Cape Town: Juta 2010

Pretorius JT (General Editor), Delport PA, Havenga M and Vermaas M, *Hahlo's Company Law through the Cases*, 6 ed, Cape Town: Juta & Co Ltd 1999

Stein C with Geoff Everingham, *The New Companies Act Unlocked*, Cape Town: Siber Ink 2011

Van der Linden J, *Koopmans Handboek 4.1.12*

Van der Merwe JG, Appleton RB, Delport PA, Furney RW, Mahony DP and Koen M, *South African Corporate Business Administration*, Cape Town: Juta & Co Ltd 2005 (loose-leaf format)

Journal articles

Cassim MF 'The introduction of the statutory merger in South African corporate law: majority rule offset by the appraisal right (Part I)' (2008) 20 *SA Merc LJ* 1 and (Part II) (2008) 20 *SA Merc LJ* 147

Coetzee L and Kennedy-Good S 'The business judgment rule' (Part 2) (2006) 27 *Obiter* 277

Finch V 'Company directors: who cares about skill and care?' (1992) 55(2) *The Modern Law Review* 179

Havenga M 'Company directors – fiduciary duties, corporate opportunities and confidential information' (1989) 1 *SA Merc LJ* 122

Havenga M 'Directors' fiduciary duties under our future company law regime' (1997) 9 *SA Merc LJ* 310

Henning JJ and Snyman E 'Revision of the law of partnership in the United States: a commendable precedent?' (1997) 114 *SALJ* 684

Henning JJ and Snyman E 'Die regsaard van die vennootskap: die entiteitsteorie seëvier in die Verenigde State' 1993 *TSAR* 306

Kiggundu J and Havenga M 'The regulation of directors' self-serving conduct: perspectives from Botswana and South Africa' (2004) 37 *CILSA* 272

Mackenzie AL 'A company director's obligations of care and skill' 1982 *Journal of Business Law* 460

Odendaal EM and De Jager H 'Regulations of the auditing profession in South Africa' (2008) 8 *The Southern African Journal of Accountability and Auditing Research* 1

Oosthuizen MJ 'Die Turquand-reël as reël van die verenigingsreg' 1977 *TSAR* 210

Sealy LS 'Reforming the law on directors' duties' (1991) 12(9) *The Company Lawyer* 175

Trebilcock M 'The liability of company directors for negligence' (1969) 32 *The Modern Law Review* 499

Vermaas M 'Dematerialisasie van die genoteerde aandeel in die Suid-Afrikaanse reg (Deel 2)' (1997) 9 *SA Merc LJ* 171

Other publications

Blackman MS 'The Fiduciary Duty Doctrine and its Application to Directors of Companies' PhD thesis, University of Cape Town 1970

Department of Trade and Industry (dti) South African Company Law for the 21st Century: Guidelines for Corporate Law Reform (2004) *Government Gazette* 26493 GN 1183

Itzkin R and Tregoning A (Bell Dewar Incorporated) 'The insider trading regime in South Africa' *www.executiveview.com/knowledge_centre.php?Id=10499*, 2 October 2009

King Committee, King Report on Corporate Governance for South Africa and the King Code of Governance Principles (King 3), Johannesburg: Institute of Directors in Southern Africa 2009 (King 3)

Rob Rose 'Liberty bonuses queried' *Sunday Times Business Times*, 16 May 2010

Webliography

AJML Group Public Accountants & Tax Agents, *www.ajml.com.au*

Congress of South African Trade Unions, *www.cosatu.org.za*

Contemporary Gazette, *www.gazette.co.za*

Executive View, *www.executiveview.com/knowledge_centre*

Fin24 – Business and Finance News, *www.fin24.com*

Grindrod Limited, *www.grindrod.co.za*

Independent Regulatory Board for Auditors, *www.irba.co.za*

Institute of Directors, *www.iod.com*

Institute of Directors in Southern Africa, *www.iodsa.co.za*

Johannesburg Stock Exchange, *www.jse.co.za*

Mpumalanga Agricultural Development Corporation, *www.madc.co.za*

National Economic Development and Labour Council, *www.nedlac.org.za*

Parliamentary Monitoring Group, *www.pmg.org.za*

South Africa Government online, *www.info.gov.za*

South African Institute of Chartered Accountants, *www.saica.co.za*

Strate, *www.strate.co.za*

Webber Wentzel Attorneys, *www.webberwentzel.com*

Table of cases

Table of legislation

Codes and Guidelines

Foreign law

Glossary

accounting period the period for which a business prepares its accounts; the period covered by its financial statements; usually a company prepares financial statements on an annual basis and the accounting period is for 12 months up to the company's financial year-end

Accounting Practices Board (APB) the Board established by, inter alia, the South African Institute of Chartered Accountants, the Independent Regulatory Board for Auditors, the Johannesburg Stock Exchange and the Association of Chambers of Commerce of South Africa; the purpose of the APB is to establish and to procure the recognition and acceptance of what the Board considers is or should be generally accepted accounting practice

actual authority the legal power in fact given by a principal to an agent to represent and bind the principal; actual authority may be contrasted with ostensible authority in that an apparent agent may have ostensible authority while lacking actual authority

affected person in the context of business rescue, a person falling within the scope of the definition of 'affected person' in s 128(1) *(a)* of the Companies Act, 2008 and refers essentially to a shareholder, creditor and/or employee of a company who has the right under the Act to apply for the commencement of business rescue proceedings

affected transaction a transaction defined as an 'affected transaction' in s 117(1)*(c)* of the Companies Act, 2008 and refers to a number of different transactions, such as a merger, takeover or disposal of the major parts of the assets of a company; an 'affected transaction' does not refer to business rescue provisions and has nothing to do with an 'affected person'

agent a person who has been given the authority to represent and legally bind another person (the principal) in relation to a third person

aggregate assets/liabilities the assets and liabilities of a company that are required to be valued for the purposes of the solvency test laid down in s 4(1)*(a)* of the Companies Act, 2008

aggregate theory of partnership the legal theory in terms of which a partnership is regarded, in law, not as a legal entity in its own right, but as a mere association of the persons who are its partners

allotment (of shares) the issuing of shares by a company to an applicant pursuant to an offer of shares to the public

alterable provisions provisions of the Companies Act, 2008 whose effect on a company may be negated, restricted, limited, qualified, extended or otherwise altered in substance or effect by that company's Memorandum of Incorporation (MOI); if any alterable provision is not altered by a company's MOI, the default provisions contained in the Companies Act will automatically apply; there are approximately 60 alterable provisions in the Companies Act

alternate director a person who stands in for a member of the board of directors during the latter's temporary absence, and who is entitled to attend and vote at meetings of the board of directors during that period

alternative dispute resolution (ADR) the resolution of disputes otherwise than by litigation in the ordinary courts, such as by way of mediation or arbitration

amalgamation an amalgamation or merger of two or more profit companies, as envisaged in s 113 of the Companies Act, 2008; such a transaction connotes that, by agreement, the assets and liabilities of one company are amalgamated or merged with those of another company, thus effectively merging their corporate identities

annual financial statements a report giving information about a company (in accordance with the requirements of the Companies Act and the Regulations thereto), which, in the case of a listed company gives information about a company on a triple bottom-line basis: (1) economic performance and position; (2) societal impact; and (3) environmental effect; regarding economic performance and position, the three basic financial statements are (1) the balance sheet (statement of financial position), which shows the company's assets, liabilities, and its net worth on a stated date, (2) the income statement, which shows the performance of a company and whether it has made a profit or a loss during the period in question, and (3) a cash flow statement, showing the inflows and outflows of cash from the company's activities over the period in question

annual general meeting the meeting of shareholders that the Companies Act requires every company to hold in each calendar year as envisaged in s 61(7) of the Companies Act, 2008

annual return the yearly statement filed – that is, delivered to the Companies and Intellectual Property Commission – by every company, in the prescribed form, as required by s 33 of the Companies Act, 2008; if a company or close corporation fails to submit an annual return, that company or close corporation can be deregistered by the Commissioner in accordance with the provisions of s 82(3) of the Act

anonymous partnership a partnership in which one or some of the partners, by agreement between them, do not take an active role in the partnership business, are not disclosed to the public as being partners, and who consequently do not incur the liabilities of an ordinary partner to creditors of the partnership, but are liable only toward their co-partners; one of the more-used anonymous partnerships is the *en commandite* partnership

AP Act (Auditing Profession Act) the statute that provides for the establishment of the Independent Regulatory Board for Auditors for the education, training and professional development of registered auditors, for the accreditation of professional bodies, the registration of auditors, and the regulation of the conduct of registered auditors

appeal (differentiated from review) an application to a superior court by a litigant (who was unsuccessful in legal proceedings that were adjudicated by a lower court) to set aside the decision of the lower court on the grounds that it was wrong in law or wrong on the facts; by contrast, an application to court for a review is an application to set aside a decision of a lower court, not on the grounds that the decision was wrong in law or wrong on the facts, but on the grounds that it was reached by a process that was unfair or irregular

application proceedings an application to court in relation to a situation in which there is no dispute with regard to the facts, and the only dispute between the parties is with regard to issues of law

appraisal rights/remedy (of dissenting shareholders) the remedy available to shareholders in terms of s 164 of the Companies Act, 2008

arbitrage the simultaneous or near-simultaneous purchase and sale of the same commodity in different markets in order to profit from price discrepancies between those markets

arbitration the determination by an impartial referee (the arbitrator) of a dispute between parties by way of a legally binding ruling

arrangement an agreement between a company, on the one hand, and its shareholders or any class of shareholders on the other, as envisaged in s 114 of the Companies Act, 2008, with the purpose of 're-arranging' the rights of those shareholders in some way (e.g. by dividing some shares into shares of a different class)

articles (articles of association) the founding document required for the formation of a company under the Companies Act, 1973; in terms of the 1973 Act, the founders of a company had to lodge both a Memorandum and Articles; in terms of the Companies Act, 2008 there is now only one document, the Memorandum of Incorporation (MOI)

association agreement a voluntary agreement entered into by all the members of a close corporation as envisaged in s 44 of the Close Corporations Act and which determines the rights and obligations between members, in much the same way that a partnership agreement determines the rights and duties of partners in a partnership; just as there are alterable and default provisions in the Companies Act, certain provisions of the Close Corporations Act will automatically apply if they are not altered by an association agreement

audit has the meaning as set out in the Auditing Profession Act, 2005 and essentially is a systematic examination of financial or accounting records by an auditor in order to verify the accuracy and truthfulness of the financial statements that have been based on those records; the purpose of an audit is to form an audit opinion on whether the financial statements are a fair presentation of a company's performance and position; the word 'audit' does not include (in terms of s 1 of the Companies Act) an 'independent review' of annual financial statements as envisaged by s 30(2) of the Act

audit committee a committee appointed annually by shareholders as envisaged in s 94 of the Companies Act, 2008 and which must nominate an independent external auditor and deal with other matters concerning the external auditor, such as fees

auditor has the meaning set out in the Auditing Profession Act, 2005 and refers to a person who has the professional qualifications and the requisite registration as an auditor to carry out an audit

authorised shares the number and the classes of shares that a company is permitted, in terms of its Memorandum of Incorporation, to issue to investors; to be distinguished from a company's 'issued' shares (shares actually issued)

authorised user (in terms of the Financial Markets Act) a person authorised by the rules of a stock exchange to perform securities services

balance sheet (also known as a statement of financial position) is a concise and condensed statement (which must comply with the requirements of the Companies Act and the Regulations thereto) showing the financial position of an entity (assets, liabilities and equity), as at a specified date, usually the last day of its accounting period

beneficial interest a right (conditional or unconditional) to the profits or other benefits of a contract or trust where the person so entitled is not the owner of those assets; thus, in an ownership trust, the trustees have legal ownership of the trust assets but no beneficial interest in the trust, in that they do not have any right to the distribution of trust income or capital; by contrast, the trust beneficiaries have a beneficial interest in the trust in that the benefits of the trust flow through to them, even though they are not the owners of the trust assets; the owner of securities that are held in the name of a nominee is the beneficial owner of the securities

beneficiaries (of a trust) the persons who stand to benefit from a trust, usually through a distribution of trust income or capital to them

bewind trust a trust in which the trust beneficiaries are the owners of the trust assets, but those assets are administered by and are put under the control of the trustees of the trust for the benefit of those beneficiaries

blank share a class of shares in respect of which (as envisaged in s 36(1)(d) and s 36(3)(d) of the Companies Act, 2008) the company's Memorandum of Incorporation does not specify the preferences, rights, limitations or other terms applicable to such shares, and where the directors (or others as specified in the MOI) have the power to allocate rights to those shares in the future

board of directors the body of persons who have the overall responsibility for the direction and control and the activities of a company

book value the amount/value that an asset is disclosed at in a statement of financial position (i.e. in a balance sheet) as determined by accounting rules and concepts

business judgement rule the common-law principle that a director is not in breach of his or her statutory duties if he or she had taken reasonably diligent steps to inform him- or herself of the matter in question, had no personal financial interest in the matter, and had a rational basis for believing that his or her decision was in the best interests of the company; this common-law principle has now been codified in s 76(4) of the Companies Act, 2008

business rescue the procedure created in Chapter 6 of the Companies Act, 2008 for the supervision of a financially distressed company

business rescue plan a business rescue plan as envisaged in Part D of Chapter 6 of the Companies Act, 2008

business rescue practitioner a person appointed as a business rescue practitioner, as envisaged in Chapter 6 of the Companies Act, 2008, to oversee a company during the business rescue process

business trust a trust in which the trustees are given the power to trade and to carry on business activities; also known as a 'trading' trust

capacity (related to *ultra vires*) the competency to perform a legal act; the capacity of a company refers to its competency, in law, to perform an act, such as entering into a contract; an act by a company that is outside the scope of its capacity is said to be *ultra vires*

capitalisation shares capitalisation shares as contemplated in s 47 of the Companies Act, 2008, and which are also referred to as 'bonus' shares, are shares that are issued by a company in lieu of dividends, and effectively arise as a result of the capitalisation (not distribution) of the profits of a company

capital maintenance the concept (now abolished by the Companies Act, 2008) that the issued share capital of a company constitutes a guarantee fund or a permanent fund, which is, in the last resort, the source from which the claims of the company's creditors can be paid, and that its value should be maintained; in order to protect the company's creditors, the concept of capital maintenance requires

that the issued share capital of a company may not be reduced, nor may it be returned to shareholders, except to the extent permitted by the common law or in the manner authorised by the Companies Act

cautionary announcement (regarding price-sensitive information) a notification by a company that negotiations are in process (such as for a takeover or merger), the outcome of which may affect its share price

central securities depository (CSD) the body that provides a platform for the custody and administration of securities to facilitate the buying and selling of securities

certificated security a security that is evidenced by a certificate – that is, a document – as distinct from a mere electronic record

civil proceedings legal proceedings involving a civil dispute – that is, a dispute between two or more persons (e.g. a claim by one person against another for damages); in other words, a claim for monetary compensation; by contrast, criminal proceedings are legal proceedings in which the State prosecutes a person for committing a criminal offence

clearing house the entity appointed by an exchange to provide services for the clearing and settling of transactions

close corporation a legal entity formed in terms of the Close Corporations Act

codification a systematic and comprehensive compilation of the entire body of law (including case law) of a particular country, or of a specific area of law

commodity derivatives derivatives whose value derives from the price of a commodity

Companies and Intellectual Property Commission (the Commission) the body established in terms of s 185 of the Companies Act, 2008

Companies and Intellectual Property Registration Office (CIPRO) the body resulting from the merger, as from 1 March 2002, of two former directorates of the Department of Trade and Industry – namely, SACRO (the South African Companies Registration Office) and SAPTO (the South African Patents & Trade Marks Office)

Companies Tribunal the tribunal established in terms of s 193 of the Companies Act, 2008

company secretary the chief administrative officer of a company; a company secretary is usually not regarded as a 'prescribed officer' of a company as envisaged by and defined in the Companies Act

compliance order/notice an order or notice issued by the Takeover Regulation Panel or the Companies and Intellectual Property Commission

compromise an agreement between two or more parties in which one or both give up part of what is due to them for the sake of settling their differences (e.g. an agreement between a company and its creditors in which the creditors agree to accept less than what is owing to them by the company)

conciliation the process of settling disputes through extra-judicial means – that is, without recourse to the courts, by way of an agreed settlement or compromise between the disputing parties

concurrent creditor an unsecured creditor who is neither secured nor preferred/preferent

consent order an order made by a court in terms that have been agreed upon by the litigants

consideration a *quid pro quo* – that is, something given or taken in return for something else; the word is defined in s 1 of the Companies Act, and s 40(2) provides that before a company issues shares, the board must determine the consideration for which those shares will be issued

consolidated assets and liabilities the aggregated assets and liabilities of a group of companies that are required to be taken into account for the purposes of the solvency and liquidity test in s 4 of the Companies Act, 2008

constructive notice knowledge that a person is, by a legal fiction, treated as possessing (whether or not the person has actual knowledge of the matter in question)

contingent (assets and liabilities) assets and liabilities that are reasonably foreseeable as likely to accrue to or be incurred by the person in question

control (in the context of relationships between holding and subsidiary parties) the dominating influence exerted by one company over another as envisaged in s 2(2)*(a)* of the Companies Act, 2008

convertible preference shares a class of shares in which the shareholders have the right to convert their shares into shares of another class

corporate finance is the manner by which assets are funded (by a combination of equity and debt) and which determines the capital structure of a company; it also refers to the decisions taken by managers to use those assets in the best and most profitable manner. Corporate finance is therefore about the sources of finance of a company, and the investment decisions made by managers

corporate governance is aimed at the conduct of the directors of a company and is a code and set of principles by which companies ought to be directed and controlled in the interests of all of their stakeholders (such as customers, employees, suppliers and the community in which they operate) and including their responsibilities to society in general as good corporate citizens

corporate rescue see business rescue

corporate veil (lifting/piercing the corporate veil) the metaphorical barrier that separates a company, as a legal persona in its own right, from its shareholders and directors

cumulative preference share a preference share in which, if a dividend is not declared in a particular year, the right to the dividend for that year is not forfeited but is carried forward and accumulated

curator *ad litem* a person appointed by a court to initiate or defend legal proceedings on behalf of another person

deal (and dealing) (in terms of the Financial Markets Act) conveying or giving an instruction to buy or sell shares or encouraging someone to do so

debenture a long-term loan owed by a company as evidenced by a document issued by a company acknowledging and showing the amount of a monetary debt owed by it to the holder of the debenture

debt finance/instrument debt finance (also referred to as external equity) is capital raised by a company by borrowing money, as distinct from capital raised through issuing shares (referred to as internal equity); the instrument is the document recording the borrowing

declaratory order an order of court that makes a determination of a hitherto uncertain, doubtful or contentious issue

deferred shares a class of shares commonly issued to the founders of a company that defers (delays) the right of the holders to receive dividends until dividends have been distributed to all the other classes of the company's shareholders

delict (delictual) relating to legally wrongful and blameworthy conduct that has resulted in injury to a person or damage to property

delinquency (declaration of) a declaration by a court of law in terms of s 162 of the Companies Act, 2008 or in terms of s 47 of the Close Corporations Act that a particular director is delinquent

dematerialisation the process whereby a paper share certificate is replaced by an electronic record of ownership

demutualisation the process whereby a mutual company – that is, a company owned by its members for their own benefit – becomes a public company in which the members give up their prior rights and, in return, receive shares in the company which can be publicly traded

derivative short for derivative instrument; a contract whose value is based on the performance of an underlying asset

derivative action a lawsuit brought by a shareholder of a company on the company's behalf to enforce or defend the company's legal rights in circumstances where the company has failed to do so

director a member of a company's board of directors

discretionary trust (in the context of a trust) a trust in which the beneficiaries have no vested right to the trust's income or assets, and have only such rights as the trustees, in their discretion, choose to give them; a

discretionary trust is to be contrasted with a vesting trust in which some or all of the beneficiaries have vested rights to the trust income or assets

dissenting shareholder's appraisal right the right of dissenting shareholders, in terms of s 164 of the Companies Act, 2008, to require the company to acquire their shares for fair value

distribution as defined in s 1 of the Companies Act, 2008, a transfer by a company of money or property, other than its own shares, to its shareholders or the shareholders of another company in the same group

dividend a distribution by a company to its shareholders of part or all of its profits

domesticated company a foreign company whose registration has been transferred to the Republic in terms of s 13(5)–(9) of the Companies Act, 2008

donor (of a trust) the person who, on the formation of a trust, donates property to the trustees to be administered by them in terms of the trust; sometimes called a founder

double-dummy structure a particular structure for a merger of equals (also called a top hat structure) in which a new holding company (Newco) creates two merger subsidiaries, each of which merges into one of the two pre-existing merging companies, with the result that each of the merging companies survives as a wholly owned subsidiary of Newco, and all of the shares of both merging companies are converted into shares of Newco

ejusdem generis Latin term meaning 'of the same kind'; the *ejusdem generis* rule is used in the interpretation of legislation when general words follow a list of specific and particular persons or things – the general words should not be given a wide meaning but should be regarded as applicable only to persons or things of the same kind or class as those specifically mentioned

employee share scheme an arrangement, put in place by a company, in terms of which shares in the company are held in trust on behalf of and for the benefit of the company's employees, with the intent that the employees then have a stake in the company's prosperity and thus an incentive to work hard

en commandite partnership see partnership *en commandite*

entity theory of partnership the legal theory in terms of which a partnership is, for certain limited purposes, treated as though it were a legal entity or persona in its own right, separate from the partners

equity in the broadest (non-company law) sense, means fairness; in a narrower sense, the money value of property in excess of claims and liabilities on the property; in the context of company law, it is a residual amount of what remains of a company's assets once all liabilities have been deducted from those assets; if the company is wound up, whatever remains of the assets of a company once all liabilities have been paid is 'equity' and can be paid to shareholders; equity is to be contrasted with debt – a person who has lent money to the company is merely owed a debt by that company, but has no equity in the company itself

equity:debt ratio the ratio derived by dividing a company's total liabilities by its shareholders' equity to indicate the relative proportions of equity and debt the company is using to finance its activities

equity insolvency the inability to pay debts as they fall due

estoppel the legal principle that prevents a person from subsequently denying the truth of a representation made by him or her, in reliance on which another person has acted; the representor is thereby estopped from denying the truth of his or her representation

exchange (as in stock exchange) an entity that provides trading facilities for stockbrokers and traders to trade shares and other securities

executive director a director who is not only on the board of directors, but is also an employee of the company (e.g. a managing director); an executive director usually works for the company, so to speak, in a full-time capacity; to be contrasted with a non-executive director whose only involvement with the company is to attend meetings of the board of directors

ex officio director a person who holds the office of director purely by virtue of occupying some other formal position or office

external company a foreign company that carries on business or non-profit activities within the Republic of South Africa

external equity debt finance – that is, borrowed money – as distinct from internal equity, namely the capital raised when a company issues shares

extraordinary partnership a partnership in which some partners are anonymous or *en commandite* partners

family trust a trust established for the benefit of the members of a particular family

fiduciary duty the duty, imposed by law on directors and other persons in a fiduciary position, to act in the best interests of the person or persons to whom they owe the duty; section 76 of the Companies Act deals with 'standards of directors' conduct' which include the fiduciary duty

financial derivative a financial instrument whose value is based on the value of one or more underlying assets

financially distressed in relation to a company, a company that is 'financially distressed' as defined in s 128(1) of the Companies Act, 2008 in the sense that its liabilities exceed its assets, or it cannot pay what it owes and is due in the normal course of business

Financial Reporting Standards Council (FRSC) the body of that name established in terms of the Corporate Laws Amendment Act 24 of 2006

financial statements – see annual financial statements

financial year an accounting period that can start on any day of a calendar year, and which comprises 12 consecutive months, at the end of which books of account are closed, profit or loss is computed, and financial reports are prepared; a financial year may or may not coincide with a calendar year

FMA (Financial Markets Act 19 of 2012) the Act whose purpose is, inter alia, to regulate financial markets, to license and regulate exchanges, to regulate and control securities trading and to prohibit insider trading and other market abuses

founder (of a trust) the person who formed the trust; also sometimes called the settlor or (where the formation of the trust included a donation by the founder) the donor

founding statement the founding statement of a close corporation, as envisaged in ss 12 and 13 of the Close Corporations Act; the constitution of a close corporation in the same way that the MOI is the constitution of a company

fundamental transaction a transaction falling within the scope of Part A of Chapter 5 of the Companies Act, 2008

Generally Accepted Accounting Practice (GAAP) a widely accepted set of rules, conventions, standards, and procedures for reporting financial information

general voting rights voting rights in relation to a company's issued securities as contemplated in s 3(2) of the Companies Act, 2008

going concern an accounting concept connoting a business that is operational and sustainable in that it is expected to continue to operate for the foreseeable future

group of companies two or more companies that share a holding company or a subsidiary relationship

historic-cost accounting financial accounting that is based on the original cost of an item and which ignores subsequent inflationary increases or values

holding company in relation to a subsidiary, a juristic person or undertaking that is a shareholder in, and controls the subsidiary

income statement a summary (which must comply with the provisions of the Companies Act and the Regulations thereto) for accounting purposes consisting of (1) the revenues and (2) expenses of a business, thus showing the performance of a business by measuring its profitability or otherwise over a given period

incorporation the act of forming an incorporated legal entity – in other words, an entity (such as a company or close corporation) that is a

legal persona in its own right and which exists separately and apart from its shareholders and directors

incorporeal property property that has no physical existence and exists only in the eyes of the law, such as a share or copyright

indemnify to agree to compensate another person if he or she suffers financial loss from a specified cause

independent accounting professional a person who complies with the requisite criteria, as laid down in the regulations to the Companies Act, 2008, to issue a report, known as an independent review, which is an alternative to an audit issued by a registered auditor

Independent Regulatory Board for Auditors (IRBA) the regulatory board established by the Auditing Profession Act

independent review (as opposed to an audit) the process, mandated by the regulations to the Companies Act, 2008, for the financial statements of all non-owner-managed companies to be independently reviewed

index (in the context of a stock exchange) an index of the market prices of a particular group of stocks, such as the S&P 500 and the Nasdaq Composite Index

indoor management rule (Turquand rule) see Turquand rule

initial public offering the first offering on the stock market for subscription by members of the public, of a firm's shares which were previously held only by a select group of shareholders; often abbreviated to 'IPO'

inside information information falling within the scope of the definition of inside information in s 77 of the Financial Markets Act and refers to information that is only known by insiders (such as directors of a company) and which is not available to the investing public at large

insider a person who has acquired inside information as contemplated in s 77 of the Financial Markets Act

insider trading is an offence and involves the trading of securities by an insider as more fully described in s 78 of the Financial Markets Act

insolvency the situation of a company that arises when the liabilities exceed the assets of that company (so-called 'factual' or 'balance sheet' insolvency) or (according to some court judgments) when a company cannot pay its debts in the normal course of business (so-called 'commercial' insolvency)

interest rate instruments documents evidencing a debt carrying a fixed or a variable rate of instrument

internal equity capital raised by a company through issuing shares

International Accounting Standards Board (IASB) an independent regulatory body, based in the United Kingdom, that aims to develop a single set of global accounting standards

International Financial Reporting Standards (IFRS) guidelines and rules set by the International Accounting Standards Board (IASB) that companies and organisations can follow when compiling financial statements

inter vivos **trust** a trust formed by a person (the founder or settlor) during his or her lifetime; in contrast to a testamentary trust, which is established in terms of a person's will and which comes into existence on that person's death

issued share capital the amount of a company's share capital that has actually been issued to its shareholders in the form of shares; a company's issued share capital cannot exceed the company's authorised share capital; the Companies Act, 2008, unlike the previous Act, does not use the word 'capital' but merely refers to 'shares' of a company, the reason being that the Act has abolished the capital maintenance concept in favour of liquidity and solvency

joint and several liability liability imposed (by law or by agreement) on two or more debtors, both jointly and severally, with the result that the creditor can claim the full amount of the debt from any of the debtors, and the debtor so paying is then entitled to reclaim their proportionate share of the debt from each of the other debtors

JSE the Johannesburg Stock Exchange

judicial management the process envisaged in Chapter XV of the Companies Act, 1973 whereby a company that is unable to pay its debts is, by an order of court, placed under the management of a judicial manager in the hope that, under the latter's management, it will be restored to solvency and viability; judicial management has now been abolished and is replaced by the new concept of business rescue

jurisprudence the study of the fundamental structure of a particular legal system or of legal systems in general; the philosophy of law

juristic personality a legal fiction whereby a non-human entity is regarded as being endowed with the capacity to have legal rights and obligations in the same way as a natural person (individual), in other words, as being a legal persona in its own right

King 3 the revised code for and the report on corporate governance principles for South African companies, released on 1 September 2009

leave (of the court) 'with the leave of the court' means with the permission of the court

letter of allocation the document that makes a rights offer as provided for in s 95(1)(*h*)(ii) of the Companies Act, 2008, read with s 96

lifting the corporate veil the situation where a court, in terms of the common law or under a particular statute, ignores the legal identity of a company as a legal person in its own right that is separate from its shareholders and directors; by contrast, piercing the corporate veil refers to the situation where the law treats the rights or duties of a company as the rights or liabilities of its shareholders or directors

limited liability the liability of a person to pay no more than a specified ceiling amount; thus, a shareholder has limited liability in that, in his or her capacity as shareholder, once he or she has paid for shares in full, he or she has no further monetary liability toward the company and cannot be held liable to pay any further amount even if the company becomes bankrupt and is unable to pay all its debts

liquidation see winding-up

liquidity the ability of a debtor to pay debts as and when they fall due

liquidity and solvency test the criteria that are applied to establish a company's solvency and liquidity as laid down in s 4(1) of the Companies Act, 2008

listed company a company that has fulfilled the listing requirements of a stock exchange and whose shares are quoted on, and can be bought and sold on, that stock exchange

listed securities shares or other securities that are bought and sold on a stock exchange

listing a place on the official list of securities of a stock exchange obtained by a company that has applied for such listing and has fulfilled the listing requirements

majority rule principle the broad principle that, in the affairs of a company, the will of those holding a majority of shareholders' votes must ultimately prevail

mandatory offer the offer that the law requires to be made by a person or related persons acting in concert who have acquired the prescribed percentage of the voting securities in a particular company and are consequently required by law to make an offer to acquire the remaining securities of that company on the terms laid down by the Companies Act and the Takeover Regulations

market abuse (in the context of the Financial Markets Act) the abuse of a securities market by way of insider trading or market manipulation

market capitalisation the aggregate value of a company, derived by multiplying the number of its issued shares by their current price per share (e.g. if a company has 15 000 000 issued shares and a share price of R20 per share, the company's market capitalisation is 15 000 000 × R20 = R300 000 000)

mediation the process of attempting to achieve an agreed settlement or compromise between disputing parties with the assistance of a neutral intermediary, called a mediator, who attempts to facilitate such an agreement; unlike an arbitrator, a mediator cannot impose a settlement on the disputing parties; the mediation, to be successful, must result in an agreement between the disputants

member (of a company) in terms of the Companies Act, 2008 a shareholder of a non-profit company; in terms of the 1973 Act, a member was any shareholder, whether of a 'for profit' or 'not for profit' company

member's interest (in a close corporation) the interest, expressed as a percentage, held by a person in a close corporation

Memorandum of Incorporation (MOI) the document envisaged in s 1 and s 15 of the Companies Act, 2008, which amounts to the constitution of a company, and which inter alia sets out the rights, duties of shareholders and directors, the authorised share capital of the company and other matters

merger a combination of two companies, as a result of which one of them is completely absorbed by the other; the less important company loses its identity and becomes part of the more important company, which retains its identity; a merger results in the extinction of the merged company and the surviving company assumes all the legal rights and liabilities of the merged corporation; see also amalgamation

minor a person who has not attained legal majority

minute (of a meeting) the written record of the meeting, including any resolutions passed

negotiable instrument a transferable, signed document that promises payment of a sum of money at a future date or on demand, e.g. a cheque or promissory note

nominee (in the context of the Financial Markets Act) a person who is approved to act as the holder of securities on behalf of another person or persons

non-executive director a director who does not, concurrently with the directorship, have a contract of employment with the company; the Companies Act does not distinguish between 'executive' and 'non-executive' directors

non-profit company a company formed for a purpose other than the making of a profit, and any incidental profits, which cannot be distributed to its members or directors except to the extent permitted by the Companies Act, 2008

offer for subscription an offer of its shares by a company that can be accepted in writing by a person who undertakes to take and pay for such shares

off-market transaction the buying and selling of shares and other securities otherwise than through a stock exchange; an off-market transaction is conducted through negotiation rather than through an auction system

option in the context of share transactions, a contract that gives the holder of the option the right to buy or sell a specified quantity of a particular share or debenture within a specified period of time at a stated price called the strike price

ordinary partnership a legal relationship for the carrying on of a business for the purposes of profit in which each of the partners is entitled to participate in the management of the business and is jointly and severally liable for all of the debts of the partnership

ordinary resolution a resolution passed by a majority of votes as determined by a company's MOI, or by the default provisions of the Companies Act

ordinary shares the residual category of a company's shares that does not carry any special class rights, such as special voting rights or preferential rights to a dividend

ordinary trust a trust in which the trustees have legal ownership of the trust assets, but must administer the trust for the benefit of the trust beneficiaries

ostensible authority authority as it appears to the outside world; the authority of an agent that is based on estoppel and which may exceed the scope of the agent's actual authority

over-the-counter trading a system for the trading of securities in which brokers or dealers negotiate by telephone or on computerised networks and not through a stock exchange

participating preference share a class of preference shares in which the holders are entitled to share in the distribution of the company's surplus profits (if any) in addition to their preferential dividend

particular partnership a partnership that is not a universal partnership

partnership a legal relationship for the carrying on of a business by the partners for their joint benefit with a view to making and sharing profits and sharing any losses

partnership *en commandite* a partnership in which, by agreement, the partnership business is carried on in the name of one or more ordinary partners, while the *en commandite* partners are not disclosed to the public; the *en commandite* partners are not liable to creditors of the partnership, but only to their co-partners, and their liability is limited to the amount of capital that they have contributed to the partnership

par value (in relation to shares) the face value of shares when initially offered by the company, as opposed to their market value; in contrast to no par value shares; the Companies Act, 2008 has abolished the concept of 'par value' and 'no par value' and simply refers to 'shares'; companies formed prior to this Act can still retain this distinction

passing off the delict committed by a person who, in the course of trade, misleadingly states or implies that certain goods and services are his or hers, whereas they are, in fact, the goods or services of another person

perpetual succession the concept that a company is capable of continuing in existence indefinitely, despite changes in its shareholders and/or directors

personal liability company a company in which the directors and past directors are jointly and severally liable, together with the company, for such contractual debts and liabilities of the company as are contracted during their respective periods of office, as envisaged in s 19(3) of the Companies Act, 2008

post commencement finance (in the context of business rescue) amounts falling within the scope of s 135 of the Companies Act, 2008

pre-emption right the right, when the property in question is offered for sale, to purchase it before anyone else

preference share a class of share that accords its holder a preference over the other classes of shares with regard to the payment of dividends, and sometimes with regard to the return of capital on a winding-up

preferred/preferent creditor a creditor whose claim is unsecured but ranks ahead of those of concurrent creditors

prescribed officer the holder of an office in company whose office has been designated as such by the Minister

price-sensitive information as yet unpublished information that, when published, will or may affect the price of a company's shares

prima facie on first appearance; a *prima facie* case is that which is supported by sufficient evidence to establish a claim if it is not contradicted by other evidence

primary offer of securities an offer to the public by a company of securities to be issued by that company, as envisaged in s 95(1)*(i)* of the Companies Act, 2008

principal (as opposed to agent) the party on whose behalf an agent acts

private company a profit company whose Memorandum of Incorporation prohibits the offering of its shares to the public and restricts the transferability of its shares

probation (as in to declare a director to be under probation) the status of a person whom a court has declared, in terms of s 162 of the Companies Act, 2008, to be under probation as a result of some contravention of the Companies Act, and can involve that person being unable to act as a director for the period of probation, and can involve some type of punishment such as the performance of a community service

proper plaintiff rule the legal rule, laid down in the case of *Foss v Harbottle*, that where a company suffers a wrong, only the company can institute legal proceedings as plaintiff for a remedy in respect of that wrong

prospectus an invitation or advertisement offering securities to the public for subscription, which is in the prescribed form, has the content prescribed by regulations, and has been registered by the Companies and Intellectual Property Commission

proving a claim the formal process of lodging, in the prescribed manner, a claim or proof of a debt against an insolvent estate

proxy a person who is duly authorised to represent another at a meeting, where that other cannot be present

public company a profit company that is not a state-owned company, a private company or a personal liability company

quorum the prescribed minimum number of persons, as determined either by a company's MOI or by the default provisions of the Companies Act, who must be present at a meeting for it to be competent to transact business

ratify to approve after the event; it is not possible to ratify something that was void from the start (void *ab initio*)

rebuttable presumption a legal presumption (conclusion) as to the existence or non-existence of a fact that holds good unless and until it is rebutted – that is, unless and until evidence is placed before the court to prove that the presumption is wrong; by contrast, an irrebuttable presumption is a legal presumption that holds good even if it transpires that the presumption is factually incorrect (e.g. the Turquand rule establishes an irrebuttable presumption)

redeemable share a share that a company is either entitled or obliged to redeem – that is, to re-acquire from its holder

registered auditor an individual or firm registered as an auditor with the Independent Regulatory Board for Auditors (IRBA)

registered office the office of a company or external company that is registered as envisaged in s 23 of the Companies Act, 2008

regulated company a company within the scope of s 118(1) and (2) of the Companies Act, 2008

regulated market a regulated market for the purchase and sale of listed securities, such as the Johannesburg Stock Exchange

related company a company in the same group of companies

related person a person who is related to another in the manner contemplated in s 2(1)*(a)–(c)* of the Companies Act, 2008

resolution (of shareholders or directors) a formal decision taken by way of a vote at the relevant meeting as envisaged by a company's MOI or by the default provisions of the Companies Act

reverse triangular merger a merger in which company B creates a merger subsidiary (S) that merges into T, with T surviving the merger as a wholly owned subsidiary of B, and with T's shareholders receiving shares in B

review (differentiated from appeal) see appeal

right of pre-emption see pre-emption right

rights offer an offer for subscription of a company's securities that is made to the current holders of the company's securities, as defined in s 95(1) of the Companies Act, 2008

ring-fenced company a company whose Memorandum of Incorporation contains certain restrictions with the result that the name of the company must be followed by the abbreviation 'RF' (ring-fenced) as envisaged in s 11(3)(b) of the Companies Act, 2008

sale in execution a sale by public auction of a judgment debtor's goods, effected by the sheriff under the authority of a writ of execution

scheme of arrangement an arrangement proposed by a board of directors and entered into between the company and holders of any class of its securities, as envisaged in s 114(1) of the Companies Act, 2008

secondary offering of securities an offer for sale to the public of any of a company's issued securities made by or on behalf of a person other than the company itself or its subsidiary, as envisaged in s 95(1) of the Companies Act, 2008

secured claim a claim by a creditor against a debtor for which the creditor holds a valid form of real security

secured creditor a person who holds a valid form of real security over the property of another for his or her claim against a debtor

securities register the register of its securities that a profit company is required to maintain in terms of s 24(4) read with s 50 of the Companies Act, 2008

Securities Regulation Panel the predecessor of the Takeover Regulation Panel now established in terms of s 196 of the Companies Act, 2008

security (as in a share of a company) shares and other securities issued by a company as envisaged in the definition of security in s 1 of the Companies Act, 2008

security (as in to provide security) a recognised form of real security over the property of another (such as a suretyship, mortgage or pledge) for the due payment of a debt

sequestration the formal procedure where the estate of an insolvent debtor who is an individual, partnership or trust is liquidated and the proceeds used to pay the debts

settlor (of a trust) the person who, in the course of creating a trust, 'settles' property on the trustees; also called the founder

share a bundle or conglomerate of personal rights entitling the holder to a defined interest in a company as set out in a company's MOI

share buyback/repurchase the acquisition/ repurchase by a company of its own shares

share capital the authorised or issued share capital of a public or private company

shareholder a person who holds a share in a company and whose name is recorded in its share register

share/stock index a statistical indicator that measures changes in the market value of a group of underlying stocks (e.g. the FTSE/JSE Top 40 Index measures the change in value, as represented by share price, of the top 40 companies (or 40 largest companies by market capitalisation) listed on the JSE)

small and medium-sized enterprises (SMEs) a small or medium-sized business; there are several different criteria (but no such criteria in the Companies Act, 2008) to determine whether a particular business qualifies as an SME

solvency and liquidity test the criteria of a company's solvency and liquidity laid down in s 4(1)(a) of the Companies Act, 2008

special partnership a special partnership registered under the now-repealed Special Partnerships Limited Liabilities Act of the Cape Province and Natal

special resolution a resolution passed by a company's shareholders, supported by at least 75 per cent of the voting rights exercised on the resolution, or such different percentage as is specified in the particular company's Memorandum of Incorporation, as envisaged in the definition of special resolution in s 1 of the Companies Act, 2008

squeeze-out transaction a transaction where a person or offeror who has obtained at least 90 per cent of any class of securities in a company exercises his or her right to acquire all the remaining shares of that class, as envisaged in s 124(1) of the Companies Act, 2008

SSA (Securities Services Act 36 of 2004) the Act whose purpose was, inter alia, to regulate and control security exchanges and to prohibit insider trading. This Act has now been repealed by the Financial Markets Act, 2012

stakeholder (in the context of companies) a party that can affect or be affected by the actions of the business as a whole, including government, employees, shareholders, customers, suppliers, trade unions and the broader community including the environment

state-owned company (SOC) a company envisaged in the definition of state-owned company in s 1 of the Companies Act, 2008

Strate Strate Ltd – South Africa's only central securities depository (CSD) for equities and bonds, licensed in terms of s 32 of the Securities Services Act to operate the electronic system for the holding and transfer of uncertificated securities; Strate is an acronym for Share Transactions Totally Electronic

strike price the price at which an option holder has the right to buy or sell a specified quantity of a particular share or debenture

subscriber for shares a person who has declared him- or herself willing to acquire shares in a company pursuant to an offer from the company itself

subsidiary a company that falls within the definition in s 3(1) of the Companies Act, 2008; in essence, a company that is controlled by a holding company as envisaged in s 2(2)(a) of the Companies Act, 2008

surety a person who guarantees the payment of a debt of another person

takeover the gaining control of a company by another company, generally by the purchase of a controlling interest in the former's shares

Takeover Regulation Panel a regulatory institution established in terms of the Companies Act, 2008 to regulate affected transactions as required by Chapter 5 of the Act and the Takeover Regulations

testamentary trust a trust formed in terms of a will and which comes into existence on the death of the testator; also called a will trust

top hat structure see double-dummy structure

trading trust a trust formed for the purpose of carrying on a business, also known as a 'business trust'

treasury shares fully paid shares of a company that have subsequently been reacquired by the company by way of a share repurchase, and which the company is permitted to re-sell or re-issue; the Companies Act, 2008 has largely abolished the concept of treasury shares, and simply requires shares that have been repurchased to be cancelled and to become part again of authorised (but unissued) shares

trial (as opposed to application proceedings) see application proceedings

triple bottom-line in the context of accounting, an expansion of the traditional reporting framework to take into account ecological and social performance in addition to financial position and performance – that is, taking account of the three pillars of 'people, planet and profit'

trust an arrangement in terms of which assets are held by trustees and administered for the benefit of the trust beneficiaries

trust account an account to hold funds that are not owned by the account holder, but are held in trust for another person, such as a trust account held by an attorney for the safekeeping of a client's funds

trust deed the document that creates and records the terms of a trust, also known as the trust instrument

trustee a person vested with the administration and management of a trust

trust instrument the document that records the creation and terms of a trust, also known as the trust deed

Turquand rule the rule in *Royal British Bank v Turquand*; the legal rule that, where an outsider deals in good faith with a company, there is an irrebuttable presumption that all aspects of the company's internal management have been duly complied with

***uberrimae fidei* contract** a contract in which the law requires one or more of the parties to act toward the others in the utmost good faith

***ultra vires* doctrine** in the context of company law, the rules relating to the consequences of a company's acting outside the scope of its powers and competency

unalterable provisions provisions of the Companies Act, 2008 whose effect cannot be negated, restricted, limited, qualified, extended or otherwise altered in substance or effect by a company's Memorandum of Incorporation; a company's MOI can make the unalterable provisions more onerous by providing for greater requirements, but an MOI cannot make them more lenient or abolish them

uncertificated securities securities that are not evidenced by a document and which are held and transferred electronically

underwriter a person who, in the context of a share issue by a company, undertakes to subscribe for such securities as are not taken up by the public

underwriting agreement an agreement entered into between a company and an underwriter, in which the latter undertakes, in the context of a forthcoming issue of shares by a company, to subscribe for such securities as are not taken up by the public

universal partnership a partnership to which the partners contribute all of their property

unlawful competition actions that infringe the legally protectable interests of a trade competitor

unlisted securities securities issued by a company that are not listed on an official stock exchange

unsecured claim a debt for which the creditor holds no recognised form of security

unsecured creditor a creditor who holds no security, such as a mortgage over the debtor's property

usufruct the right to use, enjoy, and have the benefit of income derived from the property owned by another person

vested rights (in context of a trust) the rights of a trust beneficiary that are not merely contingent, but have vested in him or her and are enforceable by him or her against the trustees, and which give rise to a personal right held by a beneficiary which can be legally enforced against the trustees

vindicate the right of an owner to assert his or her ownership and thereby recover possession of his or her property, which is being held by another person

voting power in the context of a company, the power determined by the voting rights that may be exercised by a person in a particular matter expressed as a percentage of all voting rights, as defined in s 1 of the Companies Act, 2008

voting rights the right of the shareholder of a company to vote at meetings of shareholders

wholly owned subsidiary a company, all of whose issued voting shares are held or controlled by its holding company

will trust see testamentary trust

winding-up the procedure during which the assets of a company that is often, but not necessarily, insolvent, are liquidated so that the proceeds may be distributed to creditors and/or shareholders, whereafter the entity's existence is terminated (dissolution)

Index

Page numbers in italics indicate information contained in tables or diagrams.